As the year 1782 opened, Americans hoped eagerly but in vain for word from overseas that the surrender of Cornwallis had forced Great Britain to admit defeat in the war. During the spring and summer the British sought to crush the rebellion by enticing the United States to desert France, by using British wares to lure war-weary Americans back to their old allegiance, and by destroying their merchant shipping. Among the leaders who were foremost in resisting this policy of subversion and in upholding the treaty of alliance with France was James Madison.

The outstanding domestic problems emphasized in this volume include the legitimate scope of congressional authority, the ownership of western lands, the independence of Vermont, and the shortage of money and troops. On several of these and other issues Madison reconciled considerations of "the general welfare" and the use of "implied powers" with the best interests of Virginia. The growing internal discord and neglect of Congress by the states warranted his concern lest the life of their fragile union depended upon a continuance of the common peril and therefore would not outlast the war.

THE PAPERS OF

James Madison

SPONSORED BY

The University of Chicago

AND

The University of Virginia

BATTLE OF THE SAINTS

THE PAPERS OF
James Madison

VOLUME 4

1 JANUARY 1782—31 JULY 1782

EDITED BY

WILLIAM T. HUTCHINSON AND WILLIAM M. E. RACHAL

EDITORIAL STAFF

JEAN SCHNEIDER   ROBERT L. SCRIBNER

THE UNIVERSITY OF CHICAGO PRESS

Library of Congress Catalog Card Number: 62-9114

The University of Chicago Press, Chicago & London
The University of Toronto Press, Toronto 5, Canada

 Published 1965. Composed and printed by The University of Chicago Press, Chicago, Illinois, U.S.A.

CONTENTS

ILLUSTRATIONS

INTRODUCTION

The documents published in this volume treat of the principal issues confronting the Continental Congress and the Commonwealth of Virginia between 1 January and 31 July 1782. War complicated even the simplest problems, while the winning of independence transcended all else. As the year opened, Americans eagerly awaited news from Europe that the surrender of Lord Cornwallis had made Great Britain willing to acknowledge defeat.

The first reports from London gave little reason for optimism. Though buffeted by a storm of criticism, Lord North for a time maintained his government by revising the means, but not the ends, of his policy. At length overthrown, he resigned on 20 March and was succeeded as prime minister by the Marquis of Rockingham (d. 1 July), but news of these events did not reach Philadelphia until 11 May 1782. It was late summer before Congress learned of the determination of Rockingham to end hostilities.

During the first seven months of 1782 Madison believed that, although Great Britain was still resolved to use her powerful navy to humble Spain, France, and the Netherlands, and to destroy the seaborne commerce of the United States, she counted above all upon enticement and subversion to persuade the former colonies to abandon their struggle. This "insidious" policy, as he characterized it, might well become a more serious threat than the army of Cornwallis had been the year before. Madison's concern over the course of the war in American waters reached a peak early in June, when he could doubt no longer the truth of the report that Sir George Brydges Rodney had decisively defeated and captured the Comte de Grasse on 12 April in the Battle of the Saints. In the future French men-of-war might no longer be available to protect American merchant ships or to co-operate again with the army, as during the Yorktown campaign. Many Americans who had joyfully hailed the triumph in October 1781 as the herald of peace were reduced to despondency by the likelihood that the calamity in the Caribbean would prolong the struggle.

During the spring and summer British frigates seized an appalling number of American merchantmen. Thereby the patriots were deprived of indispensable military matériel from Europe and of their profitable commerce with the West Indies. These maritime losses heightened the pressure by merchants and shipowners for peace, even on terms unfavorable to the United States. The interruption of overseas commerce further depressed the value of the redundant paper currency, accelerated the erratic fluctuation of prices, and increased the temptation to exchange such specie as remained for the luxuries and other goods offered for sale by the British. Madison recognized that the enemy was using these wares to seduce war-weary patriots, to foster domestic discord, and to open a breach between France and the United States.

Hoping to weaken the Confederation by encouraging a relaxation of effort, the British suspended offensive warfare on the mainland and confined their troops within narrow perimeters around New York City, Charleston, S.C., and Savannah, Ga. A *de facto* truce existed, except for desultory fighting in the far South and British-aided Indian raids in northern New York and the Ohio Valley.

In May Sir Henry Clinton was replaced as commander-in-chief by the able and accommodating Sir Guy Carleton. The new commander's courtesies soon alarmed Washington, who feared that they would undermine patriot morale. Carleton tried without success to draw Washington or the Continental Congress into negotiations for an armistice. Simultaneously overseas, agents of North and later of Rockingham sought to disrupt the alliance between France and the United States by luring representatives of each into separate parleys. The outcome of these maneuvers was the opposite of that for which they had been designed. Both Congress and the court of Versailles reaffirmed the indivisibility of their goals.

To the maintenance of this entente Madison was enthusiastically committed. He warned his colleagues in Congress and his correspondents in Virginia against the blandishments of Great Britain and advocated stern measures of retaliation for mistreatment of American prisoners of war, stricter prohibitions against trade with the enemy, unqualified refusal to negotiate with Carleton, and more vigorous measures to bring the conflict to a successful conclusion.

Because influential Dutch merchants and shipowners obviously were eager to supplant their British counterparts in the American market, Madison believed that the Netherlands would recognize the independence of the United States before the end of the war. Dutch recognition was extended on 22 April, but official confirmation was not to reach Congress until 11 September.

Although Spain continued to remain aloof, recognition by her became less important during 1782. The brightening outlook led Madison to urge Congress, unsuccessfully, to retract its offer to Spain to yield the "right" of Americans to navigate freely the full length of the Mississippi River in exchange for the long-sought alliance.

Madison's view of foreign relations chiefly reflected his firm belief in the binding force of the treaty of alliance with France and his appreciation of the vital aid given by Louis XVI to the United States. His position was not always supported by his fellow delegates from Virginia.

Among the fundamental and often complex domestic issues discussed in Madison's papers were the nature of the union of states as a legal construct, the extent of the "implied power," the breadth of control which Congress could exercise in each of its assigned fields of jurisdiction, and the authority of Congress over matters of "general interest" not specified in the Articles of Confederation, such as the admission of Vermont as a state and the ownership and administration of land west of the Appalachians. These issues were the more controversial because they stimulated competition among men for wealth or political power and rivalry among individual states or between geographical blocs of states.

In terms of the limited scope of power assigned to Congress by the Articles of Confederation, Madison was usually nationalistic in outlook, even though he still regarded Virginia as "my country." Commissioned by her General Assembly to represent her interests, he could not support policies which he deemed advantageous to the general welfare unless convinced that their adoption would benefit Virginia.

The frequent thinness of attendance at Philadelphia, combined with the stipulation of the Articles of Confederation that no ordinance on an important subject could be enacted without the approval of at least nine states, often relegated Congress to the status of a debating society. State delegations which fell below the required minimum of two delegates, or which divided equally on an issue, could not cast an effective vote. Of the five members of the Virginia delegation Madison, Joseph Jones, and Edmund Randolph were closely attuned in position, but they were often opposed by Theodorick Bland, Jr., and Arthur Lee. For this reason the long absences of Jones and Randolph during the first seven months of 1782 sometimes handicapped Madison.

A shortage of sound money complicated most domestic issues and accounts for the prominence of Robert Morris, the superintendent of finance, in the present volume. The inability or unwillingness of many states, including Virginia, whose treasury was bare, to honor the financial requisitions of Congress, and the antagonism of a few states toward a proposed amendment to the Articles of Confederation authorizing Congress to levy a 5 per cent duty on imports made it impossible for Morris to pay military and civilian personnel or to purchase the food and clothing needed by the continental army.

The necessity for a bank to serve as a fiscal agent of Congress was obvious, and the profit its shareholders might expect made it popular with men of substance. Morris' plan for the Bank of North America to be chartered by Congress put Madison in a quandary. He recognized the urgent need for the institution, but he believed that the charter should be issued by the General Assembly of Pennsylvania, then adjourned, rather than by Congress. Faced with the alternative of supporting or opposing a measure which, in his view, was essential to the general welfare but unauthorized by the Articles of Confederation, Madison accompanied his affirmative vote on 31 December 1781 with a statement of his constitutional scruples.

On the issue of the western lands, as on the issue of the bank, considerations of practical politics, state rights, and national interest were too interwoven to permit him to be wholly logical or constitutionally consistent in his course of action. He defended the title of Virginia to the territory north and west of the Ohio River against the conflicting claims of New York, Massachusetts, Connecticut, and various land companies. He denied that a committee of Congress had authority to judge between the claimants. On the other hand, while assuming this rigid posture in behalf of state sovereignty, he was also an arch nationalist in assuming that Congress could own and govern a vast domain, even though no power to do so had been conferred by the Articles of Confederation. Although this compact amply justified his opposition to the admission of the "state" of Vermont to the Confederation by Congress, his stand on the issue almost certainly was based less upon constitutional principles than upon his unwillingness to encourage separatist movements in Kentucky, or to add to the number of state delegations which denied the legitimacy of Virginia's title to the Old Northwest.

During the first seven months of 1782 the growing internal discord, financial stringency, public apathy, and neglect of Congress sharpened Madison's concern lest the winning of independence result in the losing of the union of states. He recognized the magnitude of the problem but not the means whereby it might be solved. Many of the papers in this volume reflect his constitutional dilemma. Although he hoped that the members of Congress would be animated by a "spirit of accom[m]odation," he also believed that they should always "appear to follow rather [than] lead the sentiments of their constituents" and not yield to the "poisonous tendency of precedents of usurpation" of power. As the prospect of Great Britain's recognizing the independence of the United States brightened, the danger that each of the constituent sovereign states would assert its independence of the other twelve, at least in domestic affairs, increased. How then could the divisive issues be compromised? And what was "usurpation"? "Nothing is more distressing," wrote Madison, "to those who have a due respect for the constitutional modifications of power than to be obliged to decide on them."

EDITORIAL NOTE

Only thirty-five of the two hundred eleven papers in this volume have been printed, either in whole or in part, in the earlier editions of the writings of James Madison. Ninety-three of the documents are altogether or partly in his hand, while an additional seventeen, not in his hand, record what he said or wrote. He signed or otherwise approved nineteen dispatches which were prepared by his colleagues on the Virginia delegation in Congress. Incoming mail comprises fifty-two letters addressed to Madison personally and twenty-four directed to the Virginia delegation in Congress. The remaining items consist of three motions or committee reports, each on a subject with which he was closely associated and drafted by a group of which he was a member, and three editorial notes on misdated or missing documents.

Many scholars assisted in the preparation of this volume, either by pointing out pertinent material or by answering questions which troubled the editors. Mr. Humbert S. Nelli of Chicago translated Philip Mazzei's letters of 13 March and 5 April, written in Italian. We especially thank Professor Atcheson L. Hench, of the University of Virginia, who was indefatigable in his search for the source of Edmund Pendleton's obscure allusion to the "Irish Treasurer's Waggons" in his letter of 25 February 1782 (*q.v.*, and n. 12).

During the preliminary stage of preparing this volume for publication, Donald O. Dewey and Harold E. Kolling were members of the editorial staff. In the autumn of 1963 we had the good fortune to enlist the services of Mrs. Elena Arguelles and Miss Mary Gae Porter as project assistants. Their expert typing and fine spirit have made them very welcome.

EDITORIAL METHOD

ABBREVIATIONS

FC File copy. Any version of a letter or other document retained by the sender for his own files and differing little if at all from the completed version. A draft, on the other hand, is a preliminary sketch, often incomplete and varying frequently in expression from the finished version.

JM James Madison.

LC Library of Congress.

MS Manuscript. A catchall term describing numerous reports and other papers written by Madison, as well as items sent to him which were not letters.

NA National Archives.

PCC Papers of the Continental Congress, a collection in the National Archives.

RC Recipient's copy. The copy of a letter intended to be read by the addressee. If its handwriting is not that of the sender, this fact is mentioned in the headnote.

Tr Transcript. A copy of a manuscript, or a copy of that copy, usually handwritten, made considerably later than the date of the manuscript and ordinarily not by its author or by the person to whom the original was addressed. The "Force Transcripts," made under the direction of Peter Force in the mid-nineteenth century, are those most frequently used in the present series.

SHORT TITLES FOR BOOKS

Only those books used very frequently, and a few whose titles are so long as to necessitate an abbreviation, have been given short titles. This list applies only to Volume IV.

Acomb, *Journal of Closen*. Evelyn M. Acomb, trans. and ed., *The Revolutionary Journal of Baron Ludwig von Closen, 1780–1783* (Chapel Hill, N.C., 1958).

Boyd, *Papers of Jefferson*. Julian P. Boyd *et al.*, eds., *The Papers of Thomas Jefferson* (16 vols. to date; Princeton, N.J., 1950—–).

Brant, *Madison*. Irving Brant, *James Madison* (6 vols.; Indianapolis and New York, 1941–61).

Burnett, *Letters.* Edmund C. Burnett, ed., *Letters of Members of the Continental Congress* (8 vols.; Washington, 1921–36).

Calendar of Virginia State Papers. William P. Palmer *et al.*, eds., *Calendar of Virginia State Papers and Other Manuscripts* (11 vols.; Richmond, 1875–93).

Cambridge Modern History. A. W. Ward, G. W. Prothero, Stanley Leathes, eds., *Cambridge Modern History* (13 vols.; Cambridge, England, 1902–12).

Fitzpatrick, *Writings of Washington.* John C. Fitzpatrick, ed., *The Writings of George Washington, from the Original Sources, 1745–1799* (39 vols.; Washington, 1931–44).

Gwathmey, *Historical Register of Virginians.* John H. Gwathmey, *Historical Register of Virginians in the Revolution: Soldiers, Sailors, Marines, 1775–1783* (Richmond, 1938).

Hansard's Parliamentary Debates. William Cobbett, ed., *The Parliamentary History of England from the Earliest Period to the Year 1803* (36 vols.; London, 1806–20; continued as *Hansard's Parliamentary Debates*).

Heitman, *Historical Register Continental.* F. B. Heitman, *Historical Register of Officers of the Continental Army during the War of the Revolution* (Washington, 1893).

Hening, *Statutes.* William Waller Hening, ed., *The Statutes at Large; Being a Collection of All the Laws of Virginia, from the First Session of the Legislature, in the Year 1619* (13 vols.; Richmond and Philadelphia, 1819–23).

JCC. Worthington Chauncey Ford *et al.*, eds., *Journals of the Continental Congress, 1774–1789* (34 vols.; Washington, 1904–37).

Journal of the House of Delegates. Journal of the House of Delegates of the Commonwealth of Virginia; Begun and Held at the Capitol, in the City of Williamsburg. Beginning in 1780, the portion after the semicolon reads, *Begun and Held in the Town of Richmond. In the County of Henrico.* The journal for each session has its own title page and is individually paginated. The edition used, unless otherwise noted, is the one in which the journals for 1777–1786 are brought together in two volumes, with each journal published in Richmond in 1827 or 1828, and often called the "Thomas W. White reprint."

Journals of the Council of State. H. R. McIlwaine *et al.*, eds., *Journals of the Council of the State of Virginia* (3 vols. to date; Richmond, 1931——).

McIlwaine, *Official Letters.* H. R. McIlwaine, ed., *Official Letters of the Governors of the State of Virginia* (3 vols.; Richmond, 1926–29).

Madison, *Letters* (Cong. ed.). [William C. Rives and Philip R. Fendall, eds.], *Letters and Other Writings of James Madison* (published by order of Congress; 4 vols.; Philadelphia, 1865).

Madison, *Papers* (Gilpin ed.). Henry D. Gilpin, ed., *The Papers of James Madison* (3 vols.; Washington, 1840).

Madison, *Writings* (Hunt ed.). Gaillard Hunt, ed., *The Writings of James Madison* (9 vols.; New York, 1900–1910).

Minute Book, House of Delegates, May 1782. Minute Book, House of Delegates, May 1782, MS in Virginia State Library.

New Jersey Archives. William S. Stryker *et al*., eds., *Documents Relating to the Revolutionary History of the State of New Jersey* (2d ser.; 5 vols.; Trenton, 1901–17).

Papers of Madison. William T. Hutchinson, William M. E. Rachal, *et al*., eds., *The Papers of James Madison* (4 vols. to date; Chicago, 1962—).

Pennsylvania Archives. Samuel Hazard *et al*., eds., *Pennsylvania Archives* (9 ser.; 138 vols.; Philadelphia and Harrisburg, 1852–1949).

Swem and Williams, *Register*. Earl G. Swem and John W. Williams, eds., *A Register of the General Assembly of Virginia, 1776–1918, and of the Constitutional Conventions* (Richmond, 1918).

Thomson, "Debates." Charles Thomson, "Debates in the Congress of the Confederation from July 22d to September 20th, 1782," *Collections of the New-York Historical Society*, XI (1878), 63–169.

Virginia Gazette. *Virginia Gazette, or, the American Advertiser* (Richmond, James Hayes, 1781–86).

Wharton, *Revolutionary Diplomatic Correspondence*. Francis Wharton, ed., *The Revolutionary Diplomatic Correspondence of the United States* (6 vols.; Washington, 1889).

MADISON CHRONOLOGY

1782

January–July	JM continues to reside in Philadelphia as a delegate to Congress.
7 January	Report on Instructions on Peace Negotiations.
1 February	Declines appointment to commission on Pennsylvania–Virginia boundary.
11 February	Congress approves contract with British merchants-capitulant at Yorktown.
19 February	Committee recommends conditional acknowledgment of independence of Vermont.
19 February	Arthur Lee re-enters Congress as a delegate from Virginia.
20 February	Congress asks states to sanction apportionment of costs of war in manner not prescribed by Articles of Confederation.
20 and 27 February	Report on settlement of accounts between Congress and each state.
4 March	House of Commons resolves against "farther prosecution of offensive war" in North America.
8 March	Virginia Admiralty Court condemns the British flag-of-truce ship "Three Friends."
18 March	Edmund Randolph leaves Congress to return to Virginia.
20 March	The ministry of Lord North falls in Great Britain.
27 March	The Marquis of Rockingham becomes prime minister.
1–20 April	The Vermont issue is again prominent in Congress.
9–12 April	The Battle of the Saints.
15 April	Theodorick Bland, Jr., returns to Congress as a delegate from Virginia.

16 April–6 May	The issue of the western lands is frequently debated in Congress.
22 April	The Netherlands acknowledges the independence of the United States.
22 April	Report on John Jay's negotiations with Spain.
23 or 24 April	Arthur Lee leaves Congress to return to Virginia.
27 April	The British release Henry Laurens.
30 April	Motion to approve John Jay's negotiations adopted.
1 May	JM drafts "Observations Relating to the Influence of Vermont and the Territorial Claims on the Policies of Congress."
2 May	Joseph Jones leaves Congress to return to Virginia.
2 and 14 May	Motions on protection of commerce adopted.
5 May	General Sir Guy Carleton takes command of British armies in North America.
11 May	News reaches Philadelphia that Parliament had requested King George III to make peace with the "revolted colonies."
13 May	Birth of the Dauphin of France announced to Congress by La Luzerne.
15 May	Credible news of French defeat in Battle of the Saints reaches Philadelphia.
20 May	Virginia House of Delegates protests against contract with merchants-capitulant at Yorktown.
20 May	Motion to inform states of financial crisis adopted.
24–25 May	Virginia General Assembly instructs its delegates in Congress to support negotiating peace only in association with France.
27 May	Motion on instructions to Francis Dana adopted.
27 May	Motion urging states to send full delegations to Congress adopted.
28 May	Report on salaries of representatives abroad.
31 May	Resolutions on fidelity to alliance with France adopted.

1 June	Virginia General Assembly appoints committee to prepare defense of Virginia's title to western lands.
5 June	Motions on German prisoners of war adopted.
9 June	Public letter written anonymously by Barbé-Marbois with JM's help.
14–15 June	Virginia General Assembly rescinds disapproval of contract with merchants-capitulant at Yorktown.
15 June	JM re-elected a delegate to Congress.
17 June	Motion on peace negotiations rejected.
17 June	Resolutions on inspection of administrative departments adopted.
19 June	Report on illicit trade with enemy.
27 June	Arthur Lee returns to Congress.
1 July	Death of the Marquis of Rockingham.
1 July	Rochambeau's army begins northward march from Williamsburg, Va.
1 July	Virginia General Assembly provides for commissioners to join with those of Maryland to protect and regulate commerce of Chesapeake Bay.
2 July	Virginia General Assembly authorizes seizure of all British goods entering state after 31 August 1782.
2 July	JM is named as chairman of committee to examine work of department of foreign affairs.
5 July	Report on revising John Adams' instructions.
11 July	The Earl of Shelburne becomes prime minister.
11 July	British troops evacuate Savannah, Ga.
12 July	Report on proposed treaty with the Netherlands.
17 July	Enactment of ordinance prohibiting trade with enemy.
19 July	Washington and Rochambeau confer in Philadelphia.
19 July	Unofficial word of Dutch recognition of American independence reaches Philadelphia.

24 July	JM's remarks on instructions to peace commissioners.
29 July	Robert Morris' "Report on Public Credit" received in Congress.
30 July	JM's remarks on public faith and credit.

THE PAPERS OF

James Madison

Virginia Delegates to Benjamin Harrison

RC (Virginia State Library). Written and franked by JM. Addressed to "His Excellency Benjamin Harrison Esqr. Governor of Virginia[.] Public service."

PHILADA. Jany. 1st. 1782

SIR

A Letter from Genl Heath[1] who commands the army on the North River, dated the 26th. Ulto: informs Congress that an intelligent person from N. York had reported to him that an embarkation of troops was taking place there, that he saw a part of them going on board, and a number of dragoon horses hoisted into the Vessels, that he was told by a Captain with whom he was well acquainted that Genl Leslie had written to Genl Clinton that unless he was reinforced with nine hundred men he could not defend Charlestown,[2] that a much larger number than that were to embark, that besides Charleston they were destined to Georgia & Augustine. The person did not know all the corps that were to embark but was informed there were to be some British, some Hessians, & the new-raised corps, of which Robinsons[3] & the N. York Volunteers were particularly mentioned. They appeared to be bringing down much baggage to the wharves. It was said they expected to have the whole on board by the sunday preceding the date of the letter.[4]

Although the general plan of our official correspondence excludes unauthenticated intelligence, the successful enterprize of the Marquis de Bouilli agst. the island of Eustatius, is attended with so many marks of reality that we can not well omit it. The article in the inclosed gazette under the Antigua head in particular, is little short of confirmation of it.[5]

We have the honor to be with the highest respect & esteem Yr Excellency's Obt. & very hble Servts.

JOS: JONES
J. MADISON JR.
EDM: RANDOLPH

[1] The entire first paragraph of the present letter is nearly a verbatim copy of a large portion of William Heath's dispatch of 26 December, read in Congress on 31 December 1781 (NA: PCC, No. 157, fols. 435–36).

[2] In a report of 30 November 1781 to Lieutenant General Sir Henry Clinton, Major General Alexander Leslie stated that, having only about 3,500 troops fit for duty, he could do little more than hold Charleston, unless reinforcements reached

him. By this date Clinton was resigned to maintaining merely a few coastal positions in South Carolina, Georgia, and northern Florida (William B. Willcox, ed., *The American Rebellion: Sir Henry Clinton's Narrative of His Campaigns, 1775–1782* [New Haven, Conn., 1954], pp. 588–89, 591–92).

[3] Colonel Beverley Robinson (1722–1792), a native of Middlesex County, Va., moved in 1748 to New York, where his wife possessed much valuable property. A veteran of the French and Indian War, Robinson conspicuously manifested his allegiance to Great Britain during the Revolution by organizing the Royal American Legion. Also engaged in secret service, he tried to win Ethan Allen and his Vermont followers to the British cause. Following the war, he lived for a time in Canada before making his home in England.

[4] That would be 23 December 1781. According to a contemporary New York newspaper, quoted in the *Pennsylvania Packet* of 26 January 1782, the reinforcements sailed on 25 December. These reinforcements, "amounting to about 550 men," belonged to the "corps in the southern district" who, being for various reasons on leave in or near New York City, were returning to their commands (William B. Willcox, ed., *American Rebellion*, pp. 356, 592).

[5] Word received from Antigua of the bloodless conquest of St. Eustatius on 26 November 1781 by a small force led by the governor of Martinique, François Claude Amour, Marquis de Bouillé (1739–1800), appeared in the *Pennsylvania Packet* of 1 January 1782. More complete accounts are in the *Packet* of 3, 10, and 31 January. Upon returning home from the West Indies at the close of the war, Bouillé was promoted to the rank of lieutenant general and, at the outset of the French Revolution, commanded an army on the eastern frontier of his country. Owing to his conspicuous role in the unsuccessful attempt in 1791 of Louis XVI and Marie Antoinette to escape from France, Bouillé necessarily became an émigré. He served for three years in the forces of the Prince of Condé and the Duke of York before retiring to spend the remainder of his life in England. He and Lafayette were cousins (Louis Gottschalk, *Lafayette Joins the American Army* [Chicago, 1937], pp. 69, 194).

Report on Instructions on Peace Negotiations

MS (NA: PCC, No. 20, I, 75–85). The report, entirely in JM's hand, is docketed: "Report of a comee on the instructions to the delegates of Massachusetts relative to the fisheries Delivered Jany 7, 1782 Order of the day for tuesday Jany 8. 1782. Jany 22 Referred to Mr Carroll Mr Randolph Mr Montgomery."

EDITORIAL NOTE

Urged by Conrad Alexandre Gérard, then French minister to the United States, Congress in 1779 debated at length about the terms of peace to be imposed upon Great Britain after her defeat in the war. That she must acknowledge the independence of the United States as a prerequisite to negotiating peace terms was stipulated without difficulty, but the proposed "ultimata" concerning boundaries, the navigation of the Mississippi River, and the Newfoundland fisheries revealed sharp differences of opinion within Congress, marked by a fairly definite cleavage between the New England and the southern delegates.

The "struggle over the fisheries, which was begun in early February [1779] and continued almost without cessation until the middle of August, was," according to Edmund Cody Burnett, "one of the most protracted, as it was probably the most hotly contested parliamentary battle ever waged in Congress. Without question no other contest stirred so violently the great deeps of Congressional bile" (*The Continental Congress* [New York, 1941], p. 433). Before this struggle lapsed into quiescence during the first days of autumn, Congress had agreed that, although a guarantee by Great Britain of "the common right to the fisheries" was of the utmost importance and must be included in any commercial treaty made with her, this right would not be asserted "on the present occasion" as unalterably controlling the American peace commissioners. The delegates from Virginia supported this decision. Although those from New England naturally opposed it, they probably abandoned their earlier uncompromising stand because of their assurance that John Adams, one of their own number, would be elected by Congress to negotiate the treaties of peace and commerce with Great Britain. Congress further agreed in 1779 that: (1) the *sine qua non* concerning boundaries would omit Canada and Nova Scotia, although the peace commissioners must endeavor strenuously to gain both territories for the United States; and (2) if Spain would join the Franco-American alliance and drive Britain from East and West Florida, the United States would guarantee the future possession of the Floridas to Spain, provided that she would reciprocally guarantee to the United States "the free navigation of the river Mississippi into and from the sea." See index to *JCC*, XV, under Boundaries of United States; Fishing rights in treaty; Florida, East, cession; Mississippi, navigation of; and Nova Scotia, cession of.

Although the terms of a peace treaty with Great Britain were not an important subject of debate in Congress during 1780, the issue of the navigation of the Mississippi was prominent throughout the autumn of that year in connection with the much hoped for alliance with Spain. Contrary to JM's wishes, the Virginia General Assembly on 2 January 1781 released its delegates from the directive to insist that Spain acknowledge the right of Americans to employ that river freely, including the use of a port of deposit at the mouth. Thereupon, on 15 February, Congress modified the earlier instructions to John Jay by authorizing him to conclude a treaty with Spain, even at the cost of relinquishing the right of the United States to the unrestricted use of the Mississippi and of a free port south of 31° north latitude (*Papers of Madison*, II, 92, n. 4; 108, n. 9; 127–34; 202–4; 273; 302–3).

Informed by La Luzerne, the French minister to the United States, that Great Britain might accept as mediators the empress of Russia and the Holy Roman emperor, or either of them, Congress between May and September 1781 reconsidered the peace "ultimata" with exhausting thoroughness and joined four other men with John Adams to constitute a peace commission (n. 3, below). These debates also produced a reaffirmation that a treaty of commerce with Great Britain must acknowledge the "right" of American and French citizens, under the terms of the Franco-American Treaty of Amity and Commerce of 1778, to use the offshore fishing banks of North America. On the other hand, in spite of JM's opposition, Congress left the matter of western boundaries largely to the discretion of the American peace commissioners, as guided by the French foreign office, and declined to designate the freedom of navigation of the Mississippi from its source to its mouth as indispensable (*Papers of Madison*, III, 133, editorial note; 148, and n. 2; 149, n. 3; 150–51; 151–52 nn.; 168, editorial note; 265, n. 2; 273–74).

Although the members of the Massachusetts General Assembly were heartened in the autumn of 1781 by the declining military fortunes of the British in the South, climaxing in the surrender of Lord Cornwallis, they were disturbed because the interests of New England were no longer solely entrusted to John Adams. At the same time, the lessened need of aid from Spain convinced JM that Congress could and should take a more positive stand on what the western boundaries of the United States must be and, above all, on the necessity of a guarantee by Great Britain in the treaty of peace, or by Spain in a treaty of alliance, of the right of Americans to navigate the entire length of the Mississippi River. Moreover, with the danger from the enemy at least temporarily reduced, the sectional and factional controversies within Congress became more acute, the attendance of its members more irregular, and the states even more laggard than before in supplying their quotas of money and troops. In a word, there was good reason to fear lest the union of states would not survive the end of the war. This union, in JM's view, must continue at least until the attainment of peace. If Congress could agree upon the indispensable terms which Britain must accept, the need of standing firm to obtain them would help to maintain the union until the treaty provided all the states with a common territorial domain and other guarantees.

Amid these circumstances, the Massachusetts legislature on 27 October 1781 directed its delegates in Philadelphia "to Represent to Congress the importance of the Fisheries to this State, and to use their utmost influence that instructions be given to the ministers appointed by Congress for negociating a Peace, in the most pressing manner to insist, that the Free and unmolested Exercise of this right be continued and Secured to the Subjects of the United States of America, in a future settlement of Peace" (NA: PCC, No. 74, fols. 189–92). The printed journal of Congress makes no mention of a session on 17 November, but the directive, according to a note on its docket, was submitted to Congress on that day and referred to a committee comprising James Lovell (Mass.), Daniel Carroll (Md.), and JM. JM's colleagues on the committee allotted to him the task of drafting the report. By joining the stipulations in regard to the western boundary and the Mississippi River, demanded by southerners, with the stipulation about fishing rights, demanded by New Englanders, JM sought in these instructions to reconcile sectional differences and thereby to check the ominous drift of the Union toward disintegration.

In the Ford collection in the New York Public Library is an undated manuscript, five pages in length, written by Elias Boudinot (N.J.) and docketed by him, "Proposed Instructions to Ministers of Peace." The contents of the first paragraph, together with the many corrections and interlineations on the first three pages of the document, strongly suggest that Boudinot was preparing, or at least copying, the draft of a letter upholding the claim of the United States to the Mississippi River as its "western & North western Boundary." Two brief passages on Boudinot's first page, two on his third page, over half of his fourth page, and all of his fifth are identical or approximately identical in phraseology with passages in the present report. Whether JM copied from Boudinot or vice versa obviously depends upon ascertaining the exact date when Boudinot wrote his manuscript. This date has eluded the editors. Unlike JM's, Boudinot's committee assignments between 23 July and 9 November 1781, the period when he last attended Congress prior to the date of the present report (Burnett, *Letters,* VI, xlvii), had not included any bearing upon instructions to the peace commissioners. For this reason, although clearly inconclusive, the editors assume that Boudinot's manuscript postdates the one given below.

[7 January 1782]

The Committee to whom was recommitted[1] the several papers relative to the fisheries having duly considered the same & being of opinion that the best security for this object short of admitting it into the Ultimatum for peace will be a representation to his M. C. M.[2] thro' our Ministers[3] for negociating peace, of its great importance to the U. S. & of the grounds upon which it is claimed & expected; & being also of opinion that a like representation touching the other claims of the U. S. excluded from the Ulti[ma]tum would have a tendency no less salutary, they have prepared instructions to the sd. Ministers on this comprehensive plan & report the same as follows for the consideration of Congress.

That the Ministers plenipotentiary for negociating a peace, or in case they should not be convened, the Minister Plenipo: at the Court of Versailles,[4] be instructed to acquaint his M. C. M. *that notwithstanding the occasion presented* to the U. S. by the signal & various advantages gained over the Enemy, of enlarging their Ultimatum for peace, the firm reliance which Congress have on the friendship and influence of his Majesty, has determined them not to depart from their resolutions of the day of last [5] by which all the objects of their desires & expectations, excepting only the Independance of the U. S. & their Alliance with his M. are eventually submitted to his Councils: But[6] that in order to make him more fully sensible of the extent & foundation of these desires & expectations they have thought it expedient that some observations should be made to him relative to the several objects which are most likely to fall within the compass of negociation.

One of these objects & which is intimately connected with the independance of the U. S. is the exterior boundary by which their extent is to be defined. On this occasion it is to be observed, that our contest will be with his Britanick Majesty alone.[7] Under his authority the limits of these States, while in the character of Colonies, were established; to these limits the U. S. considered as independt. sovereignties, have succeeded. Whatsoever territorial rights therefore, belonged to them before the revolution, were necessarily devolved upon them at the aera of independence.

Those grounds support the assertion, that the U. S. are bounded, as they are declared to be in the instructions given to Mr. Adams on the   day of August 1779.[8]

As the efforts of his Britannick Majesty will be principally directed agst. the Western & N. Western boundary, the observations on this subject may be confined thereto.

The treaty of Paris in 1763 to which his M. C. M. and the British King were parties, restricted those Colonies wch. were before extended by their Charters to the Sea, to the river Mississippi.[9] To this river then these States will still extend in the same manner unless by some subsequent constitutional & rightful act, their limits have been abridged.

The negociations on this head will probably assume a variety of forms. None perhaps will be more strenuously urged than those which arise from his Britannick Majesty's proclamation on the 7th. day of October 1763, the treaty of Fort Stanwix in 1768 between him & the six nations, and the British Statute in 1774, establishing among other things the boundaries of Quebec.[10]

1. If it can be supposed, that the purpose of the Proclamation was to affect the boundaries of the U. S. it must be remembered to be the act of the very Prince against whom we contend; that it preceded a short time only the manifestation of those wicked & oppressive measures which gave birth to the Revolution, and that it directly interfered with the rights accruing to the Colonies by the antient & more solemn acts of his predecessors.

But by the prohibition to the Governors of the other Colonies than of Quebec, E. Florida or W. Florida, to grant warrants of survey, or pass patents, "for the present, and untill his (the Britis[h] King's) farther pleasure sd. be known," for any lands beyon[d] the heads or sources of any of the rivers which fall into the Atlantic ocean from the West & North West, is strongly shewn an opinion that there were lands beyond the heads of those rivers, within the grants of the Governors.[11]

By the prohibition too to grant warrants of survey or pass patents for any lands whatever, which "not having been ceded to or purchased by the British King were reserved to the Indians or any of them," a restriction of territory could not have been designed by a King, who granted the Charters to the Colonies,[12] knowing that they would interfere with the rights of the Indians—who has always considered a cession or purchase from the Indians, not so much the source of a title as a milder means of preventing their hostility—who since the date of the proclamation has granted through the prohibited Governors themselves, large quantities of land beyond the heads of those rivers,[13] & whose own Geographer in a map describing and distinguishing the British, Spanish & French dominions in America according to the aforesaid Treaty of Paris, carries the States of Georgia, N. Carolina, S. Carolina & Virginia as far as the Mississippi.[14]

In a word this part of the Proclamation seems to have been intended merely to shut up the land offices, not to curtail limits, to keep the Indians in peace, not to relinquish the rights accruing under the charters, & particularly that of preemption.[15]

2. The Treaty of Fort Stanwix is susceptible of a similar answer by viewing it as an instrument of peace, not the conveyance of a title. For there is reason to believe, that the British King has never ratified it; and yet it is notorious that his Governors have granted lands within the Cession then made.[16]

If it be said that the authority to grant those lands was derived from the Treaty of Lancaster in 1744, here then is a forcible illustration of our Doctrine. For on what principle, but on account of peace, could the British King have attempted to procure a new Cession of the same Country? on the other hand, if the authority to grant those lands was not derived from the Treaty of Lancaster, it can rest on no other foundation than that of his Charters.[17]

3. The Quebec Act is one of the multiplied causes of our opposition & finally of the revolution. No stress therefore ought to be laid on it, even if in its operation it abridged the boundaries of the States. But the provision that nothing therein contained, relative to the boundary of the province of Quebec should in any wise affect the boundaries of any other Colony, excludes such an operation, & confirms chartered rights.[18]

Should G. B. retain that portion of the U. S. bordering on the Mississippi, the neighbourhood of her possessions will be imminently dangerous to our peace. Should she also retain Canada & W. Florida, or even Canada alone, by applying herself to the settlement of that Country, and pushing on her trade there with vigor, a new nursery for her marine will speed[il]y be established.

From a full confidence that the Western territory now contended for lay within the U. S. the British posts therein have been reduced by our Citizens and American government is now exercised within the same; large bounties of land have been promised to the army, and we have relied on it as an important source for discharging the debts incurred during the war.

For a considerable distance beyond the Apalachian Mountains & particularly on the Ohio American Citizens are actually settled at this day. By the surrender therefore of the W. territory to G. B. a large number of fencible men,[19] men too who have not been behind any of their fellow Citizens in the struggle for liberty, would be thrown back within her power.

But a decisive objection exists against this mutilation of our Country, that the principle by which it would be limited to the distance of a Mile only from the Mississippi, would justify mutilations to an immense extent.

Another claim is the common right of the U. S. to take fish in the N. American seas & particularly on the banks of N. foundland. With respect to this object the sd. ministers are instructed to consider & contend for it as described in the instructions relative to a treaty of Commerce given to J. A on the 29th of Sepr. 1779,[20] as equally desired & expected by Congress with any of the other claims not made ultimata in the instructions given to the Ministers plenipo for negociating a peace on the day of last,[21] & are therein referred to as objects of the desires & expectations of Congress. They are also instructed to observe to his M. C. M. with respect to this claim, that it does not[22] extend to any parts of the sea lying within three leagues of the shores held by G. B. or any other Nation. That under this limitation, it is conceived by Congress, a common right of taking fish cannot be denied to them without a manifest violation of the freedom of the seas, as established by the law of Nations & the dictates of reason; according to both which the use of the sea, except such parts thereof, as lye within the vicinity of the shore & are deemed appurtena[nt] thereto, is common to all nations,[23] those only excepted, who have either by positive convention, or by long & silent acquiescence under exclusion, renounced that common right; that neither of these exceptions militate against the claim of the U. S. since it does not extend to the vicinity of the shore, and since they are so far from having either expressly or tacitly renounced their right, that they were prior to the war, though indeed not in the character of an independt. nation, in the constant, & even during the war, in the occasional exercise of it; that although a greater space than three leagues has in some instances been, both by public Treaties & by customs, annexed to the shore as part of the same dominion, yet as it is the present aim of the Maritime powers to circumscribe, as far as reason will justify, all exclusive pretensions to the sea,[24] and as that is the distance specified in a treaty to which both G. B. & his Majesty are parties, & which relates to the very object in question,[25] it was supposed that no other distance cd. in the present case, be more properly assumed; that if a greater or an indefinite distance should be alledged to be appurtenant by the law of Nations to the Shore it may be answered that the fisheries in question, even those on the banks of Newfoundland, being of so vast an extent, might with much greater reason be deemed appurtenant to the whole Continent of N. America, than to the inconsiderable portion of it held by G. B; that Congress expect with the greater assurance the concurrence of his Majesty in these ideas, since his own claim to the fisheries wd. by a contrary doctrine be suspended on[26] the mere concession of G. B. instead of resting on the solid & honorable basis of the law of Nations & of right; that if G. B. cannot by virtue of her occupancy of the shore claim an exclusive use of the fisheries beyond the vicinity thereof, and a right to the common use is incident to the U. S. as a free & independent community, they cannot admit that they have no such right without renouncing an attribute of that sovereinty which they are bound as well by respect for his Majesty's honor as for their own interests & dignity to maintain entire; that this right is no less indispensable in its exercise than it is indisputable in its principles, the inhabitants of a considerable part of the U. S. being dependent thereon both for a material proportion of their subsistance, & for the means of their commerce; and as they were in the full enjoyment of this resource prior to the revolution, the loss of it by an event from which very different expectations have been cherished, and which ought to bestow as far as possible equal advantages on all who have laboured equally for its accomplishment, could not fail to be attended with disappointment & mortifying comparisons: that from these considerations Congress have the most earnest desire as well as the most sanguine hope that his Majesty's efforts will obtain for his Allies a stipulation on the part of G. B. not to molest them in the common use of the fisheries as above stated; or if insuperable difficulties should oppose a positive stipulation in their favor, that his Majesty will in every event find means to avoid a surrender of that common right; that whilst however this latter expedient is suggested to his Majesty it cannot escape his discernment, that it is so pregnant with dangerous consequences, that the former cannot be contended for with too much urgency & zeal.

That with respect to the confiscated property of those who have adhered to the interests of the Enemy, & which may possibly be claimed for the former owners the aforesaid Ministers are to observe to his Majesty, that these confiscations having taken place more or less in *almost* all the States,[27] and having undergone various transfers from individual to individual, a specific restitution is absolutely impracticable; and when the vast amount of them is compared with the ravages & burdens which the war will leave behind it, an equivalent restitution wd. be little less than impracticable, that as the general usage of nations, as well as the particular law of G. B. excludes aliens from holding real & immoveable estates, the moment our national independence was assumed, the titles of all those who on or prior to that event espoused the side of the Enemy, became under strict construction, extinct: and that such as afterwards deserted to them falling under the denomination of Traytors, have forfeited not only their estates but their lives to their Country; that although it were to be admitted that the peculiarity of circumstances which distinguish the present war between the U. S. & G. B. from a war between two nations seperate & independent at its origin, affords some plea for reversing the confiscations, this consideration is far outweighed by the great value of which the Citizens of these States have, contrary to the laws of war, been despoiled by the Enemy, and the still greater losses which they have suffered from wanton destructions; in both which, those who have fled or been expelled from their Country, have been often the chief instigators & instruments, and by the first of which many of them have enriched themselves greatly beyond their losses.[28]

That the Ministers further observe to his Majesty that any stipulation authorizing such fugitives & exiles from their Country to return into it wd. not only be dishonorable to the Governments of these states, but so obnoxious to the people at large, and especially to such as have been the objects of their outrages, that it is the particular wish of Congress that it may be most strenuously opposed; that such a permission is the more to be dreaded as it cd. only be intended for such as are totally devoid both of honor & sensibility who alone wd. avail themselves of a privilege that wd. subject them to the indignation & resentments which they had provoked.

That as it is not improbable the subject of commerce will among others be introduced into the negociation, the Ministers be instructed to observe thereon to his M.C.M that the U.S. as a free & sovereign nation being the absolute masters as well of their Commerce as of their Government, no claim of right can, nor probably will, be pretended with respect to the former, by those who relinquish such pretension with respect to the latter; that it is the wish & the policy of the U. States to preserve their commerce as unfettered as possible with stipulations in favor of nations with which they are now unconnected, and particularly of that with which they are now at war; that this policy can not but coincide with the sentiments of his Majesty since it alone will leave to his Allies the future opportunity of manifesting their preference of his interests to those of his Enemies & rivals:[29] that Congress do for these reasons most earnestly desire, expect & intreat that his Majesty will spare no efforts that may be necessary to exclude from a Treaty every article which wd. restrain the U. S. from imposin[g] on the trade of G. B. any duties, restrictions or prohibitions which may hereafter be judged expedient; Unless & so fa[r] only as, a relaxation in this point may be essentially necessary for obtaining peace, or the several objects above mentioned.[30]

[1] The docket, quoted in the headnote above, omits mention of the submission of the committee's report to Congress on 12 December 1781, when it was "debated and re-committed" (*JCC*, XXI, 1166). As originally drafted by JM, the report probably began with the word "Resolved," which is crossed out in the manuscript. The introductory paragraph is squeezed above the deleted "Resolved" at the top of the first page. JM's use of the word "recommitted" most likely signifies that he added this preamble on some date between 12 December 1781 and 7 January 1782.

[2] His Most Christian Majesty King Louis XVI of France.

[3] John Adams, John Jay, Benjamin Franklin, Thomas Jefferson, and Henry Laurens (*Papers of Madison*, III, 154, n. 5). On 14 February 1783 Congress excused Jefferson from his assignment to proceed to France as a peace commissioner (Boyd, *Papers of Jefferson*, VI, 240; *JCC*, XXIV, 132).

[4] Benjamin Franklin. On a separate line immediately preceding this paragraph, JM wrote and deleted "Resolved."

[5] The resolutions were those of 15 June 1781 (*JCC*, XX, 651–52). That they were of much humbler tone than the present report no doubt mirrors the effect of "the signal & various advantages gained over the Enemy." See *Papers of Madison*, III, 154, n. 3.

6 The portion of this paragraph, beginning with the first italicized word and ending here, is enclosed in brackets. What the brackets connoted to the person who inserted them is unknown.

7 The implication of this forthright statement is clear: differences which eventually might arise between Spain and the United States over their common boundary in the West and South were irrelevant to the peace negotiations of the United States with Great Britain. Probably the peace commissioners were also expected to infer that they must not tolerate an attempt by France to advance the territorial claims of her other ally, Spain, in opposition to those of the United States.

8 For the instructions of 14 August 1779, see *JCC,* XIV, 956–60.

9 JM here accepts as a matter of course the right of the king, when exercising his prerogative of making treaties, to alter the boundaries of a colony as defined in a royal charter. JM apparently assumed that this right was so generally understood that he did not need to mention it when, on other occasions, he insisted that a charter was contractual in nature and hence could not be annulled or modified by the grantor except with the consent of the grantee. For this view, see JM to Randolph, 9 April 1782. Article VII of the Treaty of Paris of 10 February 1763 between France and Great Britain stated that "for the future the confines between the dominions of his Most Christian Majesty and those of his Britannic Majesty in this part of the world shall be irrevocably fixed by a line drawn along the middle of the river Mississippi from its source to the river of Iberville, and from thence by a line drawn along the middle of this river and the lakes Maurepas and Pontchartrain to the sea" (Frances Gardiner Davenport and Charles Oscar Paullin, eds., *European Treaties Bearing on the History of the United States and Its Dependencies* [4 vols.; Washington, 1917–37], IV, 94).

10 The Royal Proclamation of 1763 created the British provinces of Quebec, East Florida, West Florida, and Grenada and defined the boundary of each. The proclamation also forbade, "for the present," outside Quebec and the two Floridas, any further survey or purchase of, or settlement on, "any lands beyond the heads or sources of any of the rivers which fall into the Atlantic Ocean from the west or northwest. The "British Statute in 1774" (Quebec Act of 22 June 1774), by extending the limits of the province of Quebec west to the Mississippi River and south to the Ohio River, traversed the alleged western boundaries of Massachusetts, New York, Connecticut, and Virginia and jeopardized the land claims of many individuals and companies resident on the eastern seaboard and in Great Britain itself (Henry Steele Commager, ed., *Documents of American History* [2d ed.; 2 vols. in 1; New York, 1940], I, 47–50, 74–76). Although the Six Nations of the Iroquois, in the Treaty of Fort Stanwix, concluded in February 1768 with Sir William Johnson of New York, the superintendent of Indian affairs in the northern department, again ceded their claims to all land south of the Ohio River (n. 17, below), many Virginians were offended by this assumption of jurisdiction over their own affairs and were alarmed lest the treaty foreshadow the granting of lands within the province's western limits directly by the Crown to "outsiders" and the creation of a new colony there (Thomas Perkins Abernethy, *Western Lands and the American Revolution* [New York, 1937], pp. 43–46, 189, 221, 242, 363–65; *Papers of Madison,* II, 176–78).

11 This argument is vulnerable. A government is not "strongly shewn" to have possessed rightfully a field of power by virtue of a subsequent denial of that field to that government. If this were true, JM would have been obliged to admit about a decade later that, prior to the ratification of the first ten amendments, the federal government could have exercised lawfully the fields of powers denied to it by those amendments.

[12] See n. 9, above. The approximately accurate quotation is taken from the tenth paragraph of the Proclamation of 1763.

[13] JM probably had in mind sizable grants made west of the Proclamation Line by John Penn, governor of Pennsylvania; by Lord Dunmore, governor of New York (where his successor, William Tryon, also became involved) and later of Virginia; and by James Wright, governor of Georgia. The Georgia grants alone were authorized by the British government, and then only after purchase from the Indians directly in the name of the Crown (Clarence Walworth Alvord, *The Mississippi Valley in British Politics* [2 vols.; Cleveland, 1917], II, 113, 203–7).

[14] The reference is to the work of Thomas Jefferys, the British royal geographer from 1760 until his death in 1771 (Robert M. Lunny, *Early Maps of North America* [Newark, N.J., 1961], p. 27). His *General Topography of North America and the West Indies*, published in partnership with Robert Sayer in London in 1768, contained "An accurate map of North America. Describing and distinguishing the British, Spanish and French dominions on this great continent; according to the definitive treaty concluded at Paris 10 feb. 1763." This map shows the Mississippi River as the western boundary of the southern colonies.

Subsequent editions of Thomas Jefferys' *The American Atlas* were published in London by Sayer and John Bennett from 1775 to 1782, inclusive (Justin Winsor, ed., *Narrative and Critical History of America* [8 vols.; Boston and New York, 1884–89], V, 618). JM may have used one of these editions.

[15] JM means that American subjects, whether as individuals or as corporations, had a pre-emptive or prior right in law to acquire title to the public lands within their respective colonies before those lands could be offered on the same terms to anyone else. JM may have intended this appended phrase to be a subtle thrust at the land speculators in Congress whose pretensions to land within Virginia were not acknowledged by that Commonwealth.

[16] Although the territory ceded by the Iroquois in the treaty was west of the Proclamation Line, grants had been made within the cession between 1768 and 1775 (above, n. 13). Sir William Johnson had violated his instructions by acquiring more land from the Iroquois than the Crown desired. For this reason, the Earl of Hillsborough, who was secretary of state for the colonies and president of the Board of Trade, opposed the treaty. Late in 1769 the Privy Council nevertheless accepted the cession but rejected the article validating the Indiana Company's purchase from the Indians (Thomas P. Abernethy, *Western Lands and the American Revolution*, pp. 43–44).

[17] By the Treaty of Lancaster (Pa.) in 1744 and that of Logstown (near Ambridge, Pa.) in 1752, the Iroquois had relinquished all claim to land south of the Ohio River. At Fort Stanwix they did so again, ignoring the protests of the dependent Delawares and Shawnees and professing to act even for the powerful and independent Cherokees (*ibid.*, p. 34; *Calendar of Virginia State Papers*, I, 278).

[18] JM's position is unconvincing. True, the assurance mentioned by him is in the Quebec Act, but it also reaffirmed the existence of the Proclamation Line south to the Ohio River. Hence his contention had no force except in relation to the claims of states to territory south of that river and west of the Appalachians.

[19] Men capable of defending themselves. A "fencible" was a militiaman enlisted solely to defend his own neighborhood.

[20] John Adams' instructions were adopted by Congress on 14 August 1779 (*JCC*, XIV, 960–62).

[21] 15 June 1781 (n. 5, above; *Papers of Madison*, III, 154, n. 5).

[22] To this point in the paragraph JM had at first written: "Another object in which these States are no[t unin]terested is their common right of fishing in the

[North] American seas & particularly on the banks of N. foundland. With respect to this claim of the U.S. the sd. Ministers are instructed to observe to his M. C. M. that it does not. . . ." It seems reasonable to conclude that New England delegates were not satisfied with this negative, halfhearted approach and insisted that JM affirm more forcibly the position of the United States with relation to the fisheries.

[23] In view of the stress by JM upon natural law, natural rights, the rights of nations, and the dictates of reason, he in all likelihood derived his references to international law largely, if not entirely, from Emmerich de Vattel, *Le droit des gens, ou principes de la loi naturelle appliqués à la conduite et aux affaires des nations et des souverains* (1758), an authority which he had consulted before drafting the instructions to John Jay, 17 October 1780 (*Papers of Madison,* II, 132; 135, n. 12). In the present instance Vattel's Book I, chap. xxiii (James Brown Scott, ed.; 2 vols.; Washington, 1916), supported JM's position upon the fisheries. Perhaps JM had also read Book II, chap. ii, sec. 3 of Hugo Grotius, *De iure belli ac pacis* (1625).

Also on 7 January 1782, Robert R. Livingston covered the same ground in a letter to Franklin. For Livingston's reference to Grotius and Vattel, see Wharton, *Revolutionary Diplomatic Correspondence,* V, 91. The similarity between Livingston's letter and JM's document suggest that they had exchanged views on the subject.

[24] JM stated accurately the general purpose of the League of Armed Neutrality, even though its more particular concern was to preserve a maximum freedom of action at sea by neutral nations in wartime. JM's subject, on the other hand, was the rights of every nation, and especially those of the United States, at sea in time of peace. See James Brown Scott, ed., *The Armed Neutralities of 1780 and 1800: A Collection of Official Documents, Preceded by the Views of Representative Publicists* (New York, 1918), pp. 273–405, *passim.*

[25] By Article V of the Treaty of Paris of 1763, the French were accorded "the liberty of fishing in the Gulf of Saint Lawrence, on condition that" they "do not exercise the said fishery but at the distance of three leagues from all the coasts belonging to Great Britain, as well those of the continent, as those of the islands situated in the said Gulf of Saint Lawrence," but because of the important military installation at Louisbourg, they were barred from fishing within fifteen leagues of Cape Breton Island (Frances G. Davenport and Charles O. Paullin, eds., *European Treaties,* IV, 94).

[26] Used in the sense of "dependent upon."

[27] JM could have said that every state had confiscated the property of Tories (Claude Halstead Van Tyne, *The Loyalists in the American Revolution* [New York, 1929], pp. 194, 277–78). Parliament finally compensated some of the Loyalists to an amount totaling about $15,500,000, a sum far less than the total extent of their losses (George Bancroft, *History of the United States of America, From the Discovery of the Continent* [author's last revision; 6 vols.; New York, 1887], VI, 101).

[28] In setting off the value of property taken from Loyalists against the value of patriots' property unjustifiably destroyed by the enemy, Madison was reflecting a resolution of Congress on 18 October 1780, adopted for the guidance of John Adams in negotiating with Great Britain. This resolution read in part: "That with respect to those persons who have either abandoned or been banished from any of the United States, since the commencement of the war, he is to make no stipulations whatsoever for their readmittance; and as to an equivalent for their property, he may attend to propositions on that subject only on a reciprocal stipulation, that Great Britain will make full compensation for all the wanton destruction which the subjects of that nation have committed on the property of the citizens of the United States" (*JCC,* XVIII, 949).

[29] In Articles II, III, and IV of the Treaty of Amity and Commerce between

France and the United States, each of the contracting parties assured the other of "most favoured" nation rights and privileges. By this, each power engaged "not to grant any particular favour to other nations in respect to commerce and navigation, which shall not immediately become common to the other party" (*JCC*, XI, 423). See *Papers of Madison*, III, 189, n. 6.

[30] Granting the accuracy of the note on the docket, this report was presented to Congress on 7 January. For the next two weeks the printed journal omits any mention of the report. The motion of William Ellery (R.I.) on 8 January, "That it is now expedient that Congress should enlarge their ultimata for concluding a treaty of peace," presumably voiced the discontent of some of the New England delegates because the recommendations of JM did not make the right to fish on the Newfoundland Banks a *sine qua non*. The Ellery motion was defeated by a vote of five states to two, with only the Massachusetts and Georgia delegates solidly for it and with the delegations from New Jersey, Pennsylvania, Maryland, Virginia, and South Carolina unanimously opposed (*JCC*, XXII, 11).

On 22 January Ellery again failed to have the right to fish on the Banks of Newfoundland made an indispensable provision of a treaty of peace with Great Britain, but Congress adopted a resolution, without a recorded vote, adding emphasis to the provisions of JM's report by expressing "the most sanguine expectations that his Majesty's [Louis XVI's] friendship and influence will obtain for his faithful allies stipulations in their favour by which the peaceable enjoyment of their common right to take fish in the American seas, and particularly on the Banks of Newfoundland[,] and the boundaries of the United States as described in the instructions [of 14 August 1779 to John Adams, including the line of the Mississippi from its source to 31° north latitude] . . . may be secured to them." At the same time, as a matter of record for the information of the delegates rather than as a directive to the peace commission, Congress agreed to Randolph's explanation "That nothing contained in the preceding instruction shall be construed to affect any territorial dispute, at any time subsisting between the United States and an individual state or between individual states" (*JCC*, XXII, 44–45). Also on 22 January JM's report was referred to a committee whose members were Daniel Carroll, Edmund Randolph, and Joseph Montgomery (Pa.) (see headnote). JM and three other delegates were added to this committee on 5 August, eleven days before its recommendations were submitted to Congress (*JCC*, XXIII, 481, 524 n.). The present report by JM, together with the communication of 27 October 1781 from the legislature of Massachusetts, were included among those recommendations and printed for the first time in the journal of Congress for 20 August 1782 (*JCC*, XXIII, 471–81). See also Motion Concerning Peace Negotiations, 17 June 1782, and n. 1.

Perhaps in connection with drafting these instructions, JM made a copy of a long letter written on 15 November 1781 by Brigadier General Lachlan McIntosh of Georgia to Edward Telfair and Noble Wymberley Jones, two of the delegates in Congress from that state (LC: Madison Papers). JM docketed his transcript, "Extent & foundation of the territorial claim of Georgia stated by Genl. McIntosh Jany. 1782." By a detailed tracing through charters, peace treaties, and royal proclamations, beginning with the charter of 1662 to the Carolina proprietors and ending with the Proclamation of 1763, McIntosh sought to demonstrate that the correct boundary between Georgia and East Florida was the St. Mary's River and that the considerable number of people living north of 31° north latitude along the Mississippi River were, as most of them wished to be, within his state rather than in West Florida. He also stressed that Georgia's southern frontier line was of much more than local concern, because wherever that boundary was drawn in a treaty of peace with Great Britain would fix the southern limits of the United States.

Virginia Delegates to Benjamin Harrison

RC (Virginia State Library). Written by Edmund Randolph. Docketed: "Lre from Delegates in Congress Dated Jany 8th. 1782[.] Inclosing Mr D Murrays papers[,] Also facts and reasons respecting the incorporation of the National Bank."

PHILADELPHIA Jany. 8. 1782.

SIR

Your excellency's favor of the 28th. Ulto, not having acknowledged the receipt of our despatches by Capt. Irish, we shall repeat them, unless the next post should announce his arrival.[1]

We cannot but lament the distressing and degrading situation, in which we are placed, from the scantiness and uncertainty of our supplies, in which our own private credit can avail us nothing, and prices are immoderate and ruinous. We beg the attention of the executive to this point, important to ourselves, and perhaps important to our country.[2]

The inclosures (No 1. & 2) were received from a Mr. Murray.[3] He has painted his services to Virginia at the Illinois, in strong terms, and his sufferings on her account in stronger. We have therefore undertaken to transmit to your board his state of both; requesting, that some answer may be given to his application.

Being disposed to advance, on every proper occasion, the views of our ally, and to demonstrate to Great Britain, how practicable it is to renounce her manufactures and produce, we rendered every aid in our power to the resolution, which the president has sent on, recommending more effectual provision against the introduction of British merchandizes. As these considerations were the grounds of the resolution, we cannot doubt, that our legislature will execute the recommendation.[4] It will be remembered, that the late ordinance, respecting captures, which has been forwarded to the judges of the court of the Admiralty thro' your excellency, relates to this species of commodities, when found on water only.[5]

The superintendant of finance is instructed to transmit to the several states copies of the act, incorporating the national bank. He probably will be explicit on the benefits to be expected from such an institution. To him we shall consign this part of the subject.[6]

But some scruples having been entertained as to the authority of congress to grant a charter of incorporation, we cannot forbear to mention the predicament, in which this body stood.

When the establishment of a bank was proposed to congress on the 26th. day of May last, its utility was immediately seen. They accordingly approved the plan, and promised to support it in the most effectual manner. Among other things, they stipulated to pass an act of incorporation; altho' objections were suggested against such an engagement. After a vote to this effect, subscriptions were made upon the expectation of a charter from congress, the president and directors chosen, and we were required to fulfil our contract. The same doubts upon congressional power were again urged; but nothing decisive was done, until a committee, appointed to confer with the bank, reported the result of the conference. They informed congress that they had communicated to the bank the difficulties, which occurred in granting a charter; but that they were answered, that the promise of a preceding congress was binding on a subsequent one; that the subscribers would be free to withdraw their subscriptions, unless a charter should pass from congress, and that tedious and expensive arrangements had been made for commencing the operations of the bank. The financier added, that a delay in these operations would injure him in his attempt towards a payment to the army. Pressed as they were by these representations, congress did incorporate the bank; some of those, who voted in the affirmative thinking themselves obliged by the engagement in may, others contending for a constitutional power in these cases, and others assenting to it from absolute necessity. The resolution subjoined to the act will therefore, we hope, be complied with by the several legislatures.[7]

We have the honor, Sir, to be with great respect yr. excellency's mo. ob. servts.

EDM: RANDOLPH
J. MADISON JR.
JOS: JONES

[1] See *Papers of Madison*, III, 309, n. 1. Benjamin Harrison's letter of 28 December 1781 has not been found. For Harrison's receipt of "the packet by Captain [Nathaniel] Irish," see Harrison to Virginia Delegates, 11 January 1782.

[2] On the day after this letter was written, through the good offices of Thomas Pleasants, Jr., the agent of David Ross, JM borrowed £100, Pennsylvania currency, from Haym Salomon, a Philadelphia broker (Harrison to Virginia Delegates, 9 February; and Expense Account as a Delegate in Congress, 20 March 1782). See also *Papers of Madison*, III, 327.

[3] Daniel Murray. See *Papers of Madison*, III, 342–44.

[4] See *Papers of Madison,* III, 338; 339, nn. By "An act for seizure and condemnation of British goods found on land," passed on 2 July 1782, the Virginia General Assembly complied with the request of Congress but stipulated that "the operation of this act shall be, and is hereby suspended until the rest of the United States shall have passed similar laws on this subject" (Minute Book, House of Delegates, May 1782, p. 86; Hening, *Statutes,* XI, 101–3; Harrison to Virginia Delegates, 18 May and 6 July 1782).

[5] See *Papers of Madison,* III, 217–19; 235–41; 338; 339, n. 2. The editors have been unable to determine when Governor Harrison received a copy of the "late ordinance" for transmission to Benjamin Waller, Richard Cary, and William Roscow Wilson Curle, judges of the Court of Admiralty of Virginia, sitting at Williamsburg. Immediately after its enactment on 4 December, this ordinance had been issued as a broadside by David C. Claypoole of Philadelphia (*JCC,* XXI, 1200). On the date of the present letter, Congress adopted "an Ordinance for amending the Ordinance, ascertaining what captures on water shall be lawful" (*JCC,* XXII, 10–11). As soon as this ordinance was printed by Claypoole, it was dispatched to the executive of each state (*JCC,* XXIII, 885; *Pennsylvania Archives,* 1st ser., IX, 479–80). The measure is in the *Virginia Gazette,* 16 February 1782.

[6] In his circular letter of 8 January 1782, addressed to the executive of each state and enclosing a copy of the ordinance of 31 December 1781, incorporating the "Subscribers to the Bank of North America," Robert Morris enthusiastically pointed out the vital services which the institution, if "conducted on the principles of equity, justice, prudence and economy," could render to the United States, each state, and to "all the Traders of every State" (*Pennsylvania Archives,* 1st ser., IX, 477–78). For the ordinance of incorporation, see *JCC,* XXI, 1187–90.

[7] Robert Morris' plan for a bank provided that "the subscribers shall be incorporated under the name of the President, Directors and Company of the Bank of North America" (*JCC,* XX, 546 n.). Thus the expected source of the charter of incorporation was not designated, but Morris implied that it would be Congress, since his plan allotted to the superintendent of finance the prime role of overseeing the proposed institution.

Laid before Congress on 21 May 1781, the plan was referred three days later to the committee, with John Witherspoon (N.J.) as its chairman, which had been appointed over two weeks earlier "to devise further ways and means to defray the expences of the ensuing campaign and what farther measures may be adopted for the better regulation of the public finances" (*JCC,* XX, 487, 519, 530–31). On 26 May the committee's report, comprising four resolutions in Morris' handwriting, was submitted to Congress. All four resolutions were apparently agreed to on that day, although only the first was adopted by a tallied vote. This first resolution, after stating that Congress approved the plan of the bank and pledged to "promote and support the same by such ways and means, from time to time, as may appear necessary for the institution and consistent with the public good," continued by affirming "That the subscribers to the said bank shall be incorporated agreeably to the principles and terms of the plan, under the name of *The President, Directors and company of the bank of North-America,* so soon as the subscription shall be filled, the directors and president chosen, and application for that purpose made to Congress by the president and directors elected." The final clause of this resolution obviously removed whatever doubt was warranted by the language of Morris' plan that Congress would be asked to issue the charter of incorporation. At the instance of Thomas Smith (Pa.), each delegate's vote on this resolution was recorded in the journal. Twenty delegates approved the resolution and only Smith, James Lovell, Artemas Ward (Mass.), and JM, unsupported by his three colleagues from Virginia, opposed it (*JCC,* XX, 546–48).

Clearly, the premise of the resolution was that Congress had the authority to issue the charter, even though the vote did not pledge Congress to do more than receive a petition asking for a charter. JM's disagreement with the premise almost certainly accounts for his adverse vote. In other words, he recognized that considerations of the general welfare made a national bank an urgent necessity, but he believed on constitutional grounds that it should be chartered by a state rather than by Congress. A decade later in the House of Representatives he would stress the same point in arguing against the proposal of Alexander Hamilton to have Congress charter a national bank. The following sentences, allegedly summarizing what JM said in the course of his speech of 8 February 1791 on the subject, must be read in the context of this position to avoid the impression that he had opposed the Bank of North America itself. "The Bank of North America he had opposed, as he considered the institution as a violation of the Confederation. The State of Massachusetts, he recollected, voted with him on that occasion" (*Annals of the Congress of the United States,* 1st Cong., 3d sess., col. 1959).

On the same day that the present dispatch was written, JM further clarified his position in a letter to Edmund Pendleton (*q.v.*). In this he pointed out that, when adopting the ordinance of incorporation on 31 December 1781, Congress deferred to the constitutional scruples of many delegates by hinging the success of the institution upon the willingness of the legislature of each state to grant the Bank of North America a monopoly of the banking business within that state for the duration of the war and to enact statutes providing for the condign punishment of counterfeiters of the notes of the Bank and of its officers or employees who were guilty of embezzlement or other fraud (*JCC,* XX, 545–48; XXI, 1190). Congress further guarded the sovereignty of each state by inserting near the close of the ordinance of incorporation an amendment by Abraham Clark (N.J.) reading, "Provided, always, that nothing herein before contained, shall be construed to authorize the said corporation, to exercise any powers in any of the United States, repugnant to the laws or constitution of such State" (*JCC,* XXI, 1189; NA: PCC, No. 59, III, 309–11). Congress also, at the instance of Edmund Randolph, resolved, "That it be recommended to the legislature of each State, to pass such laws as they may judge necessary, for giving the foregoing ordinance its full operation" (*ibid.,* No. 59, III, 315; *JCC,* XXI, 1190). Whether these safeguards of state sovereignty led JM to vote for the ordinance of incorporation is not known, because the votes of the members of Congress were not entered in the journal. In all likelihood JM was among those who, as he remarked in his letter of this day to Pendleton, cast "an acquiescing rather than an affirmative vote." By this subtle distinction JM probably meant that many delegates, in spite of their conviction that they were supporting an act in violation of the Articles of Confederation, voted to have Congress charter the bank because of the extreme and immediate need for it at a time when the Pennsylvania General Assembly, which constitutionally should have been the incorporator, was not in session. Although the analogy is not exact, JM's argument of "necessity" suggests his position in the 1790's, when he upheld the exercise of "implied powers," provided that it was a requisite rather than merely a possible means of making effective a field of authority clearly delegated to Congress by the Constitution of the United States.

Before Morris' circular letter (n. 6, above) reached Governor Harrison, the Virginia General Assembly had adjourned. At the opening of the session of May 1782, the governor forwarded to the speaker of the House of Delegates, without recommendation, Morris' letter and a copy of "the resolution of Congress establishing a public bank" (McIlwaine, *Official Letters,* III, 214). These documents were laid before the House on 15 May, the first day enough members assembled to make a quorum. There being no known extant journal of the House, such consideration as was given to the subject must be traced in the manuscript minutes kept by the clerk, whose entries are frequently too cryptic to be understood. The bank proposition was discussed in committee of the whole on 16 and 17 May and on the latter day assigned to a committee comprising twelve of the ablest delegates with Mann Page, Jr., as chairman (Minute Book, House of Delegates, May 1782, pp. 44, 46, 48). Beyond that, evidence is negative, strongly suggesting that neither report nor recommendations ever reached the floor. Hening's *Statutes* contains no law relating to the Bank of North America enacted by that session.

To Edmund Pendleton

RC (LC: Madison Papers). Docketed by Pendleton, "James Madison, Esq. Jan. 8, 1782."

PHILADA. Jany. 8th. 1782

DEAR SIR

I have before me your favor of the 31st. Ulto.[1] I regret much the refusal of Mr. J. to become a member of the Virga. delegation, not only as it deprives his country of that particular service, but as I fear it proceeds from a fixed disinclination to all public employments.[2]

Yesterday was opened for the first time the bank instituted under the auspices of Congress. Its principal founder is Mr: R. M who has certain prerogatives wth. respect to it in his quality of superintendant of finance.[3] It is pretty analagous in its principles to the bank of England. The stock subscribed is 400,000 dollars.[4] When the scheme was originally proposed to Congress for their approbation & patronage, a promise was given that as soon as it was ripe for operation the company sd. be incorporated. a few days ago[5] the fulfilment of the promise was claimed. The competency of Congress to such an act had been called in question in the first instance, but the subject not lying in so near & distinct a view, the objections did not prevail. On the last occasion, the general opinion though with some exceptions was that the Confederation gave no such power and that the exercise of it would not bear the test of a forensic disquisition[6] & consequently would not avail the institution. The bank however supposing that such a sanction from Congress wd. at least give it a dignity & preeminence in the public opinion, urged the engagement of Congress; that on this engagement the subscriptions had been made; & that a disappointment would leave the subscribers free to withdraw their names. These considerations were reinforced by the Superintendt. of finance, who relyed on this institution as a great auxiliary to his department, and in particular expected aid from it in a payment he is exerting himself to make to the army. The immediate interposition of Congress was rendered the more essential too by the sudden adjournment of the Assembly of this State,[7] to whom the bank might have been referred for the desired incorporation, which it was the opinion of many would have given them a sufficient legal existence in every state. You will conceive the dilemma in which these circumstances placed the members who felt on one side the *importance* of the institution, and on the other a want of power and an aversion to assume it. Something like a middle way finally produced an acquiessing rather than an affirmative vote. A charter of incorporation was granted, with a recommendation to the States to give it all the necessary validity within their respective jurisdictions.[8] As this is a tacit admission of a defect of power I hope it will be an antidote against the poisonous tendency of precedents of usurpation.

In the ordinance lately passed for regulating captures, which I presume you have seen, a clause was inserted, exposing to capture all merchantizes produced in G.B. if coming into these States, & within three leagues of the coast, altho the property of a neutral nation. Congress have now recommended to the States to subject them to seizure during the war, if found on land within their respective limit[s.] These measures had become necessary to check an evil which was every day increasing, and which both enabled & encouraged G. Britain to persevere in the war, at the same time that it mortifyed our ally with daily seeing the fruits of his generosity to us remitted in payment to the rival of his nation & the enemy of both.[9]

The success of the Marquis de Bouilli agst St. Eustatius is sufficiently confirmed. about 700 prisoners were taken. As we have good reason to believe strong reinforcements are on the way from France to the W. I. this loss may be considered as a presage of much greater misfortunes.[10]

I am Dr Sir Yrs. sincerely

J. MADISON JR.

[1] See *Papers of Madison*, III, 347–48.

[2] For Thomas Jefferson's election to Congress and refusal to serve, see *ibid*., III, 338, n. 3.

[3] See Virginia Delegates to Harrison, 8 January 1782, n. 6. According to Articles XI and XII of the plan for the Bank of North America, Robert Morris as superintendent of finance was authorized "at all times, to examine into the affairs of the Bank, and for that purpose shall have access to all the books and papers." On every day except Sundays he was to be provided with a statement "of the cash account and of the notes issued and received" (*JCC*, XX, 545–46 n.). In his extended com-

ment on each of the seventeen articles of the plan, Morris justified these "prerogatives" as a way to prevent fraud and mismanagement, and as a substitute for frequent inspection by private citizens whereby "the National Enemies would be apprized of our resources & operations" (NA: PCC, No. 137, I, 25–27).

[4] Article I of the plan provided that "a subscription be opened for four hundred thousand dollars, in shares of four hundred dollars each, to be paid in gold or silver" (*JCC*, XX, 545 n.).

[5] Possibly on 29 December 1781 when the "Committee appointed to confer with the Bank" reported to Congress (*JCC*, XXI, 1185). The preamble of the ordinance of incorporation of 31 December 1781, which closely followed a draft written by Edmund Randolph as a member of this committee, includes the words, "and, whereas, the subscription thereto [the bank stock] is now filled from an expectation of a charter of incorporation from Congress" (*JCC*, XXI, 1188, 1189 n.).

[6] Probably meaning a constitutional debate, with the victor chosen by an impartial judge or judges. If JM had in mind a test before a court, it would be interesting to know what tribunal, in his opinion, was competent to exercise jurisdiction.

[7] On 28 December 1781, only one day before the ordinance of incorporation was given its first reading in Congress. The Pennsylvania General Assembly fixed 10 February 1782 as the opening date of its next session (*Pennsylvania Gazette, and Weekly Advertiser*, 2 January 1782).

[8] See Virginia Delegates to Harrison, 8 January 1782, and n. 7.

[9] *Ibid.*, and nn. 4 and 5.

[10] See Virginia Delegates to Harrison, 1 January 1782, n. 5. The "misfortunes" befell the French rather than the British. Early in December 1781 a formidable fleet, convoying transports loaded with troops, sailed from Brest and Bordeaux. Soon after losing nineteen ships as prizes captured by British men-of-war, this French armada was further weakened by a severe storm. Eventually, in March 1782, two war vessels and five transports reached the West Indies (W[illiam] M. James, *The British Navy in Adversity: A Study of the War of American Independence* [London, 1926], pp. 312–15, 331).

Benjamin Harrison to Virginia Delegates

FC (Virginia State Library). In the hand of Charles Hay, assistant clerk of the Council of State.

In Council January 11th. 1782[1]

Gentlemen

We have the honor to acknowledge the receipt of your favor of the 1st instant and to inform you that the packet by Captain Irish did not get to hand time enough for the assembly which rose on the fifth.[2] They have passed a bill for raising 3000 men. We have no doubt of getting them provided Congress will forward the Continental bounty which in addition to twenty dollars given by the State we consider very sufficient for the purpose and gives us every reason to hope for the speedy Completion of our Quota, but ready money alone can give Success to this business.[3]

They have laid a Tax of one per Cent. on land, ten Shillings on all negroes ten shillings two pounds of bacon and half a bushel of wheat on all white Titheables—besides an heavy duty on all imported Articles.[4]

Armands Corps and all the Continental Staff are unprovided for, nor has the State any means of supporting them. The well known disorders and Irregularities of that Corps are much to be dreaded; We have therefore to press in the most earnest manner that they be immediately furnished with such necessaries as they may want or that they be removed out of the State.[5]

We have also to request that you forward the journals for the years 1777 & 78 also from the 10th of May 79, to the 17th; from the 20th of June to 26 of July; from the 2d of October to 11th Do. from the 31st July 80 to this day and also the regulations respecting the promotion of Officers.[6] I am &c

BENJAMIN HARRISON

1 This letter was not approved in Council until 12 January (*Journals of the Council of State*, III, 25).

2 See *Papers of Madison*, III, 305, n. 1.

3 "An act to recruit the Virginia line on the continental establishment" became a law on 5 January 1782 (*Journal of the House of Delegates*, October 1781, p. 74; Hening, *Statutes*, X, 499–500). By an ordinance of 3 October 1780, as amended eighteen days later, Congress had promised a bounty of "not exceeding fifty dollars" to each recruit who enlisted for the duration of the war and fixed Virginia's quota as eight regiments of infantry, one of artillery, and two of cavalry. On 10 December 1781 Congress decided to retain this quota for the next year, but the delinquencies of the states in paying their money quotas left Congress unable during the early months of 1782 to fulfill the pledge of a $50.00 bounty to each recruit (*JCC*, XVIII, 894–95, 959; XXI, 1163–64; Jameson to JM, 23 February 1782; McIlwaine, *Official Letters*, III, 214).

4 This paragraph mentions merely a few provisions of two comprehensive and complicated statutes—one entitled "An act for laying taxes in certain enumerated commodities," and the other "An act for ascertaining certain taxes and duties, and for establishing a permanent revenue." They were enacted on 5 January 1782. Harrison would have been more accurate if he had mentioned that masters were exempted from taxation on aged and infirm slaves and that free Negroes paid the same taxes as whites (*Journal of the House of Delegates*, October 1781, p. 74; Hening, *Statutes*, X, 490–92, 501–17).

5 By this date Charles Armand Tuffin, Marquis de La Rouërie, usually known in America simply as Colonel Charles Armand (1750–1793), had exasperated Governor Harrison by his complaints about unco-operative Virginia officials and by his arbitrary impressment of wagons and horses for the use of his partisan legion. In a letter of 6 December 1781, Harrison had acceded to the request of Armand to recruit troopers in Virginia but had bluntly told him that, if he needed wagons, he should seek them from the continental quartermaster. Although the differences of opinion between the governor and the colonel were to continue for many months, Harrison no doubt hoped even at this time that Armand and his legion would be

removed from the state (McIlwaine, *Official Letters*, III, 106–7, 120, 127, 137, 196, 315).

Ever since Armand had entered the continental service as a colonel on 10 May 1777 (*JCC*, VII, 346), he had commanded cavalry-infantry units, mostly comprising "Deserters from the Enemy's foreign Troops, French men, and others not owing Allegiance to the King of Great Britain" (*JCC*, XI, 642–45; XIV, 755; XVI, 187, 203). Although this miscellaneous personnel, frequently of dubious antecedents, was hard to discipline, it had served effectively in the field, except at the Battle of Camden (Henry Lee, *Memoirs of the War in the Southern Department of the United States* [2 vols.; Philadelphia, 1812], I, 181 n.). Armand had often threatened to resign unless he was made a brigadier general—a rank finally awarded him by Congress in 1783—but his undoubted devotion to the cause led him to return to France for about eight months in 1781, seeking there at his own expense to collect better equipment for the men and horses of his command (*JCC*, XIII, 148; XVI, 72, 78, 187; XVIII, 1010–11, 1058; XIX, 75–76; XXIV, 343–44). When he returned to the United States in September of that year, he found that his corps had been reduced by attrition during his absence to about sixty-five men, of whom over half had no mounts (*JCC*, XX, 682; NA: PCC, No. 164, fols. 454, 466). Authorized by Congress to rebuild his legion to its full strength of about 250 troopers, Armand set about doing it in Virginia with his customary vigor and disregard of civilian officials (*JCC*, XXI, 976, 994, 1024).

[6] Beginning with its first meeting in May 1775, the Second Continental Congress employed a succession of printers, including William and Thomas Bradford, Robert Aitken, John Dunlap, and David C. Claypoole, to publish its non-secret proceedings, or extracts from them on particular subjects. Except between April and December 1779, when a weekly edition was provided for, Congress tried to have the journal appear in monthly installments, followed by an edition embracing a full calendar year. Regularity of publication was interrupted by the British occupation of Philadelphia and frequently by shortage of money or paper. Article IX of the Articles of Confederation stipulated that copies of the monthly edition should be supplied to the members of Congress for the use of the legislatures of their states. The appendix of the concluding volume of each year of the *JCC* lists early editions of the journal. As samples of the attention given by Congress to the publication of its proceedings, see *JCC*, III, 393; V, 829; XI, 416; XII, 1115–16; XIII, 179, 395; XV, 1459–62; XVIII, 1237. Upon his return to Virginia in March 1782, Edmund Randolph apparently delivered the journals requested by Governor Harrison in the present letter (Virginia Delegates to Harrison, 15 February and 19 March 1782).

On 25 May 1781 Congress had adopted rules to regulate the promotion of army officers (*JCC*, XX, 539–42), but on 16 November 1781, by an almost unanimous vote, including JM's, Congress decided that these regulations should not bar the promotion of "any officer, on account of extraordinary merit or eminent services, contrary to the rule of succession therein mentioned" (*JCC*, XXI, 1119).

From David Jameson

RC (LC: Rives Collection of Madison Papers). The cover is missing, and the letter is undated. Probably many years later, JM wrote "[1782?]" at the top of the first sheet.

[*ca.* 12 January 1782][1]

Dr. Sir

By last Post I told you Mr Stark had written to you about your Accot. in a conversation with him since on the subject, I find I was mistaken, he intended to write but did not, because he could not fill up the blanks. He expected the Assembly would have fixed the allowance but they have not done so.[2] He wishes you to send a state of the whole Accot. at one view We have put into Mr Ross's hands a Bill of Exchange for about £900 sterling. that, or the value, he will send to the Delegates.[3] I shall be glad to know how long this will last, that some method may be fallen on to procure more in time—what this method will be I do not now know, as the assembly have with the stroke of a pen put it out of the Agents power to do *anything*. After encouraging him to make large contracts in behalf of the State, they have repealed all the Laws by which he was to make good those Contracts.[4] And they have put nothing in the power of the Executive, until the Revenue and *new* Specific Acts can be enforced.[5] I hope however you will somehow or other be better supplied than you have been, for let us at home suffer what we may it is cruel, it is shameful, to let those who serve the State abroad suffer. for the quarters Salary due to the Council the first day of April, they recd. as much paper Money as would purchase only £72 Specie. Since that time, no officer of Government has been paid a shilling. the last Assembly fixed their pay in Specie,[6] but as there is no Specie, nor any thing in hand that will raise it, some of them (I am told) have within these few days taken Auditors Warrants to the amount of their pay, and sold for less than a third of their nominal Value Some who have more paper Money than will pay their arrears of taxes, are selling it for Specie at 3000 for one,[7] rather than carry it into the Treasury & take certificates. There is but little Specie in the state—not any in the Treasury—and those whose services are required by the State, will not take certificates, so that the meanest Coblar can now obtain Credit where the State cannot. how humiliating, how hurtful to the feelings of every friend to his Country: And where it will end God only knows. While the tax payable in Tobacco continued in force, the State had some Credit, but that being set aside we are now quite Bankrupt.[8] I write this only to yourself. Can any method be fallen on to releave us by a loan or otherwise? On looking over the dispatches by Irish recd. while I was below, I find you understood that the Bill drawn in his favour, was to be paid out of the 4/10 of the 18t. of March money. The Bill is not now in Town, therefore I cannot speak possitively, but I am pretty sure it was drawn on our Treasurer[9] And we never did conceive ourselves or the Treasurer of the State to have any controul of that money—nor ever ordered the payment of a shilling of it on any occasion[10] You some time ago asked why we desired the British prisoners to be removed. it was on supposition we must guard and feed them if they remained in the State, which it was not in our power to do, unless Congress would have furnished Specie for the purpose; and that we had no reason to expect. The people in that part of the Country supposing they were to have their provisions taken from them & to receive certificates as usual; expresly refused to supply them. Had we known Congress intended to feed them by contract and to pay Specie, the people would have been very glad to keep them. it would indeed have been a considerable benefit to the State, and particularly to the Counties near Winchester[11]

We are again disapointed by having no Mail from the Northward. I suppose you have had hard frost. We too have had some severe Weather. Tuesday last was I think as cold a day as I ever felt, the frost continued, and thursday evening it began to Snow, & contd Snowing all yesterday. however it is not very deep

I am Yrs sincerely

DAVID JAMESON

[1] The clue to the exact dating of this letter is chiefly in its final paragraph. As was his custom, Jameson was writing on a Saturday and, in this instance, it was on the closing day of a week in Richmond that included an unusually cold Tuesday and a snowy Thursday evening and Friday. The particular Saturday could not have been earlier than 12 January, for, until he resumed his seat on the Council of State on Thursday the tenth, after an absence from Richmond of about three weeks, Jameson had had no access to "the dispatches by Irish" that had arrived on the fifth. By stating in his letter of 26 January to JM (*q.v.*) that "In my last I mentd Gen Greenes requisition," Jameson eliminated the nineteenth of that month from consideration, because the "requisition" is not mentioned in the present dispatch.

Lacking a daily report of Richmond's weather in January and early February 1782, the latest Saturday when he could have written this letter is more problematical. The reasons for excluding 2 and 9 February are somewhat complicated. At the outset of the present letter Jameson remarks that "By last Post" he had mentioned

"Mr Stark." This eliminates 2 February as a possible date, because "By last Post" would then have been 26 January, and his letter to JM on that day makes no reference to Stark. Jameson's statement in the present letter that the "Bill [of Captain Irish] is not now in Town" removes 9 February from consideration, because this bill was before the Council of State three days earlier, and Jameson had attended that session (*Journals of the Council of State,* III, 40). Since no letters from JM to Jameson are known to exist, acknowledgments in them of letters from Jameson are obviously unavailable for help in fixing the date in this instance.

[2] Bolling Stark was an auditor of public accounts for the Commonwealth of Virginia. By "the blanks," Jameson meant those left by JM on his expense accounts of 20 June, 20 September, and 20 December 1781 because he did not know his per diem salary and allowances (*Papers of Madison,* III, 163, 264, 334). Before adjourning on 5 January 1782, the General Assembly had provided for many state officials, not including the delegates in Congress, a revised salary scale which, much more realistically than the one it superseded, recognized the depreciation of paper currency (Hening, *Statutes,* X, 493–94).

[3] See Expense Account as Delegate, 20 March 1782.

[4] Besides the law mentioned in his letter of 26 January (*q.v.*), Jameson probably also referred to another statute enacted by the General Assembly on 5 January 1782 whereby the legal-tender quality of all currency issued by Virginia was voided for "payment of any debt or contract whatsoever, except in payment of taxes due" in 1781 (*Journal of the House of Delegates,* October 1781, p. 74; Hening, *Statutes,* X, 456). Although David Ross, in a letter of 2 April 1782, notified the governor that his expected election to the General Assembly as a delegate from Fluvanna County would legally bar him from continuing as commercial agent of Virginia, he may have been the more willing to resign that office because of the legislation mentioned above (*Calendar of Virginia State Papers,* III, 118). On 24 May, William Hay replaced Ross as commercial agent (*Journals of the Council of State,* III, 97).

[5] For these laws, see Hening, *Statutes,* X, 456–57, 501–17.

[6] By the statute mentioned in n. 2, the eight privy councilors, taken together, were to receive annually £3,200, "to be divided amongst them according to their attendance." Whatever salaries under the old scale had been due to the councilors since 1 July 1781 were to be paid in specie "after the rate of twenty shillings for each hundred pounds of tobacco."

[7] The Virginia General Assembly, in its session of October 1781, had set one thousand to one as the depreciation rate for the paper currency of the state in relation to gold (Hening, *Statutes,* X, 473).

[8] Although Jameson does not qualify his statement, he must have intended it to apply only to the tax on land. According to "An act for ascertaining certain taxes and duties, and for establishing a permanent revenue," passed by the General Assembly on 5 January 1782, all other taxes could be paid "in specie, tobacco, hemp, or flour," in certain stipulated proportions (*Journal of the House of Delegates,* October 1781, p. 74; Hening, *Statutes,* X, 508).

[9] George Brooke (1728–1782) of King and Queen County served as treasurer of the Commonwealth from his election to that office by the General Assembly in December 1779 until his death in April 1782 (*Journal of the House of Delegates,* October 1779, pp. 105, 106; *Journals of the Council of State,* III, 76; *Virginia Gazette,* 13 April 1782).

[10] Upon receiving a statement of account from Captain Nathaniel Irish, the Council of State on 6 February requested John Hopkins, Jr., in charge of the continental loan office in Virginia (*Papers of Madison,* III, 325, n. 2.), "to pay a bill drawn by Michael Hillegas esqr. Continental Treasurer on . . . the State of Virginia in

favor of Samuel Hodgden Dep: Com: Gen: of mil: Stores bearing date July 10th 1781 for ten thousand Dollars of the new emission of Continental Money; it appearing from the face of the said Bill that it was intended to be paid out of the four tenths received for continental uses" (*Journals of the Council of State*, III, 40). But Hopkins quickly convinced the governor that the charge had been assessed against state rather than continental funds. The former being exhausted, the bill remained unpaid. See Harrison to Virginia Delegates, 9 February 1782. As already pointed out, the ordinance of Congress of 18 March 1780, providing for the exchange of continental currency for a new issue of paper money at the rate of forty for one, stipulated that Congress should have for its own use four-tenths of the new issue, the amount in dollars depending upon the quantity of the old currency which each state redeemed of its quota (*Papers of Madison*, II, 49, n. 2).

[11] See *ibid.*, III, 313, n. 2; 319, n. 1; 335–36. When JM asked "why we desired the British prisoners to be removed" is not known to the editors.

Virginia Delegates to Benjamin Harrison

RC (Virginia State Library). Written by Edmund Randolph and addressed to "His excellency the governor of Virginia Richmond."

PHILADELPHIA Jany. 15. 1782.

SIR

Having informed your excellency in our last letter, that we should repeat our dispatches, transmitted to Capt. Irish, unless you should announce the receipt of them by yesterday's post, and hearing nothing from the executive, we shall prepare them for the mail of the next week. We unfortunately supposed, that he would convey them in the most expeditious manner. But we have now reason to believe, that his delay on the road has been occasioned by sickness.[1]

The inclosure contains an answer to the letter, addressed to General Washington by the speaker of the house of delegates on the subject of thanks. We beg leave to consign it to your excellency's care.[2]

We have the honor, Sir, to be with great respect and esteem yr. mo. ob: servt's

JAS. MADISON JR.
JOS: JONES.
EDM: RANDOLPH.

[1] See *Papers of Madison*, III, 309, n. 1.

[2] On 17 December 1781 the Virginia House of Delegates unanimously passed a resolution praising Washington "for his late glorious services at Yorktown" (*Journal of the House of Delegates*, October 1781, p. 42). John Tyler (1747–1813) of

Charles City County, the speaker of the House of Delegates, forwarded the resolution on 21 December to the Virginia delegates for transmission to Washington. Washington's acknowledgment of 8 January was relayed in the present letter to Governor Harrison for delivery to Tyler (Fitzpatrick, *Writings of Washington*, XXIII, 435). He is usually referred to as Judge John Tyler in order to distinguish him from his son, President John Tyler. After 1784, except between 1808 and 1811, when Judge Tyler was governor of Virginia, he served again as speaker of the House and successively as a judge of the Court of Admiralty, the Supreme Court of Appeals, and the General Court of his state, and, for the two years before his death, of the United States District Court for Virginia (E. Griffith Dodson, *Speakers and Clerks of the Virginia House of Delegates, 1776–1955* [Richmond, 1956], p. 23).

Benjamin Harrison to Virginia Delegates

FC (Virginia State Library). In the hand of Charles Hay.

IN COUNCIL January 15th. 1782

GENTLEMEN

The inclosed resolution of the Assembly just came to hand directing no money to be paid or specifics[1] delivered but by special order of Congress or the Financier General You will please therefore to put it in such a train that Congress may avail themselves of any supplies we may be able to furnish them.[2] I am &c

BENJA HARRISON[3]

[1] That is, specific commodities, such as food, other military matériel, or tobacco.

[2] On 5 January 1782 the Virginia General Assembly resolved, "That the Executive are hereby directed not to pay any money or specifics on continental account, except to the financier general or his order, or other person specially appointed by Congress to receive the same; and that particular accounts of such payments and their vouchers for the same, be laid before the General Assembly, at the beginning of every session" (*Journal of the House of Delegates*, October 1781, p. 73). For an explanation of this resolution, see Harrison to Virginia Delegates, 1 March 1782. The delegates assured Harrison in their letter of 12 March (*q.v.*) that they had delivered a copy of the resolution to Robert Morris. See also Harrison to Morris, 27 March 1782 (McIlwaine, *Official Letters*, III, 184–85).

[3] On 1 February 1782 Edmund Randolph acknowledged to Harrison, "in behalf of the Virginia delegation," his dispatch of 17 January. The journal of the Council of State usually made note of letters which were to be or had been written by the governor to the delegates, but no entry of this kind appears in the record for 17 January (*Journals of the Council of State*, III, 28). Randolph may have meant to acknowledge receipt of the present letter rather than one dated two days later; but if he did receive a letter of the seventeenth, it is now missing. See Virginia Delegates to Harrison, 8 February 1782, n. 1.

To Thomas Jefferson

RC (LC: Madison Papers). The cover is missing, but the letter was docketed by Jefferson, "Madison Jas. Jany. 15. 1782."

PHILADA: Jany. 15th. 1782

DEAR SIR

Your favor of the day of written on the eve of your departure from Richmond came safe to hand by the last week's post.[1] The result of the attack on your administration was so fully anticipated that it made little impression on me.[2] If it had been consistent with your sentiments & views to engage in the new service to which you were called, it wd. have afforded me both unexpected & singular satisfaction, not only from the personal interest I felt in it but from the important aid which the interests of the state would probably have derived from it.[3] What I particularly refer to is her claim to Western territory. The machinations which have long been practised by interested individuals agst. this claim are well known to you. The late proceedings within the walls of Congress in consequence of the territorial cessions produced[4] by their recommendations[5] to the States claiming the Western Country were many weeks ago transmitted for the Legislature by a Capt. Irish. By the same conveyance I wrote to you on the subject.[6] We have the mortification to find by our latest letters from Richmond that this Gentleman had not at the date of them appeared there.[7] As it is uncertain whether that information may not have totally miscarried it will be proper to repeat to you that the States besides Virga. from which the cessions came were Connecticut & N York. The cession of the former consisted of all her claim west of N. York as far as the Missippi. That of the latter of all her claims beyond a certain western limit drawn on the occasion. The cession of Cont. extended to the soil only expressly reserving the jurisdiction. That of N.Y. made no reservation.[8] These cessions with that of Virga. & sundry memorials from the Inda. & other land Companies were referred to a Committee composed of a Member from N.H. R.I. N.J. Pa. & Maryld. The ingredients of this composition prepared us for the complexion of their proceedings.[9] Their first step was to investigate & discuss the respective titles of the States to the territory ceded[.] as this was directly in the face of the recommendation of Congress which professed to bury all such discussions & might prejudge future controversies between individual members of the Union, we refused to exhibit any evidence in favor of the title of Va.

and endeavoured though in vain to prevail on Congress to interdict the Committee from proceeding in the enquiry.[10] The next step of the Committee was still more obnoxious. They went fully into a hearing of the Memorialists through their Agents, & received all the evidence adduced in support of their pretensions. On this occasion we renewed our remonstrances to the Committee & our complaints to Congress, but with as little effect as on the first occasion. The upshot of the whole was a report to Congress rejecting the Cessions of Virga. & Cont. and accepting that of N.Y.; disallowing also, the claims of the Companies N.W. of the Ohio but justifying that of the Inda. Compy. The report seems to distrust the doctrine hitherto maintained, of territorial rights being incident to the U.S. Collectively which are not comprehended within any individual State; substituting the expedient of recognizing the title of N.Y. stretching it over the whole country claimed by the other ceding States, & then accepting a transfer of it to the U.S.[11] In this state the business now rests, the report having never been taken into consideration, nor do we wish it should, till it shall have undergone the consideration of Virga.

In whatever light the policy of this proceeding may be viewed it affords an additional proof of the industry & perseverance with which the territorial rights of Virga. are persecuted, & of the necessity of fortifying them with every precaution which their importance demands. As a very obvious & necessary one we long since recommended to the State an accurate & full collection of the documents which relate to the subject. If the arrival of Capt. Irish had taken place before the adjournt. of the Assembly & during your stay with it we flattered ourselves that this recommendation wd. have been attended to[12] & that the task wd. have fallen on you. As this was not the case we have no hope at present of being enabled from any other sources than the voluntary aids of individuals to contradict even verbally the misrepresentations & calumnies which are daily levelled agst. the claims of Va. & which can not fail to prepossess the public with errors injurious at present to her reputation & which may affect a future decision on her rights. Col. Masons industry & kindness have supplied us with some valuable papers & remarks. Mr. Jones has also recd. from Mr. Pendleton some judicious remarks on the subject.[13] We are still notwithstandg. far from possessing a complete view of it. Will you permit me to ask of you such information as your researches have yielded, with the observations which you have made in the course of them. I would not obtrude such a request on you if the subject were not of public importance & if it could have been addressed with equal prospect of advantage elsewhere. Indeed if you cd. prevail on yourself to spare as much time as would Survey the whole subject, beginning with the original charter, pursuing it thro' the subsequent charters & other public acts of the crown thro' the Govs. of Virga., & referring to all the transactions with the Indians which have been drawn into the question, the public utility I am persuaded wd sufficiently reward you for the labor.[14]

pray did you ever receive a letter from me inclosing a proposition declaratory of the coercive power of Congress over the States? It went by an Express while you were at the head of the Exec.[15]

We have not a word of new[s] from Europe. The French are assemblg a force in the W. Indies which presages further calamities to the English. The Spaniards are also in motion but their Object will probably be both a small & a selfish one.[16] I shall cheerfully send you a line as often as I have a subject for it, tho' I shall be so selfish as to hope for some return for it.

I am Dr Sir Yrs sincerely

J. MADISON JR.

[1] The letter which Jefferson wrote before leaving Richmond on 24 December 1781 for Monticello has not been found.

[2] See *Papers of Madison*, III, 338, n. 3; 347–48; 348, n. 1. Many years later JM, or someone at his direction, inserted a bracket at the beginning of this sentence and another at the close of the second from the last paragraph of the letter, thus indicating the portion to be published. See Madison, *Papers* (Gilpin ed.), I, 106–8.

[3] See *Papers of Madison*, III, 338, n. 3. JM's use of the word "unexpected" may reflect his surprise that the General Assembly had elected to a seat in Congress a man whose weariness with public life had been so positively stated (*Papers of Madison*, III, 45–47). Probably even more "unexpected," this confidence in Jefferson had been expressed only four days after the General Assembly set the date for investigating his administration as governor and nearly two weeks before exonerating him (*Journal of the House of Delegates*, June 1781, p. 15; October 1781, pp. 17, 23–24, 37).

[4] Between "cessions" and "produced," JM at first wrote, then deleted, "offered by several States."

[5] Following this word, JM crossed out "on the subject."

[6] See *Papers of Madison*, III, 307–8; 309, n. 1.

[7] See Virginia Delegates to Harrison, 8 January; and Harrison to Virginia Delegates, 11 January 1782. Of course, this latter dispatch, reporting the receipt of the material sent by Captain Nathaniel Irish, had not reached the delegates when JM wrote the present letter.

[8] On 19 February 1780 the New York legislature had empowered its delegates in Congress "to limit and restrict the boundaries of this State, in the western part thereof, by such line or lines, and in such manner and form, as they shall judge to be expedient; either with respect to the Jurisdiction as well as the right or pre-

emption of soil." Upon laying this offer of cession before Congress on 1 March 1781, the New York delegation "recited, proceeded and executed in due form in behalf of their State," a written "instrument" defining the boundaries of the area to be relinquished solely for the "use and benefit of such of the states as are or shall become parties to the Articles of Confederation" (*JCC,* XIX, 208–13). When Congress finally accepted the offer on 29 October 1782, JM and Theodorick Bland, Jr., the only Virginia delegates then in Congress, voted "no" (*JCC,* XXIII, 694). In October 1780 the General Court of Connecticut, in order to help remove "the obstacle that prevents a Ratification of the Articles of Confederation," ceded to Congress its claim to land situated "westward of the Susquehannah Purchase, so called, and eastward of the river Misisipi." Although in this statute, which was laid before Congress on 31 January 1781, Connecticut relinquished title to the property, she explicitly reserved political jurisdiction over it (Charles J. Hoadly, ed., *The Public Records of the State of Connecticut* [3 vols.; Hartford, Conn., 1894–1922], III, 177–78; *JCC,* XIX, 99). A prolonged and acrimonious boundary dispute between Pennsylvania and Connecticut kept Congress from accepting Connecticut's offer of cession until 1786.

[9] The five members of this committee were Elias Boudinot, James Mitchell Varnum (R.I.), Daniel of St. Thomas Jenifer (Md.), Thomas Smith (Pa.), and Samuel Livermore (N.H.). Except for Livermore, they were hostile to Virginia's western claims and disposed to favor the memorials of land-speculator companies asking Congress to recognize as valid their alleged titles to much of the territory embraced within Virginia's offer of cession. See *Papers of Madison,* III, 210, n. 4; 283, n. 5. The latter footnote cites the many references in *Papers of Madison,* II, which trace the long background of the land problem up to 1 March 1781.

[10] JM here refers to the decision of Congress on 6 September 1780 not to discuss or attempt to decide the validity of Virginia's title to the West or the merits of Maryland's arguments against that title, because "such questions" could not "be now revived with any prospect of conciliation" (*JCC,* XVII, 806). On 26 October 1781 Congress by a vote of five states to three had defeated Randolph's motion to forbid the Boudinot committee "to admit counsel" or to "hear documents, proofs, or evidence, not among the records, nor on the files of Congress, which have not been specially referred to them" (*JCC,* XXI, 1077–78).

[11] The latter half of this paragraph summarizes the course and nature of the discussions of the western lands problem in Congress and at the hearings of the Boudinot committee between 2 October 1781 and the close of the year. See index of *Papers of Madison,* III, under Continental Congress, actions on western lands; Madison, James, Jr., views of western lands of Va. and their government.

[12] See *Papers of Madison,* III, 286–88. JM implies that the delegates had repeated their recommendation in the dispatch, now missing, of 17 November 1781 to Governor Nelson (*ibid.,* III, 305, n. 1).

[13] On 27 July 1780 George Mason had written at length to Joseph Jones on "the Subject of our back Lands" and asked Jones to share the letter with his colleagues from Virginia in Congress (*Papers of Madison,* II, 52–53, and n. 3). Insofar as is known, Mason did not correspond further about this matter with Jones or any of his colleagues at Philadelphia during the next eighteen months. Pendleton's letter to Jones has not been found. Judging from JM's reply, Pendleton had commented on the western issue in his now missing letter of 5 November, as he would do again when writing to JM on 3 December 1781 (*ibid.,* III, 301–3, 324–25).

[14] In his letter of 24 March 1782 (*q.v.*), Jefferson explained why, at that time, he could not accede to JM's request.

[15] See *Papers of Madison,* III, 71–72. On five separate occasions between 16 April

1781 and 15 January 1782, either JM or Jones tried in vain to elicit from Jefferson an opinion about JM's proposal to empower Congress to use naval vessels to force a recalcitrant state to fulfill its financial or other obligations to the United States (Brant, *Madison*, II, 110, and n. 9).

[16] See JM to Pendleton, 8 January 1782, and n. 10. In the Caribbean at this time, the French and Spanish naval commanders were planning a combined operation against Jamaica. They were unable to launch this expedition because of the decisive defeat in April of the French fleet by the British in the Battle of the Saints and the subsequent loss of many troops from illness. See JM to Pendleton, 23 April, n. 3; Pendleton to JM, 20 May 1782, n. 10. The *Pennsylvania Packet* of 15 January 1782 reported that early in December the Spaniards in Cuba were about to attack the "infernal nest of pirates" in the Bahama Islands and probably would also try to drive the British from St. Augustine, Fla. See also *ibid.*, 19 January 1782. The same newspaper in its issue of 31 January included an item from Norwich, Conn., under a 10 January date line, stating that New Providence Island in the Bahamas had "lately" been captured by Spain. See Report on Foreign Dispatches, 20 March 1782, n. 6.

From Edmund Randolph

Letter misdated.

EDITORIAL NOTE

15 January 1782[3]. The contents of this manuscript in the Madison Papers of the Library of Congress make certain that Randolph inadvertently dated it one year before he wrote it.

Amendment to Report on War Department

MS (NA: PCC, No. 27, fol. 153). In JM's hand.

[16 January 1782]

*That at all times in the absence of the Secretary at War, the Assistant be authorised to transact all such business within the department as shall be assigned to him by the said Secretary, who shall be responsible for the conduct of the Assistant[1]

[1] By letters of 11 and 14 January, respectively, addressed to the president of Congress, Secretary at War Benjamin Lincoln sought permission to visit briefly his home in Massachusetts and to appoint an assistant, a secretary, and two clerks (NA: PCC, No. 149, I, 97–104). Each letter, received by Congress on the day it was written, was referred to a committee consisting of Ezekiel Cornell (R.I.), Richard Law (Conn.), and JM. The docket of the report notes that it was submitted to Congress on 16 January. This fact is not mentioned in the printed journal. Congress adopted the report on the following day (*JCC*, XXII, (35–37).

Besides recommending the additions of office personnel and the leave of absence requested by Lincoln, the committee in the original draft of the report included the statement "that at all times in the absence of the Secretary at War the business in the War Office shall devolve on his assistant subject to the orders of the Secretary at war Who shall be responsable for the transaction of the business in his absence in the same manner as when present." In view of the asterisk at the beginning of JM's suggested substitute for this portion of the report, he most probably offered the amendment in committee rather than in Congress.

In February General Lincoln appointed as assistant secretary his former aide-de-camp, Major William Jackson (1759–1828) of Philadelphia. Jackson, who recently had been the assistant of John Laurens during his mission to France, served later as secretary of the Constitutional Convention of 1787 and as a private secretary of President Washington during his first administration (Fitzpatrick, *Writings of Washington*, XX, 323 n.; XXXII, 499 n.; Wharton, *Revolutionary Diplomatic Correspondence*, IV, 417).

From Benjamin Harrison

RC (Maine Historical Society, Portland). In the hand of Archibald Blair, clerk of the Council of State. Addressed to "The Hon. Mr. Jas. Madison."

In council Jany. 19th. 1782[1]

Sir

The Executive have appointed Mr Madison and Mr Andrews commissioners to meet those of Pensylvania,[2] to run and finally settle the boundary line betwixt this State and that; in order to do it with accuracy, some astronomical Observations are necessary, Mr Madison will make them in the back Country and Mr Andrews some where near Philadelphia, we think it necessary least any accident should happen to either of those Gentn. to give each an assosiate, and we have to beg the favor of you to assist the latter, you will be so kind as to excuse our making this request, we well know your usefulness in your present employment, but as it is a matter of consiquence to this State, and ought to be trusted to none but men of Honor and abilities and perhaps a Virginian, we earnestly request you to undertake it; if you should not be able to comply with this desire be so kind as to recommend some person to act in your stead, we know of no one here capable of the business that will undertake the journey.[3] I have never yet heard one word from that raskal Bringhurst about the Chariot will you be so obliging as to call on him again and let me know whether I am ever to get it or not[4] I am

Dr Sir Your most Obedt. Humble Servant

Benj Harrison

[1] Under this date in the "Council Minute Book, 1781–1782" in the Virginia State Library is a canceled entry mentioning the consideration of a letter "to Delegates in Congress" (*Journals of the Council of State*, III, 31, n. 34). Probably the deletion signifies that the Council of State decided against sending a dispatch. None of that date from the governor to the delegates has been found.

[2] As commissioners of Virginia, the Reverend James Madison and the Reverend Robert Andrews, both of the College of William and Mary, had met in the summer of 1779 in Baltimore with their counterparts from Pennsylvania (Hening, *Statutes*, X, 520–34). For their agreement, see Randolph to JM, 26 April 1782, n. 2.

[3] H. R. McIlwaine concluded that Blair had erred in addressing this letter to JM rather than to "the gentleman appointed as Mr. Robert Andrews's assistant" (*Official Letters*, III, 130 n.). The journal of the Council of State for 16 January exonerates the clerk by recording the appointment of "James Madison junr. and James McCorcle esquires [as] Associates to the Commissioners who are, on behalf of this State, to run the boundary line between it & the State of Pennsylvania" (*Journals of the Council of State*, III, 28). The executive of Virginia experienced great difficulty in filling these two positions. JM declined on 1 February 1782 (*q.v.*) and was replaced by John Page. After McCorkle and Thomas Lewis refused to serve, Governor Harrison received an acceptance from Andrew Ellicott of Maryland in June 1784, shortly before the surveyors began their work (*ibid.*, III, 59, 295, 345–46, 377, 401; *Calendar of Virginia State Papers*, III, 592).

[4] John Bringhurst (1726–1795) was a coachmaker in Germantown, Pa. (*Pennsylvania Magazine of History and Biography*, V [1881], 377; VI [1882], 139; LV [1931], 317, 320 n.).

To Edmund Pendleton

RC (LC: Madison Papers).

PHILADA. Jany. 22d. 1782

DEAR SIR

The post having not yet come in I have not the pleasure of acknowledg[in]g yours which I make no doubt he brings for me.[1]

Congress[2] are much occupied & perplexed at present with the case of Vermont. The pretensions of that settlement to the character of an independt. State, with the grounds on which they are made & the countenance given them by Congress are I presume pretty well known to you. It has long been contended that an explicit acknowledgment of that Character and the admission of them into the federal Union was an act both of Justice & policy.[3] The discovery made through several channels & particularly by the intercepted letters of Ld. G. Germaine[4] added such force to the latter of these considerations that in the course of last summer preliminary overtures were made on the part of Congress for taking them into the confederation, containing as one condition on the part of Vermont that they sd. contract their claims within the bounds to which they were originally confined, & guaranting to N.Y. & N.H. all the territory without those bounds to which their encroachments had been extended. Instead of complying with this condition they have gone on in their encroachments both on the N.Y. & N.H. sides & there is at this moment every symtom of approaching hostility with each of them.[5] In this delicate crisis the interposition of Congress is again called for, & indeed seems to be indispensable; but whether in the way of military coercion, or a renewal of former overtures, or by making the first a condition of a refusal of the last, is not so unanimously decided. Indeed with several members & I may say States in Congress a want of power either to decide on their independence or to open the door of the confederacy to them is utterly disclaimd,[6] besides which the danger of the precedent,[7] & the preponderancy it wd. give to the Eastern scale deserve serious consideration.[8] These reasons nevertheless can only prevail when the alternative contains fewer evils. It is very unhappy that such plausible pretexts if not necessary occasions of assuming power should occur. Nothing is more distressing to those who have a due respect for the constitutional modifications of power than to be obliged to decide on them.[9]

We have nothing fresh from Europe. We are informed by the way of N.Y. that the Earl of Dunmore has arrived at Charleston to claim from Earl Cornwallis the fulfilment of his promise. No individual[s] in his Suite are named.[10]

I am Dr Sir Yr Sincere friend & hbl servt

Js. Madison Jr.

We have fresh & indubitable confirmations of the apostasy of Deane from the Independence of his Country[11]

[1] Insofar as the editors have been able to determine, Pendleton's next letter to JM after the one of 31 December 1781 was that of 28 January 1782 (*q.v.*).

[2] Late in life JM, or someone at his direction, bracketed all of the letter from the opening of this paragraph through the next to last paragraph, thereby designating the portion to be published (Madison, *Papers* [Gilpin ed.], I, 109–11).

[3] For the congressional background of this controversy during 1781, see *Papers of Madison*, III, 223–24; 225, n. 11; 309, n. 4.

[4] See *ibid.*, III, 226, n. 12.

[5] JM probably gleaned his information from several sources–resolutions of the New York legislature presented to Congress on 5 December, evidence arriving a week later from Thomas Chittenden, "Governor of the State of Vermont," documents received on 18 December from President Meshech Weare of New Hampshire, and papers sent by Governor George Clinton of New York and laid before Congress on 31 December 1781. Upon the arrival of the Weare dossier, Congress referred it and the other papers on the Vermont crisis (and later the many more received from Clinton) to a committee with Daniel Carroll as its chairman and Joseph Jones as one of the other three members (NA: PCC, No. 40, II, fols. 105–17, 119, 123, 137–39, 173; *JCC*, XXI, 1159–60, 1166 n., 1179 n., 1185 n., 1190 n.). In Hugh

Hastings and J. A. Holden, eds., *Public Papers of George Clinton, First Governor of New York* . . . (10 vols.; Albany and New York, 1899–1914), VII, 484–632, *passim*, are copies of many documents dating in November and December 1781, describing the highly explosive situation and purporting to supply incontrovertible proof of "a Treasonable Intercourse between the Leaders of the usurped Government on the [New Hampshire] Grants and the Enemy" (*ibid.*, VII, 624).

[6] Here JM refers to the report of the Carroll committee, not mentioned in the printed journal but laid before Congress on 7 January, first debated three days later and heatedly discussed on several other occasions both before and after the date of JM's letter (NA: PCC, No. 40, II, 241–45; Burnett, *Letters*, VI, 291, 294–95). The committee's recommendations were equivalent to an ultimatum. They reaffirmed the boundaries of Vermont as defined by Congress on 21 August 1781 and summarily rejected by the governor and legislature of the self-styled "independent State of Vermont" about three months later (*Papers of Madison*, III, 225, n. 11). According to the committee's recommendations, Congress should dispatch a commissioner to Vermont authorized to pledge that, if the inhabitants accepted the boundaries specified, appointed delegates to Congress, and ratified the Articles of Confederation, Congress would recognize Vermont (if that was the name which the people preferred) as "a free Sovereign & Independent State." On the other hand, if the Vermonters rejected the offer or expressed no opinion about it before a date fixed by the commissioner, they must "utterly disclaim all pretensions to Independence" and peaceably submit to the jurisdiction of New Hampshire or New York, depending upon the place of residence of each inhabitant and how the territory should eventually be divided between those two states. Should they refuse to do this, Congress would conclude that they had "hostile designs against the United States" and hence must be subdued by continental troops, whose commander, by imposing "martial law," would "bring to condign punishment such as prove refractory."

Apparently unwilling either to accept or reject this report, but of a mind to make it less belligerent in tone and to delay a decision upon so delicate a matter as long as possible, Congress softened the recommendations and committed them on 28 January to a "grand committee," upon which each state had one delegate, including Edmund Randolph for Virginia. Samuel Livermore of New Hampshire was the chairman. Jonas Fay and Ira Allen, the agents of Vermont, returned to Philadelphia about two days later after five months' absence (*JCC*, XXII, 57–60, 66, n. 1; NA: PCC, No. 40, II, 207; Burnett, *Letters*, VI, 297–98). See JM to Pendleton, 7 February 1782.

[7] See *Papers of Madison*, II, 87; III, 226, n. 13.

[8] Writing here as a southerner, JM assumes that the attention given by Congress to the legitimate needs of his section will decline in direct proportion to the number of northern states admitted to the Confederation. Within two decades he would find Vermont, unlike the rest of New England, usually controlled by Jeffersonian Republicans rather than by Federalists.

[9] Although obviously in a constitutional quandary, JM appears in these three sentences to favor an assumption by Congress of undelegated powers, if consonant with the general welfare, if not merely for partisan or sectional advantage, and if a greater evil would clearly result from an inflexible adherence to state sovereignty.

[10] Although the *Pennsylvania Journal* of 19 January 1782 included a report that the Earl of Dunmore, along with troop reinforcements from Great Britain, had reached Charleston late in December, Congress first read the news officially on 22 January in a letter written by General William Heath eight days earlier (NA: PCC, No. 157, fols. 439–40). With the blessing of Lord Germain, Dunmore had embarked about the time of Cornwallis' surrender to resume the governorship of

the province of Virginia, from which the rebels had ousted him in 1776. The document, if any, containing Cornwallis' "promise," presumably to restore Dunmore to his office, has not been found. See *Pennsylvania Packet*, 29 January and 23 April 1782; William Emmett O'Donnell, *The Chevalier de La Luzerne, French Minister to the United States, 1779–1784* (Bruges, 1938), p. 213, n. 108; Boyd, *Papers of Jefferson*, VIII, 329. On the other hand, when Cornwallis was about to invade Virginia, he expressed the hope that he would be able "to possess the country sufficiently to overturn the Rebel government" (Charles Ross, ed., *Correspondence of Charles, First Marquis Cornwallis* [3 vols.; London, 1859], I, 87). Dunmore's aim evoked much humorous comment in the *Virginia Gazette*. After labeling his return to the United States "a laughable circumstance," the issue of 26 January continues, "As he seems, however, to be unwilling to come among us for the purposes for which he was sent out, it will be well for him if his masters, the British ministers, do not avail themselves of the circumstances, and strike him off for neglect of duty." On 9 February 1782 the *Virginia Gazette, and Weekly Advertiser* notes that Dunmore "brought out with him, his charriot and horses, servants, and a large pack of hounds, in order to enjoy all the pleasures that the conquered state of Virginia could afford him."

[11] See *Papers of Madison*, III, 301–2; 303, n. 7; 328–29. On 17 January 1782 Congress listened to two letters allegedly written by Silas Deane in Paris in September 1781 to friends in Connecticut and intercepted in France. Finding that these two dispatches "contained matters injurious to the public," Congress referred them for authentication to the secretary for foreign affairs. If he concluded that they were what they purported to be, he was authorized to send certified copies of them to the governor of Connecticut and, at the secretary's discretion, other copies or extracts from the letters to Robert Morris, superintendent of finance, to La Luzerne, and to the envoys of the United States in France and Spain (*JCC*, XXII, 37–38). On 19 January 1782 JM was named to a committee, with Daniel Carroll as its chairman, to consider a resolution which directed that the powers of Thomas Barclay, the American consul in France, "so far as they relate to the settlement of the accounts" of Deane, be revoked and that Robert Morris order "Deane to repair to Philadelphia with his accounts and vouchers against the United States in order that they may be there liquidated and settled" (*JCC*, XXII, 39–40, and 40, n. 1). If this committee ever reported, Congress must have adopted a greatly altered resolution. Deane remained abroad and, as late as 3 April 1784, wrote to one of his brothers, "Mr Barclay the Consul has been with Me, examining my Accts, for some time, but his Instructions are so drawn up, that every thing, any way doubtful, must be referred to Congress" (*Collections of the Connecticut Historical Society*, XXIII [1930], 198). For the background of "the apostasy of Deane," see *Papers of Madison*, III, 303 n. 7.

To Edmund Randolph

Letter misdated.

EDITORIAL NOTE

22 January 1782[3]. The manuscript of this document is now missing. A printed copy is in Madison, *Papers* (Gilpin ed.), I, 111–12. Many years after writing the letter, JM selected at least a portion of it for inclusion in the earliest edition of his papers. Either JM misdated the letter a year too early, or Gilpin mistook JM's "3" in "1783" for "2."

Virginia Delegates to Benjamin Harrison

RC (University of North Carolina Library: Southern Historical Collection). The letter was written by Edmund Randolph. It is docketed: "Lre from our Delegates in Congress Janry 24. 1782. Reced Febry 7th:"

PHILADELPHIA Jany. 24. 1782.

SIR

The minister plenipotentiary of France communicated to us this afternoon the inclosed extract from a letter of Count de Vergennes. We are happy to find, that the supplies, which your excellency negotiated with the minister, are ready for transportation to our country.[1] Being informed, that the last letter, which you received from Mr. Luzerne on this subject, threw a damp on the prospect of obtaining them, we conceive that no particular steps have been taken for the forwarding of them.[2] Fearing too, lest a delay in sending them on might prove injurious, if not fatal, to Virginia, we answered the communication by the inclosed letter.[3] We trust, that, howsoever we may have passed beyond the bounds of our authority in this matter, it is justified by the present situation of things: since it is probable, that, unless the Hermione, which is now ready to sail from Virginia, should be the bearer of some direction for the conveyance of these stores, they may be witholden from us for a twelvemonth, and the express cannot wait, or indeed call at Richmond for an answer from the executive.[4]

If, however, we have counteracted any scheme, which your board may have adopted in this business, it is possible, that the mischief may be corrected, by contradicting our dispatches, in a letter, addressed to count de Vergennes and sent by the Hermione.[5]

We have the honor, sir, to be with great respect your excellency's mo. ob. servts.

JOS: JONES.
J MADISON JR.
EDMUND RANDOLPH.

[1] When Benjamin Harrison had reached Philadelphia in February 1781 as special envoy from the General Assembly of Virginia, he found La Luzerne ready to help that Commonwealth procure military stores from France, to be paid for by Virginia after the war (*Journal of the House of Delegates*, October 1780, pp. 76, 77; *Papers of Madison*, II, 269, n. 5; 299, n. 4). On 23 November 1781 Congress was informed that France had responded favorably to applications by Virginia and

Maryland for arms and other military supplies, "subject however to the order of Congress" and at congressional expense (*JCC*, XXI, 1139–40). Thereupon, Robert Morris refused to let the cash resources of the Confederation in Europe be drawn upon for debts incurred by a state (William E. O'Donnell, *Chevalier de La Luzerne*, pp. 187–89). "The idea of making advances for any individual State from the funds of the United States," he declared in a letter to Franklin on 27 November 1781, "must never be admitted by any servant of Congress" (Wharton, *Revolutionary Diplomatic Correspondence*, V, 25). If the delegates knew of Morris' stand, they did not mention it in the present letter; nor did La Luzerne in his dispatch of 25 January 1782 to Governor Harrison. When Charles Gravier, Comte de Vergennes (1717–1787), the French minister of foreign affairs, learned of the position of the superintendent of finance, he informed La Luzerne in a letter of instructions dated 23 March 1782 that the goods would not be sent to either Virginia or Maryland (n. 2, below; William E. O'Donnell, *Chevalier de La Luzerne*, pp. 188–89, and 189, n. 19).

The brief extract from Vergennes' instructions of 8 October 1781 to La Luzerne, which accompanied the present dispatch, is in the Virginia State Library. The excerpt includes nothing about the mode of payment and states merely that, because the supplies would be ready for shipment on or about 1 April at the latest, the Comte should be informed before that date whether the consignee would send vessels or expected French men-of-war to transport the cargo. See *Calendar of Virginia State Papers*, III, 47.

[2] How the delegates had been "informed," and when La Luzerne wrote his "last letter" to Harrison, are unknown to the editors, although Harrison's dispatch of 29 December 1781 to La Luzerne makes clear that he was addressing the French minister for the first time since assuming the governorship and possibly for the first time since 29 May 1781 (McIlwaine, *Official Letters*, III, 117–18). La Luzerne's reply of 25 January 1782 to Harrison is in French (Virginia State Library). The English equivalent of the text is written in the left-hand margin of each of the three pages of this letter. The first three and one-half sentences of the translation are in a hand which closely resembles JM's; but if he wrote them, he departed from his usual style—perhaps because he was cramped for space—by designating each "the" with a thorn. Most of the translation is by someone whose penmanship contrasts markedly with that of JM. Obviously, if JM shared in making the English version, he must have been asked to do so by La Luzerne before the letter was forwarded. In this dispatch, after acknowledging receipt of Harrison's letter of 29 December 1781, which stressed Virginia's pressing need for the supplies, La Luzerne reported that the delegates, hoping to expedite the delivery of the goods, had asked that the cargo be brought across the Atlantic in French warships. La Luzerne cautioned Harrison to empower an agent in France as soon as possible to acknowledge the debt and agree with the "company," which apparently was willing to advance the purchase price of the supplies, about the terms of repaying principal and interest after the war. La Luzerne closed by assuring Harrison of Louis XVI's great satisfaction, because Virginia was determined to make a vigorous military effort to prevent the British from again ravaging the state as they had done in 1781.

[3] See Virginia Delegates to La Luzerne, 24 January 1782.

[4] Judging from the tenor of Vergennes' letter of 23 March 1782 to La Luzerne, mentioned in n. 1, above, the latter's dispatch to Vergennes, no doubt including a report of the mode of conveyance selected by the Virginia delegates, was borne across the Atlantic by "L'Hermione," which sailed from Yorktown on 2 February and reached her destination early the next month (Acomb, *Journal of Closen*, p.

173; *Virginia Magazine of History and Biography*, VIII [1900–1901], 24). After Cornwallis' surrender, Grasse had ordered this warship, together with the "Romulus" and "Diligente," to remain in Chesapeake Bay (Boyd, *Papers of Jefferson*, VI, 236 n.).

[5] The meaning of this paragraph and of the last sentence of the preceding paragraph can be harmonized only by concluding that La Luzerne's dispatch for transmittal on "L'Hermione" to Vergennes and the delegates' letter to Harrison were taken to Virginia by different couriers. Randolph evidently assumed that the governor, if he disagreed with what the delegates had told La Luzerne, would still have time to send Vergennes an amendatory message aboard the vessel, even though she was "now ready to sail from Virginia." See n. 4, above.

On 8 February 1782, after listening to the present letter, the Virginia Council of State expressed its disagreement with the delegates by resolving that the Commonwealth vessels "Cormorant" and "Oliver Cromwell" should proceed to France as soon as possible to bring back the goods (*Journals of the Council of State*, III, 41–42). By the next day, when Harrison wrote La Luzerne, this decision had been reconsidered, perhaps because the executive had been informed either that the two vessels were weakly armed or that an insufficient amount of tobacco was available for them to carry overseas. "I . . . intreat your Excellency," the governor wrote, "to have the Loan brought over in one of the Kings Ships. . . . We could send Merchants Ships for them but the Stake is too great and we have too much Dependency on their safe Arrival to risk them in such Vessels" (McIlwaine, *Official Letters*, III, 148–49). See also Harrison to Virginia Delegates, 9 February 1782.

On 21 May, when the "Cormorant" and "Oliver Cromwell" were "about to sail for france," Harrison apprised the House of Delegates of the fact and laid before that body his letter of 25 January 1782 from La Luzerne (*Journals of the Council of State*, III, 94; McIlwaine, *Official Letters*, III, 229). Thereupon, the General Assembly prevented the departure of the ships by resolving that they "should not be sent on trading voyages but that they be manned and fitted with all possible expedition to cruise in" Chesapeake Bay and the rivers "for the protection of commerce and security of the Inhabitants," and "that the Governor be desired to inform the Minister of France at Philadelphia, that this Assembly rely on the goodness of his most Christian Majesty for the supplies . . . as well as for their being transmitted in ships of France, as . . . communicated to the delegates in Congress from this State by the Minister of France on the 24th of January 1782" (see first sentence of present letter; also Minute Book, House of Delegates, May 1782, p. 44; and Hening, *Statutes*, XI, 42–44). The journals of the General Assembly for this session being apparently destroyed and the minute book being merely a sketch of procedures, these resolutions seem to exist only in the copy filed in the Virginia State Library with La Luzerne's letter to Harrison, mentioned above. The copy of the resolutions was made by the unidentified person, referred to in n. 2, above, who had translated most of that dispatch into English. On 31 May 1782 Harrison sent a copy of the resolutions to La Luzerne (*Journals of the Council of State*, III, 100; McIlwaine, *Official Letters*, III, 238–39). See also *JCC*, XXII, 357; Randolph to JM, 10 May, and n. 21; Harrison to Virginia Delegates, 11 May, and n. 1; Virginia Delegates to Harrison, 4 June 1782.

Virginia Delegates to La Luzerne

FC (Virginia State Library). Probably made by a clerk.

PHILADELPHIA January 24th. 1782

SIR

We have taken into consideration the Communication which you were pleased to make us this afternoon of that part of his Excellencys Count de Vergennies late Letter which relates to the mode of forwarding the supplies furnished by his Court to the State of Virga.[1] Being Sensible of the difficulties under which our Country labours from the want of Military Stores, we cannot do otherwise than recommend that those which our generous Ally has directed for the use of Virginia, should be forwarded in French bottoms without delay. We are confident that every measure tending to the secure transportation of these Stores will be adopted, and particularly that they will be sent under a convoy of a convenient force, if it be practicable.

We shall inform the Governor of Virginia of the Steps, which we have now taken, and doubt not that they will prove acceptable.

Altho' Mr. Harrison who negociated these Supplies with you mentions in his Letter of the 29th. of May last, the propriety of sending them to the Delaware, yet we beg leave to refer you to his preceding Letter of the 17th. of Feby. in which he observes "that it would add greatly to the obligation if the Stores could be transported in a Frigate to York Town in Virginia." The latter Letter having been written at a Season when our ports were infested by British vessels we conceive that the former suggests, for our present circumstances, the most convenient & advantageous plan.[2]

But should the position of the Enemy make it unsafe to enter Chesapeake bay, we are convinced that due precaution will be taken.

[1] See Virginia Delegates to Harrison, 24 January 1782, and nn.

[2] These letters from Harrison have not been found. He evidently had no copies of them at hand when he wrote on 9 February 1782 to the Virginia delegates (*q.v.*). La Luzerne apparently showed the letters to the delegates during their conference with him on 24 January. The "latter" and "former" clearly should be interchanged.

From David Jameson

RC (LC: Rives Collection of Madison Papers). Docketed by JM, "Jany 26. 1782."

RICHMOND Jan 26. 1782

DR SIR

I am sorry to inform you we have had no Mail this week from the North of Potowmack In my last I mentd. Gen Greenes requisition and I believe told you the Executive have no power to send Militia out of the State nor have they power to raise supplies of any sort. I expected they would call the Assembly but that is not determined on[1] Cap Ragsdale went to Count Rochambeau who has consented to send the Legion of Lauzun (about 600 Horse & foot) to Peytonsburg, there to wait Gen. Washingtons orders whether they shall proceed to So. Carolina or not[2]—they are to leave Wmsbg. early in next Week. Febigers Batallion is still in this state also Col Armands Legion— I am very sorry they are not in motion. the Officers of the former it is said will not march without money, the latter waits for their clothes *to be made up*[3]

I send you one of the Acts of last Session on Acct of the scale of depreciation, wch. if I may give an opinion is not an equitable one.[4] I send you Nicholson & Prentis's paper— they ask the favour of you to give them now & then pieces of intelligence in exchange for this paper wch. I will convey to them while I am in this place. if you wish to have Hayes's paper sent to yourself let me know it.[5] Did I tell you that there is an act to collect 2 lb Bacon & half a bush. Wheat p[er] tithable but they may be commuted for at 6d. the pound & 3/ the bushel Speice— this act is not yet printed. I sent you the Revenue act last post[6]

adieu Yr obt Ser

DAVID JAMESON

[1] Jameson's earlier letter, probably written on 19 January, has not been found. Two days later Governor Harrison answered Nathanael Greene's dispatch of 27 December 1781 before forwarding it to Congress (McIlwaine, *Official Letters,* III, 132–33). Declaring that unless he was speedily reinforced he would have to withdraw from South Carolina and Georgia, Greene asked Virginia for at least two thousand well-equipped militia, as many fat cattle, and as much salt and rum as possible. Even if the considerable force of Tory troops were left out of the reckoning and even if the contingent of Pennsylvania continentals, marching to join him, were taken into account, Greene estimated that the enemy would soon outnumber

his soldiers three to one. He had been told that the British, holding Charleston and other posts southward to Savannah, were expecting momentarily an increase in strength of over 100 per cent by the arrival of four thousand reinforcements from Ireland and New York City (NA: PCC, No. 172, I, 327–32; George Washington Greene, *The Life of Nathanael Greene* [3 vols.; New York, 1871], III, 423–25; Acomb, *Journal of Closen*, p. 174). Although Harrison at once tried to start salt and rum on their way to the southern army, he replied to Greene that he could do no more, because the executive no longer had the authority to impress supplies or to order militia to serve outside the state; and that Virginia lacked sufficient funds to fill its continental troop quota. "We are at this Time," he lamented, "the poorest and the most impotent Executive perhaps in the world. The credit of the State is lost and we have not a Shilling in the Treasury." "I think," Harrison continued, "of immediately calling the Assembly, laying before them your Letters and pressing for their exertions. These I am sure you might expect, but our situation is such that their best Endeavours will be but feeble Efforts" (McIlwaine, *Official Letters*, III, 132; *Journals of the Council of State*, III, 32).

Not long after writing in this vein, Harrison probably heard that the reinforcement of the enemy in the South was far less than Greene had feared. Although in February the governor urged every county lieutenant and sheriff to collect taxes before their due date in order to enable recruiting agents to enlist soldiers (McIlwaine, *Official Letters*, III, 154–57), he did not summon the General Assembly to meet in special session. He included in his message to the legislature, when it convened early in May, a reference to Greene's letter of 27 December 1781 and added that if the British reinforcements expected by Greene had arrived, the executive "could only have remained the dejected Spectators of that great man's fall & the total ruin of a Sister State." Would "it not be better on such great occasions," Harrison inquired, "to put a little confidence in the Executive? who are amenable to the Legislature and may be easily called to a severe account for the misapplication of power" (*ibid.*, III, 213). Although the General Assembly provided by law on 2 July 1782 for "recruiting this state's quota of troops in the continental service," the members apparently believed that the military crisis had ended, for they conferred no emergency powers upon the executive (Minute Book, House of Delegates, May 1782, p. 86; Hening, *Statutes*, XI, 14–20).

[2] Drury Ragsdale, Jr., of King William County, Va., was captain of a continental regiment of artillery with Greene's army. The troops of the Comte de Rochambeau were still encamped near Yorktown. Having been selected by Rochambeau to carry the news of Cornwallis' surrender to the court of Versailles, the Duc de Lauzun had embarked on the frigate "Surveillante" in November and did not arrive back in the United States until September 1782 (François Barrière, ed., *Mémoires du Duc de Lauzun, Bibliothèque des mémoires, relatifs à l'histoire de France, pendant le 18e siècle*, XXV [Paris, 1882], 203–4). To be more readily available in the event that Greene needed help, Lauzun's legion moved its winter quarters from the Virginia Tidewater to Peytonsburg in Pittsylvania County, about twenty miles above the North Carolina border (Fitzpatrick, *Writings of Washington*, XXIII, 493–94; XXIV, 1, 152, 157).

[3] The recruits of the continental line, assembled at or near Cumberland Old Court House (a town no longer extant, in western Powhatan County) by Colonel Christian Febiger, continental chief recruiting officer, suffered from a lack of provisions, pay, and adequate clothing. He was obliged to help quell a small mutiny on 14 February before the four hundred troops under Lieutenant Colonel Thomas Posey would consent to begin their long march to the southern army. As late as May, Febiger was still engaged in the difficult business of bringing recruits to the

same place of rendezvous and starting them on their way to General Greene (*ibid.*, XXIV, 2, 35, 61; McIlwaine, *Official Letters*, III, 134–35, 149; *Calendar of Virginia State Papers*, III, 67, 73–74, 93–95, 127, 154). See also Harrison to Virginia Delegates, 1 March 1782.

For Governor Harrison's troubled relations with Colonel Armand, see Harrison to Virginia Delegates, 11 January 1782, n. 5. In August 1782 Washington ordered Armand to move his legion from Virginia to reinforce Greene in South Carolina (Fitzpatrick, *Writings of Washington*, XXIV, 469–70).

[4] "An act directing the mode of adjusting and settling the payment of certain debts and contracts, and for other purposes," passed on 5 January 1782 (*Journal of the House of Delegates*, October 1781, p. 74; Hening, *Statutes*, X, 471–74). This statute defined a "scale of depreciation," in terms of silver and gold, for the settlement of all debts or contracts incurred or entered into between 1 January 1777 and 1 January 1782, and for the discharge of which the debtor had not pledged to pay with specie, tobacco, or "other specific property." Although Jameson does not make his position clear, he may have believed that the depreciation scale was inequitable to creditors. The act also included a stay-law provision whereby, except for sums owed to the Commonwealth, creditors were barred until 1 December 1783 from instituting suits for the recovery of debts.

[5] Insofar as the editors know, JM did not comply with the request of Nicolson and Prentis. Both the *Virginia Gazette, and Weekly Advertiser* (Nicolson and Prentis) and the *Virginia Gazette, or, the American Advertiser* (James Hayes, Jr.) were published in Richmond. Thomas Nicolson and William Prentis (*ca.* 1740–*ca.* 1824) also printed for the Commonwealth until 1785, when their partnership was dissolved. Quitting Richmond, Prentis in 1786 established (with Miles Hunter, who died in 1788) the pioneer *Virginia Gazette, and Petersburg Intelligencer*, which, shortened in title to *The Petersburg Intelligencer* in 1800, he continued to publish until his retirement four years later. He had also published (in partnership with Daniel Baxter) the *Norfolk and Portsmouth Chronicle* between 1789 and 1792. Prentis was mayor of Petersburg for several terms between 1793 and 1806 (Petersburg City Records, Hustings Court Deed Book, No. 7, p. 199; Petersburg Personal Property Tax Book, 1823, microfilm and MS, respectively, both in the Virginia State Library; Clarence S. Brigham, *History and Bibliography of American Newspapers, 1690–1820* [2 vols.; Worcester, Mass., 1947], II, 1123–24, 1131, 1134; Edward A. Wyatt IV, ed., "Preliminary Checklist for Petersburg, 1786–1876; Virginia Imprints Number 9" [mimeographed, Richmond, 1949], pp. 209, 211).

[6] See Harrison to Virginia Delegates, 11 January, and n. 4; Jameson to JM, *ca.* 12 January 1782, n. 8.

From Edmund Pendleton

Tr (LC: Force Transcripts). Another copy taken from the original is printed in the *Proceedings of the Massachusetts Historical Society*, 2d ser., XIX (1905), 145–47. An extract is given in Stan. V. Henkels Catalogue No. 694 (1892).

VIRGA Jany 28th 1782

DEAR SIR.

I have yr favr of the 8th. The Objections[1] yr Bank was to encounter had not occurr'd to me, since if such a measure was useful, it seems necessary that Congress should have power over the Regulations which were to direct its operations, it being of General & not local concern, and as the confederation had not given such a power, the medium adopted appears to be the proper & indeed the only recourse[,][2] to call for the Individual confirmation of the States, to the granting which I se[e] no possible objection, but on Account of the restriction[3] in your scheme upon the Institution of State Banks, which at some future day may become very[4] useful & necessary.[5] Whatever evils may have been experienced & ever will be, from a Redundancy of paper Credit, yet my opinion is that the History of all Countries, as well as the reason of the thing, prove that the circulation of a moderate quantity of paper may be made in every Countrey without danger of depreciation & with many advantages to Commerce & business even Superior to the precious metals. Its locality, the principle[6] source of Objection, has its use in preventing that stagnation in a circulating medium, which in the Flux & reflux of the Metals will unavoidably happen, especially since the Marchants have practiced the import and export of those[7] as a subject of trade, as they rise at one Market and fall at another, instead of a mere Medium or representative of Ballances in Barter:[8] Of all kinds of paper circulated as the representative of money, That of a Bank has undoubtedly the preference, because it has a real constituent,[9] a stock of Cash deposited & kept always ready to take its place when any foreign purpose[10] shall make it necessary, whereas if we were ask'd what our late paper represented?[11] Candor would compel us to answer, what it has come to: Nothing. I can foresee that when the Mass of paper is totally anihilated, and before a general free trade takes place, we may be distressed for a sufficient medium of Commerce & might prefer a Bank scheme to any other, & why should we be restrained[?][12] If it be said that the States might increase their Bank so as to answer the purposes of all the States in the Union, I answer that a general & equally valuable circulation of Bank notes can only prevail to a certain distance from the Bank; as the difficulty of Access to that is increased so will the Value diminish, til a total stop is put to its circulation—for instance suppo[s]e a Man at Charles Town with a Bank note applying to a foreign Mercht to purchase goods, he would refuse it, since in Vain would the holder say you may have gold for it by going to the Bank, since that would require another Voiage, not a very short one, to accomplish; In Philadelphia the note would be taken with Avidity.[13] The notes of the Bank of England circulate indeed to a great distance, but so does the trade which centers in London; and yet that Bank has no such exclusive restrictions,[14] a multitude of other Banks subsist & with other mediums supply all Occasions of Commerce without experiencing inconvenience; that is not the Case in America. Phila. is not nor ever will be the centre of its trade, tho' a considerable Branch, and remittances from the different states, will be much oftner wanted to other parts than to that City.

I hope the states comply with the recommendation respecting the forfeiture of British Goods, since tis a most ungrateful & Impolitic abuse of the kindness of our Allies to throw the money they so generously supply us with, into the hands of their & our Enemy, to the neglect of their trade.[15] Wisely & Prophetically did honest Genl Gadsden say to Congress in 1774, "Take care, or yr liberties will be traded away."[16]

By letter just received from Genl Green's camp of the 28th past I find he was alarm'd for his Situation, having certain & Authentic Accts that the Cork fleet with 4 Regiments of Infantry & two of dismounted Dragoons, Victulars & Store Ships, & 3 Regts from New York, were seen on the Coast going into[17] Charles Town, wch would give the Enemy a Superiority, that would oblige him to abandon the Countrey to their ravages, Or Sacrifice the remains of his brave little Army: a dreadful alternative.[18] I am

Yr very affc

EDMD. PENDLETON

[1] In the *Proceedings of the Massachusetts Historical Society* and in Henkels Catalogue, this word is "objection."

[2] The versions in the *Proceedings of the Massachusetts Historical Society* and in Henkels Catalogue have "resource." Pendleton probably intended to write "recourse." For the background of his observations about the Bank of North America, see JM to Pendleton, 8 January 1782; and Virginia Delegates to Harrison, on the same day. See JM to Pendleton, 25 February 1782, for JM's comments upon Pendleton's remarks.

[3] In Henkels Catalogue, the word "restitution" instead of "restriction" is obviously a copyist's error.

[4] This word appears also in the Henkels Catalogue copy but is omitted in the *Proceedings of the Massachusetts Historical Society*.

[5] Pendleton's meaning would have been clearer if he had placed a period after "recourse" and followed it with a new sentence of this tenor: "Although I am completely in accord with having the states ratify the ordinance establishing the Bank, I believe state banks will be necessary in the future, and hence I cannot support the request of Congress that each state grant to the Bank of North America a banking monopoly as long as the war continues." See Virginia Delegates to Harrison, 8 January 1782, n. 7.

[6] This word and "Marchants," which appears later in the sentence, are spelled correctly in the Henkels Catalogue and *Proceedings of the Massachusetts Historical Society* copies. By "Its locality," Pendleton meant that, as compared with specie,

bank notes or other paper currency circulated only within a small circle of territory, having as its center the place where this money was issued.

[7] The word is "these" in the *Proceedings of the Massachusetts Historical Society*.

[8] Since this phrase appears in both the Force transcript and the Massachusetts Historical Society copy, Henkels' meaningless "Balance and Barter" is most probably an error.

[9] If Pendleton had followed "constituent" with an expression like "back of the bank notes," he would have clarified his meaning. As he used the word "constituent," the reader is reminded of the same word when it is employed to signify a member of the constituency of a public officeholder.

[10] Pendleton meant that, because of the cash reserve behind bank notes, a holder of them who wished to pay a debt in another country or even in another state where these bank notes would be unacceptable could readily exchange them for specie at the bank of issue. Further along in this paragraph, he comments on this matter at greater length.

[11] Probably a reference to an act of 5 January 1782 of the Virginia General Assembly, declaring that, since the greatly depreciated paper currency of the state was "neither a proper medium of circulation nor a just standard whereby to settle and adjust debts and contracts," it "shall no longer pass current" (Hening, *Statutes*, X, 471).

[12] See n. 5, above.

[13] See n. 10, above.

[14] That is, "monopoly"; see n. 5, above.

[15] See *Papers of Madison*, III, 338; 339, n. 2; Virginia Delegates to Harrison, 8 January 1782, and n. 4.

[16] Pendleton probably was recalling what he heard the Charleston merchant and fiery patriot, Christopher Gadsden (1724–1805), later a brigadier general in the continental army, say in the First Continental Congress. In that body, Gadsden, an uncompromising opponent of continuing economic relations between the colonies and the mother country, championed the Association and was a member of the important committee "to examine & report the several Statutes, which affect the trade and manufactures of the Colonies" (*JCC*, I, 26, 29; Burnett, *Letters*, I, 30, 49, 86).

[17] The copy in the *Proceedings of the Massachusetts Historical Society* has this word as "in."

[18] Pendleton almost certainly derived most of this information from Greene's letter of 27 December 1781 (Jameson to JM, 26 January 1782, n. 1).

To Benjamin Harrison

RC (Maine Historical Society, Portland). Franked "public Service" and "J. Madison Jr." Addressed to "His Excellency Benjamin Harrison Esqr. Governor of Virginia." Docketed, "J Madison Recd. 14h. Febry 1782."

PHILADA. Feby. 1st. 1781. [1782][1]

SIR

Your Excellency's favor of the 19th. Ult. notifying to me the desire of the Executive to associate me with the Revd. Mr. Andrews in settling the boundary between Virga. & this State, came to hand this moment. That no disappointment may retard the business I embrace the immediate return of the post to inform the Executive that although I am duly impressed with this mark of their confidence & am much disposed to render every service to my Country, yet I am constrained to decline the one to which I am now called. Mathematics & astronomy did not make the principal branch of my academic studies, they have made no part of them since I have been engaged in a different sphere, & the little knowledge I originally had of them was merely theoretical. I find myself therefore not qualified even for the office of an auxiliary to Mr. Andrews, much less to step into his place in case of accident. The skill of the Commissioners on the part of Pennsylvania[2] requires that Virginia should oppose to them none but men who are masters of the subject. I am sorry that it is not in my power to point out any one here who is entitled to this description & otherwise unexceptionable. I will however make enquiry, & communicate the result by the next post.[3] In the mean time the Executive will be sensible of the expediency of providing if possible some person within the State to accompany Mr. Andrews.

I will endevour to obtain the decisive information you wish for relative to Bringhurst.[4]

I am Sir with great respect & esteem yr. Excellys. Most Obt. & humble Servt.

J. MADISON JR.

[1] JM mistakenly dated his letter 1781, but it is clearly an answer to Harrison's dispatch of 19 January 1782. Footnotes 2, 3, and 4 of the governor's letter will clarify this reply.

[2] By authorization of the General Assembly, the president and Supreme Executive Council of Pennsylvania in February 1781 had appointed John Lukens (1720–1789), surveyor general of Pennsylvania, and Dr. Archibald McClean (1736–1786), mathematician and surveyor of York County, Pa., as commissioners of their state to join with a similar commission representing Virginia in completing the survey of the boundary between the two commonwealths (*Calendar of Virginia State Papers*, I, 532).

[3] See JM to Harrison, 7 February 1782.

[4] *Ibid.*

Virginia Delegates to Benjamin Harrison

RC (Virginia State Library). Franked by Edmund Randolph. Docketed, "Virga Delegates recd 14 Febry 1782."

PHILADELPHIA Feby. 1. 1782.

SIR

The post of the present week having failed to arrive in this city on its usual day (Tuesday) and our letters not coming to hand until this morning (Friday) we can answer your excellency's favor of the 17th. instant[1] only by acknowledging the receipt of it.

We have the honor sir to be with great respect yr. excellency's mo. ob. sers:

EDM: RANDOLPH in behalf of the Virginia delegation

[1] See Harrison to Virginia Delegates, 15 January, n. 3; and Virginia Delegates to Harrison, 8 February 1782, n. 1.

Benjamin Harrison to Virginia Delegates

FC (Virginia State Library). In the hand of Charles Hay.

COUNCIL CHAMBER February 2d 1782.

GENTLEMEN

We have received none of your Favors by the last two posts, nor has any Northward Mail come in. I suppose the Badness of the Weather as usual stopped them on the road.[1]

On looking over your letter by Captn Irish[2] I find that you suppose the bill drawn payable to him was for part of the four tenths of the new Congress money as it is called; in this I fancy you are mistaken, as the Gentlemen of the Council assure me it was drawn on the State Treasurer,[3] which I think must have been the Case or it would not have been presented to them. I shall look into the matter and if you are not mistaken, order the money to be paid, tho' it is out of my line as this board have never yet interfered in any manner with it. I have called on the Loan Officer[4] in whose hands that money is, and been informed by him that he has a pretty considerable Sum by him which I have ordered him to retain till he hears from me; which will be as soon as I can get an Answer from Irish.[5]

We have not one Syllable of news stirring except that the French Legion will move in a few Days for Peytonsburg to be in readiness to join Genl Green if Genl Washington should so order it.[6]

I am &c

BENJAMIN HARRISON

P S. You will please to forward the inclosed Letters to Monsr Mazzei by different Opportunities[7]

[1] The Richmond *Virginia Gazette* of 2 February reported, "The late cold weather has almost entirely cut off our communication with the northward and southward, as the river at this place and all to the north of us, are full of ice." See also Richmond *Virginia Gazette, or Weekly Advertiser*, 26 January and 2 February, and *Pennsylvania Packet*, 29 January and 5 February 1782.

[2] The delegates' letter to Harrison on 17 November 1781, carried by Captain Nathaniel Irish, on his return from Philadelphia to Richmond, finally reached the governor on 5 January 1782 but has been missing for many years (*Papers of Madison*, III, 309, n. 1).

[3] George Brooke.

[4] John Hopkins, Jr.

[5] See Jameson to JM, *ca.* 12 January 1782, n. 10.

[6] See Jameson to JM, 26 January 1782, n. 2.

[7] Harrison's letter of 31 January 1782 to Philip Mazzei, relieving him, on grounds of needed economy, of his duties as an agent of Virginia in Tuscany, is printed in McIlwaine, *Official Letters*, III, 142. See *Journals of the Council of State*, III, 34; *Papers of Madison*, I, 287, n. 2. To assure that Mazzei would receive the letter, the governor evidently sent several copies of it—each to be dispatched overseas in a different ship.

To Benjamin Harrison

RC (Harvard University Library). Although the cover is missing, the contents permit no doubt that Governor Harrison was the recipient.

PHILADA. Feby. 7th. 1782

SIR

According to my promise by the last post & to your Excellency's request I have made enquiry for some person fit for the service which my unfitness obliged me to decline, but with as little success as I expected. If skill in the business alone were requisite, it would perhaps be not easy to find one duly qualified & willing to undertake it, but as some particular tie to the State with whose interest he is to be charged is equally indispensable, a proper associate for Mr. Andrews can not be sought for with any hope of success out of the State itself.

I have had no opportunity yet of seeing or hearing from Bringhurst.[1]

I am Sir with great respect & esteem yr. most obt & hble Servt.

J. MADISON JR.

[1] For clarification of the matters mentioned in this letter, see Harrison to JM, 19 January; JM to Harrison, 1 February 1782.

To Edmund Pendleton

RC (LC: Madison Papers). The cover is missing, but the contents of the letter permit no doubt that Pendleton was the recipient.

PHILADA. Feby. 7th. 1782.

DR. SIR

The post has been very irregular for several weeks past & this week the Mail South of Annapolis has failed altogether;[1] by which means I lose the pleasure of your alternate favor.

A vessel from France informs us that the frigate freigted with the event at York had arrived there in 22 days.[2] We are hourly & anxiously expecting the echo of it from Europe & particularly from England. Unless some revolution in the councils of the latter should result from it, our last intelligence with respect to them justifies our suspicion that they will continue to be as bloody as ever.[3]

Congress are still occupied with the thorny subject of Vermont.[4] Some plan for a general liquidation & apportionment of the public debts is also under their consideration, & I fear will be little less perplexing. It is proposed that untill justice & the situation of the States will admit of a valuation of lands[5] the States should be applied to for power to substitute such other rule of apportioning the expenditures as shall be equitable & practicable, and that Commissrs. be appointed by the concurrent act of the U.S. & each State to settle the accts. between them. The scheme is not yet matured, and will meet with many difficulties in its passage thro' Congress.[6] I wish it may not meet with much greater when it goes down to the States. A spirit of accomodation alone can render it unanimously admissible; a spir[it] which but too little prevails, but wch in few instance[s] is more powerfully recommended by the occasion than the present. If our voluminous & entangled accts. be not put into some certain course of settlemt. before a foreign war is off our hands it is easy to see they must prove an exuberan[t] & formidable source of intestine dissentions.[7]

The Alliance a Continel. frigate carrying the Marquis to France, has sent a fine prize to Boston with 5 or 600 Hhds of Sugar on board.[8]

I have had so short notice of the arrival & departure of the post, that I not only write in haste but with brevity.

Adieu

J. Madison [Jr.]

[1] See Harrison to Virginia Delegates, 2 February 1782, n. 1.

[2] See Jameson to JM, 26 January 1782, n. 2. The Duc de Lauzun, bearing Rochambeau's dispatches telling of Cornwallis' surrender, reached Brest on 19 November 1781 (*Pennsylvania Journal*, 13 February 1782).

[3] On 25 November 1781, two days before Parliament convened, London first heard of the disaster at Yorktown. The *Pennsylvania Packet* of 12 February reported a rumor that George III had taken refuge in the Tower of London because of riots occasioned by the bad news. Military and civil officers in the United States expected, and the king and Parliament at first were determined to make, a fresh attempt in the spring of 1782 to suppress the rebellion. See JM to Pendleton, 25 February 1782, n. 7. The loss of Cornwallis' army, however, was an important cause of the fall of Lord North's ministry on 20 March of that year.

[4] See *Papers of Madison,* III, 223–24; 225, n. 11; 226, n. 13; JM to Pendleton, 22 January 1782, and nn. 5, 6. Samuel Livermore, as chairman of the grand committee, reported on 19 February in favor of statehood for Vermont, provided that its inhabitants, after agreeing to the stipulated boundaries without delay, would elect delegates to Congress authorized to sign the Articles of Confederation. On 1 March the delegates from New York, Virginia, South Carolina, and Georgia unanimously combined to defeat this proposal (*JCC*, XXII, 80, 105–8). On the same day, over the opposition of six state delegations including the delegation from Virginia, Congress refused to return the remainder of the report to the Livermore committee. Except for the provision that continental troops, as well as militia of New Hampshire and New York, would, if necessary, compel the inhabitants of Vermont to obey the will of Congress should they spurn the proposed boundaries, this portion of the committee's report was approximately the same as that summarized in n. 6 of JM's letter of 22 January to Pendleton (*JCC*, XXII, 108–14). After 1 March the Vermont issue did not come importantly before Congress until 17 April 1782, but see Motion Concerning Documents on Vermont, 3 April 1782.

[5] Article VIII of the Articles of Confederation provided that all charges "for the common defence or general welfare . . . shall be defrayed out of a common treasury, which shall be supplied by the several states in proportion to the value of all land within each state, granted to or surveyed for any Person, as such land and the buildings and improvements thereon shall be estimated according to such mode as the united states in congress assembled, shall from time to time direct and appoint" (*JCC*, XIX, 217).

[6] On 9 January 1782 a committee of five delegates, with Joseph Jones as chairman, submitted in amended form to Congress an ordinance, drafted by Robert Morris, "respecting the settlement of public accounts." The committee recommended that

each state be asked to send an agent to Philadelphia and that these men decide by majority vote, or by the affirmative votes of at least seven if merely the quorum of nine should be present, "the proportion to be paid by each State of the expence which has accrued during the present war . . . excepting such part thereof as now is or may hereafter become a funded debt of the United States." If this suggestion was adopted, Congress should then, upon the nomination of the superintendent of finance and the subsequent approval of each state, name for each state a commissioner who would have "full power and authority finally to settle (in such form as by the Comptroller of the Treasury shall be directed) the accounts between the State for which he shall have been appointed and the United States" (*JCC*, XXII, 12–14, and 14, n. 1). After being debated on 11 and 16 January, these recommendations were referred to a grand committee with Samuel Livermore as chairman and Jones as the member from Virginia (*JCC*, XXII, 34, 36).

On the date of the present letter Congress heard, debated, and recommitted the report of this committee (*JCC*, XXII, 68). Thirteen days later Congress adopted the revised proposals of the committee—by then with George Clymer of Pennsylvania rather than Livermore as its chairman—touching upon the two chief recommendations summarized earlier in this footnote. Although the provision for a commissioner in each state remained essentially unaltered, the suggestion of a meeting in Philadelphia of agents from the states was discarded. In its place, the legislature of each state was asked "without delay, to authorise and empower the United States in Congress assembled, in the final settlement of the proportions to be borne by each State, of the general expences of the war, . . . to assume and adopt such principles as, from the particular circumstances of the several states, at different periods, may appear just and equitable, without being wholly confined to the rule laid down in the eighth Article of the Confederation, in cases where the same cannot be applied without manifest injustice." See above, n. 5. To aid Congress in arriving at these "proportions," the states were requested to send "as soon as may be, all such documents and information as they may judge most proper" (*JCC*, XXII, 82–84). The exceedingly complicated problem of adjusting the cost of the war among the states would not be solved, of course, for almost a decade, but the efforts to solve it were to ease Alexander Hamilton's task as secretary of the treasury. Over five months elapsed after 20 February 1782 before the issue again came before Congress—and then as the result of a resolution of the Virginia General Assembly on 28 May and 1 June 1782 refusing "to authorise Congress to alter the mode appointed by the Confederation, for apportioning the quotas of the respective states" (NA: PCC, No. 75, fols. 363–65; *JCC*, XXII, 413). See also Virginia Delegates to Harrison, 11 June 1782, and n. 2.

[7] Once more, as when the ratification of the Articles of Confederation was the issue, JM feared that an agreement might never be reached unless it were effected before the termination of the war served to break the only important bond between the states.

[8] The "Alliance," with Lafayette as one of its passengers, sailed from Boston on 25 December 1781. JM probably derived his information about the "fine prize" from either the *Pennsylvania Gazette* of 6 February or the *Pennsylvania Packet* of 7 February 1782. The latter paper on 12 February corrected the news item by saying that the captor of the large vessel bound from Jamaica to New York City had been a Philadelphia privateer rather than the "Alliance."

Virginia Delegates to Benjamin Harrison

Printed extract (Stan. V. Henkels Catalogue No. 1170 [2 June 1916], p. 34). The catalogue states that this letter, four pages in length, is dated as below and signed by JM, Joseph Jones, and Edmund Randolph. The dispatch is apparently in JM's hand.

PHILADELPHIA, Feb. 8, 1782.

It was found that great quantities of British goods, were brought by circuitous commerce into these States, that this trafic tending to strengthen the Enemy both policy and interest required should be suppressed during the War, that the money lent us by the French nation to support our credit and enable us more vigorously to prosecute the War ag't the Common Enemy was chiefly employed in this injurious Commerce, that France seeing her aid of money applied to such nefarious purposes and no effectual measures taken by the United States to prevent it, complained of this trafic so hurtfull to both nations, . . . we wish to retain the French nation as friends, but not to admit them into our Councils. . . . The establishing of a National Bank under our particular circumstances appeared to Congress a desirable object, and if properly supported by the authority of the several States, promises to be generally useful,[1] &c.

[1] If all of this letter were available, it most likely would refer to a dispatch, now missing, written by Governor Harrison on 17 January to the delegates in reply to their letter of 8 January 1782 (*q.v.*), concerning the two subjects discussed in this excerpt (Harrison to Virginia Delegates, 15 January 1782, n. 3). The text of the letter of 8 January and its nn. 4, 5, 6, and 7 will clarify the present remarks of the delegates.

Benjamin Harrison to Virginia Delegates

FC (Virginia State Library). In the hand of Charles Hay.

VIRGINIA IN COUNCIL February 9th: 1782

GENTLEMEN,

You will find by the inclosed[1] that the Executive have had under their Consideration the Situation of the Continental Troops and the Staff Departments now in this State, which is so truly distressing both to them and us, that I want Words to give you a just Idea of it. The

State you will know from my former letters and your own Sufferings is altogether unable to assist them, not having the Command of a Shilling for the present, nor the least prospect of obtaining money for several Months to come, and what is still worse its Credit is so lost that little or no Support can be obtained from it.[2] This Situation we have reduced ourselves to by blindly furnishing every Thing that has been demanded of us either by purchase or the oppressive mode of Impressment; fatal experience has taught us to act with more wisdom, and to endeavour by Prudence and Oeconomy to set about a Reformation before our Affairs get beyond redress. If we let slip the present opportunity, we are undone, we shall part with the Substance for the empty Boast of having deserved a better Fate.

What we have to ask of you is to call on Congress and to insist that they deal by us as they have done by other States, that is to feed their Troops and to support their Post by Contracts and to furnish their Quartermasters and Commissaries with money to support their several Departments and to fall on Means to give us Credit for whatever we have or may furnish out of the money Demands that are made on us. We wish not to exonerate the State from a single Farthing of its due Proportion of the American Burdens but we have a Right to share Benefits in common with the other States and can not support the Southern Army alone any longer[3]

I am in great Hopes this Business will be in a proper Train before this reaches you as I have written pretty fully to General Washington on the Subject by Colo. Carrington, and the Colo. himself is perfectly acquainted with our Situation and possessed of my Sentiments on the Subject.[4] Should this be the Case we would leave you to your own Discretion either to make the demand or not as you shall think most adviseable, but by no Means to omit it if you find such Steps are not taken as will bring about the desired End.[5]

Since my last Irish's Bill has been presented. At first Sight I thought as you did, that the Money was to come out of the four tenths of the new Continental Money, and gave orders to the Commissioner of the Continental Loan Office[6] to pay it. He called on me yesterday and satisfied me I was under a Mistake, and that the Money was expected from our Treasurer, out of our Proportion of three Millions of that kind of Money demanded by Congress by a Resolution of the 22d: of May 1781, which Money we truly say has been long since expended for Continental Purposes, and therefore that we are not able to pay it again[7]

We are made extremely happy by your favor of the 24th: ulto. and much approve of what you have done. I do not remember exactly what I wrote to [the] Chevalier on the Subject from Charlottesville and have no Copy of the Letter to refresh my Memory having destroyed it when I betook myself to the Mountains,[8] however I recollect that I accomodated my Letter to the then Situation of the Country as I did indeed when in Philadelphia; at both of these Periods the Enemy were in Possession of Portsmouth. York Town was therefore the only Place where the Stores could be landed or the Ship lay in any Kind of Safety. It was therefore my first Wish that she should get to that Port if it should be found practicable, but if not that they should be landed in the Delaware, but as the Face of Things is so happily changed, I now wish that they may be brought as high up James River as Hoods[9] where the Ship may be in perfect Safety and be dispatched in a very short time; and I beg you to make this Alteration if it is in your Power. No Steps have hitherto been taken in this Business for a variety of Reasons, but one alone suffice[s], viz, we were able to take none, but as that is not altogether the Case at present and a Delay must not take Place, Youl please to inform us from what port the Stores will be shipped and what pro[s]pect you have of getting one of the King's Ships to bring them over.[10]

I have called on Mr Ross[11] tho' with the worst grace in the World, he being already greatly in Advance from the State and has no prospect of being shortly paid[,] to know what Steps he was taking for your Support and received for Answer that he was taking up some of your Bills and would exert himself to serve you. This Gentleman has great merit I hope he will meet with suitable returns from the State. I am &c

BENJAMIN HARRISON

[1] On 8 February the Council of State had advised the governor "that our Delegates be instructed to move in Congress for the supplying the Southern Army and the Continental posts in this State in the same mode as has been adopted in Pennsylvania and other Northern States." According to the council's journal of 9 February, this instruction was enclosed in the present letter (*Journals of the Council of State*, III, 41, 42).

[2] See Virginia Delegates to Harrison, 8 January; Jameson to JM, *ca.* 12 January, and n. 2; and Harrison to Virginia Delegates, 15 January 1782, and n. 2.

[3] See Virginia Delegates to Harrison, 15 February 1782. Soon after Robert Morris assumed the office of superintendent of finance in July 1781, he greatly improved the methods of procuring and forwarding supplies to the northern army by centralizing the administration of these operations and by engaging the services of private contractors (Louis Clinton Hatch, *The Administration of the American*

Revolutionary Army [New York, 1904], pp. 113–21). See Virginia Delegates to Harrison, 25 February 1782, and n. 3, for the delegates' justification of Morris' failure to extend the contract system to the southern department.

4 Lieutenant Colonel Edward Carrington (1749–1810) of Cumberland County had been a member of the county Committee of Safety in 1775 and a lieutenant colonel of the continental artillery since November 1776. Following service under Washington, he was Virginia state supervisor and director for the repair of arms, 1780–1781. In the latter year he became Greene's deputy quartermaster general and chief of artillery. As an artilleryman, he participated with distinction in the battles of Guilford Court House and Hobkirk's Hill, and, being temporarily withdrawn from Greene's command, he directed the Virginia artillery at Yorktown. While on his way in Greene's behalf to consult with Robert Morris at Philadelphia, Carrington bore a letter of 4 January 1782 from Harrison to Washington. In this dispatch the governor portrayed the "embarras'd situation of the finances and other public matters" of Virginia and complained because the Commonwealth, although denied remunerative contracts for rationing the southern army, was being pressed by Morris to contribute more for its sustenance than her just share. Washington's reply, dated 6 February, which had not come to hand at the time Harrison signed the present letter, disclaimed any jurisdiction over the allotment of quotas "of Men and Money" and reminded the governor that the war could only end speedily by "making early and vigorous preparations for the next Campaign." Provision contracts, Washington added, could not be expected "unless the Financier is enabled by the States to pay the Contractor regularly" (Fitzpatrick, *Writings of Washington,* XXIII, 485–86).

Carrington served as a delegate for Cumberland County to the General Assembly, 1784–1786, as a congressman, 1786–1788, and as a delegate for Powhatan County, 1788–1789. Removing to Richmond, he was in 1789 appointed United States marshal for the District Court of Virginia, and in 1791 federal supervisor of the district of Virginia for the collection of the excise tax on liquors. Although an ardent Federalist, he declined the secretaryship of war in 1795. In 1806 and 1809 he was mayor of Richmond, and in 1807 foreman of the jury at the trial, presided over by his brother-in-law, Chief Justice John Marshall, of Aaron Burr for treason (Garland Evans Hopkins, "The Life of Edward Carrington, a Brief Sketch," *Americana,* XXXIV [1940], 458–74, and "Colonel Carrington of Cumberland" [mimeographed, Winchester, Va., 1942]). See also Report of Delegates of Pennsylvania, Maryland, and Virginia on Carrington's Memorial, 20 April 1782, editorial note.

5 Although, as mentioned in n. 1, the Council of State had advised that "our Delegates be instructed," the governor here entrusts the matter to their discretion. Judging from their letter of acknowledgment of 25 February (*q.v.*) and the printed journal of Congress, they decided against following the instruction of the Council of State.

6 John Hopkins, Jr.

7 See Jameson to JM, *ca.* 12 January, and n. 10; and Harrison to Virginia Delegates, 2 February 1782. Congress had resolved on 22 May 1781 that "the treasurer of the United States is directed immediately to draw orders on the treasurers of the several states, payable at thirty days' sight, for their respective quotas of the three millions of dollars, called for on the 26 day of August, 1780, and which was to have been paid into the continental treasury on or before the last day of December last" (*JCC*, XX, 525).

8 Harrison's dispatch of 29 May 1781, mentioned in the delegates' letter of 24 January 1782 to La Luzerne (*q.v.*), was written at Charlottesville, because the Virginia General Assembly had moved there from Richmond to escape the British.

At that time Harrison was speaker of the House of Delegates. Before the end of May, once again to avoid capture by the enemy, the government fled to Staunton ("the Mountains"). See *Papers of Madison*, III, 121, n. 3.

[9] See map between pp. 212 and 213 of *Papers of Madison*, I.

[10] See Virginia Delegates to Harrison, 24 January 1782, and nn.

[11] David Ross. See Jameson to JM, *ca.* 12 January 1782.

From Edmund Pendleton

Tr (LC: Force Transcripts). Addressed to "The Honble James Madison Esqr Philada." Another copy of the original is in the *Proceedings of the Massachusetts Historical Society*, 2d ser., XIX (1905), 147.

VIRGA Feby 11. 1782

DEAR SIR

I have missed two Posts to get a letter from you, which proceeds from the Susquehanah being frozen which stopd the passage of the Post;[1] the Mail however came to Fredg. but only brought an old letter from Mr Jones.[2]

We have been amused with contrary Reports concerning the arrival of a large reinforcement to the British Army at Charles Town. Genl Green's account of their amount, near 5000, has since been contradicted by officers from his camp, who say [no][3] Troops came from Ireland, & all who got there were the 3 Regiments from New York. I yet think these Gentn were under a mistake, and that Green's relation was too well founded.[4] We are just now told by a Gentn. from Phila. that the Enemy had certainly evacuated New York.[5] I am impatient to have a confirmation of this, & to hear their destination which I suppose is[6] either to the Southern States, or to the West Indies. We are just going to celebrate this anniversary of the General's birth,[7] & I cannot but add[8] that I am

Dr Sr Yr mo. affe friend

EDMD PENDLETON

[1] See Harrison to Virginia Delegates, 2 February 1782, n. 1. On his way from Philadelphia to Baltimore, the postrider crossed the Susquehanna River opposite Havre de Grace, Md. From Baltimore he proceeded by way of Annapolis, Alexandria, and Fredericksburg to Richmond and Petersburg, Va.

[2] Joseph Jones. The letter has not been identified.

[3] Although the Force transcript shows this word as "the," Pendleton almost certainly wrote, or intended to write, "no," as appears in the version printed in the *Proceedings of the Massachusetts Historical Society*.

[4] For Greene's dispatch telling of the expected reinforcements, see Jameson to JM, 26 January 1782, n. 1. According to a letter of that date from Washington to Greene, the British in Charleston had been strengthened from New York City by merely "five to seven hundred" German troops rather than by three regiments of the royal army (Fitzpatrick, *Writings of Washington,* XXIII, 465). Writing on 18 February 1782, Washington assured Greene that the Charleston garrison was unlikely to be reinforced with troops from Ireland in the near future (*ibid*., XXIV, 2). Who these "Gentn" were is not known to the editors, but one of them was likely Lieutenant Colonel John Eager Howard (1752–1827) of the Maryland line, who was at this time returning from the southern army to his home in Baltimore County (Maryland Historical Records Survey Project, Works Progress Administration, comp., "Calendar of the General Otho Holland Williams Papers in the Maryland Historical Society" [mimeographed, Baltimore, 1940], p. 60). On 23 February the Richmond *Virginia Gazette, and Weekly Advertiser,* after mentioning a rumor which had "been prevailing here for several days past" of about 8,000 enemy troops in Charleston, added that the number was "generally thought" to be "exaggerated."

[5] In his reply to Pendleton on 25 February (*q.v.*), JM called the unknown purveyor of this story "an impudent liar." Perhaps, however, the informant had heard in Philadelphia that nineteen transports were in New York Harbor preparing to sail. On 25 February Washington wrote to President John Hanson that these empty troopships had almost certainly gone to sea on the eighteenth for the not unlikely purpose of bringing the Charleston garrison back to New York (Fitzpatrick, *Writings of Washington,* XXIV, 20). Their real mission was to transfer about one thousand British soldiers from the coastal areas of South Carolina and Georgia to the West Indies (Theodore Thayer, *Nathanael Greene: Strategist of the American Revolution* [New York, 1960], p. 395; William B. Willcox, ed., *American Rebellion,* p. 594).

[6] The copy in the *Proceedings of the Massachusetts Historical Society* omits "is."

[7] Washington was born on 11 February, old style, but most "Almanack-makers" as late as 1780, even though they used the new-style calendar in their almanacs, still showed his birthday opposite that date rather than that of 22 February (*Pennsylvania Magazine of History and Biography,* XLIII [1919], 146–47; *Papers of Madison,* I, 3). The first public recognition of the anniversary appears to have been accorded, not on the eleventh but on the twenty-second, by Washington's troops at Valley Forge in 1778. Three years later the Comte de Rochambeau designated 12 February as a holiday for the French troops to honor Washington, since the day before had fallen on Sunday (John C. Fitzpatrick, *The Spirit of the Revolution: New Light from Some of the Original Sources of American History* [Boston, 1924], pp. 94–95). In Richmond the celebration to which Pendleton alludes was such that "the gratitude of the People towards their Great Deliverer could not be restrained." There were bonfires, illuminations, and cannon salutes. Governor Harrison entertained at dinner a "number of officers of the army and other Gentlemen" who drank many toasts "expressive of the warmest attachment to our illustrious Commander." These festivities culminated with an "elegant Ball" (*Virginia Gazette,* 16 February 1782).

[8] The version in the *Proceedings of the Massachusetts Historical Society* reads, "add but."

To James Madison, Sr.

RC (LC: Madison Papers). Years later, JM docketed the letter, "Madison Js Feby 1782." Following the signature at the close of the letter, JM's father added, "This letter was wrote about the 12th. of Feby. 1782."

[*ca.* 12] Feby 1782

HOND. SIR

A conveyance by a waggon returning to your neighbourhood this moment presenting itself I make use of it to forward you a collection of papers which have accumulated since the last supply. If there are any deficiencies be so good as to point them out to me. By the same conveyance I send to Mr. W. Maury 4 English grammars the price of which is 3 dollars which he is to remit thro' you.[1]

The disappointment in forwarding the money by Mr. Brownlow[2] has been sorely felt by me, and the more so as the Legislature has made no provision for the subsistance of the Delegates that can be relyed on.[3] I hope some opportunity will soon put it in your power to renew the attempt to transmit it, & that the delay will have made considerable addition to it. Besides the necessity of this supply for the common occasions I have frequent opportunities here of purchasing many scarce & necessary books at 1/4 of the price which if to be had at all they will hereafter cost me.[4] If an immediate conveyance does not present itself for the cash, I wd. recommend that a bill of exchance on some merchant here be got of Mr. Hunter, Mr. Maury[5] or other respectable Merchant; & forwarded by the post. This is a safer method than the, first, and I make no doubt is very practicable. I wish at all events the trial to be made & that speedily.

I recollect nothing new which is not contained in some of the late papers. present my affectionate regards to all the family. I have not time to add more, than that I am your dutiful Son

J. MADISON JR.

[1] In his letter of 1 August 1781 to his father, JM had also mentioned forwarding Philadelphia newspapers, along with six English grammars for the Orange County schoolmaster, Walker Maury (*Papers of Madison,* III, 206–7). Apparently JM was endeavoring to accumulate at Montpelier for his own reference in the future, as well as for his father's more immediate use, a complete file, probably of the *Pennsylvania Packet,* and wished to be informed of any missing issues. In the left-hand margin of the letter, opposite JM's sentence about the grammars, appears in his father's hand, "Mr. Maury pd. 18/ & 2d for Bal. of the other Dollars."

[2] Probably John Brownlow (1753–1816), a Fredericksburg commission merchant whose connections in times of peace were with mercantile houses in Liverpool, England (Fredericksburg City Records, Hustings Court Will Book B, pp. 3–4, microfilm in Virginia State Library).

[3] See Jameson to JM, *ca.* 12 January 1782, and n. 2.

[4] See JM to James Madison, Sr., 30 March 1782, and n. 4.

[5] James Hunter, Jr., whose business interests were now directed from Richmond (*Virginia Magazine of History and Biography*, LVI [1948], 18), and James Maury, a prominent Fredericksburg merchant.

Virginia Delegates to Benjamin Harrison

RC (Virginia State Library). Written by Joseph Jones. Docketed, "Virga. Delegates Letters, Feby. 15th. 1782. inclosg. resolution of Congress respectg Beef & men."

PHILA: 15th. Febry 1782.

SR.

We have your favor of the 2d. with the inclosures. those for Monsr. Mazzei shall be delivered to the minister of foreign affairs with request to forward them in the manner desired.[1]

Although general Greenes information of the number of Men reported to reinforce general Lessly at Charles Town may be exagerated,[2] yet it cannot be doubted the Enemy intend to prosecute the ensuing Campaign with all the vigor in their Power, and should considerable reinforcemts. get to Charles Town before general Greene is properly supported, we fear he will be obliged to abandon his present position and the blame fall chiefly on Virginia, whose line that should be first on the list of the southern Army for Numbers, is, we are informed, greatly short of that of Maryland.[3] Duty as a Member of the foederal union and interest as more intimately involved in the fate of the southern States, cannot fail to operate as powerfull incentives to Virginia to use every means in her power to recruit her continental line and afford every other reasonable support to the southern Army. As we are unacquainted with the supplies of Beef furnished by the State upon former requisitions we are at a loss to know how far it wod. be necessary to ascertain the terms of the supply now called for to enable the State to charge it in acct. with the united States in part of the quota of the present year. If therefore any thing further is necessary to be done You will please to communicate your desires and they shall be attended to.[4]

The Chevr. Luzerne has received intelligence from the Wt. Indies that the Count de Grasse with the fleet under his command and a large body of Troops commanded by the Governor of Martinique had invested the Island of St. Kitts, landed the Troops on the 7th. of last month and in ten days subdued the whole Island except the Fortress on brimstone Hill, to which place part of the British troops and some Militia had retired–that this place was closely invested and it was thought could not long withstand the force of the assailants–about one hundred Merchant Ships and Vessells with a large quantity of naval and military stores had fallen into the Counts hands–that Adml. Hood with nineteen Sail of the line lay at Barbadoes but hearing of the Counts movements had quited that place and gone to Antigua.[5]

Mr. Randolph intends shortly to Virginia[.] by him we will endeavour to send the journals you wrote for and also the Cypher so long promised.[6] we are with great respect

Sr. yr. obed. hum. servs.

J. Madison Jr.
Edmd. Randolph
Jos: Jones

[1] See Harrison to Virginia Delegates, 2 February 1782, and n. 7. Robert R. Livingston was secretary for foreign affairs.

[2] See Jameson to JM, 26 January 1782, n. 1; and Pendleton to JM, 11 February 1782, nn. 4, 5. General Leslie commanded the British southern army, which at this time probably numbered about thirty-five hundred men fit for duty (William B. Willcox, ed., *American Rebellion,* p. 588).

[3] On 7 December 1781 Greene had established his headquarters at Round O, about thirty-five miles from Charleston and athwart Leslie's most feasible line of communication between that city and Savannah–a line rendered more precarious for the British about six weeks later when Greene's pressure obliged them to evacuate James and Johns islands. By then, although the enlistment period of the Virginia troops had expired and most of them were on their way home, Greene's army was approximately as large as the enemy's, because he had been reinforced by a contingent led by Anthony Wayne and by weary and discontented Maryland and Delaware troops commanded by Major General Arthur St. Clair (Theodore Thayer, *Nathanael Greene,* pp. 387–90; George W. Greene, *Life of Nathanael Greene,* III, 421–22, 428–29, 430–32, 445–46). Thus the Virginia delegates had been correctly informed about the few soldiers from their state in Greene's army as compared with those from Maryland. See Jameson to JM, 26 January 1782, n. 3.

[4] Congress on 6 February, upon receiving Harrison's letter of 21 January to President Hanson enclosing a copy of Greene's letter of 27 December 1781 to the governor, referred the two dispatches to a committee of which Joseph Jones was a member and the draftsman of its report. This report, adopted by Congress on 13 February, not only directed Robert Morris "to take immediate measures" to send salt and rum to Greene and to expedite for service with him whatever troops Washington felt able to detach from his own army, but also "earnestly recommended to the executive authority of the State of Virginia to take decisive and

effective measures to furnish the men and beef required by General Greene in his letter of 27 of December last" (*JCC*, XXII, 67 n., 74). A copy of this latter recommendation was enclosed by the delegates in the present dispatch. See Harrison's reply of 1 March.

Before receiving the present dispatch, Harrison and the Council of State had been embarrassed by the failure of some county courts to appoint commissioners of taxation and by the negligence of the commissioners in other counties to report collections of beeves (*Journals of the Council of State*, III, 46, 48). Probably adding to the confusion was the act of the General Assembly on 5 January 1782, directing the executive, where "necessary," to discontinue the "state quarter-masters and commissaries, and put into the hands of the continental staff officers the disbursement of the state resources" (Hening, *Statutes*, X, 415). On 18 February the resignation of William Armistead, Jr., was accepted, after he had pointed out that his role as state commissary of stores had become superfluous, the public stores being "almost destitute of every necessary Supply for the Army" (*Calendar of Virginia State Papers*, III, 66; *Journals of the Council of State*, III, 47).

[5] Disembarked on St. Kitts (St. Christopher) from Grasse's ships on 11 January, the Marquis de Bouillé, governor of Martinique, and his troops soon had the much smaller British force confined to Brimstone Hill. In a sharp engagement on 25–26 January, Rear Admiral Sir Samuel Hood's twenty-two ships forced the twenty-nine of Grasse to abandon the anchorage of Basseterre Roads, about twelve miles from the hill, but Hood was unable to prevent the surrender of the garrison on 12 February, along with ten pieces of artillery, six thousand cannon balls, and fifteen hundred mortar shells. Having sailed from St. Kitts the next day, Hood effected a junction about two weeks later near Antigua with Admiral Sir George Brydges Rodney's fleet, recently arrived from Great Britain (Karl Gustaf Tornquist, *The Naval Campaigns of Count de Grasse during the American Revolution, 1781–1783*, trans. and ed. by Amandus Johnson [Philadelphia, 1942], pp. 81–82). On 20 March the *Pennsylvania Journal*, which had reported Bouillé's victory in its issue of 27 February, printed the Articles of Capitulation, dated fifteen days earlier at St. Kitts.

[6] The sending of the cipher would be a tardy fulfillment of the intention expressed by the delegates to Governor Thomas Nelson, Jr., in their letter of 23 October 1781 (*Papers of Madison*, III, 293). Harrison had requested the journals in his dispatch of 11 January 1782 to the delegates (*q.v.*).

Report on Settlement of Accounts

MS (NA: PCC, No. 19, IV, 347–49). Docketed: "Report of Mr Cornell Mr Montgomery Mr Madison On a letter of 18 from superintendant of finance[.] Read Debated 26. The two last paragraphs recommitted[.] Passed Feby 27th 1782." JM wrote all of the report except two passages mentioned below in notes 4 and 5.

[20 and 27 February 1782][1]

The Committee to whom was referred a letter from the Superindt. of Finance of the 18th. instant[2] recommend the following resolutions,

That five Commissioners be appointed for the Settlements of accounts under the direction of the Superintendant of the Finances namely one for the Quarter Master's Departmt one for the Commissary's Department, one for the Hospital Department, one for the Cloathier's Department, and one for the Marine Department; each of which commissions shall have full power & authority to liquidate & finally settle the accounts of the departments respectively assigned to them up to the last day of December 1781 inclusive[3]

That the Superintendant of Finance be authorised and directed to appoint the said five Commissioners, and that he report the names of the same to Congress. & in order that they may disapprove such appointment if they shall think proper.[4]

That each of the said Commissioners be allowed one Clerk for his assistance in the execution of his Trust: or[5] in case more sd. be found necessary, that he be authorised to add such number as the Superintendt. of Finance shall approve.

That a Salary be allowed to each of sd. Commissioners at the rate of 1500 Dollars per Annum, during the time in which he shall be employed in the duties assigned to him; and that each Clerk be allowed a Salary at the rate of 500—Dollrs per annum during the time of his Service. to be in full to Each for their Services and Expences.[6]

That it be recommended to the several Legislatures of the States to empower the said Commissioners to call for Witnesses & examine them on oath or affirmation touching such accounts as are respectively assigned to them for settlement; and that it be also recommended to the said Legislatures to make provision by law for the speedy & effectual recovery from individuals of debts due & effects, belonging to the U. States[7]

[1] Although not mentioned in the printed journal of Congress, Robert Morris' letter of 18 February was referred the next day to Ezekiel Cornell, Joseph Montgomery, and JM. This committee rendered a report on 20 February. See Charles Thomson's committee book in NA: PCC, No. 186, fol. 13.

[2] The first two pages of this letter are in *ibid.*, No. 137, I, 333–34. The final page is missing. Morris recommended that the accounts of the commissary, quartermaster, hospital, and marine departments be settled by special commissioners, appointed by Congress, who should have "a Degree of Vigor and Decision in the Conduct of the Business which few men possess, a knowledge of Business which is not commonly to be found, and such uncorrupted and uncorruptible Integrity as will give Security to the United States." Morris warned Congress that, in all likelihood, the commissioners would uncover "many fraudulent Practices" by the personnel of those four departments.

[3] Except for changing Morris' "four" to "five" at the opening of this paragraph, so as to include the "Cloathier's Department," and adding the provision that the commissioners should be under the direction of the superintendent of finance, the

committee up to this point made merely minor textual alterations in Morris' own draft.

[4] As adopted by Congress, the words "and he is hereby" appear between "be" and "authorised." Furthermore, the portion of this paragraph beginning with "&" is in Charles Thomson's hand and was probably an amendment made during the debate of 26 or 27 February on the report.

[5] The word "and" replaces "or" in the version adopted by Congress.

[6] Morris had asked for authorization to reach an agreement with the commissioners respecting their services and "the Allowances to be made to their Clerks" (NA: PCC, No. 137, I, 334). The last clause of this paragraph, which may have been written by John Hanson, was probably appended during the debate mentioned in n. 4, and "of them" was inserted between "Each" and "for" prior to the adoption of the report.

[7] JM wrote this paragraph as a substitute for two paragraphs which Congress evidently asked the committee to reconsider as a result of the debate on 26 February. The two paragraphs read:

"That it be recommended to the States to empower the said Commissrs. to send for such persons & papers as may be found necessary in the course of their business.

"That a Committee be appointed to prepare a bill to be recommended to the States, providing for an effectual recovery from individuals, of effects belonging & debts due to the U. States."

JM crossed out these recommendations, wrote "turn over" at the bottom of the manuscript, and penned the substitute on the reverse of the page. Possibly the alteration had been required by a majority in Congress who felt that the committee's original recommendations had shown too little deference to state sovereignty.

Morris had difficulty in finding men sufficiently well qualified to hold the five new positions (nn. 2 and 3, above). Congress accepted his departmental appointees on the following dates: commissary, 22 April; quartermaster, 1 August; hospital, 11 October; clothing, 14 October 1782; and marine, 19 June 1783 (*JCC*, XXIII, 204, 425; XXIII, 645, 648; XXIV, 402). For another report on the subject of this item, insofar as it related to the quartermaster general's department, see Report on Personal Liability of Officers of the United States, 13 March 1782.

From David Jameson

RC (LC: Rives Collection of Madison Papers). Docketed by JM at the beginning of the letter, "Jameson D.," and at the close, "Feby. 23. 1782."

RICHMOND Feb 23. 1782

DR SIR

I am favoured with yours of the 7th. and am very sorry (as you will not under take to join Mr Andrews in the necessary observations for ascertaining the boundary line yourself) to find that you have not succeeded in your endeavours to engage a proper person.[1] It is of consequence to be sure to have a person capable of making astronomical observations, but I think it of much more, to have a person well skilled in the Grants, Charters &ca. that have been obtained, And who is from a general knowledge of the subject equal to the task. I wish Mr Page would undertake the business. we had him in contemplation when the first appointment was made, but supposed he could not then conveniently leave his Family, and at that time he had not had the small pox, which disorder he much dreaded. I am told he is now inoculated, and I intend to write to him on the subject[2] I imagine you must ere this have recd. my several Letters, acquainting you with the Auditors answer[3]

Mr Ross is not in Town. I am unable therefore to say what steps have been taken to supply the wants of the Delegates so necessary for their peace and the honour of the State.[4]

We have not recd. a tittle of News from any quarter since my last I much fear your answer to the Govr. about the Continental Bounty will impede the recruiting business.[5] We are about to ask of the good Citizens an advance of their land Tax to enable us to pay the Bounty by Act of Assembly. the circular letter &ca. I will send you in my next. I much fear the people cannot find Specie enough to pay the 9/10 of the land Tax wch by the Revenue Act you will observe is directed to be pd in Specie[6] with great regard

I am Dr Sir Your Obedt hb Ser

David Jameson

[1] Jameson, as lieutenant governor, was probably referring to JM's letter of 7 February to Governor Harrison (*q.v.*). The governor was ill and, except on 18 and 22 February, did not attend meetings of the council between the fourteenth and twenty-eighth of that month (*Journals of the Council of State*, III, 45–51). If, on the other hand, JM wrote to Jameson on 7 February, the letter is now missing.

[2] See Harrison to JM, 19 January 1782, n. 3. Smallpox was rife during the winter of 1782 in the Virginia Tidewater, including Gloucester County, where John Page lived (*Calendar of Virginia State Papers*, III, 19, 35, 55, 56; Hening, *Statutes*, X, 458).

[3] Of these "several letters," the editors have found only the one of *ca.* 12 January 1782 (*q.v.*).

[4] See *ibid.*, and n. 4; and Harrison to Virginia Delegates, 9 February 1782.

[5] See Harrison to Virginia Delegates, 11 January 1782, and n. 3. By his remark, Jameson makes clear that the delegates had answered this letter. The reply, probably dated *ca.* 31 January, is now missing, and no mention of it occurs in the journal of the Council of State.

[6] See Jameson to JM, *ca.* 12 January 1782, and n. 8. To procure the money necessary for the payment of bounties to recruits, the Governor in Council on 12 February decided to empower "proper persons" in their respective counties "to receive from each of our patriotic Citizens whose zeal may incline them to aid their Country on this important occasion whatever monies they may think proper to advance on account of their Taxes for the current year" (*Journals of the Council of State*, III, 44). In accord with this plan, Governor Harrison drafted a circular letter, predated 1 March, to be sent to the county lieutenants and other prominent individuals. After amending the draft on 28 February, the Council of State directed the public printer to make eighty copies of the letter (*ibid.*, III, 52; McIlwaine, *Official Letters*, III, 154–57). See Jameson to JM, 2 March 1782, and n. 3.

Virginia Delegates to Benjamin Harrison

RC (Virginia State Library). Written by Joseph Jones. Docketed, "Virga. Delegates Letter recd March 7. 1782. Feby: 25th."

PHILA: 25th. Febry 1782

SIR

We have your Excellencys favor of the 9th. of this month. Since our last the plan for the final settlement of the public accounts from the commencement of the War to the 1st. of Janry. 1782, which we formerly mentioned to be under consideration has been adjusted and agreed to by Congress and will be fully explained to your Excellency by the superintendant of finance to whose department it properly belongs. the want of the rule prescribed by the articles of Confederation and which from the particular situation of some of the States could not now be obtained rendered the adoption of any mode very difficult,[1] the one proposed when the variety of circumstances and interests to be combined upon the occasion are considered will perhaps be found as free from exception as any that could be devised and will it is to be hoped meet the approbation of the States.[2]

We have reason to believe it has not proceeded from partiality to the Eastern and middle States that contracts for the southern department have not been proposed, as previous to the receipt of your Letter we had shewn attention to this business, and found the Financier disposed to take that course for supplying the southern department so soon as Taxes were laid and likely to be collected in those States to enable him to comply with such engagements as he should enter into for that purpose. If any preference appears to have been given to the State of Pensylvania in the benefit of Contracts we are assured it has proceeded from the money supplied by that State to enable the superintendant of Finance to fullfil them. This money was supplied in commutation for the specific requisitions due to the united States. It may with truth be said that the States as Virga. which supplied the specifics did their duty as much as Pensylvania wch. commuted for money, but unhappily the latter mode only has put into the hands of the superintendant the means of fullfiling future contracts.[3] we must beg leave to refer to the inclosed paper for the news and are very respectfully

Sr. yr. Excellencys obed hum: servts.

JAMES MADISON JR.
EDM: RANDOLPH.
JOS: JONES.
A. LEE

[1] See JM to Pendleton, 7 February, n. 6; and Report on Settlement of Accounts, 20 and 27 February 1782, and notes. Contrary to the delegates' assurance, "the plan" was not "fully explained" in Robert Morris' brief circular letter of 9 March to the executive of each state. In this letter, received by Governor Harrison and the Council of State on 21 March 1782, the superintendent of finance merely asked that the public accounts of Virginia be prepared for settlement and promised to send later "a general and comprehensive point of View" about the matter. In Morris' opinion, an adjustment of "these intricate and almost obsolete Transactions" was essential to the relief of creditors, to the restoration of public credit, "to the Consolidation of our federal Union, to the Promotion of general Harmony and generous Confidence throughout the United States, and to the Establishment of our glorious Independence on the Solid Base of Justice" (*Pennsylvania Archives*, 1st ser., IX, 512–13; *Journals of the Council of State*, III, 62). The executives of the states were not officially furnished with copies of the ordinances of Congress of 20 and 27 February until they were enclosed by Morris on 15 April 1782 in his second circular letter dealing with the subject (Wharton, *Revolutionary Diplomatic Correspondence*, V, 309–10).

[2] By the ordinance of 20 February, the commissioner for each state was authorized to estimate "all accounts of moneys advanced, supplies furnished, or services performed," by that state to the United States or by the latter to that state, according to the Board of Treasury's table of depreciation of 29 July 1780. In cases not covered by a directive of Congress, the commissioner was empowered to follow "principles of equity and good conscience" when settling, "in specie value, all certificates given for supplies by public officers to individuals, and other claims against the United States by individuals for supplies furnished the army, the transportation thereof and contingent expences thereon" (*JCC*, XXII, 85).

[3] See Harrison to Virginia Delegates, 9 February, and n. 3; Randolph to JM, 16–17 May 1782, and n. 18. In a lengthy circular letter of 15 February addressed to the state executives, Robert Morris had defended his allocation of contracts for supplying the army (Wharton, *Revolutionary Diplomatic Correspondence*, V, 164–69).

Although Virginia had had little or no money in her treasury for months past, Governor Harrison believed that she had nearly, or more than, filled her stipulated quota–not in cash, to be sure, but in many kinds of supplies and services to the southern army and to the continental line within her own borders. She had extended these aids upon her own initiative, or in response to requests from Congress, or from commanders of continental troops.

For this reason Harrison could hardly have relished the delegates' exoneration of Morris in the present letter. On 7 February the governor had written him, challenging the merits of his "plea" that Virginia fill a requisition for tobacco, and bluntly observing that neither Congress nor any of its officials had the constitutional competence to tell a state how to meet its financial quota. Moreover, Harrison had added, Virginia was "the only State that has not had large Advances made to it by Congress" and, as would become clear "whenever this States Account with the Continent comes to be settled," was "far from being indebted" to the Confederation (McIlwaine, *Official Letters*, III, 144–45). Upon receiving Morris' sharp rejoinder, Harrison answered in kind, asserting to the superintendent that his "Stile . . . savours much more of that passion and ignorance you so obligingly attribute to me, than that calmness and decency ever the Characteristic of the great Minister" (*ibid.*, III, 184; *Calendar of Virginia State Papers*, III, 77–78).

To Edmund Pendleton

RC (LC: Madison Papers). The cover is missing, but the letter was docketed by Pendleton, "James Maddison jr. Feb. 25th. 1782." In another hand, "E. Pendleton Esq Caroline County Va" appears at the bottom of the second page of the letter.

PHILADA. Feby. 25th. 1782

DEAR SIR

The irregularity of the post has again left me two of your favrs. to acknowledge at once, the first of which is of the 28th. Ultimo & the other of the 11th. instant. My two last it seems have miscarried altogether.[1]

You[2] have been misinformed I find with respect to that article in the scheme of the bank which claims for it the exclusive privilege of issuing circulating notes. It is true Congress have recommended to the States to allow it such a privilege, but it is to be continued only during the present war. Under such a limitation it was conceived both necessary to the success of the scheme, & consistent with the policy of the several States; it being improbable that the collective credit & specie of the whole wd. support more than one such institution, or that any particular State wd. during the war stake its credit anew on any paper experiment whatever.[3]

We have letters from Cadiz as late as the 7 of Jany. which impart that a Spanish fleet composed of 41 Sail of the line sailed from that port on the 3d. of the same month which had under their convoy transports with 4000 troops supposed to be destined for the Havanna. It was said the fleet was to cruize off Madiera & to await the junction of the Cr. de Guichen who had sailed from Brest on the 11th. of December with 19 ships of the line convoying 15,000 troops wch. with a part of the fleet it was supposed would also proceed for the W. Indies. It was reported however that an action, the issue of wch. was unknown, had taken place between de Guichen and a British squadron of 13 Ships under Admiral Kempenfeldt. This it was apprehended might disconcert the arrangement with the Spaniards.[4] Nothing definitive had happened at Minorca, but the reports continued to be flattering.[5]

The fate of Brimstone Hill the only remaining post on St. Kitts is not yet known here. A flag which came in a few days ago, with prisoners from Antigua confirms a preceding rumor of an engagement between Hood & de Grasse the former of whom had made an essay to relieve St. Kitts. An Antigua paper labours to make it probable that Hood had succeeded & that the French had lost a ship of the line, but the private information reverses the probability. The next post I hope will remove the uncertainty in which this must leave you.[6]

The inclosed papers will at length gratify you with the speech of the British King & the address of the two Houses of Parliament. The debates to which they must have given birth are either not arrived at N. York or they are backward in publishing them. The amendment proposed to the Address in the Upper House could not well fail to have produced an interesting skirmish between the oratorical combatants.[7]

The Gentleman from this place who reported the certain evacuation of N. York was an impudent liar. There has not existed here a whisper to palliate his offense.[8]

I am Dr. Sir with very sincere regard Yr. &c

J. MADISON JR.

[1] These were JM's letters of 22 January and 7 February 1782. When Pendleton received the earlier of these is unknown to the editors, but he acknowledged the one of the seventh in his letter of 25 February (*q.v.*).

[2] Late in life JM, or someone at his bidding, bracketed this paragraph to designate it for publication. See Madison, *Papers* (Gilpin ed.), I, 113–14.

[3] See Pendleton to JM, 28 January 1782, and n. 5.

[4] JM's information came from two letters, written at Cadiz on 7 and 8 January, respectively. Carried in the brigantine "Fox" to Philadelphia, extracts of them appeared in the *Pennsylvania Packet* of 19 February, with the names of writer(s) and addressee(s) omitted. JM probably saw the full text of these dispatches, because he mentions here a few details not found in the published excerpts. Commanding a fleet of thirteen war vessels and outmaneuvering Comte de Guichen with his nineteen ships of the line, Rear Admiral Richard Kempenfelt (1718–1782) in mid-December 1781 captured twenty French transports, manned by about five hundred sailors and carrying over one thousand troops. In consequence of this loss and of further damage suffered shortly thereafter in a heavy gale, Guichen was obliged to sail back to Brest, his port of departure. The reinforcement of Grasse in the West Indies with ships and soldiers was necessarily delayed for several months. Don Luis de Córdova's Spanish fleet, which Guichen had intended to join, returned to Cadiz (David Hannay, *A Short History of the Royal Navy, 1217–1815* [2 vols.; London, 1898–1909], II, 272–73; W. M. James, *British Navy in Adversity*, pp. 312–15, 366). See JM to Pendleton, 9 April 1782.

[5] A combined force of French and Spanish troops, led by the Duc de Crillon, had forced the British to surrender Castle St. Philip and Port Mahon, Minorca, on 4–5 February 1782 (Wharton, *Revolutionary Diplomatic Correspondence*, V, 171, 175).

[6] See Virginia Delegates to Harrison, 15 February 1782, n. 5. JM is reporting what would appear in the *Pennsylvania Packet* of 26 February. This issue admits that the British, instead of losing two frigates in Basseterre Roads, St. Kitts, as reported in the *Packet* of 23 February, had captured or destroyed one of Grasse's warships there. This report was also erroneous. In the operations around St. Kitts

between 23 January and 1 February, the small British frigate "Solebay" was wrecked on the coast of the neighboring island of Nevis, and the "Alfred" was damaged in a collision. British cannon balls obliged Grasse to make extensive repairs to the hull of his flagship "Ville de Paris" (Wm. Laird Clowes, *The Royal Navy: A History from the Earliest Times to the Present* [7 vols.; Boston, 1897–1903], IV, 112; David Hannay, *Short History of the Royal Navy*, II, 274). On 28 February the *Pennsylvania Packet* announced that the Brimstone Hill garrison had surrendered to the French.

[7] JM probably enclosed the *Pennsylvania Packet* of 19 and 23 February. The latter issue reported that the following amendment by the Earl of Shelburne on 27 November 1781 to the "Address to the King" in the House of Lords had been voted down: "And we will without delay apply ourselves with united hearts to propose and digest such councils, as may in this crisis excite the efforts, point the arms, and by a total change of system, command the confidence of all his majesty's subjects." After "united hearts," the official version reads, "to prepare and digest such councils to be laid at his royal feet, as may excite the efforts, point the arms, and command the confidence of all his subjects." The amendment was rejected by a vote of 75 to 31 (*Hansard's Parliamentary Debates*, XXII, cols. 649, 679).

[8] See Pendleton to JM, 11 February 1782, and n. 5.

From Edmund Pendleton

Tr (LC: Force Transcripts). Addressed to "The Honble James Madison jr Esqr Philadelphia." Another copy of the original manuscript is printed in the *Proceedings of the Massachusetts Historical Society*, 2d ser., XIX (1905), 147–48.

VIRGA. Feby 25th 1782

DR SIR

I have yr favr of the 7th and regret the Irregularity of the Post which has deprived me of some & delayed others of yr agreeable letters.[1] However I comfort myself with the reflection that the Frosty season is nearly over, and that our correspondence will soon become more regular as well as Interesting. I shall anxiously expect every future post to bring some account of the effects in Europe of the great event at York, which I think the first arrival from that quarter must certainly bring.[2] nothing of the sort has yet reached us. we have a loose report of a severe engagement between Genl Green and the Enemy, in which both sustain'd great & pretty equal loss, but it wants credibility & probability.[3] We are marching our drafts to reinforce him.[4]

I wish you out of the Thorny tract into which the Vermontiese have led you; I fear they are more like to produce that kind of fruit, than olives, and may require severe amputation.[5] Why should any Alteration be made at present in yr scales of contribution for each State?[6] since it is in its nature temporary and subject to adjustment, according to that rule which shall be established, when peace shall afford time and Opportunity for a proper investigation. the attempt now to change the Rule which can't be made a definition,[7] if it is not suggested by some Party Views, is calculated to produce dissentions, of which we have enough. If indeed the rule could now be finally fixd, it might be probably done with more temper[8] than when we are freed from the dread of a foreign Enemy, and I am persuaded that it would have been more justly and peaceably settled in 1776, as was intended by Congress the year before,[9] than it can be now, or at any future period, as the true spirit of Union was then more predominant than it has been since, or will be;[10] But as it was then put off, and a mode adopted subject to a future Account and Regulation, I cannot think it prudent to change that mode for another temporary one. In the meantime, I do not see why the Accounts should remain unexamined; The several Articles furnished by each State, may be exam[in]ed by the Vouchers and fairly entered in a General Account with that state, and be ready when ever the Proportion is fix'd, to form the Aggregate sum to be proportion'd, when in one Article each state may-be debited for its share, and the Ballance discover'd.[11] If this Minutia of the Account is neglected 'til the end of the War, I prophecy it will never be settled, but like the Contents of the Irish Treasurer's Waggons, will affrighten Congress out of the attempt, especially as it will probably be the Interest of some states to drop all Accounts & to burn Books, as the saying is. since I am reduced to the borrowing an expression from old Bonniface,[12] it is time to stop, & tell you that I am

Dr Sr Yr mo affe

EDMD PENDLETON

[1] See JM to Pendleton, 25 February 1782, n. 1.

[2] See Harrison to Virginia Delegates, 2 February, n. 1; and JM to Pendleton, 7 February 1782, n. 2. The *Pennsylvania Packet* of 19 February reported how gratified the court of Madrid had been to hear the news of Cornwallis' surrender.

[3] See Virginia Delegates to Harrison, 15 February 1782, n. 3. Although the "severe engagement" had never occurred, the rumor of it probably arose from the abortive attempt, during the night of 13–14 January, of a portion of General Greene's army to launch an attack against the enemy on James and Johns islands, a few miles south of Charleston.

[4] The version in the *Proceedings of the Massachusetts Historical Society* reads "making" rather than "marching." See Jameson to JM, 26 January, n. 1; and Harrison to Virginia Delegates, 1 March 1782, and n. 9.

[5] See JM to Pendleton, 7 February 1782, n. 4. In this letter JM had called Vermont a "thorny subject." By putting "olives" in opposition to thorns, Pendleton may

have had a particular passage of the Bible in mind or may have blended separate portions of several of its verses. For example, Matthew 7:16-19, Luke 6:44, and Judges 9:8-15 suggest Pendleton's metaphor.

[6] See Virginia Delegates to Harrison, 25 February 1782, and n. 2. The copy of the present letter in *Proceedings of the Massachusetts Historical Society* has "your scale," not "yr scales."

[7] The word "definitive" appears *ibid.*, but if Pendleton wrote "definition," he used it in the sense of "precise judgment."

[8] Used in the sense of "equanimity" or as an equivalent of the "justly and peaceably" appearing later in this sentence.

[9] Pendleton probably refers to the resolution of Congress of 29 July 1775 fixing a temporary quota of money to be contributed by each colony, with the understanding that the sums would "undergo a revision and correction" after "the number of Inhabitants, of all ages, including negroes and mulattoes" in each colony became known (*JCC*, II, 221–22). On 17 February 1776 a standing committee was directed, among other duties, to have each colony make an enumeration of its people. This, however, was not done either in that year or in any other year prior to 1783, even though the matter came before Congress occasionally, and Article IX of the Articles of Confederation stipulated that each state's troop quota should be proportionate to "the number of white inhabitants in such State," as compared with their total number in all the states (*JCC*, XI, 651; XIX, 219–20; XXI, 1129–30; XXV, 953).

[10] See *Papers of Madison*, III, 307–8; 309, n. 8; JM to Pendleton, 7 February 1782, n. 7.

[11] Pendleton was recommending that, although steps should be taken immediately to draw up a "General Account" for each state, listing its debits and credits as evidenced by relevant vouchers held by that state's and Congress' administrative officers, or by individuals who had furnished goods or services to civil or military agencies of the Confederation government, the preparation of a consolidated balance sheet ("one Article") for all the states taken together should or perhaps must await the end of the war, when the quota of each state could be determined in accordance with the "mode" prescribed by Article VIII of the Articles of Confederation. See JM to Pendleton, 7 February, nn. 5 and 6; Jones to Pendleton, 19 March 1782, in Burnett, *Letters*, VI, 319–20.

[12] The editors have been unable to identify the "Irish Treasurer's Waggons." See above, p. xix. Boniface, the innkeeper in the comedy *Beaux' Stratagem* by George Farquhar (1678–1707), rarely speaks without using the expression "as the saying is."

Benjamin Harrison to Virginia Delegates

FC (Virginia State Library). In the hand of Charles Hay.

VIRGINIA IN COUNCIL March 1st: 1782.

GENTLEMEN

The resolutions of Congress you inclosed me respecting the beef to be provided by this State, for Genl Greene's Army,[1] is by no means as full as it ought to be, and cannot be complyed with, even if our Circumstances were much more flourishing than they are.

I some time ago forwarded a resolution of our Assembly, forbidding any specific Supplies being furnished by the Executive, unless by special order of Congress, or the Financier;[2] the meaning of which is, that the State may get credit for their amount on the money demand made on us; if Congress intend this they must say so in explicit terms. You seem to doubt whether we have furnished the beef demanded from us in the last year; I beg you to calculate the rations of five or six thousand men for a year, to give us some Credit for what has been sent to the Southward; the supply furnished the Continental Army at York,[3] and the Support of the Several posts in this State, and you will have all your Doubts on that Subject cleared up.[4] True it is the Account is not yet settled, but as the troops have been supported by this State, the fact speaks for itself, and amounts to almost positive proof.[5]

You are by this time fully informed of our distressed Situation, my late Letters[6] being filled with scarce any thing else, notwithstanding which my endeavours to comply with the requisition of Congress if amended, shall not be wanting, and I have hopes of their proving successful, but without the alteration I can not stir a Step.

The Virginia Line in the field is weak, but not quite so much so as you think it is; between four & five hundred men from Cumberland Courthouse, will join the army, before this reaches you, and there are ninety three more on the Eastern Shore—that body of men[7] has amounted to nearly double the number they now are, but they have been so banded[8] about, and the time of their march so protracted by one means or other, that nearly one half of them are lost; those on the other Side of the Bay have been detained there, without any order from the State that I can hear of, and Colo Febiger now makes such Demands on us, for money & necessaries which he know[s] we have not, that I apprehend their terms of enlistment will expire, before he marches them.[9]

I have a Letter from Genl. Greene dated the 8th: ulto, all was quiet then and had been so for some time. The Enemy were within their lines of Charlestown and Savannah, and had not been reinforced with more than three hundred men both from Europe & New York.[10]

A Gentleman of this Town has received a letter of late date from the West Indies, informing him that the French had attempted Brimstone Hill by Storm; that they were repulsed with the loss of seven hundred men, that Hood had been so reinforced as to make him nearly equal to the French Fleet, and that they were in Sight of each other, both seeming determined to fight.[11] If this should prove true & the old Count can give him a good Drubbing, it will bring about what we much want—a good Peace. I am &c

BENJAMIN HARRISON.

P S. Inclosed you have a Copy of the resolution of the Assembly.[12]

[1] See Virginia Delegates to Harrison, 15 February 1782, n. 4.

[2] See Harrison to Virginia Delegates, 15 January 1782, and n. 2.

[3] Yorktown, Va.

[4] On 28 February, in a letter to Harrison, Robert Morris urged that cattle be forwarded speedily to General Greene. Morris added that if he was mistaken in his belief that "a considerable Ballance is due from the State of Virginia on the Requisitions for Specific Supplies," the value of the cattle would be accounted a part of the state's quota of 1782 (*Calendar of Virginia State Papers*, III, 79).

[5] See Report on Settlement of Accounts, 20 and 27 February, and n. 7; Virginia Delegates to Harrison, 25 February 1782, and notes.

[6] See Harrison to Virginia Delegates, 11 January and 9 February 1782.

[7] Judging from Harrison's specific mention later in this paragraph of "those on the other Side of the Bay," he was referring here to the recruits then at Cumberland Old Court House.

[8] Harrison probably intended to write "bandied."

[9] See Jameson to JM, 26 January 1782, and nn. 1 and 3. For the dearth of money, food, liquor, clothing, and military equipment, handicapping the efforts to recruit soldiers, encouraging their desertion, and retarding the dispatch of Virginia continentals to Greene's army in South Carolina, see *Calendar of Virginia State Papers*, III, 65–95, *passim*. On 11 February, in a letter to Colonel Christian Febiger, chief continental recruiting officer for Virginia, Harrison stressed that "perfect Oeconomy is absolutely necessary" and added, "I am extremely anxious to hear of the March of the Detachments ordered to the Southward" (McIlwaine, *Official Letters*, III, 149). Instead of making a direct reply to a letter from Febiger, the Governor in Council referred the dispatch on 26 February to Colonel William Davies, commissioner of the war office, with a directive to inform Febiger "That the Executive do not think themselves authorized to give any Instructions with respect either to the stay or removal of the troops on the Eastern Shore, they being a part of this States Quota raised for the continental army, are subject to the orders of the commander in chief only" (*Journals of the Council of State*, III, 50–51). Unable to accept Harrison's contention that the contingent on the Eastern Shore enjoyed a special status, Davies on 5 March advised the governor that he considered those troops available for Greene's use (*Calendar of Virginia State Papers*, III, 84).

[10] On 4 March, in acknowledging Greene's dispatches of 8 and 24 January, Harrison expressed "great Pleasure to find the boasted reinforcements of the Enemy dwindled down to a mere handful of men," but in response to a plea for reinforcements, Harrison stated that "it is not in my power to send you Aid of militia" and reiterated his complaints concerning the unreasonableness of Febiger's demands (McIlwaine, *Official Letters*, III, 169–70). See JM to Pendleton, 22 January, n. 10; Jameson to JM, 26 January, n. 1; and Pendleton to JM, 11 February 1782, n. 4. In a letter to President John Hanson on 10 February, read in Congress on 13 March, Greene derived from the "very wretched condition" of his troops the lesson that "If we cannot learn to feel for one another's suffering, and be more ready to succour

the distressed, or be brought to it by some co-ercive Power . . . we cannot long continue a United People" (NA: PCC, No. 172, II, 17, 18).

[11] A report to this effect, appearing in the *Pennsylvania Packet* of 2 March as an excerpt from the *Royal Gazette* of New York City, was false. See Virginia Delegates to Harrison, 15 February 1782, n. 5. After Rodney and Hood united their fleets on 25 February, they had more ships and heavier armament than the squadron of Grasse, "the old Count," who was then fifty-nine years of age.

[12] The resolution is quoted in n. 2 of Harrison to the Virginia Delegates, 15 January 1782.

From David Jameson

RC (LC: Rives Collection of Madison Papers). Docketed by JM, "Jameson D."

RICHMOND Mch 2. 1782

DR SIR

It was very unfortunate that Count de Grasse did not succeed in his designs agt. Barbadoes and Hoods fleet.[1] had they fallen I think it must have shortened the War. however we will be content if St Kitts is reduced, but by information we have had, the French failed in an attempt to Storm Brimstone Hill, and lost a considerable Number of Men.[2] I mentioned to you in my last that the Executive intended to address the people in hope of an advance of part of the land tax to recruit our line. the letter &ca. is not yet come from the press.[3] I am truly sorry it is not now in our power to send Gen. Greene a greater reinforcement. By his last letter[4] the Enemy's force is not so formidable as he had supposed it would be, when he sent off his former dispatches. Yet I wish we could give him aid, I wish indeed our whole line was compleat. would it not be proper to have all the troops of our line together? I fear those at Pittsburg we have no credit for. The Govr. has been advised to write to the General on that head.[5] Gen. Greene has again mentd. the Beef Cattle. the Governor has written to the Delegates on the occasion.[6] Mr Ross is expected here in a day or two and you may depend every thing that can be will be done to keep you supplied.[7] I am told Dr. Lee was provided with Money. when Col Bland means to return I have not heard[8]

Mr Stark is out of Town and the other Auditors[9] know nothing of your Accots. by next post you shall have a full answer on that head

We are told the Lottery is drawing, if so be so kind as send a list of the prizes as soon as published[10]

I have desired Mr Hayes to inclose a paper to you every week wch.

he has promised to do. Messrs Nicholson & Prentis assure me they do so.[11] I gave these directions, that you may meet with no disapointment in my absence[12] with very great esteem I am

dr Sir Yr Obedt hb Servt

DAVID JAMESON

[1] See JM to Pendleton, 25 February 1782, and nn. 4 and 6. Adverse weather in the West Indies, Hood's skillful maneuvering of his fleet, and Kempenfelt's capture of many French troops on their way to the Caribbean were among the reasons why Grasse and Bouillé failed to capture Barbados and other British islands (W. M. James, *British Navy in Adversity*, p. 321).

[2] See Virginia Delegates to Harrison, 15 February, n. 5; and Harrison to Virginia Delegates, 1 March 1782, n. 11.

[3] See Jameson to JM, 23 February 1782, n. 6. On what date the copies of Harrison's circular letter of 1 March were sent out is indeterminable, except that one had been received at Norfolk before 27 March (*Calendar of Virginia State Papers*, III, 112). Jameson's "&ca." probably refers to printed "Certificates or Receipts" which were to accompany each letter. When "signed by certain persons authorized by the executive to give the same, for monies advanced on account of the Land tax," each certificate would be accepted by the state treasurer as equivalent to the sum of money entered on the paper (*Journals of the Council of State*, III, 52).

[4] See Harrison to Virginia Delegates, 1 March 1782, and n. 10.

[5] In a letter of 8 February Governor Harrison proposed to Washington that he transfer the personnel of the 7th Virginia Regiment at Fort Pitt, numbering about 120, to Greene's army (McIlwaine, *Official Letters*, III, 146). Unknown to Jameson, Washington's reply of 28 February, although assuring Harrison that those troops would not be merged with the Pennsylvanians in the garrison to form a single regiment, declined to adopt the governor's suggestion. On the contrary, in a letter of 8 March to Brigadier General William Irvine directing him to assume command at Fort Pitt, and in a dispatch four days later to Brigadier General Peter Muhlenberg ordering him to supersede Febiger as chief continental recruiting officer in Virginia, Washington made clear that he expected to send to the fort an unspecified "proportion" of the continental recruits then being raised in his native state (Fitzpatrick, *Writings of Washington*, XXIV, 28, 48, 61).

[6] See Jameson to JM, 26 January, and n. 1; Virginia Delegates to Harrison, 15 February, and n. 4; and Harrison to Virginia Delegates, 1 March 1782.

[7] David Ross. See Jameson to JM, *ca.* 12 January; and Harrison to Virginia Delegates, 9 February 1782.

[8] See *Papers of Madison*, III, 161, n. 2. Arthur Lee re-entered Congress on 19 February 1782. Theodorick Bland was not in Congress from about 9 October 1781 to 15 April 1782 (*JCC*, XXI, 1043; XXII, 77–78, 180).

[9] Bolling Stark, Harrison Randolph, and John Boush (*ca.* 1752–1792).

[10] The drawings of the winning tickets in the national lottery had begun on 2 April 1781 and were still continuing (*Papers of Madison*, II, 290, n. 9; III, 5, n. 8). On 26 March 1782 Congress was informed that the drawing of the remaining tickets, numbering about thirty thousand, would be completed in a month. Appearing intermittently in Philadelphia newspapers was an advertisement inviting "lottery adventurers" to learn the "fate of their tickets" by applying to a clerk in Robert Morris' office (e.g., *Pennsylvania Packet*, 14 March 1782).

[11] See Jameson to JM, 26 January 1782, n. 5.

[12] Jameson retired from the Council of State on 30 March 1782 (*Journals of the Council of State*, III, 68–69).

From the Reverend James Madison

RC (LC: Madison Papers). Letter has an appended note by Carlo (Charles) Bellini. Docketed by JM, "Madison Js. Revd. Mar. 1782."

[*ca.* 2] March. 1782.
WM. & MARY COLL.

After so long a Silence, my Friend, where shall I begin? Like Cain, I have been a Vagabond, since August last.[1] But have at Length returned to this Place, for little else indeed, than to be a Spectator of Misery & Ruin. Our Friend Bellini, who has withstood all the Calamities which surrounded him with a Fortitude worthy of an old Roman Descent, affords me now an Asylum to write you a few Lines: otherwise I know not that I could here scarce find a Place,[2] even to beg you to reassume a Correspondence, which I so highly esteem, but which my Situation has hitherto rendered almost impracticable. We have spent the Winter in Botetourt, with not such Scenes as Philada. affords—and have often regretted that one of the Inconveniences of so distant a Corner was, the Interruption of some Kind of friendly Intercourse between us. But soon hope to be resettled here. As it is probable the French Army will evacuate their *Hospital* in the Spring.[3]

I congratulate you with all my Heart upon the many glorious Events which America has lately experienced. But when, will this Devastation of every Thing necessary to human Felicity cease. When shall we once more enjoy the Blessings of Peace, & behold the cruel Sword beaten into the blessed Plowshare.[4] If you can afford me any Consolation upon this Head, pray communicate it. For I am tired of war, & every Thing relative to it. I believe the most perfect Quietist, the most rational Being.[5] You mentioned in one of your Letters formerly the name of Chastellux.[6] I have now the Pleasure of knowing him. he has been presented with the most honourable Mark of Distinction wch. our University can confer, & promises to be very useful to it—And also to be active in having a Compensation given for our great Losses here.[7] He seems indeed a distinguished Character.

I must leave Room for Mr. B. so that I shall only at present beg to be remembered by yourself, the Atty Mr R. & M[?][8]

Yr. affe. Friend

J. MADISON

Carmo. Sige. Giacomo: Nonostante ch'io abbia moltissimo sofferto relativamente a ciõ che i mici Amici, ed in particolare il Sigre. Presidente, e La povera Università, io non ni sono impiccato: S'io posso rivedere, a Lei e gli altri, e L'Università nel Loro Stato primiero, io Sarò immortale certamente; per ora io sono col piu dipinto ossequio, e La Stima piu perfetta.

Suo Divosmo, Obbtmo. Serve ed Amico

C. Bellini

Dearest Mr. James: Notwithstanding the great deal which I may have suffered with regard to my friends, and in particular the President, and the poor University, I have not hanged myself: If I could see you, and the others again, and the University as it once was, I would be forever grateful; for now I am with the highest respect and esteem,

Your most devoted, obedient Servant and friend,

C. Bellini

[1] Genesis 4:12–14. Beginning in March 1781 the College of William and Mary was closed for about a year, because Williamsburg was successively occupied during much of that period by the British and the Franco-American armies.

[2] See *Papers of Madison,* III, 182, n. 18. Evidently Carlo (Charles) Bellini was again living in his own house, which he seems to have vacated in October 1781, at Washington's request, for use as a military hospital (Fitzpatrick, *Writings of Washington,* XXIII, 234–35).

[3] On 21 July 1781 the Reverend James Madison had written his brother William, then sheriff of Botetourt County, that, because the "College is entirely broke up" and "Nothing but a lucky Accident" had kept most of his few slaves from "joining the Enemy," he had decided to move to Botetourt and hoped that "any kind of House of my own" could be found there (Pierpont Morgan Library, New York City). Although the location of the clergyman's temporary home in the county is unknown to the editors, it probably was close to his brother in or near the present town of Cloverdale (Robert Douthat Stoner, *A Seed-Bed of the Republic: A Study of the Pioneers in the Upper (Southern) Valley of Virginia* [Roanoke, Va., 1962], pp. 112, 456). The French used the college buildings as a hospital (*William and Mary Quarterly,* 2d ser., VIII [1928], 246). When the vanguard of the French army left Williamsburg on 1 July, followed the next day by Rochambeau and his staff, the French left behind the hospital corps and an artillery contingent numbering about four hundred men in all (Acomb, *Journal of Closen,* pp. 207–8). See also Randolph to JM, 5 July 1782, and n. 7.

[4] Micah 4:3.

[5] A Quietist is a mystic who, through prolonged contemplation, transcends all selfish desires and thus attains a state of perfect peace.

[6] In the missing letter of February 1781 to his cousin, which Captain Thaddy Kelly carried to Williamsburg, JM may have mentioned that he had dined on 13 December 1780 with François Jean, Chevalier de Chastellux, in Philadelphia (*Papers of Madison,* II, 226, n. 7; III, 11, n. 1).

[7] Chastellux received the degree of doctor of civil law from the College of Wil-

liam and Mary on 2 March 1782. Shortly after the surrender of Cornwallis, when the leaders of the college sought to regain possession of their campus, Chastellux encouraged their efforts. Writing of the institution, Chastellux remarked: "The beauty of the edifice is surpassed by the richness of its library, and that, still farther by the distinguished merit of several of the Professors, such as the Doctors *Maddison, Wythe, Bellini,* &c. &c. who may be regarded as living books, at once affording precepts and examples" (*Travels in North-America, in the Years 1780, 1781, and 1782* [2 vols.; Dublin, 1787], II, 209). See also *William and Mary Quarterly*, 1st ser., XV (1906–7), 264–65.

In a letter of 23 February 1782, Washington thanked Rochambeau "for your generous donation to our Hospital at Williamsburg" (Fitzpatrick, *Writings of Washington*, XXIV, 19; Boyd, *Papers of Jefferson*, VI, 144). Indeed, most of the townspeople were sorry when the army left, because the French had spent much hard money in the community, destroyed little private property, and recompensed owners who had suffered losses during the occupation. For the generosity of the French toward the Reverend James Madison, see Edmund Randolph to JM, 18 July 1782; Acomb, *Journal of Closen*, p. 166. Baron Hans Christoph Friedrich Ignatz Ludwig von Closen-Haydenburg (*ca.* 1754–1830) was an aide-de-camp of Rochambeau.

[8] "Mr R." was Edmund Randolph, and if this indistinct letter is "M," it probably signifies "Mrs" or "Mistress" Randolph.

Motion on Secretary for Foreign Affairs

MS (NA: PCC, No. 25, II, 81).

[4 March 1782]

That the Scy. of F: Affairs have permission to be absent from the public service for the time requested in his letter of day of [1]

[1] A letter, now missing, from Robert R. Livingston, secretary for foreign affairs, to the president of Congress was referred to Arthur Lee, John Morin Scott (N.Y.), and Thomas Bee (S.C.). To this committee's report, recommending that the secretary's request for a leave of absence of "a few weeks" be granted "if in the opinion of Congress the business of his Department will admit of it," JM evidently moved the above addendum, after hastily writing it on a scrap of paper. Congress accepted this amendment along with the committee's report (*JCC*, XXII, 114–15).

Livingston's "excursion to the state of New York" lasted for over a month (Burnett, *Letters*, VI, 330 n.). At this time he was discontented because Congress accorded his office little prestige, assigned tasks to him which he deemed menial, and denied him much independence of action in the shaping of foreign policy. In New York his political rivals were seeking to remove him as chancellor on the grounds that he should not simultaneously occupy a high position under each of two governments (George Dangerfield, *Chancellor Robert R. Livingston of New York, 1746–1813* [New York, 1960], pp. 144–45, 177, 477, n. 28; Report on Form of Public Audience for La Luzerne, 7–9 May 1782, n. 7).

Virginia Delegates to Benjamin Harrison

RC (Virginia State Library). Written by Joseph Jones. Docketed, "Virga Delegates Lr. recd. March. 1782. March 5th."

PHILA: Mar: 5th. 1782

SIR.

This weeks Post has brot. us no Letter from your Excellency.

Mr. Ross has directed Mr. Whiteside a mercht. of this City to pay us £200 each,[1] which will enable those of us who have been sometime here to discharge our outstanding balances but will leave a small sum only for future occasions.

We impatiently expect a confirmation of the very interesting intelligence received from the Wt. Indies respecting the entire reduction of the Island of St. Christophers by the Forces of his most christian Majesty and advantage gained by the Fleet of the Ct. de Grasse over that of Sr. Saml. Hood. this last circumstance, if true, will give the Count so decided a superiority, that it is probable other Islands of the Enemy will soon share the fate of St. Christophers.[2]

The Chevr. de la Luzerne will we expect, in a few days set out for Virginia on a visit To Ct. Rochambeau, you will probably see him at Richmond.[3] very respectfully we are

Yr. Excellencys obed Servts.

JAMES MADISON JR.
EDM: RANDOLPH
ARTHUR LEE
JOS: JONES

[1] See Expense Account as Delegate, 20 March 1782. Probably in 1777, after serving for "about three years" as a clerk in Willing, Morris and Company's office, Peter Whiteside (1752–1828) became a Philadelphia merchant under the firm name Peter Whiteside and Company. Thereafter Congress occasionally had business dealings with the company (NA: PCC, No. 19, IV, 247–48; *JCC*, XI, 738, 837; XIII, 164–66; XVI, 136–37; Clarence L. Ver Steeg, *Robert Morris: Revolutionary Financier, with an Analysis of His Earlier Career* [Philadelphia, 1954], p. 31; *Harper's Encyclopedia of United States History from 458 A.D. to 1905, based upon the Plan of Benson John Lossing* . . . [10 vols.; New York, 1905], X, 348). By 1784 Whiteside had acquired 50,000 acres of land in Kentucky (Willard Rouse Jillson, comp., *Old Kentucky Entries and Deeds: A Complete Index to All the Earliest Land Entries, Military Warrants, Deeds and Wills of the Commonwealth of Kentucky* [Louisville, 1926], p. 159).

[2] See Virginia Delegates to Harrison, 15 February, n. 5; and JM to Pendleton, 25 February 1782, n. 6. The *Pennsylvania Packet* of 7 March reported that Grasse's ships outnumbered Hood's and that an early engagement between the two fleets was almost certain to occur.

[3] La Luzerne left Philadelphia about 8 March and returned by 13 April, but he did not visit Richmond while in Virginia (Wharton, *Revolutionary Diplomatic Correspondence*, V, 229, 302–3; Randolph to JM, 11–13 April 1782). In his dispatch of 7 March 1782 to Vergennes, La Luzerne wrote that, besides seeking to persuade Rochambeau to come north for a conference with Washington on military affairs, he hoped to ascertain in Virginia "the causes of the languor which the state has shown for the last three or four years, and rouse the government officials, as best I can, to adopt more vigorous measures" (William E. O'Donnell, *Chevalier de La Luzerne*, p. 202). Having this objective, it is strange that La Luzerne did not include the state capital in his itinerary. Harrison explained in his letter of 4 May 1782 to the Virginia delegates (*q.v.*) why he could not go to Williamsburg before 29 March to call upon La Luzerne. On that day the French minister left the town to return to Philadelphia (*Pennsylvania Packet*, 16 April 1782).

Motion To Amend Articles of Confederation and a Rule of Congress

MS not found.

EDITORIAL NOTE

6 March 1782. In Charles Thomson's committee ledger under this date appears, "Mr Madison Mr Scott Mr Carroll[,] Motion of Mr. Madison for repealing the 16th. rule for the conduct of business & to revise the 8th article." A marginal note records that the committee reported on 18 March 1782 (NA: PCC, No. 186, fol. 15).

Neither the motion nor the report has been found. Thomson's entry is apparently the only extant reference to an action which would seem to have been of sufficient importance to deserve mention in other contemporary documents. The printed journal of Congress is very brief for 6 March and a complete blank for the eighteenth of that month. The vote, if any, on JM's proposals must have been adverse. By a coincidence, exactly one year later on 6 and 18 March 1783, Congress devoted attention to a committee report, drafted by JM, which included among the recommendations a revision of the eighth article of the Articles of Confederation. The fact that JM was the only member who served on both committees and that John Morin Scott was not in Congress in 1783 obviates the possibility that Thomson entered the wrong year in his ledger.

The sixteenth rule "for conducting business in the United States in Congress assembled" was: "The previous question (which is always to be understood in this sense that the main question be not now put) shall only be admitted when in the judgment of two states at least, the subject moved is in its nature or from the circumstances of time or place improper to be debated or decided, and shall therefore preclude all amendments and farther debates on the subject, until it is decided" (*JCC*, XX, 479).

In what respects JM wished to revise the eighth article of the Articles of Confederation is the more interesting question because of the phrase "common defence or general welfare" in that article. In its wording, if not also in its intent to limit the purposes for which Congress might levy "taxes, duties, imposts, and excises," this phrase was incorporated unchanged, except that "and" was substituted for "or," in Article I, section 8, paragraph 1 of the Constitution of the United States. In later years JM often challenged the accuracy of nationalists who contended that this phrase was a separate and substantive grant of authority to Congress rather than merely a limitation upon the tax power. By 1826 he would advocate an amendment to expunge the phrase from the Constitution (Madison, *Writings* [Hunt ed.], VI, 354–55; IX, 255, 417, 428 n.).

No reference has been found in JM's surviving papers to his effort in 1782 to amend the eighth article of the Articles of Confederation. This fact may signify either that his proposed change had no bearing upon the phrase "common defence or general welfare" or was inconsistent with his later position. The first of these two possible explanations is more likely the correct one, because his recommendations a year later, mentioned above, left the phrase unaltered. Probably in March 1782, as in March 1783, his motion sought only to make the provisions of the eighth article harmonize with the plan adopted by Congress on 20 February 1782 for the "settlement of public accounts" with each state. See JM to Pendleton, 7 February 1782, and especially nn. 5 and 6.

From David Jameson

RC (LC: Rives Collection of Madison Papers). Docketed by JM, "March 9. 1782."

RICHMOND Mch 9, 1782

DR SIR

I am to acknowledge the rect. of your favour of the 25th. ult.[1] You are right in your observation of the person proper to be entrusted with transcribing letters & papers to replace our loss by Arnold, but God knows when we shall have money to employ such person.[2] Mr Ross is not returned[.] I therefore cannot give you proper information of what is likely to be done for the Delegates. Agreable to the promise in my last I again waited on the Auditors[3] and am sorry it is not in my power to give you more satisfaction in that business. Mr Stark gave me two Accots. sent by you, and assures me these are all that can be found.[4] I inclose copies of these accots. & am in hope you can if it is necessary from them be able to judge of any others that have miscarried. the Auditors have not filled up the allowance, their reason I think good, it is, that the Assembly have made no alteration in that, since the Octob. session of 1779, which was 20 dollars P day. they have expected every Session that an alteration would be made, and therefore have not settled the two Accots. above mentd. they can as the law stands allow only the 20 dollars P day wch. for the last year was not worth accepting[.] it was a trifle indeed when the act passed[.] I cannot suppose but the Assembly will at their next meeting make the pay good for the two last years.[5] I have told the printers you had not recd. their papers. they assure me they were put up. I have now desired them to send the papers to M Ambler or myself to be inclosed[6]

I am Dr Sir Yr. afe. hb Sert

D. JAMESON

[1] This letter is missing, but JM probably wrote in much the same tenor as to Pendleton on the same day (*q.v.*).

[2] See *Papers of Madison*, III, 119, and n. 4. Whom JM recommended for the task is not known, but the governor and council on 21 March 1782 appointed Foster Webb, Jr., whose private business was taking him to Philadelphia, to transcribe "all Letters of importance which have passed prior to the first of January 1781, between the Executive of this State, Congress, his Excellency General Washington, and the Continental Boards of War & Treasurer" (*Journals of the Council of State*, III, 62, 86; Harrison to Virginia Delegates, 23 March 1782).

[3] See Jameson to JM, 2 March 1782, n. 9.

[4] See Jameson to JM, 2 March 1782. The "two Accots" were probably those of 20 September and 20 December 1781 (*Papers of Madison*, III, 264, 334), since there was a long delay before the state fully paid the balances due to JM on these reckonings.

[5] By laws to be enacted in the session of May 1782, the General Assembly would stipulate that a portion of the revenue derived from the tax on land and certain "articles" should be used to pay each delegate in Congress from Virginia "eight dollars per day" in the future and in settlement of all arrears of salary owed to him (Hening, *Statutes*, XI, 12–14, 31–32).

[6] See Jameson to JM, 26 January, and n. 5, and 2 March 1782, and n. 12. Jacquelin Ambler continued to attend the meetings of the Council of State until 12 April, when he assumed his duties as ad interim treasurer of the Commonwealth (*Journals of the Council of State*, III, 76).

From Edmund Pendleton

Tr (LC: Force Transcripts). Addressed to "The Honble James Madison junr Esqr Philadelphia." Another copy of the original manuscript is printed in the *Proceedings of the Massachusetts Historical Society*, 2d ser., XIX (1905), 148–49.

VIRGA March 11. 1782

DEAR SIR

I am to thank you for yr favr of the 25th past, in which you have removed by Objection[1] to the Bank scheme by proving that it was founded in error. The King of Britain's Speech and its doubted Echo, do not breathe the spirit of Peace with America, yet I think they tread that ground very tenderly & suddenly fly off at a tangent to the East Indies in search of a subject of Consolation.[2] If your Intelligence be true respecting the present state & prospect of their affairs in the West Indies,[3] I think no success they can have in the East will save them from the Necessity of peace.

I have a letter of the 24th January from Genl Green's Camp at Jacksonborough 36 Miles West of Chas Town—all was quiet, & no re-inforcement to the Enemy: What gave rise to the report of such, was the return of some convalescents who had been to New York to better their Health.[4] The Assembly was then sitting & had pass'd a law for confiscating British Property, and that of the Torys who had joined & remain'd with the Enemy;[5] most of those of note who had taken protection, have joined Us—& some of the refugees to Charles Town have ship'd themselves and property to Britain, an Omen that they at least have small hopes of being relieved. 30 sail of ships under convoy of a Frigate had just sailed with that sort of Cargoe.[6]

I have no doubt but the debates on the Speech and Addresses must be entertaining, the event at York was too good a subject for the Opposition to gall Administration with, for them to let slip, and no doubt they shone in it though they cut no figure in the vote.[7] I have nothing to add worth turning over so will only say that I am

Dr Sr Yr very affe friend

EDMD PENDLETON

[1] In the *Proceedings of the Massachusetts Historical Society* version, "by Objection" appears as "my objections." Pendleton probably wrote, or intended to write, "my."

[2] The version mentioned in n. 1 also has "doubted"; hence Pendleton must have written the word inadvertently instead of "undoubted." In all likelihood, his remark was prompted by JM's mention, in his letter to Pendleton on 25 February 1782 (*q.v.*, and n. 7), of the king's speech of 27 November 1781. The "Humble Address" of each House of Parliament, in reply to this speech, echoed its comment about the "favourable appearance" of the situation in India contrasting happily with the state of affairs in the American colonies. Excerpts from the debate in Parliament, occasioned by the king's speech, are in the 2 March issues of both the *Pennsylvania Packet* and *Pennsylvania Journal*. See Mazzei to JM, 13 March 1782, n. 15.

[3] See JM to Pendleton, 25 February 1782, and nn. 4 and 6.

[4] See Jameson to JM, 26 January 1782, n. 1. Jacksonboro was only nineteen miles west of Charleston. The reinforcements were the troops ordered in December 1781 to return from New York to their southern commands (Virginia Delegates to Harrison, 1 January 1782, n. 4). Although the letter to which Pendleton refers has not been identified, it may have been from his nephew, Judge Henry Pendleton,

who had returned to South Carolina and would be reimprisoned on 26 March by the British for violating his parole (*Papers of Madison*, II, 105, n. 5; *Pennsylvania Packet*, 18 and 25 April 1782). On 16 January Greene established his headquarters at Pon Pon, a plantation on the east bank of the Edisto River near Jacksonboro, where the General Assembly of South Carolina convened two days later. Although "all was quiet" in regard to military operations in the Charleston neighborhood, the expression inaccurately described Greene's state of mind. In a dispatch to Congress, written on the date of the present letter, he commented at length upon the "deplorable situation of our troops," who, he feared, must soon face a new British offensive (NA: PCC, No. 155, fols. 433–38).

[5] An "Act for Disposing of Certain Estates and Banishing Certain Persons" was passed by the General Assembly on 26 February (A. S. Salley, Jr., ed., *Journal of the House of Representatives of South Carolina: January 8, 1782–February 26, 1782* [Columbia, S.C., 1916], pp. 112, 121). Pendleton's informant was obviously misinformed about the date when this bill became a law.

[6] An account from Camden, S.C., dated 5 February, told of many Tories leaving Charleston to go behind American lines, and of "daily and great" British desertions (*Pennsylvania Packet*, 14 March 1782). The convoy and the frigate may have been the homeward-bound Cork fleet and its escort of either the 28-gun frigate "Grana" or the 32-gun "Quebec" (*ibid.*, 2 and 7 February 1782).

[7] See JM to Pendleton, 25 February 1782, and n. 7.

Virginia Delegates to Benjamin Harrison

RC (Virginia State Library). Written by Joseph Jones. Docketed, "Del: in Congress March 12th 1782."

PHILA: 12th. Mar: 1782

SR.

We are honoured with your favors of the 22d. ult.[1] and 1st. instant the last covering a resolution of the House of Delegates of the 5th. of Jan[ua]ry last which we had before received[2] and lodged a Copy with the supertendt. of Finance. We cannot at present return a full answer to your request respecting the supply of Beef required from Virga. for the Southern Army.[3] It is probable we shall be able to do it by Mr. Randolph, who will set off in a few days for Virga.[4]

respectfully we are yr. most hum. Sevts.

J. MADISON
JOS. JONES

[1] Not found. See Jameson to JM, 23 February 1782, n. 1.

[2] See Harrison to Virginia Delegates, 15 January, and n. 2; 1 March 1782.

[3] See Virginia Delegates to Harrison, 15 February 1782, and n. 4.

[4] See Virginia Delegates to Harrison, 19 March 1782. Edmund Randolph left

Philadelphia on 18 March and never resumed his seat in Congress. The General Assembly re-elected him as a delegate on 15 June 1782 (Minute Book, House of Delegates, p. 72), but he declined in a letter received by the House of Delegates on 11 December (*Journal of the House of Delegates*, October 1782, p. 61). On 1 June 1782 he was appointed to a committee of five "to collect all Documents and Proofs necessary for establishing the Right of this State to it's Western Territory as stated by the Act of Government in 1776" (Boyd, *Papers of Jefferson*, VI, 189), a project he believed to be of sufficient significance to engage his unremitting attention (Burnett, *Letters*, VI, 559, n. 2). See also Randolph to JM, 22 November 1782, quoted in excerpt by Moncure Daniel Conway in *Omitted Chapters of History Disclosed in the Life and Papers of Edmund Randolph* (New York, 1888), p. 47.

Report on Personal Liability of Officers of the United States

MS (NA: PCC, No. 19, V, 171–73). Docketed in JM's hand: "Report of the Committee on the letter from Colo. Pickering—Mr Livermore Mr Madison Mr Clarke[.] Passed March 19. 1782." A copy of the report is owned by Charles M. Storey of Boston.

MARCH 13th. 1782.

The Committee to whom was referred the report of the Committe[e] on the letter of day of from Coll. Pickering submit the following report.[1]

It being represented to Congress that divers suits have been & that others probably will be brought agst. the officers & servants of the U. States, for debts contracted by them with individuals for supplies furnished, or services rendered to the U. States, whereby such officers & servants may be exposed to great trouble & expence, in cases[2] where the failure to discharge their contracts hath proceeded from the deficiency of the advances recd. by them from the public treasury: And Congress having by their Resolution of the 2d. of Novr. last provided for the redemption of certificates for supplies & services afforded to the U. S. by resolving to accept the same from the States producing them in payment of balances due on former requisitions; & by subsequent resolutions[3] having directed the appointment of Commisers. for liquidating & settling[4] all such certificates & other demands agst. the U. S. as also Commisers. for settling finally the Accts. of the aforesaid officers & servants, whereby it will appear in what cases non payment of the debts contracted by them hath proceeded from misapplication of public monies advanced to them; & Congress having moreover recommended to the several Legislatures to make the necessary provision for the speedy & effectual recovery in behalf of the U. States of all balances which shall be found due from such officers & servts.

Resolved

That it be & hereby is recommended to the Legislatures of the several States to make suitable provision for staying all suits wch. have been brought & preventing future suits by individuals agst. the aforesaid officers & Servants for debts contracted by them for supplies furnished or services rendered to the U. States.[5]

[1] The copy owned by Charles M. Storey begins: "By the United States in Congress Assembled–March 19th. 1782–On a report of a Committee, consisting of Mr. Livermore, Mr. Madison and Mr. Clark to whom was committed a report on a Letter of the twenty fifth of February from Colonel T. Pickering Quarter Master General." Although no mention of the fact appears in the printed journal, Congress referred Timothy Pickering's letter (NA: PCC, No. 192, fol. 89) to a committee of five members, with John Morin Scott as chairman. Following the submission of their report on 7 March, Congress named a new committee to rewrite the recommendation (*ibid.*, No. 192, fols. 93–96). The present version bears little resemblance to Scott's report, but the resolutions at the close of the two drafts are alike in their general tenor. Pickering's request that state courts be barred from entertaining suits against him or his agents when, through no fault of their own, they were unable to fulfill their contracts for the purchase of military supplies recalls JM's committee report to Congress about Quartermaster General Nathanael Greene's liability for the financial dealings of members of his staff whom he could not closely supervise (*Papers of Madison*, II, 44–46).

[2] At first JM wrote "even in cases."

[3] For the resolution of 2 November 1781, see *JCC*, XXI, 1091. For the "subsequent resolutions," see Report on Settlement of Accounts, 20 and 27 February 1782; and *JCC*, XXII, 83–86, 102–4.

[4] After "settling," JM wrote and deleted "the accounts of the aforesaid officers & servants."

[5] The following addendum was moved by Abraham Clark and accepted by Congress: "Provided always that nothing in said Resolution contained shall be construed to imply an Opinion in Congress that the af[oresai]d. Officers & Servants of these united States are personally liable for any debts contracted by them for the Use & Benefit of the said States" (NA: PCC, No. 19, V, 175). Although Governor Harrison was not officially notified of the present resolution (an omission he attributed to "accident"), he invited the attention of the Virginia General Assembly on 4 June to the resolution as printed in the journals of Congress. Again on 21 October, following his receipt of Robert Morris' letter of 17 August 1782 on the subject, Harrison followed the same course (McIlwaine, *Official Letters*, III, 242, 348). The legislature declined to act. On 17 May 1783 William Finnie, stating that he was being sued "in his private character" for obligations incurred during his service as deputy quartermaster general of the southern army, petitioned the Assembly to adopt the congressional resolutions as state law. His petition was rejected by the House of Delegates (*Journal of the House of Delegates*, May 1783, pp. 10, 34).

From Philip Mazzei

RC (LC: Madison Papers). Docketed, "March 13. 1782[.] Mazzei," by JM, probably early in June 1782 when he received the letter (JM to Edmund Randolph, 4 June 1782, and n. 41).

FIRENZE 13. Marzo 1782.

CARISSIMO AMICO

Eccovi La mia terza in risposta alla sola gratissima vostra pervenutami data di Filadelfia di 25. 8bre 1781, e diretta a me in Firenze. Quelle che dite avermi scritte anteriormente, non mi son pervenute. Vi ringranzio delle nuove favoritemi tanto in essa, che nel P. S. alla gazzetta; ma son giunte troppo tardi, forse per non aver voi inclusa La Lettera in una sopraccarta diretta a Mr. Mark Lynch Mt. in Nantes, conforme desiderai nella prima mia de' 30. 9bre 1780, La quale io comprendo aver voi ricevuta, perchè fate menzione d'un paragrafo in cifra, e nella 2da. de' 7. 10bre. dell'istesso anno non vi era cifra. Poichè mi dite avervi scritto Mr. Jameson, che La cifra è persa, il detto Paragrafo resterà sotto chiave finchè io abbia il desiderato piacere di rivedervi. La mia 2da., che non sento aver voi ricevuta, conteneva La nuova della morte della Regina d'Ungheria, e alcune reflessioni sul sistema politico delle Potenze del Nort, che credevo doversi comunicare al Congresso, considerata La Fonte dalla quale ricevevo, come ricevo, i dati certi che mi autorizzano a congetturare con qualche fondamento. Dopo quel tempo è seguito un cambiamento stupendo, che allora non era neppur da sognarsi. Questo è il distacco della Russia dalla Prussia per collegarsi strettissimamente coll'Imperatore. Molti ne congetturano i principj politici, ma s'ingannano, quantunque Le operazioni future potranno forse far Loro credere d'aver bene indovinato. Il vero motivo è tale, che fornisce delle serie reflessioni, molto consolanti per chi à La sorte di esser cittadino di Patria Libera; ma senza cifra non posso scriverlo. Questo inaspettato, e sorprendente evento comincia ora ad esser pubblico. Son però più d'otto mesi che ne avevo dei forti indizj, e più di quattro che Lo sapevo di certo. Desideravo che fosse partecipato al Congresso; ma non sapendo se voi eri tuttavia in Filadelfia, ne scrissi al nostro Governatore nella mia 27ma. Lettera d'Officio il 1mo. 9bre 1781, e da quel che dissi in quella, e quel che aggiunsi nella 30ma. dei 18. Gennajo passato, si può rilevare un prospetto assai chiaro della presente situazion politica d'Europa. Si pretende che La Russia, e L'Imperatore abbian convenuto di cacciare il Turco d'Europa; i preparativi Loro, come pure quei del Turco par che avvalorino La Supposizione; e si teme da per tutto di una guerra universale. Per Le ragioni indicate nella detta Lettera 30ma., e per altre ancora, io continovo a credere che L'Imperatore procurerà di evitar La guerra. Se poi La Russia e L'Imperatore convenissero col Rè di Prussia di dividersi La Turchia Europea, come fecero di una porzione della Pollonia, La cosa riescirebbe senza strepito, e non produrrebbe altra consequenza che L'ingrandimento dei dominj di quelle tre Potenze. Ma volendo far ciò senza il consenso del Rè di Prussia, o volendo L'Imperatore tentare di ricuperar dal medesimo La Slesia, confidando nell'alleanza della Russia, ne seguirebbe una Lega tra il Turco Prussia e Francia contro Inghilterra Russia e Imperatore, colla superiorità dei primi (secondo La mia opinione) per tutti i capi. Le Finanze di questi sono in molto miglior situazione di quelle degli altri; il numero degli uomini maggiore, poichè L'Inghilterra non potrebbe somministrarne; megliore il comando stante che i Turchi medi. agirebbero sotto Generali prussiani; e tra gli altri stati piccoli, e mediocri, che prenderebbero partito quando seguisse una guerra universale, preponderebbe La forza di quegli che si unirebbero a questi. La Svezia non si staccherebbe dalla Francia, e il corpo Germanico preponderà di molto in favore del Rè di Prussia. A me pare dunque, che qualunque piega prendano Le cose in Europa, La nostra Causa sia stabilmente assicurata, e che i nostri affari debbano andare di bene in meglio.

Per La via di Francia sarete informato prima dell'arrivo di questa della presa del Forte S. Filippo, per cui L'Isola di Minorca è ora intieramente in possesso degli Spagnoli. Ci è qualche apparenza che Gibilterra possa subire L'istessa sorte. Il Governo Inglese pretende d'aver buone nuove dall'Indie Orientali, ma oltre il non farcene parola, i fondi della compagnia all'arrivo delle meda. caddero dal 139. al 134. I 3 per 100. consolidati erano cogli ultimi avvisi a 54⅝. Danno fuori che son per fare gran preparativi contro di noi, ma io son persuaso che, non ostante tutti i Loro sforzi faranno poco più del *parturiens mons.*

Coll'ultima mia degli 8. del corrente al nostro Governatore, che è La 31ma. d'Officio, gli mandai 3. di quei miei scritti, che ò procurato di render più pubblici che ò potuto, non solo in Italia, come in altre parti d'Europa. Avrei piacere che gli vedeste; ne ò mandate 2. copie; se giungessero ambedue a salvamento potreste farvene mandar'una. Il primo, che scrissi al principio dell'anno passato, à per titolo *Ragioni per cui non può darsi agli Stati Americani La taccia di ribelli.* Avendo io scritto per questo Sovrano, affinchè Lo facesse Leggere all'Imperatore suo Fratello, conforme Lo pregai, feci valere unicamente quelle ragioni, che possono sodisfare La Sovranità. Il secondo, che scrissi L'Aprile seguente, L'intitolai *Reflessioni tendenti a prognosticar L'evento della presente guerra.* Siccome per quel che gli avevo detto prima di venire in America, e per quel che d'America gli avevo scritto, al mio arrivo in Firenze mi disse che io *avevo predetto tutto quello che è seguito,* Leggendo Le dette Reflessioni voi vedrete, che non à potuto, e non può far di meno di convenire che Le mie profezie continovano ad avverarsi. Il terzo, che scrissi nel passato gennajo, è intitolato *Istoria del principio, progresso, e fine del denaro di Carta degli Stati Uniti d'America.*

Nella vostra dei 25. 8bre non facendomi voi menzione del contenuto nella mia di 30. 9bre 1780, devo supporre che mi ci abbiate risposto sufficientemente nelle precedenti, che non ò ricevute; il che probabilmente non sarebbe seguito se ne aveste fatte d'ognuna 3. duplicate, come fo io, e a tutte aveste fatta una sopraccarta diretta a Mr. Lynch. Sappiate per tanto che io son tuttavia nell'istesse circostanze che ero allora. Non so nulla riguardo ai Nostri *Loan-Officies,* e non mi è stato rimesso un soldo. Mr. Penet protestò fin La Cambiale di 300. Luigi, che il Governatore mi ordinò di trargli fin dai 31. Maggio 1780. A quest'ora saprete gl'imbroglj di quel soggetto, il carattere del quale avevo già bastantemente dimostrato nella mia 12ma. d'Officio data di Parigi ai 20. Aprile 1780. Se vedeste tutte Le mie Lettere al nostro Governo, son persuaso che vi sentireste scuotere dalla pietà della mia Situazione, e dallo sdegno di vedermi tanto crudelmente negletto. La vostra amicizia per me, La premura che dovete avere per il decoro dello Stato, e L'amor del giusto e dell'onesto v'impegnano ad adoprarvi premurosamente, affinchè senza ulterior dilazione si pensi a trattarmi come è di ragione. Voi non ignorate, Amico, il mio carattere in quanto all'attività, e allo zelo. Sappiate dunque, che La mia bocca, La mia penna, i miej pensieri, tutte Le mie azioni sono state dal punto in cui ricovrai La Libertà costantemente, e quasi unicamente impiegate in promuovere (per quanto Le mie circostanze permettevano) gl'interessi della nostra Patria, e in far comparire nel più Luminoso aspetto La giustizia della nostra Causa. Questo è ben noto in Italia e in Francia, e non s'ignora totalmente in altre parti. Finora ò potuto mediante il mio credito tener celato il trattamento che ò ricevuto, ma il tempo della crise è imminente. Finirò col rammentarvi, che siccome doveva esservi a cuore, che L'amico vostro si comportasse in maniera Lodevole, così dovete per quanto è in poter vostro adoprarvi, affinchè egli non sia strapazzato. Nelle mie Lettere al Governo potete vedere, che quel che non ò fatto, è derivato unicamente dal non avermene il Governo medesimo conferito il potere. Addio.

Vostro Affezmo: Servo e Amico

FILIPPO MAZZEI

FLORENCE 13 March 1782

DEAREST FRIEND

Here is my third letter in response to your most gracious one dated Philadelphia, 25 October 1781 and addressed to me in Florence.[1] The letters that you said you had previously written to me have not arrived.[2] I thank you for the encouraging news and for that in the P.S. to the gazette;[3] but they arrived so late, perhaps because you did not enclose the letter in an envelope addressed to Mr. Mark Lynch Mt. in Nantes in accordance with the instructions in my first letter of 30 November 1780.[4] I believe that you have received the letter, because you mention a paragraph in code, and in my second letter of 7 December of the same year there was no code for you. Since you indicate that Mr. Jameson has informed you that the code is lost,[5] the said paragraph will remain under lock and key until I shall have the pleasure of seeing you again. My second letter, which I feel you have not received, contained the news of the death of the Queen of Hungary and some reflections on the political system of the Northern Powers, which I believed ought to be sent to the Congress, considering the source from which I received it, how I received it, and certain data which permits me to conjecture with some confidence.[6] Since that time a stupendous change has happened, which was not even dreamed of then. This is the estrangement of Russia from Prussia in order to ally herself very closely with the Emperor.[7] Many are speculating on the political principles involved, but they deceive themselves, although future events may perhaps cause them to believe that they have guessed well. The true motive, which comes from serious reflection, gives much consolation to one who has the good fortune of being a citizen of a free country; but without code I cannot write about it. This unexpected and surprising event is now becoming known publicly. I had a strong inkling of it more than eight months ago, however, and I knew about it for certain more than four months ago. I wanted Congress to be informed, but not knowing if you were still in Philadelphia, I wrote about it to our Governor in my 27th official report of the first of November 1781. A very clear view of the present European political situation can be drawn from that report and from what I added in my 30th report of last January 18.[8] It is said that Russia and the Emperor have joined together to drive the Turk from Europe; their preparations, as well as those of the Turk, tend to strengthen the supposition; and everywhere there is fear of a universal war. For the reasons indicated in my 30th report, and also for other reasons, I continue to believe that the Emperor will endeavor to avoid war.[9] If Russia and the Emperor should then unite with the King of Prussia to partition Turkey-in-Europe, as they did with a portion of Poland,[10] it would pass without serious incident and would produce no consequences other than the aggrandizement of the dominions of the three Powers. But if they wish to do this without the concurrence of the King of Prussia, or if the Emperor, relying on an alliance with Russia, wanted to try to recover Silesia from the King of Prussia,[11] there would arise a league between the Turk, Prussia, and France against England, Russia, and the Emperor. All the advantages would be held by the former (in my opinion). The finances of the former are in much better condition than those of the other group; the number of men greater, since England would not be able to provide any; the command better because the Turks would move under Prussian generals; and the small and mediocre states that would take part when a general war developed would join forces with the states to which they are allied. Sweden would not detach herself from France, and the body of Germanic states would throw their weight in favor of the King of Prussia.[12] It appears to me, however, that whatever course things may take in Europe, our Cause is firmly secure and our affairs must get better and better.[13]

You will probably have been informed via France before this letter arrives of the capture of Fort St. Philip, and that as a result, the entire island of Minorca is in the hands of the Spaniards.[14] There is some indication that Gibraltar might suffer the same fate. The English Government claims to have had good news from the East Indies, but it has not been clarified and the stocks of the company fell from 139 to 134. At last notice the 3 per 100 consolidateds were at 54⅝.[15] It is rumored that they are making great preparations against us, but I am convinced that in spite of all their efforts they will do but little more than *parturiens mons*.[16]

With my last letter to the Governor of the 8th of this month,[17] which is my 31st report, I sent him three of my own written works, which I am trying to make more widely known than I have been able to in Italy or elsewhere in Europe. I should be pleased if you could see them. I have sent two copies, and if both have arrived safely you can have one copy delivered to you.[18] The first work, which I wrote at the beginning of last year, is called *The reasons why the American States cannot be given the stigma of rebels.* Having written it for this Sovereign I asked him to persuade his brother, the Emperor, to read it; in accordance with this I stressed only those reasons which might uphold Sovereignty. The second work, which I wrote the following April, is entitled *Reflections tending to forecast the results of the present war.* In view of what I had said about this subject before coming to America and what I had written from America, he remarked on my arrival in Florence that *I had predicted every occurrence.* On reading the said Reflections you will see this for yourself, and you can do no less than agree that my predictions continue to prove true. The third work, written last January, is called *History of the origin, progress, and purpose of the paper money of the United States of America.*[19]

Since you did not mention the contents of my letter of 30 November 1780 in your letter of 25 October, I must assume that you have referred to them in your previous letters, which I have not received. This probably would not have happened if you had made three duplicates of each letter, as I do, and above all if you had used an envelope addressed to Mr. Lynch. Notwithstanding, be it known that I am still in the same circumstances as before. I know nothing regarding our Loan-Offices, and not one soldo has been remitted to me. Mr. Penet even protested the Bill of Exchange of 300 Louis d'or that the Governor directed me to draw after 31 May 1780. By now you will know of the imbroglio surrounding this subject, the nature of which I have amply demonstrated in my 12th report dated Paris, 20 April 1780.[20] If you were to see all of my letters to our Government, I am certain that you would be moved to pity by my situation and angered to see me so cruelly neglected. Your friendship for me, the zeal which you have for the honor of the State, and your love of justice and honesty oblige you to take immediate action so that I may receive just treatment without further delay. You know full well, my friend, how active and enthusiastic I always have been. Be it known, then, that ever since I regained my freedom, my mouth, my pen, my thoughts, all of my actions, have been constantly employed, and that I have labored almost solely (whenever my circumstances permitted) to promote the interests of our Country and to illuminate the justice of our Cause. This is well known in Italy and in France, and it is not totally unrecognized elsewhere. Up to now I have been able to keep the treatment I have received concealed by means of my credit, but the time of crisis is imminent. As it should give you heart to know that your friend conducts himself in a laudable way, I shall conclude by reminding you that you must find it within your power to take action so that he may not be rebuked. You can observe in my letters to the Government that what I have not done stems only from the fact that the Government itself has not granted me the authority.[21] Farewell.

Your most Affectionate Servant and Friend

PHILIP MAZZEI

[1] JM's letter of 25 October 1781 has not been found.

[2] Apparently only JM's letter of 7 July 1781 is extant (*Papers of Madison*, III, 176–80). According to the "Daily Journal or Despatch Book of the Office of Foreign Affairs, 1781–1783" (NA: PCC, No. 126, fols. 6 and 15), JM also wrote Mazzei about 16 November and 18 December 1781.

[3] Besides writing of the campaign in Virginia, JM in his missing letter of 25 October 1781 probably had enclosed a copy of the "Postscript" of the *Pennsylvania Journal* of 24 October, which published, by authorization of Congress, the Articles of Capitulation agreed upon by Washington and Cornwallis at Yorktown five days earlier.

[4] See *Papers of Madison*, II, 216, and n. 11.

[5] *Ibid.*, II, 216, n. 10; 230; III, 267–68.

[6] *Ibid.*, II, 229–30, and n. 1.

[7] The death of Queen Maria Theresa on 29 November 1780 left the Emperor Joseph II sole ruler of the Hapsburg dominions. His efforts to extend his control in Bavaria alienated King Frederick the Great of Prussia. At the same time Tsarina Catherine II of Russia found Joseph receptive to her proposal that they join forces to drive Turkey out of Europe, so that Joseph could bring the western Balkans under his sovereignty, and Catherine could create a "new Greek empire" in the eastern Balkans for her grandson Constantine. With Austria, Prussia's rival, moving into the Russian orbit, and with the relations between Prussia and Russia increasingly strained by their conflicting interests in Poland, the rift between Prussia and Russia gradually widened until in 1788 Prussia allied with Great Britain, and in 1790 with Turkey and Poland (*Cambridge Modern History*, VI, 634–35, 646–48, 674–75, 709, 734).

[8] Neither of these two letters appears to be extant.

[9] Without the aid of Austria and in spite of Prussia's diplomatic opposition, Russia forced Turkey to give up its claim to the Crimea in 1783. Five years later Austria joined Russia in her war against Turkey (*ibid.*, VI, 675–76, 709).

[10] The first partition of Poland by Austria, Prussia, and Russia was provided for by a treaty signed in February 1772 (*ibid.*, VI, 357, 669).

[11] By the Treaty of Hubertusburg on 15 February 1763, Prussia had been confirmed in possession of most of Upper and Lower Silesia, wrested from Austria between 1740 and 1742 (*ibid.*, VI, 229–35, 346).

[12] As one counterpoise to the rapprochement between Austria and Russia, mentioned in n. 7, Frederick the Great sought to draw the German states into a confederation under his leadership—an effort which led to the formation of the Fürstenbund in July 1785 (*ibid.*, VI, 708).

[13] Prone to prophesy, Mazzei tended to exaggerate his accuracy as a seer. In the present instance he was, of course, partially correct, but, as on an earlier occasion

(*Papers of Madison,* II, 230, and 231, n. 4), the crises did not come as early as he predicted.

[14] See JM to Pendleton, 25 February 1782, n. 5.

[15] See Pendleton to JM, 11 March 1782, n. 2. Probably the latest "good news" from India was that of the British capture on 11 November 1781 and 11 January 1782, respectively, of the Dutch fortress of Negapatam on the Coromandel Coast and of Trincomalee in Ceylon. On the other hand the treasury of the East India Company "was nearly empty, the military forces were greatly diminished, an expensive and bloody war was being fought against Hyder Ali and the Mahratas, and most of the other native states were openly or secretly hostile to the British." Although almost certainly unknown to Mazzei, a British fleet on 16–17 February had suffered heavily in an indecisive engagement with French men-of-war which were under orders to co-operate with Haidar (Hyder) Ali in driving the British out of India (*Papers of Madison,* III, 298, n. 4; W. M. James, *British Navy in Adversity,* pp. 386–89). The "consolidateds" or "consols" were bonds of the British government with no definite maturity date but yielding 3 or 3½ per cent interest, annually, to the owner.

[16] Mazzei refers to Horace's "parturient montes, nascetur ridiculus mus" ("the mountains are in labor, and will give birth to an absurd mouse," *De ars poetica,* line 139).

[17] This letter, reproduced in Richard Cecil Garlick, Jr., *Philip Mazzei, Friend of Jefferson: His Life and Letters* (Baltimore, 1933), pp. 73–76, was addressed to Jefferson in the erroneous belief that he still was governor.

[18] See n. 8, above. These writings by Mazzei apparently reached neither Jefferson nor JM (E. Millicent Sowerby, comp. and ed., *Catalogue of the Library of Thomas Jefferson* [5 vols.; Washington, 1952–59], V, 356).

[19] Mazzei might have added a reference to his pamphlet, "The Importance of engaging in Trade with Virginia," which he also presented to "this Sovereign," Leopold I, grand duke of Tuscany and younger brother of Joseph II, Holy Roman Emperor (Richard C. Garlick, Jr., *Philip Mazzei,* p. 72; Howard R. Marraro, trans., *Memoirs of the Life and Peregrinations of the Florentine, Philip Mazzei, 1730–1816* [New York, 1942], p. 256, n. 9). Mazzei's correspondence with the grand duke is printed in the *William and Mary Quarterly,* 2d ser., XXII (1942), 275–301, 361–80. See also n. 13, above.

[20] For J. Pierre Penet and his shipping firm at Nantes, France, see *Papers of Madison,* I, 294, n. 2. A "soldo" is an Italian small copper coin, worth about one-twentieth of a lira. The French "louis d'or" was worth at least twenty francs. Mazzei wrote to John Page on 2 August 1782 that he had received the promissory note, which Penet had refused to cash, in a letter from Jefferson on 31 May 1780 (Howard R. Marraro, ed., "Unpublished Mazzei Correspondence during His American Mission to Europe," *William and Mary Quarterly,* 2d ser., XXIII [1943], 432). Jefferson may have enclosed the warrant in the letter cited by Mazzei, but there is no mention of it in the text (Boyd, *Papers of Jefferson,* III, 405–6).

[21] Although many letters from or to Mazzei were lost or intercepted in transit, he appears to have had good reason to complain because governors Nelson and Harrison, beset by financial stringency and the enemy, had neglected him. On the other hand, Mazzei's mission to Tuscany as a commercial agent of Virginia had produced many words from his pen but no loans of money or shipments of military supplies. Even as he was writing the present letter, a dispatch from Governor Harrison was en route to him, thanking him for his "good intentions towards us" but canceling his commission because of the need for "the most rigid Econemy" (McIlwaine, *Official Letters,* III, 142; Harrison to Virginia Delegates, 2 February, and n. 7; and Virginia Delegates to Harrison, 15 February 1782).

To Thomas Jefferson

RC (LC: Madison Papers). Docketed by Jefferson, "Madison Jas. Mar 18. 1782."

PHILADA. MARCH 18th. 1782

DEAR SIR

In my last to you on the subject of the map in the hands of Dr. Smith I informed you of the little chance of getting a copy of it for you.[1] Nothing has since occurred wch. affords the least expectation from that quarter, but I have met with a bundle of old pamplets belonging to the public Library here in which is a map published in 1650 which from this & other circumstances I am pretty confident is of the same impression with that of Doctr. Smith's. It represents the South sea at about 10 days travel from the heads or falls I forget which of James River.[2] From the tenor however of the pamphlet to which it is immediately annexed & indeed of the whole collection there is just ground to suspect that this representation was an artifice to favor the object of the publications which evidently was to entice imigrants from England by a flattering picture of the advantages of this Country, one of which dwelt on in all the pamphlets is the vicinity of the S. Sea, and the facility it afforded of a trade with the Eastern World.[3] Another circumstance wch. lessens much the value of this map to the Antiquary is that it is more modern by 25 years than those extant in Purchase's pilgrim,[4] wch. are referred to in the Negociations between the British & french Commissaries touching the bounds of N. Scotia as the first of Authenticity relating to this part of the world.[5] If notwithstanding these considerations you still desire that a copy be taken from the map above described I shall with pleasure execute your orders, or if you wish that a copy of the map of Virga. or of the whole country may be taken from those in Purchase, your orders shall be equally attended to. I much doubt however whether that book be so extremely scarce as to require a transcript from it for the purpose you seem to have in view.[6]

You will find in the inclosed gazette all our latest intelligence both from Europe & the W. Indies. The Ministerial speeches in Parliament as well as other considerations render it pretty certain that the system for recovering America will be changed. A peace with Holland & a suspension of the expensive operations in America, are to give their resources full play agst. France & Spain, whilst all the arts of division & seduction will probably be practised on the U. States.[7]

Congress have taken no step in the business of the Western territory since the report of the Committee of which I have already given you an account, & which we hear arrived at Richmond on the day of the Ajournment of the Assembly.[8] We wish it to undergo their consideration, & to receive their instructions before we again move in it. Mr. Randolph by whom this goes, will probably be present at the May Session[9] & will be possessed of every information that may be necessary. I refer you to the interview with him which I hope that occasion will afford you for other congressional intelligence.[10]

I am this moment told that pretty certain information is come to hand of the final reduction of St. Kitts.[11]

With great regard I am Dr. Sr. Yr. obt. friend & Servt.

J. MADISON JR.

[1] JM last wrote to Jefferson on 3 April 1781 about the map owned by Dr. William Smith (*Papers of Madison*, III, 45).

[2] The Library Company of Philadelphia owned a copy of the pamphlet, cited in n. 3, in which appears a reproduction of the "Faithfull Map of Virginia in America," drawn by Virginia Ferrar (Farrar) in 1651. This chart assures its users that the "happy shore" of "The Sea of China and the Indies" may be "discovered to the exceeding benefit of Great Brittain and joys of all true English" by "a ten dayes march with 50 foote and 30 horsemen from the head of James River, over those hills and through the rich adjacent Vallyes beautyfied with . . . proffitable rivers, which necessarily must run into the peacefull Indian Sea." For a facsimile of this map, see Coolie Verner, "The First Maps of Virginia, 1590–1673," *Virginia Magazine of History and Biography*, LVIII (1950), facing p. 9.

[3] E[dward] W[illiams], Gent., *Virginia in America, Richly Valued: More especially the southern Parts. With the Tendure of the Vine and Silkworms, etc. Together with a Compleat Map of the Country from 35 to 41 Degrees of Latitude discovered, and the West Sea* (London, 1651). Either through a lack of geographical knowledge or of scruples, English colonial promoters often had sought to attract settlers and financial backing by minimizing the width of North America. The lure of the Orient was, of course, a potent force in European history for many centuries.

[4] A map drawn about 1612, utilizing information supplied by Captain John Smith, appears in Samuel Purchas, *Purchas his Pilgrimage* (4 vols.; London, 1625), IV, facing p. 1690. For a description of this map, see pp. 9–10 of Coolie Verner's article, cited in n. 2.

[5] JM evidently derived his comments from *The Memorials of the English and French Commissaries Concerning the Limits of Nova Scotia or Acadia* (London, 1755), p. 267. This volume describes the map as "the first antient Map of this Country which has the Marks of Knowledge and Correctness in it; it was published within about Twenty Years after the earliest Settlements made in this Country by the *English* and *French*, which gave Geographers an Opportunity of getting a Knowledge of it."

[6] Although Jefferson's probable "purpose" was to gather data for inclusion in his *Notes on the State of Virginia*, JM still hoped that his friend would draft a historical brief upholding the western claims of Virginia (JM to Jefferson, 15 January; and Jefferson to JM, 24 March 1782).

[7] The *Pennsylvania Packet* of 14 and 16 March, and the *Pennsylvania Journal* of the latter date, published much news from overseas and the West Indies, including an extract from the journal of the House of Commons for 12 December 1781. Although Lord North, defending the policy of the ministry, declared that he planned "to change the form of the war altogether," neither he nor Lord George Germain, who also spoke, was explicit about what the "change" would be. Apparently they contemplated extending more help to the Loyalists than ever before, confining British occupation of the Atlantic seaboard to Halifax, New York, Charleston, and their environs, possibly driving the French from Rhode Island, and giving priority to military operations against France and Spain in the West Indies and Europe. The above newspapers further reported the probability that Holland would soon withdraw from the war as a result of the mediation of the tsarina of Russia. JM's comments also suggest that he had read John Adams' dispatches of 4, 13, and 18 December 1781, received by Congress on 18 March (Report on Foreign Dispatches, 20 March 1782; Wharton, *Revolutionary Diplomatic Correspondence*, V, 36–38, 43–44, 55).

[8] See JM to Jefferson, 15 January 1782, and nn. 8, 9, 10; also *Papers of Madison*, III, 307–8; 309, nn. 1, 4, 7).

[9] See Virginia Delegates to Harrison, 12 March 1782, n. 4; and Pendleton to JM, 15 April 1782.

[10] See Randolph to Harrison, 22 April 1782 (*Calendar of Virginia State Papers*, III, 133–36).

[11] The capitulation of St. Kitts and Nevis on 12 and 19 February 1782 was reported in the *Pennsylvania Packet* of 19 March.

Virginia Delegates to Benjamin Harrison

RC (Virginia State Library). Except for the signatures of JM and Joseph Jones, the letter was written, franked, and addressed by Arthur Lee to "His Excellency Benjamin Harrison Esqr. Governor of Virginia." Docketed, "Virga. Delegates Lr. March 19th 1782."

PHILADELPHIA March 19th. 1782

SIR

The Motion we made for Congress to accept the Beef, that might be supplied by the State for the southern Army above her former quota of that article, in discount for its value in the last Quota; is referrd to the Super-intendant of Finance, who has not yet reported upon it.[1] If our accounts are true, touching the evacuation of Charlestown, which is said to have taken place on the 24th. ult.[2] it will hardly be an object for us to press, considering the precedent it will establish.[3]

The capture of Cornwallis and of his Army, has made a great impression on the European Courts in our favor;[4] & the evacuation of the southern parts of the U. S. will probably raise such an opinion of the establishment of our Independancy beyond the power of G. B. to shake, as to incline some of those Courts to an Alliance, that may make our Enemies dispair of ever succeeding against us. The alarm in England is very great. Strong & pointed Petitions have been presented against continuing the war,[5] the opposition in the House of Commons has reachd within 41 of the ministerial majority,[6] & the accounts from N. York are, that the Lords North, Germaine & Sandwich are actually displaced.[7] Vigorous preparations, on our part, for the ensuing campaign, will give such efficacy to these impressions, as may probably put a period to the war.

We enclose the Paper, which will shew the success of our Ally in the W. Indies.[8]

Our Colleague Mr. Randolph, who left this place for Richmond yesterday, will give you a more particular account of the contents of our latest Dispatches,[9] & of the proceedings here, than it is proper for us to commit to Paper.

We have the honor to be, with the greatest respect, Sir, Yr. Excellency's most obedt. & most Humb. Servts.

J MADISON JR.
JOS. JONES
A. LEE

[1] On 15 March 1782 Congress "*Ordered*, That the motion of the Delegates of Virginia to be credited out of requisition of quota of 8 Millions for Beef she may furnish more than required in the Act for Specific Supplies be referred to the Superintendant of Finance" (*JCC*, XXII, 136). The meaning of this order is highly ambiguous unless it is borne in mind that the "8 Millions" stand for the entire quota of money requisitioned by Congress from the thirteen states during 1782—"to be paid quarterly in equal proportions, the first payment to be made on the first day of April" 1782 (*JCC*, XXI, 1087–88). When Congress on 2 November 1781 decided what portion of the "8 Millions" each state should pay, it allotted Virginia $1,307,594. Although on that day Congress empowered Robert Morris, the superintendent of finance, to decide what percentage of this sum might be discharged with food "and other articles of supplies for the army," Congress quickly prohibited these payments in kind, probably at Morris' own suggestion (*JCC*, XXI, 1090–92, 1112). Viewing taxes in kind as "vicious," he aimed to make the notes of the Bank of North America and the notes issued under his own signature ("Morris notes") a "national" currency and to oblige every state to pay its financial quotas in those media or in specie rather than in "specifics" or in its own depreciated paper money. He was determined to press toward this goal, even though it was unrealistic in terms of the economic situation in Virginia and other war-ravaged southern states in 1782 (Clarence L. Ver Steeg, *Robert Morris*, pp. 79, 87, 134–36, 141, 151–56). For this reason, although his reply to the order of Congress of 15 March, quoted above, has not been found, he probably thwarted the effort of the Virginia delegates to have an "Act for Specific Supplies" passed in 1782. Morris,

of course, was the more opposed to state quotas paid in "specifics" because they conflicted with the private-contractor system, inaugurated by him in 1781, for supplying the continental army outside the South (Harrison to Virginia Delegates, 9 February, n. 3; Virginia Delegates to Harrison, 25 February 1782, n. 3). See also Virginia Delegates to Harrison, 15 February, and n. 4, and 12 March; Harrison to Virginia Delegates, 1 March 1782, and n. 4.

[2] Although British troops remained in Charleston until 14 December 1782, rumors of their leaving were often current in Philadelphia during the nine months preceding that date (Burnett, *Letters*, VI, *passim*).

[3] The implication is that if the news from South Carolina was true, need for meat in Greene's army would be reduced and Virginia's economic situation would improve. The exception requested of Congress would, therefore, be less urgent, and pressure should not be exerted to establish a "precedent" which might sanction a resort to a barter economy by the Confederation even after the close of the war.

[4] This statement reflects a comment by John Adams in his letter of 4 December 1781, read in Congress on 18 March 1782 (*JCC*, XXII, 140). In his dispatch of 18 December, Adams also remarked that the French ambassador to The Hague had advised him, in view of "the late *Cornwallization*," to "assume a higher tone" in his dealings with the Dutch government (Wharton, *Revolutionary Diplomatic Correspondence*, V, 36, 55).

[5] The *Pennsylvania Packet* of 16 March 1782 printed a petition from residents of Westminster, asking for a cessation of the American war.

[6] See JM to Jefferson, 18 March 1782, n. 7. A division of the Commons on 12 December 1781, although on an order of the day, had the effect of defeating, 220 to 179, an opposition motion, the crux of which was that "all further attempts to reduce the revolted colonies to obedience are contrary to the true interests of this kingdom, as tending to weaken its efforts against its ancient and powerful enemies" (*Hansard's Parliamentary Debates*, XXII, cols. 802–3, 831).

[7] The source of these reports is unknown. Lord George Germain was secretary of state for colonies, and John Montagu (1718–1792), fourth Earl of Sandwich, first lord of the admiralty. The North ministry fell on 20 March, following the adoption by the House of Commons on 4 March 1782 of a resolution denouncing as "enemies to His Majesty and this country" all who should advise or attempt "the farther prosecution of offensive war on the continent of North America, for the purpose of reducing the revolted colonies to obedience by force" (*Hansard's Parliamentary Debates*, XXII, cols. 1064, 1085; Ian Ralph Christie, *The End of North's Ministry, 1780–1782* [London, 1958], pp. 367–69).

[8] Probably the *Pennsylvania Packet* of 19 March 1782, in which appears the Articles of Capitulation, whereby the British surrendered St. Kitts and Nevis to the French, and reports that both the British and French fleets in the West Indies had been strengthened.

[9] See Virginia Delegates to Harrison, 12 March, n. 4; JM to Pendleton, 19 March, n. 4; and Report on Foreign Dispatches, 20 March 1782.

To Edmund Pendleton

RC (LC: Madison Papers). Addressed to "The Honble Edmund Pendleton Esqr. Caroline County Virginia."

PHILADA. March 19th. 1782

DEAR SIR

Yesterday's post brought me your favor of the 11th instant, which if my recollection does not fail me is an act of supererogation, the terms of our contract entitling Mr Jones alone to your correspondence of the present week. To show you how acceptable it is to me I have selected the inclosed gazette published here last week[1] as containing the greatest portion of entertaining & interesting matter which we have of late recd. I leave it to Mr. Jones to transmit you the gazette of this morning.[2]

The Ministerial Speeches with other circumstances place it beyond a doubt that the plan for recovering America will be changed. A separate peace with the Dutch, a suspension of the offensive war here, an exertion of their resources thus disencumbered against the naval power of France & Spain and a renewal of the arts of seduction & division in the U. States will probably constitute the outlines of the new plan. Whether they will succeed in the first article of it can not be ascertained by the last intelligence we have from Holland. It is only certain that negociations are on foot under the auspices of the Empress of Russia.[3] Mr. Randolph set off this morning[4] & will probably reach you nearly as soon as this. I leave it to him to make known other particulars. I am &c.

J. MADISON JR.

[1] Almost certainly this was the *Pennsylvania Packet* of Saturday, 16 March 1782, which included a lengthy account of the debate in the House of Commons on 12 December as reported in the *Whitehall Evening Post* (London) of 13 December 1781.

[2] The *Pennsylvania Packet* of 19 March contained the speech of the Earl of Shelburne on 27 November 1781 in the House of Lords, reviewing the seven years of war which had accomplished a "great deal worse than nothing." Joseph Jones began his dispatch of 19 March to Pendleton by writing, "I know not whether it is my turn regularly to answer you this week or not as your Letter [of 25 February] was to Mr. Madison, but be that as it may I shall take the liberty of troubling you with a Letter" (Burnett, *Letters*, VI, 319–30).

[3] See JM to Jefferson, 18 March 1782, n. 7. On 29 July 1782 William Lee wrote from Cleves to his brother Richard Henry Lee: "Last spring Russia, whose object is to have the war continue as long as possible, to keep the parties nearly equal, threatened the Dutch, if they did not make a separate peace with Great Britain. The Dutch

however refused, and since the disaster [Battle of the Saints] of the 12th of April in the West Indies was known, Russia has been quiet; for the English have revived their old ideas, and talk of nothing less than totally annihilating the navies of France and Spain" (Worthington Chauncey Ford, ed., *Letters of William Lee, Sheriff and Alderman of London; Commercial Agent of the Continental Congress in France, and Minister to the Courts of Vienna and Berlin, 1766–1783* [3 vols.; Brooklyn, N.Y., 1891], III, 871). The preliminary peace between Great Britain and the Netherlands was not signed until 2 September 1783 (Samuel Flagg Bemis, *A Diplomatic History of the United States* [4th ed.; New York, 1960], p. 62).

[4] JM erred. In their letter of this date to Governor Harrison (*q.v.*), the delegates wrote that Edmund Randolph had left on 18 rather than 19 March. In a letter to JM on 5 May 1782 (*q.v.*), Randolph stated that "on the morning of my departure," Congress referred foreign dispatches to a committee of which JM was chairman. This occurred on 18 March (*JCC*, XXII, 140).

John Bradford to Virginia Delegates

Copy (Virginia State Library). This copy, in JM's hand, is docketed by him, "Letter from J. Bradford Boston March 20th. 1782 to J Madison & J Jones relating to certain Stores belonging to Virginia No. 1. 1782. March 20th." The Virginia delegates enclosed the copy in their letter of 23 April 1782 to Harrison.

BOSTON 20th. March 1782

GENTLEMEN

Your favor under the 5th. currt.[1] reached me last evening by the post, to which I beg leave to reply that the Stores[2] lye unsold tho' nothing has been wanting in my power to get them off, the most I coud obtain for the Shot was the price of old Iron and but one or two articles among the whole that would sell to greater advantage. I found if I had risked them at vendue they wd. scarcely have sold for enough to pay charges. Our Governor[3] gave me hopes that great part of them might be purchased for the use of our Castle,[4] and when the Court met I preferred a memorial, offering the Articles at prime Cost, but in vain. they gave me for answer they were not wanted, if the spirit of privateering sd. again revive they may be in demand in part & with that prospect its possible there may be those who might speculate. If you chuse to have them sold at auction you will please to signify & it shall be done on the best terms possible.

I have &c.

(signed) J. BRADFORD[5]

[1] Apparently the delegates' letter of 5 March 1782 is not extant.

[2] See *Papers of Madison,* II, 308, and n. 3. The revival of interest in Virginia's consignment of military stores, which had been landed at Boston over two years before, after being shipped by Penet, d'Acosta Frères et Cie of Nantes, may reflect the recent decision of the governor and council of Virginia to reach a financial settlement with that firm and dispense with its services as foreign commercial agent (*Journals of the Council of State,* III, 34).

[3] John Hancock.

[4] Castle William was an island fortress in Boston Harbor.

[5] Captain John Bradford was the continental agent at Boston (*Papers of Madison,* II, 9, n. 4).

Expense Account as Delegate in Congress

MS (Virginia State Library). In LC: Madison Papers are notes by JM written on four sheets of paper. All of these notes, except for one entry mentioned below, relate to the present account. Although the writing on one of these pages is largely illegible because of fading and water stains, the jottings evidently served JM as a rough draft for a more orderly listing of his debits and credits, grouped one above the other on a separate page. On a third he recorded the sums received by him from Peter Whiteside and Company on 2, 6, 9, and 23 March 1782. The last of these payments, of course, does not appear on the present tally. Finally, JM retained in his files a copy of the account sent to the Board of Auditors of Virginia. This file copy is docketed, "Expenses from Decr 21 1781 to March 20 1782." In the footnotes, the first three of these pages will be referred to as No. 1, 2, and 3, in the order listed above.

[1] See Virginia Delegates to Harrison, 8 January 1782, n. 2.

[2] Haym Salomon (1740–1785), who spelled his name "Solomons" until late in 1781. Of Polish birth, he emigrated to New York City about 1772 and was a money broker and merchant there until 1778. In that year, after being condemned to death by the British as a spy, he allegedly bribed his way out of prison and escaped to Philadelphia. At his office on Front Street, between Market and Arch streets, he bought and sold on commission "Bills of Exchange on France, or any other part of Europe: Likewise all kinds of Merchandize. He also, discounts inland Bills or Drafts, and has it often in his power to procure Money on Loan for a short time" (*Pennsylvania Packet,* 12 January 1782). On 20 January 1827, replying to an inquiry from Salomon's son, JM wrote, "Among other members of Congs. from Virginia whose resources public & private had been cut off, I had occasion once perhaps twice myself to resort to his pecuniary aid on a small scale for current wants. We regarded him as upright, intelligent and friendly in his transactions with us" (LC: Madison Papers).

From Decr. 20–1781—to March 20–1782

Date		Pena. Curry.	Date		£
1781. Decr 28.	To Cash recd. of T. Pleasants[1]...........	£ 75		By balance on Decr. 20th. 1781[4].........	
1782. Jany. 9.	To do. recd. of Haym Solomons[2] by order from do................................	100	March 20	By Board & Lodg. includg. liqrs. &Ca...	96..10..6[5]
				By incidental expences not included in the above..........................	4.. 7...[6]
March 2d–9	To do recd. of Peter Whitesides in consequence of directions from Mr. Ross......	106..5[3]		By expence of 2 Horses	18.. 5..4[7]
				By Washing..........................	6..11..2[8]
		£281..5		By Wood abt. 4 Cord..................	10..12..6[9]
				By allowance for 90 days at [10]...........	
					[11]

E. Excd.[12] J. Madison Jr.

[3] See Virginia Delegates to Harrison, 5 March 1782, n. 1. According to page No. 3, mentioned in the headnote, this sum was received from Peter Whiteside and Company in the following installments:

2 March	$50 or	£18 15*s.*
6 March	50 or	18 15*s.*
9 March	150 or	56 5*s.*
1 case of Claret		12 10*s.*

At the above ratio of $2.66⅔ to £1, a case of imported wine in lieu of $33.33 was probably a bargain.

[4] See *Papers of Madison,* III, 333, n. 3; 334. JM could not know the balance due him from Virginia, because the General Assembly had not yet determined the per diem allowance to be paid to a delegate from the state in Congress.

[5] Page No. 2 (see headnote) reveals that this amount is a consolidation of "By Bd. & Logg, £61 . . 15" and "By Liqrs &Ca. 34 . . 15 . . 6."

[6] This item probably includes the indistinct jotting on page No. 1 (see headnote), apparently reading, "12[?] Jany By expences on a party to Frankfort, £2." What official business this entry connotes is unknown. Frankford, Pa., was five miles north of Philadelphia, on the highway to Trenton, N.J.

[7] On page No. 1 (see headnote), a few of the several entries making this total appear to be £5 for stablage, 33*s.* 4*d.* for oats, and £2 2*s.* for oats. Together these add to £8 15*s.* 4*d.*, or about £10 less than is shown on the expense account.

[8] The four entries for washing on page No. 1 (see headnote) are 8*s.* 4*d.*, £1 16*s.* 5*d.*, 18*s.* 9*d.*, and £3 7*s.* 8*d.* These add to £6 11*s.* 2*d.*

[9] The only purchases of wood which can be read on page No. 1 (see headnote) are for £2 5*s.*, £3, and £2 7*s.* 6*d.* These add to £10 12*s.* 6*d.*, or £3 short of the entry on the expense account.

[10] See n. 4, above.

[11] On page No. 2 (see headnote) the five entries in this credit column are totaled correctly as £136 6*s.* 6*d.*

[12] Errors excepted.

Report on Foreign Dispatches

MS (NA: PCC, No. 25, II, 91). Written by JM. Docketed: "Report of Committee on foreign Despatches[.] Passed March 20h 1782."

[20 March 1782]

The Committee to whom were referred the foreign despatches read in Congress on the 18th. instant[1] report

That the letters from Mr. Jay & Mr. Carmichael be referred to a

1 Special Committee & that the Committee be authorised & instructed to communicate to the Superintendant of finance, such parts thereof as relate to his Department & to the committee on ritaliation such parts as relate to that Subject.[2]

2d. That the letters from Docr. Franklin & Mr. Adams be referred to another Committee[3] & that the same in like manner communicate the proper extracts to the Superintendt. of finance, & to the Committees on Subjects to which they relate

3d. That the Protest of Capt: Ary de Neuf of the Brigantine Berkenboesh be referred to the preceeding Committee[4]

That the letter from Ct. de Vergennes with the Memorial from Creditors of Capt Gillon be referred to the Delegates of S. Carolina[5]

That the letters of Capt. Gillon & Mr. Searle be referred to the Superindt. of finance[6]

[1] The printed journal for 18 March 1782 is a blank, but on that day Charles Thomson's committee ledger records that JM, Samuel Osgood (Mass.), and Daniel Carroll were named a committee to report upon "sundry letters from Ministers at Versaill[es,] Madrid & Hague" (NA: PCC, No. 186, fol. 17). These dispatches were (1) Benjamin Franklin's of 13 September and 5 November, enclosing a protest of Captain Ary de Neef (Neeff, Neif, Neuf) and Vergennes' letter of 28 October 1781 to Franklin about the debt of 51,291 livres owed by Commodore Alexander Gillon to the mercantile house of La Marque and Fabre in Paris; (2) John Adams' of 4, 13, 14, and 18 December; (3) William Carmichael's of 20 December; (4) John Jay's of 20 September and 3 October, enclosing Gillon's letter of 28 September justifying his conduct to Jay, and Colonel James Searle's of 26 September 1781 to Jay, accusing Gillon of misconduct (NA: PCC, No. 95, fols. 198–209; No. 185, III, 20, 21; No. 186, fols. 17–19, 22).

[2] The "Special Committee," comprising JM, John Morin Scott, and Daniel Carroll (*JCC*, XXII, 141, n. 1), appointed to review Jay's negotiations with Spain, reported on 22 April 1782 (*q.v.*). The financial difficulties, discussed at considerable length by Jay and Carmichael in their letters mentioned above, were tersely summarized by Jay near the close of his long dispatch of 3 October 1781 to the president of Congress. "I have now," Jay wrote, "bills to the amount of between seventy and eighty thousand dollars to pay, and no funds provided. What am I to do? Dr Franklin writes me that so far from being able to give me further aids, he does not expect to have it in his power even to pay our salaries in future.

"From the facts stated in this letter Congress will perceive that this court neither refuse nor promise to afford us further aid. Delay is their system" (Wharton, *Revolutionary Diplomatic Correspondence*, IV, 738–65, and especially 764; V, 61–65).

Although Jay recommended in his letter of 3 October 1781 that Congress retaliate against British captives in the United States as a possible means of compelling the enemy to stop trying to force American "distressed seamen" to enlist in the British navy by mistreating them "in English gaols," his mention of the matter was brief and mild compared with Franklin's bitter reflections, in his dispatch of 5 November 1781, upon the "upwards of eight hundred" of "our poor brave countrymen" who in some instances "have been in that cruel captivity now near four years" (*ibid.*, IV, 764, 825–26). On 20 November 1781 Congress had appointed a committee on retaliation, with Daniel Carroll as chairman and Ezekiel Cornell, Samuel John Atlee (Pa.), Edmund Randolph, and Nicholas Eveleigh (S.C.) as the other members. By the date of the present report, Atlee and Randolph had been replaced on this committee by Abraham Clark and Arthur Lee (NA: PCC, No. 186, fol. 4). See also *Papers of Madison*, III, 271–72; 322–23; 323 nn. 3, 5.

[3] Congress referred the letters of Adams and Franklin to William Ellery, Arthur Lee, Arthur Middleton (S.C.), Thomas McKean (Del.), and "Mr. Jones," who was probably Noble Wymberley of Georgia, not Joseph of Virginia. This committee reported on 26 March 1782 (*JCC*, XXII, 150–51).

[4] On 9 January 1780 the continental frigate "Alliance," commanded by John Paul Jones, intercepted at sea the brigantine "Berkenbosch," a Dutch merchantman commanded by Captain Ary de Neef and loaded with British goods. Jones permitted the vessel to continue on her voyage but only after obliging Neef to exchange with him the ships' cooks and several other members of the crews. By ill chance, the "Berkenbosch" was owned by a member of an influential Dutch family which had been friendly to the American cause. After the Netherlands entered the war as a belligerent, the British captured the "Berkenbosch" in the West Indies and confiscated seven-eighths of her cargo. This misfortune appeared to aggrieve Neef less than his alleged mistreatment by Jones. According to Neef's deposition, the cook Jones had forced on him was a prize master whose poor seamanship led to the capture of the brigantine by the British (NA: PCC, No. 167, fols. 271–81). On 26 March 1782 Congress accepted the recommendation of a committee that Neef's protest be referred to the secretary for foreign affairs (*JCC*, XXII, 150–51, and 151, n. 1). Jones's own account of the incident, together with Neef's admission that his cargo had been British-owned, convinced Livingston that "at first view," Jones had acted with "sufficient justification" (Wharton, *Revolutionary Diplomatic Correspondence*, IV, 826; V, 313, 461–62, 478; Charles Henry Lincoln, comp., *A Calendar of John Paul Jones Manuscripts in the Library of Congress* [Washington, 1903], pp. 149, 163, 181; Samuel Eliot Morison, *John Paul Jones: A Sailor's Biography* [Boston, 1959], pp. 269–70).

[5] See n. 1, above. Alexander Gillon (1741–1794), a merchant shipowner of Charleston and a prominent South Carolina patriot on the eve of the Revolution, was commodore of the navy of his state from February 1778 until the close of the war. Between late 1778, when he reached France to purchase military supplies and frigates for South Carolina, and 28 May 1782, when he finally arrived in the port of Philadelphia, he amply demonstrated, by his many adventures and misadventures, his bravery and resourcefulness, as well as his penchant for becoming embroiled with civil authorities.

Thanks to the exploits mentioned in the last paragraph of n. 6, below, Gillon returned to South Carolina a hero. After the war he was a delegate in several sessions of the state legislature, a commissioner for "erecting the new town of Columbia," a member of the convention which ratified the Federal Constitution, and a representative in the Third Congress of the United States.

[6] While in Paris on his special mission for Congress, Lieutenant Colonel John Laurens of South Carolina persuaded Franklin to aid Gillon with an advance of £10,000 sterling (Wharton, *Revolutionary Diplomatic Correspondence*, V, 514). Thus the commodore was enabled to charter and rename as the "South Carolina," a 44-gun frigate which the Chevalier (later Prince) de Luxembourg had leased from the French government. Gillon's failure to abide by the terms of his agreements with his crew and with the Chevalier would lead to litigation, prolonged even until 1855 (D. E. Huger Smith, "The Luxembourg Claims," *South Carolina Historical and Genealogical Magazine*, X [1909], 92–115).

In Paris and Amsterdam, at a cost far exceeding the money promised by Franklin, Gillon purchased more military supplies than could be stowed in the hold of his frigate. Thereupon, without Franklin's knowledge, Gillon chartered two smaller ships to accommodate the surplus. In August 1781, beset by debts and unable to fulfill his contract with the owners of the merchantmen, Gillon left their vessels at the dock in Amsterdam and put out to sea from that port in the "South Carolina" (NA: PCC, No. 82, II, fols. 61–69; Wharton, *Revolutionary Diplomatic Correspondence*, IV, 705, 781, 827–28, 836–38; V, 8–10, 37). Unable to reach Gillon and realizing that to repudiate his business transactions would still further injure the already shaky credit of the United States, Franklin assumed the unwelcome task, with the help of John Adams, then at The Hague, and Thomas Barclay, consul of the United States, of effecting settlements with Gillon's creditors (*ibid.*, IV, 835, 857; V, 46–48, 54, 159–60, 190, 218–19, 231, 278, 296, 510, 726; *JCC*, XXIII, 591, 702–6). John Laurens' secretary, William Jackson, shared in many of Gillon's transactions in the Netherlands. See Motion on Laurens' Mission, 12 July 1782, editorial note.

Although the troops of South Carolina greatly needed the supplies aboard the frigate, Gillon cruised in European waters for some six weeks after leaving Amsterdam, endeavoring to capture enemy cargo vessels. Among his passengers were Jackson and James Searle (1730–1797), who was anxious to return home from his unsuccessful mission to France and the Netherlands in quest of loans and military supplies for Pennsylvania (*Pennsylvania Archives*, 1st ser., IX, 311, 519–20, 564, 589–95). A prominent merchant-shipowner of Philadelphia, Searle had been a lieutenant colonel of militia, a manager of the United States lottery (1776–1778), a member of the Navy Board in 1778, and a delegate in Congress from 1778 to 1780 (Mildred E. Lombard, "James Searle: Radical Business Man of the Revolution," *Pennsylvania Magazine of History and Biography*, LIX [1935], 284–94).

Late in September 1781, when a shortage of food and water obliged the "South Carolina" to drop anchor at Corunna, Spain, Searle and Jackson left the frigate. By then they were much at odds with Gillon, and all three recorded their grievances in letters addressed to John Jay at Madrid (n. 1, above; Wharton, *Revolutionary Diplomatic Correspondence*, IV, 765, 769–70, 835–38; V, 340–41). Although these protests are now missing, they most probably were "the letters" referred by Congress to Morris upon the recommendation of JM's committee. A lengthy defense of Gillon's conduct with relation to Jackson and Searle appeared in the *Pennsylvania Packet*, 25 July 1782.

When Gillon sailed from Corunna, he left behind him a budget of problems for Jay and Carmichael to solve, including bills unpaid, Searle and Jackson marooned, and a controversy with Spanish authorities over the recruitment of alleged deserters from the Spanish army for the crew of the "South Carolina" (Wharton, *Revolutionary Diplomatic Correspondence*, V, 66, 338–40). Upon reaching the Caribbean, Gillon captured "five rich Jamaica ships" and brought them into Havana harbor on 13 January 1782. Easily persuaded by the captain general of Cuba, Don Juan Manuel de Cagigal, to lead an expedition of fifty-nine Spanish and American vessels against the British garrison at New Providence, Gillon and Spanish troops effected a bloodless conquest of the Bahama Islands on 8 May 1782 (*ibid.*, V, 219, 298; *Pennsylvania Packet*, 11 April and 2 June 1782; *JCC*, XXII, 378 n.; NA: PCC, No. 72, fols. 139, 143–50). Thereafter, accompanied by "a part of the Havana fleet," the "South Carolina" proceeded to Philadelphia (JM to Randolph, 29 May 1782; Wharton, *Revolutionary Diplomatic Correspondence*, V, 463; *Pennsylvania Packet*, 30 May 1782; D. E. Huger Smith, "Commodore Alexander Gillon and the Frigate South Carolina," *South Carolina Historical and Genealogical Magazine*, IX [1908], 189–219).

Benjamin Harrison to Virginia Delegates

FC (Virginia State Library). In the hand of Charles Hay.

VIRGINIA March 23d: 1782

GENTLEMEN

A privateer belonging to this State has seized a flag in one of the Ports of North Carolina, and brought her into this Country, libelled and condemned her in our Court of Admiralty, which has given such offence to Govr Burke that he once intended to send an armed force to carry her back. I hope he has given over this rash design on a promise made him by the Executive to give all the satisfaction in their power to his State which can only be by depriving the Captn. of his Commission and prosecuting him on his Bond; this we have requested Congress to do, as you will see by the enclosed Letter to the President, to which and the proceedings of the Court of Admiralty I refer you for full information of this troublesome affair.[1] It appears to us necessary that Congress should amend their marine law, and declare explicitly how far the rights of each State extend, with respect to vessels in Port, if it is not done we shall certainly get to Blows soon, we therefore request you at some proper time to bring the matter on.[2]

By a vessel just arrived from the West Indies, we are informed that Count de Grasse has totally defeated the British Fleet, and taken or destroyed four sail of the line and a hundred sail of transports with 3,000 Troops on Board. If this should prove true all the English West India Islands must fall into his hands.[3] The Enemy are still quiet in the lines of Charlestown, and General Greene and his brave fellows enjoying what they have long wanted, ease and refreshment about thirty miles from them.[4] Mr Foster Webb has agreed to transcribe the Letters written by our Governors to Congress, General Washington and the Delegates, and their answers which have been destroyed by the Enemy. We request the favor of you to procure him the means of doing it.[5] I am &c

BENJ. HARRISON

[1] The British schooner "Three Friends," sailing under a flag of truce, entered the harbor of Edenton, N.C., late in February 1782 and duly reported to the naval officer of that port. While awaiting his permission to "be admitted as a flag," the vessel was seized by the Virginia brig "Grand Turk," commanded by Captain Cornelius Schermerhorn, and the South Carolina brig "Dolphin," commanded by Captain Madet Engs, and taken to South Quay on Blackwater River, Va. Thereupon, the captors, who were operating under letters of marque and reprisal issued through the governor of Virginia, appeared before the admiralty court of Virginia, in session at Williamsburg, to have the judges condemn the "Three Friends" as a

lawful prize on the grounds that the schooner had violated the ordinances of Congress of 23 March 1776 and 27 March 1781 by trading illegally while operating under a flag of truce (*JCC*, IV, 229–32; XIX, 314–16; *Virginia Gazette, and Weekly Advertiser*, 2, 23, and 30 March 1782; George F. Emmons, comp., *The Navy of the United States, from the Commencement, 1775 to 1853 . . . To Which Is Added a List of Private Armed Vessels . . .* [Washington, 1853], pp. 135, 165). After overruling the plea of the captain of the "Three Friends" that the issue could be tried only in North Carolina, the court condemned the ship on 8 March 1782 and ordered that the vessel and her cargo be sold at public auction for cash to the highest bidder and that the owners, captain, and crew of the "Grand Turk" and the "Dolphin" each receive one half of the net proceeds. These amounted to £3,840, but the issue of dividing this sum was being negotiated as late as 30 April 1783 between attorneys representing the two captors (*Calendar of Virginia State Papers*, III, 88; "Agreement of Thomas Walker and Henry Tazewell, 30 Apr. 1783," MS in Virginia Historical Society).

Governor Harrison knew nothing of the capture until 7 March 1782, when he received an indignant letter from Governor Thomas Burke (*ca.* 1747–1783) of North Carolina in which the writer charged Captain Schermerhorn with insulting a sovereign state and threatened to repossess "Three Friends" by force if she were not returned at once to Edenton.

Besides dispatching Burke a conciliatory reply, Harrison urged Admiralty Judge Benjamin Waller to stay proceedings against the vessel and forward copies of the depositions made by the parties concerned (*Journals of the Council of State*, III, 56, 60–61; McIlwaine, *Official Letters*, III, 173, 174, 175–76). Waller complied immediately with the latter request but could not halt the trial, since the court had already rendered judgment and adjourned (*Calendar of Virginia State Papers*, III, 90–91).

The depositions permitted no doubt that the "Three Friends" was justly condemned because of her illicit trading. Upon reviewing the evidence to this effect, sent to him by Harrison, Burke admitted that "the principle on which I have interposed in behalf of this State has been mistaken." On the other hand he insisted that Schermerhorn must be punished for affronting "the dignity" of North Carolina by removing the schooner to Virginia, thereby obliging North Carolina "to rely on the maritime court of a neighboring state for taking care of our most Material Interests, Vizt., those of Sovereignty and Commerce" (Walter Clark, ed., *The State Records of North Carolina* [26 vols.; Goldsboro, N.C., 1886–1907], XVI, 556–57).

As the present letter shows, Harrison believed that the punishment of Schermerhorn could be imposed only by Congress, since the Articles of Confederation (Articles VI and IX) conferred the exclusive power to regulate privateering upon that body. The instructions to commanders of privateers, adopted by Congress on 7 April 1781, had not pointed out "how far from the Shores of each State it should be lawful for Privateers to take and carry vessels to other States to be tried, without which they will be preying on & oppressing the trade continually" (*JCC*, XIX, 361–64; XX, 645–47; McIlwaine, *Official Letters*, III, 215). Harrison's letter to President Thomas McKean, enclosed in the present dispatch, is dated 22 March 1782 (*ibid.*, III, 177; *Journals of the Council of State*, III, 63). For Edmund Randolph's comments about the Schermerhorn case, see Randolph to JM, 19 April 1782. For JM's opinion of Governor Burke's conduct, see JM to Randolph, 1 May 1782.

[2] Harrison evidently did not know when he wrote the present letter that a committee of Congress, with Randolph as chairman, had reported an ordinance on 1 February 1782 embodying "instructions to the captains of armed vessels." On 13 February the report was returned to the committee with instructions to confer on the subject with Robert Morris in his capacity as agent of marine (*JCC*, XXII, 65–

66, 74). A recommendation on 23 April of a committee appointed nineteen days earlier to consider Harrison's dispatch to McKean (above, n. 1; also NA: PCC, No. 186, fol. 20; No. 191, fol. 13) has not been found, but Congress, on 21 May, "*Resolved,* That the executives of the several states be, and they are hereby authorised, on information of illegal intercourse, which hath taken place or shall take place between the captains of any private armed vessels belonging to these states and the enemy, or of any other mal-conduct, to suspend the commission of such captains until the executive shall have examined into the offence; and if upon enquiry it shall appear that the information was well founded, they are requested to report their proceedings to the United States in Congress assembled, and in this case the commission shall stand suspended until Congress shall have taken order thereon" (*JCC*, XXII, 280–81; *Calendar of Virginia State Papers,* III, 175). This penalty could hardly be assessed retroactively; hence Harrison probably did not suspend the commission of Captain Schermerhorn.

Born in New York in 1756, Cornelius Schermerhorn was a member of a family long engaged in business as ship chandlers and merchant shippers, especially to and from New York City, Charleston, and other ports on the southern seaboard. From the close of the Revolution until his death about 1816, Schermerhorn continued in his profession as a captain of merchant vessels (*New York Genealogical and Biographical Record,* XXXVI [1905], 146–47, 200–205; Alice Barnwell Keith, ed., *The John Gray Blount Papers* [2 vols. to date; Raleigh, N.C. 1952——], I, 193).

Evidently the missing committee report of 23 April, mentioned above, was referred by Congress to a new committee composed of John Morin Scott, John Lowell (Mass.), and JM. Although its recommendation of 29 May seems also to be lost, it may have urged Congress "to devise and report ways and means to prevent an illicit trade with the enemy"—an increasingly menacing commerce of which the "Three Friends" provided only one of many examples (NA: PCC, No. 186, fols. 31, 36; No. 191, fol. 13). Whether the Scott committee did or did not so recommend, Congress on 14 June appointed a committee of eleven members, including JM, to consider the general problem. Three days later, upon his motion, Congress transferred the matter to a five-man committee, with JM as its chairman (*JCC*, XXII, 333 n.). See Report on Illicit Trade with the Enemy, 19 June 1782.

[3] The *Virginia Gazette, and Weekly Advertiser* of 23 March mentioned letters from Grasse to Rochambeau, carried by a ship that had "arrived in York river," which told about the French capture of St. Kitts and Nevis, along with three thousand British troops. The same issue of the *Gazette* reported an overwhelming French naval victory in the Caribbean, marked by the British loss of 4 ships of the line, 2 frigates, 3 sloops, and 115 transports. This may have been an exaggerated account of the capture by a 5-ship French squadron of three ports in British Guiana, together with 5 small warships and 11 "private vessels of different sizes," between 30 January and 2 February 1782 (Wm. L. Clowes, *Royal Navy,* IV, 77; *Pennsylvania Packet,* 9 and 11 April 1782). See also Jameson to JM, 23 March 1782.

[4] Harrison was relaying information contained in an extract of a letter of 6 February 1782 "from an officer in the Southern army," printed in the *Virginia Gazette, and Weekly Advertiser* of 23 March 1782. Although the military outlook in the South was brightening, especially since about one thousand of the British troops pent up in Charleston would soon be transferred to the West Indies, the American forces still suffered from an insufficiency of food, clothing, and arms (Pendleton to JM, 11 February, n. 5, and 11 March 1782, n. 4; George W. Greene, *Life of Nathanael Greene,* III, 447–49).

[5] See Jameson to JM, 9 March 1782, n. 2.

From David Jameson

RC (LC: Madison Papers). Docketed by JM, "March 23d. 1782."

RICHMOND Mch 23. 1782

DR SIR

I have your favour of the 12t.[1] and have reason to suppose I did not express my meaning, properly when I mentioned the Associate to Mr. Andrews. there cannot be a doubt but a person skilled in Astronomy ought to be preferred. I intended to say, if such a person could not be got, a Man of Integrity & Abilities in other requisites would be necessary, and the Astro. observations must then rest with Mr Andrews only. I wrote on the occasion to our friend Page (the Man among us I should prefer, and who as you justly observe is in every point qualified)—and although he did not positively say he would go to Phila., yet he left me room to believe he would not refuse: And he was appointed.[2] But the matter is now cut very short. The Governor recd. a letter by Post this Week from the President of Pena. desiring to postpone the final adjustment of the Boundary, and proposing a temporary line to be run, which is agreed to. the reason assigned for defering the Astro. observations, is the disturbances & dangers likely to be occasioned by the Indians to the Westward[3]

I am very glad Congress have determined to name Commissioners to settle the Accots. in the different States.[4] I shall now hope the prejudices conceived against Virginia will be soon removed[.] I fear very few Men will be brought into the field by our endeavours to enforce the draft in the (last years) delinquent Counties. In several of them Assessments were not made, or divisions laid off. And I fear there is some obstacle in each of them that cannot be removed but by the Legislature.[5] I have some hope from the Circular letter,[6] but I confess not great. Some Substitutes will be got. the people are well aware that if Men cannot be recruited under the last law, a draft must take place as soon as the Assembly meets; and I think a good number will guard against the draft by hiring substitutes

My Nephew[7] writes me that he has recd. no letter from me for some Months past. I was in hopes those I took the liberty to trouble you with would get to him[.] I again take the liberty to inclose a letter for him. he will I expect be in Philadelphia by the time this gets to hand We have no News worth relating. You are told in the paper that a French

Frigate was arrd. in York River and brot. several interesting Accots. No Frigate was arrd., but we hope the intelligence said to be brot. by her is true.[8]

I am with great esteem D Sir Yr obt hb Set

DAVID JAMESON

If Col Jameson does not soon come to Phila. be so kind as put the letter under Cover & forward it to him.

[1] Not found, but portions of it can be surmised from the present letter.

[2] See Harrison to JM, 19 January, and n. 3; JM to Harrison, 1 and 7 February; and Jameson to JM, 23 February 1782. On 14 March the Council of State advised Governor Harrison to request John Page, a graduate of the College of William and Mary, 1763, to accept the assignment. Page apparently agreed at once, because he was one of the four commissioners of Virginia when Harrison wrote to him nine days later (*Journals of the Council of State*, III, 59; McIlwaine, *Official Letters*, III, 179–80). The Reverend Robert Andrews a decade before had been tutor to Page's children (*Papers of Madison*, III, 312, n. 2).

[3] On 2 March the Pennsylvania General Assembly had resolved that "from the great expences necessarily attending the compleating the Line between this State and Virginia, it would be most prudent to defer it for the present. And that a temporary Line during the Continuance of the present War, or till times are more settled on the Frontiors, may be made and agreed on at a small expence, which will answer every purpose expected,–and to effect which Council will take the necessary measures" (*Pennsylvania Archives*, 1st ser., IX, 506–7). The letter from President William Moore of Pennsylvania to Governor Harrison has not been found, but Harrison's answer, dated 22 March, is printed *ibid.*, 1st ser., IX, 518–19, and in McIlwaine, *Official Letters*, III, 176–77. See also *Journals of the Council of State*, III, 63.

[4] See JM to Pendleton, 7 February, and n. 6; Report on Settlement of Accounts, 20 and 27 February; and Virginia Delegates to Harrison, 25 February 1782, and n. 1.

[5] See *Papers of Madison*, III, 317–18; 318, n. 3; Jameson to JM, 26 January, and n. 1; and Virginia Delegates to Harrison, 15 February 1782. The Virginia General Assembly enacted on 2 July 1782 a new statute providing for the recruitment of three thousand continental troops. Of this number, each county was allotted a quota equal to one-fifteenth of its quota of militia (Minute Book, House of Delegates, May 1782, p. 86; Hening, *Statutes*, XI, 14–20). See Randolph to JM, 20 June 1782, and n. 48.

[6] See Jameson to JM, 23 February 1782, n. 6.

[7] Lieutenant Colonel John Jameson of Culpeper County, second in command of the 2d Continental Dragoons, then stationed under General Heath on the lower Hudson River (Gwathmey, *Historical Register of Virginians*, p. 413).

[8] See Harrison to Virginia Delegates, 23 March 1782, and n. 3.

From Thomas Jefferson

Draft (LC: Jefferson Papers).

MONTICELLO Mar. 24 1782

DR SIR

I have recd from you two several favours on the subject of the designs against the territorial rights of Virginia.[1] I never before could comprehend on what principle our right to the Western country could be denied which would not at the same time subvert the rights of all the states to the whole of their territory. what objections may be founded on the Charter of N. York I cannot say, having never seen that charter nor been able to get a copy of it in this country.[2] I had thought to have seised the first leisure on my return from the last assembly to have considered & stated our right and to have communicated to our Delegates or perhaps to the public so much as I could trace, and expected to have derived some assistance from antient M.S.S. which I have been able to collect. these with my other papers & books however had been removed to Augusta to be out of danger from the enemy[3] & have not yet been brought back. the ground on which I now find the question to be bottomed is so unknown to me that it is out of my power to say any thing on the subject. should it be practicable for me to procure a copy of the charter of N Y. I shall probably think on it, and would cheerfully communicate to you whatever could occur to me worth your notice. but this will probably be much too late to be of any service before Congress who doubtless will decide ere long on the subject. I sincerely wish their decision may tend to the preservation of peace. If I am not totally deceived in the determination of this country the decision of Congress if unfavourable, will not close the question.[4] I suppose some people on the Western waters who are ambitious to be Governors &c will urge a separation by authority of Congress: but the bulk of the people Westward are already thrown into great ferment by the report of what is proposed, to which I think they will not submit. this separation is unacceptable to us in form only & not in substance. on the contrary I may safely say it is desired by the Eastern part of our country whenever their Western brethren shall think themselves able to stand alone. in the mean time on the petition of the Western counties a plan is digesting for rendering their access to government more easy.[5]

I trouble you with the inclosed to Monsr. Marbois.[6] I had the pleasure of hearing that your father & family were well yesterday, by your brother who is about to study the law in my neighborhood.[7] I shall alwais be glad to hear from you; & if it be possible for me, retired from public business to find any thing worth your notice, I shall communicate it with great pleasure. I am with sincere esteem Dr Sir

your friend & sert

[1] JM's "two several favours" were those of 18 November 1781 and 15 January 1782. For the latter, see above; for the former, see *Papers of Madison*, III, 307–8; 309, n. 7.

[2] The territory granted in the charter of 1663/64 from King Charles II to his brother James, Duke of York, did not overlap the western claims of Virginia. For the basis of New York's alleged title to land in the Old Northwest, see *Papers of Madison*, II, 73–74.

[3] That is, to Staunton, Augusta County, to which the Virginia General Assembly had fled about 1 June 1781, to avoid capture by British troops (*Papers of Madison*, III, 120; 121, n. 3).

[4] This sentence was interlineated by Jefferson.

[5] Many circumstances contributed to the discontent of the men "on the Western waters." The earlier victories of George Rogers Clark over the British and their Indian allies had been largely nullified by the winter of 1781–1782. Having under his immediate command only a small force of state troops, poorly equipped and long unpaid, Clark could not maintain a garrison at Vincennes or more than a "few spys" at Kaskaskia and Cahokia. His belief that the British at Detroit were preparing a spring and summer assault by many Indians against Kentucky and the Kanawha Valley area of Virginia was supported by the unusual number of small raids into those regions from north of the Ohio River during the winter months (*Calendar of Virginia State Papers*, II, 529–31, 562–64, 651; III, 68, 87–88). Blockhouses were useless as a means of protecting outlying settlements against these forays. Determined to defend their families, the scattered militiamen naturally refused Clark's summons to garrison a fort or share in an expedition far from their homes.

Probably of even more importance in stimulating movements for separate statehood in Washington County and in Kentucky were the remoteness of the capital and the inadequacies of civil government on the frontier, the inability of pioneers to secure titles to acres which they had improved and defended, absentee ownership of huge tracts, competitive land speculation, and, as Jefferson remarks in the present letter, people "ambitious to be Governors." On 8 April 1782 John Floyd of Kentucky commented in a letter to John May that "the new invented Ideas of a separate State, calculated on purpose for disaffection & an Evasion of duty . . . seems to threaten us on all sides with Anarchy, Confusion & I may add Destruction" (*ibid.*, III, 121; Thomas P. Abernethy, *Western Lands and the American Revolution*, pp. 258–65, 302–3).

As Jefferson foresaw, at least two petitions from residents of the "three counties of Kentucky" were presented to the Virginia General Assembly at its session of May 1782. The forty-one signers of one of these memorials asked the Assembly to compel all absentee owners either to cultivate their huge acreages of Kentucky land or to dispose of them to settlers. If their request was granted, the petitioners continued, Kentucky would advance "towards that stage of maturity when the tenderness of a kind parent to a departing child, will direct us to form a constitution and act for ourselves." On 1 June 1782 the House of Delegates ordered that this petition "lie on the table" (Kentucky Petitions, MSS in Virginia State Library). A considerably longer memorial, signed by fifty-seven Kentuckians, had already been received by the House of Delegates. After portraying their hard lot because of inadequate defense against Indians, scarce or almost worthless money, and the lack of homestead and pre-emption laws, the petitioners prayed "you to take into Consideration and Create them a power Sufficient for their Controul and better Government" or to intercede "with the Honourable the Continental Congress for their Incorporation with them." Aside from a rather lengthy résumé of the contents, the docketing of this memorial reads, cryptically: "Kentuckey petition May 30th: 1782. referred to Courts of Justice June 13th 1782. Some parts Reasonable. Other parts Rejected[.] Reported" (Kentucky Petitions, MSS in Virginia State Library). Evidently the legislature did not grant the alternative request of the petitioners by asking Congress to admit Kentucky to the Union as a state. On the other hand, the General Assembly provided "a supreme court of judicature of original jurisdiction" for the three Kentucky counties (Jefferson, Fayette, and Lincoln) and directed the register of the land office to "issue pre-emption warrants" for a maximum of four hundred acres to Kentuckians whose claims to land should be uncontested within the period specified by the law (Hening, *Statutes*, X, 431–32; XI, 85–92, 103). See *Papers of Madison*, III, 349, n. 9.

Following 23 August 1780, when the earliest petition "from sundry inhabitants of Kentucke" reached Congress, two years elapsed before another memorial from that area "was filed in the office of the Secretary of Congress" (NA: PCC, No. 48, fols. 237–44; *JCC*, XVII, 760; XXIII, 532; *Papers of Madison*, II, 65, and nn.).

[6] In this letter of 24 March to François, Marquis de Barbé-Marbois, Jefferson explained why he had delayed so long to reply to the Marquis' questions about Virginia (Boyd, *Papers of Jefferson*, VI, 171–72). Jefferson's answers were the basis of his well-known *Notes on the State of Virginia* (*Papers of Madison*, III, 330, n. 1; JM to Jefferson, 18 March 1782, n. 6).

[7] Although JM's brother William visited Charlottesville to determine whether he could study law there, he evidently did not come under Jefferson's tutelage until several months later (JM to James Madison, Sr., 20 May 1782). Late in the following November this arrangement necessarily ended when Jefferson consented to be "a minister plenipotentiary for negotiating peace with Great Britain" (*JCC*, XXIII, 720–21; Boyd, *Papers of Jefferson*, VI, 202, 206).

Report on New Hampshire Requisition

MS (NA: PCC, No. 20, I, 19–21). Written and docketed by JM: "Report of Committee on the Letter from President Weare of 23d. of Feby. 1782[.] 25th. March 1782. Monday next assigned[.]" Between "Feby. 1782" and "25th. March," Charles Thomson, secretary of Congress, later inserted "Agreed to May 22d. 1782."

March 25th. 1782

The Committee to whom was referred the letter of the 23d. of Feby last from the President of N. Hamshire[1] submit the following report:

That so much of the said letter as relates to 5 Millions of Dollars of the old emission remaining in the Treasury of N. Hamshire, as a surplus of the quota allotted to that State for redemption, be referred to the Superintendt of Finance to report thereon.[2]

That in answer to the remaining part of the letter which represents that the State of N. Hamshire was overated in the requisition made by Congress on the 2d. of Novr. last, and contains a return of its inhabitants, amounting to 82,200 only the President of the said State be informed;[3]

That as a valuation of land throughout the U. States wch. the instrument of confederation prescribes as the rule for apportioning the public burdens on the several States,[4] was under present circumstances manifestly unattainable, Congress were obliged to resort to some other rule in fixing the quotas in the requisition of Novr. last:

That the number of inhabitants in each State, having been a rule observed in previous requisitions of money naturally presented itself as the most eligible one;

That as no actual numeration of the inhabitants of each State hath yet been obtained by Congress, the computed number which formed the basis of the first requisition made on the States the 29th. of July 1775,[5] was adhered to:

That although the particular numeration of the Inhabitants of N. Hamshire, as stated in the letter, should have been made with due accuracy, still a reduction of its quota in conformity thereto, might produce injustice to the other States; since the computation of July 1775 may as far exceed their real number as it has been found to exceed that of New Hamshire:

That if the justice of the application from N. Hamshire were less uncertain, it would at this season be impossible to superadd to the quotas of the other States, any deduction from that of N. Hamshire; and to make such deduction without superadding it to the quotas of the other States, would leave a deficiency in the revenue which has been found on calculation to be essential for the exigencies of the current year.

That the other facts stated by him in his letter,[6] however well founded they may be, are not peculiar to N. Hamshire, and if admitted for the purpose to which they are applied, would authorize, and produce similar demands from other States:

That for these considerations, and more especially as, the apportionment in question, if hereafter found to be erroneous will be subject to correction, Congress cannot comply with the request made in behalf of

N. Hamshire; and confide in the justice and public spirit of the sd. State for those exertions which may be necessary to prevent a deficiency in the public revenue.[7]

[1] Meshech Weare's letter, addressed to Samuel Livermore, the only New Hampshire delegate then in Congress, was read on 13 March and referred to JM, Abraham Clark, and Ezekiel Cornell (*JCC*, XXII, 128, n. 2).

[2] Weare pointed out that, subsequent to the ordinance of 18 March 1780 providing for the cancellation of the "old emission" of continental currency, notes of that emission had depreciated more slowly in New Hampshire than in most of the other states. Hence, late in the spring of 1781, when these bills suddenly became almost worthless along the middle Atlantic seaboard, they naturally flowed in large quantities to New Hampshire, which until 23 July continued to receive them for taxes at the legal exchange rate of $40.00 of the old for $1.00 of the new currency. As a result, his state had drawn over double its quota of these bills into its treasury but could not use them to pay domestic debts or the annual allotment of money to Congress. In view of this situation and the fact that some states had not retired their full quotas of the old emission, Weare asked that Congress direct these delinquent states to make up their shortages by purchases from the surplus held by New Hampshire, or that Congress agree to receive this continental currency "in part payment of our Taxes for the current year" (NA: PCC, No. 64, fols. 218–20). See also *JCC*, XV, 1150; XVI, 262–66; *Papers of Madison*, II, 49, n. 2; III, 108–9; 109–10, nn. As the present report recommended, Weare's request was referred to Robert Morris on 22 May. Morris' proposed solution was rejected by Congress on 26 November 1782. Thereafter the matter at issue was merged with the much larger problem of effecting financial settlements among the states and between each state and Congress (*JCC*, XXIII, 854–56).

[3] By the requisition of 2 November 1781, New Hampshire was asked to supply $373,598 or 4.67 per cent of the $8 million total. Lacking both a reliable population census for most of the colonies and similar tables of property values, Congress on 29 July 1775 had apportioned its first requisition in sums assumed to reflect the relative populations, "including negroes and mulattoes," of the thirteen colonies (*JCC*, II, 221–22; XXI, 1090). When requisitioning money thereafter, Congress adhered approximately to the ratio agreed upon in 1775. The cover of Weare's letter contains docketing that notes the number of New Hampshire's "Inhabitants taken on Oath in 1775" was 82,200. Only three other colonies had taken a similar census in that year; hence the total population at the outset of the Revolution can only be estimated. If the people in the thirteen colonies then numbered about 2,507,180, as one careful scholar has concluded, New Hampshire's percentage of the total should have been 3.24 rather than 4.67 (Stella H. Sutherland, *Population Distribution in Colonial America* [New York, 1936], pp. xii, 271). Therefore it seems Weare had good reason to believe that New Hampshire was "overated." Although he did not specify in his letter by how much the population of his state had been overestimated, an opinion on this point was at least implied by Livermore on 1 April 1782, when he succeeded merely in postponing the adoption of JM's report by offering a substitute motion to lessen New Hampshire's quota by $66,512 (*JCC*, XXII, 158–61). If Congress had consented to this reduction, the state's percentage of the $8 million would have dropped from 4.67 to about 3.84.

[4] Article VIII of the Articles of Confederation (*JCC* XIX, 217). See JM to Pendleton, 7 February 1782, n. 5.

[5] See n. 3, above.

[6] Among these "other facts" stated by Weare were "little Trade," many new, unproductive farms, no "hard Money," and "the great difficulties and embarrassments we are under, on account of the disputes subsisting in the western Parts of this State" (NA: PCC, No. 64, fol. 220). For the Vermont or New Hampshire Grants disputes, see JM to Pendleton, 22 January, and nn. 3, 5, and 6; and 7 February 1782, and n. 4.

[7] In a letter on 16 April to Weare, Livermore mentioned his "utmost efforts" to defeat the report and sarcastically characterized it as "wise," according to "the wisdom of this world, and savours of the mammon of unrighteousness" (Burnett, *Letters,* VI, 328–29; see also *ibid.*, VI, 317). Although unmentioned in the printed journal, Congress on 22 April referred the report to Joseph Montgomery, Thomas Bee, and Oliver Wolcott (Conn.) for review (NA: PCC, No. 186, fol. 22). In a letter written to Weare on that day, Livermore expressed the hope that the report "will be well considered and set right" by the new committee (Burnett, *Letters,* VI, 332). The hope was in vain. On 22 May 1782 Congress adopted JM's original report without alteration (*JCC,* XXII, 290).

Virginia Delegates to Benjamin Harrison

RC (Virginia State Library). Written and franked by Arthur Lee. Docketed: "Virga. Delegates Lr. recd. Apl 82[.] March 26h 1782[.] Latest advices from Europe indicate determination of British Cabinet to continue the War."

PHILADELPHIA, March 26th. 1782

SIR

The Superintendant of Finance informs us, that he has sent a proposition to our Executive which he conceives will answer the object of our motion relative to the supply of Beef.[1]

The latest Advices from Europe assure us of the determination of the british Cabinet to continue the war, & it is believd that the distressing our Commerce will be their principal object with regard to the United States.[2] France & Spain are sending strong re-enforcements to the W. Indies; & it is probable they will maintain the superiority in those Seas, in spite of all the efforts of the Enemy[3]

It is two posts, since we had the honor of a line from your Excellency.[4]

We have the honor to be with the greatest respect Yr. Excellency's most obedt & most Humle Servts

JOS: JONES.
J. MADISON JR.
A. LEE

[1] See Virginia Delegates to Harrison, 19 March 1782, n. 1.

[2] To what "latest Advices" Lee refers is unknown, but they may have been from his brother William, then stationed in Brussels. The debates in Parliament, reprinted in issues of Philadelphia newspapers, could have led Arthur Lee readily to conclude that in 1782 Great Britain planned to rely more heavily upon its navy than its army to subdue the American rebellion (JM to Jefferson, 18 March 1782, and n. 7). In his letter of 18 December 1781, read in Congress on 18 March, John Adams had suggested that the British might "try their skill in intercepting our trade" (Wharton, *Revolutionary Diplomatic Correspondence*, V, 55). See the preamble of Report on Illicit Trade with the Enemy, 19 June 1782.

[3] Lee may have derived this information from William Lee or, perhaps less likely, from William Carmichael's letter of 20 December 1781, read in Congress on 18 March (Wharton, *Revolutionary Diplomatic Correspondence*, V, 63; and Report on Foreign Dispatches, 20 March 1782, n. 1). Carmichael, of course, could not have heard of Admiral Kempenfelt's victory over the fleet of the Comte de Guichen (JM to Pendleton, 25 February 1782, and n. 4).

[4] See Harrison to Virginia Delegates, 6 April 1782.

To Thomas Jefferson

Printed text (Madison, *Papers* [Gilpin ed.], I, 116). The letter has not been found.

PHILADELPHIA, March 26, 1782.

DEAR SIR,

A letter has been lately received from you by the President of Congress, accompanied by a bundle of papers procured from the Cherokees by Colonel Campbell.[1] As it appears that these papers were transmitted at the request of the late President, it is proper to apprize you that it was made without any written or verbal sanction, and even without the knowledge of Congress; and not improbably with a view of fishing for discoveries which may be subservient to the aggressions meditated on the territorial rights of Virginia.[2] It would have been unnecessary to trouble you with this, had it not appeared that Colonel Campbell has given a promise of other papers; which if he should fulfil, and the papers contain any thing which the adversaries of Virginia may make an ill use of, you will not suffer any respect for the acts of Congress to induce you to forward hither.

[1] See *Papers of Madison*, III, 250, n. 7; 299, n. 1. The letter was Jefferson's of 20 December to President Thomas McKean, complying belatedly with President Samuel Huntington's request of 27 April for a number of documents which Colonel Arthur Campbell had taken from the Cherokee Indians in January 1781. According to Huntington's letter, Jefferson might deem some or all of the manuscripts worthy to be included in a "Collection of American State Papers" being assembled for publication by Ebenezer Hazard (Boyd, *Papers of Jefferson*, V, 562–63; VI,

141 n.). The committee, to which Congress on 22 March 1782 referred Jefferson's reply and its enclosures, apparently never submitted a report (NA: PCC, No. 186, III, 18). Whether any of these documents were ever in Hazard's possession is not known. His *Historical Collections; Consisting of State Papers, and Other Authentic Documents; Intended as Materials for an History of the United States of America* (2 vols.; Philadelphia, 1792–94) does not encompass southern affairs so late as the 1780's.

Arthur Campbell (1743–1811) of Washington County, Va., was a frontiersman all his life, which included three years as an Indian captive in his youth. He served in the Virginia Convention of 1776 and in the House of Delegates during six sessions between that year and 1788. Involved in many western land speculations, he prominently supported the movement to separate Kentucky from Virginia and to cut off a part of southwestern Virginia for inclusion with the Watauga district of North Carolina in the "State of Franklin" (Thomas P. Abernethy, *Western Lands and the American Revolution*, pp. 79, 102, 124, 131–32, 166, 191, 255, 258, 261–62, 290–338, *passim;* Jefferson to JM, 24 March 1782, n. 5).

[2] Although Huntington had not been specifically directed by Congress to approach Jefferson on Hazard's behalf, he was complying with the resolution of Congress of 20 July 1778 (*JCC*, XI, 705). JM was concerned, of course, lest there might be material in Campbell's documents which would be useful to Huntington, McKean, or other delegates in Congress who were strenuously opposing Virginia's title to the West.

To James Madison, Sr.

RC (LC: Madison Papers). The cover is missing, but JM, Sr., docketed the letter, "Madison Js. cop. March 30. 1782."

PHILADA. March 30th. 1782

HOND SIR

Mr. J. Walker[1] has safely delivered to me three letters from you attended with the money therein specified. He has also been so obliging as to undertake the conveyance of the several articles of Medecine you wanted with a Gallon keg filled with good Port: wine, to all which I add a large packet of Newspapers, and an Almanack. The last packet I sent was by a waggon returning to your neighbourhood which brought me a letter from Mr. W. Maury;[2] By which I sent at the same time a small supply of Bark[3] for my Mother.

I mentioned to you in one of my former letters that I had a prospect of getting on very favorable terms a few scarce books from a library brought hither for sale by Col. Zane.[4] My purchases of him have amounted in the whole to Nineteen pounds three shillings of this currency.[5] As I had not the money here for him, & he could not conveniently wait till it would be convenient for me to pay him, I was obliged to give him a draught on you. I hope you will be able to find means to satisfy it. If it can not be otherwise done than by a deduction from the further supply you have in contemplation for me I must submit to it How far I shall depend on you for the resources necessary for my expences here not included in the legal provision, and for the arrearages into which I have unavoidably fallen, will be known as soon as the Assembly have finally decided on our accounts & the allowance which is to be made to us. This I suppose will be done at their Session in May next.[6] Unless liberal principles prevail on the occasion, I shall be under the necessity of selling a negro

I have not time to provide for this opportunity the information relative to the Copper plates.[7]

The newspapers give you in general the intelligence we have from Europe. As far as we are enabled to Judge of the views of the British Cabinet, the misfortunes of one more campaign at least will be necessary to conquer their obstinacy. They are attempting a separate peace with the Dutch & talk of suspending their offensive war agst. us, & directing their whole resources agst. the naval power of France & Spain.[8] If this be their real plan we may be sure they do not mean by it to abandon their pretensions to the U. States but try another mode for recovering them. During their offensive exertions agst. our Ally, they can be practising insidious ones agst. us:[9] and if in the first they should be successful, & in the latter disappointed, a renewal of a vigorous war upon us will certainly take place. The best security agst. every artifice & every event will be such military preparations on our part as will be sufficient either to resist or expell them as the case may require.

With my affectionate regards for the family I am Kind Sir Yr. dutiful son

J. MADISON JR.

[1] Probably James Walker of Orange County. The three letters have not been found.

[2] Walker Maury's letter is missing.

[3] Cinchona bark (quinine) or a substitute for it.

[4] See JM to his father, 12 February 1782. Colonel Isaac Zane, Jr., had come to Philadelphia from the Shenandoah Valley to sell some of the valuable books which he had bought in March 1778 from the estate of William Byrd III (*Virginia Magazine of History and Biography*, XXXVIII [1930], 52).

[5] In the margin JM, Sr., wrote "£15 . . 6 . . 5," possibly to indicate the price in Virginia rather than Pennsylvania currency.

[6] See Jameson to JM, 9 March 1782, n. 4.

[7] See JM to James Madison, Sr., 20 May 1782.

[8] See JM to Jefferson, 18 March, and n. 7; Virginia Delegates to Harrison, 19 March, and nn. 4, 6, 7; and JM to Pendleton, 19 March 1782, and n. 3.

[9] See Virginia Delegates to Harrison, 26 March 1782, and n. 2.

Virginia Delegates to Benjamin Lincoln, and Benjamin Lincoln to Virginia Delegates

Copy (Virginia State Library). Made by Arthur Lee on a single page and enclosed in Virginia Delegates to Harrison, 2 April 1782 (*q.v.*).

IN CONGRESS April 1st. 1782

SIR,

The success of recruiting in Virginia will very much depend on the State having Arms & Clothing for the Men that may be raisd. We therefore beg you will inform us, what supply of these Articles the State may depend upon from your department.

We have the honor to be &c

To the Honble Maj. G. Lincoln
Minister at War } signd J. JONES
J. MADISON
A. LEE

ANSWER.

WAR-OFFICE April 1st. 1782

I have this morning, Gentlemen, been honord with your favor of this date; intimating your wish, to be informd what supply of Arms & Clothing the State may depend on from the War department.

On the 1st. Sepr. last Congress took upon themselves the whole business of clothing the Army & made provision accordingly.[1] As soon as the State of Virginia shall fix on a place of general rendezvous from which Recruits shall march to join the Army; an Officer of rank will be appointed to attend that post, to receive & forward them, to whom Clothing & Arms will be sent, on his return, from time to time, sufficient fully to clothe & equip the Troops[2]

I have the honor to be &c &c

signd B. LINCOLN

THE HONBLE
JOS. JONES
J. MADISON
A. LEE } ESQRS.

[1] On 18 June 1781 Congress resolved that "all state purchases of cloathing on continental account, and all state appointments and regulations in the cloathing department on continental account, be abolished on the first day of September" (*JCC*, XX, 663).

[2] According to the detailed regulations adopted by Congress on 18 June 1781, the clothier general would call upon the quartermaster general or the latter's deputies in the several states to "furnish the means of transportation of all articles of cloathing from the places where imported, received, or purchased, to the places of deposit" (*JCC*, XX, 666). The legislation of 7 February 1781 establishing the Department of War obliged Lincoln to account for the disposition of weapons. Not until 24 July 1782 would Congress empower him to appoint and issue direct orders to the commissary of military stores (*JCC*, XIX, 126–27; XXII, 415).

Virginia Delegates to Benjamin Harrison

RC (Virginia State Library). Written by Arthur Lee. Docketed, "Letter from Delegates April 2d 1782."

PHILADELPHIA April 2d. 1782

SIR,

We had the honor of receiving your Excellency's letter of the 23d. ult. with the Papers for Congress[1] which we shall present.

We are obliged to your Excellency for your intelligence from the W. Indies, which we hope will be confirmed. Mr. Foster Webb will receive every assistance we can give him.[2]

The Copies enclosd[3] will inform your Excellency of the arrangement made at the war-Office, relative to the arms and clothing for the Recruits of our line. We are apprehensive, that in the present state of things, it will not be enough for the recruiting Officer to assure the People that Clothing will be ready at the Rendezvous, for those that enlist; but that he must have some uniforms with him to convince it is not an imposition, & that they will not suffer, as others have done, for want of Cloths. But your Excellency will be better able to judge whether this is necessary; & therefore we shall not press for the Clothing to be sent previous to the Recruits being raisd, 'till we have the honor of hearing from you.[4]

We enclose a Resolution of Congress, for retaking such of the british Prisoners as may have escapd from confinement.[5]

With the greatest respect, We have the honor to be Yr. Excellency's most Obedt. & most Humbe. Serts.

J MADISON JR.
A LEE
JOS: JONES

[1] See Harrison to Virginia Delegates, 23 March 1782, and nn. 1 and 2.

[2] See *ibid.*, and n. 3; Jameson to JM, 23 March 1782.

[3] See Virginia Delegates to Lincoln, and Lincoln to Virginia Delegates, 1 April 1782.

[4] For Harrison's answer, see his letter of 12 April 1782 to the Virginia delegates.

[5] The enclosure was an "Extract from the Minutes," attested by Deputy Secretary of Congress George Bond, of the resolution of 30 March 1782 recommending that the states grant a reward of $8.00 at continental expense for the recapture of each enemy prisoner and that they provide for the punishment of any person "harboring, secreting, assisting, abetting, or comforting, any prisoner of war" (*JCC*, XXII, 154–56). Also filed with the delegates' letter in the Virginia State Library is another copy of the resolution, which was made on 9 April 1782 by Major William Jackson, assistant secretary at war, and sent to Governor Harrison.

The resolution was particularly applicable to the situation in Virginia. Not only were numbers of convention captives moving about freely within the state, but soon after Cornwallis' surrender at Yorktown many enemy soldiers had begun to roam the countryside, work for the inhabitants, or even conduct businesses of their own. Governor Harrison's directives to county lieutenants and militia officers to round up these prisoners and return them to their cantonments were either unenforceable or unheeded. At Harrison's urgent request, the Virginia General Assembly in its session of May 1782 enacted a measure "for apprehending British prisoners of war, and for other purposes," but the statute has been lost (William M. Dabney, *After Saratoga: The Story of the Convention Army* [Albuquerque, 1954], pp. 76–77; *Virginia Gazette*, 6 July 1782).

To Edmund Pendleton

RC (LC: Madison Papers). That Pendleton was the addressee is made clear by his letter of 15 April to JM (*q.v.*).

PHILADA. April 2d. 1782.

DEAR SIR

The only event with which the period since my last has enabled me to repay your favor of the 25th. Ulto.[1] is the arrival of four Deputies from Vermt. with a plenipotentiary commission to accede to the confederacy. The business is referred to a Committee who are sufficiently devoted to the policy of gaining the Vote of Vermont into Congress.[2] The result will be the subject of a future letter.

The thinness or rather vacancy of the Virginia line, & the little prospect of recruiting it are subjects of a very distressing nature. If those on whom the remedy depends were sensible of the insulting comparisons to which they expose the State,[3] & of the wound they give to her influence in the General Councils, I am persuaded more decisive exertions would be made. Considering the extensive interests & claims which Virga. has, & the enemies & calumnies which these very claims form agst. her She is perhaps under the strongest obligation of any State in the Union to preserve her military contingent on a respectable footing,[4] and unhappily her line is perhaps of all in the most discraceful condition. The only hope that remains is that her true policy will be better consulted at the Ensuing assembly, & that as far as a proper sense of it may be deficient, the expostulations of her friends and clamours of her enemies will supply the place of it.[5] If I speak my sentiments too freely on this point, it can only be imputed to my sensibility to the honor & interest of my Country[6]

I am Dr Sir Yrs. very sincerly.

J MADISON JR

[1] Not found.

[2] See Motion Concerning Documents on Vermont, 3 April, and n. 2; and Motion on Letter of Vermont Agents, 20 April 1782. Congress on 1 April 1782 referred the "business" to George Clymer, Daniel Carroll, Abraham Clark, Samuel Livermore, and Richard Law. With the exception of Livermore, these men were known to favor adding to the number of small states or, as in the cases of Carroll and Clymer, forming Vermont from parts of New York and New Hampshire so as to establish a precedent warranting Congress to assert title to and jurisdiction over Virginia's territory in the Old Northwest (*JCC*, XXII, 157–58, 185; Burnett, *Letters*, VI, 312, 323, 324, 326, 329).

[3] Examples of these "calumnies" that found their way into print are a letter in the *Pennsylvania Packet* of 6 April taking Virginia severely to task for neglecting to reinforce General Greene's army, and an article by "A LOVER OF JUSTICE" in the same newspaper on 27 April 1782. "The claim, or rather the pretentions of Virginia," wrote this scribe, "to lands which can only belong to the United States, has debased her mind[;] it has taught her to do dishonourable things. . . . Has her monopoly enriched her? No. Has it enabled her to send more men into the field? No. Has it filled her treasury and forwarded her share of supplies? No. It has aggrandized a few; but it has left her without troops in the service; without money in her coffers, and without honour in the Union."

[4] See *Papers of Madison*, III, 317–18; 318, n. 3; 349, n. 9; Harrison to Virginia Delegates, 11 January, and n. 2; 9 February; and 1 March; Jameson to JM, 26 January, n. 1; 23 February, n. 6; 2 March; and 23 March; Virginia Delegates to Harrison, 15 February 1782, and n. 3.

[5] See Jameson to JM, 23 March 1782, n. 5. In his message of 6 May 1782 to the General Assembly, Harrison mentioned the complete failure of the recruiting act then in force to raise more than "a few substitutes." If, continued the governor, "we wish to be at ease at home it will be necessary to Keep the enemy fully employed at a distance, to do which part of the strength of this country must be applyd as it is certain the States of North & South Carolina are too much exhausted by the ravages of the enemy to confine them long to Charles Town with the Troops they now have or can expect from any other quarter; indeed it appears to me to be a duty incumbent on us as friends, neighbors & confederates to send them powerful assistance. Justice seems to call for it, and our own honor and importance in the American scale will be lost without it" (McIlwaine, *Official Letters*, III, 214–15).

[6] Virginia.

Motion Concerning Documents on Vermont

MS (NA: PCC, No. 36, I, 273). Written by JM. At the bottom of the document is Charles Thomson's recording of the roll call on the motion. In his note on the document, Thomson incorrectly stated that Madison's motion, seconded by Scott, had "passed April 4h 1782" (n. 8, below).

EDITORIAL NOTE

The relation of Congress during January and February 1782 to the issue of the Vermont, or New Hampshire Grants, has already been summarized (JM to Pendleton, 22 January, and nn. 5 and 6; and 7 February 1782, n. 4). Except for a long discussion of the problem on 1 March, the matter is not mentioned in the printed journals of Congress for that month. This interlude in the debate on a subject which, in Samuel Livermore's words, had "worn a little thread-bare," signified that none of the competing solutions could be adopted until the delegations of at least nine states should agree.

By March the delegates from Massachusetts, Rhode Island, Connecticut, New Jersey, Pennsylvania, Delaware, and Maryland were ready to acknowledge the independence of the "state" of Vermont, provided that the *de facto* government should accept the boundaries stipulated by Congress on 7 and 20 August 1781 (*JCC*, XXI, 836–39, 887–88). If this bloc of seven should be joined by two more states, it could work its will. On 12 March a rumor, soon confirmed, was current in Philadelphia that the "General Assembly" of Vermont had rescinded its earlier rejection of Congress' offer and now accepted it (Burnett, *Letters*, VI, 312).

The members of Congress from New Hampshire, New York, Virginia, North Carolina, South Carolina, and Georgia, with varying degrees of firmness and for varying reasons, stood together in opposing a recognition of the sovereignty of Vermont. Livermore, for example, although doubting the constitutional competence of Congress to encourage a separatist movement at the expense of his state and New York and much preferring that those states on their own initiative amicably partition between them the land comprising Vermont, was willing for the sake of settling the divisive issue to vote for the independence of Vermont whenever the New Hampshire legislature should authorize him to do so (*ibid.*, VI, 312, 317–18, 327 n. 3, 331–32).

The New York delegates in Congress, led by John Morin Scott, were in a difficult position. Their uncompromising stand against Vermont's independence enlisted only a minority support, which, they feared, would decrease during the coming weeks. Under these circumstances they could do no more than try to prevent a vote on the issue as long as possible and urge Governor George Clinton to have the New York legislature back them speedily in such unqualified terms that the pro-Vermont bloc in Congress might hesitate to defy so important a state as theirs (*ibid.*, VI, 310, 313–14, 321–22).

The New Yorkers and their allies, including Joseph Jones and probably JM, held that Vermont's rejection of Congress' offer of 7 and 20 August 1781 in October of that year had released Congress from its alleged guarantee. Hence, Vermont's reconsideration and acceptance in February 1782 of the stipulated boundaries were of no effect unless Congress agreed to re-extend the same terms. This Congress should not do, since the attendant circumstances had drastically altered. In the summer of 1781, unlike the winter of 1782, the United States had been in dire peril from the enemy, not only in Virginia and the Carolinas–but even in Vermont itself, because of the machinations of the Allen brothers and other Green Mountain men. In short, the generous offer of August 1781 had been extended in considerable degree for reasons of expediency. Furthermore, during the ensuing six months, menacing separatist movements, which the recognition of Vermont's independence would serve to encourage, had appeared in other parts of the Confederation. These movements, in Joseph Jones's view, "so strongly mark a hostile disposition in some States to invade the rights of others, that, I believe, it will be very difficult to obtain the concurrence of nine to give them [Vermont] independence and privileges of the Union, at least before some great political questions are decided respecting the united States, their individual and general rights" (Jones to Pendleton, 19 March 1782, *ibid.*, VI, 319).

Earlier in his letter Jones had expressed doubt whether the affirmative votes of nine states should be sufficient to bring Vermont into the Confederation. By a vote of nine, Congress might acknowledge Vermont's independence, but the assent of all thirteen ought to be required to admit a sovereign state to their company (see n. 5, below). Yet Article XI of the Articles of Confederation explicitly provided that another "colony" might join if invited "by nine states." Jones did not explain why unanimity should be a prerequisite, but apparently he considered Article XI irrelevant, because the Green Mountain area had never been a separate "colony." In the unlikely event that Congress should accept this technical distinction, New York could bar Vermont indefinitely from membership in the Confederation.

In their letter of 31 March 1782 to President John Hanson of Congress, with an enclosed copy of their appointment and of the resolutions of the "General Assembly" of Vermont accepting the boundaries defined by Congress, the four Vermont commissioners confidently asserted, "We assure ourselves that not the least obstacle remains to our admission into a foederal union with the United States of America." On the following day, although Scott seconded Abraham Clark's motion to refer to a committee the letter of the commissioners and its enclosures, "together with the several papers on the files of Congress, relating to the same subject, and received since the 20th of August last," Scott voted against Clark's motion. JM's affirmative vote was offset by the adverse votes of Jones and Lee. As previously noted, upon the adoption of Clark's motion the papers were referred to a committee dominated by Vermont's friends (NA: PCC, No. 40, II, 187–89, 269–75; *JCC*, XXII, 158; JM to Pendleton, 2 April 1782, n. 2).

Although the journal of Congress of 1 April explicitly characterizes some of "the papers" turned over to this committee as favorable to Vermont's request, the journal fails to specify that the other documents referred to the committee were of a contrary nature (*JCC*, XXII, 157–58). Opposing a recognition of Vermont's independence, JM and Scott sought by the present motion to have the printed journal make clear that "the several papers on the files of Congress" strongly argued against creating a new state by taking territory from New York and New Hampshire without the consent of those two states (see below, n. 5).

1782 April 3[1]

Congress having by a resolution of the first instant referred to a Committee sundry papers recd. from Jonas Fay &c, together with the other papers on the files of Congress relating to the same subject, recd. since the 20th. of Augst. last,[2] the yeas & nays having been required on the question And of the papers so committed, Such part only having been entered on the journal of the said day, as purports on the part of the New Hampshire grants[3] a compliance with a preliminary requisition contained in the resolution of Congress of the 20th. of Augst. last;[4] The proceedings of Vermont from the 16th. to the 19th. of October last rejecting the same and sundry resolutions of the State of N. York of the 15th. & 19th. day of November last,[5] both included among the papers referred, being omitted: And an entry on the journal thus partially stating the case, having a tendency to misinform & mislead the public judgment, as well as to defeat the purpose of calling for the yeas & nays as authorised by the 9th. Article of the Confederation;[6] And Congress having adjourned on the 2nd. instant whilst the Journal of the preceding day was under consideration, whereby the opportunity of then supplying the omission was lost,[7] Resolved that the Secy. be authorized & directed to enter on the Journal of the first instant as of the proceedings of that day the sd. proceedings and the sd. resolutions of the State of N. York which are in the words following—to wit[8]

[1] Charles Thomson entered this date at the head of the motion. He then wrote, "A motion was made by Mr Madison second by Mr Scott, in the following words." See *JCC*, XXII, 161–63.

[2] See JM to Pendleton, 2 April 1782, and n. 2. Jonas Fay (1737–1818), leader of the Vermont commission whose other members were Moses Robinson, Paul Spooner, and Isaac Tichenor, had prominently shared in the efforts to achieve separate statehood for the Green Mountain region. Fay had attended the convention of January 1777, which declared the independence of Vermont, and had served as secretary of its constitutional convention in July of that year. From 1778 to 1785 he was a member of the executive council of his "state" and in 1782 became one of the judges of its supreme court.

[3] After the comma JM at first wrote, "as states on the part of Vermont."

[4] See editorial note, and *JCC*, XXI, 887–88. The "preliminary requisition" defined the boundaries which must be accepted before Congress would (or might) recognize "the independence of the people inhabiting the territory called Vermont" and admit them into "the federal union," but whether by the resolution of 20 August 1781 recognition and admission had been guaranteed, once the "indispensible preliminary" was fulfilled by Vermont, is debatable.

[5] Before JM amended his draft, the wording after the semicolon read, "A previous act of Vermont of the 20th of Nov last, rejecting the same and sundry resolutions of the State of N. York of the 20th day of October [inserted over a deleted 'Aug'], last." Copies of these documents appear in *JCC*, XXII, 164–73. A letter of 20 November from Governor Thomas Chittenden of Vermont, enclosing a report of the proceedings of the General Assembly rejecting the offer of Congress of 7 and 20 August, had been read in Congress on 12 December 1781 (*JCC*, XXI, 1166 n.). A letter of 24 November from Governor Clinton of New York, transmitting resolutions of its legislature concerning Vermont, had been laid before Congress on 5 December 1781 (*JCC*, XXI, 1159–60). One of these resolutions declared that the unanimous consent of the thirteen states would be required "to create a new state by dismembering" any of the thirteen and that "Congress have not any authority by the Articles of Confederation, in any Wise, to intermeddle with the former territorial Extent of Jurisdiction or Property of either of these United States, except in Cases of Dispute concerning the same, between two or more States in the Union" (Hugh Hastings and J. A. Holden, eds., *Public Papers of George Clinton*, VII, 518).

[6] That is, the reason for the "yea" or "nay" vote of a delegate on Clark's motion would not be clear as long as the printed journal left the impression that all the documents referred to the Clymer committee were favorable to Vermont (see last two paragraphs of editorial note). The final paragraph of the long ninth article of the Articles of Confederation makes no mention of "the purpose" which JM here ascribes to it. According to the article, Congress should "publish the Journal of their proceedings monthly, except such parts thereof relating to treaties, alliances or military operations, as in their judgment require secrecy; and the yeas and nays of the delegates of each state on any question shall be entered on the Journal, when it is desired by any delegate" (*JCC*, XIX, 220). Probably "their proceedings" was meant to include "all questions agitated and determined," as Congress had stipulated on 2 August 1777 (*JCC*, VIII, 599).

[7] Here JM explains why he had been unable to observe the rule of Congress requiring "That the journals of a preceding day be open to correction during the whole of the next day" (*JCC*, XIV, 638). In other words, if this regulation were strictly adhered to, JM's motion to amend the journal could only be rejected.

[8] JM intended the two documents, mentioned in n. 5, above, to follow "to wit" and to be made a part of Clark's motion of 1 April. Although Congress refused to accede to this motion, by a vote of six state delegations to four (New York, Virginia, South Carolina, and Georgia), Congress on 4 April, upon Livermore's motion and without a recorded division, consented to print the two documents as a part of JM's own motion of 3 April. Hence, by getting the texts of these documents spread upon the printed journal (*JCC*, XXII, 164–73), JM won his main point. Moreover, by yielding to JM's insistence in this regard, and by not printing in the journal the letter from the four Vermont commissioners of 31 March 1782, with its enclosures, Congress even showed partiality to the opponents of Vermont independence. For more on the Vermont issue, see Motion on Letter of Vermont Agents, 20 April; and Observations Relating to the Influence of Vermont and the Territorial Claims on the Politics of Congress, 1 May 1782.

From Philip Mazzei

RC (LC: Madison Papers). The cover is only a fragment, reading, "Hble: James Madi . . . of the Virgi." Letter unsigned.

2da. Copia
FIRENZE 5. Aprile 1782.

CARMO: AMICO

A norma di quanto vi scrissi nella mia quarta lettera dei 28. del passato, vi mando l'incluse pregandovi di aggiungere a quella di Mr. Lomax il suo nome di battesimo, che non ò mai saputo. Da quella, e dall'altra che v'inclusi p[er] Mr. Man Page, voi vedete quel che penso degl'Inglesi, e del metodo che a mio giudizio noi dovremmo tenere con essi. Nelle 2. lettere a Mr. Blair avete una conferma della mia dura situazione. Se il Governo fosse renitente a rendermi giustizia, mi pare che il decoro almeno dello Stato dovrebbe indurre qualcheduno a proporre nell'Assemblea, che si esaminasse il mio carteggio, e si ordinasse poi quel che è di ragione, e non si permetesse che un Cittadino fosse costretto, p[er] salvare il proprio onore e per trovare da sostentarsi, a pubblicar l'indiscretezza della sua Patria.

Mi pare che il Congresso dovrebbe cominciare a pensare ad aver dei Ministri o Agenti ad alcune altre Corti Europee. Voi già sapete che a motivo del nostro Commercio questa è da considerarsi moltissimo. Qua si crede generalmente che io abbia le credenziali del Congresso. Il Principe lo gradirebbe, ma egli solo sa che io sono Agente del solo Stato di Virginia. Vi parlerò francamente. Se codesti Sigri: mi credono capace e degno di servirgli, credo che potrò più facilmente d'un'altro incanalare una corrispondenza utile e piacevole; ma bramerei che seguisse presto, p[er]chè mi par mill'anni di ritornare in Virginia. Intanto potrei appianar la strada p[er] chi dovesse venir dopo di me.

Addio.

Second copy
FLORENCE, 5 April 1782

DEAREST FRIEND

With regard to what I wrote to you in my fourth letter of the 28th of last month,[1] I am sending you an enclosure asking that you add Mr. Lomax's[2] Christian name, which I have never learned. From the contents of that letter, and from another one which I sent to you through Mr. Man Page,[3] you see what I think of the English and of the method which in my judgment we must employ regarding them.

In the two letters to Mr. Blair[4] you have a confirmation of my difficult situation. If the Governor is unwilling to act justly toward me, it seems to me that the honor of the state should at least induce someone in the Assembly to propose that my correspondence be examined, that orders then be given for that which is just, and that it not be permitted that a citizen may be forced to reveal the indiscretions of his country in order to sustain himself and save his own honor.

It seems to me that the Congress must begin to think of having Ministers and Agents in some other European Courts. You probably already know that this is a very important consideration with respect to our Commerce. It is generally believed here that I possess credentials from the Congress. The Prince[5] would welcome this, but he alone knows that I am an Agent of the single state of Virginia.[6] I shall be frank with you. If these Gentlemen believe that I am capable and worthy of serving them, I think that I will be able to supply an agreeable and useful correspondence more easily than anyone else. But I hope that it comes to pass soon because I yearn so much to come back to Virginia. In the meantime, the path could be smoothed for whoever might follow after me.

Farewell.

[1] Not found. By "fourth letter," Mazzei meant the fourth of a series rather than the fourth letter written on 28 March. See Mazzei to JM, 13 March 1782.

[2] Thomas Lomax (1746–1811), a prominent planter of Port Tobago (Porto Bago) on the Rappahannock River in Caroline County, Va. From 1774 to 1776 he had served on the Committee of Safety of his county and from the latter year until after the Revolution as a member of the county court. He represented his district in the state Senate in 1776, and his county in the House of Delegates in 1778, 1779, and 1781–82 ([Edward Lloyd Lomax], *Genealogy of the Virginia Family of Lomax* [Chicago, 1913], p. 19; T[homas] E. Campbell, *Colonial Caroline: A History of Caroline County, Virginia* [Richmond, 1954], pp. 234, 266, 343–45; Swem and Williams, *Register*, pp. 3, 5, 8, 13). Between 1 December 1781 and 22 December 1783 he was a member of the Council of State, although he occasionally was absent for many weeks (*Journals of the Council of State*, III, 1, 272, 314, 318). In JM's papers in the Library of Congress a fragment of the cover of a letter of 5 April 1782 from Mazzei, reading, "[Mr. Lo]max, Esqre. in Caroline County, Virginia," evidently connotes that JM put a new cover on the letter before forwarding it. For Mazzei's letter to Lomax, see Richard C. Garlick, Jr., *Philip Mazzei*, pp. 81–82.

[3] Not found. Probably Mann Page, Jr. (*ca.* 1749–*ca.* 1810), a planter and lawyer of Mannsfield, Spotsylvania County, Va. (MS, Spotsylvania County Personal Property Tax Book, 1810; microfilm, Spotsylvania County Court Records, Minute Book, 1810–1812, p. 210, both in Virginia State Library). After serving in the Convention of 1776, he was a member of the House of Delegates in most of its sessions between 1776 and 1787, during one of which he acted as speaker pro tempore (*Journal of the House of Delegates*, October 1783, p. 4), and again a member in 1795 and 1796

(Richard Channing Moore, *Genealogy of the Page Family in Virginia* [New York, 1893], p. 81; Swem and Williams, *Register*, pp. 2–25, *passim*, 45, 47). Having been elected on 4 December 1776 by the General Assembly as a delegate from Virginia to the Continental Congress, he sat in that body for about four months, beginning on 30 January 1777 (*JCC*, VII, 71–72, 369). In the following November he declined re-election (*Journal of the House of Delegates*, October 1777, p. 35). Writing in his memoirs about his travels in Virginia in 1784, Mazzei recorded: "I crossed the York River to see the good, too good, Mr. John Page. The following day, I went to call on his [half-]brother, Mann, on the Rappahannock River, where Mr Lomax, his brother-in-law, came to visit me and dine with us" (Howard R. Marraro, trans., *Memoirs of Philip Mazzei*, pp. 284–85).

[4] John Blair of Williamsburg, who at this time was a judge of the High Court of Chancery. Blair acted on Mazzei's behalf in matters relating to his financial affairs in Virginia. Mazzei's letters of 22 March and 5 April 1782 to Blair are in JM's papers in the Library of Congress and may have been returned to JM after he forwarded them to the addressee. In the dispatch of 22 March, Mazzei complained of his "unmerited neglect" and added, "I can hardly undertake to write a letter, but it turns out a Lamentation." He also remarked that no letter had reached him from any friend in Virginia "Except one from Col: Maddison, lately rec'd. by the way of Spain."

[5] Leopold I, Grand Duke of Tuscany.

[6] Mazzei, of course, did not know that he was no longer an overseas agent of Virginia (Mazzei to JM, 13 March 1782, n. 21). In a letter of 31 May 1783 Governor Harrison was to express surprise because of the Florentine's professed hesitation "to act for Congress if they requested it," since the termination of his commission from Virginia removed any possibility of a conflict of interest (Executive Letter Book, 1783–1786, p. 147, MS in Virginia State Library).

From Jacquelin Ambler

RC (LC: Madison Papers). Docketed by JM, "Apl. 6. 1782."

VIRGINIA RICHMOND April 6th. 1782

DEAR SIR

Our friend Mr. Jameson resigned his seat in Council on saturday last:[1] before he left this place he desired I would acknowledge the receipt of your favors as they come to hand: I shall do so with much pleasure, and transmit our Weekly papers, while I continue here:[2] those of the present day contain very little of importance. Indeed there have been no very late arrivals from the West Indies, nor any thing new from the Southward thro' which channels alone foreign intelligence can come wh. you have not heard before.[3]

With every aid that Mr. Ross could give, the difficulty of making you remittances, adequate to your expences at Philaa., was insurmountable. What shall we do now that he has quitted the Commercial department.[4] It is in vain for the Assembly to pass resolution after resolution directing the Executive to make remittances, unless they will put the Means in their hands also. I am really much distressed on this subject; to say nothing of the injury done the feelings of our Delegates, our national Character will be grieviously wounded.[5]

Would it not be prudent for you to send a spirited Memorial to the Assembly as soon as they meet, insisting on some particular funds being set apart for this purpose.[6] As long as our financies remain without system, and the hand of every Department is to dip in one common purse, so long will our perplexities continue to multiply, and our distresses be encreased.[7]

I am with very great esteem & regard Your affect Servt

J: AMBLER

[1] This was 30 March. On 6 May Governor Harrison forwarded Jameson's letter of resignation to the House of Delegates (McIlwaine, *Official Letters*, III, 220).

[2] See Jameson to JM, 2 March, n. 12, and 9 March 1782, n. 6.

[3] Of the two Richmond papers issued on 6 April only the *Virginia Gazette, or, the American Advertiser*, mentioned "accounts from the Southward of the 10th ult.," which it correctly summarized as "containing nothing very capital." Neither paper alluded to events in the West Indies.

[4] See Jameson to JM, *ca.* 12 January 1782, n. 4. As Ross had expected, he was elected to represent Fluvanna County in the House of Delegates in the two sessions of 1782. He was re-elected in 1783 (Swem and Williams, *Register*, pp. 15, 17).

[5] That is, the reputation of Virginia with other Americans. See Virginia Delegates to Harrison, 8 January 1782.

[6] This was done by the General Assembly in the May session, apparently without the prod of a "spirited Memorial" from the delegates (Jameson to JM, 9 March 1782, n. 5).

[7] See Randolph to JM, 11–13 April 1782.

Benjamin Harrison to Virginia Delegates

FC (Virginia State Library). In the hand of Charles Hay.

VIRGA. IN COUNCIL Apl. 6th. 1782.

GENTLEMEN

My letters that you miss[1] were sent to the Post Office, and I suppose must have been either mislaid or taken away by Some curious Tory, who will meet with but little gratification in reading them, as they containd nothing of consequence, indeed that Seems to be the Case on both Sides. When I came to the government I found the correspondence establishd and most willingly agreed to keep it up in hopes of knowing what was doing in Congress, except when Secresy was injoin'd; I am disappointed in my expectations & I suppose for good reasons, tho' when I had the honor of a Seat there I look'd on it as a part of my duty to give Such information.[2] I wish you to transmit me, if to be procured the Sum paid in from each State of the forty for one money, for the use of Congress, and to inform me whether any of them continue to pay it in; This State is much in arrear on that Score.[3] There is in the hands of the Loan Officer[4] and Continental Paymaster[5] a considerable Sum, which I understand is ordered to Philadelphia by the Financier, from which I conclude it will be hoarded up, and a demand of redemption made on us to exchange it dollar for dollar; Should this be the Case you may easily see how injurious it will be to the State: what little we have in circulation is from four to five for one.[6] I am &c

1 See Virginia Delegates to Harrison, 26 March 1782.

2 See Randolph to JM, 11–13 April 1782, and n. 14. Harrison had been a delegate to the Second Continental Congress from 1776 until 1778, although he did not attend in the latter year.

3 On 25 July 1781 Robert Morris had dispatched a circular letter to the executive of each state, requesting information speedily about the "moneys, supplies, transportation, &c." advanced to the Confederation since 18 March 1780, as well as about "the amount of the several paper currencies now circulating in your State, the probable increase or decrease of each, and the respective rates of depreciation" (Wharton, *Revolutionary Diplomatic Correspondence*, IV, 601–4). The military crisis in Virginia had prevented Governor Nelson from doing more than to promise his co-operation (*Papers of Madison*, III, 281; 282, n. 4). His successor, Governor Harrison, had either overlooked the request or decided to ignore it. See Virginia Delegates to Harrison, 25 February 1782, and n. 1. In the present letter he asked, in effect, to be informed of what the executives of the other states had done to comply with Morris' request. Obviously they had done little, for as late as 12 July 1782 Morris commented to Alexander Hamilton, "The Answers I have received here have been very few and very short of the Objects so that I have not been able to Act as I wished for want of necessary information" (Harold C. Syrett and Jacob E. Cooke, eds., *The Papers of Alexander Hamilton* [7 vols. to date; New York, 1961—], III, 107).

4 John Hopkins, Jr.

5 Harrison's son Benjamin, Jr., continental paymaster of the southern department and, since 1776, a business correspondent of Robert Morris (Clarence L. Ver Steeg, *Robert Morris*, pp. 14–15).

6 See Virginia Delegates to Harrison, 23 April; and Motion for Financial Reports, 30 April 1782; also *Papers of Madison*, II, 49, n. 2. For Morris' determination to centralize the funds of Congress in its treasury, see his letter of 15 April 1782 to Alexander Hamilton (Harold C. Syrett and Jacob E. Cooke, eds., *Papers of Alexander Hamilton*, III, 72–74). In expressing his concern, Harrison overlooked the fact that the resolution of Congress of 2 November 1781 had merely recommended that

the states "pass acts" to enable Morris to achieve his purpose (*JCC*, XXI, 1091). Morris required the receiver of continental taxes in each state to publish monthly the amount of money derived from taxes which he had transmitted to the treasury of the United States. The continental receiver for Virginia stated in the *Virginia Gazette* of 29 June 1782 that no money had been received to forward during April, May, and June. Although an act of the Virginia General Assembly in its session of May 1782 stipulated that certain tax income "shall be appropriated to continental purposes," the measure included no provision for sending the money to Morris or even for transferring it to the custody of his fiscal agent in Virginia (Hening, *Statutes*, XI, 12–14).

To Edmund Pendleton

RC (New York Public Library). The cover is missing, but Pendleton docketed the letter, "James Madison Esqr. Apl: 9. 1782."

PHILADA. April 9th. 1782

DEAR SIR

The paper of this morning will make a small but high seasoned addition to the treat afforded you by our last parliamentary intelligence.[1] A French frigate is lately arrived at Rhode Island which has brought despatches for the Chevr. de la luzerne, the contents of which are not yet disclosed. The Cargo of the Frigate is said to be coin for their army. She was destined for Chesapeak, but unluckily chased into another port.[2] It is added that she sailed from Brest with a large fleet under de Guichen who had repaired the havoc of Kampenfelt & the storm and was proceeding for the West Indies. Our Intelligence from this last quarter seems to authorize an expectation that a powerful descent has before this been made on Jamaica, by the combined armaments of France & Spain.[3]

A more authentic copy of the Capitulation of Brimston[e] Hill supplies an omission which excited some little surprize. The Garrison is expressly restrained from serving agst. the *Allies* of France as well as against the King himself whose name alone was inserted in the copy first brought hither. Whether this omission was mere mistake in the English Printer or one of those little dirty frauds which they have so often practised is uncertain.[4]

A Flag from N. York with Cloathing for the British Prisoners is just arrived here. On a search into the Contents Unlicensed goods to the amount it is said of several thousand pounds value have been discovered. Other Flags we are told are gone on to Maryland & Virginia. I hope equal vigilance will be employed with respect to them.[5]

I have nothing to add from within doors. No step is yet taken on the subject of Vermont.

With great regard I am Dr Sir Yr. Obt Friend & servt.

J. MADISON JR

[1] For the "treat," see JM to Pendleton, 19 March 1782, and nn. 1 and 2. The *Pennsylvania Packet* of 9 April 1782 afforded the "addition" by allegedly quoting from Charles James Fox's philippic in the House of Commons on 27 November 1781. In characterizing the speech, composed by the ministry and delivered from the throne at the opening of Parliament, the *Packet* quoted Fox as saying: "It is the language of traitors who have ruined us, and who have left us but the hope of seeing them one day expiate on the scaffold the enormity of their crimes. This day I hope is not distant." Although Fox's indictment was devastating, the *Packet* may have erred in claiming that he branded the members of the ministry as "traitors." According to *Hansard's Parliamentary Debates* (XXII, cols. 692, 705), he stated that both in Parliament and "at the tribunal of justice" the ministers must hear about the outcome of their "disgraceful and ruinous measures" and "expiate them on the public scaffold." In Fox's view, the war was "accursed and abominable."

[2] See Virginia Delegates to Harrison, 5 March 1782, n. 3. This was the frigate "Émeraude," which reached Newport on 26 March, forty-two days out of Brest, bearing dispatches, dated in February, to La Luzerne (Acomb, *Journal of Closen*, pp. 193, 195; *Pennsylvania Packet*, 9 April 1782). The French minister may have decided not to divulge the content of the dispatches to Congress lest the news of additional financial aid from France increase American lethargy. He wrote to Washington concerning alternate possibilities in waging the campaign of 1782 and requested the General's estimates of both the American and British forces (Wharton, *Revolutionary Diplomatic Correspondence*, V, 302–3). In two letters on 28 April, Washington supplied these data and also informed La Luzerne that the "Treasure which came in the Frigate" had been safely moved inland (Fitzpatrick, *Writings of Washington*, XXIV, 178–82).

[3] See *Pennsylvania Packet*, 6 April 1782; and JM to Pendleton, 25 February 1782, n. 4. The Comte de Guichen remained in France, but two warships of his former command reached Fort Royal, Martinique, on 20 March, after convoying a large number of troop transports and store ships from Brest. Having at long last a sufficiently strong land force and expecting assistance from the Spanish soldiers and squadron at Hispaniola, the Comte de Grasse was enabled to launch an expedition against the British in Jamaica. With his freedom to maneuver severely limited by the necessity of escorting 150 transports loaded with troops, Grasse sailed from Martinique on 8 April. On the following day—the date of the present letter—Hood, commanding the forward division of Rodney's fleet, closed upon Grasse's van in the St. Lucia channel and opened the first phase of the Battle of the Saints (W. M. James, *British Navy in Adversity*, pp. 330–35).

[4] See Virginia Delegates to Harrison, 19 March 1782, n. 8. The Articles of Capitulation had appeared in the *Pennsylvania Packet* of 20 March. This version omitted from the second of the seventeen "Articles" the rectification printed by the *Packet* in its issue of 9 April.

[5] The particular episode mentioned by JM has not been identified. With increasing frequency, British flag-of-truce ships were smuggling goods of enemy origin into American ports. See Harrison to Virginia Delegates, 23 March 1782, and nn. 1 and 2.

To Edmund Randolph

RC (LC: Madison Papers). The cover is missing, but the contents permit no doubt that JM was writing to Randolph.

PHILADA. Apl. 9th. 1782

DEAR SIR

I had promised myself the pleasure of a line from you by this post but find by a letter from Mr. Jameson that you had not arrived at Richmond at the time of writing for it. I have inclosed to Mr. J. the paper of this morning which contains all the news current without doors.[1] Within doors nothing worth particularizing has taken place. The Committee on the affair of Vermont have made no report as yet.

I perceive by a passage cited in the "Examination of the Connecticut claim to lands in Pennsa.["] that we have been mistaken in supposing the acquiescence of Virginia in the defalcations of her Chartered Territory to have been a silent one. It said that "at a meeting of the Privy Councell July 3. 1633. was taken into consideration the Petition of the Planters of Virginia remonstrating that some grants had lately been obtained of a great proportion of the lands & territoriees within the limits of the Colony there, and a day was ordered for further hearing the parties (to wit Ld. Baltimore & sd. Adventurers & Planters)."[2] The decision agst. Virga. is urged as proof that the Crown did not regard the Charter as in force with respect to the bounds of Virga. It is clearly a proof that Virga. at that time thought otherwise & made all the opposition to the encroachment which cd. then have been made to the Arbitrary Acts which gave birth [to] the present revolution. If any monuments of the transactions of Virga. at the period above [mentioned] or any of the successive periods at wch. these encroachmen[ts had] been repeated you will have an opportunity of searching [more] minutely into them. It is not probable however that after a fa[ilure] in the first opposition any further opposition will be found [to] subsequent grants out of Virga.[3]

Present my sincere respects to your amiable lady & [believe] me &c &c.

J. MADISON JR.

Col Carrington will not fulfill his intentions on se[tting] off for Virga.[4] Docr. Lee will [set] off in 5 or 6 days & I shall [take] that conveyance for the proposed *report.*[5] Mr. Jones will [follow] the Docr. abt. the last of this month.[6] I hope you will a[dd] due weight to these considerations in deciding on the tim[e for] your return.

[1] Neither David Jameson's letter—probably of 30 March—nor JM's response of 9 April has been found. The "paper" must have been the *Pennsylvania Packet.*

[2] See JM to Pendleton, 2 April, n. 2; and Motion Concerning Documents on Vermont, 3 April 1782, editorial note. Many years later JM or someone at his direction enclosed this paragraph in brackets to designate it for publication (Madison, *Papers* [Gilpin ed.], I, 118).

JM here refers to the Reverend William Smith's *An Examination of the Connecticut Claim to Lands in Pennsylvania. With an Appendix, Containing Extracts and Copies Taken from Original Papers* (Philadelphia, 1774). The passage which JM quotes with approximate accuracy appears on page 160 of the reprint of the pamphlet in *Pennsylvania Archives,* 2d ser., XVIII, 125–214. For obvious reasons, he welcomed this evidence that Virginians had immediately protested the grant of a charter by King Charles I to "Caecilius Calvert, Baron of Baltimore, in our Kingdom of Ireland" for territory traversing that conferred by charter in 1609 upon "The Treasurer and Company of Adventurers and Planters of the City of London for the first Colony in Virginia," even though JM could not accept the constitutional principle upon which Smith based his main argument (Instructions on Peace Negotiations, 7 January 1782, n. 9). Smith contended that, because the king in Privy Council was sovereign, a charter could not be a contract, irrevocable except by the consent of both the grantor and grantee. Hence, since the charter given to Connecticut was postdated by that given to William Penn, the latter automatically superseded the former insofar as the territories specified in both overlapped.

[3] The bracketed words and parts of words in this paragraph are from Gilpin's edition of the Madison papers. The right edge of the manuscript's second page is now torn. Since Gilpin did not print the letter beyond this point, the remaining brackets enclose what the editors surmise JM wrote. In a letter of 22 April 1782 to the governor (MS in Virginia State Library), Randolph remarked, "I was instructed by my brethren in the delegation to obtain access to the entries of the council before the revolution." See also Randolph to JM, 5 May 1782, and n. 6. JM's assumption that there probably had been no "further opposition" was erroneous. Virginians in 1673 received with "unspeakable griefe and Astonishment" the news that King Charles II had granted jurisdiction over the "Northern Neck" to certain courtiers, and proprietary rights over all Virginia for thirty-one years to Henry Bennet, Earl of Arlington, and Thomas, Lord Culpeper. About a decade later, having bought out the other claimants, Culpeper sold back to the Crown all of his rights except to quitrents outstanding and to the proprietorship of the Northern Neck. This area, encompassing at its greatest extent over five million acres or twenty-three future counties, including five now in West Virginia, was inherited in 1719 by the Scot Thomas, Baron Fairfax of Cameron, the sixth of his line. He died at Greenway Court near Winchester in December 1781. Legislation respecting the Fairfax lands was for years, even so late as 1796, necessarily of a special nature (Samuel Shepherd, ed., *The Statutes at Large of Virginia* [new ser.; 3 vols.; Richmond, 1835], II, 22–23, 140; Thomas J. Wertenbaker, ed., "The Virginia Charter of 1676," *Virginia Magazine of History and Biography,* LVI [1948], 261–66; Josiah Look Dickinson, *The Fairfax Proprietary: The Northern Neck, the Fairfax Manors, and Beginnings of Warren County* [Front Royal, Va., 1959], p. 1).

[4] See Harrison to Delegates, 9 February, and n. 4; and Motion on Carrington, 26

April 1782. Colonel Edward Carrington was in Philadelphia primarily to arrange with Washington, Quartermaster General Timothy Pickering, and Robert Morris for outfitting with clothing and other equipment the continental recruits being raised in Virginia and neighboring states for service in Nathanael Greene's army in South Carolina (Fitzpatrick, *Writings of Washington,* XXIV, 28, 35, 61, 66). As early as 27 March, Carrington was "hourly expected" at Fredericksburg, but two weeks later Colonel Christian Febiger, at Cumberland Old Court House, Va., exclaimed, "What in the name of God, keeps Carrington." He apparently left Philadelphia on 1 May and reached Richmond on 14 May 1782 (*Calendar of Virginia State Papers,* III, 112, 127, 143–44, 167; McIlwaine, *Official Letters,* III, 225; Randolph to JM, 16 May 1782).

[5] Congress granted Arthur Lee a leave of absence on 9 April, but he remained in Philadelphia until either the twenty-third or twenty-fourth of the month (*JCC,* XXII, 177; JM to Pendleton, 23 April 1782, and to Randolph on the same day). The "report" almost certainly was the one adverse to Virginia's title to the Old Northwest, submitted by a committee to Congress on 3 November 1781, tabled eleven days later, and about to be debated again (*JCC,* XXII, 184). Although the delegates from Virginia had sent Governor Nelson a copy of this report, along with other relevant documents, on 17 November 1781, Randolph may have wanted it for his own use. Jefferson probably possessed a copy already, since Arthur Lee in a letter of 13 March had enclosed for him one which Randolph undertook to forward to Monticello (*Papers of Madison,* III, 304–5 nn.; *JCC,* XXII, 184; Boyd, *Papers of Jefferson,* VI, 164–65, 560–61; JM to Randolph, 1 May, n. 6; Randolph to JM, 10 May 1782). In view of the hostile attitude of a majority of Congress, the matter probably would be of grave concern to the Virginia General Assembly at its spring session. On 6 May 1782, upon sending the documents mentioned above to the speaker of the House of Delegates, Governor Harrison emphasized the need for a "speedy and decisive determination" of the issue (McIlwaine, *Official Letters,* III, 213).

[6] Joseph Jones was absent from Congress between 2 May and 4 September 1782, both inclusive (*JCC,* XXII, 233; XXIII, 547).

From Edmund Randolph

RC (LC: Madison Papers). Docketed, "Apl. 11th. 1782," by JM. The cover is missing, and the letter is unsigned. The handwriting of the letter is Randolph's, and its contents permit no doubt that JM was the recipient.

RICHMOND April 11. 1782

DEAR SIR

We announced to you from Bush-town[1] the difficulties, which we had encountered on our journey. Whether the roads were really better, as we advanced southwardly, or seemed so from our approach towards home, I cannot tell; but the fact was, that we appeared to travel from Baltimore with scarcely any friction. My family are now fixed at an humble cottage, about six miles distant from hence; which forms a contrast with Philadelphia, that nothing can reconcile me to, [but?]

the presence of my domestic triumvirate, and the pleasures of my library.[2] I might add another cause of consolation, when I address myself to you, who are at this moment perhaps suffering under the severe anguish of the want of money:[3] altho we have only coarse fare, we wish for much less, than we did, whilst surrounded by the luxuries of Philadelphia, and have therefore less occasion for cash.

I hope, that my draught on you for the 20£ did not distress you. I trust, that it could not, as it was made in consequence of your own friendly offer. Tell me the mode, in which I shall account for it. It shall be remitted to you, or charged in the auditors' books against me, at your choise.[4]

The business of the court has hitherto prevented me from waiting upon the executive. I shall probably confer with them in a few days: but my communications will be short, in comparison to the thirst, which some of the gentlemen of the board may have for a full knowledge of our political situation.[5]

When I inquired into the state of our treasury, I found that 100£ had been the extent of receipts; and that the whole of that sum was immediately appropriated to the quartermaster's department. Judge then what my present sensations are, after having bound myself to repay to Whiteside about 200£, which he lent to me on my private credit, but which I took up from a confidence that I should reimburse him out of the public coffers?[6]

April 13th.

On saturday last Colo. Brooke quitted our exhausted treasury to reap those treasures, which he had laid up in heaven. The apoplectic stroke, which brought him to his end, gave him a warning of but five minutes.[7] It is believed, that Mr. J. Ambler will succeed him in office, until the meeting of the assembly; and it is probable, that they will confirm him.[8]

It is a matter of some wonder, that the minister of France did not visit our governor. Was there any misunderstanding on the score of etiquette? or has the suspicion, which some people entertain here, reached the ears of *the minister*, that *Harrison* is *an enemy* to *the French?*[9] By accident yesterday the resolution of congress, recommending the confiscation of british manufactures, came into conversation at the governor's table. It seemed to me to be a fit season to ascertain the objections, which had been conceived against it, but an improper one to answer them. Our discourse, however, was too short for the discussion, and was concluded by a general assertion, on the part of Mr. Harrison, that the legislature would not adopt it.[10]

Mr. Madison, who is with us, informs me of an incident, which caused much discontent in Williamsburg, about a month since, and argues little in favor of the prudence of *count Rochambeau.* A waggoner from the back country had been detected in the robbery of a french soldier. Summary justice was administered; for he was flagellated by military authority, as some say, without the form of trial, and according to others, with no other than before a tribunal of officers. This harsh punishment, thus inflicted, gave a keener edge to the acrimony of those, whose principles are abhorrent from the alliance. But I hope, the clamour has subsided for the present, and that our citizens will not be driven to indecent expressions of their indignation by a repetition of this ill-judged exercise of power.[11]

I shall obey the commands of your favor of the 2d. instant.[12] But it is probable, that the havock of war will prevent me from making any territorial inquiries, later than the abolition of regal government.

The governor complained yesterday of the sterility of your correspondence; saying, that you did not communicate the circulating news, and that he should cease to write on every other subject than business.[13] I reminded him of the ter[ms] stipulated with governor Nelson: but these have not been put into his hands. It might not be amiss to transcribe the regulations, and send them to him.[14]

If you have an opportunity, pray ask Mr. Morris, whether he has received my letter of last week.[15] Entre nous, there will probably be a *paper war* between *him and the Governor.* You remember a letter, which I mentioned to you. This will perhaps blow up a flame.[16]

My best respects attend all your family. Mrs.[17] carries her good wishes farther, and *prays* for their and your happiness.

Assure Mr. Jones of my affectionate esteem, and present me in the most acceptable manner to his lady.

Charge yourself with my compliments to Mr. Lee & Mr. Bland. This being done, I give you a carte blanche to assume any portion of the for-ment.[18] regard of

Your friend, & serv:

Can you send a copy of the journals for 1781?[19]

[1] Probably from the Bush stone tavern (erected *ca.* 1750), about seventeen miles northeast of Baltimore. See JM to Pendleton, 19 March 1782. Randolph's letter to JM from Bushtown (Bush), written about 24 March, has not been found.

[2] By "triumvirate," Randolph apparently meant himself, his wife Elizabeth Carter

Nicholas (d. 1810), daughter of Robert Carter Nicholas, and son Peyton (1779–1828). In his letter of 10 May 1782 to JM (*q.v.*), Randolph designated the "humble cottage" as "Pettus's." He seems to have rented from Dabney Pettus (d. 1788) a house situated north and slightly west of Richmond in Henrico County (R[obert] A[lonzo] Brock, ed., *The Vestry Book of Henrico Parish, Virginia, 1730–1773* [Richmond, 1874], p. 141; Clayton Torrence, ed., *The Edward Pleasants Valentine Papers* [4 vols.; Richmond, n.d.], I, 28; III, 1661).

[3] See Jameson to JM, 2 March 1782.

[4] See JM to Randolph, 23 April 1782, and n. 5; and Account with Randolph, *ca.* 1 May 1782.

[5] See Randolph to JM, 19 April 1782. Randolph meant that, when conferring with the governor and Council of State, he would be careful not to reveal information which, as a member of Congress, he was pledged to keep in confidence. In a letter of 8 April Randolph informed Harrison: "Most of the late letters from the Virginia delegates in Congress have referred to me for particular communications. But I do not recollect anything which I am at liberty to communicate of very great consequence. Should the executive however conceive, that I can give them any information, I shall be ready to wait upon them, whenever I am called upon" (*Calendar of Virginia State Papers*, III, 125–26).

[6] Peter Whiteside individually or in connection with his Philadelphia company. On 9 May, in his reply to a letter of 22 April 1782 from Randolph asking for £200 so that he could pay a personal debt of that amount owed to Whiteside, Harrison stated, "I assure you Sir, I am greatly distressed at not having it in my power to comply with your money demand" (*ibid.*, III, 134; McIlwaine, *Official Letters*, III, 207).

[7] George Brooke's death occurred on Sunday, 7 April. See Jameson to JM, *ca.* 12 January 1782, n. 9.

[8] See Jameson to JM, 9 March, n. 6; Pendleton to JM, 22 April; *Virginia Gazette*, 20 April 1782. Ambler was confirmed as treasurer on 29 May (Resolution of the General Assembly, 28–29 May 1782, MS in Virginia State Library).

[9] See Virginia Delegates to Harrison, 5 March, n. 3; JM to Randolph, 23 April; and Harrison to Virginia Delegates, 4 May 1782. The italicized words in this letter, with the exception of "prays" near the close, are written in the delegates' official cipher. On his return from Philadelphia, Randolph had brought the key to the cipher, which he thought to be "inscrutible," but he did not give it to Foster Webb, Jr., for transmission to Governor Harrison until 21 April 1782 (*Calendar of Virginia State Papers*, III, 133–34).

[10] See Virginia Delegates to Harrison, 8 January, and n. 4; and 8 February 1782.

[11] The Reverend James Madison must have regarded this episode as exceptional, because he praised the general conduct of the French troops during their stay in Williamsburg (the Reverend James Madison to JM, *ca.* 2 March, and n. 7; and 15 June 1782).

[12] Not found. Someone other than JM wrote "9th" over the date, for Randolph seems to be referring to JM's request, made in his letter of the 9th (*q.v.*), that a search be made for documents supporting Virginia's title to the West. Since more than four days would at least normally be required for a letter to reach Richmond from Philadelphia, JM probably also included "the commands" in a letter, now missing, dated 2 April 1782.

[13] See Harrison to Virginia Delegates, 6 April 1782.

[14] Although the regulations have not been found, the Virginia delegates stated in their letter to Governor Harrison on 1 January 1782 (*q.v.*) that "the general plan of our official correspondence excludes unauthenticated intelligence." Perhaps as a

result of the occasional interception by the enemy of correspondence containing confidential information, Governor Nelson and the delegates had agreed to omit matters of this sort from their letters until they had arranged to use a cipher (*Papers of Madison*, III, 293; 294, n. 6).

15 See JM to Randolph, 23 April 1782, and n. 6.

16 See Virginia Delegates to Harrison, 25 February 1782, n. 3. Randolph may refer either to Morris' letter of 26 February to Harrison or the latter's dispatch of 27 March to Morris (*Calendar of Virginia State Papers*, III, 77–78; McIlwaine, *Official Letters*, III, 184–85). In the correspondence relating to Virginia's financial obligations, the two writers indulged in personalities.

17 Randolph wrote "Mrs." above a blank space in which he appears to have erased a much longer word. Following "Mrs.," he added what seems to be a capitalized initial, possibly an "R," but now indistinct because he, JM, or someone else drew four ink lines across it. The missing name may have been "Randolph."

18 Probably an abbreviation of "before mentioned."

19 See JM to Randolph, 4 June 1782.

Benjamin Harrison to Virginia Delegates

FC (Virginia State Library). In the hand of Charles Hay.

In Council April 12th. 1782

Gentlemen.

It certainly would forward the recruiting service much to have cloths lodged with every person appointed to that business, but as it would be attended with great trouble and expence and perhaps some loss to send them into every County, I think it will be sufficient if an order can be obtained from the War Office permiting the Executive to call for them as they may be wanted at the several places of rendezous[1] There are nine fixed on in the first instance from which they are to be marched to the general one (which is at Cumberland old Court House) or to the Army when it is more convenient to do so.[2] I am continually apply'd to for Commissions for vessels fiting out in and belonging to North Carolina which from some abuses that have been practiced I have refused.[3] Will you inform the Delegates of that State of this, and request them to forward Commissions immediately; if they send them to my care I will contrive them to their Governor.[4] I am, &c

1 See Virginia Delegates to Lincoln and his reply, 1 April, and n. 2; Virginia Delegates to Harrison, 2 April; and JM to Randolph, 9 April 1782, n. 4.

2 On 2 April 1782 the Virginia executive had "appointed the following places at which the men that are raised under the Act for recruiting the Virginia Line on the Continental establishment may be received to wit: Richmond, Fredericksburg, Winchester, Staunton[,] Cabin point, Prince Edward Courthouse, Cumberland old

Courthouse, Peytonsburg, & Montgomery Courthouse." Cumberland Old Court House in Powhatan County was "appointed the place of General rendezvous" (*Journals of the Council of State*, III, 70).

[3] In view of the delicate relations between Virginia and North Carolina resulting from the episode of the "Three Friends" (Harrison to Virginia Delegates, 23 March, and n. 1; Randolph to JM, 19 April 1782), Harrison was probably taking particular care to refrain from any further action which Governor Alexander Martin, a brother of JM's former teacher Thomas Martin (*Papers of Madison*, I, 43, n. 2), might regard as another infringement upon the sovereignty of North Carolina. For the "abuses" committed by privateers, see the resolution of Congress of 21 May 1782 (*JCC*, XXII, 280–81). On that same day an unsuccessful attempt was made in Congress to forbid any state executive to issue letters of marque and reprisal except to citizens of his own state.

[4] The delegates were unable, at least immediately, to honor this request, because North Carolina was unrepresented in Congress from about 4 March until 19 July 1782 (*JCC*, XXII, 114, 401).

Motion on Chairman of Congress

MS (NA: PCC, No. 36, I, 283). The slip of paper used by JM is neither docketed nor dated.

[15 April 1782][1]

The President being indisposed,[2] Resolved that a Membe[r] be now chosen to preside in Congress[3] until th[e] President shall attend & resume the chair.[4]

[1] The Articles of Confederation explicitly authorized Congress "to appoint one of their number to preside" for a period of one year but were silent about what should be done if he did not resign when illness or other cause obliged him to be absent for a considerable time during his term. "Rules for conducting business," adopted on 4 May 1781, failed to anticipate that emergency (*JCC*, XX, 476–82).

Although the printed journal of Congress for 15 April 1782 does not refer to JM's motion, he almost certainly drafted it on that date during the discussion occasioned by the illness of President John Hanson. This debate was interrupted by a request to tally the vote on a solution offered by John Morin Scott. When Scott's motion was rejected, JM and Jones apparently left the room, possibly with Samuel Wharton of Delaware, in order to prepare the above resolution. It may be inferred from the printed journal that the motion was never introduced, because when they returned to their seats after missing the roll call on a second proposal, also defeated, they found Congress ready to vote, viva voce, on Thomas Bee's suggestion that "whenever the President for the time being, shall be prevented, by sickness or otherwise, from attending the house, one of the members present be chosen by ballot to act as chairman for the purpose of keeping order in the house only, but that all official papers shall nevertheless be signed and authenticated by the President as heretofore." This was acceptable to JM and Jones, and also to every member from each of the eight states which, being represented by at least two delegates, could cast an effective vote. Since Daniel Carroll was then chosen as "chairman" by an unrecorded ballot, there is no entry in the journal of how each member voted (*JCC*, XXII, 180–83). JM and his three colleagues could hardly have favored Carroll in view of his staunch opposition to Virginia's title to the Old Northwest.

[2] When John Hanson (1721–1783) next attended Congress after 15 April is uncertain. Bearing in mind that as temporary presiding officer Carroll's correct title was "chairman of Congress," and assuming that the journal reflects titles accurately, Hanson returned after 7 May, when Robert R. Livingston addressed a letter to the "Chairman of Congress," and before 13 May, when the "President of Congress" shared in the audience accorded to La Luzerne (Wharton, *Revolutionary Diplomatic Correspondence*, V, 396; *JCC*, XXII, 262). Hanson probably had not resumed the chair by 9 May, because on that day he did not vote in the three polls recorded (*JCC*, XXII, 251–53).

[3] After first writing "execute the functions of the chair," JM neglected to strike it out when he interlineated "preside in Congress" above it.

[4] The word "chair" appears above an undeleted "same."

From Edmund Pendleton

Tr (LC: Force Transcripts). Another copy, also taken from the original manuscript, is in the *Proceedings of the Massachusetts Historical Society*, 2d ser., XIX (1905), 149–50.

VIRGA. April 15th 1782.

DEAR SIR

I have your favr of the 2d & agree with you that the expostulations of the friends to Virginia will be properly interposed, and the Clamours of her Enemies well applied, if both together will effect the rousing her to proper exertions for recovering her consequence in the united Scale.[1] The Executive have pd Attention to this important Subject, & having an empty Treasury, have circulated a request for the prompt advance of half the land tax payable some Months hence for the purpose of recruiting our line;[2] Our County,[3] which yields to none in alacrity on such Occasions, appear willing to comply, but from conversing on the Subject with several Gentlemen, it is the general Opinion that there is not in the County Specie Sufficient to pay 1/4th of that tax, & I se[e] no prospect of our being able to pay it at the time, tho' specific Commodoties where the Alternative is allowed (as is the case in all but the land tax) may be had.[4] the little Cash, which is pick'd[5] by Us, at the distance we are from the French Army, immediately goes to the Merchants at Port Royal or Fredg[6] who chiefly trade on Commission from the Eastern States, whither I suppose it is sent for we se[e] it no more, very few of them offer to buy our commodities, & when they do, 'tis at such a price that only makes us angry. Tho' there is some reason for complaint agt Virginia, yet the Clamours are carried to excess in respect of her line;[7] she has contributed more than her proportion of men, and formerly devoted herself to exertions in the cause, to the neglect of trade, which other states pursued wth Avidity not consistent with their proportion of duty. this circumstance wch enables them to Vaunt & shew away now at the 11th hour, prevents the present resources of Virga. to recruit her line when by an ill judged inclination to save Charles Town, a respectable Corps of them were lost;[8] however we must bear these Insults with patience 'til time shall enable us to prove that the resources of Virga. tho' they can't be called forth at every[9] moment, are great & Permanent, and that we never want inclination to employ them for the common Interest.

Reports continue of the evacuation of Charles Town, and the last is said to come from the Frigate arrived as an Express from Count de Grasse to Ct Rochambeau,[10] with the Additional circumstance of the Troops being carrd. together with a detachment from New York to the West Indies.[11] You'l have a better Account of these things than we can have, as also whether there be grounds of truth in other Accounts circulating here, that Jamaica & Antigua are both Invaded by our Ally and their Troops here called thither, at the same time that the Marquis d'Fayette is arrived at Boston with 4000 others.[12]

Mr Jones tels me he is coming away & the future burthen of my correspondence will fall upon you.[13] should any letter to him reach Phila after he leaves it, you'l consider it as Address'd to you. Our Elections run much into New Members, amongst others are Monroe & John Mercer formerly Officers, since fellow Students in the law & said to be clever.[14] The Attorney might as well have stay'd with you. the Genl Court sat but 6 days in Criminal business only, & I am told very little will be done in the other Courts the approaching terms.[15] Our Treasurer, Colo. Brooke, died suddenly last week I suppose with an Appoplectic stroke. I have not heard who is his successor.[16]

I am Dr Sir Yr Affe friend

EDMD PENDLETON

[1] See JM to Pendleton, 2 April 1782, and n. 3.

[2] See Jameson to JM, 23 February, and n. 6; 2 March, and n. 3; 23 March 1782, and n. 5. On 5 January 1782 the Virginia General Assembly had enacted a law "for ascertaining certain taxes and duties, and for establishing a permanent revenue." The second section of this lengthy statute fixed the land tax at £1 for every £100 valuation, to be paid on or before 1 July. Nine-tenths of this tax had to be paid in specie, equating a Spanish milled dollar as six shillings, and the remainder might be discharged "in the bills of credit emitted on the funds of this commonwealth

and the faith of the United States as pledged by the resolutions of congress" of 18 March 1780 (Hening, *Statutes,* X, 501–8; Harrison to Virginia Delegates, 11 January 1782, and n. 4).

[3] Caroline County.

[4] By the act mentioned in n. 2, above, and by another passed on the same day and entitled "An act for laying taxes in certain enumerated commodities," the taxes on polls, slaves, horses, mules, cattle, carriages, billiard tables, and taverns might be paid in grain, flour, bacon, tobacco, or hemp, or in specie at rates stipulated in the measures. Which commodity or commodities would be accepted varied, depending upon whether the tax was assessed upon a person, beast, or article. The dearth of specie, not only in Caroline County but throughout almost all of Virginia, obliged the General Assembly in its October 1782 session to permit the payment of the land tax and all other taxes in specie, specified commodities, or in bills of credit emitted by the Commonwealth (Ambler to JM, 11 May 1782; Hening, *Statutes,* X, 490–91, 504, 508–9; XI, 112–29, and especially 117–19).

[5] The version in the *Proceedings of the Massachusetts Historical Society* has "picked up."

[6] Port Royal in Caroline County is about fifteen miles southeast of Fredericksburg in Spotsylvania County. Both front the Rappahannock River. Using silver livres to purchase provisions and pay their soldiers and sailors, the French had greatly relieved the shortage of specie in the neighborhood of Williamsburg and Yorktown (*Papers of Madison,* III, 261–62; 263, n. 9; the Reverend James Madison to JM, *ca.* 2 March 1782, n. 7).

[7] See Harrison to Virginia Delegates, 9 February, and n. 4, and 1 March, n. 9; Jameson to JM, 23 February, and n. 6; JM to Pendleton, 2 April 1782, and n. 5.

[8] The Board of War reported to Congress on 21 August 1780 that, when Charleston fell to the British on 12 May of that year, they captured "245 officers and 2,326 non comd officers and privates" (*JCC,* XVII, 753). About 40 per cent of this number appear to have been from Virginia (Hamilton J. Eckenrode, "List of the Revolutionary Soldiers of Virginia," *Eighth Annual Report of the Library Board of the Virginia State Library, 1910–1911* [Richmond, 1912], pp. 6–7). See also JM to Pendleton, 2 April 1782, and n. 5.

[9] The copy in the *Proceedings of the Massachusetts Historical Society* has "any" instead of "every."

[10] See Virginia Delegates to Harrison, 19 March, n. 2; and Harrison to Virginia Delegates, 23 March 1782, and n. 3. The rumored evacuation of Charleston was reported in the *Virginia Gazette* of 13 April 1782.

[11] See Harrison to Virginia Delegates, 23 March 1782, n. 4.

[12] These reports were erroneous. See JM to Jefferson, 15 January, n. 16; and JM to Pendleton, 9 April 1782, n. 3. The *Virginia Gazette* of 13 and 20 April 1782 stated that the French had landed on Antigua. The source of the rumors about Jamaica and about Lafayette reaching Boston has not been identified. Although on 20 April 1782 the same newspaper mentioned that Lafayette expected to return to America soon, he did not arrive until 4 August 1784. This, his third visit, lasted until 21 December of that year (Louis Gottschalk, *Lafayette between the American and the French Revolution, 1783–1789* [Chicago, 1950], pp. 84, 141).

[13] See JM to Pendleton, 19 March, and n. 2; and JM to Randolph, 9 April 1782, n. 6.

[14] Although 59 of the 150 delegates elected had not served in the legislature before, Archibald Cary, the speaker of the Senate in the May 1782 session, was of the opinion that "we have a better assembly than we have had for several years" (Swem and Williams, *Register,* pp. 15–16, and *passim;* Cary to Washington, 25 May 1782 [MS

in LC: Washington Papers]; Fitzpatrick, *Writings of Washington*, XXIV, 347). James Monroe, a future president of the United States, began his tenure of about sixteen months as a member of the Virginia Council of State on 8 June 1782, after resigning as a delegate from King George County to the General Assembly (*Journals of the Council of State*, III, 104, 296).

In 1778, after two years of service in the continental line, John Francis Mercer (1759–1821) of Stafford County was a major and aide-de-camp to General Charles Lee. The misconduct of Lee at the Battle of Monmouth and his subsequent suspension from the service led Mercer to resign his commission in October 1779. In the following year, and again in 1781, he took the field briefly as a lieutenant colonel of militia. During the intervals of his military career, Mercer studied law under Jefferson and practiced the profession for a short time in Fredericksburg. In 1782 and 1785–1786 Mercer was a member of the House of Delegates. Between these terms he attended Congress as a delegate from Virginia. In 1785 he moved to Maryland, where he quickly rose to political prominence. Besides serving frequently in the legislature, he was a member of the delegation to the Constitutional Convention of 1787, one of the Maryland congressmen from 1791 to 1794, and governor from 1801 to 1803.

[15] See Virginia delegates to Harrison, 12 March 1782, n. 4.

[16] See Randolph to JM, 11–13 April 1782, and nn. 7 and 8.

To Thomas Jefferson

RC (LC: Madison Papers). Addressed, "Ths. Jefferson Esqr." Jefferson wrote "Madison Jas." above the date at the beginning of the letter.

Phila. April 16th 1782

Dear Sir

Your favor of the 24 of March[1] with a letter inclosed for Mr. Marbois came to hand yesterday.

I[2] intreat that you will not suffer the chance of a speedy and final determination of the territorial question by Congress to affect your purpose of tracing the title of Virga. to her claims.[3] It is in the first place very uncertain when a determination will take place, even if it takes place at all; & in the next it will assuredly not be a final one, unless Virga. means to be passive & silent under aggression on her rights. In every event therefore it is proper to be armed with every argument & document that can vindicate her title. Her adversaries will be either the U. States, or N.Y. or both. The former will either claim on the principle that the vacant country is not included in any particular State & consequently falls to the whole, or will cloath themselves with the title of the latter by accepting its cession.[4] In both cases it will be alledged that the Charter of 1609 was annulled by the resumption of it into the hands of the Crown, and that the subsequent grants to Maryland &c. denote this to have been the construction of it;[5] that the Proclamation of 1763 has constituted the Alleghany Ridge the Western limit of Virga. & that the letter of Presidt. Nelson on the subject of a New Colony on the Ohio, relinquishes[6] on the part of Virga. all interference with the Authority of the Crown beyond that limit.[7] In case the title of N.Y. should alone be opposed to that of Virginia,[8] It will be further alledged agst. the latter that the treaties of 1684, 1701, 1726, 1744 & 1754 between the Govt. of the former & the 6 Nations have annexed to it all the Country claimed by those nations & their tributaries,[9] and that the expence of N. York in defending & protecting them[10] ought in equity to be reimbursed by this exclusive advantage. The original title of N.Y. is indeed drawn from the charter to the Duke of York in 1663–4, renewed after the treaty of Westminster in 1674.[11] But this Charter will not I believe reach any territory claimed by Virga.[12]

Much stress will also be laid on the Treaty of Fort Stanwix particularly as a bar to any corroboration of the Claim of Virga. from the Treatys of Lancaster & Loggstown. It is under this Treaty that the companies of Inda. & Vandalia shelter their pretensions agst. the claims of Virga. &c. &c. see the pamphlets entitled "Public good" & "plain facts."[13] As these pretensions can be of no avail unless the Jurisdiction of Congress, or N. York at least can be established, they no otherwise deserve notice than as sources of calumny & influence in public councils; in both which respects[14] it is the interest of Virga. that an antidote sd. be applied.

Mr. Randolph during his stay here was very industrious & successful in his researches into the territorial claims of all the States, and will be able to furnish you with many valuable hints. Your visit to Richmond in May will give him an opportunity.[15]

Our information from Europe has been peculiarly defective of late. It seems little probable that any decisive steps have been or will speedily be taken towards either a partial or general peace. The weight of the war will probably fall on the West Indies at least in the early part of the Campaign. Whither it will then be shifted is altogether uncertain.[16]

With very sincere regard I am Dr Sir Yr Obt. Servt

J MADISON JR

[1] *Q.v.*

[2] Many years later JM, or someone at his direction, inserted a bracket at the beginning of this paragraph and another at the end of the next paragraph to designate the portion of this letter to be published (Madison, *Papers* [Gilpin ed.], I, 119–20).

[3] JM probably was the more eager for Jefferson to begin preparing a defense of "the title of Virga." because the issue, which had been quiescent in Congress since 14 November 1781, was about to be revived (*Papers of Madison,* III, 304; 304–5, and nn.; 307–8; 309, nn. 4, 7; *JCC,* XXII, 191).

[4] Having ended this sentence by adding three or four words after "cession," JM crossed them out so completely that they cannot now be read.

[5] See *Papers of Madison,* II, 73–77; 138, n. 2; III, 210, n. 4; 281–95, and 304–9, *passim;* JM to Jefferson, 15 January, and nn. 8 and 10; Jefferson to JM, 24 March, and n. 2; JM to Pendleton, 2 April, and nn. 2 and 3; and JM to Randolph, 9 April 1782, n. 2.

[6] JM wrote this word above a deleted "recognizes."

[7] William Nelson (1711–1772), president of the Virginia council, had written to the colonial secretary, Lord Hillsborough, on 18 October 1770 about the colony of Vandalia, which the Walpole Company proposed to establish on the Ohio River. By stating in that dispatch, "We do not presume to say to whom our gracious Sovereign shall grant his vacant lands," Nelson appeared to view the area west of "the Alleghany Ridge" as outside the boundaries of Virginia, even though he expressed the hope "that all prior rights, whether *equitable* or *legal* may be preserved and protected" (John Pendleton Kennedy, ed., *Journals of the House of Burgesses of Virginia, 1770–1772* [Richmond, 1906], p. xxiv). Nelson, a wealthy merchant of Yorktown and the father of Governor Thomas Nelson, served in the House of Burgesses from 1742 to 1744 and on the Council of State from 1744 until his death. He was the acting governor of the province during the interim of about one year between the death of the Baron de Botetourt on 15 October 1770 and the arrival of the Earl of Dunmore.

[8] Instead of this clause, JM first wrote, "In case the title of N.Y. should be brought into the question."

[9] For the treaty of 1684, see *Papers of Madison,* II, 73–74. At Albany on 19 July 1701, at a conference with Lieutenant Governor John Nanfan of New York, representatives of the Iroquois signed a "Deed from the Five Nations to the King of their Beaver Hunting Ground." This area was said to extend west about eight hundred miles and from north to south about four hundred, including virtually all of the region known later as the Northwest Territory (E[dmund] B. O'Callaghan, ed., *Documents Relative to the Colonial History of the State of New-York* [15 vols.; Albany, 1853–87], IV, 908–11). At Albany on 14 September 1726, after William Burnet, governor of New York and New Jersey, had reminded spokesmen of the Five (later Six) Nations that they had not fulfilled the terms of the cession of 1701, three tribes executed a new deed. The western limit of land embraced in this document, however, was about at the present site of Cleveland, Ohio, and south from there to the Ohio River (*ibid*., V, 799–801). This release of title, it should be noted, was to the king rather than to the province of New York and hence did not transfer to that colony whatever valid claim Virginia may have had to any of the territory. By the Treaty of Lancaster, Pa., in July 1744, the Six Nations signed a "Deed recognizing the King's Right to all the Lands that are, or shall be, by his Majesty's Appointment in the Colony of Virginia" (Julian P. Boyd, ed., *Indian Treaties Printed by Benjamin Franklin, 1736–1762* [Philadelphia, 1938], p. 69).

At the Albany Conference in July 1754, commissioners from the four New England colonies and from New York, Pennsylvania, and Maryland reaffirmed the ancient alliance ("covenant chain") with, as well as the suzerainty of the British Crown over, the Iroquois. After the Indians withdrew from the meeting, the commissioners agreed, "That the bounds of these Colonies which extend to the South sea, be contracted and limited by the Allegheny or Apalachian mountains."

Governor Robert Dinwiddie of Virginia had declined to send representatives to the conference (E. B. O'Callaghan, ed., *Documents Relative to Colonial History of New-York*, VI, 828, 861–85, 888).

[10] JM at first wrote "those nations" instead of "them."

[11] The Dutch, after reoccupying New Netherland for fifteen months, agreed in the Treaty of Westminster to return the colony to England (Frances G. Davenport and Charles O. Paullin, *European Treaties*, II, 232, 239).

[12] See Jefferson to JM, 24 March 1782, n. 2.

[13] See *Papers of Madison*, II, 176–77; 178, nn. 1, 2, 6; 188; 190–91; 195; 196, n. 2; III, 14, n. 17; Instructions on Peace Negotiations, 7 January 1782, nn. 10, 16, 17. Thomas Paine's pamphlet, *Public Good*, was still selling in Philadelphia for "one fourth of a dollar" (*Pennsylvania Packet*, 27 April 1782). Without comment, the *Virginia Gazette* of 6 April reported Philadelphia gossip to the effect that the Indiana Company had bestowed on Paine a "requital" of 12,000 acres of land for writing the pamphlet. See also Randolph to JM, 10 May 1782, n. 7.

[14] The four words following the semicolon were substituted by JM for a deleted "in the respect of the first."

[15] See JM to Randolph, 9 April, and nn. 2 and 5; Randolph to JM, 11–13 April 1782, and n. 12. On 11 April the freeholders of Albemarle County had elected Jefferson and Thomas Walker as their representatives in the House of Delegates (Boyd, *Papers of Jefferson*, VI, 174–75, 179). JM must have taken Jefferson's re-election for granted, because five days were hardly long enough for the news to reach Philadelphia.

[16] See JM to Jefferson, 18 March, and n. 7; Virginia Delegates to Harrison, 26 March, and n. 2; JM to Pendleton, 9 April 1782, n. 3.

Virginia Delegates to Benjamin Harrison

Printed extract (Paul C. Richards Catalogue No. 11 [1964], item 266). The catalogue describes the manuscript as comprising two pages written by JM and bearing the signatures of Joseph Jones, Theodorick Bland, JM, and Arthur Lee.

[17 April 1782]

We thought it necessary to have a decision from Congress relative to the cession of our western territory, for the information of the ensuing Assembly; & therefore moved for the appointment of a day, to take up the consideration of the report on that subject. Monday last was the day assigned; but a call for an adjournment put it by for that day. . . .[1]

A vessel just arrived here from the Cape, reports that 17 Spanish Sail of the Line & 12 thousand troops were then in that port.[2] We . . . will comply with what your Excellency desires relative to the one for forty Emission. . . .[3]

[1] Congress had resumed consideration of the Boudinot committee's report on Tuesday, 16 April, "but came to no determination thereon" (*JCC*, XXII, 184). Although not mentioned in the printed journal, Congress adopted a motion, prob-

ably made by the Virginia delegates at the close of the debate, to designate this report the "order of the day" for 18 April (*JCC*, XXII, 191). See Motion To Amend Lee's Motion on Western Lands, 18 April, n. 1; Virginia Delegates to Harrison, 14 May 1782.

[2] The *Pennsylvania Packet* of 9 and 13 April 1782 reported the arrival at Cap Français, Haiti, of these ships and troops from Cadiz. Although at least most of this armament had not come recently from Spain, there were at Cap Français early in April about fourteen Spanish war vessels and 10,000 soldiers ready to join Grasse's command in conquering Jamaica (JM to Pendleton, 9 April 1782, n. 3; J[ohn Dawson] G[ilmary] Shea, ed., *The Operations of the French Fleet under the Count de Grasse in 1781–2, as Described in Two Contemporaneous Journals* [New York, 1864], pp. 126–27, 129, 199; [Louis] É[douard] Chevalier, *Histoire de la marine française pendant la guerre de l'independance américaine. . . .* [Paris, 1877], p. 287).

[3] See Harrison to Virginia Delegates, 6 April 1782, and nn. 3, 6.

Motion To Amend Arthur Lee's Motion on Western Lands

Printed text (JCC, XXII, 193).

[18 April 1782]

A motion was then made by Mr. [James] Madison, seconded by Mr. [John Morin] Scott, after the word "postponed," to insert the words "until to-morrow;"[1]

[1] The bracketed words are in the *JCC*. As already mentioned, Congress on 2 October 1781 had referred to a committee, with Elias Boudinot as its chairman, the report of another committee, of which John Witherspoon had been chairman, "on the cessions of New York, Virginia, Connecticut, and the petitions of the Indiana, Vandalia, Illinois, and Wabash companies" (*Papers of Madison*, III, 283, n. 6; 294–95; 295, n. 6; JM to Jefferson, 15 January, and n. 9; JM to Randolph, 9 April 1782, and n. 5). Debate upon the Boudinot committee's report, wholly adverse to Virginia's claim to the Northwest Territory, had opened on 16 April (*JCC*, XXII, 184; Virginia Delegates to Harrison, 17 April 1782, n. 1). Upon being resumed two days later, the discussion focused upon the initial recommendation of the committee, "That Congress do in behalf of the united States accept the Cession made by the State of New York" (NA: PCC, No. 30, fol. 2; *JCC*, XXII, 225). Arthur Lee then moved, and Bland seconded, a motion asking: "That the *first resolve in* the report under consideration be postponed *till Congress shall have determined on the following motion:* 'That previous to any determination in Congress, relative to the cessions of the western lands, the name of each member present be called over by the secretary, that on such call, each member do declare upon his honour, whether he is, or is not personally interested directly or indirectly in the claims of any company or companies, which have petitioned against the territorial rights of any one of the states, by whom such cessions have been made, and that such declaration be entered on the journals'" (*JCC*, XXII, 191).

In spite of the unanimous vote of the delegates from Georgia, South Carolina, and

Virginia to retain the words "till Congress shall have determined on the following motion," this clause was deleted—thus in effect relieving some of the congressmen from the embarrassment of appearing to oppose Virginia's title to the Northwest only because they were land speculators (*JCC*, XXII, 191–92). Against the will of the delegates of the three states mentioned above, Congress then struck from Arthur Lee's motion the words "the first resolve in" (*JCC*, XXII, 192). At this juncture in the debate, JM introduced his motion, but it failed to attract support, except from the one delegate present from New Hampshire and from South Carolina, one of the two delegates present from Connecticut and from New York, one of the four delegates from Pennsylvania, all five from Virginia, and both delegates from Georgia (*JCC*, XXII, 193). Thus, as the day's session drew toward its close, Arthur Lee's motion had been reduced to, "That the report under consideration be postponed." Before adjourning, Congress defeated, by a division of votes approximately the same as on JM's motion, an effort by Lee to have "until Monday next" follow "postponed" (*JCC*, XXII, 193–94). On 1 May, after Lee had left Philadelphia to return to Virginia, Bland tried without success to have Congress adopt Lee's original motion. Finally on 6 May, over the adverse votes of the delegates from Virginia and South Carolina, Congress decided to table the Boudinot committee report without naming any day for its reconsideration (*JCC*, XXII, 225, 232, 240–41). See also Observations Relating to the Influence of Vermont and Territorial Claims, 1 May, n. 9; Motion on Delegates' Financial Interest in West, 2 May 1782.

From Edmund Randolph

RC (LC: Madison Papers).

RICHMOND April 19. 1782.

DEAR SIR

I derive the sincerest pleasure from the prospect, which your punctuality of correspondence presents. I could not begin my part of our intercourse by letter until the last week: but the obstacles must be invincible, which shall prevent me from a weekly return in future.[1]

Our maritime code requires a small alteration. From the deference, which we paid to the ante-confederational institutions of congress, we were led into one,[2] which may produce discontent, and probably goes beyond our power. A vessel, when seized, may be carried according to the late ordinance into *any* court of admiralty.[3] Justified by this law, a privateer brought a few weeks since into our admiralty, a prize, made within the jurisdiction of North Carolina.[4] I say, that it was made within the jurisdiction of North Carolina, not because this was a point confessed, but because the court considered it as proved; and proceeded on it as a fact. The owner of the captured ship pleaded that she was not triable here. This objection, after a solemn argument, was overruled. Governor Burke being highly inflamed at this procedure, demanded restitution from our executive. They "being," as Mr. Harrison expressed their imbecility on a former occasion, "the poorest and most impotent executive throughout the continent,"[5] could not interfere in any forensic business; whereby the law was left to its operation, and condemnation took place. Mr. Burke repeated his demand of restitution, and threatened reprisal. The answer to his menace was mild and decent, but representing the danger, and confusion, which would flow from such a measure. This unlucky affair occurred before my arrival at this place, and therefore I retail it to you upon the information of another, which does not appear very distinct. However it rests here for the present. Upon these facts I submit the following queries:

1. Does the power of ascertaining, what captures on water are legal, involve a power to infringe the sovereignty of a state so far, as to authorize the withdrawing of a vessel seized within the jurisdiction of its admiralty to the inquiry of a court of another? Strictly the words of the confederation admit not such a construction,[6] and by no view of the matter can such a power be rendered necessary or subservient to the welfare of the United States.

2. Ought not the inferior courts to be placed more within the reach and controul of congress, or at least of the court of appeals? The purpose, for which the investiture of congress with a superintendence of maritime affairs was intended, will be considerably defeated, if the court of a particular state shall be free from check in great national questions.

The old solution for high prices, to wit a great demand, and a scanty supply, can scarcely account for the exorbitancy of every thing of foreign growth offered for sale here. For 1. goods are not so scarce, as to warrant a merchant to bring cloth from Phila., which is sold there for £3. by the yard and selling it here for 15 dollars: 2. money is so confined in its circulation, and credit for merchandize is so generally refused, that the number of buyers is small. I cannot but suspect, that paper-money will have a resurrection under some form or other.[7] It is talked of with much earnestness in certain parts of the country. As I do not know, in what garb or light this fiend of darkness is to be clothed, I shall not execrate it, as yet.

I can assure you, that I return to the law with a species of sorrow. It is not often, that I lament my want of patrimony; but, when obliged to exchange a pursuit, liberal and extensive, like politicks, for reports and entries, I surely do not commit an unpardonable Sin in reprehending my father for not handing down a fortune to me.[8] This melancholy reflection paves the way for an answer to your invitation to Phila. I must recover, what I expended there, and see a firm establishment for our support, before I set my face northwards. Let the assembly provide funds; I shall have immediately a violent conflict with prudence.[9]

Can you send me a copy of the examination of the Connecticut claim?[10] I believe, that I shall say something in print upon the territorial rights of Virginia, if the legislature shall not adopt the better measure of forcing Mr. Jefferson or Mr. Mason to undertake the work.[11]

Adieu my dear friend.

Pray contrive me a paper every week. I will send you the subscription by Mr. F. Webb, who will visit you soon.[12]

1 See JM to Randolph, 9 April; and Randolph to JM, 11–13 April 1782.

2 The antecedent of "one" is the "maritime code" adopted by Congress on 7 April 1781 (*JCC*, XIX, 361–64).

3 In April 1776 Congress had agreed upon the form of commission and instructions to be issued to the captain of a privateer. This commission obliged him only to bring his prizes to "some convenient ports in the said colonies, in order that the courts which are or shall be there appointed to hear and determine causes, civil and maritime, may proceed, in due form, to condemn the said captures, if they be adjudged lawful prize" (*JCC*, IV, 247–48, 253). Following the adoption of the Articles of Confederation, Congress on 7 April 1781 revised these instructions but still permitted prizes, wherever captured, to be brought "to judgment in any of the courts of admiralty that now are or hereafter may be established in any of these United States" (*JCC*, XIX, 362). In spite of Randolph's scruples that the sovereignty of each state, affirmed in Article II of the Articles of Confederation, obliged prizes to be condemned by the admiralty court of the state in whose waters the capture occurred, Congress did not modify the instructions of 7 April 1781 in this regard before the close of the war. See n. 6, below.

4 Randolph is referring to the case of "Three Friends." See Harrison to Virginia Delegates, 23 March, and n. 1, and 12 April 1782, n. 3.

5 In characterizing the executive of Virginia, Randolph approximately quoted from Governor Harrison's letter of 21 January 1782 to General Greene (Jameson to JM, 26 January 1782, n. 1). Randolph obviously used "imbecility" in the sense of impotence rather than of mental debility.

6 In his reply of 1 May 1782 (*q.v.*), JM agreed with Randolph's contention that the ninth article of the Articles of Confederation, by conferring upon Congress the authority to establish "courts for receiving and determining finally appeals in all cases of captures," assumed that each state would create a court of admiralty with original jurisdiction over captures occurring inside the boundaries of that state (n. 3, above). This assumption was in no way weakened by the further provision in the same article, giving Congress "the sole and exclusive right . . . of establishing rules for deciding in all cases, what captures on land or water shall be legal," or by the stipulation in the sixth article that privateering commissions and letters of marque or reprisal, issued by a state, must conform with "such regulations as shall be established by the united states in congress assembled" (*JCC*, XIX, 216–17).

[7] The Virginia General Assembly at its session of May 1782 did not issue more bills of credit.

[8] At the onset of the Revolution John Randolph (*ca.* 1727–1784), Edmund's father, had been the attorney general of the Crown and a burgess in the provincial assembly from the College of William and Mary. True to his allegiance to King George III, he had fled to England in 1775 with his wife and two daughters, Susanna and Ariana (Boyd, *Papers of Jefferson,* I, 240–43, 244, 268–70; III, 116). Edmund's uncle, Peyton Randolph (d. October 1775), had willed his estate to his wife (d. 1783) and, upon her death, to his brother John, with the proviso that, upon John's death, the property would descend to Edmund, except for £500 to each of Edmund's sisters. Having assumed the obligation of discharging the large debts owed by his father in Virginia and of sending money, whenever opportunity offered, to him in England, Edmund was financially embarrassed in the spring of 1782. He would soon be additionally burdened by the management of the land and slaves left by Mrs. Peyton Randolph upon her death. At the time of the present letter Edmund was dependent upon his rapidly growing law practice for most of his income (Moncure D. Conway, *Edmund Randolph,* pp. 48–50).

[9] Although the Virginia General Assembly in its session of May 1782 provided for paying the long overdue salaries and allowances of the delegates, Randolph did not return to Congress (Jameson to JM, 9 March, n. 4; Virginia Delegates to Harrison, 12 March 1782, n. 4).

[10] See JM to Randolph, 9 April 1782, and n. 2.

[11] George Mason. See *Papers of Madison,* II, 52–53; 178, n. 3; JM to Randolph, 9 April, and n. 5; Randolph to JM, 1 June 1782, and n. 3.

[12] Foster Webb, Jr. See Jameson to JM, 9 March, n. 2; Randolph to JM, 16–17 May; and JM to Randolph, 4 June 1782.

From Jacquelin Ambler

RC (LC: Madison Papers). Docketed by JM, "Apl. 20th 1782."

VIRGINIA RICHMOND April 20th. 1782

DEAR SIR

I sent on your favor which came by Post on Thursday to our friend Mr. Jameson, who is still at York; & doubt not he will replace the money immediately which was so kindly advanced his Nephew.[1] I know he lodged thirty pounds with Mr. Foster Webb, before he left Richmond; and expected Mr. Webb would have been in Philadelphia by this time. The sudden, unexpected death of the Treasurer makes it uncertain now when he can get out.[2] Mr. Jameson was unwilling to make the remittance by draft on Phila. lest any possibility of disappointment should happen, but as Mr. Webb's trip is still delayed, I have advised him to send on a good Bill as speedily as possible.

I rejoice to hear the Allies of France were included in the Capitula-

ELIAS BOUDINOT

RALPH IZARD

SAMUEL LIVERMORE

JOHN RUTLEDGE

BENJAMIN HARRISON

ROBERT R. LIVINGSTON

EDMUND RANDOLPH

RICHARD HENRY LEE

tion of St. Kitts. The omission was eagerly caught at by those who are never happier than when they meet with an opportunity of increasing the prejudices against our friends.[3]

The Executive have been exceedingly jealous for some time past on account of the great number of flag Vessels which arrive from New York and have given the most pointed Orders to have them diligently search'd and nothing permitted to be landed from them without their express license.[4]

We are quite without news from any quarter. I am Dear Sir with great esteem & regard Yours

J. AMBLER

[1] JM's letter has not been found. While in Philadelphia, Lieutenant Colonel John Jameson had evidently borrowed money from JM (Jameson to JM, 23 March 1782, and n. 7). In his missing letter to Jameson, probably written on 9 April, JM apparently mentioned the amount of the loan and included the news he had sent to Pendleton on that date (*q.v.*).

[2] The death of George Brooke, the treasurer, would naturally have delayed Foster Webb, Jr.'s, departure. Webb was on the staff of the treasurer's office and aspired to be Brooke's successor (*Calendar of Virginia State Papers*, II, 408; Pendleton to JM, 22 April 1782, and n. 12). After Ambler became ad interim treasurer on 12 April, he very likely required Webb to assist in preparing the accounts to be presented to the General Assembly in May (Randolph to JM, 11–13 April, 1782, n. 8).

[3] See JM to Pendleton, 9 April 1782, and n. 4.

[4] Although flag-of-truce ships, carrying supplies for the support or comfort of prisoners of war, served a necessary humanitarian purpose, they required close supervision lest they engage in illicit trade with the enemy or with patriots unable to forego an opportunity to profit. Acting under the ninth article of the Articles of Capitulation, concluded with the British at Yorktown on 19 October 1781, Timothy Pickering, quartermaster general of the continental army, agreed to purchase for military use many of the wares of "the British Merchants and Traders, that are within the Garrisons of York and Gloucester," and pay in tobacco made available in Virginia for shipment to New York or Charleston in British flag-of-truce ships. Washington and Robert Morris endorsed this contract (Benjamin Franklin Stevens, ed., *The Campaign in Virginia, 1781: An exact Reprint of Six rare Pamphlets on the Clinton-Cornwallis Controversy* . . . [2 vols.; London, 1888], II, 202; Octavius Pickering and Charles W. Upham, *The Life of Timothy Pickering* [4 vols.; Boston, 1867–73], I, 310–11; *Calendar of Virginia State Papers*, II, 567–68, 572–73, 652, 668–69; III, 118). By providing a market for tobacco and thus serving to lessen the outflow of Virginia's meager supply of specie, the arrangement appeared to be advantageous to the Commonwealth. Yet even before the flag-of-truce ships arrived early in May, Governor Harrison deemed "indispensably necessary" to "the honor" and "security" of the state that the "great Irregularities," of which these vessels often had been guilty, be prevented by a strict limitation upon where they could dock and what cargo they could discharge or load (*Journals of the Council of State*, III, 34, 41, 85; McIlwaine, *Official Letters*, III, 223). The constitutional issues complicating the general problem soon elicited comment from JM. See JM to Randolph, 28 May, and 29 May 1782.

Motion on Letter of Vermont Agents

MS (NA: PCC, No. 36, I, 289). Docketed: "Motion of Mr J Jones Seconded by Mr. Madison[.] Negatived April 20h 1782." This motion, presented by Jones, is in JM's hand.

[20 April 1782]

Jonas Fay. M. R. & I. T.[1] styling themselves Agents and Delegates from the State of Vermont having[2] in a letter dated the 19th. instant informed Congress "that in consequence of the faith of Congress pledged to them, in and by a resolution of the 20th. of Augst. last, and by official advice from sundry Gentlemen of the first Characters in America, the Legislature of Vermont have been prevailed upon to comply, in the most ample manner, with the resolution aforesaid"[3]

Resolved That the Secy. be directed to apply to the said J. F. M. R. & I T. and request them to communicate to him the sd. official advice together with the names of the Gentlemen from whom the same was recived.[4]

[1] Jonas Fay, Moses Robinson (1742–1813), and Isaac Tichenor (1754–1838). See Motion Concerning Documents on Vermont, 3 April 1782, editorial note, and nn. 2, 4, 5. Robinson, a lawyer, a militia colonel in Vermont, and a leader of its movement for statehood, had come to Bennington from Massachusetts in 1761. From 1777 to 1785 he served on the governor's council of the "independent republic" and, during most of the years from 1778 to 1789, as its first chief justice. While he was governor, 1789–1790, he shared prominently in the activities resulting in Vermont's admission to the federal union in 1791. He was one of his state's first two United States senators. Upon his resignation from the Senate in 1796, the General Assembly chose as his successor Isaac Tichenor, also of Bennington. A native of New Jersey and a Princeton alumnus, Tichenor had studied law in Schenectady before settling in Vermont in 1777. In 1781 he had been elected to the Vermont House of Representatives and was its speaker in 1783–1784. From 1786 to 1791 he was a member of the Council of State, and from 1791 to 1796 a judge of the Supreme Court of Vermont. Tichenor's brief term as United States senator was terminated by his election in 1797 as governor, an office which he occupied until 1807 and in 1808–1809. He served again in the Senate from 1815 to 1821.

[2] At first JM wrote, and deleted after "having," "this day day informed."

[3] The agents' letter, dated 19 April, was read in Congress on the following day (*JCC*, XXII, 203). To make the words of the opening clause of the quotation conform with the motion, JM changed "their" to "the" and "us" to "them." Otherwise, except for insignificant differences in punctuation and capitalization, he quoted correctly from the agents' letter (NA: PCC, No. 40, II, 285).

In this letter to President John Hanson, after expressing disappointment because of the "unexpected delay" by Congress in honoring its promise of 21 (not 20) August 1781, the agents requested a speedy reply, because they planned to leave Philadelphia "to morrow Morning." The "delay" had begun on 17 April, when the committee, with George Clymer as chairman, recommended that Congress acknowledge "the State of Vermont, as free, sovereign and independent" and initiate negotiations with her about "the terms and mode" of her admission into the federal union. Thereupon, the "first Tuesday in October next," "the third Tuesday in June," and "Monday next" were voted down successively as the date to be assigned for debating the committee's report. By favoring only the first of the three motions, JM made evident his wish to delay a settlement of the issue as long as possible. He apparently was as eager to postpone a recognition of Vermont's independence and to embarrass its advocates as he and his fellow delegates from Virginia had been to hasten a vote on the Boudinot committee's report and to demonstrate that its chief advocates were land speculators (*JCC*, XXII, 185–90; JM to Pendleton, 2 April, n. 2; Motion To Amend Lee's Motion on Western Lands, 18 April 1782, n. 1). The report of the Clymer committee was not again before Congress until 5 November 1782 (*JCC*, XXIII, 713–14).

[4] The roll call recorded on the back of the manuscript shows that only New York, Virginia, and South Carolina supported the motion. Theodorick Bland opposed it but was outvoted by Jones, Lee, and JM (*JCC*, XXII, 205).

Report of Delegates of Pennsylvania, Maryland, and Virginia on Edward Carrington's Memorial

MS (NA: PCC, No. 19, I, 543). The report, in an unidentified hand, is docketed: "Delivered April 20. 1782 Entd. Read. April 22 Referred to Mr. Montgomery Mr. Bland Mr. [Philemon] Dickinson [Del.] to confer with the executive of Pennsylvania."

EDITORIAL NOTE

In 1781 Lieutenant Colonel Edward Carrington was an officer of the 1st Continental Regiment of Artillery, composed largely of Virginians, and was also on detached service as deputy quartermaster general of the southern department. Upon the resignation on 9 April of Lieutenant Colonel Thomas Proctor as commanding officer of the 4th Continental Regiment of Artillery, Carrington became the senior lieutenant colonel of continental artillery. Its procedure in regard to promotions had the sanction of long usage. For this reason, Carrington confidently expected to succeed to the post vacated by Proctor. On 19 April the officers of the 4th Regiment called the attention of President Joseph Reed of Pennsylvania to the fact that Congress on 3 October 1780 had allocated six regiments of infantry, one of cavalry, one of artificers, and the 4th Continental Regiment of Artillery to Pennsylvania, and had resolved that the state thereafter should fill every vacancy in the complement of its officers up to and including the rank of lieutenant colonel commandant (*Pennsylvania Archives*, 1st ser., IX, 168–69). Furthermore, the seventh article of the Articles of Confederation, which had become effective on 4 March 1781, declared that "all officers of or under the rank of colonel, shall be appointed by the legislature of each state respectively, by whom such forces shall be raised, or in such manner as such state shall direct." Reed forwarded "the remonstrance" of the officers to Washington on 24 April.

In his reply of 5 May, which Reed called "perfect & satisfactory," the commander-in-chief stated that the procedure of promotions in the artillery and cavalry had always differed from that in the infantry and that, since the resolutions of 3 October 1780 had been designed to make operative his own recommendations, Congress had probably not intended to have its statement about promotions embrace more than the infantry. Washington added that he had requested Congress to clarify the matter (*ibid.*, 1st ser., IX, 98–99; *JCC*, XVIII, 895; Fitzpatrick, *Writings of Washington*, XXII, 45–48). Even before this exchange of letters with Reed, Washington had informed the Board of War in a letter of 20 April that, if Carrington was the senior lieutenant colonel of artillery, he was entitled by the "present mode of promotion" to the position from which Proctor had resigned (*ibid.*, XXI, 481). Evidently agreeing with Washington, the Board prepared Carrington's new commission but, with Washington's approval, delayed its delivery pending clearance by Congress (*ibid.*, XXII, 63). Although Congress on 25 May 1781 resolved that "promotions in the cavalry and artillery be regimental to the rank of commanding officer inclusive"—that is, that promotions within a particular regiment be confined to its own complement of officers—Washington assumed that this new procedure would not be retroactive. Hence he informed the Board of War by letter of 9 June, and Reed by letter of 15 June, that Carrington would become, vice Proctor, the lieutenant colonel commandant of the 4th Artillery Regiment (*ibid.*, XXII, 193–94, 223–24; *Pennsylvania Archives*, 1st ser., IX, 207).

Although the printed journal affords no help, Congress probably directed the Board of War to withhold Carrington's commission indefinitely. As deputy quartermaster general he was at General Greene's headquarters during most of the summer and in Virginia from early September until he went to Philadelphia in January 1782 (Fitzpatrick, *Writings of Washington*, XXIII, 485; *Calendar of Virginia State Papers*, II, 400, 486, 612). In the meantime the Pennsylvania Supreme Executive Council on 19 June, upon receiving Washington's dispatch written four days earlier, merely ordered that it "be filed" (*Colonial Records of Pennsylvania* [16 vols.; Harrisburg, 1851–53], XII, 761). Yet when mentioning the 4th Regiment of Artillery in a letter on 7 July to Washington, Reed wrote, "Col. Carrington, we believe, is in Virginia—we have not heard from him since his Accession to this Command" (*Pennsylvania Archives*, 1st ser., IX, 255–56). For the rest of the year the issue was quiescent, probably because it became inconsequential compared with the problems of moving the heavy cannons of the regiment to Virginia and locating them for effective use during the Yorktown campaign (Harrison to Virginia Delegates, 9 February 1782, n. 4). By January 1782 the regiment was back in Pennsylvania (Fitzpatrick, *Writings of Washington*, XXIII, 166, and n., 463, and n.).

In Philadelphia on 12 February Carrington wrote to President William

Moore of Pennsylvania, reasserting his claim to be lieutenant colonel commandant of the 4th Regiment of Artillery and explaining his persistence by remarking that "the Honorary prospects depending on this circumstance are of great consequence to me" (*Pennsylvania Archives*, 1st ser., IX, 487–88). Although the reply of Moore has not been found, he informed Carrington that, since the 4th Artillery Regiment had been allocated to Pennsylvania in 1780 and the resignation of Lieutenant Colonel Proctor had postdated the adoption of the Articles of Confederation, the appointment and promotion of officers in that regiment were within the province of the executive of that state, and the position of lieutenant colonel commandant had already been filled. In a long memorial addressed to President John Hanson of Congress, Carrington on 1 March cited Moore's reply and set forth the reasons, summarized above, which justified his own claim (NA: PCC, No. 41, II, 118–23). Three days later Congress referred the memorial to the delegates of Pennsylvania, Maryland, and Virginia, with instructions "to confer with comr. in chief and Gen'l Knox" (*JCC*, XXII, 115, n. 2). Washington and Knox were then in Philadelphia. Brigadier General (Major General, 22 March) Henry Knox was chief of artillery, continental army.

[20 April 1782]

Report of a Committee on Col. Carrington's memorial.[1]

The Delegates of Pennsylvania, Maryland & Virginia to whom the Memorial of Lieut. Colonel Carrington & the Letter of Capt. Pierce of the Artillery[2] &c were referred, beg leave to report that it is their opinion that the two regiments of Artillery—the one annexed to the Pennsylvania Line and the other to Virginia, cannot at present be incorporated without obvious injustice being done to some very deserving Officers in both Regiments.

As to the Memorial of Lieut. Colonel Carrington claiming the Command of the Artillery of Pennsylvania: your Committee do not think themselves competent to decide upon his claim; but beg leave to observe, that if Congress should be of opinion that his claim founded upon the general Practice of the Artillery-Corps in the Army, antecedent to the ratification of the Articles of Confederation, is well founded, Then they will please to Resolve,

That Lieutenant Colonel Carrington be appointed to the Command of the fourth or Pennsylvania regiment of Artillery.

The determination of Congress on the above resolution will answer Capt. Pierce's Petition.[3]

[1] Although the docket, quoted in the headnote, mentions that the report was made on 20 April and was then referred to the Montgomery committee, neither of these facts appears in the printed journal for that date (*JCC*, XXII, 201–4).

[2] The index of the printed journal for 1782 (*JCC*, XXIII, 911) identifies Pierce as Captain Thomas Pierce of Massachusetts, but the memorialist was beyond a doubt Captain William Leigh Pierce, Jr. (1740–1789), a native Georgian, of the 1st Continental Artillery Regiment, which had been allocated to Virginia by Congress on 3 October 1780 (*JCC*, XVIII, 894). For his meritorious services at the Battle of Eutaw Springs while he was on detached service as an aide-de-camp of General Greene, Pierce had been voted a sword by Congress on 29 October 1781 (*JCC*, XXI, 1085). Pierce's letter has not been found, but, in view of the last paragraph of the committee's report, he must have sought from Congress a promotion in rank on the same grounds as those advanced by Carrington. Officers, including Captain Pierce, who were under the rank of major general and had not been promoted since 1777, were brevetted one grade higher by Congress on 30 September 1783 (*JCC*, XXV, 632–33). Pierce moved to Savannah in that year. After serving briefly in the Georgia General Assembly, he was chosen in 1787 to be a delegate in the Continental Congress and in the Federal Constitutional Convention.

[3] See Motion on Colonel Edward Carrington, 26 April 1782.

Report Approving John Jay's Negotiations with Spain

MS (NA: PCC, No. 19, III, 263). Written by JM. Docketed: "No 6. Report of the Committee on the Letter of the 3d. of October 1781–from Mr Jay at Madrid–April 22. 1782[.] Referred to the Secy for foreign Affairs to report."

[22 April 1782]

The Committee to whom was referred the letter from Mr Jay of the 3d. of Octr. 1781, recommend the following answer thereto, to be subscribed by the Secy. of F. A.[1]

Sir

Your Letter of the 3d. of Octr. last was recd. by Congress on the day of [2] and I am authorized to acquaint you, that your conduct as therein detailed has met with their entire approbation.

The limitation which you have affixed to the proposed surrender of the navigation of the Mississippi in particular corresponds with the views of Congress.[3] They observe with much surprize & concern that a proposition so liberal in itself, which removed the only avowed obstacle to a connection between his C. M. & the U. S. & from which the latter had formed the most sanguine expectation,[4] should have produced so little effect on the councils of his C. M. [The perseverance of his Ministers, notwithstanding this relaxation on the part of Congress, in perplexing your negociation by multiplied & dilitory pretexts, no less inconsistent with their own professions than disrespectful to the U. S. but too well justifies your surmise as to their latent purposes.][5] The surrender of the navigation of the Mississippi was meant as the price of the advantages promised by an early & intimate alliance with the Spanish Monarchy. If this Alliance is to be procrastinated till the conclusion of the war, during a continuance of which only, it can be necessary, the reason of the Sacrifice will no longer exist. Nay, every day which the expected Treaty is delayed by the Spanish Court, detracts from the obligation & inducement of Congress to adhere to their overture, and will consequently justify you in representing in strong terms the obligation it imposes on Spain to make the Treaty the more liberal on her part.[6] This may easily be done, either by enlarging her pecuniary aids, by facilitating to the Citizens of the U. S. the use of the Mississippi, or by indulgences in the commerce of her American Colonies, particularly by following the example of his M. C. M. in establishing a free port or ports in some of them.[7] In the mean time however you will employ your utmost address in ascertaining the real views of the Spanish Cabinet with regard to a Treaty with the U. S. & communicate the result from time to time to Congress.[8]

[1] The committee consisted of JM as chairman, John Morin Scott, and Daniel Carroll. In this paragraph the word "answer" was JM's substitute for his original "letter to be sent." Although he closed the paragraph with the word "President," someone else deleted it and wrote "Secy. of F. A." Whether this change was made before or after the committee reported to Congress is unknown, but Robert R. Livingston expressed regret at the outset of his letter of 27 April 1782 to Jay transmitting the gist of the committee's recommendation, because the dispatch was not being signed by President Hanson in the name of Congress, so as to "express their approbation of your conduct, and afford you that intimate knowledge of their sentiments which the delicacy of your situation renders particularly important" (Wharton, *Revolutionary Diplomatic Correspondence*, V, 332). See also Motion Approving Jay's Negotiations, 30 April 1782, editorial note.

[2] The letter had been read on 18 March (Report on Foreign Dispatches, 20 March 1782, and nn. 1 and 2).

[3] In his letter of 3 October Jay included a copy of his proposals of 22 September 1781 to José Moniño y Redondo, Conde de Floridablanca, which plainly but tactfully reminded the Spanish minister that the United States would not surrender its claims to the navigation of the Mississippi River if Spain withheld its consent to an alliance until the "vicissitudes, dangers, and difficulties of a distressing war" were at an end (Wharton, *Revolutionary Diplomatic Correspondence*, IV, 761–62).

[4] See *Papers of Madison*, II, 133; III, 101–4.

[5] The brackets enclosing this sentence do not appear in the printed journal and may have been inserted by Charles Thomson during the debate on the report, or by Livingston after its adoption by Congress, to call attention to an indictment of King Charles III's ministers which should be conveyed by Livingston to Jay in more diplomatic language. Unlike the committee's report, Livingston included in

his dispatch, possibly for the eyes of Spanish agents who very likely would open it before it reached Jay, flattering references to Charles III and expressed "the grateful sense that Congress entertain of the disinterested conduct of Spain in rejecting the proffers [of peace] of Great Britain" (Wharton, *Revolutionary Diplomatic Correspondence*, V, 332–35).

In his letter of 3 October 1781 to Congress, Jay had commented that, in his opinion, "the king is honestly disposed to do us good," and that a posture by Congress of "prudent self-respect" would "prosper more here than that of humility and compliance." The devious policy of the Spanish ministers, continued Jay, reflected their "wish to see our independence established, and yet not be among the first to subscribe a precedent that may one day be turned against them. They wish not to exclude themselves by any present engagements from taking advantage of the chances and events of the war, not choosing, on the one hand, that in case we sink, that we should be fastened to them by any political ties; nor, on the other hand, in case we survive the storm, to be so circumstanced as not to make the most of us. I think it is their design, therefore, to draw from us all such concessions as our present distress and the hopes of aid may extort, and by protracting negociations about the treaty endeavor to avail themselves of these concessions at a future day, when our inducements to offer them shall have ceased" (*ibid*., IV, 744, 762–63). Jay was writing, of course, before the surrender of Cornwallis.

[6] See n. 3, above.

[7] In Article XXXII of the Treaty of Amity and Commerce concluded in 1778, the French government promised Americans, "in Europe one or more free Ports, where they may bring and dispose of all the Produce and Merchandize of the thirteen United States; and his Majesty will also continue to the Subjects of the Said States, the free Ports which have been and are open in the french Islands of America" (Hunter Miller, ed., *Treaties and Other International Acts of the United States of America* [8 vols.; Washington, 1931–48], II, 27).

[8] For further action on the subject of this report, see JM's Motion Approving Jay's Negotiations with Spain, 30 April 1782.

From Edmund Pendleton

Tr (LC: Force Transcripts). Addressed to "The Honble. James Madison Esq Philadelphia." Another copy, also taken from the original manuscript, is in the *Proceedings of the Massachusetts Historical Society*, 2d ser., XIX (1905), 150–51.

VIRGA. April 22d. 1782

DEAR SIR

Taking up the Pen to acknowledge the receipt of yr favr of the 9th an Idea struck me that I had written to you last week,[1] again transgressing the rotine which intitled Mr Jones to that letter; should it have been so, & he then & yet remaining in Phila.,[2] pray present him my Complts and tel him it was the unintentioned defect of a bad memory;

perhaps I ought rather to appologize to you for giving you more trouble than was your share.

I am sorry fortune sent the Frigate into Rhode Island instead of the Chesapeak, as her Cargoe is a scarce Commodity here, however her escape & safe arrival any where, is matter of joy, as is the Account of her companions from Brest, of whom I think we shall soon hear something agreable.[3] The discovery of a mistake in the Capitulation of Brimstone hill pleased me much, as the Copy I first read, corresponding with that of the Spaniards in Florida,[4] struck me with Astonishment, which almost shook my faith & confidence in our noble Ally, which their liberal & generous conduct however preserved, & made me suppose some latent cause had produced it, rather than an intention to let them loose upon us, to whom they had given so very material Assistance, if the omission was a designed fraud at New York, it was a Cobweb Artifice of an hour, too Contemptible almost for Hottentots.[5]

I am glad the trade intended to be commenced under cover of Flags to supply the Prisoners, is so early detected; I believe it was pretty extensively carried on here formerly at Charlottesville & tended to poison the minds of the people in that neighbourhood by the circulation of those charms, Specie & British goods.[6] pray what is the effect of the discovery? does it forfeit the Vessel & whole Loading; or only the unlicensed goods? Or rather do Congress mean to insist on the former, which I fancy the laws of Nations intitle them to, or be content with the latter.[7] perhaps I say Congress improperly, since it may be the State of Pennsylvania, who are to determine upon it. It may be well, should any come here, to have Uniformity in the decisions upon the Subject. Governor Rutledge & Colo Jervais, passing lately to Congress,[8] I am told have contradicted the Reports of the evacuation of Charles Town[9]—from them you'l have had an Account of things in that Quarter, about which we have had many conjectures & dreams, the amusements of a day.

Mr Jacqlin Ambler is our Treasurer in the room of Colo Brooke.[10] empty as the strong Box is I am told there was a warm contest for this office, and Mr George Webb is much chagrined[11] at the disappointment of his Nephew Mr Foster Webb, a clever youth in business, but too young for the dignity & importance of that office.[12] Mr Ambler is well esteem'd & I think will be confirmed by the assembly. some elections, since my last, seem to mend the Representation, which I hope will be better than I then feared.[13]

You'l probably hear that in Caroline we have chosen a Tory & other epithets added to it, in Mr Gilchrist[14] of Port Royal. He is a *Scotch man*, "the very head and Front of his offence hath that extent, no more"[15] against which we have only to Urge in our justification that he came from that Countrey a Youth, has been in Caroline upwards of 40 years. Married & realised all his property (which is very considerable) in the county, & for upwards of 30 years has been an [active], Vigilant & upright Majestrate, as well as of irreprochable life [in][16] the Character of a private Citizen, which 19/20ths of the County (foolishly it seems) thought sufficient to purge the Sin contracted by his birth in that hostile Countrey. I am

Dr Sr Yr affe friend

EDMD PENDLETON

[1] See Pendleton to JM, 15 April 1782.

[2] See JM to Randolph, 9 April 1782, n. 6.

[3] See JM to Pendleton, 9 April 1782, nn. 2 and 3.

[4] See *Papers of Madison*, III, 196–97; 197, n. 3.

[5] See JM to Pendleton, 9 April 1782, and n. 4.

[6] See *ibid*., and n. 5; Ambler to JM, 20 April 1782, n. 4. Pendleton is referring to the period from January 1778 to November 1780, when the headquarters of the British army had provided the convention troops interned at Charlottesville with specie and supplies. On 27 March 1779 Jefferson estimated that this source was adding "30,000 dollars a week at the least" to the "circulating money" of the Charlottesville neighborhood (Boyd, *Papers of Jefferson*, II, 238).

[7] See Harrison to Virginia Delegates, 23 March, and nn. 1 and 2; Randolph to JM, 19 April 1782, and nn. 3 and 6. On 17 July 1782 Congress adopted "An Ordinance More Effectually to Prevent Illicit Trade With the Enemy" stipulating that vessels engaged in this "pernicious commerce" should, with their cargoes, be "condemned as lawful prize, to the use of the state" in which the trial was held (*JCC*, XXII, 392–93). See also Report on Illicit Trade, 19 June 1782.

[8] John Rutledge re-entered Congress on 2 May, but John Lewis Gervais (*ca.* 1741–1798) delayed taking his seat until 1 July 1782 (*JCC*, XXII, 233, 360). A native of France, Gervais had reached Charleston, S.C., in June 1764, carrying a letter of introduction to Henry Laurens. Nine years later, when he married Mary, a daughter of the merchant John Sinclair, Gervais was a planter as well as a partner in a mercantile firm. In 1775, 1776, and 1781 he shared in the activities of the council of safety and of the provincial convention and congress. Besides being a continental deputy paymaster general in 1778 and 1779, he was a continental commissioner for purchasing rice in the following year. He served in the Senate of his state in 1781 and 1782 and remained politically prominent thereafter (*South Carolina Historical and Genealogical Magazine*, XXI [1920], 14, n. 40, 65, n. 44; XXVI [1925], 208, n. 46; XXVII [1926], 1, n. 1; *JCC*, XII, 1027; XV, 1123; XVI, 16, 283, 315).

[9] See Virginia Delegates to Harrison, 19 March 1782, n. 2. If Baron Ludwig von Closen's journal is a trustworthy source, Governor Harrison repeated at Williamsburg on 27 April the assurance given him by former Governor Rutledge that the British had evacuated Charleston (Acomb, *Journal of Closen*, p. 195). Either Harrison misunderstood Rutledge or, more likely, Closen misunderstood Harrison.

[10] See Jameson to JM, 9 March, n. 6; Randolph to JM, 11–13 April 1782, and n. 7.

[11] On 22 April there were four shillings in the "strong Box" (*Calendar of Virginia State Papers*, III, 133). Pendleton probably wrote "chagreen'd," the spelling used in the copy of the letter in the *Proceedings of the Massachusetts Historical Society*.

[12] Foster Webb, Jr. (1756–1812), was twenty-six years old. His ambition to be treasurer apparently was spurred by his uncle, who had held that office from January 1777 until his resignation in December 1779. When the present letter was written, George Webb was a member of the Council of State (*Journals of the Council of State*, I, 316; III, 77; McIlwaine, *Official Letters*, II, 81).

[13] See Pendleton to JM, 15 April 1782; also *Papers of Madison*, III, 73–74; 74, n. 6.

[14] Robert Gilchrist (*ca.* 1720–1803), a prominent Port Royal merchant since 1744, represented Caroline County in the House of Delegates in 1782 and 1783. He had been sheriff of the county in 1759 and a coroner two years earlier. For almost all of the period from 1744 until the close of the Revolution he was a magistrate of the county court. During much of this time one of his fellow justices was Edmund Pendleton, whom he also named an executor of his estate. Although Gilchrist had opposed taxation of the colonists by Parliament, thereby incurring the disfavor of Governor Botetourt, he likewise had offended some of the more ardent Whigs in 1774 by refusing to serve on the county's Committee of Safety (T. E. Campbell, *Colonial Caroline*, pp. 115, 122–23, 160, 174, 182, 206, 227, 234, 269, 347, 357, 359, 389–91; Swem and Williams, *Register*, pp. 15, 17; Caroline County Court Records, Order Book, 1802–1804, p. 283, microfilm in Virginia State Library).

[15] Shakespeare, *Othello*, Act 1, scene 3, lines 80–81:

> The very head and front of my offending
> Hath this extent, no more.

[16] The bracketed words here and earlier in the sentence are taken from the version of the letter in the *Proceedings of the Massachusetts Historical Society* as replacements for "action" and "as," respectively, in the Force transcript.

Virginia Delegates to Benjamin Harrison

RC (Virginia State Library). Written by JM. Docketed, "Lr from Delegates partly in Cypher May 82[.] April 23d 1782." "May 82" probably signifies when the letter was received. Italicized words in the present copy appear in the manuscript as numbers, conforming with the so-called "official cypher." A decoding and an encoding page are in the Virginia State Library.

PHILADA. April 23d. 1782

SIR

Your Excellency's favor of the 12th. came to hand yesterday. There is at present no Delegate here from N. Carolina. As soon as one arrives, we shall apprize him of the want of Commissions suggested by you.[1]

The office of the Superintendant of Finance does not contain the information you wish relative to the amount of payments made by the

States in the new Continental bills, no regular returns having been yet transmitted thither. As far as the portion of these bills allotted to the use of Congress shall be unissued, as also as far as the requisitions made in them on the States shall be unpaid, they will constitute a charge agst. the States, respectively.[2] But the rate at which they are to be charged is yet to be determined by Congress.[3]

The Delegates have long had it in charge from the Executive to provide a conveyance to Virginia of certain Stores taken on their passage from France & carried into Boston, or if that could not be accomplished, to have them Sold. They lye in the hands of Mr. J. Bradford formerly an Agent for the U. States. We have written various letters to him on the Subject, & recd. various answers without being able to fulfill either of the alternatives. The first indeed has been long relinquished. Our last letter requested him peremptorily to sell the Stores & remit the amount. The inclosed paper No. 1. is his answer, on which we shall await the pleasure of the Executive.[4]

We have again endeavored to obtain from Congress some explicit decision on the territorial cession of Virginia that the assembly may not again be left in uncertainty on that subject. The sickness of the Presidt. which suspended the vote of Maryland furnished a pretext for postponing the business which we judged it prudent to yield to. As soon as he returns to Congress which will probably be in a few days, we shall renew our proposition and continue to urge it till we obtain in some form or other such evidence of the purpose of Congress as will be satisfactory to the State:[5]

Early in the last year a plan was formed by the Courts of Vienna & Petersburg for bringing about a general pacification under their mediation. The preliminary articles which were proposed with this view to the belligerent powers are copied in the inclosed paper No. 2.[6] Congress have just received from *the minister o[f]*[7] *France some informal communications* relative to *the* issue of this *pacific* experiment. Among *them* is *the answer of the British court given* in *June last.* It *explicitly* and *emphatically re[j]ects*[8] that part of the *plan* which *relates* to the *negotiation between her* and *the colonies* and *guaranties the result* as *incompatible* with *the relation* of *sub[j]ects* to their *so[v]ereign* and *the* essential *interests* of *the empire; alleging* at the same time that a great *part* of *the Americans are disposed* to *return* to their *held [al]legiance*[9] and *that such step* would *furnish the rebel chiefs with fresh means* of *nourishing the [re]bellion* and *confirming* their *usurpe[d] authority. The final answer* of *the me[diat]ing courts* professes *great impartiali[ty] and* delicacy *toward the beligerent partys adheres* [to] *the expediency* of the *first plan* & *hopes* that it m[ay] *st[ill]*[10] *become* under more favorable *circumstances*[11] *the basis* of *a general pacification.*[12]

We have the honor to be with great esteem and respect Your Excellency's Obt. & hble. servts.

J. MADISON. JR.
THEOK. BLAND JR.
JOS: JONES.

[1] See Harrison to Virginia Delegates, 12 April 1782, and n. 4.

[2] See Report on New Hampshire Requisition, 25 March, n. 2; Harrison to Virginia Delegates, 6 April 1782, and nn. 3 and 6. By the ordinance of Congress of 18 March 1780, "the portion of these bills allotted to the use of Congress" was 40 per cent (*Papers of Madison,* II, 49, n. 2). On 17 June 1782, because the amount of cash being paid the "receivers of Continental taxes in the several States" had become alarmingly meager, Abraham Clark introduced a motion in Congress directing Morris to have his agents stop "their publications of monies received as well as where none was received, as a measure tending to discredit our public funds, and give offence to the delinquent States" (*JCC,* XXII, 336). The committee to whom this motion was referred apparently made no recommendation, probably because on the same day Congress adopted JM's report providing for a comprehensive inquiry "into the proceedings of the department of finance." See Report on Congressional Inspection of Departments, 17 June 1782, and n. 5. Clark was one of the investigating committee named by Congress for this purpose on 2 July 1782 (*JCC,* XXII, 370).

[3] Even as late as November 1782 Congress still was discussing what "the rate" of depreciation for issues made prior to 18 March 1780 should be (*JCC,* XXIII, 855). At the close of this paragraph JM canceled about thirty-six words so heavily that only a few of them can now be recovered with assurance. The deleted passage was approximately of this tenor: "As far as the States shall redeem the old currency by emissions of their own & shall redeem the old currency beyond the emissions of their respective shares of the ten Millions of the . . . surplus[.]" Apparently not finishing the sentence, JM may have intended at its outset to cite the situation in New Hampshire. See Report on New Hampshire Requisition, 25 March 1782, and n. 2.

[4] See *Papers of Madison,* II, 308; and Bradford to Virginia Delegates, 20 March 1782, headnote and notes. Except for this one dispatch, the editors have not found the correspondence with Bradford mentioned by the delegates in this paragraph. In his reply of 4 May to them (*q.v.*) the governor disapproved their directive to Bradford. The ultimate fate of the cargo is unknown to the editors. When Penet, d'Acosta Frères et Cie, the supplier of these "Stores," became bankrupt, some of its creditors sought remuneration from Virginia, because the Commonwealth was in debt to the firm. The price of the "Stores" probably formed a part of the claims. Between 1788 and 1791 Virginia paid these claimants at least £2,000. See the following three MSS in the Virginia State Library: Resolution of the General Assembly, 21 and 22 November 1788; undated Petition of Louis Abraham Pauly to the Virginia High Court of Chancery; Ruling of the High Court of Chancery, Richmond, 28 October 1790; also a resolution of the General Assembly in 1791, printed in Hening, *Statutes,* XIII, 323. See Boyd, *Papers of Jefferson,* XII, 312.

[5] See Motion on Chairman of Congress, 15 April, and n. 2; Virginia Delegates to Harrison, 17 April, and n. 1; Motion To Amend Lee's Motion on Western Lands, 18 April, and n. 1; JM to Pendleton, 23 April 1782, and n. 7.

[6] See *Papers of Madison*, III, 133; 147; 175, n. 19; 205, n. 3. John Adams' letters of 11, 14, and 15 July, read in Congress on 3 October 1781, each contained a copy of the "Articles pour servir de base à la négociation du rétablissement de la paix," dated 21 May 1781, and dispatched jointly by the Tsarina Catherine II and the Emperor Joseph II to the courts of London and Versailles. Before receiving Adams' dispatches, Congress may have been furnished a copy of the document by La Luzerne (*JCC*, XXI, 990, 1032). JM transcribed the French text at least twice, retaining one copy for his own use (LC: Rives Collection of Madison Papers) and enclosing the other in the present letter. An English translation appears in Wharton, *Revolutionary Diplomatic Correspondence*, IV, 561. JM most likely made his two copies shortly before the delegates' letter was posted to Harrison. During the latter half of April, after receiving Vergennes' dispatches which included news about the attempted mediation, La Luzerne passed along the information to Livingston for transmittal to Congress (Report on Communication from La Luzerne, 1 May 1782, and notes).

[7] Here JM inadvertently wrote the numerical symbol for "o" rather than for "of."

[8] The code lacked symbols for "je" and "ve." Hence in this sentence, JM used the symbol for "ie" to indicate the former and the symbol for "ue" to indicate the latter.

[9] Except for those mentioned in n. 10, all the brackets from here to the end of the paragraph signify missing ciphers because of a tear in the manuscript. The letters within the brackets are taken from a decoded copy in the Virginia State Library. This copy was made by Archibald Blair, clerk of the Council of State.

[10] By mistake, JM here wrote 695, the symbol for "learn," rather than 696, the symbol for "il."

[11] After writing this word, JM heavily deleted it and designated it by the appropriate symbol.

[12] In this paragraph JM summarizes very briefly the British response to the proposed mediation and the rejoinder of the mediators to that response. This interchange and other papers bearing upon the same subject evidently interested JM greatly because, using eleven pages of folio size and omitting all personal comments, he copied for his own use the French texts of the following documents and docketed them, "Comunication relating to the issue of the proposed mediation of Vienna & Peterburg": (*a*) "Reponse de S. M. T. C. [Louis XVI] aux articles proposés par les deux Cours Mediatrices" on 16 August 1781; (*b*) "Reponse fait par la Cour de Londres aux Articles preliminaires proposés par les Cours Mediatrices" on 15 June 1781; (*c*) "Reponse au papier marqué A. remis à la Cour de Londres par Mr. Compte de Belgioso [Belgioioso]," apparently also on 15 June 1781; (*d*) "Reponse verbale du roy de la G. B. aux observations verbales remise par M. le Compte de Belgioso" on 13[?] November 1781; and (*e*) "Reponse des Mediats.," possibly on 27 October 1781 (LC: Papers of Madison; Isabel de Madariaga, *Britain, Russia and the Armed Neutrality of 1780: Sir James Harris's Mission to St. Petersburg during the American Revolution* [New Haven, 1962], pp. 267, 272–73, 278, 281, 290, 325, 328, 352–53). Count Lodovico Antonio Barbiano di Belgioioso-Este was the Austrian ambassador to Great Britain. "Compte" should be "Comte."

Although John Adams, Francis Dana, Benjamin Franklin, and La Luzerne had furnished Congress with general information about the progress of the mediation, Congress apparently lacked the texts of all five of the documents listed above until

La Luzerne gave them to Robert R. Livingston, the secretary for foreign affairs, late in April 1782 (Wharton, *Revolutionary Diplomatic Correspondence*, IV, 440–41, 720–22, 859; V, 138, 190). JM probably did not make his copies from those supplied by La Luzerne but from a slightly different version of them transmitted by Franklin. Both sets of these documents, translated into English, appear in *ibid.*, IV, 441–47, 860–66. See also JM to Randolph, 23 April; and Report on Communication from La Luzerne, 1 May 1782.

To Edmund Pendleton

RC (New York Public Library). Addressed to "The Honble Edmund Pendleton Esqr. Caroline County Virginia." Docketed by Pendleton, "James Madison Esqr. April 23d. 1782."

PHILADA: Apl: 23d. 1782

DEAR SIR

We have had here the same reports of the evacuation of Charleston which your letter of the 15. recites, but the wished for confirmation is still wanting.[1] That it will take place in the course of the Campaign cannot I think be doubted if the military succours are yielded by the states in any proportion to the call for them & the maritime superiority of our Ally in the W. I. should keep up the apprehensions of the British Garrisons from that quarter. This superiority was for a while somewhat endangered by the arrival of Rodney before the Brest Fleet. It is now said though upon very unauthentic grounds, that the latter with a large reinforcement of land troops is safe at Martinique.[2] This augmentation of the French force with that of Spain, to say nothing of the Dutch which is also said not to be contemptible, must submit every thing that is British in that quarter to the mercy of their Enemies.[3]

We have recd. some communications from Europe, but none of them are of late date. It appears from them that the pride & stubbornness of the British Court had rendered abortive the mediatory purposes of Vienna & Petersburg. Unless therefore the misfortune in Virga. sd. have broken their spirit as well as blasted their hopes, and made them suitors for a renewal of the interposition of these Courts, no immediate expectations can be retained from that quarter.[4] Nothing is said with regard to the separate negociation betwe[en] England & Holland. The recapture of the possessions of the latter with other circumstances has so entangled her with France that it will be very difficult for her to accomplish a separate pacification, even if she should be disposed to it.[5]

Vermont & the Western lands are still the themes which exercise our politics within doors. The Committe to whom the last application of the former to be admitted into the Confederacy was referred have according to expectation, reported that the measure is warranted by the Articles of Union & required by the engagements of Congress to them & expedient in itself.[6] The true secret is that the Vote of Vermont is wished for as an auxiliary agst. the Western claims of Virga. Some of the small States may indeed wish for it also as an auxiliary to their party, but no other motive can prevail with D. & M. Some of the E. States which are anxious for the admission of Vermont see this and impede the adjustment of Western boundaries on the ground of the Cessions, lest that event should be followed by a secession of those 2 States.[7] The radical impediment however is the influence of the land companies. We have in the course of the week past very sensibly experienced this influence.[8] As no answer had yet been given to the Cession of Virga. & the Legislature is shortly to meet, the Delegates thought it proper & accordingly proposed that the determination of Congress on that subject should without delay be come into. Every artifice that could perplex the case was immediately exerted: and it is extremely contingent, whether we shall be able to obtain an explicit answer to our reasonable request. We shall however continue to press it till Congress take some step which will either directly or indirectly, positively or negatively decide on the case & let the State know on what ground it is to form its measures.[9]

Mr. Lee sets off tomorrow morning in order to be ready for his duty at Richmond. Mr. Jones will follow about a week hence. I regret much that Mr. Randolph's unnecessary return to Virga. will in consequence expose her vote to the risk of division.[10] I shall urge him to face about again & wish for the co-operation of yourself & his other friends. Unless the A-y[11] remove his apprehension of pecuniary distress his past experience will it is little to be doubted render him callous to every argument on that subject.

I am Dr. Sir very sincerly yrs. &c.

J MADISON

[1] See Pendleton to JM, 15 April 1782, and n. 10.

[2] See JM to Pendleton, 9 April 1782, and n. 3.

[3] See Virginia Delegates to Harrison, 17 April 1782, and n. 2. JM's comment about the naval strength of the Netherlands in the Caribbean was probably based upon an item in the *Pennsylvania Packet* of 16 April 1782. Unknown to JM, the British fleet under Rodney had decisively defeated the French squadron commanded

by Grasse on 9–12 April 1782 in the Battle of the Saints, fought near the Îles des Saintes. By the close of the engagement Grasse was a prisoner of war, and five French ships of the line had surrendered. Two more struck their colors on 19 April. Five days earlier, in his victory dispatch to the secretary of the admiralty, Rodney mentioned that his own fleet had also "greatly suffered" in "Masts, Sails Rigging and Hulls" (*Letter-Books and Order-Book of George, Lord Rodney, Admiral of the White Squadron, 1780–1782* [2 vols.; New York, 1932], I, 358; W. M. James, *British Navy in Adversity*, pp. 333–44, 348, 354).

[4] See *Papers of Madison*, III, 197, n. 2; 205, n. 3; Instructions on Peace Negotiations, 7 January 1782, editorial note.

[5] See JM to Jefferson, 18 March, and n. 7; Virginia Delegates to Harrison, 19 March, n. 8; and JM to Pendleton, 19 March 1782, n. 3. For the expulsion of the British from St. Eustatius by the French, see Virginia Delegates to Harrison, 1 January 1782, n. 5. Early in 1782 the ministry of Lord North, which was being heavily assailed in Parliament because of British reverses in India, the Mediterranean, the Carribbean, and Virginia, sought to redeem itself by enticing France and the Netherlands to make peace separately, and by offering to acknowledge the autonomous status of the united American colonies within the empire. Rebuffed in these efforts, Lord North resigned on 20 March. By the date of the present letter, the Earl of Shelburne, secretary of state for the home office in the new ministry of the Marquis of Rockingham, had sent Richard Oswald to Paris to talk unofficially with Benjamin Franklin about peace terms between Great Britain and the United States. Their first conference was on 12 April (Samuel Flagg Bemis, *The Diplomacy of the American Revolution* [New York, 1935], pp. 191–95).

[6] See Motion Concerning Documents on Vermont, 3 April, editorial note and n. 8; Motion To Amend Lee's Motion on Western Lands, 18 April, n. 1; Motion on Letter of Vermont Agents, 20 April 1782, and nn. 3 and 4.

[7] JM meant that, in his opinion, the delegates of Delaware and Maryland ("D & M") did not support the admission of Vermont to the Confederation in order to add another member to "their party" of small states but to gain the vote of one more state against the acceptance by Congress of Virginia's qualified offer to cede her western lands. Some of the northern delegates, who supported the aspirations of Vermont, recognized this fact and hence impeded "the adjustment of Western boundaries," knowing that once they were decided upon, the delegates of Delaware and Maryland, being essentially southern in viewpoint, would oppose the entrance of Vermont into the union.

[8] JM certainly knew that several of the delegates from Pennsylvania, New Jersey, Delaware, and Maryland were prominent members of the Indiana, Vandalia, or Illinois-Wabash companies. For example, Samuel Wharton, a delegate from Delaware but a resident of Philadelphia, was heavily interested in the Indiana and Vandalia companies, while Daniel Carroll, a delegate from Maryland, was a cousin of Charles Carroll, a leading shareholder in the Illinois-Wabash Company (Thomas P. Abernethy, *Western Lands and the American Revolution*, pp. 37, 54, 122, 239).

[9] See Motion To Amend Lee's Motion on Western Lands, 18 April, n. 1; and Virginia Delegates to Harrison, 23 April 1782.

[10] Here JM apparently was not criticizing Randolph for returning to Virginia but merely referring to the opinion expressed by Pendleton in his letter of 15 April (*q.v.*). For Randolph's own view of the matter, see Randolph to JM, 19 April, and nn. 8, 9; and JM to Randolph, 23 April 1782, n. 4. From 2 May, when Jones left, until 27 June, when Arthur Lee returned, JM and Bland were the only delegates of Virginia in Congress. During these eight weeks, eighteen roll-call votes appear

in the printed journal. On five of these, Virginia's vote was lost—once because Bland was absent, and four times because he and JM cast opposing ballots. Of the latter, the issue was Vermont on one occasion, while in the other three the financial accounts of Benjamin Franklin were in controversy. Unlike JM, Bland and Lee were hostile to Franklin (*JCC*, XXII, 242, 286, 294–95).

[11] The General Assembly of Virginia. See Randolph to JM, 19 April 1782, and n. 9.

To Edmund Randolph

RC (LC: Madison Papers). The words written by JM in the official cipher are italicized in the present copy. Although the letter is incomplete, the missing portion apparently contained only a few concluding words and JM's signature.

PHILADA. Apl. 23d. 1782

DR SIR

I am at length assured of your safe arrival at your destination by your favor of the 11 continued on the 13th.[1] The little necessity I understand there was for your return to Virga. makes me [ex]ceedingly regret that you cd. not be diverted from it; as the little occasion there is likely to be according to Mr. Pendleton's idea of yr. continuance there flatters me that it will not be long before you resume your Station in Congress.[2] This duty may be the more enforced upon you, as Mr. Lee leaves us this morning & Mr Jones to follow in a few days. The vote of Virga. will in consequence be in all questions exposed to the chance of division.[3] I am sensible of the plea which may be drawn from the emptiness of the public coffers; but I hope it will not be a permanent one, & that if you can only stay a few months with us you will not think the period unworthy of the expedition.[4]

I informed you in my last that your draught was duly honored[.] The advance was by no means distressful to me but the prospect now before me obliges me to prefer repayment here to any other mode. It will not I hope make any difference with you.[5] Mr. Morris has recd. & answered your letter.[6] The return of the French Minister without visiting Richmond had no particular cause which I can explain. He expressed doubts on that point you may remember before he set out for Virginia.[7]

Congress have recd from *the minister* [of France][8] some informal communications relative to the issue of *the proposed mediation* of *Vienna and Petersburg*. The *answer* of *the British court* to *the str pre-*

li[*mina*]*ry*[9] *articles* is *among them.* It *re*[*j*]*ects*[10] explicitly that part of the *plan* which *requires concurren*[t][11] *negotiation between her* and *America* & *guaran*[ti]*es the result* as *incompatible* with *the relation* of [subj]*ects* to their *soveryreign*[12] and *the* essential *interest* of *the empire; alleging* at the same time that a *part* of *the people are disposed* to *return* to their *held alle*[giance] & that such a *treaty* wd. *suply the rebels* with *pretexts* for *misleading* them. *The final answer* of *the mediating courts* professes *great impartiality and* delicacy *toward the belige*[ren]*t partys*[,] *adheres* to the *expediency* of the *first* [plan,] & *hopes* that it may *still become* under more fa[vor]able *circumstances the basis* of *a general pacification.*[13]

Another letter has come to hand from *M*[r.] *Dana.* [His] *proposed rash* step was *probably* taken a *few* [days] *after the date* of *it* which was abt. the middle of *October*[14]

The Committee on the last application from Vermont ha[ve] reported fully in their favor. The consideration of the Report w[ill] not be called for however till the pulse of nine States bea[ts] favorably for it. This is so uncertain that the Agents have returned. The recognition of the Independence of Vermont is n[ow?] fully stated in the report as a resolution antecedent ev[en to?] authorizing a committee to treat with them on the terms of their admission.[15] You well know the object of this arrangeme[nt.]

You will be so good as to take charge of the inclosed letter [to M]r Jefferson[16] & give it a safe conveyance. Every one about me joins in

[1] *Q.v.*

[2] See Pendleton to JM, 15 April 1782. JM's meaning would be clearer if he had placed a comma before "according" and after the third "there" in the sentence.

[3] See Virginia Delegates to Harrison, 12 March, and n. 4; JM to Randolph, 9 April, and nn. 5 and 6; JM to Pendleton, 23 April 1782, and n. 10.

[4] See Randolph to JM, 11–13 April, and n. 6; and 19 April 1782, and n. 9. On 22 April Randolph described his financial embarrassment to Governor Harrison: "I am now in a situation, truly humiliating to myself, and, I might add, disgraceful to the commonwealth. I could not have rescued myself from the hands of those creditors, to whom I was indebted for my subsistance during my stay in Phila, without borrowing about two hundred pounds. My note has travelled after me, and I cannot meet it with my own purse" (MS in Virginia State Library).

[5] In his letter of 11–13 April (*q.v.*), Randolph asked JM in what manner he would prefer to be repaid the £20 he had loaned Randolph in Philadelphia. JM's "last letter," probably dated 16 April, has not been found. See also Randolph to JM, 5 and 16–17 May 1782.

[6] The dispatch of Randolph to Robert Morris has not been found. Letterbook C, among the papers of Morris in the Library of Congress, contains letters of 9 March, 16 April, and 11 June 1782 from him to Randolph (pp. 85–86, 189–90, 413–45).

These show that, after declining to be continental receiver of taxes in Virginia, Randolph was asked by Morris to recommend candidates for the position. Removed from the Council of State by vote of the General Assembly on 28 May (Minute Book, House of Delegates, May 1782, p. 55), George Webb subsequently accepted the receivership. See Randolph to JM, 1 June 1782, and n. 5.

[7] See Virginia Delegates to Harrison, 5 March, and n. 3; Randolph to JM, 11–13 April 1782.

[8] Inserted in brackets by JM many years later, when he interlineated a decoding of the cipher. JM evidently selected this paragraph and the two succeeding paragraphs for publication in the first edition of his papers (Madison, *Papers* [Gilpin ed.], I, 121–22).

[9] JM inadvertently wrote the numerical symbol for "str." Upon decoding the symbol, he wrote and then crossed out "str" but let the symbol remain. Although there is a cipher for "mina," JM indicated it only by a dash.

[10] Since there was no symbol for "je," JM generally used the symbol for "ie."

[11] This and most of the later bracketed inserts in this letter signify a tear on the right margin which eliminated ciphers and parts of words.

[12] Sovereign.

[13] See Virginia Delegates to Harrison, 23 April 1782, nn. 6 and 12.

[14] Although not mentioned in the printed journals of Congress, the dispatch of 15 October 1781 from Francis Dana (1743–1811), who had been a delegate to Congress from Massachusetts in 1776–1778, had been received on 22 April (NA: PCC, No. 89, II, fols. 598–603, docket). Dana's dispatch of 15 September, including copies of his correspondence with Charles Olivier de Saint-Georges, Marquis de Vérac, French ambassador at the court of St. Petersburg, arrived on 15 March 1782, three days before Randolph left Congress (NA: PCC, No. 186, fols. 19–20). The third article of the instructions given by Congress to Dana upon electing him as "minister to the Court of Russia" on 19 December 1780 stipulated, "If the result of your inquiries should point out a fair prospect of an honourable reception, you are to announce your publick character, and deliver your letters of credence in the usual form" (*JCC*, XVIII, 1170). In spite of the cautious policy prescribed by this article and advice of the same tenor offered by Vérac to Dana soon after Dana reached St. Petersburg on 27 August 1781, he resolved to present his credentials whenever the situation at the imperial court might seem even slightly favorable to his purpose (Wharton, *Revolutionary Diplomatic Correspondence*, IV, 683–85, 695–99, 705–7, 710–14, 773–76). This was the "rash step" to which JM refers. Unknown to him, Dana had come to accept Vérac's point of view by the close of 1781 (*ibid.*, V, 223–25).

The extremely long time-distance from St. Petersburg to Philadelphia worked greatly to Dana's disadvantage. In a letter of 2 March 1782 the secretary for foreign affairs informed Dana that not "a single line" had been received from him "since May, 1781" (*ibid.*, V, 209). Conversely, Dana's dispatch of 28 June 1782 informed Livingston that his letter of 22 October 1781 was the last which had reached St. Petersburg (*ibid.*, V, 532). In other words, lacking a more recent word from Dana than his letter of 15 October 1781, Congress would rebuke him in May 1782 for a "rash step" which he had not taken and no longer intended to take (*ibid.*, V, 411–13; Motion on Instructions to Dana, 27 May 1782). Dana remained in St. Petersburg until 8 September 1783 without being recognized by Tsarina Catherine as the minister of the United States. He disembarked at Boston on 12 December of that year (Wharton, *Revolutionary Diplomatic Correspondence*, VI, 636, 657, 739). In 1784 he returned briefly to Congress and from 1785 to

1791 was a justice of the Massachusetts Supreme Court and its chief justice thereafter until 1806.

[15] See Motion Concerning Documents on Vermont, 3 April, editorial note, and notes; Motion on Letter of Vermont Agents, 20 April, and nn. 1, 4, and especially 3; JM to Pendleton, 23 April 1782. At this point in the manuscript, a narrow strip is torn from the right-hand edge; the left-hand corner is also missing. In the Gilpin edition of JM's papers (I, 122), this sentence appears as, "The recognition of the Independence of Vermont is not fully stated in the report, as a resolution, antecedent, went to authorizing a committee to treat with them on the terms of their admission." Nothing in the manuscript, at least in its present form, obliges this to be what JM wrote or prevents the rendition given in the text above. It seems much more likely that he would summarize accurately, rather than inaccurately, the contents of a report of great interest to him on a subject which, as recently as 17 April, had been discussed at great length in Congress.

[16] No letter of this date has been found. The letter referred to may have been the one written to Jefferson by Barbé-Marbois in Philadelphia on 22 April 1782 (Boyd, *Papers of Jefferson,* VI, 177–78).

Motion on Colonel Edward Carrington

MS (NA: PCC, No. 19, I, 541½). In JM's hand.

[26 April 1782]

Resold[1] That Lt Colo. Carrington be informd that the 7th. Art: of the Confederation having reserved to the States the right of appointing all officers of & under the rank of Colonels for the forces respectively raised by them & of filling up all vacancies of such officers, Congress cannot appoint him to the vacancy in the Command of the 4th. Regt. of Artillery raisd by the State of Pesa.

Agreed to April 26. 1782

[1] See Report of Delegates of Pennsylvania, Maryland, and Virginia on Carrington's Memorial, 20 April 1782, and editorial note and n. 1. The Montgomery committee, having ascertained that the Supreme Executive Council of Pennsylvania was determined not to grant Lieutenant Colonel Carrington the commission which he sought, recommended the following resolution to Congress on 26 April 1782: "Resolved That Col Carrington cannot, at present be appointed to the Command of the 4th. Regt. of Artillery" (NA: PCC, No. 19, I, 541). Before adopting this resolution on the same day, Congress apparently consented to temper its brusqueness by agreeing also to JM's proposal (*JCC,* XXII, 215). See also JM to Randolph, 29 May 1782.

From Edmund Randolph

RC (LC: Madison Papers). Unsigned, but in Randolph's hand. Addressed to "The honble James Madison jr. of Congress Philadelphia."

RICHMOND April 26. 1782.

DEAR SIR

The principle of "timeo Danaos et dona ferentes"[1] has so powerful an effect upon the minds of our executive, that they seem fearful, lest the proposal of Pennsylvania to run a temporary line should contain an ambuscade. It offers the extension of Mason and Dixon's line three and twenty miles. To this the governor and council are ready to assent. But hearing, that this line was produced by the Pennsylvania commissioner, after the commissioner for Maryland had left him, and that this produced line also goes under the name of Mason and Dixon's, they apprehend, that the 23 miles are intended to be started from the termination of the produced line. There may be some reason for this apprehension, if the part added is to the south of the latitude of Mason and Dixon's line. But if it be not, I hardly think it of sufficient consequence to bustle about it: as the 5° of longitude must necessarily be the distance of the western boundary of Penna. from the Delaware.[2] Pray inquire into, and transmit to me the particulars of this Addition, made by the Penna. commissioner: and be sure to inform me, what Distance Mason and Dixon's line was run by the two commissioners in conjunction.[3]

I can give you no intelligence as to supplies. I fear, however, that it is the fate of the delegation to undergo anew a state of humiliation and poverty.[4]

I beg to learn, how far the Dutch are warped from the war by negotiations with Britain. When I left you, his britannick majesty seemed disposed to a separate peace with them: but nothing appeared to warrant the belief, that they would yield to the seduction. Probably you have acquired more recent notice.[5]

Yrs mo. sincerely.

[1] "I fear the Greeks, even when bringing gifts" (Virgil *Aeneid* ii. 49).

[2] See Harrison to JM, 19 January, and nn. 2 and 3; JM to Harrison, 1 February, and n. 2; Jefferson to JM, 24 March 1782, and n. 5. Contrary to Governor Harrison's belief, Charles Mason (1730–1787) and Jeremiah Dixon (d. 1773) were not employed from 1764 to 1767 by the proprietors of Pennsylvania and Maryland to favor either province but merely to survey accurately the boundary between the

two provinces. Hostile Indians compelled the surveyors to abandon their task when they were about twenty-three miles from the western end of the line. For excellent summaries of the basis and course, prior to 1776, of the controversy between Pennsylvania and Virginia over the ownership of the territory from the westernmost range of the Allegheny Mountains to, or even beyond, the Ohio River, including much of the Monongahela and Youghiogheny river valleys and also "the forks" at Fort Pitt, see Boyd, *Papers of Jefferson*, I, 234–36, 594–97; and Solon J. Buck and Elizabeth Hawthorn Buck, *The Planting of Civilization in Western Pennsylvania* (Pittsburgh, 1939), pp. 156–72. The dozen conflicting solutions, including several "temporary" lines offered by officials of Virginia or Pennsylvania between 1774 and 1779, are shown on Plate 97G of Charles O. Paullin, *Atlas of the Historical Geography of the United States*, ed. by John K. Wright (Washington and New York, 1932).

Although the issue could not be discussed without mentioning the ambiguous and apparently overlapping boundaries stipulated in the London Company's charter of 1609 and William Penn's of 1681, much more practical considerations by 1781 mainly accounted for the heat of the controversy in the disputed areas and the seeming inability to reach an equitable compromise. Among these circumstances were the following: (1) A considerable number of Virginians and a lesser number of Pennsylvanians had settled there—some as squatters, some as tenants of absentee landlords with conflicting claims to extensive acreages, and a few with patents from these landlords or from Virginia or Pennsylvania. (2) Political and military officials were in conflict, because each of these states had created counties embracing the disputed territory. (3) Indian tribes were fighting each other and allegedly were goaded by frontiersmen of each state to attack the settlers of the other. (4) Agitation by Tories added to the chronic turmoil. (5) The Pennsylvania settlers, especially, were resisting the efforts of George Rogers Clark and the local officials of Virginia to enlist volunteers or forcibly to draft militia for service against the British and Indians in the Northwest Territory. (6) A few malcontents, probably encouraged by British agents or by leaders of the Indiana Company, which claimed much of the region west of the Monongahela River, were endeavoring to have the settlers secede from both Pennsylvania and Virginia and gain statehood, along with a confirmation of land titles from Congress. These would-be seceders contended that the disputed territory, being west of the Appalachian watershed, had reverted from Pennsylvania or Virginia to the Crown in consequence of the Royal Proclamation Line of 1763. Therefore, the Declaration of Independence had transferred to Congress, as successor to the Crown, the sole jurisdiction over the region (*JCC*, II, 76; XXII, 223–32, 240–41; *Calendar of Virginia State Papers*, I, 273–74; Hening, *Statutes*, IX, 262–63; McIlwaine, *Official Letters*, I, 280, 330, 373; *Pennsylvania Archives*, 1st ser., IX, 193–94, 233–34, 315–19, 343–45; Motion To Amend Lee's Motion on Western Lands, 18 April, n. 1; JM to Pendleton, 23 April 1782, and n. 8).

At Baltimore on 31 August 1779 commissioners of Pennsylvania and Virginia had agreed to "extend Mason's and Dixon's line due west five degrees of longitude, to be computed from the river Delaware, for the southern boundary of Pennsylvania, and that a meridian drawn from the western extremity thereof to the northern limit of the said state be the western boundary of Pennsylvania forever" (Hening, *Statutes*, X, 533). Although the Pennsylvania General Assembly ratified this compact on 19 November 1779, the Virginia General Assembly delayed until 4 July 1780 before expressing an approval, qualified by provisos intended to protect the personal and property rights of Virginians who, after the delineation of the boundary, would be under Pennsylvania's jurisdiction (*ibid.*, X, 534–37). In the meantime, responding to a complaint lodged by Pennsylvania, Congress on 27 December 1779 had requested Pennsylvania and Virginia (and they soon agreed) to cease granting land within the area in controversy "until the dispute can be amicably settled by both states or brought to a just decision by the intervention of Congress" (*JCC*, XV, 1411; McIlwaine, *Official Letters*, II, 37 n., 97–100; Hening, *Statutes*, X, 239). In the background of this resolution were the Indiana Company's memorial of 14 September 1779 and the then unratified Articles of Confederation, whose ninth article designated Congress as "the last resort on appeal in all disputes and differences now subsisting or that hereafter may arise between two or more states concerning boundary, jurisdiction or any other cause whatever" (*JCC*, XV, 1063–65; XIX, 217–18).

Governor Jefferson of Virginia and President Reed of Pennsylvania desired "to establish Peace, Good Order & Government as soon as possible" in the disputed area, so that, incidentally, the inhabitants would be deprived of their customary "Pretence of unsettled Boundary" as a justification of their continuous bickering. After the two executives came to recognize the impracticality, under the existing circumstances, of running a permanent boundary line "by astronomical observations" in accord with the Baltimore agreement of 1779, they decided to resort to "a temporary line," which would serve until the making of a definitive survey in the spring of 1782. The invasion of Virginia by the British, the harassment of the controversial borderland by Indians, the opposition of some of its frontiersmen to surveyors, and lack of money prevented even this stopgap action from taking place during 1781 (Boyd, *Papers of Jefferson*, III, 586; V, 303–4, 374–75, 478; VI, 74; *Pennsylvania Archives*, 1st ser., IX, 20–21, 300–302, 304–5, 374–75, 402–3, 438–40, 444–45, 468).

Governor Harrison readily acquiesced to the resolution of 2 March 1782 of the Pennsylvania General Assembly to postpone surveying a permanent boundary until after the war, but he obviously was less eager than President Moore of Pennsylvania to have a temporary line drawn without delay. For awhile in the spring and early summer, Moore threatened to proceed with the survey, even though Virginia would not co-operate (McIlwaine, *Official Letters*, III, 176–77, 179–80; *Pennsylvania Archives*, 1st ser., IX, 506–7, 519). Harrison's hesitation reflected not only his belief that the western portion of Mason and Dixon's line had been marked too far south and, hence, by being extended would give Pennsylvania more of the disputed area than was rightfully her due, but also his conviction, shared by Randolph, that Pennsylvania should be obliged prior to the survey to guarantee the personal and property rights, and the political privileges, of Virginians who, once the boundary had been defined, would become residents of Pennsylvania. Randolph also suggested to Harrison, in a letter of 22 April, that the rights, if any, of Congress and the Indiana Company in the territory at issue should be clarified (Randolph to Harrison, 22 April 1782, MS in Virginia State Library; McIlwaine, *Official Letters*, III, 198, 206).

On 6 June 1782 the Virginia General Assembly responded to Harrison's request for instructions by directing him to appoint a surveyor to join with one of Pennsylvania in drawing a "temporary boundary" by extending Mason and Dixon's line twenty-three miles west and proceeding from its termination due north to the Ohio River (McIlwaine, *Official Letters*, III, 216, 235–36, 261, 287; *Pennsylvania Archives*, 1st ser., IX, 562). Although the Pennsylvania surveyor had arrived at the agreed starting point by 10 June and was impatient to begin the survey, President Moore deferred to Harrison's wish to postpone the work until November, when trees and undergrowth would be bare of leaves and when, very likely,

Indian war parties would have left the area (McIlwaine, *Official Letters*, III, 291; *Pennsylvania Archives*, 1st ser., IX, 562, 564–67, 585, 588). On 28 November 1782 the boundary commissioners signed a joint report to the effect that they had run the temporary line as directed. By then Governor Harrison had received a letter from JM, telling of a rumored secession movement in the western Pennsylvania-Virginia border country and encroachments there by Pennsylvanians on land held under Virginia titles (McIlwaine, *Official Letters*, III, 386–87; *Journals of the Council of State*, III, 228, 474; *Colonial Records of Pennsylvania*, XIII, 541–42; *Pennsylvania Magazine of History and Biography*, XXXVIII [1914], 407–26; JM to Harrison, 15 November 1782, MS in Princeton University Library). See also Harrison to JM, 19 January 1782, n. 3.

[3] If JM answered Randolph's request, the letter has not been found.

[4] See Randolph to JM, 19 April 1782, n. 9.

[5] See JM to Pendleton, 23 April, and n. 5; and JM to Randolph, 7 May 1782, and n. 3.

Benjamin Harrison to Virginia Delegates

FC (Virginia State Library). In the hand of Charles Hay.

Virginia Council Chamber Apl 27th. 1782

Gentlemen

By some queries that have been presented to the Attorney General there is reason to apprehend that the people who inhabit the lands that were in dispute with the State of Pennsylvania are likely to suffer, not only in the property of their lands but by a reversal of the decrees of the Courts whilst they were look'd on as subjects of this State and are also under prosecution for acts done by them under its laws.[1] The Executive beg the favor of you to enquire into these matters, and to give them such information as you can obtain, and also an account of all the proceedings of the Pennsylvania Assembly that relate to the Inhabitants of that country.[2] I am with respect &c

[1] See Randolph to JM, 26 April 1782, and n. 2. A series of seven queries was addressed to Edmund Randolph by two residents of the area that was destined to become a part of Pennsylvania. These questions, forwarded by him to the governor in a letter of 22 April 1782, are filed with that dispatch in the Virginia State Library. In addition to the objections cited by Harrison, the westerners doubted whether Pennsylvania and Virginia had "Legal right to alter Original Charters for mear Conveniency of the States to the Prejudice of the Inhabitants immediately residing on the Contested Territory and whether such alterration is not Subject to the future Discussion of Congress."

[2] See letters of Virginia Delegates to Harrison, 7, 14, and 28 May 1782.

Motion for Financial Reports

MS (NA: PCC, No. 36, I, 291). Written by JM. Docketed, "Motion of Mr Madison seconded by Mr [Joseph] Montgomery[,] passed April 30h 1782."

[30 April 1782]

Ordered, That the Superintendt of Finance do prepare & lay before Congress a State of the monies borrowed & not repaid by the U. S. prior to the 1st. day of Jany. last[1] and that he also lay before Congress every half year computing from the sd. 1st. day of Jany. a State of all monies borrowed & bills emitted during such periods respectively;–[2] that the same may be transmitted to the respective States pursuant to the direction contained in the 9th. Art. of the Confed–[3]

[1] At this point JM deleted a clause, "that the same may be transmitted to the respective States, pursuant to the direction contained in the 9th Art. of the Confederation," and transposed it, except for the last three syllables of "Confederation," to the position indicated in n. 2, below.

[2] Here JM inserted a dash and followed it by the clause quoted in n. 1, above. By so doing, he was able to delete the repetitious clause, "to be in like manner transmitted to the several States," with which he had closed the motion in its original form.

[3] By this article Congress was authorized "to borrow money, or emit bills on the credit of the united states, transmitting every half year to the respective states an account of the sums of money so borrowed or emitted" (*JCC*, XIX, 219). Robert Morris apparently never embodied in one document a full compliance with JM's motion, especially if the phrase "prior to the 1st. day of Jany. last" was intended to include the entire period of the Revolution since the first meeting of the Second Continental Congress rather than since the adoption of the Articles of Confederation on 1 March 1781. On the other hand, Morris prepared in July 1782 an elaborate report which was "the most important single state paper on public credit ever written prior to Hamilton's First Report" on that subject (Clarence L. Ver Steeg, *Robert Morris*, pp. 124, 239, n. 11; *JCC*, XXII, 429–46). Furthermore, under date of 18 November 1782, a report was published entitled *A General View of Receipts and Expenditures of Public Monies, by Authority from the Superintendent of Finance, from the Time of his entering on the Administration of the Finances, to the 31st December, 1781* (*JCC*, XXIII, 889; NA: PCC, No. 137, III, 329, 333).

Motion Approving John Jay's Negotiations with Spain

MS (NA: PCC, No. 36, IV, 7). In JM's hand. Docketed, "Motion of Mr Madison seconded by Mr Jones. That Congress approved of the Conduct of the Minister Plenipotentiary at the Court of Madrid."

EDITORIAL NOTE

In view of the Report Approving John Jay's negotiations with Spain, 22 April 1782 (*q.v.*) and the fact that between that date and 30 April Congress received no dispatches from Jay or William Carmichael, JM's reasons for introducing this motion, so similar in its contents to the report, invite comment. Both the report and this motion were in response to Jay's long dispatch of 3 October 1781 to the president of Congress (Wharton, *Revolutionary Diplomatic Correspondence*, IV, 738–65, and esp. p. 763).

Since Livingston had been on an extended "excursion" to New York (Motion on Secretary for Foreign Affairs, 4 March 1782, n. 1) when this letter was received, Congress directed a committee under JM's chairmanship to draft a reply. By failing to mention Livingston in this directive, Congress apparently assumed that Livingston would not be available for consultation (Report on Foreign Dispatches, 20 March 1782). At least a week before 22 April, when the committee submitted its recommendation to Congress, Livingston returned to Philadelphia. He then read Jay's dispatch and a preliminary draft of the committee's report. On 16 April, having heard that a vessel was to "sail in two hours for Cadiz" and believing that congressional agreement upon a reply would be delayed by extended debate, Livingston wrote a private letter to Jay summarizing the contents of the proposed report (Burnett, *Letters*, VI, 330 n.). The secretary for foreign affairs assumed in this letter that the official answer to Jay's dispatch would be signed by President Hanson. On the contrary, the Madison committee suggested in their report on 22 April that their recommendations be made the basis of an answer to Jay "to be subscribed by the Secy. of F A." Although unnoted in the journal for that day, Livingston evidently was directed not to mail his reply until it had been approved by Congress (Report Approving Jay's Negotiations with Spain, 22 April 1782, and n. 1; *JCC*, XXII, 207–8).

What took place between 23 and 30 April with regard to this matter cannot be fully ascertained from any primary sources known to the editors. Livingston appears to have been dissatisfied both because he, rather than Hanson, had been assigned the task of drafting the dispatch and because Congress decided to send the text of its resolutions to Jay. Charles Thomson noted in one of his record books that on 29 April, "Secy for For. Affairs on report of a Committee on Mr. Jays letter of 3 Oct 1781," and on 30 April, "His [Livingston's] two letters proposed were read & postponed & a motion adopted & passed in lieu thereof" (NA: PCC, No. 191, fol. 14). The first of these entries apparently means that on 29 April (Monday) Livingston submitted to Congress his draft of a dispatch to Jay, dated two days earlier, summarizing the resolutions of 22 April. Perhaps after reading this draft, JM persuaded Livingston that, since the need of Spanish aid was no longer so urgent, and since the court of Madrid patently read all correspondence between Jay and Carmichael and the officials of Congress, including the enciphered passages, the time had come to supplement the soft and diplomatic paragraphs of Livingston's proposed letter to Jay with some forthright congressional resolutions which JM was prepared to introduce (Report Approving Jay's Negotiations with Spain, 22 April 1782, n. 5). Jay had hinted in his dispatch of 3 October 1781 that he would welcome these. Under date of 28 April Livingston wrote a second letter to Jay which, as Thomson noted, reached Congress two days later, just before JM introduced his resolutions. This brief dispatch appears to be merely a covering letter for these resolutions which Livingston would enclose without enciphering them (Wharton, *Revolutionary Diplomatic Correspondence*, V, 332–35, 377; George Dangerfield, *Chancellor Robert R. Livingston*, p. 168).

[30 April 1782][1]

Resolved That the[2] the Minister Plenipo: of the U. S. at the Court of Madrid be inform'd that Congress entirely approve of his Conduct as detailed in his letter of the 3d. of Ocr. last: that the limitation affixed by him to the proposed surrender of the Navigation of the Mississippi in particular corresponds with the views of Congress: that they observe not withou[t][3] surprize & concern that a proposition so liberal in itself & which removed the only avowed obstacle to a connection between the U. S. & his C. M.[4] should not have produced[5] greater effects on the Councils of the latter: that the surrender of the Navigation of the Mississippi was meant as the price of the Advantages promised by an early & intimate alliance with the Spanish Monarchy, & that if this alliance is to be procrastinated till the conclusion of the war,[6] the reason of the Sacrifice will no longer exist: that as every day wch. the proposed Treaty is delayed, detracts from the obligation & inducement of the U. S. to adhere to their overture, it is the instruction of Congress that he urge to the[7] Ministers of his C. M. the obligation it imposes on Spain to make the Treaty the more liberal on her part: and that in particular he use his endeavors to obtain in consideration of such delay, either an enlargement of her pecuniary aids to the U. S. a facilitating of the use of the[8] Mississippi to the Citizens thereof or some peculiar indulgences in the commerce of the Spanish Colonies in America.

1 See *JCC*, XXII, 142, and n.; 219–20, and n.; *Secret Journals of the Acts and Proceedings of Congress, from the First Meeting thereof to the Dissolution of the Confederation, by the Adoption of the Constitution of the United States* (4 vols.; Boston, 1820–21), III, 98–99.

2 After "That the" JM at first wrote, and then deleted, "Secy. of Foreign Affairs be directed to inform." Above this clause he penned, and again struck out, "Minister for the United States at St [Ildefonso]." Upon starting anew, he evidently forgot that he had not eliminated the first "the."

3 JM crossed out "much" after "without."

4 His Catholic Majesty, the King of Spain.

5 At first JM wrote, "produced a little effect."

6 JM crossed out "during a continuance of wch only it can be necessary."

7 JM wrote "ally" here but then deleted it.

8 Here JM struck out "navigation of."

Virginia Delegates to Benjamin Harrison

RC (Virginia State Library). Addressed, "His Excelly. B. Harrison Esqr." Entirely in JM's hand except for the signatures of the other delegates. The words in the official cipher are here italicized. Accompanying the recipient's copy is a sheet upon which the second paragraph of the letter was decoded by Archibald Blair, clerk of the Council of State.

PHILADA. April 30th. 1782

SIR

We have not the honor of acknowledging any letter from your Excellency by yesterday's post.

Congress received yesterday some *supplemental communications* through the channel mentioned in our last.[1] They speak on the part of *our ally much regret at the thinness* of *our military ranks:* insinuate *the idea* of *cooperating with us in expelling the enemy from their remaining posts within the United States* and observe that *G. Britain* stills *reckons much on her numerous friends* in *this country* & will *spare* no *means* of *increaseing them.*[2] It is supposed in particular that *experiments may be made* to *seduce the states* [*to*][3] *separate negotiations.* The whole *concl*[*ud*]*es*[4] *with* fresh *assurances of the unalterable adherance of his Most Christi*[an] *Ma*[*j*]*esty to the principles* of *the alliance.*[5]

Our last intelligence from Europe & the West Indies comes through the British Gazette of N. York and is contained in the inclosed Gazette of this place. The fall of Minorca may be received thro' that channel without distrust. The blockade of the French Fleet at Martinique is probably an invention to soothe the distress resulting from that fresh misfortune.[6]

We have the honor to be with sentiments of great regard & esteem yr. Excelly's obt. & hble servts.

J. MADISON JR.
THEOK. BLAND JR.
JOS: JONES.

[1] See Virginia Delegates to Harrison, 23 April 1782, and n. 6.

[2] See JM to James Madison, Sr., 30 March 1782.

[3] JM wrote the cipher for "most." On the decoding sheet, "most" was crossed out and replaced by "to."

[4] By writing 413 rather than 423, JM mistakenly used the ciphers for "conclpaes." After so decoding it in Virginia, the last four letters were deleted and "udes" substituted.

[5] See Report on Communication from La Luzerne, 1 May 1782.

[6] The delegates evidently enclosed the 30 April issue of the *Pennsylvania Packet*, which furnished the news items in this paragraph by taking them from the 24 April issue of Rivington's *Royal Gazette* of New York City. See JM to Pendleton, 23 April 1782, n. 3.

Report on Communication from La Luzerne

MS (NA: PCC, No. 25, II, 95). The manuscript, written by JM, is docketed: "Report of Committee on foreign Communications. Passed May 1st 1782."

[1 May 1782][1]

The Committee to whom were referred the Communication &c laid before Congress by the Secy. of F. Affairs, submit the following resolutions.

Resolved. The Secretary of Fo. Affairs be directed to make a confidential communication to the Several States, of the intelligence recd. by Congress on the day of [2] through his Department; in order that the States may be the more fully impressed with the necessity of, such, United & determined exertions as with the co-operation of our generous Ally will expell the Enemy from their remaining ports within the U. S. and display to the world the falsehood of the assertions of the British Court that the people of these States are neither united nor determined in support of their national Independence.[3]

Resolved That the sd. Secy. be further directed to prepare and report to Congress a Manifesto exhibiting to the World the origin &

justice of our cause, and in particular the several facts & arguments which demonstrate the Unanimity & unalterable firmness of the Citizens of the U. S. therein.[4]

[1] Prefatory to this report in *JCC*, XXII, 222–23, is an entry, chiefly comprising Robert Livingston's summary of a conversation on Sunday, 28 April 1782, with La Luzerne about the latter's dispatches, dated 24 December 1781 and 22 January 1782, from Vergennes. Although unnoted in *JCC*, Congress referred the summary on 29 April to a committee consisting of JM, John Morin Scott, and Arthur Middleton (NA: PCC, No. 186, fol. 20). Accompanying the manuscript of the summary in NA: PCC, No. 79, II, 125–31, is a resolution, probably in the hand of a clerk, in which Livingston suggests what action Congress might direct him to take so as to give satisfaction to the government of France. This proposed resolution, similar to JM's report in content but rarely in phraseology, no doubt helped to guide the deliberations of the committee.

[2] 29 April 1782 (*JCC*, XXII, 222).

[3] Although partly designed to stir the state governments from their lethargy, the resolution was intended also to allay French fears that American war weariness, combined with British propaganda, might lead to an Anglo-American accommodation to the injury of France. Before his conference with Livingston, La Luzerne had written to Washington about Vergennes' disquietude. At the same time a letter from Lafayette informed the commander-in-chief that in France it was "generally thought, the exertions of America are not equal to her abilities, and that nothing could operate so much for further assistance, as pointed assurances of a good Army for the War." On 23 April Washington quoted Lafayette's comment in a letter to Livingston and added, "I wish I could say, that the States were making all the efforts, our situation demands, and which our Allies have a right to expect from us." Five days later, in a dispatch to La Luzerne estimating the probable strength of the American and British forces in the military operations expected soon to begin, Washington frankly acknowledged ignorance of what the effective strength of the American forces would be (Fitzpatrick, *Writings of Washington*, XXIV, 155–56, 178–82; William E. O'Donnell, *Chevalier de La Luzerne*, pp. 212–15).

On 2 May 1782, in accord with the tenor of the present resolution, Livingston sent an identical letter to the executive of each state. In this dispatch he more closely followed the information he had gleaned from La Luzerne and Washington than the precise terms of the directive of Congress. Besides warning against "the artifice of the enemy" and suggesting ways to counteract it, Livingston chided the executives upon the halfhearted manner in which their states had co-operated with France. "We have at no period," he declared, "been in a situation to second fully the endeavors of our ally to serve us; we either neglected to assemble our army in time or to provide the means for supporting or moving them; a feather would have turned the balance last year, notwithstanding the powerful aid we received from abroad. Providence blinded our adversaries; to their temerity we owe our success" (Wharton, *Revolutionary Diplomatic Correspondence*, V, 393–95).

[4] Congress apparently declined to adopt this second resolution. It is deleted both in *JCC*, XXII, 223, and in the manuscript copy of the committee's report. Congress may have rejected the suggestion of "a Manifesto" because Livingston had not included it in his proposed resolution, mentioned in n. 1, above.

Account with Edmund Randolph

RC (LC: Madison Papers). At the top of this undated, torn, and water-stained scrap of paper, Randolph wrote "Madison to Randolph E." On the reverse of the sheet, "J. Madison" appears twice in Randolph's hand and also a "32." What this numeral connotes is unknown. Being sharp in outline, the "3" can hardly be a vestige of an "8" which, in combination with the "2," might have represented the year 1782.

EDITORIAL NOTE

Insofar as is known, the extant correspondence of JM and Randolph does not refer to this statement of account. JM obviously prepared it after Randolph left Philadelphia on 18 March. The first entry in the "Credt." column may suggest that the statement was drafted before or shortly after Joseph Jones started from that city for Virginia on 2 May 1782. In his letter of 16–17 May, Randolph referred to his debt for the last time in his correspondence with JM (Randolph to JM, 11–13 April, 5, 10, 16–17 May 1782). This fact may indicate that at least by then Randolph had received JM's statement. JM probably had been fully remunerated by the end of May. See his letter of 4 June 1782 to Randolph.

[*ca.* 1 May 1782]

E. R. to JM.	Dr.		Credt.
To ballance pd. at Mrs Houses[1]	£14–11	By 54 ⅔ dollrs. recd. on E. R's acct. out of 130 supplied to Mr. Jones by T. P.[7]	£20–10
To share in stable	6		
	20–11		
		By old ballance 4. drs	[1–10][8]
			22
To cash lent out of J.M's share of 23 half Joes recd. from Pleasants[2]	7–		
To do. 12 Crowns[3]	5		
To do. at Bells[4] 3 Crowns	1– 5	Note	
To do. pd. for Trial per [?] pair [?][5]	1–	The 54 ⅔ drs. were drawn from the £130 in the hands of Mr Jones for the special purpose of pay to Mrs. House & for the stable[9]	
	£34–16		
	22		
	£12 16 bal: due.[6]		

[1] See Randolph to JM, 16–17 May 1782, and n. 28.

[2] Thomas Pleasants, Jr. The "23 half Joes" (about $184 or £70) may have been the money received by JM in Philadelphia on 28 December 1781 through the agency of Pleasants. See Expense Account as Delegate in Congress, 20 March; Randolph to JM, 27–29 June 1782, n. 12; *Papers of Madison*, I, 51, n. 4.

[3] A British crown is worth five shillings. The "do" in each instance stands for "cash." In this item and the one following, the sums are multiplied by 1.66 to convert them into Pennsylvania currency.

[4] This probably was either the Bell Tavern at 48 South Eighth Street or the bookshop of Robert Bell at Third Street near St. Paul's Church (*Papers of Madison*, I, 133, n. 1; John F. Watson, *Annals of Philadelphia, and Pennsylvania, in the Olden Time* [3 vols.; Philadelphia, 1927], III, 365; Joseph Jackson, *Encyclopedia of Philadelphia* [4 vols.; Harrisburg, Pa., 1931–33], I, 266–69).

[5] Perhaps "Trial," which is clearly written in the manuscript, refers to a book. If "Trial" designates a book, "per pair" may signify either that the publication was in two volumes or that Randolph had bought two copies of a single-volume work.

[6] When Foster Webb, Jr., left Richmond for Philadelphia on 15 May, he took with him from Randolph to deliver to JM "a bill for 20 £. Penna. curren[cy]." By this means Randolph may have paid the balance of his debt (Randolph to JM, 16–17 May; JM to Randolph, 4 June 1782). By applying the depreciation rate of 1.66, £20 equaled about £12 12*d.*

[7] Thomas Pleasants, Jr. Dividing dollars by 2.66 converted them into pounds. The date when Randolph received the £20 10*s.* has not been determined. The account of Joseph Jones with the state auditors shows that Jones was paid £221 by Pleasants in December 1781 and £200 in February 1782 (MS in Virginia State Library).

[8] What former account between Randolph and JM was balanced so that JM still owed $4.00 to his friend is unknown. The piece missing from the manuscript's right-hand margin opposite this entry must have noted £1 10*s.*

[9] See the first two entries in the debit column.

To Edmund Randolph

Printed text (Madison, *Papers* [Gilpin ed.], I, 90–93; and Madison, *Letters* [Cong. ed.], I, 43). The third paragraph of the letter, as here printed, is taken from the Congressional edition; the rest follows the version published in the Gilpin edition. In both of these editions the letter is misdated "May 1, 1781." See *Papers of Madison*, III, 100–101.

PHILADELPHIA, May 1, 178[2].

DEAR SIR,

The case of the vessel captured within North Carolina was some time since remitted to Congress by Governor Harrison. I am glad to find your ideas correspond so exactly with those I had advanced on the subject.[1] The legislative power over captures, and the judiciary in the last resort, are clearly vested in Congress by the Confederation. But the judiciary power in the first instance, not being delegated, is as clearly reserved to the Admiralty Courts of the particular States within which the captures are made. Captures made on the high seas must fall within the jurisdiction of the State into which it shall please the captor to carry them. It will be sufficient, I believe, to insert in the instructions to privateers, a clause for preventing the grievance complained of by North Carolina. The anger of Mr. Burke was erroneous in its principle, as well as intemperate in its degree. The offender being an officer of Congress,[2] and not of Virginia, Congress, and not Virginia, should have been resorted to for redress.

On a consultation before Doctor Lee left us,[3] it was determined that we ought to renew our attempts to obtain from Congress a decision on the cession of Virginia, before the meeting of the Legislature. The attempt was accordingly made, and produced all the perplexing and dilatory objections which its adversaries could devise. An indisposition of the President, which suspended the vote of Maryland, furnished an argument for postponing, which it was prudent to yield to,[4] but which is now removed by the arrival of Mr. Wright,[5] a new Delegate from that State. We shall call again on Congress for a simple answer in the affirmative or the negative, without going into any unnecessary discussions on the point of right; and should the decision be postponed *sine die*,[6] we hope the State will consider itself at liberty to take any course which its interest shall suggest. It happens very unluckily that Virginia will only have two Representatives present during the interesting business. Mr. Jones cannot be prevailed on to wait the event.[7] Colonel Bland thinks the validity of charters unimportant to the title of Virginia, and that the title of the natives militates against the claims of the companies.[8] Is not my situation an enviable one?

A letter which I received a few days ago from Mr. Jefferson[9] gives me a hope that he will lend his succor in defending the title of Virginia. He professes ignorance of the ground on which the report of the committee places the controversy. I have exhorted him not to drop his purpose, and referred him to you as a source of copious information on the subject. I wish much you and he could unite your ideas on it.[10] Since you left us I have picked up several pamphlets which had escaped our researches. Among them are the examination of the Connecticut claim,[11] and the charter of Georgia, bound up with that of Maryland and four others.[12] Presuming that a better use will be made of them, I will send them by Mr. Jones, requesting, however, that they may be returned by the hands of him, Dr. Lee, or yourself, as the case may be.

A further communication from the French Minister informs us, that the Court of France laments the weakness of our army; insinuates the idea of co-operation in expelling the enemy from the United States; apprehends attempts to seduce the States into separate negotiations, and hopes measures will be taken to frustrate such views. I believe, from this and other circumstances, that the Court of France begins to have serious suspicions of some latent danger. It is extremely probable, that as the enemy relax in their military exertions against this country, they will redouble the means of seduction and division[.][13] This consideration is an additional argument in favor of a full representation of the States. In a multitude of counsellors there is the best chance for honesty, if not of wisdom.

The subject of Vermont has not yet been called up. Their agents and those of the land-mongers are playing with great adroitness into each others' hands.[14] Mr. Jones will explain this game to you. Colonel Bland is still schismatical on this point. I flatter myself, however, that he will so far respect the united opinion of his brethren as to be silent.[15] Mr. Lee entered fully into the policy of keeping the vote of Vermont out of Congress.[16]

The refugees from New York have lately perpetrated one of the most daring and flagrant acts that has occurred in the course of the war. A captain of militia of New Jersey, who unfortunately fell a captive into their hands, was carried to New York, confined successively in different prisons, and treated with every mark of insult and cruelty; and finally brought over to the Jerseys, and in cold blood hanged. A label was left on his breast, charging him with having murdered one of their fraternity, and denouncing a like fate to others. The charge has been disproved by unexceptionable testimony. A number of respectable people of New Jersey have, by a memorial, called aloud on the Commander-in-Chief for retaliation;[17] in consequence of which he has, in the most decisive terms, claimed of Sir Henry Clinton a delivery of the offenders up to justice, as the only means of averting the stroke of vengeance from the innocent head of a captive officer of equal rank to the Jersey captain. The answer of Clinton was not received when General Washington despatched a state of the transaction to Congress.[18]

[1] See Harrison to Virginia Delegates, 23 March, and nn. 1, 2; Randolph to JM, 19 April 1782, and nn. 3, 6.

[2] That is, the legal status of the captain of a privateer was derived from a letter of marque and reprisal issued to him by Congress, not by a state.

[3] Arthur Lee left Philadelphia to return to Virginia on either 23 or 24 April (JM to Pendleton, 23 April; JM to Randolph, 23 April 1782).

[4] See Motion on Chairman of Congress, 15 April; Virginia Delegates to Harrison, 17 April; Motion To Amend Lee's Motion on Western Lands, 18 April, and n. 1; Virginia Delegates to Harrison, 23 April; JM to Pendleton, 23 April 1782.

[5] Turbutt Wright (1741–1783) of Queen Annes County, Md., had taken his seat in Congress on 29 April 1782 (*JCC*, XXII, 217). Besides having been a member of the General Assembly, 1773–74 and 1781–82, he had helped to draft the constitution of Maryland in 1776 and had served on the state Council of Safety in the following year.

[6] On the date of the present letter, Congress resumed consideration of the Boudinot committee report and of Arthur Lee's revised amendment thereto (JM to Jefferson, 15 January, n. 9; Motion To Amend Lee's Motion on Western Lands, 18 April 1782, and n. 1). The lengthy report opposed Virginia's offer of cession, approved New York's, viewed the land claims of the Indiana Company with favor, and recommended that "the petition of the Illinois and Wabash companies be dismissed" (*JCC*, XXII, 225–32). During the extended discussion on 1 May, the representatives of New York, Virginia, South Carolina, and Georgia defeated a motion to postpone consideration of this report, but Congress adjourned before the Virginians could ask for "a simple answer in the affirmative or the negative" on the offer of their state to cede her title to the Old Northwest (*JCC*, XXII, 223–24, 232–33). See Motion on Delegates' Financial Interest in West, 2 May, and n. 1; and Motion on Point of Order, 3 May 1782, nn. 3, 4.

[7] Joseph Jones attended Congress on 1 May, but he apparently left for Virginia early the next day, before Congress convened. Governor Harrison submitted the issue of the western lands on 6 May to the speaker of the House of Delegates for referral to the Virginia General Assembly when it convened (JM to Randolph, 9 April 1782, n. 5). On 1 June 1782 the legislature appointed George Mason, Jefferson, Randolph, Arthur Lee, and Dr. Thomas Walker as a committee to prepare and publish a defense of Virginia's western claims (Virginia Delegates to Harrison, 12 March, n. 4; Randolph to JM, 1 June 1782).

[8] Although a statement by Bland to this effect has not been found, he probably agreed with Arthur Lee. Deeming "the validity of charters unimportant," Lee based the title of Virginia and several other states to the trans-Appalachian West almost solely upon the fact that they "individually were sovereign and independent, and upon them alone devolved the rights of the Crown within their respective territories" (Burnett, *Letters*, VI, 448). See also Instructions on Peace Negotiations, 7 January, and n. 9; Randolph to JM, 10 May 1782, and n. 7. Unlike the Indiana Company, most companies speculating in western lands had not purchased their alleged holdings from Indian tribes (*Papers of Madison*, II, 178 nn.; III, 288, n. 5; 304, n. 1).

[9] If, as seems almost certain, JM refers to Jefferson's letter of 24 March (*q.v.*), he meant 15 April by a "few days ago" (JM to Jefferson, 16 April 1782).

[10] See n. 7, above; and JM to Jefferson, 16 April 1782.

[11] See JM to Randolph, 9 April 1782, n. 2.

[12] The pamphlets probably were the one by the Reverend William Smith, cited in n. 2 of JM to Randolph, 9 April 1782, and six charters comprising that of "Georgia, bound up with that of Maryland" and "four others," as listed in E. Millicent Sowerby, comp. and ed., *Catalogue of the Library of Thomas Jefferson*, III, 271, 275.

[13] JM encoded the remarks on this subject in the delegates' dispatch of 30 April 1782 to Governor Harrison (*q.v.*). He probably encoded this paragraph also.

[14] See Observations Relating to the Influence of Vermont and the Territorial Claims on the Politics of Congress, 1 May 1782, and n. 9.

[15] See JM to Pendleton, 23 April 1782, n. 10. On 21 May 1782, in a poll upon John Morin Scott's motion to refer to a special committee two statutes, recently enacted by the New York General Assembly and generally conciliatory in their offers to the Vermonters, JM voted "ay" and Bland, "no." Even if both men had voted "ay," the motion still would have failed to pass (*JCC*, XXII, 281–86).

[16] That is, to refuse even to consider admitting Vermont as a state. Between 1 March and 3 April, there were five tallied votes in Congress on the Vermont issue. In four of these, JM and Lee voted alike (*JCC*, XXII, 107–8, 114, 158, 163). During that period Bland was in Virginia. Between 17 and 20 April 1782, there were four tallied votes on the same issue. With the exception of one roll call in which Lee did not share, his stand and JM's were again the same. Bland and JM differed in viewpoint on three of the polls (*JCC*, XXII, 188–90, 204).

[17] Joshua Huddy (*ca.* 1745–1782) of Monmouth County, N.J., a captain of state artillery and at times a privateersman, had been a locally prominent leader in the internecine strife between patriots and Tories in his county. The Tories were usually called "refugees," because many of them had fled to New York City, whence their armed raids were directed by the Board of Associated Loyalists (*Papers of Madison,* III, 52–55; 55, n. 2). On 24 March a party of "refugees" captured Huddy at Tom's River, N.J., and imprisoned him in New York City. General Clinton, apparently given to understand that Huddy would be exchanged for a Tory or Tories held captive in New Jersey, delivered the prisoner to the custody of Captain Richard Lippincott (1745–1826), a refugee from Shrewsbury, Monmouth County. At Middletown Point, near his home, Lippincott hanged his prisoner on 12 April, allegedly as a reprisal for the recent "murder" by militia of Philip White, a refugee kinsman of Lippincott. Upon the arrival of Huddy's body at Monmouth Court House (Freehold) for burial, fourteen spokesmen for a large mass meeting addressed a memorial to Washington telling the story of Huddy's execution, supplying written testimony that he had been in prison when White was killed, and requesting the commander-in-chief to demand Lippincott or an officer of equivalent rank from Clinton for condign punishment (*New Jersey Archives*, 2d ser., V, 400, 424–25; Franklin Ellis, *History of Monmouth County, New Jersey* [Philadelphia, 1885], pp. 213, 216–17, 219–20, 223–25; Katherine Mayo, *General Washington's Dilemma* [New York, 1938], pp. 71–74, 82–84, 88, 94–95, 99).

[18] On 20 April, after receiving the Monmouth County memorial and the opinions of "the general and field officers" of his army, Washington wrote to Congress, enclosing a copy of the memorial, of his letter to Clinton demanding that Lippincott be delivered up for hanging, and the affidavits of sundry witnesses of Huddy's execution and of White's death from bullets fired by his captors when he tried to escape. On 29 April Congress unanimously resolved that the enemy's "unprecedented and inhuman cruelties, so contrary to the laws of nations and of war, will no longer be suffered with impunity" and that Washington's "fixed purpose of exemplary retaliation" had "their firmest support" (Fitzpatrick, *Writings of Washington,* XXIV, 135–39, 144–45, 146–47; *JCC,* XXII, 217–18). In May 1782, over three months before General Sir Guy Carleton, Clinton's successor as commander-in-chief of the British Army in North America, let Washington know that Lippincott had been obeying orders and hence had been exonerated by a court-martial, Washington took the alternative step, mentioned in his letter to Clinton, of having a British prisoner of captain's rank selected by lot to go to the gallows in case Lippincott should not be delivered for execution. Much to Washington's embarrassment, the lot fell upon Captain Charles Asgill, a prisoner under the Yorktown capitulation and a

member of an influential British family. Yielding to pressure from the government of France, Congress on 7 November 1782 directed Washington "to set Captain Asgill at liberty" (Fitzpatrick, *Writings of Washington*, XXIV and XXV, *passim; JCC*, XXIII, 652–53, 662 and n., 689–91, 695 n., 715, 718–19, 829 n., 845; Wharton, *Revolutionary Diplomatic Correspondence*, V, 462–63, 463 n., 617–18, 634–36, 833, 870, 872; VI, 64–65; Madison, *Writings* [Hunt ed.], I, 252–53 n.). A gratifying result of the Huddy episode was the dissolution of the Board of Associated Loyalists (Thomas Jefferson Wertenbaker, *Father Knickerbocker Rebels: New York City during the Revolution* [New York, 1948], p. 232).

Observations Relating to the Influence of Vermont and the Territorial Claims on the Politics of Congress

MS (LC: Madison Papers). Written by JM and docketed by him with the above title, followed by "May 1, 1782."

EDITORIAL NOTE

Why JM prepared this memorandum at this time can only be surmised. Perhaps believing that the Vermont issue, which had been quiescent since 20 April, would come importantly to the fore within a few days, he wished to organize his thoughts about the matter and its complex relationships with other interstate boundary controversies and with issues involving cessions of western territory to Congress by the landed states. He may also have desired to provide Joseph Jones, who was to depart for Virginia on 2 May, with a memorandum which would be welcomed by public officials at Richmond (JM to Randolph, 1 May 1782).

May 1st. 1782.

The two great objects which predominate in the politics of Congress at this juncture are I. Vermont.[1] II. Western territory.[2]

I The independence of Vermont and its admission into the Confederacy are patronised by the Eastern States[3] (N. Hamshire excepted) 1. from ancient prejudice agst. N York: 2. the interest which Citizens of those States have in lands granted by Vermont. 3. but principally from the accession of weight they will derive from it in Congress. N. Hamshire having gained its main object by the exclusion of its territory East of Connecticut River from the claims of Vermont,[4] is already indifferent to its independence, and will probably soon combine with other Eastern States in its favor.

The same patronage is yielded to the pretensions of Vermont by Pennsylvania & Maryland with the sole view of reinforcing the opposition to claims of Western territory particularly those of Virginia and by N. Jersey & Delaware with the additional view of strengthening the interest of the little States. Both of these considerations operate also on Rhode Island in addition to those above mentioned.[5]

The independence of Vermont and its admission into the Union are opposed by N. York for reasons obvious & well known.[6]

The like opposition is made by Virginia N. Carolina, S. Carolina, and Georgia. The grounds of this opposition are. 1. an habitual jealosy of a predominance of Eastern Interests. 2. the opposition expected from Vermont to Western claims. 3. the inexpediency of admitting so unimportant a State, to an equal vote in deciding on peace & all the other grand interests of the Union now depending. 4. the influence[7] of the example on a premature dismemberment of other States. These considerations influence the four States last mentioned in different degrees.[8] The 2. & 3. to say nothing of the 4. ought to be decisive with Virginia.

II The territorial claims, particularly those of Virginia are opposed by Rhode Island, N. Jersey, Pennsylvania Delaware & Maryland. Rhode Island is influenced in her opposition by 1. a lucrative desire of sharing in the vacant territory as a fund of revenue. 2. by the envy & jealousy naturally excited by superior resources & importance. N. J. Penna: Delaware, Maryland, are influenced partly by the same considerations; but principally by the intrigues of their Citizens who are interested in the claims of land Companies. The decisive influence of this last consideration is manifest from the peculiar, and persivering opposition made agst. Virginia within whose limits those claims lye.[9]

The Western claims, or rather[10] a final settlement of them, are also thwarted by Massachussetts and Connecticut. This object with them is chiefly subservient to that of Vermont, as the latter is with Pennsylvania & Maryland to the former.[11] The general policy and interests of these two States are opposed to the admission of Vermont into the Union, and if the case of the Western territory were once removed, they would instantly divide from the Eastern States in the case of Vermont. Of this Massachussetts & Connecticut are not insensible, and therefore find their advantage in keeping the territorial Controversy pending. Connecticut may likewise conceive some analogy between her claim to the Western Country & that of Virginia, and that the[12] acceptance of the cession of the latter, would influence[13] her sentiments in the controversy between the former &[14] Pennsylvania.[15]

The Western claims are espoused by Virga. N & S. Carolinas, Georgia & N. York, all of these States being interested therein[.] S.

Carolina is the least so.[16] The claim of N. York is very extensive, but her title very flimsy.[17] She urges it more with the hope of obtaining some advantage, or credit, by its cession, than of ever maintaining it. If this Cession should be accepted, and the affair of Vermont terminated,[18] as these are the only ties which unite her with the Southern States, she will immediately connect her policy with that of the Eastern States; as far at least, as the remains of former prejudices will permit.

[1] The background of the Vermont issue has been treated in *Papers of Madison,* III, 223–24; 225–26, nn. 11–13; 307–8; 309, n. 4; JM to Pendleton, 22 January, and nn. 5–8; 7 February, and n. 4; 2 April, and n. 2; 23 April, and nn. 7, 8; Motion Concerning Documents on Vermont, 3 April, editorial note, and nn. 4, 5, 8; Motion on Letter of Vermont Agents, 20 April, and nn. 3, 4; and JM to Randolph, 23 April 1782, and n. 15.

[2] For the background of the issue of the western lands, see JM to Jefferson, 15 January, and nn. 8–13; 16 April, and nn. 3, 7, 9; JM to Pendleton, 2 April, and n. 3; 23 April, and nn. 7, 8; JM to Randolph, 9 April, and nn. 2, 3; Virginia Delegates to Harrison, 17 April, and 23 April; Motion To Amend Lee's Motion on Western Lands, 18 April 1782, and n. 1.

[3] Those of New England.

[4] In February 1782 the "government" of Vermont had agreed to the stipulation made by Congress on 21 August 1781 that the eastern boundary of the proposed state should be "the west bank of Connecticut river" (*JCC,* XXI, 892; Motion Concerning Documents on Vermont, 3 April 1782, editorial note). See also JM to Pendleton, 22 January 1782, and n. 8.

[5] See JM to Pendleton, 2 April, and n. 2; Motion Concerning Documents on Vermont, 3 April 1782, editorial note.

[6] See Motion Concerning Documents on Vermont, 3 April 1782, editorial note, and n. 5. Besides the reasons mentioned in this cross-reference, the executive and legislature of New York charged the *de facto* government of Vermont with presuming to rule over, and grant land titles to, an area rightfully under the jurisdiction of New York and owned by her citizens. In their correspondence with Governor George Clinton, members of the New York delegation in Congress had analyzed the position of other delegates with relation to Vermont in a fashion similar to the present memorandum (Burnett, *Letters,* VI, 212, 297–98, 309).

[7] JM first wrote "tendency" and then deleted it.

[8] See JM to Pendleton, 7 February 1782, and n. 4. See also Burnett, *Letters,* VI, 327 n.

[9] Arthur Lee wrote on 21 April 1782 in a letter to Samuel Adams: "these Agents [of land companies] are using every art to seduce us and to sow dissention among the States, I think they are more dangerous than the Enemy's Arms. Every Motion relative to Vermont and the Cessions of the other States is directed by the interests of these Companies. I have in vain movd for a purifying declaration from each member that he is not concerned in them. The Motion was evaded by three days chicane, and remains undecided" (Burnett, *Letters,* VI, 331). After Lee offered his motion on 18 April, JM had supported it with his vote (*JCC,* XXII, 191–92; Motion To Amend Lee's Motion on Western Lands, 18 April 1782, n. 1). See also JM to Jefferson, 15 January, and n. 9, and 16 April; JM to Pendleton, 23 April, and n. 8; Randolph to JM, 26 April 1782, n. 2.

[10] After "rather," JM wrote and crossed out "perhaps."

[11] That is, although Massachusetts and Connecticut were more concerned about Vermont than about the "Western claims," these claims were of greater consequence than Vermont to Pennsylvania and Maryland.

[12] Here JM wrote and deleted "adjustment of the latter."

[13] At this point JM deleted "the part."

[14] JM substituted "the former &" for "Connecticut and."

[15] See JM to Jefferson, 15 January, and n. 8; JM to Randolph, 9 April 1782, and n. 2.

[16] See *Papers of Madison,* II, 73. Although each of the two charters, granted in 1663 and 1665, respectively, by King Charles II to the Carolina proprietors, specified that their domain should extend "to the West as far as the South Seas," the division of the territory into the provinces of North and South Carolina had allotted to the former all or almost all of the region now known as Tennessee. A few years later, in 1732, James Edward Oglethorpe and his fellow trustees received from King George II a charter which may have further hedged South Carolina on the west by declaring that Georgia stretched in that direction to "the south seas." In other words, South Carolina naturally was not as concerned about the western lands as were the other southern states, because her rightful jurisdiction beyond the Appalachian watershed was confined, at best, to a very narrow corridor of territory extending to the Mississippi River. Following the making of a compact between South Carolina and Georgia about their common boundaries, South Carolina's offer of her western lands was accepted by Congress on 9 August 1787 (William Macdonald, ed., *Select Charters and Other Documents Illustrative of American History, 1606–1775* [New York, 1899], pp. 121, 148, 242; *JCC,* XXXIII, 467–77).

[17] See *Papers of Madison,* II, 73–74.

[18] On 29 October 1782 Congress agreed to the cession by New York (*JCC,* XXIII, 694; JM to Jefferson, 15 January 1782, n. 8). The "affair of Vermont," of course, was not settled until her admission as a state in 1791.

Motion on Delegates' Financial Interest in West

MS (NA: PCC, No. 36, I, 293). Docketed by JM: "Motion of Mr Bland seconded by Mr Madison[.] May 2d 1782. Rejected as out of order." Although Bland presented the motion in Congress, the manuscript is in JM's hand. Also in his hand, on the page containing the docket, appear the words, "assistance from the fleets of his M C or C M as can be afforded for the like purpose." This passage was evidently a part of the first draft of JM's Motion on Protection of Commerce submitted to Congress on 2 May 1782 (*q.v.*).

[2 May 1782]

that the question be now taken on the proposition contained in the words following to wiz.[1] [that previous to any determination, &c. (as recited yesterday)][2] the same being the remainder of a proposition, on the first part of which a vote was yesterday taken on a call a division,[3] and now intitled to decision without debate.[4]

[1] JM evidently meant to write "wit" or "viz." On 1 May Congress had further altered Arthur Lee's motion of 18 April, as amended that day (*q.v.* and n. 1), by deleting the remainder of the first paragraph asking for a postponement of a vote on New York's offer to cede her western claims (JM to Randolph, 1 May 1782, and n. 6). Therefore, the present motion requested a vote on the second proposal in Lee's motion, quoted in Motion To Amend Lee's Motion on Western Lands, 18 April 1782, n. 1.

[2] See *JCC*, XXII, 223.

[3] See *JCC*, XXII, 232.

[4] As stipulated by the twenty-second rule for "conducting business," adopted by Congress on 4 May 1781 (*JCC*, XX, 480). When Bland introduced the motion, it was at once challenged as being "out of order." The "chairman," Daniel Carroll (Motion on Chairman of Congress, 15 April 1782, n. 1), in doubt about the correct parliamentary procedure, acted in accordance with the twenty-sixth rule (*JCC*, XX, 481) by calling "for the judgment of the house." As he was privileged to do by the twenty-third rule (*JCC*, XX, 480), Bland then "required" a tallied vote "on the question, is the motion in order." With the exception of the Virginia delegation, the states represented in Congress unanimously decided that Bland's motion was "out of order" (*JCC*, XXII, 234–35). On the sheet of paper containing the motion as drafted by JM, Charles Thomson recorded how each delegate voted. See Motion on Point of Order, 3 May 1782.

Motion on Protection of Commerce

MS (NA: PCC, No. 28, fol. 241). Written by JM. With a sharper quill than the one he used to draft the motion, JM penned at the top of the page, "Resolved that next be appointed to receive." Almost certainly he made this note on 2 May, when Congress agreed upon a date for receiving La Luzerne (*JCC*, XXII, 235). In the PCC, immediately following this page, is another bearing the docket, "Report of Committee on Memorial of the Merchants of Philada. referred to the Agent of Marine to take order May 2, 1782." Perhaps, in view of the comments in n. 1, below, this docket is misplaced and belongs in the PCC with fol. 243a, upon which the committee appointed to consider the memorial wrote its recommendation.

[2 May 1782][1]

Resolved That the Agent of Marine be instructed to employ the naval force of the U. States under his direction in such manner as will most effectually protect the Trade & Commerce of the U States, and that he be Directed[2] to make application to any of the Commanders of the fleets of his M. C. M.[3] or of his C. M.[4] for such assistance as they may respectively be able to afford for the like purpose[5]

[1] On 29 April 1782, after listening to the undated "Memorial of the Merchants and Traders of the City of Philadelphia in behalf of themselves and of the commercial interests" of all the states, Congress referred it to a committee of five delegates under the chairmanship of Samuel Osgood. On 2 May, although *JCC* makes no mention of the fact, JM evidently introduced his motion, and Congress sent it to the committee as a directive. Following a conference with Robert Morris, the agent of marine, the committee submitted its recommendation on 4 May, and Congress adopted it on that day (*JCC*, XXII, 218 n., 237 and nn.; NA: PCC, No. 185, III, 25; No. 186, fol. 25).

The memorial was occasioned by the grievous losses of American ships and cargoes to British men-of-war and privateers in the spring of 1782. In response to pleas from Philadelphia businessmen, the Pennsylvania General Assembly on 15 April authorized the purchase of armed ships to protect merchant vessels owned by citizens of the state (*Colonial Records of Pennsylvania*, XIII, 270; *Pennsylvania Archives*, 1st ser., IX, 531–32; *Pennsylvania Journal*, 17 April 1782; *Pennsylvania Packet*, 25 April and 15 May 1782). Unknown to the legislature when it took this action, the most devastating blow to the sea-borne trade of the city had occurred on 14 April. That day, off the Delaware capes, British ships captured from nine to eleven Philadelphia-owned cargo vessels and soon brought these rich prizes into New York Harbor, where, according to Rivington's *Royal Gazette*, their arrival was "to the unspeakable satisfaction of all who wish the annihilation of the rebel commerce" (quoted in *Pennsylvania Gazette*, 8 May 1782; see also *Pennsylvania Packet*, 2 May 1782). In Philadelphia, on the other hand, the Baron von Closen commented in his journal about "the stupid policy of sending out so many ships at once" and noted that the "merchants were furious at the loss of 9 ships loaded with wheat and beef" (Acomb, *Journal of Closen*, pp. 202–3).

The memorial was signed by eighty-seven "Merchants and Traders," who observed that the British, "finding themselves incompetent to the purpose of conquering our Territory, seem determined to destroy our Trade." The memorialists emphasized that success in the war depended upon a continuation of this commerce. Without it, there would be neither sufficient consumer goods for troops and civilians nor adequate public revenues derived from taxes, import duties, and requisitions upon the states. Expressing "the most alarming disquietudes" because of "the incompetency of the naval force of the United States to afford protection to our Commerce," the petition closed with a request that Congress extend as much "permanent relief and assistance" as possible (NA: PCC, No. 41, VI, 283–85).

[2] A substitute by JM for a deleted "authorized."

[3] His Most Christian Majesty King Louis XVI of France.

[4] His Catholic Majesty King Charles III of Spain.

[5] In his response of 4 May to this directive, Morris informed Congress that, since "the Navy of the United States is not in a situation to afford protection," he should be directed, as "Superintendant of the Finances," to "prepare a state of the Commerce of the United States together with a plan for the protection thereof," and, as "Agent of Marine," be authorized to request "the Commanders of the fleets of France and Spain in the West Indies" to provide men-of-war to convoy American cargo vessels. Congress at once acquiesced to these recommendations and also di-

rected Morris to "prepare a draught of application" for Congress to present to the French court (*JCC*, XXII, 237–38). The decisive British naval victory in the Battle of the Saints blasted hope that Admiral de Grasse might help (JM to Pendleton, 23 April 1782, n. 3; Clarence L. Ver Steeg, *Robert Morris*, pp. 138–39). See Motion To Request France To Protect American Commerce, 14 May 1782.

Motion on Point of Order

MS (NA: PCC, No. 36, I, 297). The manuscript is in JM's hand. Charles Thomson entered "Madison, Bland" at the top to signify who made and seconded the motion, and "Madison" at the bottom to indicate that JM demanded a roll call. Below the second "Madison," Thomson recorded the vote on the motion. On a cover addressed by a clerk of the War Office to "His Excellency, The President of Congress," Thomson wrote, "Motion of Mr Madison Seconded by Mr Bland May 3d 1782 Question taken & lost."

[3 May 1782]

That the sense of the House be taken whether it be in order to take into consideration a report from the Secretary of War which was read yesterday by the Secretary & has since lain on the table,[1] unless the same be called for by a member[2]

[1] On 2 May Charles Thomson had read to Congress a report by Secretary at War Benjamin Lincoln opposing a promotion in rank for Colonel Goose Van Schaick of the First New York Regiment, continental line. Daniel Carroll, chairman of Congress, sought to have the report discussed on 3 May, even though it had not been assigned a place on the calendar for that day (*JCC*, XXII, 236, 287–88; Burnett, *Letters*, VI, 323). In accordance with a procedural rule of Congress (see n. 2), JM called for a vote to determine whether the delegates would sustain Carroll's action and thereby delay consideration of "the order of the day." This had been since 1 May the report of the Boudinot committee on the petitions of the land companies and the offers of New York, Virginia, and Connecticut to cede their western lands (*JCC*, XXII, 223–35). JM should have written, "Secretary at War."

[2] This motion was another tactical maneuver by Madison and Bland to prevent the opponents of Virginia from postponing a vote until they could sufficiently recruit their strength to carry the Boudinot committee's recommendation that Virginia's offer of cession be rejected (JM to Randolph, 1 May 1782, and n. 6). JM's motion was in accord with the seventh procedural rule of Congress, reading, "An order of the day, when called for by a State shall always have the preference and shall not be postponed but by the votes of a majority of the United States in Congress assembled." This rule qualified the sixth, which begins, "When a report, which has been read and lies for consideration, is called for it shall immediately be taken up" (*JCC*, XX, 477). In the vote on JM's motion, only the delegation of Georgia sided with Virginia. Of the delegates from states north of Virginia, John Morin Scott alone supported JM (*JCC*, XXII, 236–37).

On 6 May, over the opposition of the Virginia and South Carolina delegations, Congress finally adopted a motion to postpone a consideration of the Boudinot committee report—a postponement destined to extend until 31 July 1782 (*JCC*, XXII, 240–41, 423). The decision to postpone signified that the advocates of the report recognized their inability to secure the votes of nine or more states, requisite for its adoption, until New Hampshire and Connecticut should be represented in Congress by at least two delegates each.

Benjamin Harrison to Virginia Delegates

FC (Virginia State Library). In the hand of Charles Hay. Addressed to "The Virginia Delegates in Congress."

IN COUNCIL May 4th. 1782.

GENTLEMEN

I am much obliged to you for your favor by the last post;[1] the intelligence is agreable tho' there is no immediate prospect of arriving at the wished for period; yet it will come in time. Who is fully informed of their being in an error, will open their eyes.

We wish not to have the Military Stores in Boston sold, unless they will bring something near value;[2] we shall want them hereafter and they may then be got at less expence from where they now are than they can be [by] land carriage from any of the Iron works in this country. I am extreemly sorry I had not the pleasure of seeing the Chevalier whilst in Virginia. I was so extreemly lame that I could not wait on him, as I most certainly should have done if I had been well, and I had such repeated information of his coming up, that I did not write to him, expecting to see him every hour for ten days.[3]

Will one of you Gentlemen please to make an apology to him for me and assure him that I am extreemly mortified at not seeing him here. I am with great respect &c.

1 See Virginia Delegates to Harrison, 23 April 1782. The remainder of Harrison's sentence is obviously a veiled reference to the encoded part of that letter.

2 See *ibid.*; and Bradford to Virginia Delegates, 20 March 1782, and n. 2.

3 See Virginia Delegates to Harrison, 5 March, and n. 3; Randolph to JM, 11–13 April; JM to Randolph, 23 April 1782.

From Edmund Randolph

RC (LC: Madison Papers). The letter is not signed, but it is in Randolph's hand. Addressed to "The honble James Madison jr. of congress Philadelphia." Docketed by JM, "May 5. 1782."

RICHMOND May 5. 1782.

DEAR SIR

Your flattering urgency for my return, contained in your favor of the 23. Ulto. was answered by anticipation in my letter of last week.[1] I still adhere to the same inclination to revisit you.

By the next post, I will remit a draught for the 20 £.[2] In the meantime should you wish an earlier payment, apply to Mr. Hollingsworth for the profits of two hogsheads of tobo, sent by Mr. Coan, the Jew in this town, to his care for my order.[3]

Mr. Jefferson has been forced into the legislative service of the country: and some other counties impressed by the embarrassment of the times, have elected the most able men, altho' they did not offer themselves.[4]

I have stumbled upon a treasure of Virginian antiquity. The office of the clerk of the General court[5] has furnished me with the proceedings of the treasurer and company; prior to the dissolution of the charter.[6] Perhaps this clue will lead to something pointed. Many records, subsequent to that period, but before the revolution in 1688, do also exist. The rumor increases concerning the revival of paper money: but the particular qualities to be attributed to it are still within the breast of its patrons.[7]

There was a desideratum in your letter, respecting Mr. Dana. I wish to learn, what antidote was prepared by your report on the letters, committed on the morning of my departure, to the fury of that gentleman.[8]

We hear nothing, worthy of your attention. The next week (Monday being the first day of the session)[9] will certainly generate news.

yrs. mo. sincerely.

[1] See JM to Randolph, 23 April 1782. Since the letter of Randolph to JM of 26 April is irrelevant, Randolph either wrote to him "last week" another letter, now missing, or should have cited his letter of 19 April (*q.v.*).

[2] See Randolph to JM, 11–13 April, and 16–17 May 1782. See also Account with Randolph, *ca.* 1 May 1782, and editorial note.

[3] Probably Levi Hollingsworth, a Philadelphia merchant and business acquaint-

ance of JM (*Papers of Madison,* II, 98, n. 3), and Jacob I. Cohen (1744–1823) of the Richmond mercantile firm of Isaacs, Cohen & Co. (*Virginia Gazette,* 22 June 1782). Cohen had emigrated to Pennsylvania from Bavaria in 1773. Removing to South Carolina, he fought as a volunteer against the British. In 1780 he settled in Richmond, where in 1790 he served as city recorder and in 1795 as a member of the common council. He moved to Philadelphia in 1806 and remained there until his death (Isaac Landman, ed., *The Universal Jewish Encyclopedia* [10 vols.; New York, 1939–43], III, 233–34).

[4] See Pendleton to JM, 15 April 1782, and n. 14. Jefferson's refusal to serve posed the constitutional issue of his right to disregard the will of the voters of Albemarle County, even though he had not declared his candidacy. The issue was not settled. Officially he continued to be a delegate during the May and October sessions of the legislature in 1782, but he did not take his seat, and a majority in the House of Delegates in May apparently rejected a proposal to have the sergeant at arms compel him to attend (Boyd, *Papers of Jefferson,* VI, 174–75, 179, 183–87; Randolph to JM, 16–17 May 1782). As already mentioned, the General Assembly on 1 June 1782 named Jefferson to a committee to draft a defense of Virginia's title to its western lands. His participation in the work of this group was meager at best (JM to Randolph, 1 May 1782, n. 7; Boyd, *Papers of Jefferson,* VI, 189, 652–54).

Among the notable members of the Virginia House of Delegates in the May 1782 session were Patrick Henry, Arthur Lee, Richard Henry Lee, John Marshall, James Monroe, Thomas Nelson, John Page, David Ross, Meriwether Smith, and John Tyler. Gentlemen of similar ability in the Senate included Archibald Cary, William Fitzhugh, David Jameson, and Henry Lee (Swem and Williams, *Register,* pp. 15–16).

[5] John Brown (1750–1810) of Richmond was appointed clerk of the General Court in 1781. Thereafter until his death he served almost continuously as clerk of the state District Court of Richmond and of the Virginia Court of Appeals. During many of these years he was also a successful merchant (Samuel Bassett French Papers, p. 716, and photocopy of Register, 1662–1797, of the Bruton Parish Church, Williamsburg, Va., MSS in Virginia State Library; *Virginia Argus* [Richmond], 2 November 1810).

[6] The records of the treasurer and the Virginia Company of London which Randolph saw were probably burned in the Richmond fire of 2–3 April 1865 (H. R. McIlwaine, ed., *Minutes of the Council and General Court of Colonial Virginia, 1622–1632, 1670–1676* [Richmond, 1924], p. v).

[7] The session of the Virginia General Assembly of May 1782 enacted no law either to issue more paper money or to revive the legal-tender quality of earlier emissions (Pendleton to JM, 28 January, n. 11; Randolph to JM, 10 May 1782; Hening, *Statutes,* XI, 9–103).

[8] The meaning of this sentence would have been clearer if Randolph had placed "to the fury of that gentleman" immediately after "antidote." See JM to Randolph, 23 April, and n. 14; 14 May; Motion on Instructions to Dana, 27 May 1782.

[9] The Virginia General Assembly convened on 6 May but the House of Delegates did not have a quorum until nine days later (Minute Book, House of Delegates, May 1782, pp. 43, 44).

Motion on Supplies for Southern Army

Printed text (*JCC*, XXII, 244).

[7 May 1782]

On motion of Mr. [James] Madison, seconded by Mr. [Ezekiel] Cornell,[1]

Resolved, unanimously,[2] That a committee be appointed to confer with the Superintendant of finance and Secretary at War, on the practicability and means of procuring supplies for the southern army by contracts, and report thereon.[3]

[1] The words in brackets are in the *JCC*. Ezekiel Cornell had entered Congress in June 1780 after considerable service as an officer in the continental army and the Rhode Island militia (*JCC*, XVII, 485). This experience fitted him to share prominently in the activities of Congress relating to the army. In January 1782 he helped draft a revised "Plan for Conducting the Inspector's Department." Nine months later, after long hesitation, he made Washington "exceedingly happy" by accepting the "Office of Inspector of the Contracts &c." (*JCC*, XXII, 30–33; Fitzpatrick, *Writings of Washington*, XXV, 185).

[2] These italicized words obviously were added after the adoption of the motion.

[3] See Harrison to Virginia Delegates, 9 February, and nn. 3 and 4; Virginia Delegates to Harrison, 25 February 1782, and n. 3. The motion was referred to John Rutledge, Theodorick Bland, and Samuel Osgood. David Ramsay (S.C.), who replaced Rutledge on the committee on 3 June, wrote the report which was presented on 21 June 1782. It included Robert Morris' assertion that because he lacked enough money to supply by contracts everywhere "was no reason why it should not be done where it could." Congress directed the secretary at war to "take every step in his power to discover the causes of delay, embezzlement, and other circumstances which have so frequently arrested the supplies for the southern army." Morris was ordered to report why that army could not be supplied by contracts (*JCC*, XXII, 244 n., 342–43). During the spring and summer of 1782 acrimonious disputes between high-ranking officers of the northern army and the contractors who supplied its food caused Morris much embarrassment (Clarence L. Ver Steeg, *Robert Morris*, pp. 142–49).

Report on Form of Public Audience for La Luzerne

MS (NA: PCC, No. 25, II, 99–103, 105, 105½). In small part, the report is in JM's hand. Docketed: "Report of Comtee relative to the Ceremonial on admitting the Minister of France to a Public Audience—Pass'd. May 7th 1782."

EDITORIAL NOTE

On 2 May 1782 the secretary for foreign affairs wrote to inform Congress that La Luzerne wished "a public audience" in order to deliver a letter from King Louis XVI "announcing the birth of a Dauphin" (Louis Joseph Xavier, d. 1789) on 22 October 1781 (*JCC*, XXII, 235, 262). With his letter, Livingston enclosed a summary description of the formalities attending the audience accorded on 6 August 1778 by Congress to Conrad Alexandre Gérard as the first diplomatic representative accredited by France and suggested a few alterations which would make that ceremony suitable for use at the reception of La Luzerne (NA: PCC, No. 79, II, 133–37; *JCC*, XI, 751–57; XXII, 246).

Upon receiving Livingston's notification on 2 May, Congress immediately designated 13 May as the date for the audience (*JCC*, XXII, 235). The docket of Livingston's letter states that, after it was read on 3 May, Congress referred it to John Rutledge, Elias Boudinot, and JM. Congress evidently instructed this committee to be guided by the secretary for foreign affairs' suggestions in recommending a ceremonial sufficiently elaborate and dignified to befit the importance of the occasion (William E. O'Donnell, *Chevalier de La Luzerne*, pp. 216–17, and nn.).

The committee's report, strongly reflecting Livingston's influence and mostly in the handwriting of a clerk, was laid before Congress on 7 May.

[7–9 May 1782]

The Committee to whom the Report of the Secretary of foreign affairs relative to the Ceremonial on admitting the Minister of France to a public Audience, beg leave to report the following, as proper to be adopted on this Occasion—[1]

The Minister shall come in his own coach to the state house, & shall be received at the foot of the steps by two Members of Congress deputed for that purpose, who shall conduct him to his seat in the room of Congress,

As the Minister enters, the President & the house shall rise, The president remaining covered. The Minister shall bow to the president & then to the house before he takes his seat. The President shall uncover his head as he returns his bow. The Minister shall then seat & cover himself. The Members conducting him shall sit on each side of him. The Members of the house shall seat themselves

When the Minister speaks he shall rise. The President & house shall remain sitting till he has spoken & delivered his Letter by his secretary to the secretary of Congress, who shall deliver it to be read by the interpreter in the original language. The interpreter shall then deliver a translation to be read by the secretary of Congress, after which the president shall deliver his answer standing & covered, the Minister & the house also standing but uncovered. The president & the Minister having bowed to each other, & the latter to the house, who shall be standing to receive it; he shall be reconducted to the foot of the stairs of the state house, in the same manner in which he came in

That after the Audience shall be over, the house shall adjourn,[2]

That places be assigned for the principals in the three[3] executive departments under Congress—and for the President of Executive Council of the state

That General Officers, Judges of appeals, the treasurer, Pay Master Genl[,] Comptroller, Auditor & Chaplains of Congress, the assistants & principal secretaries in each of the Departments, be admitted without the bar of the house.[4]

That the Secretary at War take order to receive the Minister with military honor, & to conclude the audience with the discharge of thirteen cannon—& a feu de joy of Musquetry[5] & for the display of fire works in the evening at 8 o'clock

That all that relates to the placing the persons particularly admitted[6] to the Audience, be under the direction of the Secretary of Congress

That each member of Congress be entitled to admit two persons & be furnished with tickets for that purpose by the Secretary.

That tickets be sent by the secretary for foreign affairs to such foreigners or other strangers as he may judge it proper to admit.

That on Monday next an entertainment be provided by Congress at the City Tavern,[7]

That a letter be written to the Commander in Chief, & to the commander in the southern department by the secretary for foreign affairs, informing them of the public annunciation of the birth of the Dauphin, that the same may be published in both armies, with such demonstrations of Joy as their commanders shall respectively direct[8]

That the Secretary for foreign Affairs also inform the Governors & Presidents of the respective States of the birth of an heir to the Crown of France,[9] that the people of each State may partake in the Joy which an event that so nearly affects the happiness of their great & generous Ally cannot fail to excite.[10]

[1] This preamble is in JM's hand.

[2] Following "adjourn," "when the president & Members shall individually pay their compliments to the Minr. of France" was crossed out. In this instance, unlike in the instances mentioned in the next four footnotes, the deletion probably represented a change made by Congress after the report was submitted.

[3] Following "That" at the beginning of this paragraph, "seats be provided" was eliminated as well as "great" after "three."

[4] In this paragraph, JM inserted "Pay Master Genl" and changed the last syllable of "within" to "out."

[5] JM interlineated "& a feu de joy of Musquetry."

[6] Apparently at JM's suggestion, "within the bar of Congress" was deleted after "admitted." He then inserted "particularly" before, and "to the Audience" after, "admitted."

[7] The State House Inn, built in 1693 and situated across Chestnut Street from Independence Hall (the State House of Pennsylvania, 1736–1799), the meeting place of Congress (Carroll Frey, *The Independence Square Neighborhood* [Philadelphia, 1926], p. 17). Following "Tavern," the words "to which shall be invited in the name of the president & Congress The Minister of France & his family" are struck out. The committee then left a broad space between the close of this paragraph and the beginning of the next. Who should be privileged to attend the "entertainment," who should arrange for it, and who should issue the invitations to it appear to have been the most difficult questions which the committee had to answer. Written on a separate piece of paper (fol. 105) by JM, or someone whose handwriting closely resembled his, is the following substitute for the deleted words given above, "tavern for the minister of france & his suite to be under the direction of the Superint of finance who may invite thereto such general Officers & foreigners of distinction in town as the president shall approve." After changing "Superint of finance" to "Secry. for F Affairs," the committee evidently accepted this emendation.

In a letter to Charles Thomson, Livingston refused to comply with the directive, declaring that the menial roles of "Presidents stewar[d]" and clerk were inconsistent with the dignity of his high office and an affront to his self-respect. Thereupon, probably as late as 9 May, Congress mollified Livingston by striking out "who may invite thereto such general Officers & foreigners of distinction in town as the president shall approve," and providing that the secretary "shall give invitations in the name of Congress to the president and council of Pennsylvania, the principals of the three executive departments under Congress, and such other persons as he may think proper" (*JCC*, XXII, 247–48; Burnett, *Letters*, VI, 346–47, and nn.). JM's share, if any, in rephrasing this paragraph to the satisfaction of Livingston and Congress is not evident. See Revised Reply of President of Congress to La Luzerne, 8–12 May 1782.

[8] Livingston complied with this portion of the resolution on 13 May, and Washington also informed Greene in a dispatch of 22 May (Wharton, *Revolutionary Diplomatic Correspondence*, V, 416–17, 436–37; Fitzpatrick, *Writings of Washington*, XXIV, 274, 276–77). The northern army celebrated the birth of the dauphin on 31 May at West Point, with more than five hundred guests present (Douglas

Southall Freeman, *George Washington, a Biography* [7 vols.; New York, 1948–57; Vol. VII, by J. A. Carroll and M. W. Ashworth], V, 416).

[9] Much to Governor Harrison's embarrassment, he did not receive Livingston's letter of 14 May on this subject until 16 July. See Randolph to JM, 18 July, and nn. 10 and 11; Harrison to Virginia Delegates, 19 July 1782.

[10] In NA: Miscellaneous Papers of the Continental Congress, 1774–1789, fols. 263–66, is another version of the committee's report. Although the report lacks the preamble and was not written by JM, he apparently added the docket, "2d Report on the Subject of the ceremonial on an audience demanded by the Minister of France May 1782." This draft includes passages which were deleted or reworded before the text reproduced above was submitted by the committee to Congress. "2d Report" possibly connotes that Livingston's suggestions, mentioned in the editorial note, were considered to be a first report and the text laid before Congress, a third version.

Virginia Delegates to Benjamin Harrison

RC (Virginia State Library). In JM's hand. Addressed to "His Excelly. The Governor of Virginia." Docketed: "Virga. Delegates Letter May 7th recd May 16. 82[.] Will soon send information as to Inhabitant[s] transfered from Jurisdiction of Virginia to that of Pensylvania. Fifty commissions forwarded by Secretary of Congress for armed Vessels. A vigorous effort to expel the enemy from our country called for." The "Fifty" should be "Twenty." Words written in the official cipher are italicized.

PHILADA. May 7. 1782[1]

SIR

Your Excellency's favor of the 27th. ulto. came to hand yesterday. There has not been since time sufficient to procure the information the Executive wish for relative to the inhabitants lately transferred from the jurisdiction of Virginia to that of Pennsylvania. We shall endeavor to obtain it for the next post.[2] The Se[c]retary of Congress assures us that 20 Commissions for armed Vessels were forwarded on the 30th. Ulto. in consequence of a letter from Mr. Blair on the subject.[3] If that number is insufficient the balance shall be supplied on the first notice.

The enclosed Gazette will furnish your Excellency with all the parliamentary intelligence by which we are as yet enabled to interpret the views of the Enemy. The perseverence of the antiministerial party in the supposed efficacy of conciliatory overtures seems to be no less obstinate than that of the Court has been with respect to military coercion, and as manifestly portends a delay of peace. The path of our duty under these circumstances cannot be mistaken. A scrupulous fidelity to our foreign engagements & a vigorous preparation for expelling the enemy from our Country must press them selves on every attention.[4]

Letters from Spain inform us that the Garrison taken at Minorca consisted of 26,00 including every description, but 1500 only of effective troops; and that this success of the Spanish arms would be followed by redoubled ardor in the siege of Gibraltar.[5] Our affairs at *this court make no progress whate*ver *toward the allyance sought for.* If it does *not take place* at *all* we shall have at *least the consolation* of *saveing the Mississippi.*[6]

We have been supplied with no news of late from the W. Indies, owing cheifly to the success of the Enemy's Cruisers on the inward as well as outward bound trade of this river, which is in a manner annihilated by them.[7]

We have the honor to be with sentiments of the highest respect Yr. Excelly's obt. & very hble servants.

J. MADISON JR.
THEOK: BLAND JR.

[1] As mentioned in the headnote, this date also appears in the docket of the letter. On 18 May the journal of the Virginia Council of State noted that "A Letter was writ to our Delegates in Congress in answer to theirs of the 7th instant" (*Journals of the Council of State*, III, 92). Yet Governor Harrison specified in his dispatch to the delegates on 18 May (*q.v.*) that he was acknowledging their letter of 4 May. Probably he or his clerk erred, because no letter from the delegates on that day, a Saturday, has been found. They usually wrote on post day, which was Tuesday of each week. Furthermore, Harrison's reply makes clear that, if the delegates wrote to him on 4 May, they must have commented on the same topics included in their dispatch three days later.

[2] See Harrison to Virginia Delegates, 27 April; and Virginia Delegates to Harrison, 28 May 1782, n. 27. The steps taken during the spring of 1782 by the legislature and executive of Pennsylvania to extend her jurisdiction effectively over the Monongahela and Youghiogheny valleys, and the strong likelihood that the boundary between that state and Virginia would soon be surveyed in conformance with the agreement reached at Baltimore in 1779, caused much unrest among the Virginia settlers in the disputed area. They feared that, once the line was determined upon, their land titles and their rights as citizens would be at the mercy of an "alien sovereign," and probably of the Indiana Company as well (Randolph to JM, 26 April 1782, and n. 2).

[3] In his letter of 18 April asking Charles Thomson for twenty more privateering commissions, Archibald Blair, clerk of the Council of State, remarked that there was "a great demand" for them in Virginia (NA: PCC, No. 71, II, 361). Thomson noted on the letter that he had received it on 30 April. Evidently he fulfilled the request the same day, but his reply has not been found.

[4] Most likely the delegates sent with their letter a copy of the *Pennsylvania Packet* of 7 May, which devoted much space to the debate of 7 February in the House

of Lords on a motion to make Cornwallis' surrender a subject of inquiry; to the debates from 27 February to 4 March in the Commons regarding the adoption of a resolution to abandon further efforts to subdue the colonies and in their stead to try conciliation as a means "to bring about peace and tranquility"; and to the response on 2 March of King George III to the address by the Commons "humbly" advocating this change of policy. The last sentence of this paragraph probably also reflects the delegates' knowledge that Vergennes and La Luzerne were disturbed lest American war weariness and British offers of generous political and economic concessions should seduce Congress to desert France and make a separate peace (William E. O'Donnell, *Chevalier de La Luzerne*, pp. 212–15). As part of the revised British strategy, Sir Henry Clinton had already ordered the royal forces on the North American mainland to suspend offensive operations (Benjamin F. Stevens, ed., *Campaign in Virginia*, I, xxvii; *Pennsylvania Packet*, 14 May 1782). On the date of the present letter General Sir Guy Carleton, who arrived in New York City on 5 May as Clinton's successor and as head of a peace commission, asked Washington by letter to inform Congress of the commission's readiness to begin negotiations. In his dispatch of 10 May forwarding to the president of Congress a copy of Carleton's overture, Washington expressed alarm at the great effect these maneuvers might have "upon the Exertions of the States which are already too feeble and void of energy." His personal belief was that "instead of relaxing we ought to improve the present Moment as the most favorable to our Wishes." That course vigorously pursued, "I think the game is our own" (Fitzpatrick, *Writings of Washington*, XXIV, 241–44).

[5] The *Pennsylvania Packet* of 7 May summarized the Articles of Capitulation of 5 February 1782, consequent upon the surrender the day before of the British garrison on Minorca to the Duc de Crillon. The delegates appear to be relaying information contained in William Carmichael's dispatch of 18 February to Livingston, which had been read in Congress on 6 May. Carmichael, however, stated that there had been 1,300 British troops fit for service on Minorca rather than 1,500 (Wharton, *Revolutionary Diplomatic Correspondence*, V, 175; JM to Lee, 7 May 1782). In the present letter JM obviously intended to write 2,600 rather than "26,00."

[6] Besides Carmichael's letter, mentioned in n. 5, Congress also listened on 6 May to his dispatch of 27 February, and to Jay's letter of the 6th of that month (JM to Lee, 7 May 1782; Wharton, *Revolutionary Diplomatic Correspondence*, V, 150–51, 204–5; NA: PCC, No. 185, III, 26). These communications emphasized the unwillingness of the court of Madrid to begin negotiations looking toward a treaty of alliance. Probably the delegates of Virginia were not made unhappy by Spain's procrastination, because the absence of an alliance, now that the military outlook had brightened, would spare Congress from sacrificing American claims to the free navigation of the Mississippi River (Report Approving Jay's Negotiations with Spain, 22 April, and nn. 3, 5; Motion Approving Jay's Negotiations with Spain, 30 April 1782, and editorial note).

[7] See Motion on Protection of Commerce, 2 May 1782, and n. 1. The *Pennsylvania Packet* of 14 May listed three dozen British ships which were infesting the American coast.

To Arthur Lee

RC (Harvard University Library). The cover is missing. JM addressed the letter to "The Hon. A. Lee, Esq.," according to the version, wrongly dated "May, 1778," published in Richard Henry Lee, *Life of Arthur Lee, LL.D.* (2 vols.; Boston, 1829), II, 331–32. In Arthur Lee's handwriting, in the right-hand margin of the manuscript's second page, appears a notation, obviously relating to the price of tobacco, reading, "Deep Creek heavy /25 pr C.wt Jas River Indian Creek." Deep Creek, in the northwestern part of Lancaster County, flows into the Rappahannock River. Indian Creek forms a small portion of the common boundaries of Lancaster and Northumberland counties and flows into Chesapeake Bay. Both creeks were the sites of tobacco-inspection warehouses. See Jones to JM, 21 May 1782, and n. 6.

PHILADA. May [7,] 1782[1]

DEAR SIR

The letter inclosed[2] herewith came to my hands from the Eastern post. I forward it not knowing how far its contents may interest you.

The parliamentary intelligence published in the gazette of this morning[3] shews that[4] some revolution in the Councils of the Legislative branch has taken place, which will probably have some effect on those of the Executive. But as the delusive idea of a federal[5] if not a political connection with this Country founded on the ruins of its connection with France, still pervades their policy, no conclusion whatever can be drawn from it that will justify the smallest relaxation in our public measures. The efficacy of conciliatory overtures seems to be as foolishly & obstinately persisted in by one party as that of Military coercion has been by the other; and if the former should be indulged in their favorite experiment, it is more probable that their disappointment & vexation will make them converts to the views of the latter, than that both parties will lay aside their prejudices & embrace the terms we hold out to them.[6]

A letter from Mr. Jay & two from Mr. Carmichael were recd. yesterday. They all speak the same language with that recd. from the former a little before you left us. The success of the Spanish arms at Minorca will we are told be followed by redoubled efforts against Gibralter.[7]

We have several times repeated our call for the order[8] on the Western Cessions, and have in every instance experienced a repetition of the same indecent obstructions & evasions of which you were a witness, & which nothing will explain but the cause to which we have from the beginning imputed them.[9] It will neither be consistent with the respect we owe to our own public characters nor with the dignity of those we serve, to persist longer in fruitless applications to Congress for an answer. We shall therefore wind up the business as well as we can in a few days,[10] and transmit a state of it for the G. Assembly, who will certainly be fully justified in taking any course with respect to their Western claims which the interest of the State shall prescribe.

I am Dr [Sr?] [yr.] sincere frd. & hble sert.

J MADISON JR

1 JM probably meant to insert "7" in the date line. The contents of this letter resemble those of the delegates' dispatch of 7 May to Harrison (*q.v.*).

2 Not identified.

3 See Virginia Delegates to Harrison, 7 May 1782, n. 4.

4 Here JM heavily deleted a word that may have been "considerable."

5 JM replaced "commercial" with "federal."

6 See Virginia Delegates to Harrison, 7 May 1782, and n. 4. For the peace terms, see Instructions on Peace Negotiations, 7 January, editorial note and nn.

7 See Virginia Delegates to Harrison, 7 May 1782, nn. 5 and 6. JM may refer to Jay's letter of 3 October 1781. Read in Congress on 18 March, this dispatch had been referred to a committee, under JM's chairmanship, which rendered its report on 22 April 1782, only a day or two before Lee left Philadelphia to return to Virginia (JM to Randolph, 9 April, n. 5; Report Approving Jay's Negotiations with Spain, 22 April 1782, and n. 2).

8 The "order of the Day" in Congress from 1 to 6 May 1782 had been the report of the Boudinot committee on the western lands (Motion on Point of Order, 3 May 1782, n. 1).

9 See Motion To Amend Lee's Motion on Western Lands, 18 April, and n. 1; Virginia Delegates to Harrison, 23 April; JM to Randolph, 1 May, and n. 6; Observations Relating to Influence of Vermont and Territorial Claims, 1 May, and n. 9; Motion on Delegates' Financial Interest in West, 2 May, and nn. 1, 4; Motion on Point of Order, 3 May 1782, and nn.

10 JM evidently viewed the vote in Congress on 6 May to postpone a consideration of the Boudinot committee report (n. 8, above) as merely another temporary decision, adverse to the wishes of the delegates from Virginia, which they might be able to reverse within a few days. As already mentioned, the issue of the western lands was not revived until 31 July (Motion on Point of Order, 3 May 1782, n. 2). See also Burnett, *Letters*, VI, 343.

To Edmund Randolph

Printed text (Madison, *Papers* [Gilpin ed.], I, 125–26).

PHILADELPHIA, May [7], 1782.[1]

DEAR SIR,

The enclosed gazette details all the information which we have received relative to the parliamentary advances towards a negotiation with the United States. The first reports which issued from the packet which brought them, were of a very different complexion, and raised high expectations of peace. We now find the ideas of the opposition, as well as the Ministry, to be far short of the only condition on which it can take place. Those who are the farthest reconciled to concessions calculate on a dissolution of the compact with France. The Ministry will yield to the experiment, and turn the result upon their adversaries. Our business is plain. Fidelity to our allies, and vigor in military preparation,—these, and these alone, will secure us against all political devices.[2]

We have received no intelligence which speaks a danger of a separate peace between the Dutch and Great Britain. Mr. Adams' request of a categorical answer was taken, *ad referendum*, prior, if I mistake not, to the knowledge of Cornwallis' fate; and it is not likely that after that event they would be less disposed to respect our overtures, or reject those of the enemy.[3]

We have letters from Mr. Jay and Mr. Carmichael of as late date as the twenty-seventh of February. They differ in nothing from the style of the former.[4] The conduct of the Spanish Court subsequent to the date of the letter received the day preceding your departure, corresponds entirely with the tenor of it as therein related.[5] Mr. Jones will inform you of the act of Congress which that letter produced.[6]

We have made no progress in the Western subject. We mean to desist, after one or two more attempts,[7] and state the matter to the Assembly by next post, expecting that they will pursue such measures as their interest prescribes, without regard to the resolutions which proposed the cession.[8]

I beg you to keep me punctually informed of every legislative step touching the Western territory. I suppose the cession cannot fail to be revoked, or, at least, a day of limitation set to it.[9] The condition relative to the companies will certainly be adhered to in every event.[10] I find that those who have been against us do not wish to lose sight of the prospect altogether. If the State is firm and prudent, I have little doubt that she will be again courted. Previous to Mr. Jones' departure, our opinions were united on the expediency of making the impost of five per cent. subservient to an honorable adjustment of territory and accounts. I have since discovered that Varnum is left out, the latter having promoted it, and that Chase is inflexible against it. Massachusetts also holds out. The expedient, therefore, would not be efficacious, and clamors would be drawn on Virginia, which it would be best should fall elsewhere.[11] Show this to Mr. Jones. He will be with you about the twentieth instant.[12]

[1] The close resemblance between the comments in the first paragraph of this letter and the second paragraph of the Virginia delegates' dispatch of 7 May to Governor Harrison (*q.v.*) permits little doubt that both communications were written on that day.

[2] See Virginia Delegates to Harrison, 7 May 1782, n. 4.

[3] Congress' latest word from John Adams had been his dispatches of 4, 13, and 14 December 1781, received on 18 March 1782, the day on which Randolph left Philadelphia to return to Virginia (Virginia Delegates to Harrison, 19 March 1782; Wharton, *Revolutionary Diplomatic Correspondence,* V, 36–38, 43–44, 49–50; *JCC,* XXII, 140).

In his letter of 4 December, written about a week after the government of the Netherlands and Adams had first heard of Cornwallis' surrender, Adams acknowledged the receipt of the resolutions of Congress of 16 August, drafted by Randolph and Thomas McKean, directing him to seek an alliance with the Netherlands for the duration of the war (*JCC,* XXI, 876–80). If such a pact should be consummated, the result would be in effect the creation of a quadruple alliance, since France was leagued with both Spain and the United States.

In his dispatch of 13 December Adams reported the willingness of the British ministry to have Tsarina Catherine II of Russia mediate a peace between Great Britain and the Netherlands, provided that the latter cease harboring "American pirates" and extending "rebel subjects" other favors equivalent to being in "a secret league" with them. The next day Adams expressed the belief that a Dutch-American alliance was inevitable. He cautioned, however, that this outcome would be "studiously and zealously slow" in coming, in part because each of the provinces as well as the Prince of Orange and Nassau would have to acquiesce to it. JM probably wrote on this subject what Randolph would recognize as irony. JM's reference to a "categorical answer" suggests Adams' memorial of 19 April 1781, in which he argued that the Netherlands "should make haste to acknowledge the independence of the United States and form equitable treaties with them." This memorial was taken *ad referendum* by the States-General (Wharton, *Revolutionary Diplomatic Correspondence,* IV, 370–77, 402–3; *Papers of Madison,* III, 281–82; 282, n. 2).

[4] See Virginia Delegates to Harrison, 7 May 1782, nn. 5 and 6.

[5] JM here refers to Jay's letter of 3 October 1781, read in Congress on 18 March 1782 (Report on Foreign Dispatches, 20 March 1782, and n. 1).

[6] See Motion Approving Jay's Negotiations with Spain, 30 April 1782. Joseph Jones left Philadelphia on 2 May for his home in Virginia (JM to Randolph, 9 April 1782, n. 6).

[7] See JM to Lee, 7 May 1782, and nn. 8, 9, 10.

[8] On 2 January 1781 the Virginia General Assembly had adopted resolutions offering to Congress most of the territory in the Old Northwest. See *Papers of Madison,* II, 300–301; and n. 10, below. For the statement intended for the General Assembly "by the next post," see Virginia Delegates to Harrison, 14 May 1782, and n. 3.

[9] See Virginia Delegates to Harrison, 12 March, n. 4; JM to Randolph, 9 April, n. 5, and 1 May 1782, n. 7.

[10] One of the provisos limiting Virginia's offer of cession was that Congress, upon accepting it, must declare "absolutely void and of no effect" any alleged land title in the ceded area derived from purchases or gifts "from any Indian or Indians, or from any Indian nation or nations" (*Journal of the House of Delegates,* October 1780, p. 80). See also Motion To Amend Lee's Motion on Western Lands, 18 April; JM to Randolph, 1 May, n. 8; Observations Relating to Influence of Vermont and Territorial Claims, 1 May 1782, and n. 9.

[11] JM, Bland, and Jones apparently had agreed, before Jones left Philadelphia on 2 May, to withhold their support from measures designed to bring pressure upon states which had not yet ratified the proposed 5 per cent impost amendment to the Articles of Confederation until Congress should make an "honorable adjustment" of Virginia's financial accounts and deal fairly with her offer to cede her lands north and west of the Ohio River. After having ratified the impost amendment in the session of May 1781, the Virginia General Assembly in its November session of that year decided to hold the ratification in abeyance until all the other states should agree to the amendment (Hening, *Statutes,* X, 409–10, 451; *JCC,* XX, 750; *Papers of Madison,* III, 349, n. 7). JM and Bland evidently expected Jones, upon reaching Richmond, to make their "expedient" known to Governor Harrison and the leaders of the General Assembly.

What occurred between 2 and 7 May to convince JM that the delegates' plan of action was no longer feasible is not altogether clear. By 7 May, unlike five days earlier, he knew that the opponents of Virginia's terms of cession had the voting strength to postpone indefinitely a decision upon the offer. Furthermore, he probably had heard that James Mitchell Varnum was not among the delegates to Congress elected in Rhode Island on 1 May (*JCC,* XXII, 320). Until he left Congress on 16 November 1781, Varnum had been a staunch advocate of the impost amendment and had supported the Virginians' effort to induce Congress to vote conclusively upon Virginia's offer of cession (William R. Staples, *Rhode Island in the Continental Congress* [Providence, 1870], pp. 325–26, 334–36, 346–50; *JCC,* XXI, 1114). Without Varnum, the delegation from Rhode Island thereafter would unanimously oppose the impost amendment and Virginia's offer of cession (*JCC,* XXII, 240–41, 424, 644–45).

Samuel Chase (1741–1811), both as a Marylander and an investor in the Illinois-Wabash Company, had fought against the terms of cession offered by Virginia (Thomas P. Abernethy, *Western Lands and the American Revolution,* pp. 171, 239). He was a member of the House of Delegates of the General Assembly of his state and a delegate-elect to Congress, but he had not attended Congress since the autumn of 1778, and although his early arrival perhaps was expected in May 1782, he would never serve in that body again (Burnett, *Letters,* VI, 366). When JM wrote on 7 May 1782, he probably knew that the Maryland Assembly was much divided on the issue of ratifying the impost amendment and appeared about to reject it as a result of the opposition of Chase and other influential legislators.

The simultaneous struggle in the Massachusetts General Court over the same issue seemed also to be going against the advocates of the amendment. For these reasons JM by 7 May had clearly decided that the onus of defeating, or at least of withholding passage of, the amendment need not, and should not, be borne by Virginia. Unknown of course to him, Massachusetts had acquiesced to the amendment three days before; Maryland and Connecticut also would do so in June 1782 (*JCC*, XXII, 333 n., 366, 388; Burnett, *Letters*, VI, 372; W[illiam] H[and] Browne *et al.*, eds., *Archives of Maryland* [65 vols.; Baltimore, 1883–1952], XLVIII, 213; J. Thomas Scharf, *History of Maryland from the Earliest Period to the Present Day* [3 vols.; Baltimore, 1879], II, 526–27, 527 n.). By that time only Georgia and Rhode Island had not ratified.

[12] JM to Pendleton, 23 April 1782, n. 10.

Revised Reply of President of Congress to La Luzerne

Draft (LC: Papers of Continental Congress Miscellany, Folder 103). Apparently in the hand of a clerk, except for the suggestions of JM.

PHILADELPHIA, May [*ca.* 8–12,] 1782[1]

SIR,

The repeated Instances of Friendship[2] which the United States of America[3] have received from His Most Christian Majesty give him too just a title to their affections to permit them to be indifferent to any event which interests[4] his happiness. Be assured Sir[5] that Congress learn with the most lively Satisfaction that it has pleased the divine giver of all good gifts to bless their august ally with an heir to his throne. Our earnest[6] prayer is that he may with it inherit[7] the virtues which have acquired to his Majesty so much glory & to his dominions so much prosperity, and which will be the means of cementing & strengthening the Union so happily established between the two[8] Nations.[9]

[1] In this line, now much faded, the unidentified writer left a space between "May" and "1782" for the insertion of the exact date. Above and to the right of the line JM wrote "[1782]" and "May 13?]," the day when La Luzerne announced to Congress the birth of the dauphin. JM and the other members of the committee appointed to recommend the nature of the ceremony evidently had the preparation of the reply of the president of Congress to La Luzerne as one of their tasks. Presumably they completed it at least a day or two before the 13th (Report on Form of Public Audience for La Luzerne, 7–9 May 1782, editorial note). See also Motion on Chairman of Congress, 15 April 1782, n. 2.

[2] "Instances of Friendship" was written by JM above a deleted "favor."

[3] JM interlineated "of America."

[4] JM's substitution for "affects."

[5] This word is in JM's hand.

[6] Following "throne," the original version read "It will be their" instead of JM's "Our earnest." He also inserted "is" after the next word, "prayer."
[7] In the original draft, "his virtues" followed "inherit" to conclude the sentence. JM interlineated "royal Father's" between "his" and "virtues," before deleting all four words and writing the rest of the paragraph after "inherit."
[8] After writing "Allied," JM replaced it with "two."
[9] The manuscript as first written ran for eighteen more lines of text. These were deleted, probably by JM. At the ceremony the president of Congress read the paragraph as given above but extended it with a passage of nearly the same length suggested by Livingston (*JCC*, XXII, 262–63; Wharton, *Revolutionary Diplomatic Correspondence*, V, 416).

Motion on Mission to Portugal

Printed text (*JCC*, XXII, 250).

[8 May 1782]

Thereupon,[1] on motion of Mr. [James] Madison, seconded by Mr. [Edward] Telfair,[2]

Resolved, That it be an instruction to Mr. Jay not to send Mr. Carmichael to the Court of Portugal in pursuance of the resolution of the 11th day of July, 1781, unless he shall have good grounds to expect that such a measure will attain the object proposed by the Superintendant of Finance.[3]

[1] This motion was a response to Robert R. Livingston's letter of 7 May to Congress. In Jay's dispatch of 3 October 1781, read in Congress on 18 March 1782 (*JCC*, XXII, 140–41, and n.), the minister to Spain had written that to send an accredited envoy to Portugal "could do no harm, and might do good; I am therefore for it" (Wharton, *Revolutionary Diplomatic Correspondence*, IV, 764). Countering this suggestion, Livingston advised that, because the possibility of an envoy's success in Lisbon was so remote, Congress should not incur the financial cost or the "loss of reputation" which would be the penalty of the mission's failure. Influenced by Great Britain, Portugal had barred American ships from her harbors and occasionally confiscated a vessel obliged by stress of weather or other emergency to disregard the injunction (*ibid.*, V, 586; *JCC*, VI, 1035–36, 1057; VII, 318). On 21 June 1780, when Arnold Henry Dohrman, a merchant of Lisbon, was appointed agent of the United States to help distressed American seamen who were stranded in Portugal (*Papers of Madison*, II, 34, n. 4), Congress directed Jay to ascertain whether "any advantageous connection" could be effected with the court of Lisbon (*JCC*, XVII, 542). Jay's inability to be sanguine in this regard, and the continuing discrimination by that court against American shipping, no doubt largely accounted for Livingston's adverse recommendation.
[2] The words in brackets are in the *JCC*. Edward Telfair (1735–1807) of Scottish nativity, had been a merchant in Savannah since 1766. His service as a delegate in Congress extended through most of the period, 1777–1783. He was governor of Georgia in 1786 and from 1790 to 1793.

3 In a letter on 9 July 1781 to the president of Congress, Robert Morris advised that, in view of the improbability that public or private sources in the United States or in France or the Netherlands could be further relied upon to relieve the desperate need of money, John Jay be extended greater discretionary powers in bargaining for a subsidy or loan from the court of Spain and be directed "to try the Court of Portugal also." Morris suggested that Lisbon might be enticed by an offer of more "Extensive unfettered" commercial privileges than were accorded to Portugal by Great Britain. If William Carmichael "can be spared from Madrid," Morris concluded, Jay would do well to send him "in his private capacity" to Lisbon, where he quickly could ascertain "what may be expected from that Quarter, and Mr. Jay can then Act Accordingly" (NA: PCC, No. 137, I, 69–76). On 11 July 1781 Congress adopted a resolution conforming fully with Morris' counsel (*JCC*, XX, 739). In his letter of 7 May 1782, mentioned in n. 1, Livingston recommended that this resolution be repealed. By adopting JM's motion, Congress qualified its acceptance of Livingston's advice. Portugal continued to bar American shipping from her harbors until 15 February 1783 (Wharton, *Revolutionary Diplomatic Correspondence,* VI, 294).

Motion on Promotion of Colonel Otho Holland Williams

MS (NA: PCC, No. 36, I, 299). In JM's hand. Charles Thomson wrote "Madison. Bland." at the top of the manuscript to signify that JM made the motion and Theodorick Bland seconded it. Docketed, "Motion of Mr Madison seconded by Mr Bland respectg the promotion of Col. O Williams passed May 9th 1782."

[9 May 1782]

General Green commandg. the Army of the U. S. in the S. Department, having represented to Congress[1] that the appointment of a Brigadr. General to command a Brigade in the Maryland line of the Army was rendered expedient by the proposed formation of the sd. line into 2 brigades, & having recommended Col. Otho Williams[2] as an officer whose distinguished Talents & services give him a just pretension to such appointment, which recommendation is also supported by the testimony of the Commander in Chief in favr. of the said officer,[3]

Resolved That in consideration of the distinguished Talents & Services of Col. O. Williams he be & hereby is appointed a Brigadr. General in the Army of the U. States.

1 On 8 May Joseph Montgomery moved that Colonel Otho H. Williams be promoted to brigadier general in accord with the recommendation of General Greene in his letter of 10 February 1782 (NA: PCC, No. 155, II, 417). Thereupon, although unanimously supported by the delegates from Massachusetts, New Jersey, Virginia,

and Georgia, an amendment by Abraham Clark to couple the name of Colonel Elias Dayton of New Jersey with that of Williams was rejected "as being out of order" (*JCC*, XXII, 248–49). On 9 May, after Clark and his colleagues from New Jersey failed to attract any backing except that of South Carolina for their resolution that "two brigadiers be appointed in the army of the United States," JM introduced his motion. Following unsuccessful efforts to postpone its consideration and strike out its preamble, the resolution was adopted by an unrecorded vote (*JCC*, XXII, 251–53). Congress delayed the promotion of Colonel Dayton until 7 January 1783 (*JCC*, XXIV, 38).

[2] See *Papers of Madison*, III, 27, n. 6. On 10 December 1776 Otho Holland Williams (1749–1794), a merchant of Frederick County, Md., was advanced to the rank of colonel and appointed to command the 6th Maryland Regiment after about eighteen months of service as an officer in the continental army. By capturing him on 16 November of that year and confining him for much of the time until 16 January 1778 in the provost jail in New York City, the British shattered his robust health. As Horatio Gates's deputy adjutant general and Nathanael Greene's adjutant general, Williams rendered distinguished service during the campaign in the Carolinas in 1780 and 1781. He resigned his commission in January 1783 to accept an appointment by Maryland as naval officer of the Baltimore district. Appointed on 4 August 1789 by President Washington to be collector for the district of Baltimore, Williams retained this post until his death, although ill health frequently kept him from his office for many weeks (*Journal of the Executive Proceedings of the Senate of the United States of America*, I [Washington, 1828], 14, 164).

[3] On 4 December 1781 in a letter to President Hanson, Washington stated that Williams had "ever stood high in my estimation" and deserved to be promoted (Fitzpatrick, *Writings of Washington*, XXIII, 370).

From Edmund Randolph

RC (LC: Madison Papers). Addressed to "The honble James Madison jr. of congress Philadelphia," but unsigned. The handwriting and contents of the letter permit no doubt that Randolph wrote it. Words encoded by him in the official cipher are here italicized.

PETTUS'S[1] NEAR RICHMOND May 10, 1782.

DEAR SIR

Yesterday I received your favor of the 1st. instant, and took Dr. Lee by the hand at almost the same moment.[2] His brother Richard Henry and himself, being members of the house of delegates, will probably give the tone to the politicks of this session, should Mr. Jefferson persist in his unpardonable rage for retirement, and Mr. Henry delay his attendance, (as he possibly may, not being as yet heard of,)[3] until the plans of the house are matured. On this event, there will be little danger of paper-money, should Mr. R. H. Lee retain his ancient abhorrence of this medium.[4]

The Dr. overflows with territorial Zeal: and something will certainly fall from the pen of the legislature.[5] Mr. Jefferson must undertake the guidance of the work; or, I fear, the deviation will be great from the path of argument, which ought to be trodden on this occasion.[6] For the Dr. seems to think, that general reasoning will be sufficient; but this, tho' powerful, does not comprehend those topics, which demonstrate the opinion of british sovereigns in favour of the existence of the charter of 1609, even after the abolition of the company's rights, and which exhibit their construction of the [nature of?] that charter.[7] I am somewhat surprized at Mr. Jefferson's "want of information of the ground, on which the report of the committee places the controversy." Dr. Lee inclosed a copy of it to him, and intrusted it to my care. The letter did, I am sure, reach him.[8]

Should an opposition be raised *to the reelection of Colonel Bland, he* will certainly *be excluded from* the *new de*[*le*][9]*gation. The governor indirectly* hints the impropriety of *his conduct* in *almost every company*. I wish, you could be delivered *from the schism*, which is likely to prevail *between you in the management* of the *controversy*. I trust however, that the evil will not have grown too inveterate for correction, *before you will receive strict instructions*. Certainly the faculties of the human mind have undergone a change with our government. Else it must be rank suicide *to oppose* the *title of* the *natives* to *the*[10] *claims* of the *companies*.[11]

There will probably be a contest for the chair between Mr. Tyler and Mr. R. H. Lee. The current runs strongly on the side of the former[.][12] [A]bout 61. members of the house of delegates have qualified:

By a vessel,[13] which arrived a few days ago, from the West Indies, we learn that the french fleet is in truth inferior to Rodney and fixed at Martinique. Not that there is not a sufficient naval force of the enemies of G. Britain, dispersed among the islands, to crush the knight:[14] for the Spaniards have 15 or 16 sail of the line at S. Domingo, and the Dutch 10 or 12. at St. Eustatius: but he continues to cruize in the track, by which a junction would be attempted, and thus renders himself equal to the whole. Perhaps then, as Rivington's account is confirmed thro' this channel, we may apprehend the probability of it.[15]

I am going to town this morning in expectation of receiving a draught on Phila. for 20 £, according to the promise of Mr. Ross's partner.[16] Should I fail to inclose it, you must attribute the omission to no neglect, nor indeed to any poverty, as far as that sum goes, on my part.

I can command the money, and will send it, should I miscarry in a bill, by the first opportunity for the conveyance of Specie.[17]

The movements of the French army are doubtless better known in Philadelphia, than here. But were we to judge from appearances, and from the engagement of [a] large number of waggons, we might infer an intention to leave the lower parts of the country at least. It is said, that the officers freely declare, that the troops are about to march from Wmsburg: but their destination is wholly secret.[18]

Governor Harrison has more than once expressed his astonishment at the application of the secretary for foreign affairs for the title-papers of Virginia. He requested an explanation of this step, supposing that he sees on every wall the shadow of a dagger uplifted *against the back-lands*. The secretary ought indeed to have attended to the jealousy entertained in Virginia of the unwarrantable claims of congress upon the subject of territory and to have been explicit in assigning the grounds of his requisition:[19] but it seems very natural, when we consider that the reason, upon which he entered into the discussion, was the suspension of the first report, and the apparent impracticability of carrying it thro' congress.[20]

[Th]e governor will inclose to you a letter from the minister of France and Mr. Morris. Surely the minister, when we conversed with him about the forwarding of the supplies, understood the payment to be postponed until the end of the war.[21]

[1] See Randolph to JM, 11–13 April 1782, n. 2.

[2] See JM to Randolph, 1 May 1782, and n. 3.

[3] See Randolph to JM, 5 May 1782, n. 4. Patrick Henry, Arthur Lee, and Richard Henry Lee were delegates from Henry, Prince William, and Westmoreland counties, respectively (Swem and Williams, *Register*, pp. 15–16). Since the journal of the General Assembly for the session of May 1782 is lost, the time of Henry's first appearance in the House of Delegates cannot be established with certainty. Although Randolph in his letter of 21–24 May (*q.v.*) informed JM that Henry had arrived "two or three days ago," the manuscript records of the House of Delegates first note his presence on 23 May (Minute Book, House of Delegates, May 1782, p. 51).

[4] Richard Henry Lee's "abhorrence" dated back at least to his service as a delegate from Westmoreland County in the House of Burgesses, 1758–1775. During his first seven years there he declined, unlike most of his colleagues, to regard the able and powerful John Robinson, speaker of the House and treasurer of the province, with either respect or affection. The immediate sequel to the death of Robinson on 11 May 1766 was the disclosure that his "humanity and good nature" had led him to violate his trust by lending over £100,000 in paper currency from the treasury to many of the principal men of Virginia. He had compounded his grave fault by requiring little or no security from them and leaving his records in confusion. At least most of the borrowers had assumed that Robinson was accommodat-

ing them from his own very extensive resources. Lee had taken a prominent part in uncovering the scandal, partly, it would seem, because he aspired to succeed Robinson as speaker and treasurer (David John Mays, *Edmund Pendleton, 1721–1803* [2 vols.; Cambridge, Mass., 1952], I, 174–86). Although the acute shortage of specie in Virginia had made paper currency almost a necessity, the excessive amount of these bills of credit invited their misuse. The Robinson affair helps to explain why Lee, when a delegate from Virginia in the Second Continental Congress (1775–1780, 1784–1787), advocated collecting more taxes, floating more loans, practicing greater economy, and fixing the prices of more commodities, in order to lessen the need for printing certificates. "The inundation of money," he had written on 9 June 1779, "appears to have overflowed virtue, and I fear will bury the liberty of America in the same grave" (Burnett, *Letters*, II, 336, 568; Edmund C. Burnett, *The Continental Congress*, p. 410).

[5] See JM to Randolph, 9 April, and n. 5, and 1 May, n. 7; JM to Arthur Lee ("The Dr."), 7 May; Randolph to JM, 1 June 1782.

[6] See JM to Jefferson, 15 January, and 16 April; Jefferson to JM, 24 March 1782.

[7] Following "the" in the manuscript, a faint mark points to a blurred interlineation of perhaps three or four short words. The "nature of" represents an editorial surmise of the sense of what is illegible.

For the action of the Privy Council to which Randolph seems to refer, see JM to Randolph, 9 April 1782, and n. 2. Randolph's observation that Arthur Lee "seems to think, that general reasoning will be sufficient" is supported by Lee's "A Concise view of tittle of Virginia to the Western lands in replication of a pamplet called Public Good," an undated seventeen-page manuscript in the Virginia State Library. For Thomas Paine's *Public Good*, see *Papers of Madison*, III, 11; 14, n. 17. Owing to Lee's mention on pp. 11 ff. of Samuel Wharton's election as a delegate to Congress and his activities there in behalf of the Indiana and Vandalia companies (JM to Pendleton, 23 April 1782, n. 8), Lee could not have prepared his defense of Virginia's western claims before March 1782. Probably he waited to draft the manuscript until his return to Virginia and hence was engaged in its composition when he talked with Randolph. Contrary to what JM and Randolph believed the historical emphasis in such a defense should be, Lee devoted scarcely one-half of his first page to the London Company's charter of 1609. A sufficient reference to this document, as he viewed it, was to state categorically, without mention of supporting authorities, that its revocation by the Crown in 1624 merely put the king in the stead of the proprietary company. Therefore, neither in "truth nor justice" could that annulment alter the boundaries or any other "rights" guaranteed to the settlers in the charter. Lee chose to rest Virginia's title to the West almost exclusively upon her expenditure of "blood and treasure" to defend the area during the French and Indian War and Lord Dunmore's War, upon a refutation of the charge that the Proclamation of 1763 had hedged, or was premised upon a much earlier restriction of, Virginia to the territory east of the Appalachian watershed, and upon numerous cessions of land in the West by Indians during the years 1744–1774 to commissioners appointed by royal governors of Virginia at the behest of, or with the retroactive sanction of, the King in Privy Council. Some of these grants, Lee took pains to point out, antedated and hence took precedence over the alleged titles of "certain companies of land mongers" to the same areas gained at the Treaty of Fort Stanwix in 1768 by disobeying the instructions of the Crown. See JM to Randolph, 1 May 1782, n. 8.

[8] Randolph is approximately quoting a sentence from JM's letter of 1 May 1782 to him (*q.v.*). Instead of "want of information," Randolph at first wrote "igno-

rance" the word used by JM. For a summary of the report of the Boudinot committee of Congress on western cessions and claims, see *Papers of Madison*, III, 304, n. 1.

[9] Randolph wrote 88, the cipher for "word," rather than 688, the cipher for "le."

[10] Instead of "to the," Randolph at first wrote "against" and then crossed it out. Above the deletion he interlineated "to" and 6, the cipher for "the."

[11] Randolph's meaning would have been clearer had he combined the last two sentences of the paragraph to state that, unless there had been a revolution in official thought, it would be political suicide for a Virginian to argue that the acquisition of Indian titles should be offered as a counter to the claims of the land companies. This, however, is what Arthur Lee, with Theodorick Bland's obvious approval, had done or would do in his "Concise view." See n. 7, above; JM to Randolph, 1 May 1782, and n. 8. Bland and JM were frequently at odds on public issues (*Papers of Madison*, II, 195–96; 196, n. 3; 203–4; JM to Pendleton, 23 April, n. 10; JM to Randolph, 1 May 1782, and nn. 15 and 16). The House of Delegates unanimously renominated Joseph Jones, JM, Bland, Randolph, and Arthur Lee on 6 June to be delegates in Congress. The delay of nine days before they were re-elected by concurrence of the Senate no doubt signifies that some of its members opposed one or more of the nominees (Minute Book, House of Delegates, May 1782, pp. 63, 72). Randolph and JM, rather than Bland, were evidently the principal targets, probably because they refused to be controlled by the Lees (Randolph to JM, 20 June 1782).

[12] John Tyler was re-elected speaker of the House of Delegates on 15 May (Lee to JM, 16 May 1782; Minute Book, House of Delegates, May 1782, p. 44).

[13] Possibly either the "Reitveld" from Curaçao, or the "May Flower" from St. Thomas (*Virginia Gazette*, 4 May; *Virginia Gazette, and Weekly Advertiser*, 4 May 1782).

[14] Admiral Sir George Brydges Rodney.

[15] See Harrison to Virginia Delegates, 1 March, n. 11; Virginia Delegates to Harrison, 26 March, and 17 April, n. 2; JM to Pendleton, 9 April 1782, n. 3. With his letter of 1 May to Randolph, JM may have enclosed the *Pennsylvania Packet* of 30 April 1782. Although Rivington's *Royal Gazette* is not specifically mentioned in this issue, it includes news items from New York City as well as elsewhere, similar in tenor to the information given by Randolph in this paragraph.

[16] Of David Ross's partners in several towns of Virginia, Randolph probably refers to Thomas Pleasants III (*ca.* 1757–1796) of Four Mile Creek, Henrico County, a nephew of Thomas Pleasants, Jr. (Clayton Torrence, ed., *Edward Pleasants Valentine Papers*, II, 1105–7; *Virginia Gazette, and General Advertiser* [Richmond, Augustine Davis], 10 January 1796; *Papers of Madison*, III, 87, n. 6).

[17] See Account with Randolph, *ca.* 1 May 1782.

[18] Rochambeau maintained his headquarters at Williamsburg until 2 July, although several contingents of his army began their long march to the north a few days earlier. During the first week in December 1782, after several prolonged periods of pause along the road, the French troops reached Boston, their port of embarkation (Acomb, *Journal of Closen*, pp. 207–8, 271–73).

[19] On 11 February 1782 Congress had adopted a resolution, introduced by Randolph, directing the secretary for foreign affairs "to endeavor to collect, in as authentic a form as possible, such papers as may tend to evidence the limits claimed by the United States" (*JCC*, XXII, 72; see also p. 89). On 18 February, in conformance with this order, Livingston addressed a "Circular Letter to the Governors of the Several States" affirming that "the territorial Rights of the United States collectively" could "only be accurately known by each State's exhibitting its claims

and the Evidence on which they found them." To this end he asked for "authentic copies from your Records of all Grants, Charters, Maps, treaties with the Natives, and other Evidences" (NA: PCC, No. 119, fols. 57–58). In his letter Livingston neglected to make clear why he wanted copies of these documents.

Harrison, who at this time was exchanging unfriendly letters with Robert Morris on monetary issues, believed that the superintendent of finance and especially the assistant superintendent, Gouverneur Morris, were close allies of Livingston and that the latter, as a prominent member of the landed gentry of New York, opposed the western claims of Virginia (Virginia Delegates to Harrison, 25 February 1782, n. 3; George Dangerfield, *Chancellor Robert R. Livingston*, pp. 160, 179, 184). Harrison, in a word, was predisposed to view Livingston's request with suspicion—a distrust which would have been much greater if he had known that the secretary for foreign affairs in a lengthy dispatch on 7 January 1782 to Franklin had suggested, "as the sentiment of an individual" rather than by direction of Congress, that the United States "perhaps" would be willing in negotiating peace to have "the course of the mountains" as her western boundary, to leave the trans-Appalachian country "to the nations which inhabit it," and to join with France, Spain, and Great Britain in guaranteeing their own freedom of trade within that vast area and the "independence" of its inhabitants. Livingston admitted that to solve the western problem in this fashion would be "restrictive of our rights," but it "would free us from the well-grounded apprehensions that the vicinity of Great Britain and her command of the savages would give us" (Wharton, *Revolutionary Diplomatic Correspondence*, V, 89–90). Possibly Livingston could have added that the idea of making the West a buffer territory had been suggested to him by La Luzerne, who, besides being obliged to voice the desire of France's ally Spain, probably shared Vergennes' hope of keeping the United States weak by confining her to the Atlantic seaboard so as to compel her to depend upon the protection of France for many years after the conclusion of peace (William E. O'Donnell, *Chevalier de La Luzerne*, pp. 99–105, 170–71; Samuel F. Bemis, *Diplomacy of the American Revolution*, p. 217; Thomas P. Abernethy, *Western Lands and the American Revolution*, pp. 281–84).

[20] The "first report" was that of the committee (Elias Boudinot, chairman) on the claims of land companies to large areas in the West and on the offers of Virginia, Connecticut, and New York to transfer to the United States their alleged titles to the Northwest. This report had been tabled on 14 November 1781. See *Papers of Madison*, III, 283, n. 5; 304–5, nn. 1, 2; JM to Randolph, 9 April, n. 5; and Motion To Amend Lee's Motion on Western Lands, 18 April 1782, n. 1.

[21] Governor Harrison wrote separate letters on 11 May 1782 to Robert Morris and La Luzerne (McIlwaine, *Official Letters*, III, 210–12). The governor's reply was in answer to a dispatch of 27 April from the superintendent of finance, enclosing a copy of a paragraph of a letter to him from La Luzerne about the military matériel which Virginia had been seeking to buy on credit in France (Virginia Delegates to Harrison, 24 January 1782, and nn.; Wharton, *Revolutionary Diplomatic Correspondence*, V, 331–32). See also Harrison to Virginia Delegates, 11 May 1782, and n. 1.

From Jacquelin Ambler

RC (LC: Madison Papers). Addressed to "The Honobl. James Madison of Congress Philadelphia." Docketed by JM, "May 11. 1782."

VIRGINIA RICHMOND May 11th. 1782

DEAR SIR

I am exceedingly obliged by the friendly sentiments in your last respecting my late appointment.[1] I have not been long enough in it to determine whether it will be attended with less inquietude than the former,[2] but I think I discover a greater degree of trouble.

Mr. Webb seems determined to set out on Monday; if so he will probably reach Phila. as soon as this gets to hand;[3] it gives me satisfaction to think you will be speedily reimbursed for the Money advanced Mr. Jameson.[4] I sincerely wish our Treasury would enable us to make you a remittance. We have not had ten pounds Specie in it since my coming into Office, and it is much to be feared there will not any come in for a long time.[5] The People begin already to complain of the burthen laid on them by the last Assembly, & make no scruple of asserting the impossibility of raising hard Money for the Land Tax.[6] Want of Commerce prevents a due circulation of what Money is in the State, so that tho' the Army of our Allies spend some with us, it remains in few hands.[7] The Officers of Civil Government have not been paid for the last ten Months; my Quarters Salary in the Spring of 1781. amounted to 9-16- at the then depreciation.[8] We don't know what to make of this intelligence under the Philaa. Head May 2. 1782[9] I hope your next will throw some light on the Subject

Yours with great esteem & regard

J: AMBLER

[1] In a letter now missing, JM must have congratulated Ambler upon his appointment as acting treasurer of the Commonwealth of Virginia. See Jameson to JM, 9 March, n. 6; Randolph to JM, 11–13 April; Pendleton to JM, 22 April 1782, and n. 12.

[2] Membership on the Council of State.

[3] Foster Webb, Jr. See Randolph to JM, 19 April, and 16–17 May; Ambler to JM, 20 April 1782, and n. 2. Webb's stay in Philadelphia lasted from about 21 May until 6 June 1782 (Ambler to JM, 18 May; JM to Randolph, 6 June 1782).

[4] See Ambler to JM, 20 April 1782, and n. 1.

[5] See Jameson to JM, *ca.* 12 January, and 9 March, and n. 4; Harrison to Virginia Delegates, 9 February; JM to James Madison, Sr., *ca.* 12 February, and 30 March; Ambler to JM, 6 April 1782.

[6] See Jameson to JM, 23 February, and n. 6; and 2 March 1782, and n. 3. On 2 May 1782 St. George Tucker, in a letter to Theodorick Bland, had commented upon the increasing opposition to the land-tax law and the "ten thousand difficulties" which would ensue if it were repealed (Charles Campbell, ed., *The Bland Papers: Being a Selection from the Manuscripts of Colonel Theodorick Bland, Jr., of Prince George County, Virginia* [2 vols.; Petersburg, Va., 1840–43], II, 79).

[7] See *Papers of Madison*, III, 261–62; 263, n. 9; 324–25; 326, n. 3; Pendleton to JM, 15 April 1782, and n. 6.

[8] Ambler refers to his salary as a member of the Council of State. According to the law defining a councilor's salary (Jameson to JM, *ca.* 12 January 1782, and n. 6), Ambler was owed about 18.3 per cent or £146 8*s*. of the quarterly stipend of £800 for all the councilors. The latter sum had to be divided among them in proportion to the number of meetings which each had attended. In the present letter, Ambler equated the £146 8*s*. as £9 16*s*. in specie by applying a depreciation ratio of about 15 to 1.

[9] Ambler had read the 11 May issue of the *Virginia Gazette*. This paper copied "Intelligence of the last Importance" from Philadelphia under a 2 May date line. The "Intelligence" comprised reports which had reached New York City by packets arriving there from Great Britain on successive days. The earlier report concerned "the full determination of the British Cabinet to pursue the War with redoubled vigour." The later report was to the effect that Parliament had acknowledged the independence of the United States of America. See Virginia Delegates to Harrison, 7 May 1782, and n. 4.

Benjamin Harrison to Virginia Delegates

FC (Virginia State Library). In the hand of Thomas Meriwether, who had succeeded Charles Hay as assistant clerk of the Council of State on 7 May 1782.

In Council May 11th. 1782.

Gentlemen

I have inclos'd for your perusal a letter to Mr Morris and one to the Chevalier, which you'l please to seal and deliver after reading, and use your endeavours to obviate any difficulties that may be started by the Minister if in your power. I am much at a loss to conjecture what could occasion such a change in him, tho' I think it clear it originated in Philadelphia on some person in power being informed that the stores were ready to be shiped; if it had come from France, the Minister would certainly be inform'd of their cost: perhaps you may be able to unravel this business; if you are I should be obliged to you for the communication.[1] Mr Ross will by this Post remit you Bills for £150 each which I hope will serve you til a way can be found to supply you fully.[2] I am &c

[1] See Virginia Delegates to Harrison, 24 January, and nn.; 28 May 1782, and nn. 11 and 13. Harrison's letters of 11 May 1782 to Robert Morris and La Luzerne, respectively, are in McIlwaine, *Official Letters*, III, 210–12. Vergennes had informed La Luzerne that the cost of the military supplies, purchased by Virginia and still awaiting shipment from France, would be charged against money loaned to Congress by Dutch bankers. To this, Robert Morris and Harrison both refused to agree. The governor felt "a sensible mortification" because the French evidently distrusted the solvency of Virginia and thereby humbled her citizens "in the eyes of the States themselves, and all the rest of the world." When they first conferred about the supplies, La Luzerne seems to have encouraged Harrison to believe that the court of Versailles would cover the cost of the goods and accept as security "a bond" pledging the Virginia General Assembly to reimburse the French government "in five annual payments, to commence from the close of the present War."

[2] See JM to Randolph, 21 May 1782.

From Edmund Pendleton

Tr (LC: Force Transcripts). Addressed to "The Honble. James Madison Esqr. Philada." Another copy, taken from the original, is printed in the *Proceedings of the Massachusetts Historical Society*, 2d ser., XIX (1905), 151–52.

VIRGA May 13th 1782

MY DEAR SIR

The last of yr favrs I have to acknowledge is that of April the 23d., a subsequent one I missed hitherto, as I was not return'd from Richmond when the Post rider pass'd my House & he carried it there, but I had left that place before his arrival, & must wait his return for the pleasure of receiving it.[1] I am however in more anxiety for your next, as I expect in that a confirmation of a piece of News Which has been brought from your City that has almost intranced Us; No less than Our darling Independancy having been acknowledged by Parliament;[2] a measure so pleasing and important, & at the same time so unlook'd for at this juncture, when the Ministry had Menaced a more Vigorous prosecution of the War than ever, that we scarce can give credit to repeated Assertions of its reality, by several credible Passengers from thence, and I must wait two days more 'til I shall have from you an Account I can depend on. If it be so, and a general Peace not in Treaty, it will become Us to be on our guard, since they must mean, whilst continuing the War against our good Ally, to trie every Art of Corruption to detach Us from them, and endeavour to seduce Us into a Seperate Peace, a more certain destruction than their Arms could ever have brought upon Us;[3] But on this head I am not uneasy, since it being impossible that any friend to America can make a proposition of that sort, I hope the Uttering such a Sentiment, will be considered as marking the author for an Enemy, and stop his influence.

Whether this great event has taken place or not, Our Eyes must be turn'd to the West Indies, as the great Theatre for playing this Campaign; whether it will be real Tragidy which may decide the fate of the War, Or a Repetition of the Farce acted for two or three seasons in the British channel,[4] time must decide; in the former case we have much to hope from the Superiority of our Allies.[5]

I left Richmond had appeared, which number 79 are Jeffer[6]

[1] When Joseph Jones and JM were together in Congress, they alternated in writing to Pendleton every week. During Jones's absence from Philadelphia between 2 May and 4 September 1782, Pendleton expected a weekly letter from JM (JM to Randolph, 9 April, n. 6; Pendleton to JM, 15 April 1782). JM probably tried to fulfill this expectation, but much of the correspondence is lost, including JM's letter of *ca.* 30 April. JM's letter of 7 May would not have reached Edmundsbury by the time Pendleton wrote the present letter. See Pendleton to JM, 20 May 1782, and n. 1.

[2] See Ambler to JM, 11 May 1782, n. 9.

[3] *Ibid.*; JM to James Madison, Sr., 30 March; JM to Pendleton, 9 April, and n. 2; Virginia Delegates to Harrison, 30 April; and 7 May, and n. 4; Report on Communication from La Luzerne, 1 May 1782, and n. 3.

[4] Pendleton's choice of the word "Farce" is well sustained by W. M. James in his three chapters devoted to the naval operations of the French, Spanish, and British squadrons in "European Waters" between 1779 and the close of 1781. Although the opposing fleets frequently maneuvered in the English Channel, and especially off the southern coast of England, they succeeded in avoiding any major, and almost any minor, engagement during that period (W. M. James, *British Navy in Adversity*, pp. 170–86, 243–51, 301–15).

[5] See Randolph to JM, 10 May 1782, and n. 15. Peter Force's clerk found the manuscript of this letter so much mutilated below this paragraph that, after writing the few words which remained, he made the bracketed comment, "the rest of the Page torn off."

[6] If in this paragraph Pendleton mentioned leaving Richmond before the House of Delegates had a quorum, he should have given 76 rather than 79 as the minimum number of delegates (150 in all) required to make a house (Minute Book, House of Delegates, May 1782, p. 44). Perhaps he added that Jefferson, although elected by the voters of Albemarle County, had written to the speaker of the House of Delegates on 6 May, stating, "I do not accept of the appointment" (Boyd, *Papers of Jefferson,* VI, 179; JM to Jefferson, 16 April, and n. 15; Randolph to JM, 5 May 1782, n. 9).

Motion To Request France To Protect American Commerce

MS (NA: PCC, No. 5, II, 652). George Bond, deputy secretary of Congress, preceded the entry of the motion in the secret foreign journal with the words, "on motion of Mr. Madison, seconded by Mr. Ellery."

[14 May 1782]

Resolved. That the Secretary for foreign affairs be and he is hereby directed to transmit the State of Commerce and plan for its protection, reported by the Superintendant of Finance, to the Minister plenipotentiary of the United States at the Court of Versailles, to be by him communicated to that Court with an application for its concurrence in the said plan.[1]

[1] See Motion on Protection of Commerce, 2 May 1782, and n. 1. In his analysis of American commerce and in his plan for its protection, Morris stressed the importance of the foreign trade in tobacco, as well as in other commodities, the certainty of injury to Great Britain, and the large economic benefit to both France and the United States if France would provide armed ships to convoy American merchant vessels (*JCC*, XXII, 264–74).

Virginia Delegates to Benjamin Harrison

RC (McGregor Library, University of Virginia). In JM's hand. Docketed: "Lr. from the Virga Delegates[.] May 23d. 1782[.] referred to the Committee appd: to prepare Instructions to the Delegates in Congress." This statement is discussed in n. 13.

PHILADA. May 14th. 1782

SIR

In our letter of the 17th Ulto. we informed your Excelly. that we had called upon Congress for a decision on the report of the Committee on the territorial cessions, a copy of which was inclosed in our letter of the 17th. of Novr last;[1] and that a day had been assigned for the consideration of that report.[2] The extract from the Journals of Congress herewith transmitted, shews the progress of the business down to the 6th. of May, when it was postponed sine die.[3]

Our revival of this subject at the time above stated proceeded from the manifest expediency of obtaining from Congress such a decision thereon, as would explain their ultimate views, and enable the Genl. Assembly at their present Session to take such measures as the case required. During a suspension of this decision of Congress, the misrepresentations & fallacies contained in the report supplied to interested persons, abundant calumny against Virginia; and the precautions which her Western interests might dictate, were exposed to be animadverted upon as premature & improper.[4] These considerations were urged upon Congress as equally obliging the State to demand and them to give a definitive answer either in the affirmative or negative to her cession. Congress were reminded too that this cession was proposed not from any interested motives on the part of Virginia, nor even originated with her, but was made at the instance of Congress themselves, who pressed it upon her as a sacrifice essential to the general Interest;[5] that the least therefore that could be expected from Congress was a speedy attention & explicit answer to it. These considerations, weighty as they were in themselves, made little impression, nor were they other wise answered, than by the evasive propositions & unseasonable adjournments stated in the extract from the Journals. The only solid objection of which the case admitted, and which on a former occasion[6] prevailed, was a thinness of the House. But on this occasion there were both at the time of assigning a day for the discussion of the report, & of the vote which finally postponed it, no less than eleven States present,[7] a number which experience has shewn to be greater than can be calculated upon at any given future period. During the course of the business the number was indeed reduced to nine States by the voluntary departure of a member for Connecticut & of another for Delaware; and advantage was taken of that conjuncture, as will be seen in the extract above referred to, to introduce the proposition made by Mr. Clarke & Mr. Ellery on the first instant.[8]

Having pursued this subject to the issue of a postponement sine die, and having found from the temper of a great part of Congress,[9] as well as the repeated declarations of individual members on the floor, that no other issue was to be expected, we thought it inconsistent with the respect due to the State we represent, to other public business, and to our friends in Congress, to persist longer in urging it. We accordingly apprized Congress that such was our determination, and that we should forthwith transmit a State of the whole proceeding to our Constituents, with whom it would remain to take such Steps as it should suggest.[10] What these Steps ought to be we presume not to point out.[11] We are persuaded that they will be the result of mature & temperate deliberation, and that they will equally tend to the honor of the State & the security of its interests. We only entreat that whatever Duties they shall assign to us may be chalked out in full and precise instructions.[12] Possessed of such instructions we shall not only speak and act with greater confidence & satisfaction to ourselves, but with greater weight and effect with respect to others. Indeed the advantage of being able to speak the declared sense of our constituents is so great that we can not but intimate the expediency of our being furnished with it on all questions which involve their important interests.[13]

Intelligence from the W. Indies renders it pretty certain that an action has lately taken place between the French and British fleets in that quarter. The result is not circumstantially known, but there is reason to believe that it was considerably in favor of the former wch. preserved its convoy and prosecuted its course to Hispaniola. At this place it is universally understood that a junction was to be made with the Spaniards, and that the combined armaments were to proceed from thence agst. Jamaica.[14]

The Gazettes which accompany this will inform your Excellency of the revolution which has taken place in the British Ministry, and of the arrival of General Carlton at N. York in quality of Commander in cheif, and joint Comissr. with Admiral Digby for treating of peace with America.[15] A letter was [received] yesterday by Congress from Genl. Washington inclosing one to him from Genl Carlton in which the latter announces his arrival, his commission, the pacific disposition of G. Britain towards this country, and his personal desire in case the war should be continued, of rendering it as little destructive as possible;[16] and finally requests a passport for Mr. Morgan his Secy. to convey a similar *letter of compliment* to Congress. Genl Washington's letter is not yet answered, but we run no risk in assuring your Excelly. that he will be directed to refuse the passport to Philada. for Mr. Morgan.[17]

The late proceedings in the British Parliamt. with the avowed repugnance of the New Ministry, particularly of Ld. Shelburne the Minister for the American Department, to a recognition of our Independence and of our Alliance with France, forbid any hope that a peace on that ground is the object of the Commission just mentioned. On the contrary we have every reason to suspect that its object is to seduce us from the latter if not from both of those essential preliminaries to peace.[18] The stile of Genl. Carlton's letter to Genl Washington perfectly coincides with this Suspicion. It gives us great pleasure to be able to observe on this occasion, that the apparent unanimity & firmness of Congress, afford every security to the honor & rights of the U. States wch. depends on their Councils.

A public Audience was yesterday given to the Minister of France in which he announced in form the birth of a Dauphin. The important light in which this event is regarded by the French Nation, and more especially the present conjuncture of public affairs rendered it proper to testify our satisfaction in it by the demonstrations specified in the Gazette of this morning.[19]

We have been disappointed in procuring the Legislative proceedings of this State relative to the Inhabitants of the district lately in dispute between it & Virga. We are assured that the whole will be printed in time to be sent by the next post.[20] The explanation & apology which your Excelly's favor of the 4th. instt. wishes to be made to the Chevr. de la Luzerne shall be duly attended to. We shall also transmit the orders you think expedient with regard to the Stores at Boston.[21]

We have the honor to be with sentiments of the highest esteem & respect Yr. Exc[e]llency's Obt. & very hbl. Servants

J. MADISON JR.
THEOK: BLAND JR.

[1] See *Papers of Madison,* III, 305, n. 1.

[2] See Virginia Delegates to Harrison, 17 April 1782, n. 1.

[3] The enclosure is missing, but it probably was a copy of the journal entries of 16 and 18 April and 1, 2, and 6 May, summarizing the unsuccessful efforts of the Virginia delegates to have Congress unambiguously accept or reject the recommendations of the Boudinot committee (*JCC,* XXII, 184, 191–94, 223–35, 240–41; Motion To Amend Lee's Motion on Western Lands, 18 April, and n. 1; Virginia Delegates to Harrison, 23 April; JM to Pendleton, 23 April, and nn. 7 and 8; JM to Randolph, 1 May, and nn. 6 and 7; and 7 May, and nn. 8, 10, and 11; Observations Relating to Influence of Vermont and Territorial Claims, 1 May, and n. 9; Motion on Delegates' Financial Interest in West, 2 May; Motion on Point of Order, 3 May, and nn. 1 and 2; JM to Lee, 7 May 1782, and n. 10).

[4] See JM to Pendleton, 2 April 1782, n. 3.

[5] Here the delegates are referring to the preamble of the resolution of Congress of 6 September 1780 (*JCC,* XVII, 806–7; *Papers of Madison,* II, 72).

[6] JM no doubt had in mind the tabling of the Boudinot committee report on 14 November 1781, when only seven states had two or more delegates in Congress (*JCC,* XXI, 1113–14; *Papers of Madison,* III, 304, and n. 1; 305, n. 2).

[7] The *JCC* does not record when Congress decided to make the Boudinot committee report the order of the day for 16 April. Eleven states were each represented by at least two delegates on 3 April, and nine or ten states were so represented during the period 15 April to 6 May, inclusive (*JCC,* XXII, 162–63, 180–241, *passim*). Although JM correctly writes that there were "eleven States present" on 6 May, when a further consideration of the report was "finally postponed," he might have

added that Connecticut, being represented by only one delegate, could not cast an effective vote.

[8] The last recorded vote of Oliver Wolcott until December 1782 was on 20 April (*JCC*, XXII, 203). Between that day and 5 May Philemon Dickinson was also absent from Congress. Abraham Clark (1726–1794), seconded by William Ellery, moved on 1 May that, since there were "but nine states represented," further consideration of the Boudinot committee report be postponed until 1 August 1782. The motion also recommended that during the interim "the executive authority of the several states be . . . furnished with copies of the said report, in order that each State may be fully represented, and their delegates properly instructed upon the subject at that time." Even though Wolcott and Dickinson were absent, enough delegates joined with those from Virginia to defeat this motion (*JCC*, XXII, 224–25). For the indefinite postponement of the issue on 6 May, see Motion on Point of Order, 3 May 1782, n. 2.

[9] JM originally wrote and then deleted "general temper of the House."

[10] The Virginia delegates may have waited several days after 6 May before apprising Congress, because JM had not immediately regarded the vote on that date as conclusive evidence that Congress could not be induced to decide definitely either for or against the Boudinot committee report (JM to Lee, 7 May 1782, and n. 10).

[11] See JM to Randolph, 7 May 1782.

[12] See *Papers of Madison*, III, 309, n. 7; JM to Randolph, 1 May 1782, n. 7.

[13] See headnote of this letter. On 6 May Governor Harrison referred to the speaker of the House of Delegates the Virginia delegates' letter of 17 November 1781 about the western lands issue in Congress. This dispatch and its many enclosures had reached Richmond too late to be considered by the October session of the Virginia General Assembly (*Papers of Madison*, III, 305, n. 1; McIlwaine, *Official Letters*, III, 213, Harrison to Virginia Delegates, 11 January 1782). On 16 May 1782 the delegates' letter of 17 November 1781 was referred to a committee of eight men, with Richard Henry Lee as chairman. The present letter was also referred to this committee on 23 May (McIlwaine, *Official Letters*, III, 233; Minute Book, House of Delegates, May 1782, pp. 46, 51). Apparently the only instructions recommended by the committee and accepted by the General Assembly were those prescribing how the delegates should stand on matters relating to the peace negotiations (*ibid.*, pp. 52, 53). For these, see Instructions to Virginia Delegates, 24–25 May 1782. The decision of the committee to suggest no instructions about the western lands may reflect the appointment on 1 June of a special committee to prepare a report which would validate the title of Virginia to the area north and west of the Ohio River. See JM to Randolph, 1 May 1782, n. 7.

[14] The delegates were reporting what they had read in the *Pennsylvania Packet* of 9 May 1782. The cheering rumor of a French naval victory intensified the shock which the *Pennsylvania Journal* caused six days later by reporting that Rodney and Hood had disastrously defeated Grasse and his fleet in the Battle of the Saints, 9–12 April 1782 (JM to Jefferson, 15 January, n. 16; JM to Pendleton, 9 April, n. 3, and 23 April 1782, n. 3). This and the next two paragraphs, slightly amended so as to conceal the addressees' and addressor's identities, appeared in the issue of the *Virginia Gazette* for 25 May 1782.

[15] For Rear Admiral Robert Digby, see *Papers of Madison*, III, 198, n 6. The delegates must have enclosed the *Pennsylvania Packet* or *Pennsylvania Journal* of 11 May, or both of them. The *Pennsylvania Gazette*, a weekly, did not print this news until 15 May. See JM to Pendleton, 23 April, n. 5; and Virginia Delegates to Harrison, 7 May 1782, n. 4.

[16] The receipt of Washington's letter of 10 May enclosing a copy of General Sir Guy Carleton's letter to him of 7 May is noted in the *JCC* for 14, not 13, May (XXII, 263). The two dispatches are in NA: PCC, No. 152, X, 525, 559. See also Fitzpatrick, *Writings of Washington,* XXIV, 243–44. JM repeated "to him" after "Carlton."

[17] In 1782 Maurice Morgann (1726–1802) served as undersecretary of state to William Petty (1737–1805), Earl of Shelburne, later first Marquis of Lansdowne. In the short-lived ministry of Charles Watson-Wentworth, Marquis of Rockingham (d. 1 July 1782), Shelburne was secretary of state for the home office, thus having domestic, Irish, and colonial affairs in his charge. In 1783 Morgann was secretary to the British commission for ratifying the peace treaty with the United States. Shakespearean scholars remember him for his *An Essay on the Dramatic Character of Sir John Falstaff* (London, 1777). See JM to Randolph, 14 May 1782, n. 8. JM underlined the italicized phrase.

[18] JM's surmise was accurate. If the Marquis of Rockingham had intended to acknowledge the independence of the United States, he would have entrusted the peace negotiations to Charles James Fox, the secretary of state for foreign affairs. Following the death of the Marquis, Shelburne became head of the government (11 July 1782), and Fox resigned.

[19] *Pennsylvania Packet*, 14 May 1782. See Report on Form of Public Audience for La Luzerne, 7–9 May, and editorial note; Revised Reply of President of Congress to La Luzerne, 8–12 May 1782.

[20] See Randolph to JM, 26 April, n. 2; Harrison to Virginia Delegates, 27 April, and nn.; Virginia Delegates to Harrison, 28 May 1782, and n. 27.

[21] See Bradford to Virginia Delegates, 20 March, and n. 2; Virginia Delegates to Harrison, 23 April, and n. 4; Harrison to Virginia Delegates, 4 May 1782.

To Edmund Randolph

Tr (LC: Madison Papers). Above the date line of his transcription, the anonymous copyist wrote "To Edmund Randolph." Someone also unknown, while checking the four pages of copy against the now missing original, interlineated two omissions (see nn. 9 and 10) and then wrote at the top of the first page, "a Duplicate letters both corrected the same Sep 14, '38." See *Papers of Madison,* I, xvii, for the probable explanation of this statement.

PHILADELPHIA May 14. 1782

DEAR SIR

The Ceres man of War we are informed by a New York paper arrived there in twenty five days on the 5th. instant having on board his Excellency Sir Guy Carleton, Commander in chief &c., and *Commissioner for making peace or war*[1] in North America. The intelligence brought by this conveyance is that the vibrations of power between the Ministry and their rivals had terminated in the complete dissolution of the former organization of the latter.[2] What change of measures will follow this change of men is yet concealed from us. The bill for empowering the King to conclude a peace or truce with the revolted Colonies in North America had been brought into Parliament on the 27th. of March. The language of it is at the same time cautious and comprehensive, and seems to make eventual provision for our Independence, without betraying any purpose of acknowledging it. The terms peace and truce are scarcely applicable to any other Conventions than National ones. And the King is authorized to annul or suspend all acts of Parliament whatever as far as they speak of the Colonies.[3] He can therefore clearly remove any parliamentary bar to his recognition of our Independence and I know of no other bar to his treating with America on that ground. All this is however very different from a real peace. The King will assuredly prefer war as long as his Ministry will stand by him, and the sentiments of his present Ministry, particularly of Shelburne are as peremptory against the dismemberments of the Empire as those of any of their predecessors. They will at least try a campaign of negociation against the United States and of war against their other enemies before they submit to it.[4] It is probable that the arrival of Sir Guy Carleton will not long precede an opening of the first campaign. Congress will I am persuaded give a proper verbal answer to any overtures with which he may insult them[5] but the best answer will come from the States in such supplies of men and money as will expel him and all our other enemies from the United States.

We have at length brought our territorial business to an issue. It was postponed sine die on the 6th. instant. We have transmitted the whole proceeding to the Governor to be laid before the Assembly.[6]

There are various accounts from the West Indies which render it pretty certain that an engagement has taken place between the two fleets. The circumstances are not ascertained. The issue seems at least to have been so far in favor of our Allies as to leave them free to pursue their course with their Convoy to Hispaniola, where a junction is to be made with the Spaniards. The object of this junction is universally supposed to be Jamaica.[7]

Since I finished the above a letter has come to Congress from General Washington enclosing one to him from Sir Guy Carleton announcing his commission in conjunction with Admiral Digby to treat of peace with this Country, and requesting a passport for his Secretary Mr. Morgan to bring a similar *letter of compliment* to Congress. The request will certainly be refused and General Washington probably directed to receive and forward any despatches which may be properly addressed to Congress.[8]

A public audience was yesterday given to the Minister of France, in which he formally announced the birth of the Dauphin. It was deemed politic at this crisis to display every proper evidence of affectionate attachment to our Ally. The Minister was accordingly received with Military honors and the audience concluded with the discharge of cannon and a feu de joi of small arms. A public entertainment followed and fireworks (at night-left out) closed the scene.[9]

The answer reported by the Committee on Mr Dana's letter (animadverted on his precipitancy and/left out) gave him a cautionary instruction. It afterwards went to the Secretary of foreign affairs and thence I suppose in his dress to Petersburgh.[10] Mr. Jones will give you more satisfactory information on this as also with respect to the answer of Mr. Jay's letter.[11]

Your surmises relative to a revival of paper currency alarms me. It is impossible that any evil can render such an alternative eligible. It will revive the hopes of the Enemy [,] increase the internal debility of the State, and awaken the clamours of all ranks throughout the United States against her. Much more to Virginia's honor would it be to rescind the taxes, altho' the consequence of that can but be of a most serious nature.[12]

[1] The italicized words here and in the fourth paragraph are lightly underlined in the transcript. For the news brought by the "Ceres," which had sailed from Great Britain on 11 April, see Virginia Delegates to Harrison, 7 May, and n. 4; and 14 May 1782, and n. 17. The facts upon which JM comments in this paragraph appeared in the *Pennsylvania Packet* of 11 May 1782.

[2] Assuming that either JM or the copyist had erred, Henry D. Gilpin rephrased this sentence after "dissolution" to read, "of the former and organization of the latter" (Madison, *Papers* [Gilpin ed.], I, 127).

Lord North's opponents were able to unite only in forcing his resignation on 20 March. One week later King George III reluctantly consented to have the Marquis of Rockingham head a new ministry. Among the chief members of the Rockingham cabinet, the Earl of Shelburne and Charles James Fox disagreed on issues of foreign policy and on the concessions which should be granted to the United States at the outset of peace negotiations. Moreover, prominent leaders who failed to gain high position after helping to unseat Lord North quickly joined former opponents to resist measures recommended by his successor (*Cambridge Modern History*, VI, 457–60; JM to Pendleton, 23 April, n. 5; Virginia Delegates to Harrison, 14 May 1782, and nn. 17 and 18).

[3] As reported by the *Pennsylvania Packet* (n. 1, above), the measure empowered the king to conclude "a peace or truce with said colonies or plantations, or any of them, or any parts thereof; any law, act or acts of parliament, matter, or thing, to the contrary notwithstanding." To this end, the king was accorded "full power

and authority . . . to repeal, annul, and make void, or to suspend, any act or acts of Parliament." JM reminded Randolph that, because in international law the words "peace" and "truce" were restricted in usage to the relations between sovereign powers, Parliament implicitly had recognized the independence of the United States or at least had granted the king the authority to do so.

4 In the *Pennsylvania Packet* of 11 May, an item dated in London about a month earlier stated that British armed forces would launch an offensive against France and Spain at once.

5 See Virginia Delegates to Harrison, 7 May, n. 4; and 14 May 1782, n. 16.

6 See Virginia Delegates to Harrison, 14 May 1782, and nn. 3, 7, 8, and 10.

7 *Ibid.*, and n. 14.

8 See n. 5, above. Later in the day on which the present letter was written, Congress resolved, "That the Commander in Chief be, and hereby is, directed to refuse the request of Sir Guy Carleton, of a passport for Mr. Morgan to bring despatches to Philadelphia" (*JCC*, XXII, 263). On 21 May Washington forwarded a copy of this resolution to Carleton, who acknowledged its receipt two days later (Fitzpatrick, *Writings of Washington*, XXIV, 270). See also JM to Randolph, 4 June 1782, and n. 37. By using the phrase, "letter of compliment," and underlining it, JM probably was referring ironically to the same expression as employed by Carleton in his letter of 7 May 1782 to Washington. Carleton had written, "I am further to acquaint you, Sir, that it was my Intention to have sent this Day a Similar Letter of Compliment to Congress" until he found that the courier would have to have a "passport" from Washington (NA: PCC, No. 152, X, 560). The adverb "properly" connotes that, in JM's view, no dispatch from Carleton would be received unless it related strictly to military matters.

9 See Report on Form of Public Audience for La Luzerne, 7–9 May, and editorial note; Revised Reply of President of Congress to La Luzerne, 8–12 May 1782; *JCC*, XXII, 261–63. The words "at night-left out" were placed in parentheses and interlineated by the person who compared the copy with the original manuscript. See headnote, above.

Although some patriots were inclined to negotiate with Carleton, Turbutt Wright very likely expressed the view of the majority when he wrote on 4 June 1782: "If any Propositions are to be made that America can listen to, the Way is open on the other side the Water, where there are Persons properly authorized to treat in Conjunction with our Allies, to them let the Applications be made" (Burnett, *Letters*, VI, 366).

10 See JM to Randolph, 23 April 1782, and n. 14. Henry D. Gilpin omitted in his edition (Madison, *Papers* [Gilpin ed.], I, 129) the words "animadverted on his precipitancy," which were inserted in parentheses in the clerk's copy by the person who checked it against the original manuscript. For Livingston's letter to Dana, see Wharton, *Revolutionary Diplomatic Correspondence*, V, 411–14. See also Motion on Instructions to Dana, 27 May 1782.

11 See Report Approving Jay's Negotiations with Spain, 22 April; JM to Randolph, 1 May, n. 7, and 7 May 1782.

12 See Randolph to JM, 5 May, and n. 7, and 10 May 1782.

From Arthur Lee

RC (University of Virginia Library). Addressed to "The Honble James Madison Esqr. in Congress Philadelphia." Docketed by JM, "A. Lee."

RICHMOND May 16th. 1782

DR.[?] SIR:

I am extremely obligd to you, my dear Sir, for yr. favor of the —— together with the letter enclosd, which you were so good as to forward.[1] It seems to me that the Party in G. Britain who flatter themselves, at this period of the contest, with being able to conciliate us; are still more weak than that which hopd to reduce us by force. To suppose we can dishonorably abandon Allies who have assisted us, for Enemies who have endeavord to destroy us, merely because those endeavors have been frustrated, to suppose we shoud of choice adopt a character of the extremest folly & perfidy, when we can with more security adhere to honorable engagements, & enjoy a reputable name; is worthy of those only, who in the whole of this business, seem to have been acting under an immediate visitation from Heaven to their shame & ruin.[2]

This is the third day that we have had a House.[3] Mr. Tyler is again our Speaker.[4] A Committee is appointed to prepare Instructions for us.[5] And when the appropriation of the taxes comes on care will be taken to provide for the support of the Delegation.[6] I am inclind to think that the flags sent here by Mr. Morris for Tobacco for the N. York Merchants, will be returnd empty; the House of Delegates not seeming disposd to suffer any such practice.[7] We are exceedingly embarrassd about raising hard-money for recruiting & other necessary purposes of Government. Not a shilling can be borrowd, distant & inadequate as the taxes are they are complaind of as oppressive; there is little money in the State, & as little prospect of more coming in.[8] That fatal article in the capitulation which allowd the British Merchants to sell their goods at York, was so speedy & effectual a drain from us of Specie, as to throw an insurmountable bar in the way of all Operations depending upon this.[9]

I shall be very much obligd to you for a continuation of your correspondence, & particularly for what is receivd from our Ministers in Europe.

May I take the liberty of requesting you to receive the Contents of the enclosd Bill, & keep them subject to my order? Please to make my Compts to the Ladies & Gentlemen of your House.[10]

Farewell.

A. LEE

[1] See JM to Lee, 7 May 1782, and n. 2.

[2] See Virginia Delegates to Harrison, 7 May, and n. 4; JM to Randolph, 14 May 1782, and n. 3.

[3] It was the second day (Randolph to JM, 5 May 1782, n. 9).

[4] John Tyler (Randolph to JM, 10 May 1782, n. 12).

[5] See Virginia Delegates to Harrison, 14 May, n. 13; Randolph to JM, 16–17 May 1782.

[6] See Jameson to JM, 9 March 1782, n. 5.

[7] See Ambler to JM, 20 April 1782, and n. 4. On 11 February 1782 Congress had adopted the report of a committee, which included JM among its members, recommending the issuance of passports to flag-of-truce vessels so as to enable them to load in Virginia for delivery in New York City to the "traders capitulants at Yorktown" an amount of tobacco equal in value to the total sales price of their property which, by the ninth of the Articles of Capitulation, these merchants had been permitted to sell following the surrender of Cornwallis (*JCC*, XXII, 70–71). Being authorized by Congress to arrange for this traffic, Robert Morris requested Governor Harrison to admit the British flag-of-truce ships "New York" and "Fame" to the ports of Virginia. The Governor in Council withheld his assent, ordered the ships to anchor in Hampton Roads, and referred the issue to Attorney General Edmund Randolph and to the General Assembly (McIlwaine, *Official Letters*, III, 222–23, 230–31; *Journals of the Council of State*, III, 34, 41, 85, 86, 88). The contract with the traders-capitulant pledged that in return for the $25,000 ($14,037⅜ Spanish milled dollars) worth of goods which they had sold to the United States at Yorktown, they would receive 685 hogsheads of tobacco averaging 1,000 pounds a hogshead (NA: PCC, No. 75, fols, 376–78). For the next mention of this long-lived issue, see Randolph to JM, 16–17 May 1782, and n. 25. See also Randolph to JM, 5 July 1782, nn. 2 and 3.

[8] In his letter of 6 May 1782 to the speaker of the House of Delegates, Harrison remarked that, although the General Assembly at its session of October 1781 had authorized the treasurer to borrow money on terms "very advantageous" to the lender, "not one shilling has been obtained" and the yield of taxes had been "too inconsiderable" to cover the necessary public expenses (McIlwaine, *Official Letters*, III, 213).

[9] Since at least part of these goods were to be paid for in tobacco (n. 7, above), this explanation of the shortage of specie in Virginia needs to be supplemented by mentioning the trade of civilians with the merchants-capitulant at Yorktown as well as indirectly with dealers in the northern states. See Fitzpatrick, *Writings of Washington*, XXIII, 354–55; Pendleton to JM, 15 April 1782.

[10] See *Papers of Madison*, II, 92, n. 8.

From Edmund Randolph

RC (LC: Madison Papers). Words encoded by Randolph in the official cipher are italicized. The letter lacks both cover and docket.

RICHMOND May 16. 1782.

DEAR SIR

Mr. F. Webb, who left this place yesterday for Phila., is the bearer of a bill for 20 £ Penna. currency. I have requested him to deliver it to you. As it was not put into my hands, after it was drawn, I wish you may not meet with some impediment in the negotiation of it. For if it was drawn in my favor, the forms of business seem to require my indorsement, to assign it to another. However, I suppose congressional reputation is not yet so low, as to render such a difficulty unsurmountable, from a suspicion of your having acquired the bill thro' fraud.[1]

Your favor of an uncertain day of may will answer, when united with your official letter to the governor,[2] an important purpose. It will reinforce the essential[3] doctrine of fidelity to our allies, and alienatio[n] from G. Britain, which seems so necessary at this day to our political salvation, and is therefore urged by me with some earnestness.

On wednesday last the house of delegates met for the first time since the new election. An opposition to Mr. Tyler, the late speaker, was rumoured, before the matter came to a crisis, but was dropped, when he was proposed for the chair. Mr. R. H. Lee was mentioned, as the competitor.[4]

Mr. Jefferson has informed the house of his election into their body and tendered[5] a resignation. This they refuse to accept, grounding the refusal upon his own principles, delivered on a similar occasion.[6]

Mr. Henry will be down on the 20th. inst. During the interregnum, occasioned by the absence of these two gentlemen, it is probable that a considerable degree of influence will run in the channel, suggested in my letter of last week.[7] On this event our resolution against British goods may be harshly treated. But, I confess, that the poison of those sentiments, by which it has been opposed, does not appear to have diffused itself so widely, as I once thought it had. The cool and unprejudiced yield to the necessity of our circumstances: and call the resolution the touchstone of our attachment to the alliance. *The governor himself* has been *moderate* making no other mention *of it* in *his public letter than mere*[ly] *by sa*[y]*ing* that *he had re*[*c*]*ieved* [it.][8] The common objections to the measure recommended are that the encouragement of free importation will produce m[o]re certain, ample and cheap supplies—that it is strange, that we should be so defective in policy, as to suppress the consumption of British commodities, when G. Britain herself, who is at least as wise as Congress, has evidenced her determination by the capture of St. Eustatius to cut off the advantages, which we otherwise should draw from her trade—and that the northern states will acquire infinite emolument, as they can cover successive importations from the British dominions under invoices of a small quantity of captured merchandize. The futility of this discourse surely proves little else, than an undistinguishing, and, in some instances, a malicious mind.[9] You must take the trouble of informing me, as soon as possible, of the yeas and nays on passing the resolution. Rhode-Island, I am sure, was at least divided: and, howsoever the vote of Penna. might have ultimately been, much disgust was discovered against the measure by one of its members.[10]

The governor's public letter was voluminous.[11] It contained, among other things, his various correspondence with Mr. Morris, and some part of his epistolary intercourse with us. The report of the commee on the cessions was the most capital figure. The whole[?] mass was referred to a commee of the whole house.[12] After the reference, Dr. Lee rose, and delivered in at the clerk's table authenticated lists of the companies' names; but I am not well satisfied, that such documents, as these, can throw much light upon the inquiry, howsoever they may furnish [*the intelligence?*] *for malice*.[13]

It is certainly the professed design *of the two Lees* to *ruin Mister Morris*. Nothing can be produced from *his office* to which some parvenu[14] construction is not given. [*The*][15] *two Lee*[*s*] [give?] a state of the *finances* much to the disadvantage of that *gentleman*, extracted, as is asserted from hi[s] *own letter to Congress*. I have *contradicted* the *malici*[*ous*][16] account. You will oblige me by forwarding the history of his *expen*[ces], which he reported soon after the *siege* of *York*. Can charity itself invent an excuse for these movements? Pray send me a short extract from this paper.[17]

Colo. Carrington arrived two days ago. He brings with him some of Mr. Morris's notes *which will* possibly *disarm his enemy*.[18]

Mr. Lee and myself yesterday presented a request for instructions upon the four great points. Being the writer of the letter, I did not fail to hint, without possible offence, to any body the absolute Necessity of the measure.[19] Our letter was referred to a committee, and this necessity seems to impress the whole assembly. As for myself, I had a decent opportunity for avoiding an examination before the house, by substituting Mr. Lee in my stead for every occurrence, which happened after his arrival at congress. I have taken care *however to procure an audience* for myself, if the *resolution* against *British goods* should be *impe[a]ched.*[20]

Governor Harrison has suggested to the assembly the propriety of subjecting the court of admiralty to the controul of the executive in cases of foreigners. There is surely great reason[21] in the idea: but I fear, our constitution forbids the execution of it.[22]

May 17. 1782.

The badness of the weather[23] has prevented me from being in Richmond to day. I have just heard, that the passports, which were granted for the tobacco, to be transported from hence to New-York came into discussion. Mr. R. H. Lee is said to have denied the power of congress to grant them. It is true, that the interdiction of the exercise of powers, not specially delegated, bears hard against this particular one. But how nearly will the impotence of congress resemble the umbra magni nominis,[24] if so natural an inference from the exclusive jurisdiction in war is protested against.[25] It astonishes me, that this business should be first discussed, as if it were the first in[26] dignity. What does it argue to your mind? I understand, that no resolution is formed upon the subject, as yet. I omit the inclosure of a newspaper, because Mr. Hayes[27] informs me, that he sends one weekly. I shall take his information to be just, unless I shall hear the contrary.

I hope Browse[28] has received his hat from Parish.[29] I left the price of it with Mr. Norton.[30]

[1] See Jameson to JM, 9 March, and n. 2; Randolph to JM, 11–13 April; Pendleton to JM, 22 April, and n. 12; JM to Randolph, 23 April, and n. 5, and 4 June 1782; Account with Randolph, *ca.* 1 May 1782, and editorial note.

[2] See JM to Randolph, 7 May; and Virginia Delegates to Harrison, 7 May 1782.

[3] Instead of "essential," Randolph at first wrote "truly important."

[4] See Randolph to JM, 10 May, and n. 12; Lee to JM, 16 May 1782.

[5] Randolph substituted "their body and tendered" for his original "the house of delegates."

[6] See Randolph to JM, 5 May 1782, n. 4. The "similar occasion" may have happened in the session of the Virginia General Assembly of May 1778, when a committee including Jefferson drafted a bill to compel the attendance of senators and delegates. Although this measure contained no provision forbidding a member to refuse to serve, Jefferson may have spoken in favor of such a prohibition during the debate preceding the rejection of the bill by a close vote. This bill, now in the Virginia State Library, was docketed by Randolph. As attorney general of the Commonwealth, he very likely would have been informed of what was said in

favor of and against the measure. Jefferson's evident embarrassment in the spring of 1782, because of the pressure upon him to attend the General Assembly, probably ended when he heard that on 28 May the House of Delegates had declined to adopt a resolution "respecting resignations." His letter to James Monroe on 20 May, arguing forcibly against the legality of denying a member of the House the right to resign, was shown by Monroe to at least some of his fellow delegates and probably contributed to the defeat of the resolution (*Journal of the House of Delegates*, May 1778, pp. 3, 21, 22; Boyd, *Papers of Jefferson*, II, 188–89; VI, 184–87; Minute Book, House of Delegates, May 1782, p. 55; Randolph to JM, 1 June 1782). Embittered by the efforts of his political opponents late in 1781 to have the General Assembly censure his conduct as governor and distressed by Mrs. Jefferson's prolonged illness culminating in her death on 6 September 1782, Jefferson remained in seclusion at Monticello during most of that year (Boyd, *Papers of Jefferson*, VI, 187 n., 196 n.; *Papers of Madison*, III, 338, n. 3).

[7] See Randolph to JM, 10 May 1782, and n. 3.

[8] See *Papers of Madison*, III, 188; 189, n. 6; 338; 339, nn. 2 and 3; Virginia Delegates to Harrison, 8 January, and nn. 4 and 5, and 8 February; JM to Pendleton, 8 January, and 9 April 1782, and n. 5. For Harrison's alleged dislike of France, see Randolph to JM, 11–13 April 1782. In his letter of 6 May to the speaker of the House of Delegates, Harrison mentioned the resolution, drafted by Randolph and adopted on 2 January by Congress, requesting the legislature of each state to confiscate all British goods, if they had been imported within its limits before 1 March 1782 or brought there after being captured at sea (*JCC*, XXII, 3; McIlwaine, *Official Letters*, III, 214, 222). For the efforts of the French to have Americans depend upon France rather than Great Britain for manufactured goods and repress illicit traffic with enemy merchantmen, see William E. O'Donnell, *Chevalier de La Luzerne*, pp. 238–39. According to Robert R. Livingston, "new habits and new fashions must be introduced" by diverting the long-established channel of American trade from Great Britain to France (Wharton, *Revolutionary Diplomatic Correspondence*, V, 73).

[9] In other words, those Virginians who favored "free importation" were, according to Randolph, either so obtuse as to want it because the enemy obviously was trying to prevent it, or so "malicious" as to hold that, if the ban were imposed, Northerners would richly profit from covering large importations of smuggled British merchandise under invoices of small amounts of enemy goods legally captured by their privateers. Randolph may have counted upon JM to understand that Richard Henry Lee and Arthur Lee, who usually and for long had supported the Massachusetts leaders in their opposition to Congress' extreme deference to France, had voiced these arguments.

[10] With his letter to Randolph on 4 June (*q.v.*), JM apparently enclosed a record of the vote of 2 January of the state delegations in Congress on Randolph's resolution mentioned in n. 8, above. What this tally showed is not known, because the enclosure is missing, and neither the printed journal nor the manuscript of the resolution lists the yeas and nays. Charles Thomson merely wrote "pass'd" on this manuscript (*JCC*, XXII, 3; NA: PCC, No. 28, fol. 243). Nevertheless, the lines of division probably conformed with those on a very similar measure which Congress had passed on 4 December 1781. In this poll Rhode Island and every other state with at least two delegates present, except Massachusetts, voted unanimously "aye." The sole delegate from New Hampshire voted "no" (*JCC*, XXI, 1153). The delegate from Pennsylvania who exhibited "much disgust" may have been George Clymer, a rich merchant and banker of Philadelphia. When on 25 February 1782 the Virginia delegation had unanimously opposed a resolution to admit British goods im-

ported in any vessel not belonging to the enemy, Clymer had voted for the measure (*JCC*, XXII, 96–98).

[11] The governor's letter, cited in n. 8, above, covered a number of subjects in a total of approximately 4,200 words.

[12] See *Papers of Madison*, III, 304, n. 1; JM to Randolph, 1 May 1782, nn. 6 and 7.

[13] See *Papers of Madison*, III, 295, n. 7; JM to Randolph, 1 May, and n. 8; Randolph to JM, 10 May 1782, and n. 7. From "The whole[?] mass" through "lists of the companies' names," Randolph was reporting in correct sequence the events of 16 May (Minute Book, House of Delegates, May 1782, pp. 45–46). In coding the first two of these four italicized words, Randolph wrote 657, the symbol for the syllable "fu," but he probably intended to use 6. 57, the ciphers for "the intelligence." He implied that Arthur Lee derived malicious pleasure by exposing some of his political enemies—particularly Franklin, Morris, and Silas Deane—as investors in the land companies which challenged the validity of Virginia's title to the West.

[14] Randolph may have meant that to the aristocratic Lees any act of Robert Morris, who in their view had risen from poverty to great wealth by unworthy means, was only what might be expected of a parvenu.

[15] Although the cipher in the manuscript is 146, standing for "do," Randolph probably should have written 6, the code number for "the."

[16] Here 751, the code figure for "ur" appears, rather than 571, the symbol for "ous."

[17] See nn. 13 and 14, above. The enmity of Arthur and Richard Henry Lee, as well as other influential members of the Lee family, toward Robert Morris dates from 1776–1778, when Congress' Secret Committee of Correspondence, dominated by Morris, had mainly supported Franklin and Deane, commissioners at the court of Versailles, in their continuous friction with their colleague Arthur Lee and his friend Ralph Izard, who had stayed in Paris instead of proceeding to his post in Tuscany. The Lees' prominent allies were John and Samuel Adams and Henry Laurens. This factionalism, often a divisive influence within Congress, basically stemmed from opposing positions on important domestic and foreign issues but was exacerbated by charges and countercharges of financial dishonesty (Clarence L. Ver Steeg, *Robert Morris*, pp. 22–27, and nn.). Aggrieved by Congress' tepid approval of his services in France, its delay in authorizing the payment of his overseas' expenses, its refusal to heed his charges against Franklin, and its deferential regard for Morris, Lee struck back by accusing the superintendent of finance of malfeasance in handling public funds (*Papers of Madison*, II, 142–43, and n. 1; 154; 217; 218, n. 2). Morris' statement of his expenses was a mystery to JM, as it is to the present editors (JM to Randolph, 4 June 1782). For JM's comment upon Arthur Lee's conduct, see JM to Randolph, 4 June, and 2 and 23 July 1782.

[18] See Harrison to Virginia Delegates, 9 February, and nn. 3, 4; Virginia Delegates to Harrison, 25 February, and n. 3; 19 March, n. 1; JM to Randolph, 9 April, n. 4; and Motion on Supplies for Southern Army, 7 May 1782. Colonel Edward Carrington brought assurances from Morris that the contract system for supplying food to the continental army would be extended "as far southwardly" as possible. This pleased Governor Harrison. On 15 May the governor recommended that the General Assembly assist Morris by agreeing to receive for taxes "the notes he may issue to enable him to fulfil his contracts" (McIlwaine, *Official Letters*, III, 224–25). The Assembly adopted this suggestion on 1 July 1782 (Minute Book, House of Delegates, May 1782, p. 85; Hening, *Statutes*, XI, 68–69). In the 18 and 25 May issues of the *Virginia Gazette*, Carrington invited bids for the award of contracts to supply rations.

[19] As shown by the remainder of the paragraph, "the measure" was the resolu-

tion mentioned in n. 8, above. The letter from Lee and Randolph has not been found. The "four great points" were probably those stated by Randolph in his letter of 16 May to the speaker of the House of Delegates–namely, the "prospect of peace," the "state of our army and navy," the "history of our finances," and the "temper of congress with regard to Virginia" (Burnett, *Letters,* VI, 352). Lee had attended Congress from 19 February to about 24 April 1782 (Jameson to JM, 2 March, n. 8; JM to Randolph, 1 May 1782, n. 3).

[20] Randolph wrote the cipher for "thirteen" instead of "a."

[21] Randolph wrote "propriety" and then deleted it.

[22] See Harrison to Virginia Delegates, 23 March 1782, and nn. 1, 2; McIlwaine, *Official Letters,* III, 215. Article IX of the Form of Government of Virginia stipulated that the governor "shall, with the advice of a Council of State, exercise the executive powers of government according to the laws of this commonwealth; and shall not, under any pretence, exercise any power or prerogative by virtue of any law, statute, or custom, of *England*" (Hening, *Statutes,* IX, 115). This emphatic prohibition barred the governor from controlling the Court of Admiralty, but Harrison evidently assumed that, even though the Form of Government contained no article defining the method of amendment, the General Assembly, with the sole power under Article XIII to appoint or remove the judges of admiralty, could delegate to him the authority requested (*ibid.,* IX, 117). This the General Assembly declined to do. Perhaps it came to this decision the more readily because of Governor Nelson's recent "usurpations" and the baffling constitutional problems involved in the present issue (*Papers of Madison,* III, 325, 326, n. 3).

[23] Written over a deleted "day."

[24] In his *De bello civili (Pharsalia),* Book I, line 135, Marcus Annaeus Lacanus (A.D. 39–65) used the words, *Stat magni nominis umbra* ("The mere shadow of a mighty name, he stood"), when describing the fading genius of Gnaeus Pompeius Magnus (106–48 B.C.) by about 50 B.C.

[25] See Lee to JM, 16 May, and n. 7; Randolph to JM, 21–24 May, and nn. 5–9, 15; JM to Randolph, 4 June 1782. Although the Articles of Confederation included no mention of ships flying flags of truce, it conferred upon Congress the power to make war and peace. This grant of authority presumably permitted the employment of all devices, including flags of truce, customarily resorted to by a belligerent. Richard Henry Lee, who less than a year before had even advocated a suspension of portions of both the Articles of Confederation and the Form of Government of Virginia for the duration of the emergency (*Papers of Madison,* III, 157–58), probably welcomed the constitutional issue in the present instance primarily as a weapon with which he again could attack Robert Morris (Ambler to JM, 20 April, and n. 4; Lee to JM, 16 May 1782, and n. 7).

[26] After "in," Randolph wrote and deleted "order of."

[27] James Hayes, Jr. See Jameson to JM, 26 January 1782, and n. 5.

[28] Hore Browse Trist (*ca.* 1778–1804). See *Papers of Madison,* II, 92, n. 8. Randolph had roomed in Philadelphia at the home of the boy's parents and grandmother, Mrs. Mary House. Jefferson, who often befriended the family, appointed Hore Browse Trist in November 1803 to be collector for the district of Mississippi and inspector of revenue at the port of Fort Adams on the Mississippi River (Boyd, *Papers of Jefferson,* X, 167, 611; XI, 178–79; *Tyler's Quarterly Historical and Genealogical Magazine,* VI [1924–25], 215; Brant, *Madison,* IV, 194, 500 n.; *Journal of the Executive Proceedings of the Senate of the United States,* I, 454–55, 464).

[29] Isaac Parrish (1735–1826) had been a Philadelphia hatter at least as early as 1749, when he was apprenticed to the trade following the death of his parents (Susanna Parrish Wharton, comp., *The Parrish Family [Philadelphia, Pennsylvania] . . .*

[Philadelphia, 1925], pp. 44, 51). He numbered George Washington among his customers (*Pennsylvania Archives*, 3d ser., XIV [1897], 187; Fitzpatrick, *Writings of Washington*, XIV, 128, 129 n.; XXX, 254 n.; XXXVII, 96).

[30] Probably Randolph's Virginia friend, John Hatley Norton (*Papers of Madison*, I, 318, n. 15), whose business firm was now located in Philadelphia. See Frances Norton Mason, ed., *John Norton & Sons: Merchants of London and Virginia . . .* (Richmond, 1937), pp. 446–48.

From Jacquelin Ambler

RC (LC: Madison Papers). The cover is missing, but the letter is docketed by JM, "May 18. 1782."

RICHMOND VIRGINIA 18th. May 1782

DEAR SIR

The paper which you were so kind to send me does indeed contain intelligence of most interesting concern to us.[1] had the lust for exorbitant power, and the prejudices of that haughty infatuated Nation been thus corrected four years ago, she would then have had good ground for the hope which some of the Members of Parliament seem now so fondly to cherish.[2] A reunion in any degree compatible with the Idea which appears to be the prevailing one there is impossible. The British Empire is shaken to its foundation; it is not at all surprizing, therefore, that her Citizens, who know and who have her real Interests at heart, think no sacrifice too great which may tend to restore her lost preeminence among the Nations: they are obliged at length to acknowledge this cannot be done but by such a connection with America as must not now be admitted. Every effort, however, which the most consummate policy can dictate will no doubt be tried to effect it, and of course to sow dissensions among the States, and seperate us from our great Ally, to whom, under Providence, we are principally indebted for the present humiliating situation of our Enemy.[3] May Heaven continue its aid, and direct our National Councils at this important Crisis. On Wednesday, and not before, a sufficient number of Delegates met to constitute a House;[4] you may imagine little has yet been done. I will endeavor to transmit you the Journals weekly if a Copy can be had. Mr. Webb will be with you early in next week.[5]

I am with very great esteem Yr. affect Servt

J: AMBLER

P.S. Since the above I hear there is an Antigua Paper come to Town which gives a dreadful Account of the Naval Engagement in the West Indies—that our Allies lost 6. Ships of the Line; & that the Count de Grasse was taken.[6] I dread a confirmation.

[1] Probably the *Pennsylvania Packet* of 7 May 1782. The contents of any letter which JM may have written to Ambler on or about that date probably resembled those in his letters of 7 May to Arthur Lee and Randolph (*q.v.*). See also Virginia Delegates to Harrison, 7 May 1782, and nn. 4 and 5.

[2] Ambler may refer to the belated efforts of Lord North in 1778 to ward off an alliance between France and the United States by dispatching to America a commission of conciliation authorized to offer "practically everything that had been asked short of independence" (Burnett, *The Continental Congress*, pp. 330–39; *Papers of Madison*, III, 272, n. 2).

[3] See Report on Communication from La Luzerne, 1 May, and n. 3; Virginia Delegates to Harrison, 14 May, and nn. 15, 16, 17; JM to Randolph, 14 May, and nn. 2 and 8; Randolph to JM, 16–17 May 1782, and n. 19.

[4] See Lee to JM, 16 May 1782, and n. 3.

[5] Foster Webb, Jr. See Ambler to JM, 11 May 1782, and n. 3.

[6] The news of Admiral Rodney's decisive victory in the Battle of the Saints would have been known by JM three days before Ambler wrote this letter (Virginia Delegates to Harrison, 14 May 1782, n. 14). On 11 May the Baron von Closen at Williamsburg had noted in his journal (Acomb, *Journal of Closen*, pp. 203–4) the arrival of "a flag from Antigua" with word about the engagement. Closen added that since "the news came from the enemy, the public refused to credit it." Perhaps this incredulity explains why, as late as 25 May, the *Virginia Gazette* published a "pretty certain" report that the outcome of the battle had been "considerably in favor" of the French. Finally, in its issue of 8 June 1782, the *Gazette* included the long account, dated 20 April in Antigua, of the engagement which had appeared on 25 May in Rivington's *Royal Gazette* of New York City. See JM to Pendleton, 23 April 1782, n. 3.

Benjamin Harrison to Virginia Delegates

FC (Virginia State Library). In the hand of Thomas Meriwether.

In Council. May 18th: 1782.

Gentlemen

We are obliged to you for your communications of the 4th. Instant;[1] I hope there can be no doubt of America's complying strictly with her engagements to our Allies; there is none here every person that I converse with seems to think it our Interest as well as duty. Our Assembly is at last doing duty and from the complexion of the house I have great hopes something clever will be done.[2] The sending Ships of the enemy here to load Tobacco for the British Merchants gives great umbrage, as indeed it ought; we have suffered too much already by an intercourse with the British. I beg of you never to countenance it again, for be assured if you do, it will be attended with bad consequences, as no means will be left untried to bring the people over to comply with the views of the British Parliament.[3] The offer that Mr Morris has accepted was in part made to me and would have been attended with great advantage to the state in her distresses but was refused as inconsistent with our duty to our Allies and to America.[4]

I am. &c.

[1] See Virginia Delegates to Harrison, 7 May 1782, n. 1.

[2] See Lee to JM, 16 May 1782, n. 3. By "clever," Harrison probably meant "satisfactory" or "positive."

[3] See Ambler to JM, 20 April, n. 4; Lee to JM, 16 May, and n. 7; Randolph to JM, 16–17 May 1782, and n. 25.

[4] The "offer" to Governor Harrison has not been identified, but it must have extended Virginians a wider opportunity to trade with the British than the Articles of Capitulation afforded. For fuller treatment of the matter as pertaining to the "duty to our Allies," see Pendleton to JM, 17 June 1782. Gratitude to the French for their indispensable aid in clearing the enemy out of Virginia in the autumn of 1781, and dependence upon the French navy to deliver the matériel which Virginia was attempting to purchase in France, may partially explain Harrison's opposition to the tobacco contract concluded with the "merchants-capitulant" at Yorktown (Virginia Delegates to Harrison, 24 January, and nn. 1 and 5; Ambler to JM, 20 April, n. 4). In Robert Morris' view, this tenderness for the feelings of the French was wholly unwarranted, since the contract was merely giving effect to the ninth of the Articles of Capitulation, to which the French had been a party. "But of all things in the world," Morris wrote on 30 May 1782 to his Virginia agent, Daniel Clark, entrusted with supervising the loading of tobacco, "the most ridiculous" was the assertion that the contract would "give cause of complaint to the king of France" (Wharton, *Revolutionary Diplomatic Correspondence,* V, 452).

Motion To Inform States of Financial Crisis

MS (NA: PCC, No. 47, fol. 339). Docketed: "Motion of Mr Madison[,] Letter 17th May 1782[, and] do 16. Circular to the States[:] May 20 referred to Mr Madison Mr Root Mr Lowell Mr Rutledge Mr Clymer to confer with the Superintendant of finance."

[20 May 1782]

Whereupon Resolved

That the Superintendt of Finance be instructed to transmit to the several Legislatures of the States, a representation of the alarming prospects which their[1] neglect to comply with the pecuniary requisitions of Congress has produced, and of the absolute necessity of immediate and adequate remittances to the Treasury of the U. States; and that he make use of such mode of transmitting the same as will[2] best ensure Secresy & dispatch.[3]

[1] JM wrote "their" above a deleted "a."

[2] After "will," JM struck out "be attended with least danger of delay."

[3] JM's motion was occasioned by Robert Morris' dispatch of 17 May 1782 to the president of Congress, enclosing a proposed letter to the executive of each state. As evidence of how "the habitual Inattention of the States has reduced us to the Brink of Ruin," Morris pointed out that since 1 January the states had paid to the treasury only $5,500, or "about one-fourth of what is necessary to support us for a single Day." Morris wanted Congress to resolve his dilemma. On the one hand, he recognized that "a faithfull Representation of our distressed Circumstances" would almost surely "fall into improper Hands," thereby producing "the most dangerous Consequences." On the other hand, if the circular letter was not sent and if disaster ensued "from the continued Negligence of the States," they could place the blame on Congress for not warning them "of their Danger" (NA: PCC, No. 137, I, 463–66). Congress apparently adopted JM's motion without tallying the vote (*JCC*, XXII, 279–80). For the recommendation of the committee appointed to consider Morris' suggested circular letter, see Report on Mission To Inform States of Financial Crisis, 22 May 1782, editorial note. John Lowell of Massachusetts entered Congress on the same day that he became a member of this committee (*JCC*, XXII, 278).

To James Madison, Sr.

RC (LC: Madison Papers). Addressed to "Col: James Madison Orange County Virginia[.] Favd. by Capt M. Walker." Probably late in his life, JM, or John C. Payne, whose handwriting greatly resembled JM's, wrote "(Biographical.)" above the salutation and "Madison, Jr" above the date line on the first page.

PHILADA. May 20th. 1782

HOND SIR

Having written a letter[1] and inclosed with it a large collection of Newspapers for you which was to have been carried by Mr. J. Smith,[2] but which I have now put into the hands of Capt: Walker,[3] whose return will be quicker, little remains for me to add here. Our anxiety on account of the West India news published at New York is still supported by contradictory reports and conjectures. The account however to which Rodneys name is prefixed renders our apprehensions too strong for our hopes. Riving[t]on has been very bold in several of his spurious publications, and at this conjuncture might venture as far to serve a particular turn as at any. But it is scarcely credible that he would dare or be permitted to sport with so high an official name.[4]

If Mr. Jefferson will be so obliging as to superintend the legal studies of Wm. I think he cannot do better than prosecute the plan he has adopted. The interruption occasioned by the Election of Mr J. altho' inconvenient in that respect, is by no means a decisive objection agst. it.[5]

I did not know before that the Letters which Mr. Walker[6] was to have carried last fall had met with the fate which it seems they did. I shall be more cautious hereafter. The papers missing in your list were I presume[,] for I do not recollect, contained in them.

The short notice does not leave me time to obtain the information you ask as to Stills. I have never heard of Iron Stills being cast here, nor do I know the price of Copper ones.[7]

If Continental money passes here at all it is in a very small quantity, at very great discount, and merely to serve particular local & temporary ends.[8]

It has at no time been more difficult for me to fix my probable return to Virga. At present all my Colleagues have left Congress except Col. Bland,[9] and it is a crisis which calls for a full representation from every State. Anxious as I am to visit my friends as long as I sustain a public trust, I shall feel a principle which is superior to it. The state of my finances also, unless the Assembly shall make a different provision for the Delegation from what has hitherto been in force,[10] will be a serious bar to my removal from this place. I shall I believe be under the necessity of purchasing a carriage of some kind besides discharging considerable arrears, & where the means for effecting either are to be found is totally without my comprehension.

Capt: Walker tells me you have a [colt?][11] which you propose to reserve for a Stu[d.] If he be not very fine, I should be exceedi[ngly gra]tified in his being prepared for the saddle. [Neither] of the Horses I have here is fit for that use, [in?] that both of them are growing too old f[or] further use of any kind. With my very affectio[nate] regards for all the family

I am yor. dutiful son

J. MADISON JR.

[1] Neither this letter nor those letters mentioned in the third paragraph have been found.

[2] Possibly Jeremiah Smith (*ca.* 1738–1801), a resident of James Madison, Sr.'s, tax district in Orange County (John Frederick Dorman, comp., "Orange County,

Virginia, Will Book 2, 1744–1778" [reproduced from typewritten copy, Washington, D.C., 1961], p. 59; Orange County, Va., Personal Property Tax Books, 1800–1801, MSS in Virginia State Library).

[3] Captain Merry Walker (*Papers of Madison*, III, 208, n. 5).

[4] Copying from the so-called "Mr. Rivington's Royal Lying Gazette" of 13 May 1782, the *Pennsylvania Packet* published five days later what purported to be Admiral Rodney's account of his "total defeat" of the French squadron in the Battle of the Saints, including the sinking of the "Diadème," and the capture of five other men-of-war, of which one was the "Ville de Paris," the Comte de Grasse's flagship. See Ambler to JM, 18 May 1782, n. 6.

[5] See Jefferson to JM, 24 March 1782, and n. 7.

[6] Probably James Walker, who had also carried letters and packages back and forth between JM and his father in March 1782 (JM to James Madison, Sr., 30 March 1782). No letter from JM to his father written after 1 August 1781 and before 12 February 1782 has been found.

[7] In the *Pennsylvania Journal* of 8 May 1782, Kaighn and Attmore, whose store was on Front Street near Arch Street, Philadelphia, advertised to sell at an unspecified price, "A new Copper Still containing 51 gallons, with a Worm." No mention of iron stills has been found among the hardware for sale by Philadelphia merchants during the first six months of 1782.

[8] See Report on New Hampshire Requisition, 25 March 1782, n. 2.

[9] See JM to Pendleton, 23 April 1782, n. 10.

[10] See Jameson to JM, 9 March, n. 5; Expense Account, 20 March, n. 4; JM to Randolph, 16 and 23 July 1782.

[11] The brackets enclosing this word and the other words or parts of words in this paragraph signify that the right-hand margin of the manuscript is missing.

From Edmund Pendleton

Tr (LC: Force Transcripts). Another copy, also made from the original manuscript, is in the *Proceedings of the Massachusetts Historical Society*, 2d ser., XIX (1905), 152–53. An extract is in Stan. V. Henkels Catalogue No. 694 (1892), pp. 89–90.

VIRGA. May 20th 1782

DEAR SIR:

Your favr of the 7th[1] brought me the debates in Parliament on which I suppose had been founded the story mentioned in my Last of their having acknowledged Our Independence, a weak ground indeed, but yet I conclude it is all they had.[2] I wish you had given me yr sentiments upon it, perhaps they might have placed the transaction in a more favourable light than it now appears to me,[3] which is that of a mere Tub thrown out to amuse that Whale,[4] the present dangerous Spirit of the Nation, in hopes time may Occasion it to evaporate, and Ministry may still pursue their beloved Object: For what does this last proceeding amount to, more than a Resolution to suspend for a very precarious time Active Operations in America, that they may be more at leisure to make effectual War agt France and Spain in other parts?[5] Oh yes, they are to make peace with Us, & we hear that General Carleton is arrived with the necessary powers:[6] what do they mean by talking of Peace with Us, & vigorous War with our ally, with whom we have solemnly engaged to make it a *Common* Cause? Are they encouraged to this Insult by any former Instance of our perfidy, the tardiness of our Ally, or the ill success of our conjunct efforts? let the unshaken firmness of America, the unbounded generosity of France and the events of the War answer. This farce of Peace then is only resolvable into that amusement before mentioned to Allay the present ferment, without quitting the War; Let them take care however that it don't recoil upon them with double force at some future day. And let Us not relax in Our preparations for repelling any Attack wch may be meditated. I had yesterday from Richmond an Account of a great Naval Action in the West Indies said to have been taken from an Antigua paper, the result of which is told me [in][7] two ways; by one the French had 4 line of battle ships taken & two sunk, according to the other only one was taken & one sunk, agreeing that Count De Grasse's ship The Ville de Paris was taken. The story is that the French Fleet of 31 sailed to join the Spanish Fleet, & were met by the British of 33, which they were compelled to engage to give the transports under their convoy, an Opportunity of escaping, the paper is silent whether that was effected,[8] but it is said the French Commandant at York has written the Governor that the transports were safe, and speaks of the Action rather as a Bagatelle.[9] I have hopes the Antigua Rivington may have Exagerated the british advantage, but fear the loss of that Valuable Officer & ship is too true. I am impatient to hear the certain Account & whether the French formed the Junction with the Spaniards after the action.[10] Mr Tyler is Speaker of the Delegates in opposition to Col. Lee,[11]

1 Not found. See Pendleton to JM, 13 May 1782, n. 1.

2 *Ibid.*; Virginia Delegates to Harrison, 7 May 1782, and n. 4.

3 The word "in" precedes this comma in the version published in the *Proceedings of the Massachusetts Historical Society*.

4 Jonathan Swift, in the preface to *Tale of a Tub* (1704), wrote, "Seamen have a custom, when they meet a whale, to fling him out an empty tub by way of amusement, to divert him from laying violent hands upon the ship."

5 Pendleton may have heard of the actions mentioned in JM to Randolph, 14 May 1782, and nn. 3 and 4.

[6] See Virginia Delegates to Harrison, 7 May, and n. 4; 14 May, and nn. 15 and 16; JM to Randolph, 14 May 1782, and n. 8.

[7] From copy in the *Proceedings of the Massachusetts Historical Society.*

[8] See Ambler to JM, 18 May, and n. 6; JM to James Madison, Sr., 20 May 1782, and n. 4. According to W. M. James, thirty-seven British and thirty French ships of the line participated in the battle. Although the 104-gun "Ville de Paris," the flagship of the Comte de Grasse, was the most formidable vessel of the two fleets, the British armament totaled 2,748 cannon and the French only 2,246. The transports carrying about 9,000 French troops succeeded in taking "shelter under the guns of Guadeloupe" before 12 April, the decisive day of the battle (W. M. James, *British Navy in Adversity*, pp. 332–33, 448–50).

[9] The Comte de Rochambeau wrote from Yorktown to Governor Harrison on 20 May, but, judging from the latter's reply, the dispatch had not mentioned the Battle of the Saints (McIlwaine, *Official Letters,* III, 230–31). On the same day the Baron von Closen noted, "M. de Rochambeau, understanding the character of the Americans among whom we were living, simply told them that according to this information [a gazette from Grenada], it was really a great success for our side" (Acomb, *Journal of Closen*, p. 204).

[10] Between the latter half of April and 10 June, "fourteen French and eleven Spanish ships of the line, 104 merchants vessels preparing for convoy" and about 19,000 French and Spanish troops assembled at Cap Français, Haiti. Perhaps in some measure because fevers and other ailments were epidemic among the soldiers, they refrained from attacking the British. On the other hand, the possibility that this force, together with other Spanish ships at Havana, would launch an offensive obliged the British to patrol the Caribbean until the end of the war (W. M. James, *British Navy in Adversity*, pp. 354–62).

[11] Randolph to JM, 10 May 1782, and n. 12; and 16–17 May. At this point, Peter Force's clerk wrote, "[The rest cut off]."

From Joseph Jones

RC (LC: Madison Papers). Addressed to "Honble James Madison jr. Philadelphia." Docketed, "May 1782."

SPRING HILL 21st. May 1782

DR. SR.

The friendly visits of my Neighbours and acquaintance[s] since my return[1] has and still continues to occupy my time[.] having not been free from Company since the day after my geting home, of course I have thought little of those matters which used while in Philadelphia to employ our attention and have not yet fixed the time of my visit to Richmond wh. will be regulated by information from there. our last accounts (whether true I know not) but your advices by the Post will inform you, say there was a House on Wednesday last.[2] if so I shall in eight or ten days pay my respects to them.[3] It is said several petitions will be presented urging a further emission of paper currency as indispensibly necessary to supply the scarsity of specie. some through folly, others from wickedness may countenance this measure but I cannot believe there can be found in the Assembly a Majority of those Characters untill the fatal adoption of the proposition shall convince me of my mistake.[4] It is certain that specie is either very scarse or if in the Country locked up as the want of it is universally complained of by the planter and merchant.[5] It must be very scarse or our commerce very languid as I am told good merchantable flour may be purchased over the mountains for 7/6 P hundred and I know Tobacco (upland too) will not produce upon this River 2d. Cash. the reason assigned [is] want of money to purchase. imported articles in general 100 PCt. higher than in Philadelphia and as the great part of the goods for sale come from that quarter and of late from N. York thu[s? i]t is easy to account for the drain of specie and what must be the consequence to these States from such a ruinous trafic and a hampered commerce.[6]

I have not been able to find your pamphlet[7] among my Books & papers. shod. I come across it you may be certain proper care shall be taken of it and conveyed by the first safe hand. did you not lend it to Mr. Lee or Col. Bland? I think you had it from me sometime before I came away and for the perusal of one of those Gentlemen? pray my friend let me have the Revolutionist from No. 4[.] I have it to that number.[8] The April packet from England may be daily expected at New York[.] by her we may probably hear the result of the proceedings in consequence of Genl. Conways motion.[9] I hear little of recruiting our line. the business, they say, is at a stand for want of money as indeed is almost every other public exertion. some military men say they could recruit our line if they had a specie bounty to offer. this cannot be furnished untill the Taxes bring it in and these, if at all, will not be productive untill October. Virga. will therefore this summer have few [m]en in the field unless for the spur of the oc[casion]. perhaps the assembly may thin[k it] necessary to order out a Body for the ti[me being?][10] Mrs. Jones[11] begs her Compliments to the Ladys and joins me in the same to Col. Bland and yourself

Yr. aff Friend & Servt.

Jos: Jones.

[1] Probably about 10 May Jones arrived from Philadelphia at Spring Hill, his estate in King George County ten miles east of Fredericksburg. See JM to Randolph, 9 April 1782, n. 6.

[2] See Randolph to JM, 5 May 1782, n. 9.

[3] Jones may have intended to make himself available for questioning by the House of Delegates, as Lee and Randolph had already done (JM to Randolph, 7 May, and n. 11; Randolph to JM, 16–17 May 1782).

[4] See Randolph to JM, 5 May and n. 7; 10 May; JM to Randolph, 14 May 1782.

[5] See Pendleton to JM, 15 April, and n. 4; Lee to JM, 16 May 1782, and nn. 8, 9.

[6] Jones's home was near the Rappahannock River. Three weeks earlier Arthur Lee evidently found that the "sweet-scented" tobacco, customarily grown in Tidewater Virginia and the "upland too," was selling along the Rappahannock River and near Chesapeake Bay at threepence a pound (JM to Lee, 7 May 1782, headnote). The reference to "N. York" signified that the avenues opened by Virginia and Tory merchants at Yorktown were still being utilized. See Lee to JM, 16 May, and n. 9; Harrison to Virginia Delegates, 18 May 1782.

[7] Unidentified.

[8] No pamphleteer or contributor to a newspaper, writing under the pseudonym, "the Revolutionist," has been identified. Jones probably meant "The Continentalist" essays of Alexander Hamilton. Of these the first four had appeared in the *New-York Packet, and the American Advertiser* (Fishkill, N.Y.) on 12 and 19 July, 9 and 30 August 1781, respectively (Harold C. Syrett and Jacob E. Cooke, eds., *Papers of Alexander Hamilton,* II, 649–52, 654–57, 660–65, 669–74). The remaining two numbers of this series appeared in the same newspaper on 18 April and 4 July 1782, respectively (*ibid.*, III, 75–82, 99–106).

[9] General Henry Seymour Conway (1721–1795), a Rockingham Whig and a member of Parliament from 1741 to 1784, had opposed Lord North's policy toward the thirteen American colonies before the Revolution. Conway's motion, which needed only one more vote to carry in the House of Commons on 22 February and passed without a division five days later, was an important step leading to the fall of the North ministry (Virginia Delegates to Harrison, 19 March, n. 7; 7 May, n. 4; JM to Pendleton, 23 April, n. 5; JM to Randolph, 14 May 1782, and n. 2).

[10] The words of this sentence were partially destroyed when the manuscript was unsealed by JM. The bracketed inserts are the editors'. For the recruitment law, adopted at the May 1782 session of the Virginia General Assembly, see Jameson to JM, 23 March 1782, n. 5. During May and June 1782 the Governor in Council ordered the militia of particular counties to perform special duties, such as guarding prisoners of war and defending the western frontiers and the Eastern Shore (*Journals of the Council of State,* III, 82–83, 84, 88, 90, 91, 104, 109).

[11] In 1779, about two years after the death of his first wife, Mary Taliaferro Jones, Joseph Jones married Mary Waugh Dawson (*ca.* 1740–*ca.* 1785), the widow of the Reverend Musgrave Dawson (d. 1763) of Caroline County, and the daughter of Alexander Waugh (d. 1793) of Orange County, Va. (George Harrison Sanford King, comp. and ed., *Marriages of Richmond County, Virginia, 1668–1853* [Fredericksburg, Va., 1964], p. 249). These data, unknown to the editors until the present volume was in preparation, render inaccurate the identification of Mrs. Jones in *Papers of Madison,* II, 108, n. 14, and oblige the insertion of "the first" before "Mrs. Jones's" in *ibid.*, III, 51, n. 4.

To Edmund Randolph

RC (LC: Madison Papers). The cover is missing, and the name of the addressee is not shown in the letter. Docketed in Randolph's hand, "J Madison May 21. 1782." JM's autograph list of letters from "JM. to E. Randolph" (*Papers of Madison*, III, 100–101, editorial note) calendars this letter as of 21 May 1782 and as dealing with "Carltons request to send Morgan to Congs. rejected."

PHILADA. May 21st. 1782

DEAR SIR

Your favor of the 10th. was recd. yesterday. I suspect that I have expressed myself ambiguously with respect to Mr. Jefferson.[1] He does not alledge ignorance of the report of the Committee, but of the title of N.Y. which is the ground on which the report places the controversy with Virga.[2]

I have no addition to make to the European intelligence contained in my last. The answer to the request of Carlton went in the negative as I anticipated.[3] The intelligence published at N. Y. relative to the action in the W. Indies, has converted our hopes into apprehensions. The evidence recd. of the favorable issue mentioned last week, appeared so clear & satisfactory that full credit was given to it. It is not even yet totally invalidated, but the opposite scale is fast preponderating.[4]

The final report of our suit to Congress for an answer to the Western Cession was sent by the last post. Mr. Jones can explain every thing relative to it[.] I feel myself much disburdened by the termination of the business. If it sd. be revived here in consequen[ce] of steps taken by the Legislature, I flatter mys[e]lf it will be under circumstances less embarrassing.[5]

We have recd. a remittance from Mr. Ross which renders it unnecessary for you to go out of the way to remit the small sum I advanced for you.[6]

I am prevented from adding another paragraph by the want of the Cypher which Col. Bland has in his possession & is making use of.

Adieu

J. M. JR.

The Govr. has not inclosed us any letter either from Mr. M. or the Minister of F. but a letter from him to each. Obtain a perusal if you can of that to the latte[r] & I shall hear from you[7] &

1 See JM to Randolph, 1 May; Randolph to JM, 10 May 1782.

2 See Jefferson to JM, 24 March 1782, and n. 2. For "the report of the Committee," see JM to Randolph, 1 May 1782, n. 6. Following "on which," JM wrote and crossed out about fifteen words so heavily that they are illegible. Late in his life he, or someone at his bidding, bracketed this paragraph and the third paragraph to signify that they should be published in the first edition of his papers. See Madison, *Papers* (Gilpin ed.), I, 130.

3 See Virginia Delegates to Harrison, 14 May 1782, and n. 17.

4 *Ibid.*, n. 14.

5 *Ibid.*, and nn. 1–13. The "sd." is an abbreviation for "should."

6 See Randolph to JM, 11–13 April and 16–17 May; JM to Randolph, 23 April and 4 June; Harrison to Virginia Delegates, 11 May 1782.

7 See Harrison to Virginia Delegates, 11 May 1782, and n. 1.

From Edmund Randolph

RC (LC: Madison Papers). This four-page letter lacks a cover and a complimentary close. In its original form the letter may have had at least one more page. The handwriting and contents permit no doubt that Randolph wrote the letter. He encoded in the official cipher the words italicized in the present copy.

RICHMOND May 21. 22. 23. 24. 1782.[1]

DEAR SIR

The information, contained in my two last letters, has appeared within these two days to be erroneous. Our resolution against British merchandize passed the committee of the whole house without opposition. An attempt was indeed made to except salt: but Mr. R. H. Lee scouted it out, as I was informed. A bill is ordered to be brought in upon it.[2]

But so strange is the revolution of things, that this very act of congress became the reason, why the passports, granted under their authority, for the transportation of tobacco to New-York, were yesterday reprobated. I intend to transmit to you a copy of the proceedings.[3] The arguments against the power of congress were first drawn from the non-enumeration of it in the confederation.[4] This ground soon appeared untenable; and resort was had to the distinction, that passports might issue under their direction for legal purposes; but not for illegal, & that the shipping of tobacco for our enemy was an illicit commerce; as contravening a law of the state.[5] But the 14th. article of the treaty of amity with France seemed to operate most strongly on the minds of the house. You will observe, that this article forbids any property of the Americans to be put into hostile bottoms.[6] I was summoned to state the matter, as it appeared to congress, when the resolution of the 13th. of february was entered into.[7] I informed them, that no debate arose on the occasion, because no distrust was harboured even by the most jealous of congressional usurpation concerning the power of granting these passports.[8] I affirmed my opinion to be, that the 2d. article ought not to be understood literally: but that the words "expressly delegated" meant an obvious and direct consequence from the general powers, briefly sketched in the confederation:[9] that the exclusive right of determining on war and peace, and the direction of military operations obviously and directly led to the power of granting passports: that a law of the state in 1776. subjected those, who exported Virginian produce to Great Britain, Ireland, or the British W. Indies to certain penalties, unless such exportation was authorized by congress,[10] and thereby plainly justified this assumption of power & that altho' we ranked ourselves among the firmest friends of the Alliance and fixed enemies to the introduction of British manufactures we did not conceive, that we derogated from either that friendship or that enmity, by asserting the right of congress on this subject. I added in answer to the objection, which the treaty of commerce presented, that nothing more was intended by it, than to restrain a trade, carried on by individuals, not to abridge the prerogative of sovereignty. It was not in my province to refute those arguments, which were adduced against the passports, my office being merely to reply to questions. But for this cause, I really think, that I should have experienced very little difficulty in overcoming the opposition. I could not however avoid the mention, that our reputation was concerned in this business; as we had been the instruments of our country in the application to congress for the passports to Bermuda last year,[11] and by this means had in a manner asserted the jurisdiction of congress in these cases. I urged the two Mr. Lees to attend to this, and at least to guard our feelings against the wound, to which the inclosed resolution exposes us. Nothing has, as yet, been done in this respect. It is impossible to say, what the fate of the act will be in the senate. But the *name of Morris makes them forget* the *good*[,] I fear, *of the public*[,] *and* common *decency*. There is more genius, and more industry, exerted *in* [an] *able matter*[12] *out of doors* than so *bad a pu*[r]*pose deserves*. Strange, that a particular state should undertake to vindicate the treaty of commerce,[13] in contradiction to an Act of congress,[14] who alone can judge; and are by the confederation appointed to judge, what its proper construction ought to be.[15] Still stranger is it, that our friend, the doctor, should have conceded so much authority to them on the discussion of the ordinance for regulating the post-office,[16] and be now anxious to restrict them in a far more necessary point of jurisdiction.

The tax-law of the last session will be assaulted.[17] Mr. Henry, who came down two or three days ago,[18] is its enemy so far, as to wish to postpone the collection of the taxes in some counties, whose poverty he says, requires the measure. Six or seven petitions depend before the house to this effect. But the torrent of opinion runs strongly against the infraction of this salutary Act,[19] and I am happy now to believe, that it runs equally strong against that weak succedaneum for specie, paper-money.[20]

The assembly avow themselves staunch to the alliance. The house of delegates yesterday passed adequate resolves, as I hear, against separate negotiation;[21] and have appointed committees to prepare bills for the security of shipwrecked property, and in general for all those objects, recommended to them by congress with respect to the consular convention.[22] Congress too do not appear unmindful of policy towards the french nation, & particularly towards the queen's party, whose force will increase upon the birth of a dauphin.[23]

A practice has prevailed of meeting the public debtors, who were bringing specie into the treasury and giving them specie warrants. By this means public necessity has been often unsatisfied, while the officer of government has received his salary. To avoid a like impropriety of conduct in future, a bill is ordered to be prepared for the appropriation of the revenue, to the various uses, for which it was designed.[24]

As soon as the senate meets, a resolution will be passed for the nomination of persons to collect documents concerning western territory.[25] A delicacy obtains in the mind of Mr. Henry, lest a rupture with congress should injure our more essential interests, and probably the repeal of the cession will be the extent of legislative proceeding at this day.[26]

I am convinced of the truth of Mr. Matlack's observation, that no part of Mason's & Dixon's line was ex parte. But if this line be 232. miles, and some perches and twenty three miles be added for the tempor[ar]y line proposed, surely the five degrees of longitude, due to Pennsa. will be overrun nine or ten miles.[27]

I shall scarcely ever be able to give you foreign intelligence. You will expect domestic only. The above therefore being the history of this week's proceedings of the assembly, I shall only repeat assurances of my friendship.

I shewed your favor of the 14th. May to Colo. Taylor,[28] and shall reserve it for Mr. Jones, when he arrives.

Pray send me the journal of 1781.[29]

[1] Randolph interlineated 22. 23. 24. above "May 21. 1782."

[2] See Virginia Delegates to Harrison, 8 January, n. 4; Randolph to JM, 16–17 May 1782, and n. 8. Randolph erred in stating that he had mentioned the resolution in his letter of 10 May. The law enacted by the General Assembly on 2 July 1782 for the seizure in Virginia of "all goods, wares or merchandize, of the growth, produce, or manufacture of Great-Britain, or of any territory depending thereon" made no exception to permit the importation of salt (Minute Book, House of Delegates, May 1782, pp. 46, 86; Hening, *Statutes*, XI, 101–3). For the shortage of salt, see *Papers of Madison*, III, 199–200; 207; 214; 222, n. 2. James Hunter, Jr., remarked in a letter of 27 July 1782 to Theodorick Bland: "I see much distress hanging over us this fall for want of the most necessary article, salt. I would wish you, therefore, and your friends in Congress, to take this matter into thought. The small quantity in hand is hoarded up to watch for an exorbitant price" (Charles Campbell, ed., *Bland Papers*, II, 87).

[3] Later in this paragraph, and in the first paragraph of his letter to JM of 1 June 1782 (*q.v.*), Randolph makes clear that he enclosed the copy. It is in LC: Madison Papers, II, 28b. This protest by the House of Delegates on 20 May was neither endorsed by the Senate nor intended to serve as instructions to the delegates of Virginia in Congress. The five resolutions comprising the protest declared that "allowing British Traders Capitulants at York to export tobacco to the amount of Monies received for their goods" was unwarranted by the terms of the Articles of Capitulation of Yorktown, and was inconsistent with the request of Congress to have Virginia confiscate British imports, with her own laws forbidding trade with the enemy, and with the Treaty of Amity and Commerce with France. For these reasons, "the vessels now arrived in this state from New York . . . ought not be permitted to load."

Having received an attested copy of these resolutions made by John Beckley, clerk of the House of Delegates, and forwarded probably by Daniel Clark, who was in Virginia as Morris' agent (*Papers of Madison*, III, 256, n. 6; Wharton, *Revolutionary Diplomatic Correspondence*, V, 448), the financier laid them before Congress. John Rutledge, chairman of a committee to which the protest was referred on 28 May, submitted an acceptable report on the next day. After expressing the opinion that the protest had been "founded on misapprehension," Congress resolved "that the members who are to repair to Virginia, be instructed to make such representations to that State as may remove every obstacle to the execution" of the contract made by Charles Thomson and Robert Morris with the "British Traders Capitulant" (NA: PCC, No. 75, fols. 367–68; *JCC*, XXII, 308, n. 1, 309–10). On 30 May Congress softened this instruction by adopting a motion, introduced by Abraham Clark and seconded by JM, authorizing the two delegates about to leave on their mission southward "to make such explanations to the legislature of Virginia as they shall deem expedient relative to the transaction which is the subject of the resolutions of the house of delegates of the said State" (*JCC*, XXII, 311). See also Randolph to JM, 1 June 1782. For "the members who are to repair to Virginia," see Report on Mission To Inform States of Financial Crisis, 22 May 1782, editorial note.

[4] That is, the Articles of Confederation.

[5] The October 1776 session of the Virginia General Assembly had enacted a law on this subject which, besides many other provisions, specifically banned trade in tobacco with the enemy (Hening, *Statutes*, IX, 162).

[6] Since Article XIV of the Treaty of Amity and Commerce dealt with merchant ships of France or the United States trading in enemy ports rather than with enemy merchantmen trading in the ports of France or the United States, it was irrelevant to the agreement between agents of Congress and the merchants-capitulant of

Yorktown. Randolph should have cited Articles XV and especially XVI of the treaty, providing for the seizure of prohibited goods, even though not contraband, on enemy ships loaded in a port of France or the United States (*JCC*, XI, 430–33). In short, the treaty banned a traffic which Congress and the Virginia General Assembly had also prohibited. The controversy involved not only a conflict between states' rights and confederation power but also between the terms of a treaty made by commissioners of Congress and the terms of an agreement, also ratified by Congress, made or endorsed by its appointees, including Washington, Morris, Charles Thomson, and Timothy Pickering, the quartermaster general.

[7] JM had been a member of the committee which had prepared the resolution, adopted by Congress on 11 (not 13) February 1782, providing for carrying out the agreement mentioned in n. 6 (*JCC*, XXII, 70–71). Although Randolph's appearance before the House on 20 May is unrecorded in the minute book, it must have been near the end of the session of that day, when the matter was considered in committee of the whole (Minute Book, House of Delegates, May 1782, p. 48).

[8] Charles Thomson, in accord with the directive of 11 February (n. 7), had issued passports about 1 April 1782 to the masters of the British merchant ships at New York City, assuring them of safe conduct as flag-of-truce vessels to proceed to Virginian ports to load 685 hogsheads of tobacco consigned to the merchants-capitulant of Yorktown (Lee to JM, 16 May 1782, and n. 7).

[9] The second of the Articles of Confederation reads: "Each State retains its sovereignty, freedom and independence, and every power, jurisdiction, and right, which is not by this confederation expressly delegated to the United States, in Congress assembled" (*JCC*, IX, 908).

[10] For this act, see Hening, *Statutes*, IX, 171.

[11] See *Papers of Madison*, III, 214; 221; 222, n. 2.

[12] Although Randolph wrote 34, the cipher for "matter," he probably should have written 816. 731. 24, standing for "manner." See Randolph to JM, 16–17 May 1782, and nn. 13 and 17.

[13] See n. 6, above.

[14] See n. 7, above.

[15] The ninth of the Articles of Confederation conferred upon Congress "the sole and exclusive right and power" of "entering into treaties and alliances, provided that no treaty of commerce shall be made, whereby the legislative power of the respective states shall be restrained from . . . prohibiting the exportation or importation of any species of goods or commodities whatsoever." The thirteenth of the Articles of Confederation declared that "Every State shall abide by the determinations of the United States, in Congress assembled, on all questions which, by this confederation, are submitted to them" (*JCC*, IX, 915, 925).

[16] The ninth of the Articles of Confederation granted to Congress complete authority to establish and regulate an interstate postal service and to determine the postage charges (*JCC*, IX, 919). When Arthur Lee had "conceded so much authority" to Congress is unknown, but he may have done so on 11 March 1782 during the debate on a proposed ordinance designed to reform the postal service and to render it profitable by centralizing the control of its operation and personnel in the postmaster general of the United States (*JCC*, XXII, 121–26).

[17] See Harrison to Virginia Delegates, 11 January, and n. 4; Jameson to JM, *ca.* 12 January, n. 8; 23 February 1782, and n. 6. See also Charles Campbell, ed., *Bland Papers*, II, 81–82.

[18] See Randolph to JM, 10 May 1782, n. 3.

[19] Contrary to Randolph's expectation, the General Assembly on 1 July extended the due dates for paying taxes because of "the late cruel ravages of the enemy and

destruction of private property, together with the great burthens already borne by the good people of this state" (Minute Book, House of Delegates, May 1782, p. 85; Hening, *Statutes*, XI, 9–12, 66–71; Randolph to JM, 1 June, and 27–29 June 1782, n. 8).

[20] See Randolph to JM, 5 May, n. 7. "Substitute" is an approximate equivalent of "succedaneum."

[21] See Virginia Delegates to Harrison, 14 May, n. 13; Lee to JM, 24 May 1782. Randolph underlined "staunch to the alliance," but the phrase is not italicized here in order to keep it distinct from the italicized portions of the letter which he wrote in code. The House of Delegates adopted these "adequate resolves" on 24 May. Hence "yesterday" connotes that Randolph, in spite of his dating of the letter, wrote this paragraph on the 25th, or had been misinformed, or had misconstrued what he had heard (Minute Book, House of Delegates, May 1782, p. 52).

[22] For the law on this subject, enacted on 1 July, see *ibid.*, p. 85; Hening, *Statutes*, XI, 51–54. See also Randolph to JM, 20 June 1782. Randolph had been the chairman of the committee to which Congress referred the recommendations from the court of Versailles of what the provisions of a consular convention might be (*Papers of Madison*, III, 201, and n.; *JCC*, XXI, 792–804; XXII, 17–26, 25–28 n.). On 9 January 1782, during the debate on the committee's report, Congress agreed to request each state to establish "a speedy mode of administrating justice" between French subjects and American citizens, and to vest "persons in the neighbourhood of the seacoast with powers to secure shipwrecked property in the most effectual manner" (*JCC*, XXII, 25). See also *JCC*, XXII, 53; and McIlwaine, *Official Letters*, III, 214. The Virginia General Assembly in the session of May 1782 adopted "An act concerning wrecks" (Hening, *Statutes*, XI, 51–54), but if the legislators considered other matters pertinent to the proposed consular convention between the United States and France, they may have concluded that the statute of 24 December 1779 "for the protection and encouragement of the commerce of nations acknowledging the independence of the United States of America" covered the subject adequately (*ibid.*, X, 202–3; *Journal of the House of Delegates*, October 1779, p. 108).

[23] See Report on Form of Public Audience for La Luzerne, 7–9 May, editorial note, and n. 7; Revised Reply of President of Congress to La Luzerne, 8–12 May 1782. Queen Marie Antoinette (1755–1793), a daughter of the Empress Maria Theresa and a sister of the Emperor Joseph II, had married the future King Louis XVI in 1770. The "queen's party" favored Austria in foreign affairs and opposed all reforms of a liberal cast in France. The enthusiasm aroused by the long-awaited birth of an heir to the throne served momentarily to lessen the queen's unpopularity (Louis Gottschalk, *Lafayette and the Close of the American Revolution* [Chicago, 1942], pp. 346, 348; Louis Gottschalk, *Lafayette between the American and the French Revolution*, pp. 153, 342).

[24] For this law, designed in part to prevent treasury clerks and other minor officials, in a time of depreciating paper currency and rising prices of commodities, from profiting personally by trafficking in the specie and specifics received by the Commonwealth in payment of taxes and duties, see Hening, *Statutes*, XI, 12–14.

[25] See JM to Randolph, 1 May 1782, n. 7.

[26] The May 1782 session of the General Assembly did not repeal the offer of cession made by the Assembly on 2 January 1781 (*Papers of Madison*, II, 300, n. 2).

[27] See Randolph to JM, 26 April 1782, and n. 2. Timothy Matlack was secretary of the Supreme Executive Council of Pennsylvania. Whether his "observation" was oral or written is not known, but it clearly was a rejoinder to Governor Harrison's protest against beginning the survey of the boundary between Virginia and

Pennsylvania from the western end of the Mason-Dixon line. In Harrison's view the western portion of that line, having been run only by the surveyor appointed by Pennsylvania after the surveyor named by Maryland had suspended his work, perhaps deviated too far south. Hence to begin at its termination and proceed due west might result in giving land to Pennsylvania which rightfully belonged to Virginia.

[28] Probably Colonel James Taylor (1732–1814) of Caroline County. He was in Richmond to represent his district in the state Senate (Louis A. Burgess, comp. and ed., *Virginia Soldiers of 1776* [3 vols.; Richmond, 1927–29], I, 440; Swem and Williams, *Register*, p. 17).

[29] See JM to Randolph, 4 June 1782.

Report on Mission To Inform States of Financial Crisis

MS (NA: PCC, No. 47, fols. 341, 343). Docketed by JM, "Report of The Committee Appointed to confer with the Superintendt of Finance on the subject of his letter of the 17 day of May 1782." Below this on the docket, the words "Delivered May 21.–Passed." appear to have been written by Charles Thomson. An incomplete copy of the report, in Thomson's hand and signed by him, is in the Henry E. Huntington Library.

EDITORIAL NOTE

The background of this report has already been presented (Motion To Inform States of Financial Crisis, 20 May 1782, and its headnote and n. 3). JM prefaced the text of the report with these words, "The Committee appointed to confer with the Superintendt of Finance on the subject of his letter of the day of report." Except for two interlineations in a hand which at least closely resembles JM's, the rest of the report was written by John Rutledge. Robert Morris had pointed out to the committee that although every state was delinquent in meeting its financial obligation to Congress, the amounts owed and the steps being taken to pay what was owed varied greatly from state to state. Rejecting his proposed circular letter to the executives of the states, which he had submitted to Congress on 17 May, the committee recommended the adoption of the alternative proposal he had made (Burnett, *Letters*, VI, 357, n. 5).

[22 May 1782]

The Committee appointed to confer with the Superintendt of Finance on the subject of his letter of the day of [1] report—That they have confer'd with the Superintendt. of Finance on the subjt. refer'd to them, &; from the Informn. recd. on this Confere. they find that some of the States have not passed Laws for levying any part of the Quota of the Contl. Estimate for this year–that some others have passed Acts for raising only a part of such Quotas; & that others have passed Laws for raising the whole, but at distant Periods, & that several of such Laws are in some respects, defective. your Comme apprehend that a circular Letter to each of the States, being inapplicable to their different Cases, is improper, but it appears to your Comme absolutely necessary that the most effectual Means be used for obtaining a general Compliance with the Requisitions of Congress.

Therefore your Comme recommend that [Mr Montgomery & Mr Root be appointed to repair to the states eastward of this & that Mr Rutledge & Mr Clymer proceed to the] States [to the southward][2] to make such Representations, as are best adapted to their respective Circumstances, & the present Situation of of publick affairs, & as may induce them to carry the Requisitions of Congress, into Effect, with the greatest dispatch & That the persons so to be sent confer with the Superintendt. of Finance, the Secretary at War, & the Secretary of foreign Affairs, who are authorised to commt. to them, such Informn:, from their respective departments, as may be most conducive to the End proposed.

[1] Robert Morris' letter of 17 May 1782.

[2] The passages enclosed within brackets by the editors may have been written by JM. These interlineations, replacing Rutledge's deleted "proper Persons be sent to the several," probably recorded an action by Congress following the submission of the report. Joseph Montgomery and George Clymer of Pennsylvania, Jesse Root (1736–1822) of Connecticut, and John Rutledge of South Carolina were possibly chosen for the mission because their states had sufficiently large delegations in Congress to permit these four men to be absent without breaking the quorum. During the debate on 22 May, the committee's report was amended by requiring the emissaries "before they leave the city" to "make the like representations to the State of Pennsylvania," and by excusing Clymer and Rutledge from proceeding to war-ravaged South Carolina or Georgia, "unless they shall for special reasons find it absolutely necessary" (*JCC*, XXII, 289–90). The trip of Montgomery and Root lasted from either 27 or 28 May until 15 July, and that of Clymer and Rutledge from about 26 May until 27 June (Burnett, *Letters*, VI, xliii, l, lii; *JCC*, XXII, 299). The two latter, however, delayed starting the southern phase of their journey until 2 June (JM to Randolph, 4 June 1782, and n. 17). On 14 June their "Communications" were heard jointly by the Virginia House of Delegates and the Senate (Minute Book, House of Delegates, May 1782, p. 71).

From Arthur Lee

Printed text (New York Book and Art Auction Company Catalogue No. 75, 1–2 March 1939). Addressed to "Honble. James Madison, Esqr., in Congress, Philadelphia." The letter is unsigned, but JM docketed it, "May 24, 1782. A. Lee."

[24 May 1782]

DEAR SIR:

The above Resolves[1] are directed to be sent to you as Instructions. They wait the confirmation of the Senate which has not yet formed a House, but will I hope effect it in a few days. The Resolves of our House for sending empty away the New York flag-Ships sent under Mr. Morris's agreement, to take away tobacco wait also the same concurrence.[2] Mr. Henry is endeavoring to overturn the tax law; but I think he will not succeed.[3] Adieu.

P.S. Mr. Izard is here and goes on in a day or two.[4] Remember me to our friends in Congress.

[1] The "Resolves" which Lee copied on the verso of his letter are printed with the letter in the catalogue mentioned in the headnote. As sent by Lee, the resolutions were in the form in which they had passed the House of Delegates only. For the resolutions as adopted by both chambers of the Virginia General Assembly, see Instructions to Virginia Delegates, 24–25 May 1782. The Senate had a quorum for the first time on 25 May.

[2] See Randolph to JM, 21–24 May 1782, and n. 3.

[3] *Ibid.*, and n. 19.

[4] Ralph Izard was elected to Congress from South Carolina on 31 January and began his service on 7 June 1782 (*JCC*, XXII, 320; JM to Randolph, 11 June 1782).

Instructions to Virginia Delegates

FC (Virginia State Library). In the hand of John Beckley, clerk of the House of Delegates, with the exception of the attestation by William Drew, clerk of the Senate.

IN THE HOUSE OF DELEGATES

Friday the 24th: of May 1782[1]

Resolved unanimously that a Proposition from the Enemy to all or any of these United States for Peace or Truce, separate from their Allies, is insidious and inadmissible.[2]

Resolved unanimously that a Proposition from the Enemy for treating with any Assembly or Body of Men in America other than the Congress of these United States is insidious and inadmissible.

Resolved unanimously that this Assembly will not listen to any Proposition nor suffer any Negotiation inconsistent with their national Faith and Foederal Union.

Resolved unanimously that this Assembly will exert the utmost powers of the State to carry on the War with Vigour and Effect, until Peace shall be obtained in a Manner consistent with our National Faith and Foederal Union.

Resolved that the above Resolutions be transmitted to the Delegates of this State at Congress, as an Instruction to the said Delegates.[3]

Teste
JOHN BECKLEY. C.H.D.

1782 May the 25th.
Agreed to by the Senate
unanimously.
WILL DREW. C.S.

[1] The copy, in Arthur Lee's hand, of these resolutions, which he enclosed in his letter of 24 May 1782 to JM (*q.v.*, and its n. 1), begins, "Moved by A. Lee and seconded by Genl. Lawson." Robert Lawson represented Prince Edward County in the House of Delegates.

[2] See Report on Communication from La Luzerne, 1 May, and n. 3; Virginia Delegates to Harrison, 7 May, and n. 4; Ambler to JM, 18 May; Harrison to Virginia Delegates, 18 May; Pendleton to JM, 20 May 1782.

[3] The delegates sent a copy of these resolutions to La Luzerne (JM to Randolph, 4 June 1782). Although the journal omits mention of the fact, the delegates probably also laid them before Congress. The resolutions are printed in the *Virginia Gazette* of 1 June and in the *Pennsylvania Packet* of 11 June 1782.

From William Sharpe

RC (LC: Madison Papers). Docketed by JM, "Sharpe Wm. May 25. 1782."

MY OWN SEAT[1]
May 25th. 1782

DEAR SIR

Your very obliging letter of the 21st. Jan'y[2] did not come to hand until late last month

We have at length had a session of the General assembly,[3] Messers. Nash, Hawkins, Blount & Docr. Williamson are appointed delegates for this State. I expect two of them will be with you in a few days. I am deeply impressed with the importance of keeping up a constant representation in Congress especially from the southern States, and flatter myself that N.C. will not be found a delinquent again.[4]

The affairs of our government are inconceivably deranged and it will be a work of some time to regulate them. We are about to raise every twentieth man of the effective militia for eighteen months in order to compleat our quota of continental troops.[5] Commerce, the source of industry, wealth and power, is in a great measure fled from us, therefore our revenue will be small.[6]

We owe our citizens an immense unfunded debt and in short all public credit at an end.

The precious metals in the interior and back parts of this State are but barely visible, under these circumstances it was impossible to lay a tax which would be a sufficient fund to give credit to Mr. Morris's proposed notes.[7]

We are making a great effort to have our accounts liquidated and ready to open a very large account against the united states and thereby fill up the chasm on the credit side of their books.[8]

For further details, I beg leave to refer you to our delegates.

I expect this will be handed you by Capt. Caldwell[9] who lives near me, and hope you will write me a long letter by him, full of news great and small, forriegn and domestic, every line of it will be read with the greatest avidity. I want nothing but intelligence to make me happy.

Now my dear sir let me intreat you to present my best compliments, my heartiest wishes to Mrs. House, Mrs. Trist, Master Browse and such gentlemen of our family as are in the city[10]—be pleased to accept the same yourself from

Dear Sir Your most Obt. Humble Servant

WM. SHARPE

1 Near Statesville, now the county seat of Iredell County, N.C.

2 Not found.

3 From 16 April to 18 May 1782 (Walter Clark, ed., *State Records of North Carolina,* XVI, 1–177). Wiliam Sharpe (1742–1818), who had been a delegate in Congress from 1779 to 27 October 1781, was a representative of Rowan County in the House of Commons of the North Carolina General Assembly in 1781 and 1782 (*ibid.*, XVI, 156).

4 The General Assembly had elected Abner Nash, William Blount (1749–1800), and Hugh Williamson (1753–1819), and re-elected Benjamin Hawkins (1754–1816) on 13 May 1782 (*ibid.*, XVI, 89–91, 94–95). Williamson and Blount took their seats in Congress on 19 and 22 July, respectively, Nash on 4 November, and Hawkins on 21 December (*JCC*, XXII, 401, 404; XXIII, 708, 823). North Carolina was un-

represented in Congress from 4 March to 19 July 1782 (Harrison to Virginia Delegates, 12 April 1782, n. 4). For about six months preceding 4 March 1782 North Carolina had been unable to cast an effective vote, because only Hawkins occasionally was present. In his missing letter to Sharpe, JM probably urged him to persuade the General Assembly of his state to dispatch a delegation to Congress. For absenteeism from Congress, see Motion Urging States To Send Delegates to Congress, 27 May 1782.

[5] See the "Act for Raising Troops To Complete the Continental Battalions of this State," passed during the April session at Hillsborough (Walter Clark, ed., *State Records of North Carolina*, XXIV, 413–17).

[6] Of the four general laws relating to revenue enacted by the April session, "An Act for ascertaining what property in this State shall be deemed Taxable property, the method of assessing the same, and collecting Public Taxes," was directed toward encouraging commerce (*ibid.*, XXIV, 429–34).

[7] Sharpe refers to the promissory notes signed by Robert Morris and given in exchange for goods or services furnished to agencies of Congress. The notes were negotiable and circulated as money. See *ibid.*, XXIV, 446; Virginia Delegates to Harrison, 19 March, n. 1; Randolph to JM, 20 June 1782, n. 42.

[8] The "great effort" was exemplified by the law for "establishing a Department for Adjusting and Liquidating the Public Accounts of this State" (Walter Clark, ed., *State Records of North Carolina*, XXIV, 442–44).

[9] Captain (later Colonel) Andrew Caldwell (1753–1828), a son-in-law of William Sharpe, was of the North Carolina militia and represented Iredell County (formed from Rowan County in 1788) in the House of Commons of the General Assembly in 1806–1808 and 1810 (*Lineage Book of the National Society of the Daughters of the American Revolution*, CXXXIV [1933], 221; Jethro Rumple, *A History of Rowan County, North Carolina* [Raleigh, 1929], p. 223; James S. Brawley, *The Rowan Story, 1753–1953: A Narrative of Rowan County, North Carolina* [Salisbury, N.C., 1953], p. 112).

[10] See *Papers of Madison*, II, 92, n. 8; Randolph to JM, 16–17 May 1782, n. 28.

Motion on Instructions to Francis Dana

MS (NA: PCC, No. 36, II, 137). In JM's hand. Docketed by him: "Motion of Mr. Madison seconded by Mr. Rutledge[.] Passed May 27 1782."

EDITORIAL NOTE

When Robert R. Livingston, secretary for foreign affairs, asked Congress to approve his proposed letter of 10 May to Francis Dana, he suggested the advisability of recommissioning Dana as minister resident rather than as minister plenipotentiary at the court of St. Petersburg (*JCC*, XXII, 259). JM apparently favored this drastic reduction in Dana's rank (JM to Randolph, 23 April, and n. 14; 14 May 1782, and n. 10). On 27 May, after JM and Rutledge succeeded in having Congress postpone a paragraph-by-paragraph discussion of Livingston's draft of a dispatch to Dana, JM introduced and Rutledge seconded the present motion (*JCC*, XXII, 301).

[27 May 1782]

That Mr. Dana be instructed not to present his letters of Credence to the Court of Petersburg untill he shall have obtained satisfactory assurances that he will be duly recd. and recognized in his public Character.[1]

[1] Immediately after adopting this motion, Congress "*Ordered,* That the copy of the letter [of 10 May] be returned to the Secretary for Foreign Affairs" (*JCC*, XXII, 301). Clearance for this dispatch to Dana probably was delayed by the discussion in Congress occasioned by the recommendations of Morris, Livingston, and the committee appointed to report on salaries, staff, and places of residence of the diplomatic personnel of the United States (Report on Salaries of Representatives Abroad, 28 May 1782, and nn. 1, 6, 12, 13). Livingston wrote to Dana on 29 May, enclosing his letter of 10 May and a copy of JM's motion (Wharton, *Revolutionary Diplomatic Correspondence,* V, 446–47).

Motion Urging States To Send Delegates to Congress

MS (NA: PCC, No. 65, II, 166). JM presented the motion, which was drafted and seconded by John Rutledge (*JCC*, XXII, 301).

[27 May 1782]

R.[1] That Inasmuch as[2] Bus: of the great. Conseqe[3] is often delayed or[4] retarded for want of sufft. rep. in Cong.[5] it be & it is Earnestly recomdd. to the[6] States which are at present unreprtd,[7] immedy to send[8] delegs. to Cong. & to all the States to keep up a constt. rep.[9]

[1] Resolved.

[2] Following "as," "the publick" was deleted.

[3] This abbreviation and "the great." were interlineated. The "great." is obviously an abbreviation of "greatest."

[4] The words "delayed or" were interlineated.

[5] Following this abbreviation, "In That" was crossed out.

[6] Following "the," "sevl States to keep up a constant rep." was inked out.

[7] An abbreviation of "unrepresented."

[8] This word was substituted for a deleted "forward a."

[9] These two final abbreviations stand for "constant representation." For JM's comment upon the reason for this motion, see his letter of 28 May 1782 to Arthur Lee. See also Report on Salaries of Representatives Abroad, 28 May, n. 1; and Virginia Delegates to Harrison, 28 May 1782, n. 15. The motion may have been timed to strengthen the pleas of the delegates who had been selected to portray the various aspects of the national emergency to the executives of the states (Report on Mission To Inform States of Financial Crisis, 22 May 1782, and n. 2).

From Edmund Pendleton

Tr (LC: Force Transcripts). Another copy is in the *Proceedings of the Massachusetts Historical Society*, 2d ser., XIX (1905), 153–54. An extract, also taken from the missing original, is in Stan. V. Henkels Catalogue No. 694 (1892), p. 90.

VIRGA May 27th. 1782

DEAR SIR

Your favr of the 14th[1] conveyed a very unexpected piece of Intelligence in the entire revolution of the British Ministry, an event which I once thought probable in the course of[2] Strugles for the loaves & fishes, but in which the old appeared about the beginning of March to be gaining ground. the Political conjectures here are busy, & much divided whether this change tends to peace or a more Active & better directed War. As it is said Ld Shelburne is to direct the Cabinet and his Opinion hath been uniform against our independance, the prospect is bad.[3] But as the Spirit of the Nation appears to be for Peace at all events, and this Spirit alone forced them into their present Offices, I think they must adopt the measure. I have no doubt but they will endeavour to detach us from our Allies, by every Seducing attempt; but when they discover the Spirit of Congress, firm to its engagements & resenting even the Idea of the least departure from them,[4] I think they will open a Treaty that shall include Our Allies and, yielding the great point to Us, put an end to a War the Nation seems so averse to—unless some flattering circumstances in foreign Treaties or sucess in Arms, should give a turn in their favour, of which there appears little probability. I am happy to hear, even from Our lowest Class of people, a becoming resolution not to purchase the peace they Ardently wish, at the expence of breaking faith with our Allies & all approve What you recommend, a preparation for continuing the War to Advantage, a conduct the most proper, even if we had a much better prospect of peace than we have; since it is best to treat with Arms in our hands.[5]

If it shall become the *inclination* of the Crown to acknowledge the Independence of America, I imagine there will be little dispute about its *Power*[6]—to remove the Shackles with which Parliament had bound the Prerogative to make peace & War,[7] was the most Constitutional & Polite way of doing the thing, as well as the most likely means of reinstating the King in the affections of the people, since peace will thus appear to be his Act, a circumstance he will probably pay some attention to, now that he is in the hands of a Whig Minist[ry.]

I hear nothing that our Assembly have done, but the refusing permission to some Vessels which came from New York wth Passports from Congress to Load tobacco under some Contract with Mr Morris, except so far as may answer the engagements of our Commercial Agent.[8] what reasons influenced this Negative, I have not heard, but they must be strong to outweigh the respect due to Congress, Our Obligation to support the credit of the Financier Genl. and our want of Specie to support our part of the War.[9] I wish Resentment for the ill treatment we have lately experienced at Philadelphia may not have entered into the deliberations on this Subject tho' I have heard nothing of the sort. What will those men have to answer for who for their private emolument have fomented these divisions.[10] I am told a Petition is circulating & signing in the Western Countrey address'd to Congress and requiring to be a seperate State, to which many there are very Averse which produces Quarels & bickerings amongst them.[11] I wish our Assembly may turn their thoughts to the Subject and endeavour to counteract the Agents of this Mischief, by a plan for administering Justice & defusing the other benefits of Government to that remote region,[12] until they shall be in a state of Acting for themselves without Injury to Us, and let us Seperate by Consent at such[13] Period, remaining good Neighbours. I want to hear the Propositions Mr Carlton hath to make, & the mode of Conducting it, as a matter of Curiosity, more than from any hope of good to be expected from it: it was Curious enough to want his Secretary to come to Philadelphia as a *Spy*, or perhaps in a more dangerous emploiment.[14] I am

Dr Sir Yr affe

EDMD. PENDLETON

[1] Not found, but its contents probably resembled those of JM's letters written on the same day to Harrison and Randolph (*q.v.*).

[2] The word "the" follows "of" in the copy in the *Proceedings of the Massachusetts Historical Society*.

[3] See Ambler to JM, 11 May, and n. 9; Pendleton to JM, 13 May; and Virginia Delegates to Harrison, 14 May 1782, and nn. 17 and 18.

[4] See Report on Communication from La Luzerne, 1 May, and n. 3; Ambler to JM, 18 May 1782.

[5] See Instructions to Virginia Delegates, 24–25 May 1782.

[6] The copy in the *Proceedings of the Massachusetts Historical Society* places a period after "Power" and capitalizes "to."

[7] See JM to Randolph, 14 May 1782, and n. 3.

[8] The "engagements" had been made by David Ross before his resignation as commercial agent (*Calendar of Virginia State Papers*, II, 668).

[9] See Ambler to JM, 20 April, n. 4; Lee to JM, 16 May, and nn. 7and 9; Randolph to JM, 16–17 May, and n. 25; and 21–24 May 1782, and nn.

[10] By "ill treatment" Pendleton undoubtedly refers to the opposition in Congress to Virginia's claims to western lands and to the terms of her offer to cede most of them to the United States (Motion To Amend Lee's Motion on Western Lands, 18 April, n. 1; JM to Pendleton, 23 April, and n. 8; JM to Randolph, 1 May, and n. 6; 7 May, and n. 10; Motion on Point of Order, 3 May 1782, n. 1). See also Randolph to JM, 16–17 May 1782, and n. 13.

[11] A "memorial and petition" seeking separate statehood for Kentucky was read in Congress on 27 August 1782 and "filed in the office of the Secretary of Congress" (*JCC*, XXIII, 532; Burnett, *Letters*, VI, 456–59, 463, 545). See also *Papers of Madison*, II, 65, and nn.; III, 275 n; Jefferson to JM, 24 March, and n. 5; Randolph to JM, 27–29 June 1782. Among those opposing separate statehood was George Rogers Clark (*Calendar of Virginia State Papers*, III, 150).

[12] See Jefferson to JM, 24 March 1782, n. 5.

[13] The version of this letter in the *Proceedings of the Massachusetts Historical Society* has an "a" after "such."

[14] See Virginia Delegates to Harrison, 7 May, and n. 4; 14 May, and nn. 15 and 16; JM to Randolph, 14 May 1782, and n. 8.

Report on Salaries of Representatives Abroad

MS (NA: PCC, No. 25, II, 205–6). Written by JM and docketed by him, "Friday May 24 1782 assigned." There are at least two other copies of this report (*ibid.*, II, 109–10, 113–16). The first of these is docketed: "Report of Comtee on *Salaries* for Ministers of the U.S. at foreign courts. Thursday May 23. 1782 Assign'd for consideration. Aug 23. 1782 Referred to Mr. Madison Mr Lee Mr. Duane." On this docket, between "consideration" and "Aug 23," the following notation was deleted: "May 28 1782 part passed and Remr postpond[.] Mr. Ramsay Mr Madison Mr Clark." The other copy is similarly docketed except that the notation deleted from the first one is omitted entirely.

[28 May 1782][1]

The Committee to whom were referred the letter of the day of from the Superintendt of Finance and the letter of the day of from the Secretary for foreign affairs[2] recommend the following resolutions; viz.

That the Minister Plenipo: of the U.S. at the Court of Versailles be instructed to take immediate measures for liquidating the accounts subsisting between the Sd. States & the sd. Ct. and report a state thereof to Congress.[3]

That a Commissr. be appointed to liquidate & finally settle the accounts of all the Servants of the U.S. who have been entrusted with the expenditure of public monies in Europe, that the Superintendt of Finance nominate to Congress a fit person for such appointment; and that the person so appointed be allowed [4]

That the Salaries & allowances to which the public Servts. of the U.S. are or shall be entitled be in future paid by the Superintt. of Finance out of the monies which shall from time to time be in his hands; and that the sd. public Servts. be authorized to make quarterly draughts on him for that purpose.[5]

That[6] the Salaries of a Minister Plenipo: from the U.S. be from & after the 1st. day of Jany. next at the rate of 3000 Dollars per annum; and of a Minister 2000 Dollars per annum; and[7] to a Secretary to a Commission 1200 Dollars P annum, but that an allowance be respectively made to them for Household expences, in which shall be included those of the Secretaries to their Embassies, and of their private Secretaries at the following rates, viz.[8]

	Dollars
To the Minister Plenipo; at the Ct. of Versailles[9]	4000
To do of Madrid[10]	4000
To do. at Hague prior to an acknowledgt. of his public Character	1500
To do. at do. subsequent to such acknowledgt.[11]	2500
To do. for negociating a peace prior to the commencement of such negociation	1500
To do. for do. subsequent thereto	4000
To Minister at Petersbg prior to an acknowledgt. &c	1000
To do. at do. subsequent thereto[12]	1500

that Francis Dana Esqr. be authorized to[13] appoint a private Secry. who shall be entitled to a Salary of 500 dollars per annum[14]

That it is unnecessary to [name] a Secry to the Comn[15]

That the appointment of Mr. Carmichael as Secry. to the Embassy to the Ct. of Madrid & his provisional appointmt. of Chargé d'affairs at the sd. Court be revoked; and that a Commission issue investing him with the like appointments at the Court of Versailles; and that his Salary from & after his arrival at the said Ct. be at the rate of 2000 Drs. per annum.[16]

That Mr. Jay be authorized to appoint a private Secy. with a Salary of 800 Dollrs. per annum.[17]

That Mr. Laurens be authorized whenever he shall enter on his Mission to the U Provinces of the low Countries to appoint a private Secry. with a Salary of 500 Dollrs. per annum.[18]

That Mr. Adams be authorized to appt. a private Secry. who shall from & after the 1st. day of Jany. next be entitled to a Salary of 500 Dollrs. per annum.[19]

[1] This apparently was the date when the report was first read in Congress and debated (*JCC*, XXII, 305–7), even though 23 and 24 May in succession had been assigned on the calendar for the submission of the report. See headnote. On the earlier of these days there seems to have been no quorum (*JCC*, XXII, 289–90), while on the latter a letter from Robert Morris rather than a recommendation by the committee led Congress to discuss one of the subjects which would be embraced in the report (*JCC*, XXII, 290–96). See n. 3, below.

[2] On 9 May 1782 Robert Morris' letter of 8 May and Robert R. Livingston's letters of 8 and 9 May were referred by Congress to David Ramsay, JM, and Abraham Clark (*JCC*, XXII, 255 n.). Having been advised by La Luzerne that the court of Versailles could no longer provide money to pay "the ministers of the United States in Europe," Morris recommended to Congress "that in future all such salaries as are payable to foreign ministers, be advanced in America." Again at La Luzerne's suggestion, Morris urged Congress to authorize Franklin "finally to settle those accounts; and in the name of the United States to execute the proper obligations for securing the debt, and fixing the periods of payment." On his own initiative Morris also reminded Congress that to settle "the publick accounts of these states with their servants in Europe" had come to be "highly necessary" (*JCC*, XXII, 253–55). In his letter of 8 May, Livingston presented to Congress the limited information at his command about prices in Madrid, Paris, Amsterdam, and St. Petersburg and the "manner of living" of Jay, Franklin, and John Adams in the first three of these capitals, respectively. Livingston's letter of the following day mainly comprised eight suggested resolutions, proposing the amount of annual salary for each of these ministers plenipotentiary, for Henry Laurens, Francis Dana, and William Carmichael, and for the private secretary of a minister plenipotentiary or a minister resident (*JCC*, XXII, 255–60).

[3] Although the committee's report first appears in the journal of Congress on 28 May (*JCC*, XXII, 305–7), the subject of this paragraph of the report had been debated four days earlier, when Morris submitted to Congress a copy of Franklin's letter of 4 March to Morris and of Vergennes' letter of 6 February to Franklin, both dealing with the "moneys obtained in Europe for account of the United States" (NA: PCC, No. 137, I, 471–82). During the debate on 24 May, Congress unanimously adopted a motion, introduced by John Rutledge and seconded by JM, reading, "That the Superintendant of finance lay before Congress an account of all money borrowed or granted in Europe, by or to the United States, antecedent to the 4 day of March last; and also a general state of the purposes to which the same has been applied" (*JCC*, XXII, 295–96). This resolution obviously dovetails in subject with the present paragraph, which was agreed to on 28 May. Livingston forwarded a copy of this resolution to Franklin on 30 May. When the latter, in a dispatch to Morris on 12 August 1782, acknowledged receipt of the directive, he commented, much too optimistically, "The liquidation of our accounts with the court was completed before the vote of Congress directing it came to hand" (Wharton, *Revolutionary Diplomatic Correspondence*, V, 462, 659).

[4] On 28 May Congress adopted this paragraph after deleting "That the Superintendt of Finance nominate to Congress a fit person for such appointment." Congress left the blank after "allowed" unfilled. Finally on 18 November 1782 Congress elected Thomas Barclay to this position and ordered Morris to "report the necessary instructions for the said commissioner, pursuant to the order of the 29th of May last" (*JCC*, XXII, 306, 308, 421, and n.; XXIII, 730). See Comment on Settlement of Foreign Accounts, 29 July 1782, editorial note and footnote.

[5] Congress adopted this paragraph on 29 May 1782 (*JCC*, XXII, 308). Two days

later Morris protested that "The tenor of this resolution would, I believe, give to every officer of the United States, both civil and military, the right of drawing upon me, which would be liable to this objection, among many others, that I should frequently be obliged to protest the bills for want of funds to discharge them. If, therefore, the object of the resolution was to provide for the foreign servants only, it might, perhaps, be proper to make some alteration in the terms." Furthermore, Morris recommended that the drafts for salary not be sent directly to him but to the appropriate "department of the civil list" to "be made up and settled at the treasury quarterly." "If this mode be pursued with respect to the Department of Foreign Affairs," Morris continued, "the moneys may be remitted to those who are abroad by the Secretary of Foreign Affairs, until they shall have appointed their respective agents to receive it from him here" (Wharton, *Revolutionary Diplomatic Correspondence*, V, 463–64).

Upon receiving Morris' letter on 3 June, Congress returned the resolution for reconsideration by the committee. JM had become its chairman, and Samuel Osgood had replaced Abraham Clark (*JCC*, XXII, 313–14, 314, n. 1). On 5 June 1782 the committee's recommendation in the form of a substitute resolution embodying Morris' suggestions was accepted by Congress. See Report on Paying Representatives Abroad, 5 June 1782.

[6] On 29 May 1782, Congress decided to postpone consideration of the remainder of the report, beginning with this paragraph. This fact is noted in the printed journal (*JCC*, XXII, 306). On the manuscript, the left edge of this paragraph and the salary table immediately following was marginated, probably by JM, with a perpendicular line and the abbreviation, "Committ." In view of this action, it is strange that the notation to this effect on one of the copies of the report (see headnote) should have been deleted. As this copy also indicates, nearly three months elapsed before most of the remainder of the report received further consideration. See *JCC*, XXII, 307, n. 1.

[7] This word and the following words through "annum" were interlineated by someone other than JM. See *JCC*, XXII, 306, n. 1.

[8] In his letter of 9 May 1782, Livingston had recommended no more than a $5,000 annual salary for a minister plenipotentiary, no more than $3,000 for a resident minister, and, as in this report, an unspecified amount for "household expences" (*JCC*, XXII, 259–60).

[9] Benjamin Franklin.

[10] John Jay.

[11] John Adams had been recognized on 22 April 1782 by "their high mightinesses, the States-General of the United Provinces" as the minister plenipotentiary from the United States (Wharton, *Revolutionary Diplomatic Correspondence*, V, 319). A copy of the document extending the recognition was first published in the United States in the *Pennsylvania Journal* of 20 July 1782.

[12] Although Congress on 19 December 1780 had appointed Francis Dana minister plenipotentiary to the court of Tsarina Catherine II, it was 1809 before a minister from the United States was accredited to, and received formally by, Russia (Samuel F. Bemis, *Diplomatic History of the United States*, pp. 44–45).

[13] Preceding "to," JM's draft of this paragraph originally read: "That the Commission of Minister Plenipo. from the U.S. to the Court of Petersbg granted to Francis Dana Esqr. on the day of unless he shall have been acknowledged in that quality, be & the same is hereby revoked; and that a Commission issue Constituting him Minister at the said Court; and that Francis Dana Esqr. be authorized, as soon as he shall be acknowledged in his public character." Although the copy in the printed journal (*JCC*, XXII, 306–7) is identical to this, except for

variations in capitalization, punctuation, and the avoidance of abbreviations, it seems plausible to assume that the paragraph had been shortened to the form shown in the text as a result of the adoption by Congress on 27 May of JM's Motion on Instructions to Francis Dana (*q.v.* and its editorial note). In the margin of the manuscript, opposite the amended form of the paragraph, "passd" is written, apparently in JM's hand. This probably took place on 28 or 29 May 1782, although the fact is not noted in the printed journal for those days (*JCC*, XXII, 306–11). See n. 6, above.

[14] Livingston had recommended $800 (*JCC*, XXII, 259).

[15] Livingston had suggested that the peace commissioners appoint a secretary with a salary of one thousand dollars per annum (*JCC*, XXII, 259).

[16] Congress had elected William Carmichael as John Jay's secretary on 29 September 1779 and as provisional chargé d'affaires on 20 April 1782. Livingston had recommended that Carmichael be appointed secretary of embassy at the court of Versailles at a salary of $4,000 (*JCC*, XV, 1127; XXII, 258; *Biographical Directory of the American Congress, 1774–1961* [Washington, 1961], p. 663). JM's committee evidently wished to pay Carmichael half that sum annually for being chargé d'affaires and secretary of embassy. This paragraph, somewhat altered in phraseology and with the salary unmentioned, was agreed to by Congress on 10 July 1782 (*JCC*, XXII, 380).

[17] Livingston had recommended $1,000 (*JCC*, XXII, 259).

[18] Livingston had suggested $1,000 (*JCC*, XXII, 259). The British had confiscated the commission and instructions of Henry Laurens when they captured him at sea while on his way from the United States to The Hague. During his imprisonment in the Tower of London, Congress elected him to be one of the commissioners for negotiating peace with Great Britain. Before naming Laurens to this office, and without canceling his appointment to the Netherlands, Congress had chosen John Adams to be minister plenipotentiary to the same country for the purpose of negotiating a treaty of alliance and treaty of amity and commerce (*Papers of Madison*, II, 225, n. 5; III, 154, n. 5; *JCC*, XXI, 876–80). Released by the British on 27 April 1782, Laurens proceeded to The Hague. Lacking his commission and finding that Adams already had been recognized by the States-General as the duly accredited representative of the United States, Laurens welcomed the opportunity of going to southern France to recover from the effects of his long incarceration. In September 1782, upon receiving his letter of 20 May declining to be a peace commissioner, Congress overrode the objections of JM and other delegates by refusing to accept Laurens' resignation. Although in "a very infirm state of health," he bowed to the will of Congress and reached Paris from Great Britain the day before the preliminary articles of peace were signed on 30 November 1782 (Wharton, *Revolutionary Diplomatic Correspondence*, V, 456–57; VI, 99, 138; *JCC*, XXIII, 593).

[19] Livingston had made no suggestion concerning the salary of John Adams' secretary except to comment in the letter of 8 May that Congress probably would consent to assume the cost of Adams' amanuensis (*JCC*, XXII, 257). From the outset of his mission abroad, John Adams had paid £100 sterling annually from his own funds to a private secretary, John Thaxter, Jr. (1721–1802). In letters of 16 May and 7 September 1782 and 1 September 1783 Adams recommended this devoted and able "clerk" to the favorable attention of Congress, which, in Adams' words, he had served by 1783 for five years "without the least reward" (L[yman] H. Butterfield *et al.*, eds., *Diary and Autobiography of John Adams* [4 vols.; Cambridge, Mass., 1961], I, 280, n. 1; Wharton, *Revolutionary Diplomatic Correspondence*, V, 421, 708; VI, 668–69).

Virginia Delegates to Benjamin Harrison

RC (Virginia State Library). Written by Theodorick Bland except for JM's signature. Docketed, "Letter from Virga Delegates recd June 6 1782." The words written by Bland in the official cipher are italicized below. Accompanying the letter are three pages upon which the cipher was decoded by Archibald Blair, clerk of the Council of State.

PHILADELPHIA May 28th 178[2]

SR

The state of News as it respects the action of the French and English Fleets in the West Indies your Excelly. will be informed of by the enclosed Paper,[1] we shall however keep the letter open to add any thing which may occur to throw a light on that important and Interesting event, concerning which we have been under such continued anxiety this fortnight Past.

The letters which came enclosed in your Excellys by last post[2] after having perused attentively, *we deliverd to the minister of France and Mister R. Morris.* no Answer or Comment on the Contents of either has yet been addressd or communicated to us. *Nor have* [*we*][3] *yet urged to either of them an explanation of the*[4] *subject of* [*them*].[5]

We shall endeavor *to investigate the motive* and *cause* of the *al*[*te*]*ration*[6] you mention *of the disposition and payment* of the *stores.*[7]

We think it proper to acquaint your Excellency that a letter *from Dr. Franklin to Mister R. Morris* read in Congress, leads to this knowledge tho not completely[.] it appears therefrom[8] that *a loan for* the *current year* has been *granted to* the *United States* of ——[9] *million of livres* and that *a deduction has been made*[10] of *seven hundred thousand livres therefrom on account* of *Virginia for stores purchased* for that *state* by the *ministry of France* whereby the *state of Virginia becomes debtor to the United States.*[11] this appears to us at present to be *the act of the ministry in France* but from what motive or by whose instigation is not clear to us. When it was *determined to sollicit that loan,* we can only find *that Congress authorized* the *minister of the war department,* of *foreign affairs and minister of fina*[*n*]*ce*[12] to explain *to the minister of France the absolute* ne[c]essity *of such a supply.*[13]

We hinted to your Excellency in our last,[14] *the distressed and critical state* of *the financees* and the measures which wd. probably be persued by Congress *in hopes of exciting the states* to all *the acti*[*v*]*ity* and *energi* they are capable of in that line[.] we have not been mistaken in our Conjecture, and congress has deemd speedy *exertions* [of] *such conseq*[u]*ence* to the *welfare of the general cause* that altho there is but *a bare representtation left*,[15] they have come to a resolution *to dispatch two* of *their members* to the *southern and two to the eastern states charged* with an *explanation* to the Executives and *such of the* [*legislature*]*s*[16] as *may be in session of the true state of our finances* and the *causes leading thereto*. They have also orderd *an exact state* of the *loans subsidies* and *monies rece*[*iv*]*ed* to be *laid before them by the minister of finanance* together *with an account* of *their application. Mis*[ter] *Rutledge and* Mr. *Clymore are deputed to the south states Mister Root and* Mr. *Montgomery to the northward* the latter *set off tomorrow*.[17] Letters from Dr. Franklin so late as the 30th. of March last[18] inform us that England is weary of the War—that she appears[19] to want to get out of it if she knew how[—]that she is nevertheless making *useless attem*[p]*ts* to *withdraw us from France by secret applications to our ministers* in *Europe* at the same time that *she* is *playing the same game by her commissioner here* and *by secret* tho' fruit*less applications to the court of France* accompanied by great and *advantageous offers to that court* which we are informd from *another quarter*[20] *France has noble re*[*je*][21]*cted and* has *categorically answerd* by declaring *she will not accept no offer but the independence of the United States*. Dr. Franklin also informs us that a Bill is on its passage through the British House of Commons for the Exchange of American Prisoners.[22] it appears that an emissary has been sent to Mr. Adams at the Hague from the British Ministry to sound him relative to peace and to know whether he had any powers from Congress to conclude a truce. A conference was held between the Emissary and him in the Presence of Mr. Adams Secry., and terminated as soon as he received information that there were powers lodged in Europe for treating of a Peace which he said no person in England could ascertain, untill then, altho, he confessd it had been announced in all the Papers of Europe.[23] we have related these facts to you but as many of them are secret in their Nature we trust they will not be divulged, but in such proportion as they may be usefull in opening the Eyes of our Constituents to the Chicane and Duplicity of our Enemy and the firmness and good faith of our Ally—and, as they may stimulate, all ranks to Energetic exertion to obtain the desired object, of an honorable peace in Conjunction with our Illustrious Ally, and Independence.[24] Mr. Adams letter to Dr. Franklin of the 26th of March also informs him that ten or eleven of the Cities of Holland, have declared for our independence and that he expects, that Province, will determine the next day to admit him to an Audience.[25] he says the Picture of England drawn by the above mentiond Emissary from G Britain is for them[26] a Gloomy one We have at length obtaind and herewith send you a copy of the Pennsylvania Act of Assembly you some time ago requested to have[27]

we are with the Greatest respect Yr. Excys. most obedt. serts.

J MADISON JR.
THEOK. BLAND JR.

[1] The *Pennsylvania Packet* of 28 May 1782 devoted its news columns mostly to accounts of the Battle of the Saints. See also JM to Pendleton, 23 April, n. 3; Virginia Delegates to Harrison, 14 May, n. 14; Pendleton to JM, 20 May 1782, and n. 8.

[2] See Randolph to JM, 10 May, n. 21; Harrison to Virginia Delegates, 11 May 1782, and n. 1.

[3] Bland wrote the cipher for "wn" rather than the cipher for "we."

[4] Bland wrote the cipher for "the," but he also interlineated the word itself.

[5] Bland wrote the cipher for "than" rather than "them."

[6] Bland wrote the cipher for "sea" rather than the cipher for "te."

[7] See Harrison to Virginia Delegates, 11 May 1782, and n. 1.

[8] Blair in decoding this paragraph erroneously copied this word as "therefore."

[9] Either the delegates in Congress had agreed to keep in secret the exact amount of the loan or else Bland could not recall the figure and forgot to put in a "six" or its cipher, 197, before posting the dispatch. If the latter, it is strange that he did not leave the space blank rather than filling it with dashes; if the former, it is evident that he was more reticent than JM, who on the same day informed Jones, Randolph, and Lee of the amount without cautioning any of these delegates that they must hold the sum in confidence (*q.v.*).

[10] Here Bland placed an "x," and encoded the next five words, except "of," in the left-hand margin of the letter.

[11] In his dispatch to Robert Morris of 4 March, read in Congress on 24 May, Franklin mentioned his "perplexity and uncertainty about our money affairs" and his difficulty in finding adequate cargo space for the goods awaiting shipment from France and the Netherlands to the United States. Morris accompanied Franklin's letter with a statement "of the moneys in France" and with a copy of Vergennes' letter of 6 February 1782 to Franklin enclosing a "Sketch of the account of Congress with the royal treasury" (Wharton, *Revolutionary Diplomatic Correspondence,* V, 218–19; *JCC*, XXII, 290–93). From this "Sketch," the Virginia delegates inferred that Vergennes expected Congress would advance from its funds in France and the Netherlands the money needed by Virginia to pay for her purchases in those countries. Morris estimated the amount at 700,000 livres, but both he and Harrison had already refused to assent to this mode of payment (Harrison to Virginia Delegates, 11 May 1782, n. 1).

[12] Bland wrote the cipher for "art" rather than for "n."

[13] See Virginia Delegates to Harrison, 24 January 1782, and nn. 1 and 2. By this statement the delegates were merely affirming what Harrison already knew at first hand. In February 1781, when Harrison had come to Philadelphia on behalf of the Virginia General Assembly, he found La Luzerne willing to recommend to Vergennes that the French government send military matériel to Virginia to be paid for

after the war. At that time neither Harrison nor La Luzerne had expected the United States to assume the cost of the goods, and certainly Congress had never offered to do so (*Papers of Madison*, II, 299, and n. 4; 314; 315, n. 3; III, 4, n. 5). As decoded by Blair, the words after "fina[n]ce," were erroneously written only "to ask such a supply."

[14] Not found, but the delegates probably mailed the dispatch on 21 May 1782.

[15] See Motion Urging States To Send Delegates to Congress, 27 May 1782. Tallied votes in Congress on 25 May 1782 reveal that only seven states were represented by two or more delegates. Of these seven, five states had only two representatives, and hence the vote of any one of these delegations would be rendered ineffective by the temporary absence of one of the delegates or by a disagreement between the two. Acquiescence by the delegations of at least seven states was required to carry a routine motion. Besides the delegations from the seven states, New York had one delegate present. New Hampshire, Connecticut, New Jersey, Delaware, and North Carolina were entirely unrepresented (*JCC*, XXII, 298–300).

[16] Here Bland erred in his encoding by writing 694,95 which symbolized a meaningless "hurs." He should have written 674,95, the ciphers for "legislatures." Harrison must have been puzzled to understand the passage, because Blair rendered it "and such of the hurs as may be in possession." Blair at first correctly wrote "session" for the ciphers 386,75, but finding "session" made no sense when taken with "hurs," he struck out "session" and compounded Bland's mistake by interlineating "possession."

[17] See Report on Mission To Inform States of Financial Crisis, 22 May 1782, editorial note and n. 2.

[18] Although Franklin's letter of 30 March was that of most recent date, the principal sources of the Virginia delegates' information were his letters of 20 March, and perhaps those of 4 and 7 March, respectively, to Livingston and Morris (Wharton, *Revolutionary Diplomatic Correspondence*, V, 214–17, 227–29, 277–79).

[19] Bland underlined this word.

[20] See Virginia Delegates to Harrison, 14 May, and nn. 16 and 17; JM to Randolph, 14 May 1782, and n. 8. The "commissioner" was Sir Guy Carleton. On the date of the present letter, Livingston reported to Congress a "verbal communication" from La Luzerne to the effect that the British had sent "Emissaries" both to Paris and to John Adams in the Netherlands to explore the possibility either of reaching an "accommodation" with Congress or of seducing Louis XVI into making "a separate peace" (*JCC*, XXII, 302–3). Franklin had stated in his letter of 20 March 1782 to Livingston (n. 18, above) that he had been "drawn into a correspondence" in a hopeless effort "to get us to treat separately from France."

[21] Bland wrote 383, the cipher for "ence," rather than 838, the cipher for "ie." The code included no cipher for "je" and hence 838 was customarily used for that combination of letters.

[22] In his dispatch of 30 March 1782 to Livingston, Franklin wrote, "I see that a bill is also passing through the House of Commons, for the exchange of American prisoners, the purport of which I do not yet know" (Wharton, *Revolutionary Diplomatic Correspondence*, V, 277). See also *Papers of Madison*, III, 233 n.

[23] The delegates derived this information from Adams' letter of 26 March, which had been enclosed in Franklin's dispatch of 30 March 1782 to Livingston (Wharton, *Revolutionary Diplomatic Correspondence*, V, 273–75, 277). The "Emissary" was Thomas Digges (1742–1821), formerly of Maryland (William Bell Clark, "In Defense of Thomas Digges," *Pennsylvania Magazine of History and Biography*, LXXVII [1953], 381–438). John Thaxter, Jr., was Adams' secretary (Report on Salaries of Representatives Abroad, 28 May 1782, n. 19).

24 See Instructions to Virginia Delegates, 24–25 May 1782.

25 By "Province," JM refers to that of Holland and West Friesland. With The Hague as its chief city and meeting place of the States-General, this was the most powerful of the seven provinces comprising the Netherlands. Adams had been permitted on 22 April 1782 to present his letter of credence to the stadholder William V, "his Most Serene Highness the Prince of Orange" and on the following day to lay a proposed treaty of amity and commerce before a committee of the States-General (Wharton, *Revolutionary Diplomatic Correspondence*, V, 319, 325).

26 Bland underlined "for them."

27 See Harrison to Virginia Delegates, 27 April 1782, and n. 1. The unspecified act passed by the Pennsylvania House of Assembly before adjourning on 16 April 1782 probably was the law "to redress certain grievances within the counties of Westmoreland and Washington." The same session further manifested its determination to exercise exclusive jurisdiction over the contested territory by providing for the establishment of ferries on the Monongahela and Youghiogheny rivers (*Pennsylvania Packet*, 18 and 24 April, and 29 May 1782). See also Harrison to Randolph, 9 May 1782, in McIlwaine, *Official Letters*, III, 206.

To Joseph Jones

RC (LC: Madison Papers). Cover missing. The words written by JM in the official cipher are italicized below.

May [28] 1782[1]

DEAR SIR

A letter from Docr. Franklin of the 4th. of March informs the Superintendt. of Finance that the *court of France had granted an aid of six million of livres to the United States* for the [*pres*]*ent*[2] *year*. It appears *however that this aid has been wholly anticipated* as well as the *aids* of the *last year* by *bil*[l]*s of exchange*[;][3] by *supplies* for *the army* particularly those *in Holland*[;] *by the debt* to *Beaumarchais* amounting to *two million* & *a half of livres*[;] by *the interest mony*[;] by the *deduction* on account of *Virginia computed* at *seven hundred thousand livres* &c.[4] The States *must therefore* by *some means* or *other supply the demands of Congress* or a *very d*[*ange*]*rous*[5] *crisis must ensue*. After the difference between the *modes of feeding the army* by *contracts* & by *the bayonet has been* experienced both *by the army and the people a recur*[r]*ence to the latter cannot be too much dreaded.*[6]

The province of Friesland has *instructed its delegates in the States general to concur in a public reception of* Mr. Adams. The *cit*[*y*] *of Dort* has done *the same to theirs in the* provincial *assembly of Holland.*[7]

The above letters came by the Alliance wch. is arrived at Rhode Island. Capt. Barry[8] I am told says that *the marquis* will *come* with *a squadron* for *the American coast* which was *equip*[p]*ing*. If *this be true* Barry is *wrong* in *discloseing it*. I *distrust it*.[9]

A French Cutter is since arrived after a short passage with despatches for the Minister[10] here. He recd. them on Saturday by an express from Salem, and has not yet communicated their Contents to Congress. I *understand th*[r]*ough*[11] *the secry* of *foreign affairs* that *the court of London has lately proposed* to *the court of France a separate peace* as the price of *which she would* place *Dunkirk in* its *former state*[,] make some *sacrifices in the East Indies and accede to a status quo in the West Indies. The answer of France was dictated by her engagements with the United States*.[12] This insidious step taken at the same moment with the agency of Mr. Carlton will I hope not long be witheld from the public. We have heard nothing from this Gentleman since the answer to his request of a passport for his Secretary.[13]

In order to explain our public affairs to *the states and to urge* the necessity of complying with the requisitions of Congress, We have determined to *depute two members* to *visit the eastern states* and *two the southern*. The first are *Root and Mon*[t]*gomery*. The others *Rutlidge and Clymer*. I put this in Cypher because Secresy *has been enjoined by Congress*. The *deputation* will probably set off in a few days.[14]

I find that *the minister of France has been informed by some correspondent in Virginia that the late intelligence from Britain has produced very unfavorable sym*[p]*toms in a large party. He seems not a little discomposed at it. The honour of the state concur*[r]*ed with my own persuasion in dictating a consolatory answer to him*.[15] For this reason as well as for others I think it would be expedient for *the legislature to enter into a unanimous decla*[ra]*tion on this point*. Other *states are doing this and such a mode of* announcing *the sense of the people may be regarded as more authentic than a declaration from Congress. The best form* I conceive will be that of an *instru*[c]*tion to the delegates*.[16] Do not fail to supply me with *accurate and full informations* on the whole subject of this paragraph.

A letter from Dr. Franklin of the 30th. of March inclosing a copy of one to him from Mr. Adams at the Hague were laid before Congress subsequent to writing the above. By these it appears not only that an essay has been made on the fidelity of France to the Alliance, but that the pulse of America has been at the same time separately felt thro' each of those Ministers. They both speak with becoming indignation on the subject, attest the firmness of our ally, and recommend decisive efforts for expelling the Enemy from our Country.[17] Mr. Adams says "*ten or eleven cities of Holland* have *declared themselves in favo[ur]*[18] *of* American independence *and* it is *expected* that to*day or tomorrow* this *province* will *take the decisive resol*[u]*tion of admitting me* to *my audience.* Perhaps some *of the other provinces may delay* it for *three or four weeks but the prince has declared* that *he has no hopes of resisting the torrent and therefore* that *he shall not attempt it. The Duke de Vauguyon has acted a very friendly and honourable part in this business without however doing any ministerial act in it.*"[19] What was said above of *Friesland* came from Mr. Berkley the Consul. Mr. Adams says *nothing of* that *province altho'* his letter is *of later date.*[20] If this sd. find you at Richmond, it will be unnecessary for you & Mr. R. both to be at the labor of decyphering, the above being copied from his letter. I made this provision for the contingency of your not having proceeded to Richmond. That you may not give me more credit for it than is due, I must confess that you owe it in part to the facility which my letter to him in Cypher afforded for repeating the intelligence to you. I believe, I have omitted one paragraph on another subject which he will communicate to you.[21] Whitesides[22] has the means remitted for taking up the note in which I am concerned. I have urged Mr. R. to return & charged him to urge you. Let me hear from you on that subject, & let it be favorably. Farewell

J. M. JR.

Yr. favr. of 21.[23] was rcd ½ after 9 OC last night.

[1] Judging from the handwriting, JM wrote "May–1782" at the top of this letter late in his life. In arranging his correspondence for editing, he probably noted the similarity between the contents of this undated letter and those of the Virginia delegates to Harrison and of his own letter to Arthur Lee on 28 May 1782. The first paragraph of the latter of these (*q.v.*), when compared with the postscript to the present letter, permits no doubt that JM wrote to Lee and Jones either on the same day or added the postscript to Jones on 28 May, after writing the rest of the dispatch on the twenty-seventh.

[2] JM inadvertently wrote 58.3, which stood for "di-car," rather than 729, the cipher for "pres." In decoding, Jones misread 58.3 as 583, and hence interlineated "within," which that number symbolized. Many years later, when JM reacquired this dispatch, he evidently checked the coding, discovered his 58.3 was an error, decided he had meant to write the cipher for "pres," and therefore wrote "present" above Jones's irrelevant "within."

[3] This and the other bracketed punctuation marks later in the sentence were probably interlineated by Jones when he decoded the letter.

[4] See Report on Salaries of Representatives Abroad, 28 May, and n. 3; Virginia Delegates to Harrison, 28 May 1782, and nn. 9, 11, and 13. In his "account of the moneys in France," read in Congress on 24 May, Morris listed, "Bills drawn by Congress in favour of Mr. de Beaumarchais three years ago, and which are payable 22 June next . . . [$]2,544,000" (*JCC*, XXII, 293). See also *JCC*, XIV, 746.

Pierre Augustin Caron de Beaumarchais (1732–1799), author of the comedies *The Barber of Seville* and *The Marriage of Figaro* as well as many other literary works, effectively befriended the American cause between 1776 and 1781. Besides giving generously from his own purse, he used his considerable influence to persuade France to ally with the United States and even from the onset of the Revolution to assist it with loans and gifts of money and military supplies. He also encouraged French officers to volunteer for service with the American army. At the close of the war he declared that the Commonwealth of Virginia owed him £42,927 and Congress 3,600,000 livres. Virginia largely discharged its obligation before Beaumarchais' death. On the other hand, his claim against the United States was complicated after 1786 by the problem of whether an unaccounted-for one million livres, which King Louis XVI in 1776 had empowered Beaumarchais to spend secretly for matériel needed by the American army, should be deducted from his bill. Finally in 1835, after the "lost million" had been a subject of repeated negotiations, including some wherein JM had supported the validity of the claim, Congress obliged the heirs of Beaumarchais either to forgo any remuneration or to accept (as they did) 800,000 livres in full settlement of the debt (*Journals of the Council of State*, III, 462, 506, 535; Hening, *Statutes*, XIII, 339–40; Samuel Shepherd, ed., *Statutes at Large of Virginia* [new ser.], III, 22; Louis Gottschalk, *Lafayette Joins the American Army*, pp. 66, 176; Louis Gottschalk, *Lafayette between the American and the French Revolution*, p. 330; Elizabeth S. Kite, *Beaumarchais and the War of American Independence* [2 vols.; Boston, 1918], II, *passim*, and especially pp. 199–211).

[5] JM wrote 501, the cipher for "bea," rather than 505, the cipher for "ange." Evidently uncertain what JM had intended, Jones disregarded the 154, symbolizing "d," immediately preceding 501, and 241. 257 symbolizing "rous," immediately following 501, and interlineated "serious."

[6] JM used "by the bayonet" to connote forcibly impressing food for the use of the army. See *Papers of Madison*, III, 325, 326, n. 5; Randolph to JM, 16–17 May 1782, and n. 18.

[7] Virginia Delegates to Harrison, 28 May 1782, and n. 25; Wharton, *Revolutionary Diplomatic Correspondence*, V, 234–35, 257–58. JM used the ciphers for "ci-ti" rather than "ci-ty."

[8] See *Papers of Madison*, II, 149, n. 5. On 10 October 1776 Congress had designated John Barry (1745–1803) as the seventh ranking captain of "the navy of the United States" (*JCC*, VI, 861). Born in Ireland, Barry migrated to Philadelphia in 1760 and was a prosperous shipmaster and shipowner at the outset of the Revolution. During the war he commanded several continental men-of-war, including the "Alliance," on which Lafayette embarked for France in December 1781 (*Papers of Madison*, III, 315, n. 2). From 1785 until 1794, when Congress named him senior captain of the United States Navy, Barry resided at his estate, Strawberry Hill, except for a mercantile voyage to China, 1787–1789. During most of the period 1797–1801 he was again at sea, especially in West Indian waters, as commodore of a squadron comprising his flagship the frigate "United States," the frigate "Constitution," and eight smaller vessels (Martin I. J. Griffin, *Commodore John Barry, "The Father of the American Navy"* [Philadelphia, 1903]).

[9] The "marquis" was Lafayette. See Pendleton to JM, 15 April 1782, and n. 12; Louis Gottschalk, ed., *The Letters of Lafayette to Washington, 1777–1799* (New York, 1944), pp. 251, 254–55. On 8 June 1782 the *Virginia Gazette* reported the likelihood that six French ships of the line and three frigates would soon arrive in American waters, and that Lafayette was "expected to be with the squadron."

[10] La Luzerne.

[11] JM used the cipher for "though" rather than the one for "through."

[12] Livingston laid this information before Congress on 28 May 1782 (*JCC*, XXII, 303). At Great Britain's insistence, France had reluctantly consented in the Peace of Paris (1763) to fulfill her earlier pledges to raze the fortifications at her Channel port of Dunkirk (*Cambridge Modern History*, VI, 331, 345, 429, 464).

[13] See Virginia Delegates to Harrison, 14 May, and n. 17; JM to Randolph, 14 May 1782, and n. 8.

[14] See Report on Mission To Inform States of Financial Crisis, 22 May 1782, editorial note.

[15] Neither La Luzerne's correspondent in Virginia nor JM's "consolatory answer" to La Luzerne is known to the editors. See Randolph to JM, 29 June, and n. 3; JM to Randolph, 9 July; Jones to JM, 22 July 1782.

[16] See Instructions to Virginia Delegates, 24–25 May 1782. The legislature of Maryland and the Pennsylvania Supreme Executive Council had already adopted resolutions of this tenor (Wharton, *Revolutionary Diplomatic Correspondence*, V, 431; *Colonial Records of Pennsylvania*, XIII, 286–88).

[17] See Virginia Delegates to Harrison, 28 May 1782, and n. 20.

[18] Here JM wrote the cipher for "resolv" rather than the cipher for "ur."

[19] Except for differences in punctuation, JM's quotation from Adams' letter of 26 March 1782 is approximately correct (Wharton, *Revolutionary Diplomatic Correspondence*, V, 275). Paul François de Quélen de Stuer de Caussade (1746–1828), Duc de La Vauguyon, was ambassador from the court of Versailles to the States-General of the United Provinces of the Netherlands between 1776 and 1784. According to Adams, La Vauguyon unofficially had used his influence at The Hague on behalf of a recognition of the independence of the United States by the Prince of Orange and the States-General. William V, Prince of Orange and Nassau and a nephew of King George III, was pro-British.

[20] Thomas Barclay (1728–1793), a Philadelphia merchant. See *Papers of Madison*, III, 201, n. 1; JM to Pendleton, 22 January, n. 11; Report on Foreign Dispatches, 20 March, n. 6; Report on Salaries of Representatives Abroad, 28 May 1782, n. 1. On 18 November 1782 Congress appointed Barclay as commissioner to settle the accounts of the United States in Europe, and on 3 January 1783 as consul general in France with authority to appoint United States commercial agents or vice consuls in that country (*JCC*, XXIII, 730; XXIV, 3). In October 1785 while holding these positions, Barclay was named by John Adams and Jefferson, who with Franklin had been commissioned by Congress to conclude a treaty of amity and commerce with the emperor of Morocco, to be their agent for carrying out this assignment. Congress complimented him upon its successful completion and ratified the treaty on 18 July 1787 (*JCC*, XXX, 259; XXXI, 923; XXXII, 355–64). In the autumn of that year Barclay returned to the United States to settle his accounts with Congress and to raise money to satisfy his insistent creditors in France. His efforts during President Washington's administration to procure a federal office in the United States were unavailing. On 31 March 1791 his friend Jefferson, then Secretary of State, named him consul for Morocco. Barclay died suddenly in Lisbon on 19 January 1793. See Boyd, *Papers of Jefferson*, XI, 493–500; XII, 114, 378; XIII, 253; XVI, 471–72. In volumes VII through XII, there are many letters from or to Barclay about his activities, 1785–1790.

[21] See JM to Randolph, 28 May 1782.

[22] Peter Whiteside. See Virginia Delegates to Harrison, 5 March, and n. 1; Randolph to JM, 11–13 April 1782, and n. 6.

[23] *Q.v.*

To Arthur Lee

Printed text (Richard Henry Lee, *Life of Arthur Lee,* II, 328–30), inaccurately dated 1778. Addressed to "The Hon. Arthur Lee, Esq." An extract, copied from the original and correctly dated, is item No. 1533 in a catalogue of the John Clark Company, Cleveland, Ohio, for January 1916.

PHILADELPHIA, May 28, 17[82]

DEAR SIR,

I received your favour of the 16th inst. between nine and ten o'clock last night, the post having been delayed by sickness. I shall pursue your commands with respect to the bill enclosed in it.[1]

The arrival of the Alliance frigate at Rhode-Island, and the subsequent arrival of a French cutter at Salem, have furnished congress and the minister of France with pretty late intelligence from Europe.[2] The latter has not yet communicated the contents of his despatches. Those from our ministers at Versailles and at the Hague inform us that British emissaries had been practising every address to each of them to feel the pulse of their constituents, and debauch them from their engagements with France. At the same time very tempting concessions were held out to the latter for a similar purpose.[3] Proper answers were given to each of these insidious applications. These circumstances afford a seasonable admonition to the credulous, of the wickedness of Mr. Cailton's mission. We have heard nothing from this gentleman since the refusal of a passport for his secretary to visit congress.[4]

Mr. Adams seems to be making considerable progress in Holland towards an acknowledgment of his public character. He says the prince had declared his inability to resist the torrent in favour of a connexion with the United States.[5]

We have received no letters from Mr. Dana very lately. If I do not forget, some have been received since you left us, which contained little more than a proof that he had not become sensible of the error which his preceding letter displayed.[6] Despatches from Mr. Jay, transmitted by Col. Livingston, have been lost to us by the capture of this gentleman by a privateer from New-York. They were not however gained by the enemy.[7] Col. Livingston is now here, but restrained by his parole from suggesting the contents of his despatches, or giving any other intelligence from that quarter.

I have written more fully in cypher to Mr. Randolph, on foreign subjects and some others, than time or prudence will permit me to repeat here. For what is omitted, I must therefore beg leave to refer you to him.[8]

The reasons which recommend an interference of the assembly in the case of the Flags, do not I confess occur to me. If the goods included in the capitulation of York, were sold, and are to be paid for, it would seem that a mode of payment, which affords to Virginia a vent for her staple, and prevents the exportation of her specie, cannot be complained of by her.[9]

The enclosed gazette contains the several obscure and contradictory advices, of the action in the West Indies, which have of late agitated our hopes and fears. The acknowledged inferiority of the fleet of our ally, gives some credulity[10] to the articles which are in favour of the enemy.[11] Should the event however have been ever so disastrous, it can only affect the duration of the war. The issue of it is fixed by causes which are superior to every particular event. Every triumph of the enemy on the ocean is rather a new argument to all Europe in favour of our independence; and I am somewhat of Mr. Adams' opinion, that if America were to betray a disposition to relapse under the dominion of Great Britain, all the maritime powers would interpose to prevent it. The tyranny which they have experienced would render any alternation preferable to a re-establishment of the superiority of power which gave birth to it.[12]

Notwithstanding the importance of the present crisis, the number of states in congress does not exceed eight, sometimes seven only, and most of these represented by only two members. The president is directed to write to the unrepresented states on the subject, and urge them to supply the deficiency.[13] I wish much for a re-inforcement to the delegation of Virginia, and have pushed Mr. Randolph to undertake that service immediately. I calculate on your return so soon as your other undertakings will permit.[14] In the present moment it is of consequence that every delegation should be tolerably full, as well as every state represented.

With great respect and regard, I am, dear sir, yours, &c.

J. MADISON, JR.

1 See Lee to JM, 16 May 1782.

2 See JM to Jones, 28 May 1782.

3 See *ibid.*; Virginia Delegates to Harrison, 28 May 1782, and n. 20.

4 JM probably wrote "Carlton" rather than "Cailton." See Virginia Delegates to Harrison, 14 May, and n. 17; JM to Randolph, 14 May 1782, and n. 8.

5 See JM to Jones, 28 May 1782, and n. 19.

[6] See Motion on Instructions to Dana, 27 May 1782, editorial note and n. 1; Report on Salaries of Representatives Abroad, 28 May, and n. 12.

[7] See *Papers of Madison*, III, 106, n. 13. While returning from Spain, Colonel Henry Brockholst Livingston had been captured by a British privateer which docked at New York City. Livingston destroyed his papers before being made a prisoner (Wharton, *Revolutionary Diplomatic Correspondence*, V, 430).

[8] See JM to Randolph, 28 May 1782.

[9] See Randolph to JM, 16–17 May, and n. 25; 21–24 May, and nn. 3, 6, 7, and 8; Harrison to Virginia Delegates, 18 May 1782, and n. 4. JM confined his remarks to the legal, tobacco-payment terms of the capitulation, overlooking the unauthorized, specie-draining trade at which Lee had hinted (Lee to JM, 16 May 1782, and nn. 7 and 9).

[10] In the catalogue mentioned in the headnote, this word is "credibility."

[11] Probably the *Pennsylvania Packet* of 28 May, which called attention to the Battle of the Saints by printing a vague French item from Martinique and a longer and more factual British account from Antigua. In view of the reports of the engagement in the *Pennsylvania Journal* of 15 May and in the *Pennsylvania Packet* three days later, Madison's uncertainty about the outcome of the battle may reflect an unwillingness to credit well-substantiated news of a severe reverse, which most likely would prolong a war already of seven years' duration. See also Virginia Delegates to Harrison, 14 May, n. 14; Ambler to JM, 18 May, n. 6; JM to James Madison, Sr., 20 May, and n. 4; Pendleton to JM, 20 May 1782, n. 8.

[12] Instead of "alternation," JM probably wrote "alternative," as in the Clark Company catalogue. JM appears to be paraphrasing remarks made by John Adams in his memorial of 19 April 1781 to the States-General of the United Provinces. Adams also tersely summarized one aspect of the same viewpoint by writing to Robert R. Livingston in a letter of 14 February 1782, "Great Britain will not cease to be the tyrant of the ocean until she ceases to be the tyrant of America" (Wharton, *Revolutionary Diplomatic Correspondence*, IV, 374–75; V, 162).

[13] See Motion Urging States To Send Delegates to Congress, 27 May 1782.

[14] See JM to Pendleton, 23 April, and n. 10; JM to Jones, 28 May 1782.

To Edmund Randolph

Excerpt (Madison, *Papers* [Gilpin ed.], I, 130–34). The manuscript has not been found. Only the last two paragraphs of the text, probably in cipher in the original, are printed here, because the rest of the letter is identical with the one which JM wrote to Joseph Jones on the same date, except for the personal portion of the latter, confined to the final thirteen lines.

PHILADELPHIA, May 28, 1782.

The Secretary of War has just given notice to Congress, that the Department of Finance is unable to supply the essential means of opening the campaign.[1] This shocks, rather than surprises, us. It will be one article in the communications of the deputies above mentioned, and adds force to the expediency of their mission.[2]

The denial to Congress of the right of granting flags is singular indeed. May not the power of Congress to agree to a truce be contested on the same grounds? The former is a partial truce, and if the silence of the Confederation reserves it to the States, the same silence reserves the latter. Admitting that Congress had the right of granting flags, was it not exercised to the advantage of Virginia in procuring a vent to her staple, and stopping the exportation of her specie?[3]

[1] The secretary at war had so informed Congress on 27 May (*JCC*, XXII, 302).
[2] See Report on Mission To Inform States of Financial Crisis, 22 May, editorial note; JM to Jones, 28 May 1782.
[3] See JM to Lee, 28 May 1782, and n. 9.

Report on Count Bieniewsky's Proposal for a Legionary Corps

MS (NA: PCC, No. 19, I, 269). Docketed: "Answer for Ct. Beniouski. Comee. Mr. Madison Mr Scot Mr. Ramsay, Passed May 29. 1782." The report is in JM's hand. In the above caption the count's surname conforms with his signature while he was in the United States. For his variant spellings of the name, see the editorial note.

EDITORIAL NOTE

In his two-volume autobiography entitled, *Memoirs and Travels of Mauritius Augustus Count de Benyowsky*, translated by William Nicholson, first published posthumously in London in 1790, and soon appearing in German, French, and Polish editions, the author recorded that he, a magnate of Poland and Hungary, had been born in Hungary in 1741. In his letter of 5 May 1782 to the president of Congress, Bieniewsky claimed to be a Pole and a cousin of Count Casimir Pulaski (NA: PCC, No. 78, IV, 299–301). According to Bieniewsky in this letter, he had served as a brigadier general in the French army and as a major general in the Austrian army. Judging from his memoirs, which recount his career until the close of 1776, he had fought in Prussia, Lithuania, and Russia, and been exiled to Siberia. From there he had escaped to China, gone to Japan, and attempted to establish a settlement in Madagascar.

In the introduction of his edition of the *Memoirs and Travels* (London, 1904), Captain S. Pasfield Oliver remarked that the memoirs were replete with inaccuracies of facts and exaggerations about the count's achievements and his rank among the nobles of Hungary and Poland. Oliver found that Bieniewsky had been born in 1746 rather than in 1741, the natal year of his choice as long as he was a soldier of fortune. He returned to Europe after his unsuccessful visit to the United States in 1782 but came back two years later. In October 1784 he sailed from Baltimore in the "Intrepid," a vessel in the foreign slave trade, and was killed in May 1786 during a skirmish with French troops on Madagascar. His alleged exploits in Kamchatka were the subject of the drama, *Graf Benjowsky* (1794), by August Friedrich Ferdinand von Kotzebue, and of the comic opera, *Beniowski ou les Exilés du Kamtschatka* (1800), by Alexander Duval and François Adrien de Boieldieu. In Warsaw in 1961 Mieczyslaw Bohdan Lipicki published *Maurycy August Beniowski.* When the count was in Hungary, he apparently spelled his surname Benyovszky; in France and Poland, Beniowski; in Great Britain, Benyowsky; in Prussia, Benjowsky; and in the United States, Bieniewsky.

Claiming the favor of Vergennes, Bieniewsky on 18 March 1782 applied for a commission in the continental army. He was informed by Washington that his request could not be honored because of the recent reduction in the number of officers (Fitzpatrick, *Writings of Washington,* XXIV, 77–78). Encouraged by the endorsement of La Luzerne and the willingness of the Baron von Steuben to sponsor him, the count then devised an elaborate plan for recruiting a legion of troops from Germany, to be under his command. This proposal, accompanied by Washington's qualified approval, came before Congress on 6 May 1782. The commander-in-chief obviously had misgivings but recognized that, in view of La Luzerne's support of the project, Congress' judgment of its merits might be influenced by considerations of political expediency (*ibid.,* XXIV, 112–15, 163–64, 175; Bieniewsky to President of Congress, 6 May 1782, in NA: PCC, No. 78, IV, 299–301; No. 186, fol. 30; *JCC,* XXII, 243 n.). The secretary at war, to whom the plan was referred, advised Congress on 9 May that the proposal involved issues beyond his authority to decide. Eighteen days later Congress rejected a committee's recommendation, written by Theodorick Bland, that Bieniewsky's plan be adopted and consigned it to the committee named in the headnote, with a directive "to report a proper answer informing him that Congress cannot accept his proposals" (*JCC,* XXII, 261, and n. 2, 296–98, 298 n.; NA: PCC, No. 186, fol. 27; No. 191, fol. 15).

[29 May 1782]

Report of the Committee relating to Ct. Beniousky

Sir

The proposal for introducing a legionary corps into the service of the U. States which accompanied your letter of the 6th. instant, has been considered by Congress with the attention due to its importance [& to the auspices under which it is presented.][1] The zeal for the American cause which the Author of it professes, and which the generous terms of the plan evince, have not failed to inspire a just esteem for his character, and a disposition to favor his wishes. Considerations however which in no respect derogate from this esteem, or this disposition render it expedient for Congress to decline the offer which has been made to them.

I have the honor &c.

J. H. Pt.[2]

[1] The words in brackets were crossed out. Above "presented," the word "made" was interlineated but also deleted. Whether the committee or Congress decided upon these excisions is not known.

[2] John Hanson, president of Congress. For Bieniewsky's effort to interest the government of Virginia in his proposal, see Count Bieniewsky to Virginia Delegates, 31 May 1782.

To Edmund Randolph

RC (LC: Madison Papers). Addressed, "Edmund Randolph Esqr. Richmond." Docketed, "J. Madison Jr. May 29. 1782."

PHILADA. May 29th. 1782.

DEAR SIR

The inclosed letter[1] was put into my hands several weeks ago. As I found by looking into it that it related to a subject decided on in the case of Col. Carrington, and which wd. be communicated by him to Majr. Pierce,[2] I thought it unnecessary to transmit it by the Post. This is the first private conveyance[3] that has offered.

I wrote to you yesterday morning by the post fully & in Cypher.[4] As I am told however the Bearer will probably be in Richmond before the Post, it may not be amiss to repeat to you that we have heard nothing from Carlton since our refusal of the passport to his Secy.[5] and that we have authentic information from Europe that insidious attempts have been made both on Dr. Franklin & Mr. Adams, by British Emissaries as well as tempting overtures employed to divide our Ally from us.[6] These Machinations have served no other end than to expose the meanness & impotence of our Enemy, and to supply fresh proofs of the indissoluble nature of the Alliance. Mr. Adams begins to advance with considerable speed towards the object of his Mission in Holland.[7]

The Action in the West Indies is still wrapt up in darkness. The inclosed paper contains a Specimen of the obscure & contradictory advices which have alternately excited our hopes & our apprehensions.[8]

A Copy of sundry resolutions of the House of Delegates touching the exportation of Tobacco in the Flags, was laid before Congress yesterday by the Superintendt of Finance & ref[erred] to a Committee.[9] On a review of the Doctrine of the 9th. art. of the Confederation I believe the right of the State to prohibit in the present case the exportation of her produce can not be controverted.*[10] Congress have no authority to enter into any Convention with a friendly power which would abridge such a right.[11] They cannot have a greater authority with respect to a Hostile power. On the other side it is equally clear that the State has no authority to grant flags for the exportation of its produce to the Enemy.[12] Armed Vessels wd. not respect them, nor would they be more respected in the Courts of Admiralty. Unless Congress & the State therefore act in Concert no Tobacco can be remitted to N.Y. and a further drain of Specie must ensue. When the matter was first opened in Congress the impression was unfavorable to the right of the State, and pretty free strictures were likely to be made on its opposition to the Constitutional power of Congress. It became necessary therefore to recur to the law & the testimony which produced an acquiescence in the contrary doctrine. Their sentiments however with regard to the policy & consistency of the Resolutions are very different. The last Resolution in particular Compared with the preliminary doctr[ines] produces animadversions which I need not recite to you.[13] There are several reasons which make me regret much this variance between Congress & Virga. of which a material one is that a great Personage[14] will be touched by it since it originates in his Act, & since in a conference between a Committee[,] him & the Superintt. he concurred in the expediency of granting the passports. Gillon is just arrived here with five sail of the Havannah fleet.[15] I have not yet heard whether he brings news or not.

Adieu

J. M. Jr.[?][16]

* The States seem to have reserved at least a right to subject foreigners to the same imposts & prohibitions as their own Citizens; and the Citizens of Virga. are at present prohibited from such an exportation as is granted in favor of the B. Merchants. This is a very interesting point and unless the division line between the Authority of Congress & the States be properly ascertained, every foreign treaty may be a source of internal as well as foreign controversy. You may call to mind one now in negotiation which may be affected by the construction of this clause in the Confederation.

1 Not found.

2 See Report of Delegates on Carrington's Memorial, 20 April, n. 2; and Motion on Carrington, 26 April 1782, and n. 1.

[3] Not identified.

[4] See JM to Randolph, 28 May 1782. Late in his life JM or someone at his direction placed a bracket at the beginning of this paragraph and another bracket at the end of the third sentence from the close of the letter, thus indicating the portion which should appear in the first edition of his papers (Madison, *Papers* [Gilpin ed.], I, 134–36).

[5] See Virginia Delegates to Harrison, 14 May, and n. 17; JM to Randolph, 14 May 1782, and n. 8.

[6] See Virginia Delegates to Harrison, 28 May 1782, and n. 20.

[7] See JM to Jones, 28 May 1782.

[8] See JM to Lee, 28 May 1782, and n. 11.

[9] See Lee to JM, 16 May, and n. 7; Randolph to JM, 16–17 May, and n. 25; and 21–24 May, and nn. 3, 6, 8, 9, and 15; Harrison to Virginia Delegates, 18 May 1782, and n. 4.

[10] Now, unlike the day before, when he wrote to Arthur Lee and Randolph (*q.v.*), JM had come to see "reasons which recommend an interference of the assembly in the case of the Flags." In the present letter he recognized that "the case" involved a conflict between the authority of Virginia as a sovereign and an action by Congress which had reasonably been implied from its "sole and exclusive right and power of determining on peace and war." Later in this paragraph JM implies that in this particular instance of conflict between two "rights," economic advantage and deference to the known wish of Washington should lead Virginia to concede and "act in Concert" with Congress to permit the agreement with the British traders to be fulfilled. The final sentence of JM's footnote probably refers to the proposed terms of a consular convention with France (*Papers of Madison*, III, 201, and n.; Randolph to JM, 21–24 May 1782, and n. 22).

[11] By the ninth article of the Articles of Confederation, Congress was forbidden to make a treaty of commerce which would bar a state "from prohibiting the exportation or importation of any species of goods or commodities whatsoever" (*JCC*, IX, 915).

[12] See Randolph to JM, 21–24 May 1782, nn. 2 and 3.

[13] In its "last Resolution," after contending that the agreement between the agents of Congress and the British traders violated an ordinance of Congress, a law of Virginia, and the Treaty of Amity and Commerce with France, the House of Delegates appeared both selfish and inconsistent by declaring that "nothing contained in these resolutions shall be construed to prevent the Execution of a Contract entered into by the Agent of this State with the Assent of His Excellency General Washington under the Capitulation with the Traders Capitulants at York for the Amount of Tobacco due for Goods received for the use of the Army" (NA: PCC, No. 75, fols. 367–68). In other words, the government of Virginia insisted, contrary to its own law, upon honoring the contract of its agent, David Ross, with the British traders, even while seeking to prevent Congress, on grounds of illegality, from fulfilling the agreement of its agent, Timothy Pickering, with the same merchants.

[14] Washington.

[15] See Report on Foreign Dispatches, 20 March 1782, and nn. 5 and 6.

[16] JM initialed rather than signed the letter, but his initials have become blurred.

Count Bieniewsky to Virginia Delegates

MS (Virginia State Library). Bieniewsky's proposals and the translation of them were enclosed by the Virginia delegates in their letter of 4 June 1782 to Harrison (*q.v.*). The document in French is docketed, "Count de Beniouskys Proposals [June 4. 1782]." The document in English is in the hand of Theodorick Bland. Having "acquired French" in his sojourns abroad, Bland was probably also the translator (Charles Campbell, ed., *Bland Papers*, I, xx, xxx), a fact seemingly borne out by his postscript in English noting that the translation is "liberal."

PHILADELPHI le 31. Mai, 1782.

Le Comte de Bieniewsky authorise Monsieur Le Colonel Bland et Deputé de L'Etat de Virginie et Membres du Congrés, de proposer a leurs dit Etat in son Nom de Statuer un Legion de Trouppe pareill qui'l a proposé au Congrés; en cas [les?] mem[es?] ou L'Etat ne voudroit operer augmentátion de Ses forces que pas [par?] degres il se Soumet de prendre le Comandement d'un Seul corps qu'il Statuera, et que l'on pourra augmenter quand besoin y Sera; mais com[m?]e les demandes qu'il a fait au Congrés ne Sont pas analogue a la Constitution de L Etat, il les reduit.—

1°—a la concession du Terrains.

2°—a la garantie du paiement pour la Levé de la Trouppe

3°—La Soldi, et entretien regulière.

4°—La garantie de la demie paie aux officiers, et de avances aux Soldats apres la guerre.

5°—a ce que cette Trouppe Soit Toujour Comande par Ses officiers et que Exercice de la Disciplin Militair Soit imediatement Subordoné au General Comandant de cette Trouppe.

6°—Que le Comte de Bieniewsky Soit emploié au Comdant de Trouppes de l'Etat, et reconu[?] en le qualité de general major, avec le rang et charge de L'inspecteur des Trouppes de l'Etat.

A ces conditions, et engagements le Comte de Bieniewsky Stipulera le Traité pour le Leve de la ditte Trouppe, et honoré[?] du Title de Citoyen de l'Etat de Virginie, et prendera serment usité.

MAURICE AUGUSTE COMTE DE BIENIEWSKY

Et en cas que Messieurs de Bland et Recevir le pouvoir de conclu Le Traité il est necessair de fai[re?] expedié en mem Temps La Comissio[n] du general Major de L'Etat de Virginie au Co. de Bieniewski;

et ses autres Pouvoirs du dit Etat de Lever la Trouppe et nomé les officiers a Leurs emploies–CM[?]

Translation of Proposals from the Count de Biniouskey to the Honbl. James Madison, & the Honble. Theok: Bland delegates in Congress from the State of Virginia. to be laid before the Said State for their Consideration and acceptance if they shd. think proper so to do, if otherwise, their refusal to be notified through their sd. Delegates in Congress to the Count de Beniouskey. viz

PHILADELPHIA May 31st. 1782

The Count de Beniouskey Authorizes Col: Bland and Mr. Madison[1] Deputies from the State of Virginia and Members of Congress to propose to their said State–in his own name to constitute a legion of troops similar to that which he has proposed to Congress.[2] But if the State, shall not see fit to Augment its troops to the number there offerd, he submits to take the Command of one of the Corps which he shall raise and which may be augmented by the addition of the other Corps or any part thereof as the sd. State shall think fit. But as the demands heretofore made to the United states in Congress assembled–may not Quadrate with the Constitution of the State of Virginia and in order to obviate any obstacles (which that might present) to the acceptance of his proposals the following are the terms which he offers to the Said State as the Basis to any agreement which may be enterd into on these proposals viz

1st.[3] the Concession or grant of the Lands to the Soldiery &.c.
2d an assurance of Payment for the expences of levying the said troops.
3d the regular pay and subsistence of the troops while in Service of the State
4th the assurance of half Pay to the officers and of the advance or loan to the Soldiers after the War
5th that the troops aforementiond shall be always commanded by their own officers, and that the Exercise of military Discipline shall be immediately subordinate to the General of those troops
6th that the Count de Beniouskey shall be employd to command the troops of the State and have the Rank of Major General with the Rank and Charge of Inspector of the troop[s] of the State

on the above Conditions and engagements the Count de Beniouskey, will stipulate the treaty,[4] for Raizing the Said troops–will become a

Citizen of the State of Virginia and will take the Usual oaths of Allegiance and fidelity to the Said State, as will his officers and soldiers on their arrival

Signd[5] MAURICE COUNT DE BENIOUSKEY

In case Messrs. Madison & Bland receives power to conclude the treaty—it will be necessary at the same time to send the Commission of Major General of the State of Virginia to the Count Beniouskey, and a power of the Said State to Levy the troops and name the officers to their respective posts therein[6]

N.B. the above is a liberal translation of his proposals in French according to the Spirit of them as explaind by Count Beniouskey to us verbally[7]

[1] In view of the fact that Bieniewsky left a blank at this point, he evidently could not recall JM's name and drafted his proposals when neither Bland nor JM was present.

[2] See Report on Bieniewsky's Proposal for a Legionary Corps, 29 May 1782.

[3] This paragraph, by including more than Bieniewsky had written, illustrates Bland's meaning of "liberal." Implicit also in Bland's statement may be the tolerance necessarily exercised by the translator in deciphering the count's penmanship and in inferring his intended meaning from his faulty French.

[4] Here and in the next paragraph the translator should have rendered "Traité" as "agreement."

[5] This is an addition by the translator.

[6] The translator omits Bieniewsky's indistinct initialing at the end of this postscript.

[7] See n. 1, above. Probably the count had conferred with Bland and JM before drafting the proposal; otherwise, he would have inserted JM's name in the two spaces he left for inserting it. For the outcome of Bieniewsky's application, see Harrison to Virginia Delegates, 22 June 1782, and n. 6.

Report on Fidelity to French Alliance

MS (NA: PCC, No. 19, II, 341, 341a, 342–44). In JM's hand. Docketed: "Report of the Committee on the Letters from Dr. Franklin &c. were referred Passed May 31 1782."

EDITORIAL NOTE

Several actions by Congress, not mentioned in the printed journal, explain the contrast in emphasis between the docket, above, and the prefatory sentence of the report, below. On 27 May Congress had referred to JM, Abraham Clark, and Jesse Root the dispatch of 30 March from Franklin to Livingston and a copy of a letter to Franklin from John Adams written on 26 March. Each of these communications reported that agents of Lord North through correspondence or conversations were seeking to entice "the Colonies" into negotiations looking toward a truce or peace with Great Britain (Virginia Delegates to Harrison, 28 May 1782, and n. 20; NA: PCC, No. 186, fol. 30; Wharton, *Revolutionary Diplomatic Correspondence*, V, 273–75, 277).

On 28 May Livingston submitted to Congress a report of what he had been told by La Luzerne. The latter, after mentioning that British "Emissaries" had sought to draw France, the Netherlands, and Adams into separate peace negotiations, emphasized that Vergennes had unqualifiedly refused to have his government dishonor its pledge in the treaty of alliance. For this reason La Luzerne suggested to Livington that "it would be useful if Congress would affirm its determination to treat with the enemy only in concert with France in Europe," thereby foreclosing the possibility of separate negotiations with Carleton in America. La Luzerne also urged Congress "to trouble the repose" of the enemy by conducting vigorous military operations during the remainder of 1782 (*JCC*, XXII, 304–5). Having listened to this communication from Livingston and noted that it related to the same subjects which Franklin and Adams had commented upon in their letters, Congress referred it on 28 May to the committee named above (NA: PCC, No. 186, fol. 30). Since Jesse Root had left Philadelphia with Joseph Montgomery to portray the critical financial situation to the legislatures of the northern states, Congress on 29 May appointed Samuel Wharton to replace Root on JM's committee (*ibid.*; see also Report on Mission To Inform States of Financial Crisis, 22 May 1782, editorial note).

[31 May 1782]

The Committee to whom were referred the Communication from the Minister Plenipo: of his M.C.M.[1] &c submit the following report:

That the Secretary of For: Affairs acquaint the Minister Plenipo: of France, that the signal proof of inviolable constancy to his engagements given by his M.C.M. in the answer to the attempts of the British Court to seduce him into a separate peace, has been recd. by Congress with the sentiments with which it ought naturally to inspire faithful & affectionate allies, & entirely corresponds with the expectations which the magninimity & good faith of his past conduct had established: That Congress embrace with particular satisfaction this occasion of renewing to his M.C.M. the assurances which they have so often & so sincerely repeated of a reciprocal & equal resolution to adhere in every event to the principles of the Alliance, & to hearken to no propositions for peace which are not perfectly conformable thereto; (That[2] the insidious steps which the Court of London is pursuing render it improbable that any propositions conformable to those principles will be made to the U.S.; but that in case such propositions should be made Congress will not depart from the measures[3] which they have heretofore taken for preventing delay[4] & for conducting the discussion of them in confidence & in concert with his M.C.M.) and that as Congress observe with the warmest approbation the purpose of his M.C.M. to oppose to the false appearances of peace held out by G.B. those redoubled efforts which may render her sincerely disposed to it, so his Majesty may be persuaded that they are no less impressed with the necessity of such concurrent exertions on the part of the U.S. as may frustrate the views of the common enemy in the new[5] system which their policy seems to have adopted on this Continent.

That the Secretary of Foreign affairs also furnish to the said Minister Plenipo: a copy of so much of the letter of the day of last[6] from the Commander in chief as relates to a letter to him from Genl. Carlton, together with copies of the latter, and of the resolution of Congress passed in consequence thereof.[7]

That the Secretary of F. Affairs transmit copies of the first of these Resolutions & of the papers referred to in the last, to the Minister Plenipo. of the U. States at the Court of Versailles and to their other public Ministers in Europe.[8]

[1] Most Christian Majesty King Louis XVI of France.

[2] The section in parentheses is a substitution written by JM on a separate sheet (fol. 341) for the following deleted passage, which includes two slanted lines: "that in case any propositions conformable to those principles should be made to them, /which the insidious steps the British Court is pursuing render very improbable at the present juncture,/ Congress will be no less attentive than they have heretofore been to the precautions necessary for preventing delays & preserving harmony & confidence in the discussion of them." Whether the substitute passage and other changes noted below were made in committee or during the discussion of the report in Congress is not known. JM wrote the substitute passage and drew the cancellation lines in the manuscript with a much blunter quill than he had used to write the first version of the report. From this fact the inference may be made, although very inconclusively, that considerably after he wrote the original, he altered his draft, perhaps to attune it to the will of Congress.

[3] This word replaced a deleted "precautions."

[4] JM at first made this word plural.

[5] Following this word JM wrote and then deleted "defensive."

[6] See Washington to the President of Congress, 10 May, in Fitzpatrick, *Writings of Washington*, XXIV, 243–44; Virginia Delegates to Harrison, 7 May 1782, n. 4.

[7] See JM to Randolph, 14 May 1782, n. 8.

[8] The final two paragraphs of this report were crossed out.

From Edmund Randolph

RC (LC: Madison Papers). Addressed to "The honble. James Madison jr. esqr. of congress Philadelphia." Unsigned letter, docketed by JM, "June 1st. 1782."

RICHMOND June 1st. 1782

DEAR SIR

The senate have amended the resolution of the house of delegates, which I inclosed to you by the last post, respecting passports for the transportation of tobacco to New-York, so as to destroy its force. The delegates disagreed to their amendment, and that disagreement remains to be discussed on monday next. There is not the least probability, that the senate will recede, their vote having passed by the voice of sixteen members against one negative. Indeed many are inclined to believe, that, should this subject be remitted to the house of delegates for consideration, they will rather abandon their disagreement.[1]

The day before yesterday, Mr. Mason, Mr. Jefferson, Mr. A. Lee, myself and Dr. Walker were appointed to state the claims of Virginia to western territory.[2] Our power extends to publication without consulting the assembly; and I presume, that two or three months will produce something.[3] I wish, I had leisure to relate to you some management, which the desire of being distinguished by an appointment of this sort has occasioned. Superior beings must surely amuse themselves with contemplating the contests, which agitate mankind for trifles, and the meanesses, to which those trifles give birth. I will shortly excite either your ridicule or indignation at some recent manoeuvres.[4]

Messrs. Webb and St. George Tucker have fallen victims to the triennial exclusion of counsellors. The former has accepted since the office of receiver of the monies, paid into our treasury for continental use.[5] I have written to Mr. Morris this week upon the subject:[6] but in addition must beg you to inform him, that, as the assembly are about to appropriate the taxes to the various uses, for which they are designed, I have suggested to Mr. Webb the propriety of deferring the publication, mentioned in his instructions,[7] lest it should irritate at a season, when the assembly intend[8] to destine for the use of the united states a portion of the public revenue; which portion will probably be affected in its quantum by the temper of the legislature.

I am afraid however, that scarcely any thing can [be] expected from the collection of taxes sooner than the latter end of the year: it having been yesterday determined to postpone it. But a blank is left for the day, to which it is to be postponed.[9]

Mr. Henry is indisposed at present to repeal the cession, desiring to wait for a fitter opportunity. This measure will be attempted next week: and will, as [I] at present think, be adopted, giving congress a day, before which they may still accept [it.][10]

The Mr. Lees[11] are the warm patrons of a r[e]formation of the general court: and have worked out a new system, which will [car]ry its own refutation with it.[12]

I saw a letter from Mr. Jefferson to Col. Monro, in which he assigns reasons for refusing his seat in the house of delegat[es.][13] The pathos of the composition is really great; and the wound, which his sp[irit] [re]ceived by the late impeachment,[14] is, as he says, to be cured only by the all-heali[ng] grave. His triumph might certainly be an illustrious one over his former enemies, were [he] to resume the legislative character: for in the constant division between the tw[o] leaders, Henry & Lee,[15] he might incline the scale to which soever side he wou[ld.]

Tell Mrs. Triste, that we remember her with affec[tio]nate regard, and present our best respects to our acquaintance under your roof[.][16]

Sincerely yours.

[1] See Randolph to JM, 21–24 May 1782, and n. 3.

[2] See Randolph to JM, 19 April; JM to Randolph, 1 May 1782, n. 7.

[3] Randolph was much too sanguine. Jefferson contributed nothing, and George Mason declined to serve, although he consented to review before publication whatever the other members of the committee might prepare. Thomas Walker and Arthur Lee, the latter of whom apparently was more interested in drafting his own separate refutation of the claims to the Northwest Territory advanced by land companies and northern states, willingly relinquished to Randolph the main burden of the committee's assignment. Helped very little by his colleagues and hampered by the dearth or confused state of "our public records," Randolph was able to "produce something" only by August 1783, or about a year later than he had expected when he wrote the present letter. Even in the autumn of 1783 he could not complete the report, because Arthur Lee, attending Congress in Philadelphia, was unavailable for consultation. Finally, on 25 November 1783, Randolph wrote to John Tyler, the speaker of the House of Delegates, to explain the long delay of the committee in rendering its report and to ask the permission of the House for "the work to go into print under the correction of Mr. Mason and myself." The House tabled Randolph's letter (Randolph to Speaker of House of Delegates, 25 November 1783, MS in Virginia State Library; *Journal of the House of Delegates*, October 1783, p. 35). See also Boyd, *Papers of Jefferson*, VI, 651–55; Randolph to JM, 10 May 1782, and n. 7.

[4] See Randolph to JM, 20 June 1782.

[5] For George Webb, see Pendleton to JM, 22 April 1782, and n. 12. St. George

Tucker (1752–1827), a Bermudian by birth, had been graduated from the College of William and Mary in 1774. He interrupted his law practice to serve in the armed forces both on sea and land and rose to the rank of lieutenant colonel of Virginia militia. Wounded at the Battle of Guilford Court House, he subsequently campaigned with Lafayette and was present at Yorktown. His later career was distinguished by his eminence as a lawyer, as a professor of law in succession to his mentor, George Wythe, at the College of William and Mary (1790–1804), as a judge of both the Virginia Court of Appeals (1804–1810) and the United States Court of the District of Virginia (1813–1827), and as an author of books and pamphlets on legal, constitutional, political, and literary subjects. Probably his best-known work is his annotated five-volume edition (1804) of Blackstone's *Commentaries on the Laws of England* (Mary Haldane Coleman, *St. George Tucker, Citizen of No Mean City* [Richmond, 1938]). George Webb had been a member of the Council of State for over two years, but Tucker had first attended a meeting of the council as recently as 22 January 1782 (*Journals of the Council of State*, II, 257; III, 32; McIlwaine, *Official Letters*, II, 123). Webb and Tucker had "fallen victims" to the operation of Article XI of the Form of Government of Virginia, which provided that two members of the Council of State should "be removed by joint ballot of both Houses of Assembly at the end of every three years, and be ineligible for the three next years" (Hening, *Statutes*, IX, 116).

[6] Robert Morris' reply of 11 June to Randolph's letter of 31 May is in Madison, *Papers* (Gilpin ed.), I, 142. After expressing his chagrin because of the slowness with which all states except New Jersey and Rhode Island were meeting their financial obligations to Congress, Morris added: "Surely a different spirit will be roused. For Heaven's sake let us owe our freedom to ourselves! We have the means, if we dare to use them."

[7] In his circular of instructions to the receiver of continental taxes in each state, Morris suggested the publication of the names of individuals who had paid their assessments promptly and from time to time the total sums received from every tax district within a state. He also importuned the state governments to authorize the receivers to hold local collectors responsible for filling their individual quotas (Clarence L. Ver Steeg, *Robert Morris*, pp. 100–101). See Harrison to Virginia Delegates, 6 April 1782, n. 6.

[8] At first Randolph wrote "are about" rather than "intend."

[9] On 1 July 1782 the Virginia General Assembly enacted a law "for appropriating the public revenue." This measure provided that the tax money "shall be appropriated to continental purposes, and shall be applied to the credit of this commonwealth, upon the requisition of congress of" 4 October 1781, but only after a half-dozen specified obligations, including the long overdue stipend of the delegates in Congress, had been paid. In view of these prior liens, the residue available for the use of Congress probably would be very small, at best (Hening, *Statutes*, XI, 12–14; Minute Book, House of Delegates, May 1782, p. 85; Virginia Delegates to Harrison, 19 March 1782, n. 1). The Assembly at the same session, by directing that the collection of taxes should be delayed, signified its refusal to heed Morris' plea for a prompt payment of the financial quota, already much in arrears (Randolph to JM, 21–24 May, and n. 19; 27–29 June 1782, n. 8).

[10] See Randolph to JM, 21–24 May 1782, and n. 26.

[11] The brothers Lee, Richard Henry and Arthur, represented Westmoreland and Prince William counties, respectively, in the House of Delegates, where the other delegate from Westmoreland County was their first cousin Richard Lee (*ca.* 1726–1795). His brother Henry (1729–1787) represented in the Senate the district comprising Prince William and Fairfax counties.

[12] On 4 July 1782 John Banister, a Lee partisan in the House of Delegates from Dinwiddie County, remarked in a letter to Theodorick Bland: "The assembly were engaged for several weeks in attempting a reform in the mode of administering justice, but, like many other essential measures, it fell through, and we remain still without credit, without the means of obtaining justice, and subject to the contempt and ridicule of all other states whose policy is better regulated" (Charles Campbell, ed., *Bland Papers*, II, 84). The nine-page bill "for regulating the General Court" was introduced on 11 June. Purportedly designed for "the more easy & speedy Administration of Justice," it divided the state into seven "Circuits or Districts" and added fourteen judges to the judiciary. This enlargement might have made the administration of justice "more diffusive," but also much more cumbersome. On 18 June the bill was "referred to the next session of Assembly on second Monday in October next" (MS bill in Virginia State Library).

[13] For Jefferson's letter to James Monroe on 20 May 1782, see Boyd, *Papers of Jefferson*, VI, 184–86, 187 n.; and Randolph to JM, 16–17 May 1782, n. 6.

[14] See *Papers of Madison*, III, 338, n. 3; 347; 348 n. 1.

[15] Patrick Henry and Richard Henry Lee.

[16] For Mrs. Nicholas Trist, see *ibid.*, II, 92, n. 8. By using the word "acquaintance" rather than "friend," Randolph may be referring sarcastically to Bland.

Virginia Delegates to Benjamin Harrison

RC (Virginia State Library). Written by Theodorick Bland, except for JM's signature. Docketed, "1782. June 4th."

PHILADELPHIA June 4th 1782

SR.

Our last of the 28th. Ultimo informed your Excelly. fully of the State of News at this place,[1] Since which nothing material has happened, except what the enclosed News Paper contains.[2] There yet remains some doubt relative to the event of the Action of the two fleets in the West Indies. Accounts from Martinique by different Channels and of a late date, appearing to render it dubious, whether Rodneys letter is spurious or real, we confess however, we have no expectation of its being the former; Yet there is great room to believe that the remainder of the French fleet will form a Junction with the Spanish at Cape François and that the Combined fleets will have a decided Superiority in the West Indies, which will enable them to proceed with the Expedition against Jamaica.[3]

We find in a Report, the Superintendt. of Finance has made to Congress the Substance of his letter to you on the Subject of Stores,[4] and have Since had a Communication with the minister of France[5] on that Subject, who, informs us he answerd your letter, to him, relative thereto, and he hopes satisfactorily, but requested us to acquaint your

Excelly., "that the Misfortune which the Count de Guichens Convoy had met with,[6] rendering it very difficult, for the Ministry to procure transports for the Supply of their own fleets and Armies and to bring out the Supplies orderd for the United States, he feard it would not be practicable to send out those which had been purchased for the State of Virginia in any short time.["] He gave us to Understand that the transfer of the Debt from the State of Virginia to the United States had been a Misunderstanding of the Ministry, or some of the Under offices, & that it would be revoked and accommodated to all parties. we think however it would not be imprudent in the State of Virginia (if they wish soon to have those Stores[)], to provide transports for them and to obtain the same Convoy as those Vessels which are to bring out those belonging to the Un: States.

The Count de Beniousky having, renewd to us, an offer which has been made to Congress and not accepted as will be seen by the Enclosed papers No. 1, 2, 3, 4, & 5.[7] We thought it a matter of too much Consequence not to transmit to your Excelly. which we have done, with copies of all the Papers, relative thereto, as above mentiond, which have been before Congress. It will rest with your Excelly. to consider the propriety of taking the Sense of the Legislature thereon. The terms offerd in the Paper No. 4 refer's to those which have been made to Congress, which Yr. Excelly. will See in the Paper No. 1, and an explanation thereof in No. 2 after having been remarked upon by Genl. Washington. We have only to add on this Subject that the Gentleman who makes the offer does it as an *Individual.* That he is a Polish Nobleman and a near relation to the late Count Pulasky.[8] That a part of the troops he offers, and many of the officers (as he informs us) are such as have followd his fortunes in the Partition of that Kingdom. That Banishd from his own Country[9] he professes a desire to become (with his followers) a Citizen of some one of these United States that he has recommendations, from the French Ministry, to their Minister here and has had his Countenance.[10] The Rejection of his offer to Congress arose from a doubt in two or three of the States concerning the Propriety or policy of their being accepted by *Congress.* It is his desire that the offer made by him—if not accepted—may be kept as secret as possible, and that the answer thereto may be transmited, through us,[11] with all possible expedition as he will be under a necessity of departing for Europe in the Course of three or four Weeks from this date—either to put himself in a state to Execute his proposals, or to take other steps with his troops, which are now in the Imperial Service,[12] and will shortly be at his own charge—his desire of Secrecy and the Expedition with which Mr. Webb[13] informs us he will travel has induced us to prefer a Conveyance by that Gentn. to one by the Post on this occasion.

Since Writing the above Genl. Washington has informd Congress in a letter read yesterday, that he had received intelligence of some movements of the Enemy at New York which indicate a considerable embarkation, as upwards of 80 transports, under a strong Convoy had fallen down to the Narrows—in order as was supposed to take in a large body of troops—that the whole of the Regular troops had been reviewd—and a very large proportion of them were under Marching orders, for what purpose not known.[14] we Submit to Yr. Excelly whether it would not be prudent, at least to be on our Guard notwithstanding the delusive appearances lately held out, at least not to relax in any preparations for carrying on the War.

The last post brought us no letter from Yr. Excelly[.] with the most perfect respect we are

Yr. Excellency's Most obedt. Humbe Serts

THEOK. BLAND JR.
J. MADISON JR.

[1] See Virginia Delegates to Harrison, 28 May 1782.

[2] Probably the *Pennsylvania Packet* of 1 or 4 June 1782.

[3] See Virginia Delegates to Harrison, 14 May, n. 14; and 28 May, and n. 1; Ambler to JM, 18 May, and n. 6; JM to Madison, Sr., 20 May, n. 4; Pendleton to JM, 20 May, nn. 8 and 10; JM to Lee, 28 May 1782, and n. 11; *Journals of the Council of State*, III, 105.

[4] See Virginia Delegates to Harrison, 24 January, and nn. 1, 2, 4, 5; Virginia Delegates to La Luzerne, 24 January; Randolph to JM, 10 May, and n. 21; Harrison to Virginia Delegates, 11 May, and n. 1; and 22 June 1782.

[5] La Luzerne.

[6] See JM to Pendleton, 25 February 1782, n. 4.

[7] See Report on Bieniewsky's Proposal for a Legionary Corps, 29 May, and editorial note; and Bieniewsky to Virginia Delegates, 31 May 1782. The four documents copied and numbered by Bland, and enclosed in the present letter, were (1) "Composition of Squadrons & companies to form corps"; (2) "Explanation of the Proposals of Ct. de Beniousky translated"; (3) "Copy of the Report of a Comme. of Congress, to whom was referrd the letter of Count Beniousky &.c. &.c."; and (4) "Translation of Proposals from Count de Beniousky to the Honble. James Madison & the Honble. Theok: Bland delegates in Congress from the State of Virginia." Bland also enclosed and probably intended to mark "No. 5," an unnumbered "Copy of a letter from General Washington to Count Beniousky," 27 April 1782. These documents are filed with the Virginia delegates' dispatch in the Virginia State Library. See Harrison to Virginia Delegates, 22 June 1782.

[8] See Report on Bieniewsky's Proposal for a Legionary Corps, 29 May 1782, editorial note. In his *Memoirs and Travels* (1790), I, 17, 27, Bieniewsky referred to Pulaski as an "old friend" and "companion." Count Casimir Pulaski (*ca.* 1748–

1779) was a Polish refugee whom Congress commissioned as a brigadier general of cavalry on 15 September 1777 (*JCC*, VII, 745). Until he was mortally wounded on 9 October 1779 during the siege of Savannah, he served with distinction in the American army.

[9] The first partition of Poland, depriving it of about one-third of its territory and population, had been concluded on 5 August 1772 by Catherine the Great of Russia, Frederick the Great of Prussia, and Maria Theresa of Austria (*Cambridge Modern History*, VI, 669). In his letter of 5 May 1782 to the president of Congress, Bieniewsky did not claim to have opposed this partition actively. He merely stated that "after the Desolation and Division of my Country, I offered my Services to France, where I was favorably received" (NA: PCC, No. 78, IV, 299).

[10] Used in the sense of aid or endorsement.

[11] See Harrison to Virginia Delegates, 22 June 1782.

[12] The service of Joseph II, Holy Roman Emperor.

[13] See Ambler to JM, 11 May 1782, n. 3.

[14] Washington's letter of 28 May, read in Congress on 3 June 1782, had three enclosures telling of the military preparations under way in New York City (NA: PCC, 152, X, 571, 575, 577, 579; Fitzpatrick, *Writings of Washington,* XXIV, 295; *JCC,* XXII, 315 n.). His informants had been misled by two occurrences at the British headquarters. On 20 and 21 May General Carleton had reviewed all the troops in New York City and on Long Island. On 28 May about thirty transports, convoyed by two frigates, left New York Harbor for Martha's Vineyard to "take on board four thousand head of cattle and an even greater number of sheep, which have been gathered together on the island from Connecticut and sold to our commissaries through go-betweens" (Bernhard A. Uhlendorf, trans. and ed., *Revolution in America: Confidential Letters and Journals, 1776–1784, of Adjutant General Major Baurmeister of the Hessian Forces* [New Brunswick, N.J., 1957], pp. 505, 509). Early in June residents of Connecticut along the north shore of Long Island Sound observed this convoy sailing toward the east and concluded that as many as 4,000 British troops must be aboard the transports (*Virginia Gazette*, 22 and 29 June 1782). On 24 June in a letter to La Luzerne, Washington remarked: "The Enemy, from the best intelligence I get from New York, have made no detachment; things remain there in Statu quo; they seem to be suspended, and are waiting for orders from their Court; which I hear they anxiously expect" (Fitzpatrick, *Writings of Washington,* XXIV, 381).

To Edmund Randolph

RC (LC: Madison Papers). In the second volume of this collection, beginning with folio 73, are four pages of a letter written by JM and dated "June 4th. 1782." Although the cover is missing, the contents permit no doubt that Randolph was the addressee. Folio 42 of the third volume of JM's manuscripts in the Library of Congress seems to be an additional page containing a postscript to the same letter and is here so treated. The extra page lacks date, complimentary close, and signature, but the final two sentences, written by JM in a hand smaller than the others, apparently to make the use of a new page unnecessary, strongly suggest that he had reached the end of his message. Madison, *Papers* (Gilpin ed.), I, 138–39, and Madison, *Writings* (Hunt ed.), I, 205–6, print a portion of this page as a separate letter to Randolph and date it "June, 1782." Note 30, below, will explain why "June 3? 1782," which is bracketed at the head of an extract from this same page in Burnett, *Letters*, VI, 363, is almost certainly incorrect. Words which JM encoded in the official cipher are italicized.

PHILADA. June 4th. 1782.

DEAR SIR

I found no difficulty in the bill remitted by Mr. F. Webb. As it was not made payable to you, even the forms of business did not require your endorsement.[1]

According to your request I send an authenticated extract from the Journals of the vote of Congress on the clause which interdicts British Manufactures.[2] It has however been for some time in print, and will probably have been at Richmond before you receive the manuscript copy. The arguments urged against the measure appear to me in the same light in which you describe them. The policy of G.B. in the capture of St. Eustatius has been constantly reprobated by some of her wisest Statesmen.[3] But whatever her policy might at that period be, it is manifest that a very different one is now pursued. British Goods are issued from the Enemy's lines with greater industry than they have ever been, and as is universally believed, with the knowledge, if not at the instigation of those in power. Indeed they would counteract their new System in doing otherwise.[4] The sense of the Eastern States will appear from the ays & nos on the question.[5] Mr. Adams in his last despatches ascribes much of the late pacific symtoms in the British Nation, and of the facilities which begin to attend his mission in Holland, to our proscription of British Merchandize.[6]

You have not sufficiently designated the papers from *M- R. Mor—s* from which you wish an extract. I do not recollect nor can I find any letter which contains a *state of the finances* except *his circular letters* which may be found either among the legislative or Executive Archives. If you should be disappointed in these researches, I will on a renewal of your demands, renew my researches. My charity I own can not *invent an excuse for* the *prepense malice* with which the *character and services of this gentleman are murdered.*[7] I am persuaded that *he accepted his office* from *motives which were honourable and patriotic.* I have seen *no proof of misfeasance.*[8] I have heard of many *charges* which *were palpably erroneous.* I have known others somewhat *specious vanish on examination.* Every *mem*ber *in Congress* must be sensible of the *benefit* which has *accrued to the public from his administeration.* No[9] intelligent man *out of Congress can be altogether in*sensible *of it.* The *Court of France has* testified *its satisfaction at his appointment* which I really believe *lessened its* repugnance to *lend us money.*[10] These considerations will make me cautious in lending an ear to the suggestions even of the impartial; to those of *known and vindictive enemys* very *incredulous.* The same fidelity to the public interest which obliges those who are[11] its appointed guardians, to pursue with every vigor a *perfidious or dishonest servant of the public* requires *them* to confront the imputations *of malice against the good and faithful one.* I have in the conduct of *my colleague here*[12] *a sure index of the sentiments and objects of one of my colleagues who is absent*[13] *relative to the department of finance.*

The Chevr. de la Luzerne tells us he has written to the Govr. on the subject of the transaction between them, and has no doubt that the difficulties which attended it will be removed.[14]

A Letter from Mr. Adams of an older date but recd. since the one mentioned in my last, confirms the article relating to Friesland in the Letter from Mr. Barkley.[15] There are some opinions & circumstances however stated in this letter which its priority will scarcely reconcile with those mentioned in the other. At the date of it which was the 11th. of March he was not sanguine as to the unaniminity of Holland, and less so as to an early concurrence of the other Provinces. What is singular is that his apprehensions with respect to the first Province were drawn from the conduct of Amsterdam, which has heretofore been the cornerstone of all his expectations. This revolution in the City is the effect he says of a revolution in the Regency[16]

The Deputies to *the s. states* set off on Sunday last.[17] Congress on a report of the Committee on the Resolutions of the House of Delegates, have authorized them to make such explanations relative to the *flags* as they shall judge expedient.[18] In a letter which I wrote by a private hand since the last post day, I have been pretty full as to the sentiments of Congress with regard to the Resolutions. I wish to hear whether this extra letter reaches you safe or not.[19]

Your favor of the 21st. came in better season than the preceding one. In the argument relating to the Flags you might have added to the passports for Salt, a case still more directly in point. A Letter from Govr. Jefferson of the 7th. of Feby. 81. refers it to the Delegates to obtain permission to send provisions to N.Y. in stead of hard money for the subsistance of the Prisoners.[20] The Enemy at that day refused to accept Tobo. but were willing to accept these more necessary articles. Congress refused to give passports for the latter. It may be sd. indeed that this was prior to the ratification of the federal Articles.[21] But it will at least justify Congress & the Viga. Delegates in particular in presuming on the concurrence of the State in the measure in question. As to the simple right of granting flags it is impossible to shake it on any principle. It is a lesser power evidently involved in the major one of making peace. A flag is a partial truce as a truce is a temporary peace.[22] I recollect that when the Committee consulted Genl. Washington & the Superintendt. it was unanimously supposed that a remittance of Tobo. to N. York wd. be less obnoxious to than of the identical money, recd. from them.[23]

The resolutions of the Assembly agst. insidious negociations are very apropos.[24] I hope all the Legislatures now sitting will enter into similar ones spontaneously & unanimously. It will always be best for Congress to appear to follow rather [than] lead the sentiments of their constituents, & particularly so in the present instance. We immediately sent a copy of them to *minister of France*.[25]

Yrs w[ith] friendship of[26]

The[27] News from the W Indies is not yet decided to the conviction of every mind. Mine is unable to withstand the evidence derived from the Jamaica Head in the inclosed Gazettes of Saturday last.[28] [The pape?]r[29] of this morning I inclose to Mr. Jones, with [w]hom you will interchange a perusal.[30] In case he sd not be at Richmond you will open the letter addressed to him. I shall give him the same provisional authority over the one addressed to you. I fear however from your silence as to your return that he will not have occasion to exercise it.[31] Mr. C. Griffin[32] who got hither on Sunday gives me some hopes on this subject.

Genl Washington has transmitted to Congress sundry informations he has recd. of preparations at N. Y. for expediting from thence, a considerable number of Ships. Whether they are to convey troops & whither, or to bring off troops from other places is uncertain.[33] He has also transmitted to Congress an answer to him from Genl Carlton on a demand[34] made at the instance of the Legislature of S. Carolina of a retransportation of the exiles at the expence of the King of G. B.[35] This demand was instituted not executed[36] during the Command of Clinton, from whom an imperious refusal was calculated upon. In pursuance of the views of the new System, his successor weeps over the misfortunes of the exiles, and in the most soothing language that cd be framed, engages to comply fully with the application. This incident at once mortifies our pride & [s]ummons our vigilance. We have n[othing] f[urther from Carlton] on the main poin[t.][37]

The communication expected in my last from the M. of F.[38] has been recd. and afforded a very seasonable occasion which was improved, of renewing the assurances suited to the present crisis.[39]

I have a letter of the 15 of March from Mazzei[40] in which he complains much of being neglected, dilates on the prospect & effects of a Turkish war & refers me to some of his patriotic publications transmitted to the Govr.

Mr. Webb will set off tomorrow or next day.[41] By him I will try to send the Journals.[42]

1 See Randolph to JM, 16–17 May; JM to Randolph, 21 May 1782.

2 See Randolph to JM, 16–17 May 1782, and n. 10.

3 JM may be referring to Charles Lennox, Duke of Richmond; Charles Watson-Wentworth, Marquis of Rockingham; William Petty, Earl of Shelburne; Charles Pratt, Baron Camden; Edmund Burke; and Charles James Fox. These men, and above all the Earl of Shelburne in the House of Lords on 25 January 1781, had scathingly attacked the policy of the ministry as exemplified by the king's "Manifesto, dated St. James's, Dec. 20, 1780," declaring a state of war to exist between Great Britain and her century-old "ally," the Netherlands. Shelburne's long indictment charged that the manifesto had been issued "to the disgrace of the country, to the total dishonour of its councils, and in direct violation of all laws, whether of nations, of nature, of public honour, and private faith," in order to permit the confiscation of all Dutch ships and their cargoes "for the joint advantage of the captors and the state" (*Hansard's Parliamentary Debates,* XXI, cols. 960–72, 1001–2, 1009–12, 1015–19, 1021–43, 1060–74, and especially col. 1032).

Although Admiral Rodney had obeyed the orders of the British Admiralty, by capturing the Dutch island of St. Eustatius on 3 February 1781, he had at the same time embarrassed the ministry and dishonored himself by seizing for his own profit much private property, including non-contraband merchandise owned by subjects of neutral powers (*Papers of Madison,* III, 28, n. 11; 30, n. 4; 298, n. 5). JM apparently agreed with the "wisest Statesmen" of Great Britain in their contention that her true policy, regardless of the outcome of the war, was to keep open her channels of trade, or at least to avoid giving mortal offense to foreigners who in peacetime had been her most valued customers.

[4] See Virginia Delegates to Harrison, 7 May, and n. 4; Randolph to JM, 16–17 May, and n. 9; and 21–24 May; Harrison to Virginia Delegates, 18 May 1782, and n. 4.

[5] See Randolph to JM, 16–17 May 1782, and n. 10.

[6] From Amsterdam on 14 February John Adams had written to Livingston: "The ordinance of Congress against British manufactures is universally approved" by the Dutch "as far as I know, as an hostility against their enemies of more importance than the exertions of an army of twenty thousand men." On 10 March 1782, again to Livingston, Adams pointed out that the same ordinance and the signs of a "sudden revival" of manufacturing by the Dutch had "raised a kind of panic" in Great Britain "and such a fermentation in Parliament as has produced a formal renunciation of the principle of the American war" (Wharton, *Revolutionary Diplomatic Correspondence,* V, 163, 233).

[7] See Randolph to JM, 16–17 May 1782, and n. 17.

[8] Instead of the correct ciphers for "misfeasance," JM used those for "misfeasach."

[9] This word replaces a deleted "Every."

[10] La Luzerne had assured Vergennes that Robert Morris was an excellent superintendent of finance. Vergennes may have agreed with this judgment, even though he remarked in a letter of 31 January 1782 to La Luzerne that Morris seemed to think "the Royal Treasury should be at his disposition" (William E. O'Donnell, *Chevalier de La Luzerne,* pp. 172, 189–90).

[11] Following "are," JM crossed out "appointed to watch over it, to the," and interlineated "its appointed" above the deletion.

[12] Theodorick Bland, Jr.

[13] Arthur Lee.

[14] See Virginia Delegates to Harrison, 4 June 1782. Governor Harrison had written to La Luzerne on 31 May, enclosing resolutions of the General Assembly giving assurance of "their intentions to pay the cost of the stores at the time stipulated" (McIlwaine, *Official Letters,* III, 238–39).

[15] Thomas Barclay. A copy of John Adams' letter of 26 March to Franklin reached Congress before Adams' dispatch of 11 March to Livingston. See JM to Jones, 28 May 1782, and nn. 19 and 20.

[16] Wharton, *Revolutionary Diplomatic Correspondence,* V, 235. In a Dutch city, according to John Adams, the patrician burgomasters, counselors, and judges comprised a "regency" (*ibid.,* V, 99). For examples of Adams' earlier letters mentioning the friendship of Amsterdam residents toward the American cause, see *ibid.,* IV, 390, 433; V, 185–86, 206.

[17] "Sunday last" was 2 June. See Report on Mission To Inform States of Financial Crisis, 22 May 1782, editorial note, and n. 2.

[18] See Randolph to JM, 21–24 May 1782, and n. 3.

[19] See JM to Randolph, 29 May, and n. 10; Randolph to JM, 15 June 1782.

[20] JM apparently refers to Jefferson's letter of that date to Benjamin Harrison, when the latter was about to arrive in Philadelphia as a special delegate from the Virginia General Assembly (Boyd, *Papers of Jefferson,* IV, 550, 656; *Papers of Madison,* II, 221, n. 7; 286, n. 3).

[21] Congress refused on 8 January 1781, nearly two months before the ratification

of the Articles of Confederation (*JCC*, XIX, 38–39, 213–14; *Papers of Madison*, II, 277; 278, n. 4).

[22] See Randolph to JM, 16–17 May 1782, and n. 25.

[23] The editors have placed this sentence, written by JM in the right-hand margin of the manuscript, where he indicated by asterisks that it should go. The third line of the sentence, penned in minute script along the extreme edge of the sheet, is indistinct and in part obliterated. Probably "our Allies" originally could be read between "obnoxious to" and "than." By the statement JM meant that the French certainly would prefer to have tobacco used to pay for the wares of the traders-capitulant rather than to be asked to supply the necessary amount of specie for this purpose. See Ambler to JM, 20 April, and n. 4; Lee to JM, 16 May, n. 7; Harrison to Virginia Delegates, 18 May, n. 4; JM to Randolph, 29 May 1782, and n. 13.

[24] See Instructions to Virginia Delegates, 24–25 May 1782.

[25] La Luzerne.

[26] JM squeezed this complimentary close in the small space remaining in the margin after writing the sentence commented upon in n. 23. He had no room left for his signature or even for his initials.

[27] The additional page mentioned in the headnote begins here.

[28] The "inclosed Gazettes" are missing, but they must have been the *Pennsylvania Packet* and the *Pennsylvania Journal*, both of 1 June 1782. Each of these papers included copies of detailed dispatches, under Kingston or St. Jago De La Vego, Jamaica, captions, describing the British naval victory in the Battle of the Saints. See Virginia Delegates to Harrison, 4 June 1782, and n. 2.

[29] At this point there is a blank, probably caused by the fading of the ink.

[30] Although JM's letter to Jones is missing, Jones in his letter of 25 June 1782 to JM (*q.v.*) acknowledged "Your favor of the 4th instant." This reference almost conclusively demonstrates that the additional page (n. 27, above) was written by JM on the fourth rather than on the third of June (see headnote). If, further, JM enclosed to Jones the Philadelphia newspaper "of this morning," it must have been the *Pennsylvania Packet* of 4 June, the only newspaper of the city appearing on Tuesdays.

[31] That is, JM feared that Randolph had decided, at least for the present, not to return to Congress. See JM to Jones, 28 May 1782.

[32] Cyrus Griffin, a judge of the continental Court of Admiralty (*Papers of Madison*, II, 54, n. 5).

[33] See Virginia Delegates to Harrison, 4 June 1782, and n. 14.

[34] This word replaces the deleted word "request."

[35] On 14 February 1782 the legislature of South Carolina had instructed its delegates in Congress to have that body communicate with General Clinton in the hope of arranging for the return at British expense of the South Carolina civilians, "particularly the women and children," whom the British army had forced to leave their homes in or near Charleston. Many of these "exiles" had been living in straitened circumstances in Philadelphia. Congress in August 1781 had sought loans from public and private sources for their support. Congress referred the request of the legislature of South Carolina to a committee including JM, and on 3 April 1782 adopted its recommendation that the request be forwarded "to the Commander in Chief, to take order in the way he shall think most proper to carry the same into effect" (*Papers of Madison*, III, 245, n. 2; Burnett, *Letters*, VI, 181; *JCC*, XXI, 782–83, 808–10; XXII, 161).

Because of the "disagreeable Circumstance" created by the Huddy-Asgill affair (JM to Randolph, 1 May 1782, nn. 17–18), Washington delayed addressing Carleton on the subject of the refugees until 21 May, when he requested that they be returned to their home state at British expense. Carleton's speedy acquiescence "with great pleasure" impressed Washington "in a very disagreeable point of Light" for, as he remarked to Lincoln in a dispatch of 28 May enclosing a copy of Carleton's reply, "I am not disposed to seek favors of, or Submit to an Idea of being under Obligations to Sir Guy, at this Moment of *concilitary War*" (NA: PCC, No. 149, I, 357; Fitzpatrick, *Writings of Washington*, XXIV, 270, 273, 296, 327).

Having referred Washington's and Carleton's letters to a committee under John Morin Scott's chairmanship on 3 June, Congress on 14 June accepted the recommendation of the committee by directing Lincoln to send Washington a list of the exiles and "the ports to which they choose to be conveyed" (*JCC*, XXII, 315 n., 330–32; Burnett, *Letters*, VI, 364). Washington forwarded this information to Carleton on 4 July and a supplementary list on 3 September 1782 (Fitzpatrick, *Writings of Washington*, XXIV, 400; XXV, 100, 114, 210).

[36] JM interlineated "not executed." Clinton had relinquished his command to Carleton on 5 May (Virginia Delegates to Harrison, 7 May 1782, n. 4).

[37] Owing to a tear in the manuscript at a fold, the bracketed portions of this sentence have been copied from Madison, *Papers* (Gilpin ed.), I, 139. For "the main point," see JM to Randolph, 14 May 1782, and n. 8. After remarking in a letter of 6 June to Congress that he had not heard from Carleton for two weeks, Washington added, "It may be in the power of Congress to account for this silence better than I can" (Fitzpatrick, *Writings of Washington*, XXIV, 320–21).

[38] The minister of France, La Luzerne. See JM to Jones, 28 May, and n. 15; JM to Randolph, 28 May 1782, headnote.

[39] See Report on Fidelity to French Alliance, 31 May 1782.

[40] Mazzei's letter to JM was dated 13 March 1782 (*q.v.*).

[41] Foster Webb, Jr., left Philadelphia on 6 June to return to Virginia (JM to Randolph, 6 June 1782).

[42] See Randolph to JM, 21–24 May 1782.

Report on German Prisoners of War

MS (NA: PCC, No. 28, fols. 67, 75–76). The report and the words, "Rept. of Committee on the German Prisoners," written parallel with the right-hand margin of the cover, are in JM's hand. The cover also bears the docket, not by JM: "Report of Comee. respectg. german prisoners Debated May 15. 1782. June 5. 1782. Referred, except the last clause, to the Comr. in chief Secry at War and Super. finance to take Order, any resolution to the contrary notwithstandg. The last clause referred to the Superintendt. of finance & Secy at War to take Order so soon as order is taken on the former part."

EDITORIAL NOTE

In a letter of 27 April 1782 to the secretary at war, Washington reported that "not a single recruit has arrived, (to my knowledge), from any State except Rhode Island, in consequence of the Requisitions of

Congress in December last." This alarming fact and the enemy's failure to provide money for the support of prisoners in American hands led him to recommend as "highly expedient that measures should be adopted, at this moment, for taking the German Prisoners of War into our Service." In Washington's opinion the German captives would "make exceedingly cheap & valuable Recruits, and being able-bodied & disciplined Men will give a Strength & solidity to our Regts. which they will not otherwise acquire this Campaign" (NA: PCC, 149, I, 309–11).

Washington's proposal was also supported by precedent. Influenced in part by a determination to retaliate against the enemy's effort to entice "our troops to desert our service," Congress as early as 14 and 27 August 1776 offered all "Hessians and other foreigners" who would "quit the British service" a land bounty of between fifty and one thousand acres, depending upon the rank of the deserter, and the opportunity to become a citizen of "any of these states" (*JCC*, V, 653–54, 707–8). Congress also had adopted Washington's proposal of 9 August 1778 by permitting Pulaski's Partisan Corps and Armand's Legion to enlist German prisoners as well as deserters from the British army (Fitzpatrick, *Writings of Washington*, XII, 305; XIII, 357; *JCC*, X, 291; XI, 642–44; Harrison to Virginia Delegates, 11 January, n. 5; Virginia Delegates to Harrison, 4 June 1782, n. 8).

The committee, under Elias Boudinot's chairmanship, to which Congress on 4 May had referred Washington's letter of 27 April, framed its recommendations of 15 May 1782 in consultation with Morris and Lincoln. The preface of the report mentioned the enemy's practice of being cruel to American prisoners "with an apparent design of forcing them" to enlist under the British flag, the "considerable number of the German Prisoners" who had "expressed an earnest desire" to serve in the American army or "to become citizens of these states," and the commander-in-chief's highly satisfactory experience with those German captives who had been formed into a separate corps. For these reasons the committee advised Congress to adopt Washington's proposal by directing Lincoln, in concert with Morris, to offer the German captives a three-years' term of service in the continental army in exchange for their release from internment, a money and land bounty, wages, and the probability of acquiring citizenship, "provided that they do not act contrary to the Laws of any State in which such prisoners may become free Citizens." On 15 May, after amending these proposals, Congress referred them to John Morin Scott, JM, and John Rutledge (*JCC*, XXII, 274–76, 276, n. 1). Although the amendments appear not to be extant, their general tenor probably is indicated by the differences between the reports of the two committees.

[5 June 1782]

Whereas the events of war have put into the possession of these U. S. great numbers of prisoners taken at different periods in the service of the King of G.B.[1]

And whereas the British Commander in cheif[2] hath[3] not as yet concurred in any measures either for liquidateg & dischargeg[4] the arrears due to the U. S. for the past subsistance of the sd. prisoners[5] or providing for their future subsistance: And Whereas a considerable proportion of the said Prisoners consists of Germans by nation, many of whom from a dislike to the service into which they have been involuntarily hired, and from a prospect of amending their condition, have expressed a desire of entering some of them into the military service of the U. S. and others into a reasonable period of common service,[6] with a view of eventually becoming Citizens & settlers within the said States: And Whereas the indulgence of the said Prisoners in their respective desires will tend to counteract the unjust & cruel designs of the Enemy and to aid the States in filling up the quotas of troops respectively required of them.[7]

Resolved (See paper annexed. A.–[8]

The Committee to whom was referred the report relative the German prisoners &. submit the following resolutions[9]

Resolved

That the Secretary at War be authorised & directed to take immediate measures for enlisting into the Army of the U. S. for the term of 3 years or of the War, at the option of the party enlisting, so many of the German prisoners of War to the said U. S.[10] as shall voluntarily agree thereto, and take the oath of fidelity prescribed by the Articles of war:[11]

That the said Secretary be authorised to allow to each recruit so enlisted a bounty of Eight[12] Dollars to be advanced from time to time on his application by the Superintendant of Finance; and to stipulate in behalf of the U. States, to all such recruits the same pay & other provisions and on the like conditions, as[13] have been stipulated to other Soldiers enlisted for the same terms into the service of the U. S.

That all recruits so enlisted be placed by the said Secretary to the credit of the several States in proportion to the quotas of troops respectively required of them by Congress; in the same manner as if the recruits had been raised by & received from them in pursuance of such requisition.

That the said recruits as fast as they shall be enlisted shall be marched to such place as the Commander in chief shall direct; and shall be arranged in the army in such manner as he shall judge most conducive to the public Service.

That the Superintendt. of Finance & Secrety. at War take order for disposing of the services of such of the said Prisoners as shall desire it for such period[14] as they shall deem reasonable not exceeding three years, and on such conditions as will secure to the same, a comfortable[15] maintenance and be most conducive to the public interest.[16]

[1] After these initials, the words "of which it appears by authentic returns that there now remain in captivity" were deleted.

[2] General Sir Guy Carleton.

[3] Following this word, "refused as well" was deleted, and "not as yet concurred in any measures either" was interlineated.

[4] The odd spelling resulted when JM replaced "to" with "for," and then added only a "g" to each infinitive.

[5] After "prisoners" JM at first wrote "as to make the necessary provision." He then crossed out the first five of these words, interlineated "or," and altered the sixth word to "providing."

[6] This clause, with its word "common" probably connoting "public," replaces the Boudinot committee's "hiring themselves out to the Inhabitants for a temporary service" (*JCC*, XXII, 275). JM may also have wished to suggest "indenturing" as well as "hiring." For what was deemed "a reasonable period," see the final paragraph of text.

[7] Preceding "States," "respective" was crossed out. JM originally wrote "fulfilling" rather than "filling up." In a letter of 27 April (see editorial note), Washington had recommended that, since the Germans who entered the service might eventually be concentrated into a separate corps, they "ought to be recruited for the Continent and not carried to the credit of the States quotas."

[8] The resolutions were written on a separate page. In the upper right-hand margin is the notation "paper A ," not in JM's hand.

[9] This introductory sentence, written by JM, is clearly superfluous and does not appear in the printed journal. The committee also decided to leave the opening paragraph as it was written. Lined out in the journal and deleted with an ink cross in the manuscript is the following paragraph, also in JM's hand:

"It being represented to Congress that a number of the Germans prisoners of war to the U. S. are desirous of becoming Citizens of the said States, and are moreover willing, on condition of being provided with future settlements in this Country, to aid in its defence by entering into the Military service of the U. S; and it being expedient that such enlistmen[ts] should be made with as little delay as possible & in such mode as will secure to the respective States a due proportion of the benefit thereof–."

[10] Following "U. S.," the words "not exceeding" are deleted.

[11] *JCC*, V, 790.

[12] Obviously an insert, this figure may have been added after the committee reported to Congress.

[13] JM substituted the next three words for a deleted "were allowed."

[14] This word replaced a deleted "time."

[15] JM originally wrote "proper" rather than "comfortable."

[16] This paragraph clarifies the meaning of "reasonable period of common service" in the second paragraph of this report. See n. 6, above.

Report on Paying Representatives Abroad

MS (NA: PCC, No. 19, IV, 357). Docketed: "Report of Mr Madison Mr Ramsay Mr Osgood On a letter of 31st. May 1782 from Supt of Finance passed June 5th 1782." JM was chairman of the committee, but its report is in Samuel Osgood's hand.

[5 June 1782]

The Committee to whom was referred the Letter from the Supirintendant of Finance of the 31st. of May report the following Resolution[1]

Resolved, that the Resolution[2] passed on the 29th of May relative to the Salaries & Allowances of the public Servants of the united States be & hereby is repealed: and that from & after the first Day of August next, Warrants be issued quarterly on the Treasurer of the united States, for one fourth Part of the annual Salaries & Allowances respectively made to the said public Servants employed in foreign Parts.

[1] For the background of the resolution, see Report on Salaries of Representatives Abroad, 28 May 1782, and n. 5.

[2] Following this word Osgood wrote and deleted "of the."

Motion To Request Report from Superintendent of Finance and Secretary at War

MS (NA: PCC, No. 36, I, 321). This motion was written by JM. At its close, "pass'd" was added, probably by Charles Thomson. Docketed in an unknown hand: "Motion of Mr Madison Seconded by Mr Bland Passed June 6th 1782."

[6 June 1782]

That the Superintendant of Finance & Secretary at War report to Congress the steps taken by them in consequence of the reference made to them on the day of [1]

[1] Congress adopted this motion after having "22d" inserted in the first blank and "April last" in the second (*JCC*, XXII, 319). The purport of the motion is difficult to establish. If, as seems most likely, it related to General Greene's plea for food, clothing, and military supplies, referred by Congress to the superintendent of finance and secretary at war "to take order," the date inserted within the blank spaces should have been 20 April (*JCC*, XXII, 202). Not only had Greene's need been

SIR GEORGE BRYDGES RODNEY

SIR GUY CARLETON

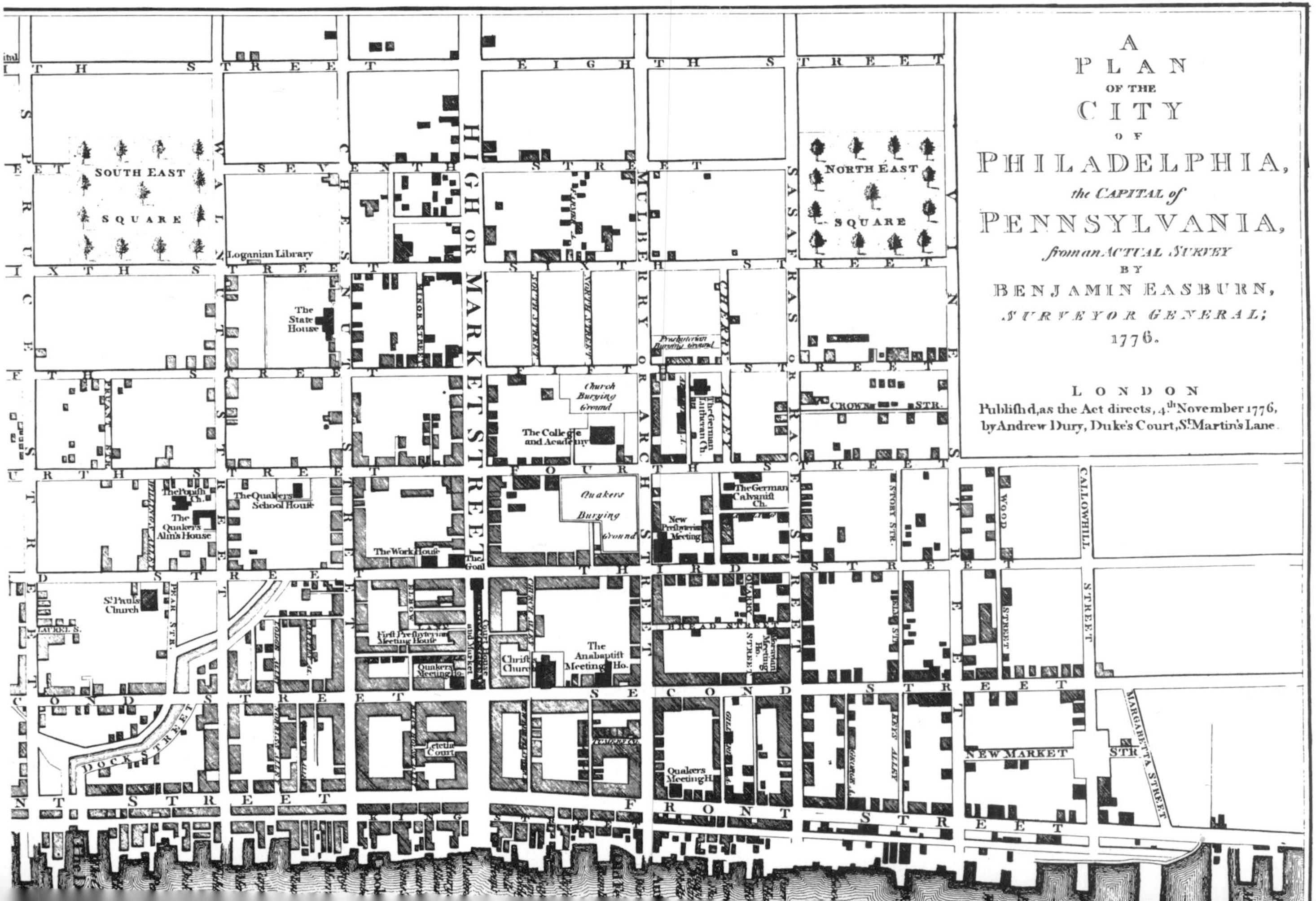

A PLAN OF THE CITY OF PHILADELPHIA, the CAPITAL of PENNSYLVANIA, from an ACTUAL SURVEY BY BENJAMIN EASBURN, SURVEYOR GENERAL; 1776.

LONDON
Publish'd, as the Act directs, 4.th November 1776, by Andrew Dury, Duke's Court, St. Martin's Lane.

EXCERPT FROM "PLAN" OF PHILADELPHIA, 1776

of concern to JM (Motion on Supplies for Southern Army, 7 May 1782), but the published journal of Congress for 6 June contains immediately below the JM-Bland motion a letter of that date stating that the secretary at war had been delayed by lack of transportation facilities from forwarding "the whole of the clothing provided for the Southern Army." Further, on 7 June Congress resolved "That the Secretary at War and Superintendant of finance be directed to take such means as they may think proper to convey in the speediest manner, by land or by water, cloathing and other necessaries to the southern army" (*JCC*, XXII, 319–21, 342–43, 363–65; NA: PCC, No. 186, fol. 33).

On the other hand, the "22d day of April last" in the printed version of the JM-Bland motion is correct if that motion related to Congress' referral on that date of a letter from Morris, written two days earlier, to a committee which was instructed to confer with the secretary at war. Although the printed journal for 22 April omits mention of this action, Thomson recorded it in his "Committee Book, 1781–1785" (NA: PCC, No. 186, fol. 23). In his letter of 20 April Morris had recommended that Washington's "Moving Army" be accompanied by a "superintendent," not subject to military discipline, who would be charged with overseeing the private suppliers of food, holding them to their contracts and providing rations himself in cases of emergency (NA: PCC, No. 137, I, 405–8; No. 185, III, 24). Congress accepted this proposal but, as already mentioned, Morris was long delayed in finding a qualified superintendent (Motion on Supplies for Southern Army, 7 May 1782, n. 1; Clarence L. Ver Steeg, *Robert Morris*, pp. 144–50). From Washington's "Moving Army," Morris excluded the units stationed mainly in the lower Hudson River valley under General William Heath's command.

To Edmund Randolph

RC (LC: Madison Papers). Lacks complimentary close and signature but is in JM's hand. Docketed, "J. Madison. June 6. 1782." Addressed: "Edmund Randolph Esqr. Richmond. Favd. by Mr. Webb."

June 6th. [1782]

DEAR SIR

Mr. Webb being detained till this morning[1] I enclose you the gazette of it. You will find a singular extract from Lord North's Butchet. The Speech was delivered on the 11th. of March.[2] It must have been Mr. Ross's Contract therefore & not Mr. Morris's which supplied this article.[3] I am just told that the Senate have put their veto on the Resolutions of the H. of Delegates agst. the latter.[4] If an existing law however prohibits the exportation, and one branch of the Legislature protests[5] agst. the authority of Congress to dispense with it, The Executive will scarcely suffer the Tobo. to be exported. If this matter should terminate in an agreement by Maryland to supply the Tobo. and Virga. should be drained of her money to purchase the Staple of the former, whilst her own Staple is left on her hands — — — — —[6] The proviso in the resolutions in favr. of the Contract of the State agent furnishes I find a copious topic for Anti-Virginian Critics.[7] It is inconsistent with the laws of the State, with the Ordinances of Congress, with the Treaty with France, with gratitude to our Allies, for Tobo. to be shipped to N.Y by Mr. M.[8] for the advantage of the U.S. But [if][9] the identical Tobo. be shipped by Mr. R.[10] for the advantage of Virga.[11] the inconsistency is done away in the eyes of The House of Delegates of Virginia.[12]

A New York paper of the 1st. Instant contains so many minute particulars touching the defeat of the French in the W. Indies, taken it is sd.[13] from an Official acct. in the St. Lucia Gazette, that Mr. de M—s.[14] himself says it is u[seles]s[15] any longer to struggle agst. the belief of it.

[1] See JM to Randolph, 4 June 1782, n. 41.

[2] The *Pennsylvania Packet* of 6 June quoted Lord North as saying in the House of Commons, in the course of his speech of 11 March 1782 on the budget, that the capitulant British traders at Yorktown had agreed to exchange their wares for about three thousand hogsheads of tobacco, priced at 2*s.* 4*d.* a pound. Lord North proposed to levy a duty of 4*d.* a pound upon this tobacco when it arrived in Great Britain (*Hansard's Parliamentary Debates,* XXII, 1154–55).

[3] The evidence available to JM for making this distinction is not clear. Possibly he meant that, although by 11 March Lord North could have heard of the amount of tobacco shipped by Virginia in December 1781 and January 1782 to the British traders to pay for David Ross's purchases from them on the Commonwealth's account, the number of hogsheads of tobacco used to settle the continental account with these merchants could not have been known to Lord North when he delivered his speech, because that consignment had not left Virginia. On the other hand, the three thousand hogsheads mentioned by Lord North certainly much exceeded the quantity used by Virginia to pay its debt (McIlwaine, *Official Letters,* III, 93; *Journals of the Council of State,* III, 34, 41; *Calendar of Virginia State Papers,* II, 571, 633, 668; Fitzpatrick, *Writings of Washington,* XXIII, 375–76, 379, 496; Lee to JM, 16 May, and n. 7; JM to Randolph, 29 May 1782, and nn. 10 and 13).

[4] See Randolph to JM, 21–24 May 1782, and nn. 3, 6, 8. As Randolph had predicted to JM in his letter of 1 June (*q.v.*), the House of Delegates was obliged on 4 June to accept the Senate's amendment of the resolutions (Minute Book, House of Delegates, May 1782, p. 61).

[5] JM wrote this word over a deleted "denies."

[6] JM's dashes signify that no comment by him was needed to make clear the absurdity of such "an agreement" or its economic injury to Virginia.

[7] See JM to Randolph, 29 May 1782, n. 13.

[8] Robert Morris.

[9] JM began this sentence before the word "identical" by writing "But the If the." He then crossed out the last two of these words. Clearly he meant only to delete the first "the" and thus to introduce his ironical statement as in the present text.

[10] David Ross. Probably unknown to JM, William Hay had replaced Ross on 24 May as commercial agent of Virginia (*Journals of the Council of State,* III, 97).

[11] JM interlineated the next nine words.

[12] JM wrote the rest of his message in the left-hand margin of the page.

13 JM apparently is referring to the 5 June issue of the *Pennsylvania Journal* and its quotation from an unidentified New York paper, most likely Rivington's *Royal Gazette*. An excerpt from Rodney's dispatch of 15 April about his decisive victory in the Battle of the Saints had appeared "by authority" in an unspecified number of the "St. Lucia Gazette Extraordinary," which had been brought by a schooner "in 17 days express" to New York City. For the battle, see JM to Madison, Sr., 20 May, n. 4; JM to Lee, 28 May 1782, and n. 11.

14 Probably François, Marquis de Barbé-Marbois, secretary of the French legation and consul general of France.

15 Upon breaking the seal of this letter Randolph tore the manuscript so that "useless" or some word of about the same length and probably of a similar purport was mostly eliminated.

Benjamin Harrison to Virginia Delegates

FC (Virginia State Library). In the hand of Thomas Meriwether.

COUNCIL CHAMBER June 8th. 1782[1]

GENTLEMEN

I am much obliged to you for your communications by the last post.[2] I hope the difficulties thrown in the way of our supplies will be removed by the resolutions of the Assembly, If they should not let me beg of you to use every endeavour to satisfy the Minister that payment will be made according to agreement and that the stores are absolutely necessary to secure our safety; you will also much oblige me by inquiring whether they are or will be shipd in men of war.[3] We are still in the dark how the naval engagements in the West Indies ended accounts differing as much so here as with you.[4] None of the great matters before the Assembly are yet finished. The delegation to Congress for the next year will remain as at present, the three years service will be computed from the confederation.[5] I am &c

BENJ. HARRISON

1 This letter apparently never reached its destination. On 15 June 1782 near Harford (Harford Town or Bushtown), Md., six armed "desperados," perhaps enemy agents, intercepted the postrider and took his mail pouch (*Pennsylvania Gazette*, 18 June; *Virginia Gazette*, 29 June 1782). See also Report on Mail Robbery, 19 June 1782.

2 See Virginia Delegates to Harrison, 28 May 1782.

3 See Harrison to Virginia Delegates, 11 May 1782, and n. 1. In his letter of 31 May to La Luzerne, the governor enclosed a resolution of the General Assembly of 23 May reaffirming Virginia's promise to pay for the military matériel ordered in France (McIlwaine, *Official Letters*, III, 238–39). The governor, of course, had not yet received the Virginia delegates' letter of 4 June (*q.v.*), reporting La Luzerne's

comment after reading Harrison's letter of 11 May to him about this issue. On 6 September 1782, in accordance with Virginia's pledge, Harrison appointed Thomas Barclay as the agent of Virginia in France to pay the debt for the "Arms, military Stores and Soldiers Clothing" and to receive them (*Journals of the Council of State*, III, 142).

[4] See JM to Randolph, 6 June 1782, and n. 13.

[5] On 1 July 1782, having determined that the fifth article of the Articles of Confederation was identical in intent and phraseology with an amended state statute passed on 24 January 1778, as well as with portions of a statute passed on 11 June 1779, in that all three limited the tenures of delegates to Congress to "three years in any term of six," the Virginia General Assembly repealed the entire first statute and pertinent portions of the second as being "unnecessary" (Hening, *Statutes*, IX, 288; X, 74–75; XI, 31–32; *Journal of the House of Delegates*, October 1777, p. 136; *ibid.*, May 1779, p. 42; Minute Book, House of Delegates, May 1782, p. 85). See also Randolph to JM, 20 June 1782, and n. 5.

Barbé-Marbois Letter Written with JM's Collaboration

Printed text (*Pennsylvania Packet*, 11 June 1782; also *Virginia Gazette*, 22 June 1782). David C. Claypoole, editor of the *Packet*, introduced the letter to his readers with this foreword, probably supplied by JM: "The following Extract of a Letter written from Philadelphia, by a Gentleman in Office to one of the principal Officers in the State of New-Jersey, cannot fail to be acceptable to the Public. We are authorized to vouch for the Authenticity of the Facts contained in it." Obviously the letter was intended for no "Gentleman in Office" but was designed to allay public concern and to strengthen sentiment in favor of the French alliance.

EDITORIAL NOTE

In his letter to Edmund Randolph on 11 June 1782 (*q.v.*), JM stated that François, Marquis de Barbé-Marbois, wrote this anonymous letter in French and then asked JM to render it into English. Neither Marbois' manuscript nor JM's handwritten translation of it appears to be extant. Unless at least the French original is found, the accuracy of JM's comment to Randolph may be challenged but not disproved.

The inclusion of the letter in this volume would seem to be warranted. As Irving Brant has remarked, if JM merely translated the letter, "Marbois had a genius for uttering Madisonian thoughts" (Brant, *Madison*, II, 171). The style of the document, the diction, and the points of view, all suggest JM. His inexpert knowledge of French would probably have led him unintentionally to depart from the original text, even granting that he had declined Marbois' invitation to be co-author as well as translator (JM to

Randolph, 11 June 1782). Late in life JM arranged some of his own papers for publication and thereby became in considerable degree the editor of the three-volume Gilpin edition of 1840 (*Papers of Madison*, I, xviii). Henry D. Gilpin prefaced his publication of the letter by remarking, "The share Mr. Madison had in this letter, and the subject to which it relates, seems to make it proper to rescue it from the files of a newspaper" (Madison, *Papers* [Gilpin ed.], III, Appendix, xxxv–xxxvii). JM may have had the clipping or even his retained copy of the translation in his files and, recalling his share in preparing the letter, have suggested to members of his family that they include it among his papers to be published.

PHILADELPHIA, June 9, 1782.

We have received no intelligence from the French islands which can remove or lessen our anxiety, with respect to the actions between the fleet of our ally and that of our enemy:[1] I am however inclined to believe, that the broken accounts published by the latter are true, but we shall learn from the French accounts only the entire damage sustained by the British fleet. There are a few among us, who, arguing from the reiterated and bold impositions of the English, and from some contradictions remarked in their accounts, still doubt the reality of the victory ascribed to them: for my own part, it appears so natural for 37 ships of the line to beat 30,[2] and the British publications are so circumstantial, that I can no longer doubt that Sir G. Rodney has gained a victory; but it is a victory which can yield him only bitter fruits, and which bestows on the conduct and courage of the unsuccessful admiral,[3] the glory of having resisted for twelve hours a force one-fifth superior to his own. Instead of multiplying conjectures on the consequences of this event; I shall content myself with informing you, that the French fleet, according to all reports, has joined fifteen French and Spanish ships of the line which awaited it at Hispaniola;[4] so that even the victory of the English has not been able to frustrate this junction, which they were resolved to spare no efforts to prevent; and we may consider this disappointment to them as an important point gained on the other side.

But the consideration most proper to console us for this event (if any thing can console us for the misfortune of a faithful and generous ally) is, that it has afforded us an occasion of displaying a national character,[5] a good faith, a constancy and firmness worthy of a people who are free, and determined to perish sooner than cease to be so. Sir Guy Carleton was presenting himself with the olive branch in his hand, at the very moment when this disagreeable intelligence arrived; perhaps he had formed so bad an opinion of us, as to suppose that this was a favourable crisis for detaching us from our allies. He has announced his plan; he has endeavoured to send his secretary, Mr. Morgan, to congress, and he has perhaps thought us so base, and so ignorant of what our duty or honour, and our interest prescribed to us, as to be ensnared by the hope of an approaching peace;[6] but although he has scarcely been a month on this continent, he must already have begun to know the Americans: four years have elapsed since the date of the happy alliance which unites us with France; we had every year received new benefits from this nation, without being able to make any other return than barren acknowledgements; and like one friend who is constantly obliged by another, without having it in his power to render reciprocal services, we waited with impatience an opportunity of demonstrating that our professions of attachment and gratitude were engraven on our hearts, and were not to be affected by the vicissitudes incident to a long war. This opportunity has happened; the enemy themselves have presented it to us, and I cannot express to you the joy with which I have seen Maryland, Pennsylvania and Virginia, with emulation and with unanimity, declare their fixed resolution to reject with disdain every offer of a separate peace, and every proposition which would throw the slightest stain on our national character or the alliance. I have just read, with the same pleasure, the resolutions passed by the assembly of New-Jersey; they breathe a true patriotism.[7] The enemy can no longer say that nine-tenths of the Americans are in their favour; they cannot even say that they have a single partizan in the thirteen states since these resolutions are all unanimous. The United States had for six years assumed their rank among independent nations; and from the present moment they will hold a distinguished place among nations the most celebrated for their generosity, their firmness and their virtues. Thanks to our enemy, who, in endeavouring to fix an indelible blot on our national character, and to ensnare us into an ignominious perfidy, have enabled us to display those qualities which are the foundation of the glory and happiness of states. Europe will at length know us: England herself will perhaps learn to judge less unfavourable of us; and finding that we are actuated by principles of justice, of constancy and fidelity, will relinquish her scheme of degrading and debasing us, that she may in the end enslave us.

But I have still to relate to you the most happy circumstance in this affair: At the time the assemblies were passing these wise and noble resolutions, congress received information, that the most seducing propositions had been made to our ally by a British agent sent to Versailles;

that concessions had been tendered, the best adapted to seduce a power influenced either by avarice, by ambition, or a sense of weakness; but the agent refused to treat at the same time of the independence of the United States. Our allies answered simply, that THIS INDEPENDENCE FORMED THE BASIS OF THEIR SYSTEM; and the negociation went no farther.[8] The conduct of the French has been so uniform, and so upright through the course of this war, that this answer excited no surprise in us; nevertheless, it is not to be denied, that a power who proceeded with a less firm step in the path of justice and wisdom, might easily have suffered itself to be led away by the dazzling offers which were made.

This was the proper conduct, both on our part and that of France, to do honour to the two nations. It is happy for their mutual glory that, without any communication, without any concert, and without any consultations, they have both, from the same innate rectitude, adopted the same resolutions against separate negotiations. What was the object of these propositions secretly and separately made to the two parties? If Great-Britain had been actuated by good faith, she ought to have apprised France that she meant to treat with us; and to acknowledge to us that she was endeavouring to treat with France: but she hoped, by sowing seeds of jealousy and distrust, to divide us: she flattered herself that the two allies, or at least one of them, might listen to her propositions; that the other would conceive suspicions therefrom; that discontent would succeed, and that a rupture would eventually take place which would terminate in our subjugation: her project has miscarried, the artifice is detected; and whilst it displays the insidious policy which still directs her councils, serves to evince the mutual fidelity and attachment of the allies; and the necessity of an unlimited confidence and constant communication of every thing which relates to our mutual interests.

I am now more proud of the title of American than I have ever been: the enemy have, without intermission, represented us as a timid and dastardly people, without faith and without honour: they are now undeceived at their own expence. But there is one point in which our national honour has too long suffered: we have sufficient firmness to abandon our houses and our habitations to an incendiary foe; we have seen without terror our houses and our farms in flames; we have seen our effects, our horses and our cattle swept away, and our sentiments have remained unshaken; we have received with contempt overtures of peace which would have covered us with shame; we have suffered all the calamities and wants which afflict exiled citizens, obliged to seek an asylum at a great distance from their own country.[9] Our wives have shewn the same firmness of soul, and sometimes their firmness and patriotism have invigorated our own. We have shed our blood in the glorious cause in which we are engaged; we are ready to shed the last drop in its defence. Nothing is above our courage, except only (with shame I speak it) except the courage to TAX ourselves.[10]

[1] See JM to Randolph, 6 June 1782, and n. 13.

[2] See Pendleton to JM, 20 May 1782, n. 8.

[3] François Joseph Paul, Comte de Grasse.

[4] See Pendleton to JM, 20 May 1782, n. 10.

[5] This expression, appearing thrice in this letter, was a favorite of JM and some of his contemporaries. He apparently used it here for the first time in his extant writings, although as a youth he had employed the term "National Characters" as a caption for some notes in his "Commonplace Book" (*Papers of Madison*, I, 6; 22; 31, n. 92).

[6] See Virginia Delegates to Harrison, 7 May, and n. 4; JM to Randolph, 14 May 1782, n. 8.

[7] See Instructions to Virginia Delegates, 24–25 May 1782; *Colonial Records of Pennsylvania*, XIII, 286–88. The resolutions of the General Assembly of Maryland on 15–16 May, of the Supreme Executive Council of Pennsylvania on 21 May, and of the General Assembly of New Jersey on 25–27 May appeared, respectively, in the *Pennsylvania Gazette* of 22 May, in the same paper of 29 May, and in the *Pennsylvania Packet* of 6 June. In the same order, these resolutions were printed in the *Virginia Gazette* of 25 May, 8 June, and 29 June 1782.

[8] See Report on Fidelity to French Alliance, 31 May 1782, editorial note.

[9] See JM to Randolph, 4 June 1782, and n. 35.

[10] See Motion To Inform States of Financial Crisis, 20 May, headnote and n. 3; Report on Mission To Inform States of Financial Crisis, 22 May 1782.

Report on Rations for Prisoners of War

MS (NA: PCC, No. 36, I, 323). In JM's hand. Docketed: "Motion of Mr Madison seconded by Mr Scott June 10. 1782 Referred to Mr Madison Mr Cornell Mr Boudinot Read June 11. 1782 postponed for the purpose of taking up a motion of Mr Midleton." Charles Thomson's "Register of Reports from Boards, Offices, and Committees of Congress, 1781–1785" notes that the report was "filed 8 Aug. 1782" (NA: PCC, No. 191, fol. 15).

[10–11 June 1782]

Report of the Committee on the Resolutions moved by Mr. Madison, &c. .[1]

Resolved, That the Secretary at War[2] be authorised & directed to make such reduction of the rations to be issued after the first day of

July next to Prisoners of war in the possession of the U. States as the interists of the U. States shall require, and the preservation of the said prisoners will admit.

That the said reduction be continued until adequate measures be taken on the part of the Enemy for liquidating and discharging the arrears due to the U. States for the past subsistence of prisoners of war; & for supplying regularly the expence necessary for their subsistence in future.[3]

That the Secretary at War be authorised to grant proper permits for the conveyance of supplies of provisions for the aforesaid Prisoners from within the lines of the Enemy.

That the said Secretary & the Superintendt of Finance[4] be authorised to take the requisite measures for remitting supplies of provisions to the Citizens of the U. States, prisoners within the lines of the Enemy.[5]

[1] JM's motion of 10 June embodying these resolutions is not mentioned in the printed journal (*JCC*, XXII, 322). The committee under JM's chairmanship, to which Congress on that day referred the motion, apparently accepted it without change and so reported to Congress on 11 June (*JCC*, XXII, 323).

[2] Benjamin Lincoln.

[3] See Report on German Prisoners of War, 5 June 1782, editorial note.

[4] Robert Morris.

[5] On 11 June Congress decided to postpone a consideration of this report "for the purpose of taking up" a substitute proposal by Arthur Middleton directing Washington to inform General Carleton, the British commander-in-chief, that, unless he would "discharge the arrears due to the United States, for the maintenance" of the prisoners and thereafter pay promptly every month the money required for their support, Congress would "take such measures respecting the prisoners as will be less burthensome, and may appear most beneficial for the public interest." Presumably after debating the merits of this suggestion, Congress referred it on 11 June to a committee comprising Elias Boudinot, Samuel John Atlee, and John Lowell (*JCC*, XXII, 323–24). At some undetermined time during the next six days this committee was relieved from its assignment, and Middleton's motion, together with JM's resolutions and the "Report of the Commissioners for settling a Cartel &c," was consigned to the original committee (see n. 1), namely, JM, chairman, Ezekiel Cornell, and Elias Boudinot. Their report, written by Boudinot without any apparent help from JM, was submitted on 17 June 1782. The report provided (1) that Carleton by August must arrange to pay for the food supplied to the prisoners or Congress would reduce its quantity; and (2) that Washington, "without appearing to be the first mover of it," should try to reopen negotiations for an exchange of prisoners (NA: PCC, No. 28, fol. 77; *JCC*, XXII, 335–36). This latter directive was designated "secret." Charles Thomson's records merely note that the report was "filed" on 8 August 1782.

Four days later, a Lowell-Cornell-JM committee, which had replaced the Boudinot-Atlee-Lowell committee on 29 July, submitted recommendations, drafted by JM, and Congress accepted them (*JCC*, XXII, 334–35, 337, and n. 2; XXIII, 461–62, 462 n.). In general the Boudinot committee, mentioned in the first paragraph of this note, concentrated upon the problem of how to readmit Loyalists, who had worn the British uniform, into the American community, while the Lowell committee reconsidered, in the light of recent developments, the subjects of a cartel and of payment by the British of the cost incurred by Americans in maintaining their captive British soldiers and sailors.

For Washington's protracted efforts to have the United States remunerated for feeding the prisoners and to effect a cartel, see Fitzpatrick, *Writings of Washington*, XXIV, 405–6, 475; XXV, 32–236, *passim*, 482–83, 485, 487.

Virginia Delegates to Benjamin Harrison

RC (New York State Historic Sites, Albany, N.Y.). Entirely in the hand of Theodorick Bland, Jr., except for JM's signature. Although the cover is missing, the title by which the recipient is addressed, along with the contents of the letter, establishes the identity of the addressee. The complete date probably should be 11 June 1782 in view of the nature of the information in the dispatch and the delegates' custom of writing to the governor on Tuesday of each week.

PHILADELPHIA June [11,] 1782

SR.

This days post brought us Your Excelly's. favor of the first of June[1] enclosing the Resolution of May 28th relative to the Commissioners for settling the Accounts of the State,[2] as also, a letter for the Chevr. de la Luzerne, and a Copy of Resolutions of the Assembly of the 23d of May, relating to the transaction of Col: Harrison with that Minister, all of which shall be duely attended to.[3]

Nothing Authentic has yet reachd this place from the French fleet in the West Indies, since the action of the 12th of April; and altho Contradictory accounts continue to arrive daily, from Various Quarters, which diminish the loss of our Ally, some of them even so far, as to reduce it, to only two ships—Yet we are sorry to give it as our opinion that there is too much reason to believe the Acct Publishd with Rodneys signature bears too many marks of Authenticity to be doubted.[4]

The Embarkation from New York, which we informd Yr. Excellency in our last was likely to take place,[5] it is reported has actually saild, but of this we have no Authentic accounts, The number of troops embarked is not ascertaind nor their destination

Nothing of moment has happend since our last. we are, with assurances of the most perfect esteem & respect,

Yr. Excellys. Most obedt. Serts.

JAMES MADISON JR.
THEOK. BLAND JR.

[1] Not found.

[2] The "Resolution," adopted by the House of Delegates on 28 May and concurred in by the Senate two days later, reads: "Resolved that the Governor with the Advice of the Council be authorized to approve the Commissioners to be appointed by Congress for settling the Accounts of this State with the United States" (MS in Virginia State Library). See also JM to Pendleton, 7 February 1782, n. 6.

[3] See Harrison to Virginia Delegates, 8 June 1782, and n. 3. Benjamin Harrison, Jr., the son of the governor, was a colonel in the continental army and at this time was also "Agent for the French Army" in Virginia (*Journals of the Council of State*, III, 122).

[4] See JM to Randolph, 6 June 1782, and n. 13.

[5] See Virginia Delegates to Harrison, 4 June 1782, and n. 14.

To Edmund Randolph

RC (LC: Madison Papers). Docketed, "J. Madison, Phil: 11. June 1782." Words written by JM in the official cipher are italicized.

PHILADA. 11 June 1782

DEAR SIR

I have your favor of the 1st. instant.[1] I hope you received mine altho you do not acknowledge them. My punctuality has not been intermitted more than once or twice since your departure, and in no instance for a considerable time past.

I have written so fully concerning the flags that I have nothing to add on that subject,[2] but that I wish the Senate may by their perseverence in this occasion exemplify the Utility of a check to the precipitate acts of a single Legislature.[3]

Having raised my curiosity by your hints as to certain maneuvres,[4] you will not forget your responsibility to gratify it. The pleasure I feel at your being included in the Commission for vindicating the claims of Virga. is considerably impaired by my fears that it may retard your return hither.[5]

Great as my partiality is to Mr. Jefferson, the mode in which he seems determined to revenge the wrong received from his Country, does not appear to me to be dictated either by philosophy or patriotism. It argues indeed a keen sensibility and a strong consciousness of rectitude. But this sensibility ought to be as great towards the relentings as the misdoings of the Legislature, not to mention the injustice of visiting the faults of this body on their innocent constituents.[6]

The fleet said to be preparing to sail from N. York has, I believe certainly left that place with a body of troops on board. The number of men as well as the destination of the fleet is very differently represented. The prevailing conjecture as to the latter is that it will go to Charlestown, and either reinforce the Garrison there, or carry off the Garrison with the troops already on board, to the West Indies.[7]

We have not yet obtained any official intelligence from the French fleet. Concurrent reports make it probable that it has made a junction with the Spanish fleet which awaited it at Hispaniola. Should this be the case, the loss suffered in the action of the 12 of April, ought not one would suppose to frustrate the expedition against Jamacia.[8]

No despatches from Europe have come to hand within the week past, nor do any of the proceedings of Congress furnish matter for a paragraph.

Sir G. Carlton still remains silent.[9] The Resolutions which the Legislatures of the States are passing may perhaps induce him to spare British pride the mortification of supplicating in vain the forgiveness of Rebels.[10]

Mr. [I]z[ard][11] warm & notorious as his predilection for *the Lees* is acknowledges and laments the opposition made *by them* to measures adapted to the *public weal.*[12]

The letter on the first page of the Gazette of this morning was written by Mr. *Marbois.*[13] In an evening of promiscuous conversation I suggested to him my opinion that the insidiousness of the British Court, and the good faith of our Ally, displayed in the late abortive attemp[t] of the former to seduce the latter,[14] might with advantage be made known in some form or other to the public at large[.] He said he would think of the matter, & next day *sent me* the letter in question, with a *request that I would revise and translate it for the press* the latter of which was done. I mention this that you may duly appreciate the facts & sentiments contained in this publication.

If Mr. Jones sd.[15] be at Richmond you will of course let him have a perusal of the inclosed papers[16] &c.

Adieu

J. M.

[1] See Randolph to JM, 1 June 1782.

[2] See JM to Randolph, 28 May, 29 May, and 6 June 1782.

[3] See Randolph to JM, 21–24 May, and n. 3; 1 June 1782.

[4] See Randolph to JM, 1 June, and 20 June 1782.

[5] See Virginia Delegates to Harrison, 12 March, n. 4; JM to Randolph, 1 May 1782, n. 7.

[6] See *Papers of Madison,* III, 338, n. 3; 347–48, n. 1; JM to Jefferson, 15 January,

and nn. 3 and 15; 16 April, and n. 15; Randolph to JM, 5 May, and n. 4; 16–17 May, and n. 6; 1 June 1782.

[7] See Virginia Delegates to Harrison, 4 June, and n. 14; JM to Randolph, 4 June 1782.

[8] See Virginia Delegates to Harrison, 17 April, and n. 2; 4 June; JM to Randolph, 4 June 1782, and n. 28.

[9] See JM to Randolph, 14 May 1782, and n. 8.

[10] See Instructions to Virginia Delegates, 24–25 May; JM to Jones, 28 May 1782, and n. 16.

[11] JM used only the cipher for "z." See Lee to JM, 24 May 1782, n. 4.

[12] See Randolph to JM, 16–17 May, and n. 17; 21–24 May 1782.

[13] *Pennsylvania Packet*, 11 June 1782. See Barbé-Marbois Letter, 9 June 1782, headnote, and editorial note.

[14] See Virginia Delegates to Harrison, 28 May, and n. 20; Report on Fidelity to French Alliance, 31 May 1782, and editorial note.

[15] JM's abbreviation for "should."

[16] Not found. One of the enclosures obviously was the newspaper mentioned in n. 13, above.

Note on Motion To Appoint Examining Committees

MS (NA: PCC, No. 186, fol. 34).

EDITORIAL NOTE

12 June 1782. In the "Committee Book, 1781–1785," cited above, an entry by Charles Thomson on 12 June reads, "A motion of Mr Madison for ap-pointg comees. to examine into the Conduct of the Officers in the three executive departments." Congress accepted this proposal and referred it to a committee consisting of JM, chairman, John Witherspoon, and Ralph Izard. See Report on Congressional Inspection of Departments, 17 June 1782.

Robert Morris, superintendent of finance, mentioned in his diary for 12 June his suggestion to JM on that day to have Congress appoint committees semiannually "to examine into the management of this and other great offices" (Ellis Paxson Oberholtzer, *Robert Morris: Patriot and Financier* [New York, 1903], p. 247).

Note on Motion of Virginia Delegates To Aid Leonard Cooper

MS (NA: PCC, No. 186, fol. 34).

EDITORIAL NOTE

12 June 1782. In his "Committee Book 1781–1785," cited above, Charles Thomson noted that a "Motion of M Bland for providing a cork leg for an Officer" had been offered on 12 June 1782 and referred to Secretary at War Benjamin Lincoln. The motion has not been found. The next day William Jackson, assistant secretary at war, made a report upon this "motion of the honorable Delegates from Virginia to provide at public expence, a cork leg for Captain Cooper of the invalids" (NA: PCC, No. 19, I, 599–601; *JCC*, XXII, 328). In view of the words used by Jackson to designate the motion, JM must have seconded it, since he was the only delegate, besides Bland, from Virginia in Congress. For Captain Leonard Cooper of the Invalid Regiment and the duel causing the loss of his right leg, see *Papers of Madison*, III, 165–66, and nn. In spite of Jackson's pointing out Cooper's ineligibility for compensation from the "public bounty," the "sense of the house" was that "the Secry: at War may advance to Capt. Cooper 16 dollars in part of his pay" (*JCC*, XXII, 328).

Credentials as a Delegate to Continental Congress

MS (NA: PCC, Credentials of Virginia Delegates, fol. 57). Docketed: "Credentials of the honr. James Madison Edmund Randolph Joseph Jones Theodk Bland Arthur Lee Delegates for the State of Virginia read & filed Novr 4th 1782."

VIRGINIA, to wit,
IN GENERAL ASSEMBLY

Saturday the 15th. June 1782.[1]

Resolved that James Madison jr., Edmund Randolph, Joseph Jones, Theoderick Bland jr., and Arthur Lee Esquires be appointed Delegates to represent this Commonwealth in Congress for one Year from the first Monday in November next.[2]

ARCHIBALD CARY S. S.
JOHN TYLER S. H. D.[3]

[1] The *Virginia Gazette* of 8 June announced that on 7 June, the General Assembly had "unanimously continued" the members of the Commonwealth's delegation in Congress for another year. The delay of eight days before issuing the credentials is explained in Randolph to JM, 20 June, and n. 5; and in Jones to JM, 25 June 1782 (*qq. v.*).

[2] Randolph declined the reappointment (Virginia Delegates to Harrison, 12 March 1782, n. 4). See also Randolph to JM, 10 May, and n. 11; 20 June, and n. 5; Harrison to Virginia Delegates, 8 June 1782.

[3] The abbreviations after Cary's and Tyler's names stand for speaker of the Senate and speaker of the House of Delegates, respectively. The submission of these credentials to Congress on 4 November 1782 is recorded in *JCC*, XXIII, 709. The retained copy of the manuscript in the Virginia Historical Society varies slightly in punctuation from the text sent to Congress and also abbreviates "junior" as "junr" after JM's and Bland's names.

From the Reverend James Madison

RC (LC: Madison Papers). Addressed: "The Hone. James Madison Esqr. Member of Congress Philadelphia." Docketed by JM: "Revd Js. [?] Madison June 15. 1782 Mahmouth-Opossum."

WILLIAMSBURG June 15h. 1782.

DEAR COL.[1]

I shd have been more expeditious in acknowledg your Favr. of 22d April,[2] had I not expected an Answer to a Short Letter I wrote you from the Attorny's by Mr. F. Webb, who intended then shortly to set out for Phila.[3] We have been all here in great Anxiety, from the Commander in Cheif[4] to the lowest amongst us, I beleive, to hear a certain Acct. of the Action in the W. I. The first Report was celebrated with a Discharge of Cannon, but it is now generally feared that the Antigua Acct. is too true.[5] What a Misfortune? How many Years may such a Disaster protract a War, hitherto continued upon a vain Opinion, by the Enemy, of their own Strength & Invincibility.

This Place affords but little Variety, for indeed there is a Sameness or Uniformity in the uncommon good Conduct of the Army here, which must ever reflect the greatest Honour upon our Allies. It is commonly said that one Company of Malitia would have done more Mischeif in a Week, than this Army has done in 9 months. indeed I know of no one, who has by Design, not even by the lowest of the Soldiery been injured to the Amount of a Penny.[6]

We had the other Day the Satisfaction of seeing the greatest Respect paid to our University. Dr. Coste, the first Physician to F. Army,[7] & who is a favourite of Gen. Chattelleux's[8] which seems alone eno' to give his Name universal Currency, delivered a latin Oration upon Medicine in general, with Applications to this Country & He met with much Applause—& you will probably soon see it in Print in Phila.[9] He was presented at the same [time] with a Degree.[10] All the Generals & principal officers attended upon this occasion which made a very brilliant Appearance. So that you see Science is not altogether neglected amongst us,—tho' it seemed to want the Arm of our Ally, as much as our unfortunate Country did some Time past. Several of the officers who have a Turn for Nat. History have made Excursions into the Country beyond the mountains. Chattelleux has visited, & ordered a Plan or View of the Natural Bridge to be taken.[11] D'abbesville[12] has examined & found out the Arcana of the Opossum—and also that the Bones of the *Mah-*

mouth, or the Incognitum[13] are common in the lower Ports. We had always taken them for Fish Bones.

You see how little I have to write about, but I expect more from you. I have not a Book left since the Conflagration of the House in wch. I lived.[14] Will you be so kind as to mention in your next, what is the Price of them generally in Phila.

By a Letter from the President of Yale Coll.[15] It seems the Phoenicians have visited Narragenset Bay, pray mention what the Litterati say upon this Head, or whether it be only the Dreams of an Antiquarian, Mr. Gibelin of Paris, who is said tho' to have a very great Reputation.[16]

Beleive me to be Yrs. sincerely

J MADISON

[1] For JM's commission as colonel, see *Papers of Madison*, I, 163.

[2] Not found.

[3] This letter, carried by Foster Webb, Jr., who left Richmond for Philadelphia on 15 May, is also missing (Ambler to JM, 11 May 1782, and n. 3). The "Attorny's" was Edmund Randolph's rented house in Henrico County (Randolph to JM, 11–13 April 1782, n. 2).

[4] The Comte de Rochambeau.

[5] That is, of the outcome of the Battle of the Saints. See JM to Randolph, 6 June, and n. 13. On 11 June, upon returning to Williamsburg from a mission for Rochambeau to Washington's headquarters, the Baron von Closen noted in his diary that "confirmation of M. de Grasses 2 battles by a flag from Antigua" had been received. Not until 20 June could he record that the "cruel uncertainty" had ended on that day, thanks to the arrival of "a gazette from Grenada, which gave the details of the battles on the 9th and 12th" April 1782 (Acomb, *Journal of Closen*, pp. 203–4).

[6] See Randolph to JM, 11–13 April 1782, and n. 11.

[7] Jean François Coste (1741–1819) had arrived in the United States with Rochambeau's army on 11 July 1780. He was mayor of Versailles in 1790–1791 and continued to serve as a high-ranking military physician and consultant until his death. For many years he was physician at the Hôtel des Invalides in Paris (John E. Lane, "Jean-François Coste, Chief Physician of the French Expeditionary Forces in the American Revolution," *Americana*, XXII [1928], 51–80).

[8] See the Reverend James Madison to JM, *ca.* 2 March 1782, and n. 7.

[9] Although the *Pennsylvania Journal* of 10 July 1782 reported the delivery of the oration, no Philadelphia edition of the lecture apparently ever appeared. The work was published in Leyden as *Oratio habita in capitolio Gulielmopolitano in comitiis Universitatis Virginiae, Die XII Juni M.DCC.LXXXII* (Lugduni, Batavorum, 1783). For an English rendition, see "The Adaptation of the Ancient Philosophy of Medicine to the New World, by Jean-François Coste," translated and edited by Anthony Pelzer Wagener in the *Journal of the History of Medicine and Allied Sciences*, VII (1952), 10–67.

[10] On 12 June the College of William and Mary conferred the degree of *Medicinae Doctor* upon Dr. Coste (*William and Mary Quarterly*, 1st ser., XV [1906–7], 266; *Pennsylvania Packet*, 13 July 1782).

[11] On 20 April 1782 François Jean, Chevalier de Chastellux, commander of the Bourbonnais regiment of Rochambeau's army, had visited the Natural Bridge,

situated in Rockbridge County and owned by Jefferson. Upon returning to Williamsburg, Chastellux persuaded Rochambeau to dispatch a French military engineer to make sketches of the bridge. Three of the five drawings were engraved and published at the close of the second volume of *Voyages de M. le Marquis de Chastellux dans l'Amérique Septentrionale dans les années 1780, 1781 et 1782* (2 vols.; Paris, 1786). See also *ibid.*, II, 90–93, 386–416; Boyd, *Papers of Jefferson*, VI, 190, 193, opp. 204; Acomb, *Journal of Closen*, p. 184.

[12] In recognition of his "judicious and spirited management" of Rochambeau's artillery during the siege of Yorktown, François Marie, Comte d'Aboville (1730–1817), had been mentioned by Washington in his "General Orders" of 20 October 1781 (Fitzpatrick, *Writings of Washington*, XXIII, 246).

[13] The Comte d'Aboville's description of the opossum appears in Chastellux, *Voyages*, II, 425–30. For the mammoth, see George Gaylord Simpson, "The Beginnings of Vertebrate Paleontology in North America," *Proceedings of the American Philosophical Society*, LXXXVI (1943), 148–50; Boyd, *Papers of Jefferson*, VI, 159–60, 204, 219–20.

[14] The fire had occurred on 23 November 1781. According to the Baron von Closen, his sovereign "got off for £12,000 in damages, in a settlement that M. de Rochambeau negotiated with the President, Mr. Madison, who had lost a large part of his library and several very fine physics instruments" (Acomb, *Journal of Closen*, p. 166).

[15] Ezra Stiles, who had initiated a correspondence with the Reverend James Madison on 12 July 1780 (*Papers of Madison*, II, 55; 56, n. 10).

[16] Antoine Court de Gebelin (1725–1784) was the author of an uncompleted work, nine volumes of which were published in Paris between 1773 and 1784 under the general title *Le monde primitif analysé et comparé avec le monde moderne*. The eighth volume, which appeared in 1781, had as its particular title *Le monde primitif considéré dans divers objets concernant l'histoire, le blason, les monnaies, les jeux, les voyages des Phéniciens autour du monde, les langues américaines ou dissertations mêlées*. See also *Pennsylvania Magazine of History and Biography*, LXIV (1940), 260–61; Boyd, *Papers of Jefferson*, XII, 264; XIII, 377–78; XV, 14–15.

From Edmund Randolph

RC (LC: Madison Papers). This letter, in Randolph's hand, lacks a cover, complimentary close, signature, and docket. Even though the final paragraph suggests that Randolph had completed his message when he reached the bottom of a single sheet of paper, the letter may have included an additional page.

RICHMOND June 15. 1782.

DEAR SIR

Mr. F. Webb, who returned yesterday, informs me, that he is the bearer of another instance of your very friendly attention to me. The letter is at some distance from the town,[1] and I shall not be able to see it, before the mail of this week is closed. I sincerely wish, that my matter could supply an equivalent for your interesting communications: but the retrograde motion of the assembly, and a toilsome employment for four days past in the trial of many unfortunate criminals are violent bars to my wishes on this head.[2]

Not having attended the assembly for the present week in person, I write from information. The tobacco, it seems, is now on float: that is, the house of delegates assented to the measure by a majority of ninety to ten or eleven, and the senate heard not a single negative.[3] Mr. Rutledge is said to have been the parent of this revolution, and effectually to have converted all the leading members, except Mr. R. H. Lee, whose perseverance remained undiminished by his arguments.[4]

The act of the legislature, which passed the delegates yesterday, for cooperating with Maryland in the defence of the bay,[5] breathes so much harmony, that something of the virulence respecting western territory ought to be abated on this account.[6] It is resolved, to unite vigorously in this important object. And that future occasions may not produce regulations of commerce, by which the one may supplant the other, it is recommended, that the imposts &c of both states shall go hand in hand.

I am called to court, and must therefore postpone a full discharge of those epistolary arrears, for which I am bound to you.[7] I beg you to present my respects to Colo. Bland, and inform him, that I received his obliging favor by the last post: and that he may be assured, that I will not remain his debtor in future.

---

[1] See JM to Randolph, 6 June 1782. Webb had apparently left the letter at "Pettus's" (Randolph to JM, 11–13 April 1782, and n. 2).

[2] As attorney general, Randolph had attended the session of the Virginia General Court terminating on the date of this letter. Two soldiers, found guilty of manslaughter, and a boy "of about twelve," convicted of grand larceny, were immediately pardoned by the court. Although six men were condemned to death—three for high treason, two for horse stealing, and one for rape—all were eventually pardoned by the governor or by the General Assembly (*Virginia Gazette*, 22 June 1782; *Journals of the Council of State*, III, 110, 122, 227; *Calendar of Virginia State Papers*, III, 194, 379; Minute Book, House of Delegates, May 1782, pp. 73, 82; *Journal of the House of Delegates*, October 1782, pp. 18–19; Hening, *Statutes*, XI, 129). See also Randolph to JM, 18 July 1782, and n. 17.

[3] For the oft-mentioned issue of the tobacco to be shipped from Virginia in British flag-of-truce vessels to New York City in exchange for the goods purchased from the traders-capitulant at Yorktown, see Randolph to JM, 21–24 May, and nn. 3, 6, 7, 8; and 1 June 1782. Randolph used the term "on float" in the sense of "free from embarrassments." On 14 and 15 June 1782 the two houses of the General Assembly, having been convinced by John Rutledge and George Clymer of "the expediency of the proceedings of congress touching the passports granted to

certain flag vessels loading" 685 hogsheads of tobacco in Virginia, asked the governor "to give every necessary assistance for carrying the views of congress and their financier into due effect" (MS in Virginia State Library).

[4] See *JCC,* XXII, 311. See also Report on Mission To Inform States of Financial Crisis, 22 May, n. 2; Randolph to JM, 21–24 May; JM to Randolph, 4 June 1782. These two letters include comments about the hostility of Richard Henry Lee and Arthur Lee toward any measure originated or favored by Robert Morris.

[5] When the "Cormorant" and "Oliver Cromwell," armed vessels of Virginia, docked at Baltimore, they were obliged by the port officials to give bond for the payment of duties. In a letter of 27 April 1782 Governor Harrison protested to his Maryland counterpart, Thomas Sim Lee, against this infringement "of the usages and customs of Nations" (McIlwaine, *Official Letters,* III, 198–99). On 23 May the Maryland General Assembly, to which Lee had referred the matter, adopted "An Act for the protection of our Bay Trade and to Defend our Citizens exposed to plunder by the Enemy's Barges." Included in this law was a provision appointing Robert Hanson Harrison as an agent to consult "the Legislature or Executive" of Virginia "on the most effectual measures for protecting the Trade of the Bay of Chesapeake, and the property of the people inhabiting the shores thereof" (MS in Virginia State Library; W. H. Browne *et al., Archives of Maryland,* XLVIII, 170–71, 173–74). Largely as a response to the above-mentioned statute and Harrison's mission to Richmond, the Virginia General Assembly on 13 and 14 June passed resolutions (MS in Virginia State Library; *Calendar of Virginia State Papers,* III, 192–93) and on 1 July 1782 an "act for defending and protecting the trade of Chesapeake bay" (Minute Book, House of Delegates, May 1782, p. 85; Hening, *Statutes,* XI, 42–44).

The resolutions requested Governor Harrison to correspond with Governor Lee on the subject of "harmonizing as much as possible in the Duties Imposts or Customs that are or may be laid on Commerce" and asked Robert Hanson Harrison to assure his government of the "Cordiality and Pleasure" with which the executive and General Assembly of Virginia had received "the very friendly Invitation of Maryland to join our Marine Forces for the Defence of the Commerce of Chesapeake Bay and its Dependencies and for protecting the Shores from the Ravages of the Enemy." Also emphasized in these resolutions was the readiness of the General Assembly to promote "the strictest Union of the two States" as conducive to their "Benefit Safety and Happiness."

Maryland, by a law of 23 May, and Virginia, by hers of 1 July 1782, respectively, allocated ships and funds and appointed commissioners "for the defence and protection of our bay trade" and for the adjustment of disputes arising over these matters. Thus the "Cormorant" and "Oliver Cromwell" incident, although merely one of many episodes illustrating the jealous regard of each state for its sovereignty during the Revolution and the frequent disagreements between Maryland and Virginia for nearly 150 years over the regulation of Chesapeake Bay commerce, helped to foster an accord which was further strengthened at the Mount Vernon Conference of 1785.

[6] Randolph expresses the hope that Maryland's opposition to the terms of Virginia's offer to cede her western lands to Congress will abate if the two states achieve harmony on matters concerning Chesapeake Bay.

[7] Of the seven letters written by JM to Randolph between 14 May and 11 June, Randolph had received five by 15 June and also knew of JM's dispatch of 6 June. During the period 16 May to 15 June, both included, Randolph wrote four letters to JM.

Note on Motion on Illicit Trade with the Enemy

MS (NA: PCC, No. 186, fol. 36).

EDITORIAL NOTE

17 June 1782. On 14 June 1782 Congress named eleven of its members, including JM, to be a committee under Samuel Osgood's chairmanship, "To devise & report ways & means to prevent an illicit trade with the Enemy." Three days later this committee was "discharged on a Motion of Mr. Madison & the business referred to a comee. of five" (NA: PCC, No. 186, fol. 36; *JCC*, XXII, 333 n.). For their recommendation, see Report on Illicit Trade with the Enemy, 19 June 1782.

Motion Concerning Peace Negotiations

MS (NA: PCC, No. 36, I, 345). In JM's hand. Docketed: "Motion of Mr Witherspoon Mr Madison. June 17. 1782 passed in the negative 5 ayes 4 noes one divd."

[17 June 1782]

That a Committee be appointed to propose & report to Congress the information & instructions proper to be transmitted to the Ministers Plenipo: for negociating peace, the better to enable them to support the several claims of the U. S. not included in their Ultimatum[1]

[1] With John Witherspoon's assistance, JM was trying to revive his Report on Instructions on Peace Negotiations of 7 January (*q.v.*, and its editorial note and nn.). This report had been dormant since 22 January, when it was referred to a committee comprising Daniel Carroll, Edmund Randolph, and Joseph Montgomery (*ibid.*, headnote). The principal "claims" omitted from the ultimata of 14 August 1779, 18 October 1780, and 15 June 1781 (*JCC*, XIV, 956–60; XVIII, 948–51; XX, 651–52) were those of free access to the fishing banks off Newfoundland and a transfer to the United States by Great Britain of her right, acquired by Article VII of the Treaty of Paris in 1763, to navigate the Mississippi River freely. The treaty having been annulled by war between the contracting powers, any effective guarantee of free navigation, together with the privilege of using New Orleans or some other site close to the mouth of the river as a port of deposit, would now have to be obtained by the United States from Spain. For JM's earlier contention that British treaty rights had "devolved" on the United States, see *Papers of Madison*, II, 132.

The tallied vote leading to the defeat of the motion does not appear in the printed journal (*JCC*, XXII, 336). Hence, which state delegations favored, which opposed, and what delegation deadlocked are not known. After several later efforts by Arthur Lee, John Lowell, Theodorick Bland, and Jesse Root also failed to achieve the aim of the present motion (*JCC*, XXII, 415, 428, 429, 458), JM and Witherspoon succeeded on 8 August in having Congress agree to a motion identical in intent to, but more specific than, this one of 17 June 1782 (*JCC*, XXII, 459–60).

Report on Congressional Inspection of Departments

MS (NA: PCC, No. 28, fol. 321). In JM's hand. The docket reads: "Report of Mr Madison Mr Witherspoon Mr Izard On a Motion of Mr. Madison. passed June 17th, 1782. Committees to be appointed to examine into the conduct of Heads of Departments & report." In the PCC there are at least two other copies of this report. One is apparently in James Duane's hand (No. 142, II, 5–6) and the other in the hand of a clerk (No. 188, fol. 1). See Note on Motion To Appoint Examining Committees, 12 June 1782.

EDITORIAL NOTE

By adopting this report, a majority of the state delegations obviously shared JM's determination to remind the administrative departments of their subordination to Congress and of their obligation to be frugal and honest in the conduct of business. Believing that the Lees were unjustifiably accusing Robert Morris of "misfeasance" (Randolph to JM, 16–17 May, 21–24 May; JM to Randolph, 4 June 1782), JM may also have introduced his motion with the confident expectation that a close scrutiny of the Department of Finance would silence Morris' enemies. If this was JM's purpose, he perhaps contrived Arthur Lee's appointment on 2 July to the committee "to enquire fully into the proceedings of the department of Finance, including the several branches of the same" (*JCC*, XXII, 370; JM to Randolph, 16 July 1782). For Lee's view of the committee, see Burnett, *Letters*, VI, 429.

On 25 July Congress named Lee to be chairman of a committee to examine and report on "the application of the moneys of the United States in France" (*JCC*, XXII, 416). Lee took full advantage of this welcome opportunity to examine and so to interpret the records of the Department of Finance as to cast suspicion, in his report of 20 November, upon the integrity of his other favorite antagonist, Benjamin Franklin (*JCC*, XXIII, 740–44). See also Amendment to Motion on Laurens' Mission, 12 July 1782.

[17 June 1782]

It[1] being expedient as well for the justification of such of the principals of the Civil Departments immediately under Congress, who duly administer the same, as for the more certain detection of such as may violate in any manner the important trusts consigned to them, that periodical & exact enquiries into their respective administrations be instituted,

It is hereby Resolved that[2] on the 1st Monday in July and the 1st Monday in Jany in every year, five Committees composed each of five members shall be appointed; which Committees shall have it in charge to enquire fully, one of them into the proceedings of the Department of Finance, including the[3] Several branches of the same, another into the proceedings of the Department of foreign affairs, another of the Department of war, another of the Department of Marine, Another[4] of the post office and to report the result of their respective enquiries to Congress.[5]

first Monday in July[6]

[1] After mentioning the members of the committee to which JM's motion of 12 June had been referred, the preface to this report in the printed journal closes by stating, "Congress agreed to the following resolution" (*JCC*, XXII, 334).

[2] Following this word, JM at first wrote "every half year beginning with the first day of August next." He then deleted the passage and interlineated "on the 3d Monday in Novr. in every year." This, too, he replaced with the words shown in the text. These alterations probably reflect the course of the debate on the report in Congress.

[3] The next five words are a substitution for JM's original "offices of Treasurer Controller & auditors of accounts."

[4] The interlineation of this word and the next four words was probably made by JM in committee so as to repair the oversight of recommending in the report that five committees be named to inspect four departments.

[5] In pursuance of this resolution, Congress on 2 July appointed five committees of investigation, each comprising five members. JM was named chairman of the committee "to enquire fully into the proceedings of the department of foreign affairs." He rendered the committee's report on 18 September 1782 (*JCC*, XXII, 370; XXIII, 586–89).

[6] The first version of this isolated note, before JM revised it, read, "last Monday in July next." He apparently jotted down these words during the debate in Congress and later inserted them in the report as a substitute for a part of the deletions mentioned in n. 2, above. The notation does not appear in either of the other copies of the report cited in the headnote.

From Edmund Pendleton

Tr (LC: Force Transcripts). Addressed to "The Honble James Madison Esqr Philadelphia." Another copy taken from the original is printed in the *Proceedings of the Massachusetts Historical Society*, 2d ser., XIX (1905), 155–57. The second paragraph of the letter, also copied from the original, appears in Stan. V. Henkels Catalogue No. 694 (1892).

VIRGA. June 17th 1782

DEAR SIR:

Your favr of the 4th[1] brought a confirmation of the unfortunate Issue of the great Naval Conflict in the West Indies on the 12th of April, unless we can suppose Adml Rodney's Letter spurious,[2] no features of which I am able to discover, unless it be an uncommon modesty, for which they have not been very remarkable in such Narrations[3] in the course of this dispute. we are yet told from Richmond, as handed to that place from Ct Rochambeau, that Degrasse is not a prisoner tho they have lost the ships mention'd, but as Rodney's letter as to that point seems confirmed by the Account brought to Baltimore by the Vessell from Hispaniola, that the Squadron *late* under Ct. Degrasse was to be commanded by Vaudruille,[4] I think that Valuable officer is a prisoner; If this Baltimore Account be true, I think we may soon hope to hear something agreeable from Jamaica, which may Ballance our former misfortune.[5]

I have a letter from Genl. Green's Camp of the 18th past wch mentions the Imbarkation of 2 Regiments near 1000 men from Charles Town on the 4th of that Month supposed for Jamaica–from whence I conjecture that the preparations at New York are for conveying troops on the like errand, unless they have some plundering plan to Execute in America.[6] there appears no Intention in the Garrison at Charles Town to evacuate it, or commence Offensive Operations. My poor nephew Judge Harry, is miserable in his Captivity there, confined in the Provost, he is afraid to take the Air of his window, lest some Refugee should be at hand to shoot him. Genl Leslie has hitherto refused his parole altho Genl Green [has][7] offer'd to pledge himself for his performing the terms of it; the present behaviour of the Refugees might Satisfie Lesly of the Propriety of his breaking his former Parole, if his letter to Ld Cornwallis had not been Satisfactory.[8] He was in bad health when taken, so that I suppose his situation & the approaching hot Season, will soon put an end to all disputes about him & gratify the wishes of his Enemies, unless no death, but that by their own hands will do so.

We have had publications of the States General having acknowledged our Independence & recognized Mr Adams as Public Minister; If they have any foundation in truth, I suppose they only mean that the Province of Holland hath acceded to that measure; but of this I doubt, as you only mention that of Friesland:[9] The whole was in a probable train, if the affair of April 12th[10] has not Interrupted it.

Your judicious decision upon the distinct Powers of Congress & the

State, respecting the Flags & Passports for carrying tobacco to New York, is unanswerable,[11] and I feel the propriety of our Assembly's joining in the necessary Concert on this Occasion, calculated to furnish a Market for our tobacco, which we much want, and save so much Specie to be sent off in discharge of our Continental proportion of expence.[12] The principal objection (and what I understand Influenced the Assembly) was a regard to our noble Ally, who 'twas thought would see with resentment our tobacco going to the Common Enemy by consent of the Governing powers,[13] a circumstance we cannot be too attentive to, from every consideration of Justice & gratitude; but besides that the Alternative of remitting the very money we Possess from their generosity,[14] could not be less displeasing, it is to be observed that they in a manner consented to this measure, when in the Capitulation at York, in which their General[15] had a part, the British Merchants were allowed to dispose of their goods here and of course tobacco must go to pay for them, since that was the only means. I heard a sensible Member say that he would have consented to the measure, if the French Minister had been consulted & approved it. The price (tho' Current here) was another Objection, for say some Gentn., if our tobacco must go to the Enemy, why should not we, rather than the united States have the whole price, wch the Enemy are willing to give. the very money lodged with Mr Morris[16] was offer'd to our Governor for tobo. at 30/ a hundred provided this Passport could be obtained to carry it to N. York,[17] and Merchants here have declared publicly that with such a passport, they would give 40/Sterling. This is indeed a Serious objection for if in consequence of this restriction in trade we are to submit to a very low price for our Staple, & must agree to wa[i]ve[18] it whenever Congress shall propose to do so, for the Interest of the United States, we may easily suppose without breach of Charity, they would soon make their Financier a Merchant to purchase up all our tobacco, and whether they would in such case continue disinterested and proper Judges to exercise the power of Flags, is pretty [e]asily determined.[19] In a general view therefore such a proceeding could not be approved, but the Inference is that in future we shall avoid all occasions of this sort, by either making the trade free & open, or not allow it in any case. As to what is past, we purchased the goods under a public & authorized Capitulation & are bound to pay for them; we must do so in Specie or tobacco; it is more convenient to part with the latter at the current price than the former, & should have been willing but for the Prohibition, to have let the Crs[20] carry the tobacco any where &

make their proffit[.] if Congress think they can without Injury to the Public allow the tobacco to go to New York, and take the proffit the Merchts would otherwise have, it would seem Virginia is not Injured, & the Union benefited. But here lies the Rub. If Virginia in payment of a debt to the Enemy contracted with the approbation & under the Sanction of the States, can avail herself of an high price for her produce, & Congress see no Injury in exporting that produce (for this is admitted in granting the Passports) why should they withold their Sanction to the export for the benefit of Virga. & compel her to purchase Passports, at the price of the whole proffit? Is not this making a Merchandise of Congressional Powers? I write my thoughts just as they occur & perhaps (like they say of the Assembly Resns.) my reasoning may be at Variance with my Opinion. Would not a Compromise be most Equitable? Let the Passports stand & be assented to here. Let the States have the benefit of the proffit, as far as the money goes Lodged wth Mr Morris (for that was gone from the State) and let Virga. have the best price she can get for tobacco for the residue of the debt, under the knowledge of these Passports & so let it end. I have given you too much trouble on this Occasion & Intreat yr Pardon. I am happy to hear the former Delegation in Congress is continued, as I suppose Mr Jones & Mr Atto[21] have agreed to return. I am with great regard

Dr Sr Your very affe friend

EDMD. PENDLETON

[1] Not found.

[2] See Virginia Delegates to Harrison, 4 June 1782, and citations in its n. 3.

[3] In the *Proceedings of the Massachusetts Historical Society* version the word is "narratives."

[4] Vice Admiral Louis Philippe de Rigaud, Marquis de Vaudreuil (1724–1802), aboard his flagship, "Triomphant," commanded a squadron in the Battle of the Saints and the French fleet in the West Indies after the capture of Grasse (W. M. James, *British Navy in Adversity*, pp. 334–35, 348–49, 450).

[5] See Pendleton to JM, 20 May 1782, n. 10.

[6] In a dispatch of 18 May, read in Congress on 24 June 1782, Nathanael Greene reported that the nineteenth and thirtieth regiments of the enemy had "lately" embarked at Charleston with the West Indies as their probable destination (NA: PCC, No. 155, II, 441–43; *JCC*, XXII, 347 n.). See also Virginia Delegates to Harrison, 4 June 1782, and n. 14. The letter to Pendleton had probably been written by his nephew, Captain Nathaniel Pendleton, Jr., aide-de-camp of Greene.

[7] Here, unlike in the two other versions of this paragraph mentioned in the headnote, the Force copyist erred by writing "his" rather than "has." General Alexander Leslie commanded the British forces in Charleston, S.C.

[8] For Judge Henry Pendleton, see *Papers of Madison*, II, 105, n. 5; and Pendleton to JM, 11 March 1782, and n. 4. In his letter of 20 July 1780 to Lord Cornwallis, Judge Pendleton justified his breach of parole on the ground that Loyalist ("Ref-

ugee") military and civilian personnel in Charleston, following its capitulation, had frequently insulted him "in the grossest manner" and threatened to kill him. The judge added, "against the pistol or dagger of a nocturnal assassin, there is no refuge but flight" (*Pennsylvania Packet*, 2 September 1780).

[9] The *Virginia Gazette* of 15 June 1782 included a purported "Translation of the Hand-bill, printed in Amsterdam," which alleged that the "United States of Holland" had recognized American independence and received Adams on 28 March 1782. See Report on Salaries of Representatives Abroad, 28 May 1782, n. 11.

[10] Battle of the Saints.

[11] From these observations, it is apparent that JM in his missing letter of 4 June to Pendleton had summarized what he had written about "Flags & Passports" to Lee and Randolph on 28 May and to Randolph on 29 May and 4 and 6 June 1782 (*qq.v.*).

[12] See Lee to JM, 16 May, and n. 9; JM to Lee, 28 May; Randolph to JM, 15 June 1782.

[13] See Harrison to Virginia Delegates, 18 May 1782, and n. 4.

[14] For the specie used by the French to buy supplies and pay their armed forces in Virginia, see *Papers of Madison*, III, 262, 263, n. 9. See also Pendleton to JM, 15 April 1782, n. 6.

[15] Comte de Rochambeau.

[16] Superintendent of Finance Robert Morris.

[17] See Harrison to Virginia Delegates, 18 May, and n. 4; JM to Randolph, 6 June 1782, n. 3.

[18] Pendleton obviously meant "waive," but whether he wrote that word, as in the version in the *Proceedings of the Massachusetts Historical Society* is not known to the editors.

[19] In the version cited in n. 18, "easily" is correctly spelled. For Robert Morris' defense of the tobacco contract against some of these objections, see his long letter of 30 May 1782 to Daniel Clark (Wharton, *Revolutionary Diplomatic Correspondence*, V, 448–54).

[20] Creditors. For "the Prohibition," see *Papers of Madison*, III, 338; Note on Motion on Illicit Trade, 17 June 1782.

[21] Edmund Randolph, attorney general of Virginia. See Credentials as Delegate, 15 June 1782, and n. 2.

Virginia Delegates to Benjamin Harrison

RC (Virginia State Library). In JM's hand except for Bland's signature. JM wrote all italicized words in the official cipher. Docketed, "Virga Dels Lr. June 18th 1782." Accompanying the manuscript in the Virginia State Library is a page upon which the second paragraph of the letter was decoded by Archibald Blair, clerk of the Council of State.

PHILADA. 18th. June 1782.

SIR

The Post having been robbed of his mail on his return through Maryland, we had not the honor yesterday of receiving any letter from Your

Excellency.[1] If it reaches us at all it will probably be through the channel of the New York Gazette.

Since our letter of the 4th. instant which inclosed a proposition from *Count Beniouski*[2] *some circumstances have come to our knowledge* which induce us to *believe* that *altho' for the reasons stated in our letter he is not to be classed with common adventurers yet his professions and undertakeings greatly exceed his resourses for fulfiling them.* In particular we have decisive evidence that [he] *cannot command the aid of the French Court in raising and transporting his legion and it is of itself evident that no private funds*[3] *can be equal to such an expence.* We do no injustice to *his character in adding that the effect of the rejection of his plan by Congress has betrayed a temper which is very far from enhancing our esteem for him.*

The destination of the fleet which lately sailed from N. York is still unknown;[4] nor have we reced. a word of intelligence from any other quarter.

We have the honor to be with the greatest respect & esteem Yr. Excellency's Obt. & hble. Servants.

J. MADISON JR.
THEOK. BLAND JR.

P.S.

The Letter from Oliver Pollock with the bill inclosed in it was put into our hands by the Gentleman in whose favor the bill is drawn, with a request that we would inclose it to the Executive.[5] As we shall probably be applied to here after for information on this subject we beg the favor of your Excellency to let us know the steps taken thereon.

[1] See Harrison to Virginia Delegates, 8 June, n. 1; JM to Randolph, 18 June; Report on Mail Robbery, 19 June 1782.

[2] See Report on Bieniewsky's Proposal for a Legionary Corps, 29 May, and editorial note; Bieniewsky to Virginia Delegates, 31 May; Virginia Delegates to Harrison, 4 June 1782, and n. 7.

[3] In the decoded page mentioned in the headnote, this word is omitted, and "private" is "privates."

[4] See Virginia Delegates to Harrison, 4 June 1782, and n. 14.

[5] Pollock's letter and the bill have not been found. The bill was returned to the delegates (Harrison to Virginia Delegates, 29 June 1782). "The Gentleman" was Thomas Irwin, a Philadelphia merchant. In a letter of 18 June to Harrison, Irwin stated that the bill, which he had asked JM to forward, was drawn on Virginia for 6,819 Spanish milled dollars owed him by Pollock for goods which the latter had purchased on Virginia's behalf—presumably for the use of George Rogers Clark and his troops (*Calendar of Virginia State Papers*, III, 196). On 31 July the Council of State, faced with a shortage of funds, authorized Harrison "to direct the State

Agent to accept the said Bill payable in Six Months from this Date, with Interest from the first Day of September next" (*Journals of the Council of State*, III, 130). See also *Papers of Madison*, III, 98, 99 n., 256, 257 nn.; Harrison to Virginia Delegates, 29 June 1782, and n. 5.

To Edmund Randolph

RC (LC: Madison Papers). The cover is missing and the letter is not docketed.

PHILADA. 18th. June 1782[1]

DEAR SIR

I recd. no letter from you yesterday nor shall[2] I receive any for that week unless it be through the channel of Rivington's Gazette, the Post having been robbed of his mail on Saturday eving last in Maryland.[3] I hope your letter did not contain anything not in Cypher which is unfit for the public eye.[4] The policy however wch. seems to direct Carlton's measures renders it probable that he will decline the mean expedient pursued on such occasions by his predecessors for giving pain to individuals.[5] It will be proper for us to take from this accident an admonition to extend the use of our Cypher.

The destination of the fleet which Sailed lately from N. York is not yet known.[6] No offical intelligence from the West Indies is yet come hand. No intelligence of any kind from Europe. The business of Congress is too un[in]teresting to merit recital.

The trade with N. York begins to excite general indignation and th[r]eatens a loss of all our hard money. The continued drains which it makes from the bank must at least contract its utility, if it produces no greater mischief to it. The Legislature of N. Jersey are devising a new remedy for this disgraceful & destructive traffic,[7] and a Committee of Congress are also employed in the same work.[8] I have little expectation that any adequate cure can be applied, whilst our foreign trade is annihilated[9] & the Enemy in New York make it an object to keep open this illicit channel

Adieu

J. M. JR.

I have written to Mr. Jones.[10] If he sd. not be at Richmond open the letter.

[1] Late in his life JM or someone by his direction bracketed the first and last paragraphs of this letter to indicate that they should be published in the first edition of his papers (Madison, *Papers* [Gilpin ed.], I, 143).

[2] JM inadvertently repeated this word.

[3] For the interception of the postrider on 15 June, see Harrison to Virginia Delegates, 8 June, and n. 1; Report on Mail Robbery, 19 June 1782.

[4] At this point JM drew a broad line of ink across a short sentence. The sentence appears to have been "I am certain it contained nothing which would be of avail to the Enemy."

[5] That is, the obvious desire of General Carleton to effect a truce in order to discuss terms of peace might lead him to abandon General Clinton's practice of publishing intercepted letters in Rivington's *Royal Gazette* for the purpose of embarrassing their authors. For Carleton's eagerness to please Washington and Congress, see JM to Randolph, 4 June 1782, n. 35.

[6] See Virginia Delegates to Harrison, 4 June 1782, and n. 14.

[7] After "new" JM crossed out "means of" and wrote "remedy." The session of the New Jersey legislature which adjourned on 24 June enacted a law "for preventing an illicit trade and intercourse between the subjects of this state and the enemy." The lengthy text of the measure is printed in the *Pennsylvania Journal* of 6 July 1782. In the 4 July issue of the *Pennsylvania Packet*, an article by "A Plain Farmer," which had recently appeared in the *New-Jersey Gazette*, stated that during the past "few weeks," no less than 40 or 50,000 pounds in specie, otherwise available for the payment of taxes, had been drained out of New Jersey by "moonlight pedlars," encouraged by General Carleton, to purchase "British gewgaws" in New York City. "Their goods are not proof against fire or water," the writer suggested. "Break up this trade root and branch," he admonished, "or it will break you up." See also the *Pennsylvania Packet* of 6 and 9 July for other articles on the same subject.

[8] See Note on Motion on Illicit Trade, 17 June; Report on Illicit Trade, 19 June 1782.

[9] With considerable success, the British pursued a policy in 1782 of avoiding military conflict with the Americans, enticing them with manufactured articles to exhaust their supply of specie, and of annihilating their trade on the seas. See Motion on Protection of Commerce, 2 May, and nn. 1 and 5; Motion To Request France To Protect American Commerce, 14 May 1782, and n. 1; Clarence L. Ver Steeg, *Robert Morris*, pp. 138–41.

[10] This letter apparently is not extant. See Jones to JM, 25 June 1782.

Report on Illicit Trade with the Enemy

MS (NA: PCC, No. 24, fols. 53–56). In JM's hand. Docketed: "recommendation to the States. Report of Committee for suppressing the illicit Trade with the Enemy—Mr Madison Mr Lowell Mr Scot Mr Wharton Mr Witherspon June 19. 1782 Read. June 20. 1782 recomd. Passed June 21."

[19 June 1782]

The Committee to whom was recomitted the Report concerning illicit trade with the Enemy,[1] recommend the following act

Whereas the Enemy, having renounced the hope of accomplishing their designs agst. the U. States by force alone, are resorting to every expedient which may tend to corrupt the patriotism, of their citizens, or to weaken the foundation of the public credit;[2] and in pursuance of this policy, are encouraging to the utmost, a clandestine traffic between the inhabitants[3] of this Country, and those who reside within the garrisons and places therein now in their possession; And Whereas some of the said inhabitants, prompted either by a sordid attachment to gain, or by a secret conspiracy with the Enemies of their country, are wickedly engaged in carrying on this illicit traffic; whereby, a market is provided for British Merchandizes, the circulating specie is exported from the U. States, the payment of taxes rendered more difficult & burdensome to the people at large, and great discouragement occasoned to honest & lawful commerce,

Resolved that it be and hereby is recommended to the Legislatures of the several States, to adopt the most efficacious measures for suppressing all[4] traffic and illicit intercourse between their respective Citizens & the Enemy

Resolved, that the Legislatures, or in case of their recess, the Executives of the several States, be earnestly requested to impress by every means in their power, on their respective Citizens at large, the baneful consequences[5] apprehended by Congress from a continuance of this illicit & infamous traffic, and the necessity of their co-operating with the public measures,[6] by such united, patriotic, and vigilant exertions, as will detect & bring to legal[7] punishment those who shall have been in any manner concerned therein.[8]

Resolved[9] that in case the Commander in chief shall be of opinion that any disposition can be made of the regular forces under his command, which will, without interfereing with military objects, aid in suppressing the pernicious traffic aforesaid, he be and hereby is authorized and directed to make such disposition, and to distribute the articles which may be captured from the Enemy, by the troops detached on such service, in such manner as he shall judge most conducive to the end proposed;[10] provided always that this resolution shall not be so construed as to affect any rule touching captures or the division thereof, contained in an ordinance entitled, An Ordinance ascertaining what captures on water shall be lawful.[11]

[1] See Note on Motion on Illicit Trade, 17 June 1782. For the background of the report, see Harrison to Virginia Delegates, 23 March 1782, n. 2.

[2] See Virginia Delegates to Harrison, 8 February; JM to Pendleton, 9 April, and n. 5; Ambler to JM, 20 April, and n. 4; JM to Randolph, 18 June 1782, and n. 7.

[3] JM interlineated this word above a deleted "people." For the alleged extent of this "clandestine traffic," see Burnett, *Letters,* VI, 374.

[4] Following this word, JM crossed out "illicit."

[5] JM inserted a cross above the last letter of this word to call attention to the next folio (55), on which he wrote an alternative passage reading, "which in the opinion of Congress will result from." Before rendering its report, the committee apparently decided that "apprehended by Congress" was preferable.

[6] The words "public measures" were a substitution by JM for a deleted "laws of this Country."

[7] JM at first wrote "due" rather than "legal."

[8] Before adjourning on 2 July 1782, the Virginia General Assembly enacted a statute "for seizure and condemnation of British goods found on land." The final proviso of the law suspended its enforcement "until the rest of the United States shall have passed similar laws on this subject" (Hening, *Statutes,* XI, 101–3). The ordinance of Congress was published in the *Virginia Gazette* of 13 July 1782.

[9] Although this entire paragraph is crossed out with heavy ink lines, it is not clear whether the committee or Congress made the excision.

[10] On fol. 56 JM also wrote the passage between "by" and "proposed," except that he penned "this service" rather than "such service."

[11] See *Papers of Madison,* III, 217–21, 236–43, and especially p. 236. As noted in the docket, Congress debated the report of the committee on 20 June and adopted it the next day (*JCC,* XXII, 340–42). Since the principal aim of this ordinance was to prevent trade with the enemy only by land, Congress on 3 July appointed John Morin Scott, Arthur Lee, and Abraham Clark as a committee to draft a bill prohibiting this "pernicious commerce" under the guise of "collusive captures on the water." Congress accepted the recommendation of the committee on 17 July 1782 (NA: PCC, No. 59, III, 427–29; *JCC,* XXII, 383, 384, 392–93).

Report on Mail Robbery

MS (NA: PCC, No. 61, fol. 507). In JM's hand. Undated and undocketed.

[19 June 1782][1]

on report of The Committee[2] to whom was referred the letter from the Post Master informing Congress of a robbery of the mail on the day of at [3] do report the following resolution Resolved that the Executives of the States of New Jersey Pennsylvania, Delaware & Maryland be & they are hereby requested to pursue the most likely measures by offering proper rewards at the Expense of the united States & otherwise for recovering the mail and bringing the Robbers to due punishment.[4]

[1] The date is taken from *JCC,* XXII, 337.

[2] As soon as he heard of the interception of the mail (Harrison to Virginia Dele-

gates, 8 June 1782, n. 1), Postmaster General Ebenezer Hazard (1744–1817) on 17 June notified the president of Congress of the "unhappy Affair" and called it "a new Inducement to wish that the Ordinance respecting the Department may be soon compleated" (NA: PCC, No. 61, fol. 113). Although this ordinance and its supplement would not be adopted until 18 and 28 October, respectively (*JCC*, XXIII, 670–78, 688–89), Congress on 17 June referred Hazard's letter to Theodorick Bland, Thomas McKean, and Turbutt Wright (NA: PCC, No. 191, fol. 16). Why JM drafted the report is unknown. The printed journal of Congress for 19 June leaves the impression that the membership of the committee had remained unchanged (*JCC*, XXII, 337).

[3] The journal errs in stating that Hazard had fixed "Sunday the 16" as the time of the robbery (*ibid.*). Hazard had merely quoted a letter of 16 June from "the Postmaster at Harford Town in Maryland," stating, "This morning the Post arrived without the Mail, being rob'd within 5 Miles of this Place" (NA: PCC, No. 61, fol. 113). Probably the robbery occurred during the evening of 15 June, as reported in the *Virginia Gazette* of 29 June 1782.

[4] In accordance with this request, President William Moore and the Pennsylvania Supreme Executive Council on 20 June issued a proclamation offering a reward of $200 for the recovery of the mail, an additional $100 for each of the robbers apprehended and convicted, and a "free pardon" to any of them who would turn state's evidence (*Pennsylvania Packet*, 22 June 1782). In Maryland Governor Thomas Sim Lee on 16 July offered $300 for recovery and $150 for apprehension and conviction (W. H. Browne *et al.*, eds., *Archives of Maryland*, XLVIII, 215). The Council and the House of Assembly of Delaware adjourned on 22 June, not to reconvene until 20 October. The brigands were captured in August (*Pennsylvania Journal*, 7 August; *Pennsylvania Packet*, 10 August 1782; *Papers of the Historical Society of Delaware*, VI: *Minutes of the Council of the Delaware State from 1776 to 1792* [1887], 743, 748). No proclamation of Governor William Livingston of New Jersey fulfilling Congress' request has been found. The legislature of the state adjourned on 24 June after scheduling 18 September as the date for reconvening (*New Jersey Archives*, 2d ser., V, 463).

From Edmund Randolph

RC (LC: Madison Papers). Unsigned letter, in Randolph's hand, addressed to "The honble James Madison jr. of congress Philadelphia." Docketed by JM, "June 20. 1782." To the left of this date and at a right angle to it, he also wrote "Rept. on Instruction." This jotting apparently bears no relation to the contents of the letter. The italicized words are those written by Randolph in the official cipher.

RICHMOND June 20. 1782.

MY DEAR FRIEND

You wound me deeply by insinuating a delinquency on my part in repeating my letters, or not acknowledging yours.[1] The latter circumstance I may have omitted in the single instance of your two favors by the express:[2] but the former charge is clearly unsupportable so far as

GEORGE WASHINGTON

ROBERT MORRIS

53

The Committee to whom was recommitted the Report concerning illicit trade with the Enemy, recommend the following act

Whereas the Enemy, having renounced the hope of accomplishing their designs agst. the U. States by force alone, are resorting to every expedient which may tend to corrupt the patriotism of their citizens, or to weaken the foundation of the public credit; and in pursuance of this policy, are encouraging to the utmost, a clandestine traffic between the ~~people~~ inhabitants of this country, and those who reside within the garrisons and places therein now in their possession; And whereas some of the said inhabitants, prompted either by a sordid attachment to gain, or by a secret conspiracy with the Enemies of their country, are wickedly engaged in carrying on this illicit traffic; whereby, a market is provided for British Merchandises, the circulating Specie is exported from the U. States, the payment of taxes rendered more difficult & burdensome to the people at large, and great discouragement occasioned to honest & lawful commerce;

Resolved that it be and hereby is recommended to the Legislatures of the several States, to adopt the most ~~efficacious~~ efficacious measures for suppressing all ~~illicit~~ traffic and illicit intercourse between their respective citizens & the Enemy.

COMMITTEE REPORT ON TRADE WITH THE ENEMY

respects the post. I have never indeed written by private opportunities, because it requires a week to collect in this barren spot intelligence enough for a letter of even a moderate length.

My last and preceding communications, which spoke of certain manoeuvres,[3] alluded to in your letter of the 11th. instant, mentioned, I believe in general terms only, that a design appeared to be formed *against the reelection of you and my self to Congress.* The attack was unexpected: and the secret suggestions which were intended to injure, had had their fullest operation, before it came to the knowledge even of *our friends.* But it may be triumphantly said, that the wicked, and malevolent did not dare to exclude from their most poisonous reports a *respect for our characters. You were* assailed under the *garb* of *friendship.* It was lamented, that the rigour of law should *cut off so*[4] *a servant* from *public employment.*[5] And to say the truth, there was such a fervency of compliment that it was unpleasant[6] to distrust its sincerity. *I too was* declared to be *ineligible*[7] after a preface overflowing with panegyrick: and indeed the manifest of hostility never could wear a milder form. However *P. Henry* propounded the question respecting *my eligibility:* for he had been informed of these clandestine operations. No man rose to assert the negative *except R. H. Lee.* He was fulsome in commendation, as I was informed, and protested against every possibility of exception, but from that quarter. He had no other coadjutor, than *the old squire.*[8] *The doctor*[9] spoke in opposition to *his brothr*[10] upon pretty much the same principle, as that which *act*[u]*ates* two *eastern delegates,*[11] when they divide; namely *an affectation of candor.* I call myself impartial, notwithstanding the *shaft* was *directed at my head:* and therefore I shall risque my reputation for charity, and affirm, that this gentleman[12] had no other motive. For he had been industrious in the circulation of the opinion, which discountenanced *my being elected.* Mr. *Jones*[13] was very warm on hearing of these doublings: and if the malicious murmur had not subsided, he would, I believe, have been very[14] pointed. Those, who defend the constitution or the laws, from principle shall never receive aught but reverence from me. But to him, who covers personal views under the pretext of public utility, I cannot be a cordial friend. Notwithstanding all this R. H. Lee wrote *me a letter today* subscribing himself "*affectionately yours.*"

The efforts of *the* [*two*][15] *Lees* seemed to have for their direct object the destruction of every man, who had not shewn himself *de*[*vote*]*d to* [*their*][16] *designs.* Within this description was included *our friend Henry.*[17] *They* disdained *not* to calumnate *him in* [*pri*][18]*vate; and* in public the younger *of the two* [*was*][19] occasionally uttered bitter things. [*Their*][20] perseverance is so much superior to *his that he will fi*[nd] *it diffi*[cult][21] *to resist* [*their*] violence, but by the most circumspect conduct. An occasion offered for giving a serious cast to his conduct: but the aspersion, tho' disadvantageous at its first representati[on] vanished upon scrutiny. An act of the assembly had reserved the land on the cape, as a common for the use of the fishermen. Mr. Henry had formed a company long before this reservation for the approp[ri]ation of them; directing the surveyor however to set apart a portion of the shore for their use. But a complaint was made to the assembly; and the Zeal of *party* mingled itself with this warfare for public good; so as manifestly to shew, that *public good was* not *the ruling motive*.[22] Mr. H—y offered to yield his pretensions: but I understand, that I am instructed to institute a suit against the patent, which he has obtained.[23]

The house of delegates have passed a bill in pursuance of the recommendation of congress concerning shipwreck.[24] The regulations, contained in it, have been principally borrowed from the british acts on the same subject. But this law is not intended to be permanent. For upon the ratification of the consular convention,[25] what it prescribes will be followed in the case of French subjects. In the meantime we imitate our ally,[26] by affording to his unfortunate people the same relief, which is extended to our own countrymen.[27]

A census is to be taken of the white inhabitants of Virginia.[28] This, when accomplished, will secure us against a repetition of the extravagant quota, assigned to us in November last.[29] It carries us too one step towards the formation of a scale of political arithmetic. But I am sorry to believe, that this measure was not dictated by a resolution to pursue system: without which the springs of government must be on a continual stretch, in order to combat occasional necessities, and the expedient of to day may destroy what may be essential to morrow.[30]

Your encomium upon the senate for preserving the reputation of the country is well-founded.[31] But I think they have been unnecessarily jealous of the incroachment attempted to be made by the house of delegates, as they suppose, on the executive. In the course of the session, the defence of our eastern frontier became a topic.[32] Two vessels, which had been purchased from the French after the capitulation of York were destined by the executive for a mercantile expedition.[33] They were actually equipped for the purpose. But it appeared to the house of delegates to be expedient to convert them into instruments of naval war.[34] The senate opposed the measure, assigning as one among other reasons, that the provision in the bill of rights against the confusion of the legislative and executive powers[35] would be defeated, if this conduct sh[ould] be tolerated. They surely were mistaken: for the distinction is, th[at] the authorities, specially delegated by the constitution to the executi[ve] cannot be exercised by the legislative; but authorities derived from the gift of the legislature, are revocable by them. Now in the present instance money was applied by the assembly to the purpose of purchasing these vessels.[36] Why then shall[37] they be precluded from rescinding their own acts? Who will Venture to deny this, when the responsibility of the representative to his constituent is peculiarly necessary in affairs of money; and when the forbidding of the legislature to recal a vot[e] for the disposal of money would be ruinous and unprecedente[d] in almost any government.?

You recollect, that confisc[ated] property has been subjected, as a fund for the discharge of the officers' certificates.[38] At the present session they have been [in] earnest for the adoption of those means, which shall give a m[ore] extensive grasp to confiscation. No man can be so unfeeling or unthankful as to deny, that their merits are great, and their sufferings deserve abundant retribution. Yet I cannot forbea[r] fearing, lest we should precipitate the U. S. into difficulties upon a negotiation, which we might possibly avoid by stoppin[g] at the point, at which we now are. But the motive is too pa[in]ful to be resisted: and I think they will be indulged.[39]

A vote passed the committee of the whole house yesterday for removing the clog on executions. It is probable too, that it will run glibly thro' the assembly.[40] I, whose interest speaks so strongly in favor of the act, do really contemplate it with apprehension.[41] Ravaged as our country has been, the little surplus over domestic want, must be drawn into the public coffers. With what are we to pay our old debts? Is the capital to be absorbed? Mr. Morris's notes, which are receivable in taxes will banish specie pro tanto:[42] and if executions are to be satisfied by specie alone, the poor man, who has disdained to avail himself of the tender law,[43] must part from his freehold at ¼ of its value to some tory, whose debt remains unextinguished because he obstinately refused paper currency. On the other hand it cannot be denied, that some of our best citizens are perhaps perishing from the want of their outstanding debts. But a general law has its eye to the body of the people, not to individuals merely: especially at a season, when they have been harrassed in property and personal service.

There may however be instances in which the suspension should be removed. Future contracts should be enforced speedily and effectually: and if an easy difference could be found in behalf of foreigners, the rights of commerce might require the removal of the suspension in their case even in past contracts. While paper-money was hastening to annihilation, it might be well to render it an object of request by Adding rapidity and sting to the law. But this stimulus is not necessary to furnish credit to the precious metals. Since the above was written, I have been informed, that executions are to be discharged in certain specifics, as well as specie.[44] But this does not lessen the evil. For one of the objections arises from the actual inability of the country: and what very great relief is it to suffer a man to pay tobacco rather than coin, when the price of that very tobacco depends absolutely upon its relation to coin? Unless I shall change my present opinion on this subject, I will certainly counteract it in the line of my profession, as far as my duty to my clients will permit.[45]

A bill is prepared for recruiting our line. The country is classed, and each class is to furnish a man by a given day, or 30 dollars. On failure in these respects it is proposed to subject the faulty class to a draught. Colo. Mercer[46] thinks, that the bill will pass in its present form. But he adds, that Capt. Marshall,[47] a young man of a rising character, will make a furious onset for the abolition of the draught.[48]

Be so good as to communicate the public intelligence, contained herein, to Colo. Bland.[49]

I will send you a copy of a succinct state[50] of the claim of Virginia to Western territory, drawn by a certain violent Anti Whartonian, together with its history[51]

[1] The meaning of "repeating my letters" is not clear. If Randolph used "repeating" in the archaic sense of "repaying," the phrase may signify "writing as often to you as you have written to me." On the other hand, the expression may signify "mentioning in each of my letters the date on which I last wrote to you." Although Randolph obviously was replying to the first paragraph of JM's letter of 11 June (*q.v.*), neither of these suggested interpretations seems to be directly relevant to the contents of that paragraph.

[2] See JM to Randolph, 29 May 1782.

[3] See Randolph to JM, 1 June 1782.

[4] Here Randolph evidently neglected to encode an adjective such as "faithful" or "excellent."

[5] See Harrison to Virginia Delegates, 8 June 1782, n. 5. Randolph is referring to the law of Virginia providing that no delegate of the Commonwealth in Congress could serve for "more than three years in any term of six years" (Hening, *Statutes*, X, 74–75). In view of the fact that JM's first appointment as a delegate was on 14 December 1779 (*Papers of Madison*, I, 318), his eligibility would appear to end in 1782 on 31 October, since the Virginia General Assembly was accustomed to elect

or re-elect its delegates in Congress annually, with the term dating from 1 November. Therefore, the "rigour of law" could be cited by opponents of JM's reappointment. On the other hand, JM's supporters argued, with evident success, that he was eligible for re-election, because his first appointment had been only ad interim to fill the place of one "of the gentlemen who hath resigned" (*Journal of the House of Delegates*, October 1779, p. 89), and that the restriction in the Articles of Confederation was irrelevant in his case, since the Articles had been in effect only since 1 March 1781. See Jones to JM, 25 June 1782.

In the General Assembly, JM was renominated to the Council of State on 3 June, but his name was withdrawn two days later (Minute Book, House of Delegates, May 1782, pp. 60, 62). Who were responsible for these "manoeuvres" is unknown to the editors. The nomination may either have been made by the opponents of JM as a way of supplanting him in Congress, or by his friends as a means of assuring his continuance in public life in the event of his defeat for re-election as a delegate. The withdrawal of his nomination may signify either the increased confidence of his friends by 5 June in the outcome of a vote to return him to Congress for a new term, or a change of opinion by his enemies to the effect that they would prefer to have him in Philadelphia rather than in Richmond.

[6] Randolph wrote this word as a replacement for a deleted "difficult."

[7] A law passed on 13 December 1779 barred a delegate of Virginia in Congress from concurrently holding any state "office judiciary or executive" (*Journal of the House of Delegates*, October 1779, p. 87; Hening, *Statutes*, X, 164). Randolph patently was not of the "executive," being neither the governor nor a member of the Council of State, but his opponents evidently claimed that, as attorney general and hence as an officer of the superior courts of Virginia, he was of the "judiciary," even though not a judge.

[8] Richard Lee, generally known as "Squire Richard Lee" of "Lee Hall" in Westmoreland County, was a member of the House of Delegates from 1777 until his death in 1795. He was a cousin of Arthur and Richard Henry Lee.

[9] Arthur Lee.

[10] Richard Henry Lee.

[11] Unidentified.

[12] Apparently Randolph meant Arthur Lee.

[13] Joseph Jones. Randolph encoded "iones." See Jones to JM, 25 June 1782.

[14] This word is interlineated above a deleted "pretty."

[15] Randolph used the cipher 210, standing for "toward," but probably intended to write 410, signifying "two."

[16] The brackets again signify errors by Randolph in coding. He obviously used an alphabetized code sheet on which "vol" and its cipher 238 immediately preceded "vote" and its cipher 604. He wrote the former rather than the latter figure. For "their," he wrote—as he would do twice again later in this letter—789 rather than 798.

[17] Patrick Henry. See n. 22, below.

[18] Although Randolph encoded 559, symbolizing "hundred," he probably meant to write 557, the cipher for "pri."

[19] After the cipher for "was," Randolph crossed out "absolutely abusive." In view of the last four words of the sentence, he should have deleted the cipher for "was." Arthur Lee was eight years younger than his brother, Richard Henry Lee.

[20] These brackets and the ones enclosing the other "their" in this sentence are explained in n. 16, above.

[21] In the case of "find," Randolph encoded merely the "fi" and neglected to add 344, the symbol for "nd." He also omitted 39 89 542 48, which together stand for "cult."

[22] On 10 October and 10 November 1781 Colonel Thomas Newton, Jr., of Norfolk wrote Governor Harrison that, notwithstanding the law of 30 May 1780 for securing "to the public certain lands heretofore held as common" (*Journal of the House of Delegates*, May 1780, p. 27; Hening, *Statutes*, XI, 226–27), Patrick Henry persisted in laying claim to "the Cape Lands." Private ownership of this acreage might "Effectually stop fishing" there and also deprive the Commonwealth of £10,000 worth of stone designed for use in erecting a lighthouse on Cape Henry (*Calendar of Virginia State Papers*, II, 543, 593). On 6 December 1781, without mentioning Patrick Henry, Harrison referred Newton's complaint against "some designing Persons" to the House of Delegates (McIlwaine, *Official Letters*, III, 106; *Journal of the House of Delegates*, October 1781, p. 29). The members of the General Assembly apparently were content to let the matter rest until the Lees revived it about six months later. Either in 1778 or early in the next year Patrick Henry and John Wilson, Willis Wilson (d. 1798), and George Kelly (d. *ca.* 1802), three residents of Norfolk County, had formed a land company and employed Andrew Stewart (d. 1789) of the same county as surveyor. Although the total expanse amassed by the company has not been ascertained, 6,800 acres on Cape Henry in Norfolk County were granted to Henry and his associates by patents signed by Governor Harrison on 1 June 1782. Nothing in the record of survey suggests that the company had designated a part of the property for the use of fishermen (Norfolk County Court Records, Will Book 3, pp. 14–20, microfilm in Virginia State Library; Virginia State Land Office Surveys, Book 6, p. 117; Virginia State Land Office Grants, Book F, pp. 466–67, 470–71, both in Virginia State Library).

[23] The act of 1 July 1782 "to amend the act for erecting a lighthouse on Cape Henry" suggests that the offer of Patrick Henry "to yield his pretensions," perhaps to the site of the proposed lighthouse and to sufficient stone for its erection, had been accepted and hence the threat to institute a suit against him had been dropped. If Randolph received instructions, they apparently do not exist. Patrick Henry's company evidently retained title to at least much of the property, for Willis Wilson in 1798 bequeathed his share, totaling 3,333 acres, to his heirs (Norfolk County Court Records, Will Book 3, pp. 204–5, microfilm in Virginia State Library). The law of 1 July 1782 provided for the appointment of six "directors," including Thomas Newton, Jr., to handle the financial aspects of "building and finishing the said lighthouse." These men were also named "trustees for the land heretofore and now deemed and held as common" (Minute Book, House of Delegates, May 1782, p. 85; Hening, *Statutes*, XI, 58).

[24] See Randolph to JM, 21–24 May 1782, and n. 22.

[25] See *Papers of Madison*, III, 201, n. 1.

[26] Following the comma, four words are inked out too heavily to be legible.

[27] See Article XX of the Treaty of Amity and Commerce, concluded between France and the United States on 4 May 1778 (*JCC*, XI, 421, 434–35).

[28] The statute, passed on 1 July, provided that on or before 10 December 1782 the clerk of each county court should deliver to the Governor in Council a census listing by families "the number of whites and blacks" in the county (Minute Book, House of Delegates, May 1782, p. 85; Hening, *Statutes*, XI, 40–41).

[29] See *Papers of Madison*, III, 301, n. 2; 328–29; 329, n. 6.

[30] What Randolph expected JM to read into this vaguely worded sentence obviously cannot be known. Enumerating the population of Virginia would enable the General Assembly to assess taxes and assign county levies of militia more equitably. If each of the other twelve states also took a census, the basis for allocating quotas of troops, as stipulated by the ninth article of the Articles of Con-

federation, would finally be provided. Perhaps, too, Randolph and JM had earlier agreed that a census would be an indispensable first step toward substituting a population-proportioned representation of each state in Congress for the existent "system" of according every state, no matter how large or small, an equal vote. See also Report on New Hampshire Requisition, 25 March 1782, n. 3.

31 See JM to Randolph, 11 June 1782.

32 See the law "for defending and protecting the trade of Chesapeake bay," enacted on 1 July 1782 (Minute Book, House of Delegates, p. 85; Hening, *Statutes*, XI, 42–44).

33 The British armed vessels sold to Virginia by the French in October 1781, following Cornwallis' surrender, were the "Cormorant" and the "Oliver Cromwell" (*Calendar of Virginia State Papers*, VI, 414–15; Gardner W. Allen, *A Naval History of the American Revolution* [2 vols.; Boston, 1913], II, 391–92). For their expected use on a "mercantile expedition," see Virginia Delegates to Harrison, 24 January 1782, n. 5.

34 For the resolution of 23 May 1782 to this effect, see *Calendar of Virginia State Papers*, III, 176; McIlwaine, *Official Letters*, III, 229, 241, 250, 252.

35 See Article V of "A Declaration of Rights" and also Article III of "The Constitution, or Form of Government" of Virginia (Hening, *Statutes*, IX, 110, 114).

36 David Ross, commercial agent of Virginia, seems to have purchased the ships, mentioned in n. 33, with funds authorized by the General Assembly on 11 and 14 June 1781 to be used by him "for particular purposes" (*Journal of the House of Delegates*, May 1781, pp. 13, 17; McIlwaine, *Official Letters*, III, 78, 144; *Calendar of Virginia State Papers*, II, 516, 525, 571, 607–8).

37 Randolph inadvertently repeated "shall."

38 This was stipulated in the fifth paragraph of a statute enacted by the Virginia General Assembly on 5 January 1782 (*Journal of the House of Delegates*, October 1781, p. 74; Hening, *Statutes*, X, 464). The certificates had been issued to officers and enlisted men in continental service to offset their loss, caused by the mounting inflation, in the real value of their pay between 1 January 1777 and 31 December 1781.

39 Randolph's expectation was fulfilled on 2 July by the adoption of "An act for providing more effectual funds for the redemption of certificates granted the officers and soldiers raised by this state" (*ibid.*, XI, 81–85; Minute Book, House of Delegates, May 1782, p. 85). To halt the depreciation of veterans' certificates and to acquire money more speedily for their redemption, the statute sought to expedite the sale of the forfeited estates of Loyalists, including property fictitiously conveyed by Loyalists to patriots for safekeeping, and to encourage Virginians in debt to Loyalists or British creditors to pay into the public treasury annually an amount of specie, tobacco, or hemp equal to "one tenth part or more" of the obligation, and thus "be so far exonerated from the same." The provisions of this law later conflicted with the fourth and fifth articles of the Treaty of Paris of 3 September 1783 between Great Britain and the United States.

40 Randolph again prophesied accurately. A law passed on 1 July 1782 and designated to take effect on 1 March of the next year, partially repealed the stay law of 5 January 1782. The new statute authorized the courts of Virginia to entertain suits for the recovery of overdue debts, provided that they had not been contracted with a British subject after 30 April 1777, and that they could be discharged until 1 December 1783 in tobacco, hemp, flour, or money, at the debtor's option (*Journal of the House of Delegates*, October 1781, p. 74; Minute Book, House of Delegates, May 1782, p. 85; Hening, *Statutes*, XI, 75–76).

41 See Randolph to JM, 19 April 1782, n. 8.

42 See Virginia Delegates to Harrison, 19 March 1782, n. 1. On 1 July 1782 the

Virginia General Assembly enacted a statute directing sheriffs and collectors to accept in payment of taxes Robert Morris' notes promising the bearer the sum written on the face of the note whenever it should be presented to the "Treasurer to the Superintendant of Finance" in Philadelphia (Minute Book, House of Delegates, May 1782, p. 85; Hening, *Statutes*, XI, 68–69). At this time Morris' notes apparently were circulating at face value in the upper South but were subject to varying degrees of discount in New York and New England. Morris decided late in August 1782 to stop issuing the notes and to destroy them as they were presented (Clarence L. Ver Steeg, *Robert Morris*, pp. 80–81, 87, 118–19).

[43] Randolph refers to the law adopted by the Virginia General Assembly on 5 January 1782 specifying a monthly scale of depreciation of paper currency from January 1777 to December 1781 for determining "the value of the several debts, contracts and demands" in silver and gold (*Journal of the House of Delegates*, October 1781, p. 74; Hening, *Statutes*, X, 471–74). This legal exchange ratio overvalued the paper currency as compared with its market value in terms of specie. The law was in part repealed by the act of 1 July 1782 cited in n. 40, above.

[44] See nn. 39 and 40, above.

[45] That is, as a practicing lawyer.

[46] John Francis Mercer, a representative of Stafford County in the House of Delegates.

[47] John Marshall, a representative of Fauquier County in the House of Delegates, late captain in the 7th Virginia Regiment, continental line, and a future Chief Justice of the United States.

[48] "An act for recruiting this state's quota of troops to serve in the army of the United States," enacted on 2 July 1782 (Minute Book, House of Delegates, May 1782, p. 86; Hening, *Statutes*, XI, 14–20). The complicated provisions of this law were designed to raise for three years or for the duration of the war three thousand able-bodied men between the ages of eighteen and fifty years. Each county was to be divided into equally populated "classes or districts," according to the number of recruits allotted to that county. Any class or district failing to furnish the soldiers required would be subject to a monetary fine. From those men upon whom this fine was imposed but who refused or were unable to pay it, one man would be drafted for military service. Each man so enlisted, whether as a volunteer or by lot or by draft "by fair and equal ballot," was promised an immediate money bounty of £12 and a bounty in land, scaled to his rank, at the termination of his service.

[49] Theodorick Bland.

[50] Randolph underlined "succinct State."

[51] Arthur Lee. See JM to Pendleton, 23 April, n. 8; Randolph to JM, 10 May 1782, n. 7.

Benjamin Harrison to Virginia Delegates

FC (Virginia State Library). In the hand of Thomas Meriwether.

VIRGA. IN COUNCIL June 22d. 1782

GENTLEMEN

The plan laid for bringing over the Stores is most unaccountably frustrated by the Assembly.[1] Our deficiency in arms and Ammunition is so truely alarming that I feel real distress, whenever I think of our situation. If you cannot get them brought over by our good friends the French[2] they will probably remain where they are til the end of the War and our country will fall a prey to the first invader. The Assembly have now entered on the Subject of recruiting the Army. I do not know the plan proposed but am sure with a good bounty men may be got[3] That the French fleet has been beaten & that they have lost their Admiral & five or Six of their ships admits of no doubt. There is a man in this Town who informs us that he was a prisoner in Jamaica & saw Count de Grass with Admiral Rodney going to dine with the Governor.[4] He also tells us that Rodneys fleet was so battered that only eighteen of them could be made fit for service for some considerable time. If this is true Jamaica may yet fall[5] I am &c

P. S. I laid the proposals of the Polish Gentleman before the Assembly immediately, they have not yet given me their determination, tho' I think it impossible for them to comply with the terms if they were ever so willing to accept them[6]

B H.

[1] See Randolph to JM, 20 June 1782, and nn. 33 and 34.

[2] See Virginia Delegates to Harrison, 4 June 1782.

[3] See Randolph to JM, 20 June 1782, and n. 48.

[4] Brigadier General Archibald Campbell (1739–1791), then lieutenant governor but to be appointed governor of Jamaica in July 1782.

[5] See JM to Pendleton, 23 April, n. 3; Pendleton to JM, 20 May, n. 10; JM to Lee, 28 May, n. 11; Barbé-Marbois Letter, 9 June 1782. Before writing the present dispatch, the governor may have read this 9 June letter, because it was printed in the *Virginia Gazette* of 22 June. The former "prisoner in Jamaica" has not been identified.

[6] See Virginia Delegates to Harrison, 4 June, and n. 7; and 18 June 1782. Governor Harrison had referred the proposal of Count Bieniewsky to the General Assembly on 13 June 1782 (McIlwaine, *Official Letters*, III, 250).

Virginia Delegates to Benjamin Harrison

RC (Virginia State Library). In JM's hand, except for Bland's signature. Docketed, "Lr. f'm Del. in Congress June 25 82."

PHILADA. 25th. June 1782.

SIR

Your Excellency's favor of the 15th.[1] came safe to hand yesterday. The loss of the mail of the preceding week[2] is the more regretted, as we understand that a packet from N. York for England which had been intercepted and carried into N. Carolina, made a part of it.

A private letter from Mr. Adams dated the 11th. of April informs his correspondent, that Friesland[,] Holland, Zealand, Overyssell and Utrecht had decided in favour of an immediate connection with the U. States and that Guelderland & Zutphen, it was expected, would follow their example in a few days. A Leyden Gazette of a posterior date says that six provinces had then concurred.[3] Their public concils seem to have been greatly stimulated to this decisive conduct, by the zeal of the Merchants who profess their fears that unless a treaty be speedily concluded with America, a pacification may exclude their commerce from some of the advantages which England may obtain. They observe also that the Ordinance of Congress against British Manufactures,[4] presents a favorable crisis for introducing those of other nations, and that commercial connection with the U. States, tending to supplant the commerce of Britain will be the most likely means of disposing her to an immediate acquiescence in the American Revolution & to a general peace.

The illicit trade with N. York under the encouragement of the enemy, and the obstruction of foreign trade has increased of late so far as to threaten great injury to the public finances.[5] The steps which have been taken by Congress on this subject will be transmitted to your Excellency by the President.[6] It is also discovered that supplies of British goods are imported under collusive captures concerted between Vessels from N. York and Vessels fitted out on the neighbouring coasts. This part of the evil is more within the jurisdiction of Congress, and a remedy for it is now under consideration.[7]

With great respect We have the honor to be Yr. Excelly's obt. & hbl. servants

J. MADISON JR.
THEOK. BLAND[8]

[1] Not found.

[2] See Virginia Delegates to Harrison, 18 June; Report on Mail Robbery, 19 June 1782, and nn. 3 and 4.

[3] John Adams' "private letter" of 11 April 1782 was to James Searle (Letter of Lyman H. Butterfield to William M. E. Rachal, 23 April 1964). The *Pennsylvania Packet* of 20 and 25 June and the *Pennsylvania Journal* of 22 June apparently do not mention the "Leyden Gazette," although they furnish news similar in tenor to that of this paragraph. JM may also have seen "a letter, dated Amsterdam, March 28," prior to the publication of an extract from it in the *Journal* of 26 June 1782. John Adams' dispatch of 19[–?] April, telling of "his reception as a Minister"

on 22 April by the States-General, was not received by Congress until 11 September 1782 (NA: PCC, No. 185, III, 41; Burnett, *Letters*, VI, 471, 473; Wharton, *Revolutionary Diplomatic Correspondence*, V, 315–19). See also Report on Salaries of Representatives Abroad, 28 May, n. 11; JM to Jones, 28 May 1782, and n. 19.

[4] See *Papers of Madison*, III, 338–39.

[5] See JM to Randolph, 18 June 1782, and n. 9.

[6] See Report on Illicit Trade, 19 June 1782, and nn. 8 and 11.

[7] The ninth of the Articles of Confederation conferred upon Congress "the sole and exclusive right and power" of "establishing rules for deciding in all cases, what captures on land or water shall be legal" (*JCC*, XIX, 217). See also Randolph to JM, 16–17 May 1782, and n. 9.

[8] The second and third paragraphs of this letter, unidentified as to sender or recipient, appeared in the *Virginia Gazette* of 6 July 1782. In the third paragraph, "you" was substituted for "your Excellency by the President" and "immediately" inserted before "transmitted."

From Joseph Jones

RC (LC: Madison Papers). Docketed, "June 25. 1782."

Spring Hill 25th June 1782

Dr. Sr.

Your favor of the 4th. instant[1] and the packet of Newspapers by Mr. Webb went to Richmond[2] and were returned to Fredericksburg where I received them the last week but no letter from you by that post. From Richmond I had written you a long letter and geting home in time for the post at Fredericksburg added a short one of some other matters that occured after my geting home.[3] these Letters I am told last night have been intercepted near Onions works in Maryland[4] and carryed (probably) to Sr. Guy Carleton before this and you will I expect have an opportunity of reading them in the royal Gazette[5] soon to which I must refer you for their contents having no Copy and not well recollecting the whole. I fear there are some observations I could wish not to be public. If any such they must relate to some transactions of the Assembly or individual members but I think none of them very reprehensible though[6] known to the parties. I was particular respecting the petition you mentioned to have been communicated to the Minister[7] and this may induce a publication. I mentd. the continuation of the old Delegates by a vote but wch. I afterwards found to be a mistake the vote being postponed untill the Bill had passed repealing the Law that rendered yourself and J. J. ineligible[8]—the allowance 8 dols. P day—no directions given for the settlement of the time past although the sense of the House asked by the Auditors respecting the daily allowance.[9]

Jefferson Mason Randolph Lee & Walker have been appointed to State the Title of Virga. to western territory—Com: to draw instructions for Delegates respecting western territory.[10]

Ct. Beneouski had not reached Richmond when I left it but hear since he was there but not likely to succeed this days post will I expect communicate the result of his application.[11]

In the intercepted Letter I transmitted you a Bill of Mr. Ross's on whitesides in my favor for two hundred and some dollars to pay Mr. C Griffin or if he was not in immediate want a Messr. Baker & Co. wch. Mr. Solomon could inform you of.[12] I that week recd. a line from my friend Griffin requesting a remittance of the money. I have wrote to day to Mr. Ross to renew the draft & forward it to me & it shall go forward as soon as I receive it.[13] pray present my Compliments to Mr. Griffin and acquaint him wth. this circumstance. I have not yet concluded on my return to Philadelphia but think I shall do it at least for the fall if I can prevail upon Mrs. Jones to accompany me with Joe. she is now up in Orange on a visit to her Father.[14] If I visit Phila: it will be about the middle or twentieth next month you will therefore be so obliging as to inquire abt. a lodging furnished, with two lodging rooms servts. room, and two entertaining rooms & the use of the Kitchen or a convenient House furnished that if I come up you may be able to engage me one upon as moderate terms as you can. as soon as I make up my mind upon the Journey you shall be informed. Mr. Lee[15] has I expect joined you as he was to set out in a few days after my leaving him in Richmond. pray make my compliments to Col. Bland & Mr Lee if present & believe me

yr. Friend

JOS: JONES

[1] Not found. See JM to Randolph, 4 June 1782, and n. 30.

[2] Foster Webb, Jr., arrived in Richmond from Philadelphia on 14 June. See JM to Randolph, 6 June; and Randolph to JM, 15 June 1782.

[3] Neither the long nor the short letter has been found. The duration of Jones's visit to Richmond is obscure. On 21 May (*q.v.*), writing to JM from Spring Hill, Jones stated that he probably would be in Richmond in "eight or ten days." Jones's stay in the town was evidently brief, because he left there ahead of the postrider who carried Governor Harrison's letter of 8 June 1782 to the delegates in Congress (*q.v.*, n. 1; also the third sentence of the present letter).

[4] The mail had been intercepted as the postrider was "passing Gravely-Hill in the forest between Onions's old iron-works and Harford-town" (*Virginia Gazette*, 29 June 1782).

[5] Rivington's *Royal Gazette* of New York City. See JM to Randolph, 18 June 1782, and n. 5.

[6] The meaning would be clearer if, instead of "though," Jones had written, "even though they should become." See Randolph to JM, 20 June 1782, for Randolph's comment about how Jones, when in Richmond, had been "very warm" in his criticism of the Lees.

[7] La Luzerne, French minister to the United States. See JM to Jones, 28 May 1782, and n. 15.

[8] Jones ("J. J.") viewed the attack as being directed against him and JM rather than against JM and Randolph (Randolph to JM, 20 June 1782, and n. 5). The constitutional or statutory limitation upon the duration of a delegate's tenure in Congress applied equally to JM and Jones. Since 14 December 1779, when the General Assembly had elected both of them, their terms as delegates had been of the same duration (*Papers of Madison*, I, 318; III, 161).

[9] The auditors were Bolling Stark, Harrison Randolph, and John Boush. Their letter requesting a scale of depreciation whereby the long overdue per diem allowance of the delegates from Virginia in Congress could be determined had been received by the House of Delegates on 4 June 1782 (Minute Book, House of Delegates, May 1782, p. 61).

[10] See Randolph to JM, 1 June 1782, and n. 3.

[11] See Harrison to Virginia Delegates, 22 June, and n. 6; 29 June 1782, and n. 2. When, if ever, Count Bieniewsky visited Richmond has not been ascertained.

[12] David Ross, Peter Whiteside, Cyrus Griffin, and Haym Salomon. Jones's letter to JM on 16 July 1782 (*q.v.*) identifies "Baker & Co." as "Baker Potts & Co. Iron-mongers" near the corner of Second and Arch Streets, Philadelphia. Baker may have been Hilary Baker (1750–1798), an "iron merchant" (*Pennsylvania Magazine of History and Biography*, X [1886], 450). Potts was probably Thomas Potts (1735–1785), an ironmonger (*ibid.*, IV [1880], 226).

[13] See Jones to JM, 1, 8, and 16 July 1782.

[14] See Jones to JM, 21 May 1782, n. 11. "Joe" (1780–*ca.* 1808) was the son of Jones and his second wife, Mary Waugh Dawson (George H. S. King, comp. and ed., *Marriages of Richmond County, Virginia*, p. 249).

[15] Arthur Lee, who resumed his seat in Congress on 27 June 1782 (*JCC*, XXII, 354).

To Arthur Lee

RC (Harvard University Library). Cover missing. About one-third of the last four lines on the left-hand side of the first page of the manuscript, and about the same fraction of the last four lines on the right-hand side of the second page of the manuscript, are missing.

PHILADA. 25th. June 1782.

DEAR SIR

The bill which you lately inclosed to me[1] was duly honored, and the contents of it are in my hands subject to any order which you may wish to give.

A private letter from Mr. Adams of the 11th. of April, informs his correspondent that Friesland Holland, Utrecht, Zealand & Overyssel had taken decided resolutions for a treaty with the U. States; and that like resolutions might be expected in a few days from the two remaining provinces.[2] A Leyden paper of posterior date, says that six provinces had concurred in this measure. This revolution[3] ap[pear]s t[o have] been exceedingly stimulated by the [int]erest which apprehended that if th[e] was lost, they might be excluded tion from some of the commercial privileges which England may obtain.[4] It is observed in a long memorial from the Merchants to the States General that, the importance of the American trade was experienced by them very sensibly prior to the loss of St. Eustatius,[5] as it has been throughout the war by France; that the Ordinance of Congress agst. British Manufactures[6] presents a precious season for substituting those of other nations, & that this season ought the rather to be improved as nothing will be so likely to open the ears of G. B. to the demands of the U. S. & to a general peace, as the prospect of being supplanted in the commercial preference, which she still expects from the habits of America.

The trafic with the Enemy's lines, had increased to so great a degree that it was thought necessary for Congress to renew their exhortations to the States upon this subject,[7] and to summ of the people in aid of the public Resolutions will be laid before you tive character. We also understand cious intercourse with the Enemy is carryed on under collusive captures preconcerted between Vessels from N.Y. & vessels fitted out on the neighbouring coasts This abuse lies more within the purview of Congress and a remedy for it is now under consideration. If the trade with N.Y. cannot be suppressed by some means or other it will very shortly steal from us all our hard money, and render our taxations abortive.[8]

I am Dr. Sir with much respect Yr obt friend & servt.

J MADISON JR.

[1] See Lee to JM, 16 May; and JM to Lee, 28 May 1782.

[2] See Virginia Delegates to Harrison, 25 June 1782, and n. 3.

[3] See JM to Randolph, 7 May 1782, n. 3. By "revolution," JM apparently meant that the sudden and strong trend in the Netherlands toward recognizing the independence of the United States had come as a surprise in view of John Adams' pessimistic comments expressed in his letter of 11 March, the latest received from him by Congress until 11 September 1782 (NA: PCC, No. 186, III, 29, 31, 35, 41).

[4] The purport of these fragmentary sentences is clearly the same as that of the corresponding portion of the second paragraph of the Virginia delegates' letter of 25 June to Governor Harrison (*q.v.*).

[5] See *Papers of Madison*, III, 28, n. 11. JM refers to the memorial of Dutch "merchants, manufacturers, and other inhabitants living by commerce in this country"

to the "States-General of the United Provinces." A copy of this memorial, together with copies of other petitions and letters of the same tenor, was enclosed by Adams in his dispatch of 19 March 1782 to Robert R. Livingston (Wharton, *Revolutionary Diplomatic Correspondence*, V, 251–54). Congress must have received copies of the memorial by 25 June from another correspondent, because this letter of Adams did not reach Livingston until 12 November 1782 (NA: PCC, No. 186, III, 48). Extracts from the memorial appeared in the *Pennsylvania Packet* of 2 July 1782.

[6] See *Papers of Madison*, III, 338–39.

[7] See JM to Randolph, 18 June, and n. 7; Report on Illicit Trade, 19 June 1782.

[8] See the third paragraph of the Virginia delegates' letter of 25 June to Governor Harrison; also Report on Illicit Trade, 19 June 1782, n. 11.

To Edmund Pendleton

RC (New York Public Library). Docketed by Pendleton, "James Maddison Jr. Esq June 25th. 1782." The cover is missing.

PHILADA. 25th. June 1782

DEAR SIR

Your favor of the 17th. escaped the accident which befel that of the preceeding week.[1] The loss of the mail is the more regretted as we now understand that a packet from N.Y. to England, which had been intercepted & carried into N. Carolina, made a part of it.

No authentic account of the fleet which sailed from N.Y. is yet come to hand.[2] The prevailing & I fancy the true conjecture now is that it contained a parcel of miserable Refugees who are doomed to exchange the fancied confiscations of their countrymen for the bleak & barren settlement in Nova Scotia or Penobscot.[3]

The illicit trade with N.Y. has under the auspices of the new system of the Enemy, been carried to such an extent, that the interposition of Congress in some form or other seemed to be called for. The only form which seemed to consist with constitutional propriety, was a renewal of their exhortation to the States, to exert their utmost legislative skill in suppressing it by land; & to impress on people the fatal effects of a continuance of it, and the necessity of their patriotic cooperation with the public measures in bringing transgressors to due punishment.[4] This trade is also carried on by water, under collusive captures of Vessels from N.Y. by little vessels fitted out on the neighbouring Coasts. The remedy for this part of the evil is more within the authority of Congress, and an application of it is now agitating.[5] Nothing can prevent the evil by land but a voluntary combination among the people at large to find out & prosecute the authors of it.

How far this will take place is uncertain. As it is dictated by the interest of the army, and of the Farmers, who feel the loss of the specie which goes to the Enemy, and by the fair traders who are undersold by the smugglers; as well as by every principle of Duty,[6] some efforts may justly be expected.

Congress have received no letters of very late date from Mr. Adams, but there is a private letter here of the 11th. April, in which he informs his correspondent, that all the Provinces except two had with astonishing unanimity & rapidity decided in favor of a connexion with the U. States; and that no doubt was entertained that the remaining two would in a few days follow the example of the others. Some Gazettes of later date have reduced the exception to a single province.[7] Upon the whole we have suffi[ci]ent ground to expect in a little time, a full & formal recognition of our Independence in that quarter. Their public councils are stimulated much by the zeal of the Merchants, who fear that unless commercial stipulations are speedily concluded, a peace with Britain[8] may place their trade under a disadvantageous competition with that both of England & of France.[9]

I am Dr Sir with sincere regard Yr. obt friend & Servt.

J. MADISON JR.

The Gazette of this morning[10] is so barren that I thought it wd. be less interesting that[11] one of wednesday last, which contains a very singular production of the American Loyali[s]ts.[12]

---

[1] Pendleton's letter, probably dated 10 June, may have been in the mail intercepted in Maryland on 15 June (Report on Mail Robbery, 19 June, n. 3; Pendleton to JM, 1 July 1782).

[2] See Virginia Delegates to Harrison, 4 June 1782, n. 14. JM mentioned this matter in his letter of 11 June to Randolph (*q.v.*) and probably wrote to the same effect on that day to Pendleton.

[3] Under orders from General Clinton, a British force from Nova Scotia in June 1778 had taken "post on the River Penobscot, by way of securing a place of reception and a permanent establishment in the Province of Maine for the King's loyal American subjects who had been driven from their habitations and deprived of their property by the rebels" (William B. Willcox, ed., *American Rebellion*, pp. 134–35). On 23 May 1782 Sir Guy Carleton directed the evacuation, with all possible secrecy, from Savannah and St. Augustine of as many civilian Loyalists as wished to depart with the British garrisons (Historical Manuscripts Commission, eds., *Report on American Manuscripts in the Royal Institution of Great Britain* [4 vols.; London, 1904–9], II, 494), but no mass movement of Loyalists from New York was to take place until after the signing of the peace treaty in 1783.

[4] See JM to Randolph, 18 June, and n. 7; Report on Illicit Trade, 19 June 1782, and n. 8.

[5] See Report on Illicit Trade, 19 June, n. 11; Virginia Delegates to Harrison, 25 June 1782, n. 7.

[6] Following this comma, JM crossed out about four words so heavily that they are illegible.

[7] See Virginia Delegates to Harrison, 25 June 1782, n. 3.

[8] "Britain" is followed by a heavily inked-out passage of perhaps five words which cannot now be read.

[9] See JM to Lee, 25 June 1782, n. 5.

[10] The *Pennsylvania Packet* of 25 June 1782.

[11] JM obviously meant to write "than."

[12] The *Pennsylvania Gazette* of 19 June reprinted from the *London Chronicle* of 9 March 1782, "The humble and dutiful DECLARATION and ADDRESS of his Majesty's American LOYALISTS To the King's Most Excellent Majesty, to both Houses of Parliament, and the People of Great Britain." After stressing their unfaltering allegiance in spite of the loss of property and other severe hardships to which they had been subjected, the petitioners devoted most of their lengthy memorial to a criticism of British military policy on three principal grounds: (1) for stationing Loyalist soldiers far from their homes or merging them into the British regular army; (2) for successively occupying and evacuating one American city after another—a "desultory manner" of waging war which could not subdue the rebels but merely incited them to inflict harsh punishments upon the Loyalists in those cities; and (3) for not recognizing that a maintenance of naval superiority in American waters would speedily crush the rebellion. The memorial closed with an affirmation that "our cause is the cause of legal and constitutional government throughout the world." In view of this fact, the petitioners believed that if European monarchs were appealed to for aid, they would assist Great Britain in her hour of great need.

To Edmund Randolph

RC (LC: Madison Papers). Unsigned letter in JM's hand. The cover is missing. Randolph wrote his own name in the lower left-hand margin of the first page of the manuscript. Probably many years later JM or someone at his bidding placed a bracket at the beginning of the first paragraph and another bracket at the close of the fifth paragraph to designate that portion of the letter for publication. See Madison, *Papers* [Gilpin ed.], I, 144–45.

PHILADA. 25th. of June 1782

DEAR SIR

Your favor of the 15th. being more fortunate than the preceding one came safe to hand yesterday. The loss of the mail is the more provoking as it is said to have contained a packet from N.Y. which had been intercepted on its passage to England & carried into N. Carolina.[1]

The illicit trade with the British lines has been pushed so far under the encouragement of the enemy as to threaten a deep wound to our Finances. Congress have renewed their exhortation to the States on this subject and recommended to the people, through them, a patriotic co-operation with the public measures.[2] This trade we have also discovered is carried on with considerable effect, under collusive captures. This branch of the iniquity falls properly within the purview of Congress and an ordinance for its excision is in the hands of a Committee.[3]

A private letter from Mr. Adams of the 11th. of April informs his correspondent that 5 of the 7 provinces had decided in favor of a Treaty with the U. S. and that the concurrence of the remaining 2 might be expected in a few days. A Leyden paper of a subsequent date, reduces the exception to a single Province. It would seem from a Memorial from the Merchants to the States General, that this revolution had been greatly stimulated by an apprehension that a sudden pacification might exclude their commerce from some of the advantages which England may obtain.[4]

The Memorial appeals to the effect of the American trade on the resources of France, & to the short & indirect experience of it which Holland enjoyed before the loss of St. Eustation,[5] as proof of its immense consequence. It observes also that the Ordinance of Congress agst. British Manufactures presented a precious crisis for introducing those of other nations; which ought to be the rather embraced, as nothing would be so likely to dispose Britain to the Independence of America & a general peace, as the prospect of her being supplanted in the commercial preference expected from the habits of her lost Provinces.

The present conjecture with regard to the fleet mentioned in my late letters, is, that it conveyed a parcel of miserable refugees who are destined to exchange the fancied confiscations of their rebellious Countrymen, for a cold and barren settlement in Nova Scotia or Penobscot.[6]

A Foreign paper has reinstated Hyder Ally in his superiority over Sr. Eyre Coote. Major General Monk is numbered among the slain in the battle which produced this reverse of fortune to the British arms.[7]

I hear nothing from Mr. Jones.[8] Tell him if he is at Richmond that this is the reason why he does not hear directly from me. Instead of the paper of this morning which is uncommonly barren, I send you one of wednesday last which contains a very curious remonstrance from the disconsolate Loyalists.[9]

[1] See Report on Mail Robbery, 19 June 1782, n. 3.

[2] See JM to Randolph, 18 June, and n. 7; Report on Illicit Trade, 19 June 1782, and n. 8.

[3] See Report on Illicit Trade, 19 June, n. 11; Virginia Delegates to Harrison, 25 June 1782, n. 7.

[4] See Virginia Delegates to Harrison, 25 June, n. 3; JM to Lee, 25 June 1782, n. 5.

[5] See *Papers of Madison*, III, 338–39; for the capture of the island of St. Eustatius by the British, see *ibid.*, III, 28, n. 11.

[6] See JM to Pendleton, 25 June 1782, n. 3.

[7] See *Papers of Madison*, III, 298, n. 4. The source of JM's information is unknown. The *Pennsylvania Packet* of 2 July reported a speech made in the House of Commons on 9 April presenting a "gloomy picture" of the situation in India. Following Lieutenant General Sir Eyre Coote's (1726–1783) defeat of Haidar Ali (1722–1782) at Porto Novo in July 1781, the course of the Second Mysore War in India favored now the one and now the other of these antagonists until the autumn of 1782, when ill health obliged each of them to relinquish his command to a less able successor (E[ric] W[illiam] Sheppard, *Coote Bahadur: A Life of Lieutenant-General Sir Eyre Coote, K.B.* [London, 1956], pp. 136–70, *passim*). Major General Monk has not been identified. No officer with that surname and rank served in the Second Mysore War. The *Virginia Gazette* of 6 July 1782 repeated the misinformation and stated that it accorded with what had appeared in "Late European papers."

[8] See Jones to JM, 25 June 1782.

[9] See JM to Pendleton, 25 June 1782, n. 12.

Report on Maritime Prizes

MS (NA: PCC, No. 28, fols. 235, 237). The first of these folios is in Samuel Wharton's hand, the second in JM's. Docketed: "Ordinance respecting prizes–The Committee consisting of Mr. Wharton, Mr. Madison, Mr. Osgood to whom was referred a letter of the 20 of June from the Agent of Marine, propose the inclosed ordinance–Read June 26, 1782 Ent'd. July 3d. 1782 Fryday next assigned for Second reading. July 5, 1782 Recommitted July 9. Read a first and second time. To morrow assigned for the 3d reading Passed July 10. 1782." The meaning of "No. 12.," which Charles Thomson added to the docket, is unknown.

EDITORIAL NOTE

Congress appointed the above committee on 21 June, after listening to a letter to President Hanson written the day before by Robert Morris, agent of marine (*JCC*, XXII, 344, n. 2; NA: PCC, No. 137, I, 559–66). Morris pointed out that although the U. S. frigate "Deane," commanded by Samuel Nicholson, had captured during April and May 1782 a total of five British naval vessels, privateers, and merchantmen, the money accruing to the treasury from these prizes would equal only about one-half of what it had cost the United States to make this successful cruise possible by outfitting the frigate and paying the wages of her officers and crew. On the other hand, the same ordinances of Congress which restricted the United States to so small a return from these captures assured to the complement of the frigate a handsome bonus in prize money and bounties (*JCC*, III, 386–87; IV, 36–37; VI, 954; XIX, 314–16; XXI, 1153–58; XXII, 10–11).

In Morris' view, the intent of Congress in providing these generous rewards had been to encourage American sailors to attack and conquer the enemy's armed vessels "of equal or superior force." The prizes of the "Deane," on the contrary, were "taken with no other trouble than what attended the chase, nor any other risque than the firing of one or two of the frigates guns, as a signal for the prizes to haul down their colours." For this reason and to make "the expense of supporting the marine" less burdensome, Morris suggested that hereafter the United States keep one-half of the prize money, except in instances of unusual heroism when Congress should decide to give officers and crew a special award in the form of a larger percentage of the net return from a captured ship.

JM's membership on the Board of Admiralty between 22 March and 6 June 1780 and his subsequent interest in maritime affairs probably account for his appointment to the present committee (*Papers of Madison*, II, 4, and n. 2; III, 25, n. 27; 217, editorial note; 218–19, and nn.; 236, editorial note). In August and September 1781, when suggesting changes to the proposed congressional ordinance on captures at sea, JM evidently had not foreseen the inequities that were now being pointed out by Morris (*ibid.*, III, 237–41, and nn.).

[26 June–10 July 1782]

An Ordinance for[1] the better distribution of prizes in certain cases.

Be it ordained by the United States in Congress Assembled that so much of the Ordinance entitled "An Ordinance ascertaining what captures on water shall be lawful," as ordains that upon the capture of a vessel commissioned as a man of war or a privateer, by any of the Vessels of war of the United States of America, the whole of the property condemned shall be adjudged to the Captors, be and the same is hereby repealed;[2] and that in all such cases of capture;[3]

And Be it further ordained by the authority aforesaid that the Resolution of the 15th. of Nov. 1776 giving[4] to the Commanders, officers & men of ships or Vessels of war, a[5] bounty for every cannon, and for every man belonging to British Ships or vessels of war, captured by them,[6] be & the same is hereby repealed.

Done by the U. S. in Congress Assembled &c

[1] After this word, JM at first wrote and deleted "rendering the support of the Marine less expensive." He then interlineated "the better distribution" and completed the title with "of prizes in certain cases." Whether this alteration and the other alterations noted below were made within the committee or represent amendments by Congress has not been ascertained. As indicated in the headnote and the first paragraph of the editorial note, nearly twenty days intervened between the appointment of the committee and the adoption of its revised report. The exact sequence of the alterations in time is unknown.

[2] The ordinance of 4 December 1781, principally drafted by Edmund Randolph. See *JCC*, XXI, 1153–58, and especially pp. 1156–57.

[3] Following this semicolon JM wrote and deleted: "the property condemned shall be decreed;—one half thereof to the United States, and the other half to the Captors, to be divided among them in the proportions as within said Ordinance are directed, unless the U. S. in Congress Assembled shall in reward of conspicuous valour and exertions otherwise specially direct."

Perhaps Congress' refusal to accept this passage explains why the report was recommitted on 5 July, following its second reading on that date (see headnote). It may have been then that JM interlineated an asterisk above the semicolon, repeated the asterisk in the margin of the manuscript, and wrote: "of the property condemned one half only shall be adjudged to the Captors, and the other half to the U. S. to be appropriated to their use; unless the Vessel taken be of equal or superior force, in which case the whole shall be adjudged to the Captors; and unless the U. S. in Congress Assembled shall in reward of distinguished valour & exertion otherwise specially direct."

Possibly at the same time, Samuel Wharton tried his hand at redrafting the passage by writing on a separate sheet (fol. 235): "the whole of the Property condemned shall be adjudged to the use of the Captors if the Vessell taken shall be of equal or Superiour Force to the Vessell making the Capture; otherwise one Half only shall be adjudged to the Captors & the other Half to the use of the united States & shall after Condemnation be so appropriated unless the U. S. in Congress assembled in Reward of distinguished Valour & Exertion shall otherwise specially direct." Whether the committee chose Wharton's version rather than JM's before submitting its revised report on 9 July, or decided to let Congress select one or the other or reject both, is not known. The ordinance as adopted the next day embodied what Wharton had written (*JCC*, XXII, 379–80). JM's marginal emendation has lines drawn across it.

[4] Following this word, JM wrote and struck out "a bounty of."

[5] Here JM interlineated and deleted "an indiscriminate."

[6] *JCC*, VI, 954. By this resolution Congress had promised a bounty of $20.00 "to the commanders, officers and men of such continental ships or vessels of war, as shall make prize of any British ships or vessels of war, for every cannon mounted on board each prize, at the time of such capture, and 8 dollars per head for every man then on board and belonging to such prize."

From Edmund Randolph

RC (LC: Madison Papers). Unsigned and undocketed letter in Randolph's hand. The cover is missing.

VIRGINIA June 27. 1782.

DEAR SIR

The capture of the mail, announced in your favor of the 18th. instant,[1] cannot thro' my means avail the enemy, nor give pain to either of us. It is impossible indeed to recollect the contents of my letter, as it was leng[thy] but I believe, that the cypher was scarcely necessary for the evelopment of any of them. But The[2] accident is an irrefragable reason against parsimony in using it in our future confidential intercourse.

I wrote to Colo. Bland and yourself fully by the last post, gleaning for your information every scrap of legislative intelligence.[3] Since that date Mr. Henry and Mr. R. H. Lee have left the assembly: the members of which seem resolved to adjourn the day after tomorrow.[4] In order to accomplish this, they have discharged the standing committees from the business, referred to them, meet at nine o'clock, and confine themselves to Matters of real weight.

A bill has passed the house of delegates for the appropriation of the public revenue.[5] No particular sum is allotted for the treasury of the U. S. But the balance, after certain objects shall be satisfied, is destined for Phila. I shall endeavour to obtain a more accurate knowledge of the probable amount of this balance;[6] and will therefore only remind you at present of two data for calculation, which I mentioned to you in a former letter,[7] the division of the payment into two instalments, and the commutability of the taxes for tobacco at 25s/pr. ct. wt. Rappahannock tobacco does not now exceed 16/. nor James river 20/.[8]

The assembly seem disposed to indulge the inhabitants of Kentucky with a separate court. I think the measure is wise; as it may retard the separation, at least until a fitter day. It is enormous to bring criminals from the distance of 400 miles for trial, and to oblige the poor settlers to travel hither for the adjustment of their disputes, at the expence perhaps of an half of their little capital.[9]

June 29.

The legislature will not rise before tuesday.[10]

The recruiting bill will pass the delegates today. The men are to be demanded from each county according to the number of militia, and the property of each division in a county is to [be] assessed for raising a bounty. With this bounty, which is not yet decided, indeed with less, if it be possible, a man is to be raised by voluntary inlistment. But a draught is to be adopted with respect to the divisions, which [s]hall fail to raise a man or the bounty.[11]

The mode of settling our past accounts has been changed; I am to[ld] much to the advantage of you, whose frugality brought your disbur[se]ments within so small a compass. We are allowed a ½ Johs. by the day. The new provision for future support is the same.[12]

1 See Report on Mail Robbery, 19 June 1782, and n. 3.

2 After interlineating "But," Randolph neglected to change the succeeding "T" to lower case.

[3] See Randolph to JM, 20 June 1782.

[4] Although Patrick Henry's last recorded appearance in the House of Delegates was on 19 June, he evidently continued there until some day between 20 and 27 June. On 20 June Richard Henry Lee was given "leave for remainder" of the session. On 28 June the Senate was notified by the House of Delegates of its determination to adjourn on 2 July and reconvene on 21 October 1782 (Minute Book, House of Delegates, May 1782, pp. 75, 76, 83).

[5] On 22 June (*ibid.*, p. 78).

[6] See Randolph to JM, 1 June 1782, n. 9.

[7] Probably in the intercepted dispatch mentioned in the first paragraph of this letter.

[8] Randolph refers to "an act to amend 'the act for ascertaining certain taxes and duties, and for establishing a permanent revenue,'" which became law on 1 July 1782 (Minute Book, House of Delegates, May 1782, p. 82; Hening, *Statutes*, XI, 66–71). Although this measure left unaltered the provision of the parent statute of 5 January 1782, specifying that tobacco would be accepted in payment of taxes at the rate of twenty-five shillings a hundredweight (*Journal of the House of Delegates*, October 1781, p. 74; Hening, *Statutes*, X, 501–17), it required only 50 per cent of the obligation, rather than 100 per cent as in the original law, to be met on 1 July. The remaining half would be due on 1 November 1782.

[9] See Jefferson to JM, 24 March, n. 5; Pendleton to JM, 27 May 1782, and n. 11.

[10] See n. 4, above.

[11] See Randolph to JM, 20 June 1782, and n. 48.

[12] In his letter of 25 June to JM (*q.v.*), Jones had cited the daily allowance of a delegate as $8.00, the equivalent of Randolph's one-half johannes, a Portuguese coin. The statute, passed on 1 July 1782, defined the delegates' stipend as "eight dollars per day for every day they shall be travelling to, attending on, and returning from congress, to be paid them quarterly" (Minute Book, House of Delegates, May 1782, p. 85; Hening, *Statutes*, XI, 32).

Benjamin Harrison to Virginia Delegates

FC (Virginia State Library). Written by Thomas Meriwether. Addressed to "Virginia Delegates. Congress."

RICHMOND. June 29th. 1782

GENTLEMEN

There was nothing in my Letter taken from the post that can be of any service to the Enemy nor any thing that can amuse the public[.][1] I confess to You the Buisness you mention in cypher in your last has turn'd out much as I expected it wou'd do.[2] It has never been attended to here. the Assembly will rise about the middle of next Week.[3] they are buisy on the recruiting Bill, and by what I hear of it will I think answer our expectations.[4] I return you Mr. Pollocks Bill and with it an answer to Mr. Irwins Letter which you'll please to deliver. Pollock may have suffer'd by the State[;] if He has I am sorry for it. but from what I hear if His Bills are all paid the State will suffer much more by Him.[5] I can know but little of this Buisness as all the Council Journalls and papers to Arnolds Invasion are lost,[6] but from what I hear and do know there has been very great abuses, or if you please frauds somewhere. I have ever heard a good Character of Mr. Pollock and therefore think He must be innocent as to the fraud, but sure I am he has been vastly imprudent for which He will probably loose considerable Sums. great Sums have been paid on His Account to Mr. Clark. the Gentlemen who were in Council at the Time the Debt was contracted think they will amount to full as much as He has a right to claim.[7]

I am with respect Your most obt. Servt.

1 See Virginia Delegates to Harrison, 18 June; Report on Mail Robbery, 19 June 1782, and n. 3.

2 The governor is referring to Count Bieniewsky's proposal of a legionary corps. See Virginia Delegates to Harrison, 4 and 18 June; Harrison to Virginia Delegates, 22 June 1782, and n. 6.

3 The General Assembly adjourned on Tuesday, 2 July 1782.

4 See Randolph to JM, 20 June 1782, and n. 48. The clerk inadvertently wrote "it it" after "of."

5 See Virginia Delegates to Harrison, 18 June 1782, and n. 5. In his reply of 29 June to Thomas Irwin, Harrison refused to accept any bill of Oliver Pollock "til a final settlement of His account with the State" (McIlwaine, *Official Letters,* III, 260). On 26 June, in a letter enclosing to the speaker of the House of Delegates all the available "accounts and orders respecting the Illinois and the back Country," Harrison stated, "immense sums are still demanded of the State from that Country, but the Executive had come to a resolution long before I came into the administration to pay none of them til the truth had been investigated and the Accounts settled by Commissioners on the Spot" (*ibid.*, III, 256). For the decision to which Harrison refers and the background of Pollock's claim, see *Papers of Madison,* III, 98; 99, n. 1; 256, and n. 6; 344 n. 2.

6 A force of British troops, commanded by Benedict Arnold, had occupied Richmond on 5 and 6 January 1781. See *ibid.*, II, 288, n. 3; III, 119, and nn.; 120, n. 6; Jameson to JM, 9 March 1782, n. 2. Governor Harrison's proclamation of 5 June, appealing for the return of the Commonwealth's lost records or for copies thereof, was printed in the *Virginia Gazette* of 8 June 1782.

7 See *Papers of Madison,* III, 256, and n. 6. Those who had been members of the Council of State in the summer of 1781, when warrants for considerable sums of money were issued to Daniel Clark, and who were available for consultation with Harrison were Jacquelin Ambler, state treasurer, and David Jameson, a state senator (*Journals of the Council of State,* II, 362–63, 364–65; *Papers of Madison,* III, 337, n. 7; Swem and Williams, *Register,* p. 17).

From Edmund Randolph

RC (LC: Madison Papers). Unsigned letter, in Randolph's hand. Besides being so badly water(?)-stained that portions of the brief text have disappeared, the paper is torn unevenly across the lower edge. Although the message ends abruptly, it apparently is complete, because the margin at the bottom is sufficiently wide and free from stain to show additional words if Randolph had written them.

VIRGA. June 29. 1782

DEAR SIR

[After?] writing to you this morning, I find, that the paper[1] of the h[as] se[t fo]rth to the public a report respecting Wmsburg., & the governor's letter, therein published, mentions your name. [This?] reminds me, that I heard it supposed some time ago, [tha]t you had written to some correspondent here a circulating rumour of the disaffection of that city; and that I read to Major Jos.[2] Southall the paragraph in your favor of the 28th. Ulto: which was absolutely satisfactory, I believe, to him.[3] My intercepted letter[4] was intended to [y]ou that there was not any thing like disaff[ection?] and I am sure, that Wmsburg. has[5] staunch for the suspicion.

[1] Unidentified. Randolph was not referring to the *Virginia Gazette* (Hayes) of 29 June 1782. No copy of the *Virginia Gazette, and Weekly Advertiser* (Nicolson and Prentis) of that date appears to be extant.

[2] Randolph should have written Jas. rather than "Jos." James Barrett Southall (1726–*ca.* 1801) of Williamsburg, owner of the Raleigh Tavern and major of militia, was superintendent of flag-of-truce ships on the James River and custodian of public property in and near Williamsburg (Land and Personal-Property Tax Books, Williamsburg and James City County, 1782–1802, MSS in Virginia State Library; McIlwaine, *Official Letters*, III, 248–49, 282, 284, 298, 309, 411; *Journals of the Council of State*, III, 88; Letter from Edward M. Riley, Colonial Williamsburg, to William M. E. Rachal, 16 June 1964).

[3] See Jones to JM, 22 July 1782. Early in June Governor Harrison evidently had been told by Major James Southall that JM had charged residents of that town with being unpatriotic. On 11 June 1782 Harrison assured Southall by letter: "The Report you have heard of Mr Madison, or any other of the Delegates writing to me on the subject is false, I assure you I have never had a Line on the subject from any Person breathing." The rumor had included a story about citizens of Williamsburg signing a paper favoring acceptance of "the terms offered by Great Britain to the United States," and about Count de Rochambeau destroying this document after convincing the signers of their error.

When Harrison's dispatch to Southall reached Williamsburg, Rochambeau certified that the entire story was "utterly false" and "ridiculous." Mayor William Holt of Williamsburg called the canard "Infamous" in his letter of 20 June, enclosing for publication "in both the Virginia Gazettes" Rochambeau's certificate and a

"Letter from the Inhabitants of this City expressive of their political principles" (McIlwaine, *Official Letters,* III, 248–49). Randolph appears to have seen printed copies, perhaps in broadside form, of these four documents before writing the present note to JM. In the *Virginia Gazette* of 6 July 1782 Hayes published the "just tribute of gratitude" of the Williamsburg officials to Rochambeau, along with his reply. This interchange does not mention the incident to which Randolph refers in the present letter.

Harrison had begun his letter of 11 June to Southall by writing, "I some time ago heard that some of the Inhabitants of Wmsburg had entered into an instrument of writing expressing their satisfaction at the terms offered by Great Britain." This statement, together with the sentence from the same dispatch quoted earlier in this footnote, makes clear that the report about the "disaffection" of Williamsburg had been made to him orally rather than in writing. In his letter to Joseph Jones on 28 May (*q.v.*), JM had mentioned sending a "consolatory answer" to La Luzerne because of the minister's disquietude occasioned "by some correspondent in Virginia" telling him "that the late intelligence from Britain has produced very unfavorable symptoms in a large party." When in Richmond early in June, Jones mentioned to acquaintances JM's interest in gaining more precise information about the matter. Whoever told Southall of Jones's inquiries evidently reported that JM had accused Williamsburg citizens of "disaffection." If Jones's "long letter," written to JM from Richmond, could be found, it probably would help to clarify this episode. See Jones to JM, 25 June, and n. 3; JM to Randolph, 9 July 1782.

[4] See JM to Randolph, 18 June 1782.

[5] Perhaps the blurred passage was "remained too," or words of equivalent meaning.

Report on Fish and Fuel for Naval Prisoners

MS (NA: PCC, No. 27, fols. 169–70). Written by JM and docketed by him: "Report on the Letter from the Secy at War respecting a supply to the Minine [Marine] prisoners of fish & fuel." A second docket in an unknown hand reads: "Report of Mr Madison Mr Lowell Mr Scott Mr Wharton Mr Witherspoon On Report of Secy at War June 28h. 1782. Passed July 1st. 1782."

[1 July 1782]

The Committee to whom was referred the letter of the 28 of June from the Secretary at war, with an extract of a letter from the Commissary of Prisoners[1] report that the said extract be referred to the Commander in chief, and that he be authorised to take[2] order thereon[3] so far as he shall judge the indulgences applied for can be guarded from abuses;[4]

[1] On 12 June 1782 Abraham Skinner (d. 1826) of Pennsylvania, commissary general of prisoners, had written from Newburgh, N.Y., to Benjamin Lincoln, secretary at war, stating that the British commissary of prisoners at New York City favored permitting groups of American seamen held captive within his jurisdiction to supple-

ment their meager supply of fresh food by fishing under guard in the waters near Sandy Hook. The British commissary also sought to buy wood within the American lines solely for use as fuel by American prisoners. If this were permitted, their supply of wood probably would be larger, for its price was much higher within the British perimeter. Reminding Lincoln of the deplorable condition of these men and of the slight likelihood of their exchange, because very few enemy seamen were held captive by the American army, Skinner strongly supported the proposals of his British counterpart (NA: PCC, No. 149, I, 433–35). In his letter of 28 June to Congress, Lincoln endorsed Skinner's recommendations and suggested that Washington "be directed to take order in the matter" (*JCC*, XXII, 360). For the appalling conditions aboard British prison ships in New York Harbor, see Thomas J. Wertenbaker, *Father Knickerbocker Rebels*, pp. 165–71.

[2] After this word, JM wrote "such" and then partially erased it.

[3] Following "thereon," JM deleted "as he shall."

[4] After "abuses," the words "particularly from a commercial intercourse with the Enemy" were deleted, either by the committee or by an amendment in Congress. Although Washington was "willing to allow the indulgence of Fishing Boats for the use of the marine prisoners, if no abuses are made of such indulgence," he refused to agree to the proposal about fuel. In his view, whatever amount of wood was needed by the prisoners could be sent to them under passports from the British (Fitzpatrick, *Writings of Washington*, XXV, 197, n. 1, 417–18).

From Joseph Jones

RC (LC: Madison Papers). Undocketed and cover missing.

FREDERICKSBURG 1st. July 1782

DR. SR.

I have no Letter from you by this Post. expecting to receive from Mr. Ross a duplicate of the Bill which fell into the hands of the Robbers[1] and forward it to you this week I came to Town to day but have no letter from him. Col. Monroe writes me he promised to send it. my friend Griffin will therefore be obliged to wait longer than I intended and hoped he would.[2] Mr Ross was also to have sent me a further draft on Philaa. for my present supply if I went forward wch. it was my intention to do abot. the middle of this month or the 20th. at furthest.[3]

Be kind enough to have the enclosed advertisement inserted twice or thrice in the Packet and inform Mr. Solomon of it that in case Cyrus is apprehended he may receive him and have him confined untill I come up or give directions abot. him. he was seen in the City since my departure.[4]

I must refer you to our friend Randolph for the News of Richmond who is on the Spot and can give it you truly. We have a report here that a large fleet had passed the Capes Steering Eastward and it is said to be fren[ch,] but the story is so vague I regard it not.[5] Mr. He[nry] and Col. Lee have left the Assembly wch. is still sitting.[6] something has been done for recruiting t[he] Army but what I cannot certainly inform you. it is expected it will bring men into the field.[7] we heard great complaints before I left Phila: of the scarsity of mony in this State,[8] they were well founded and increase every day. If there is not a real scarsity those who possess the money lock it up which produces all the inconveniences of a scarsity. should I pay you a visit I shall find it difficult to procure cash sufficient for my expences.[9]

Yr. friend & Servt

Jos: Jones.

[1] See Report on Mail Robbery, 19 June, and n. 3; Jones to JM, 25 June 1782, and n. 12.

[2] James Monroe's letter to his uncle, Joseph Jones, has not been found. For Jones's debt to Cyrus Griffin, see Jones to JM, 25 June 1782.

[3] See Jones to JM, 8 and 16 July 1782. Jones resumed his seat in Congress on 5 September 1782 (*JCC*, XXIII, 547).

[4] "Solomon" was Haym Salomon (Expense Account, 20 March 1782, n. 2). No advertisement for Jones's runaway slave Cyrus has been found in the *Pennsylvania Packet* or any other Philadelphia newspaper.

[5] For a similar report, see Charles Campbell, ed., *Bland Papers*, II, 84. Perhaps the basis of the rumor was the departure on 28 June from Hampton Roads of a convoy of about fifteen vessels loaded with flour and other food for the French West Indies (Acomb, *Journal of Closen*, pp. 206–7). On the other hand, the *Virginia Gazette* of 29 June 1782 printed a report, already several days old, that British ships bearing three thousand troops from New York to Charleston had been sighted "south of the capes."

[6] See Randolph to JM, 27–29 June 1782.

[7] See Randolph to JM, 20 June, n. 48; Harrison to Virginia Delegates, 6 July 1782.

[8] See, for example, Pendleton to JM, 15 April 1782, and n. 4.

[9] See Jones to JM, 8 July 1782.

From Edmund Pendleton

Tr (LC: Force Transcripts). Addressed to "The Honble James Madison Esqr Philada." Another copy made from the manuscript is in the *Proceedings of the Massachusetts Historical Society*, 2d ser., XIX (1905), 157.

Virginia July 1st 1782

Dear Sir

I am sorry to find by yr favr of the 18th past[1] that the Southern Mail had been made prize of, & probably carried to New York. I don't remember the contents of my letter,[2] but dare say it can produce no Injury Public or personal, unless it be such to myself to be detected, by those not so Indulgent as my friend, in being a dul[l] unmeaning Correspondent. If it had contained Asperity of expression towards them,[3] I had been the more pleased with it[;] however such as it is let them make the most of it.

Nothing amazes me so much as that we should be so long without a certain official Account of the Engagement in the West Indies,[4] about which people here continue divided in Opinion, and the event is the frequent subject of Wagers; we are told that Mr Harrison, yr Commercial Agent in that quarter, is lately arrived, and no doubt brings some Account which may be depended on.[5] They tell us a strange story from Baltimore that after the junction of the French & Spanish Fleets at Hispaniola, they again seperated & were gone no one could say wither.[6]

I can't say whether our Assembly have adjourned, no[r] what they have done? They were to have ended their Session on Saturday, but did not I believe.[7] I fancy they have pass'd a law for raising our men, most other important Bills I am told are put off 'till next Session.[8] We have had [a][9] long drought, yet our Corn has suffered less than we expected. I am

Dr Sr Yr affe friend

EDMD PENDLETON

[1] Although this letter has not been found, its contents very likely resembled those of JM to Randolph, 18 June 1782 (*q.v.*).

[2] Pendleton probably wrote his intercepted letter about 10 June 1782.

[3] That is, the enemy.

[4] The Battle of the Saints. See JM to James Madison, Sr., 20 May 1782, n. 4. If Pendleton expected the court of Versailles or Congress to issue an "official" statement, he was destined to be disappointed. The first "official" allusion to the defeat seems to have been made by La Luzerne to a committee of Congress on 23 September 1782 (*JCC*, XXIII, 594, 596–603; Wharton, *Revolutionary Diplomatic Correspondence*, V, 757–62).

[5] Richard Harrison (*Papers of Madison*, II, 53, n. 2) had been a merchant in Martinique and also commercial agent there, from 1776 to 1778, for Virginia and Maryland (*Journals of the Council of State*, I and II, *passim;* W. H. Browne *et al.*, eds., *Archives of Maryland*, XXI, *passim*). In the summer of 1779, as a partner in, and foreign representative of, a mercantile firm based at Alexandria, Va., and Port Tobacco, Md., Harrison settled in Cadiz (I[saac] Minis Hays, ed., *Calendar of the Papers of Benjamin Franklin in the Library of the American Philosophical Society* [5 vols.; Philadelphia, 1906–8], II, 90, 128; IV, 300, 323; *Pennsylvania Packet*, 22 November 1781; Curtis Carroll Davis, *The King's Chevalier: A Biography of Lewis Littlepage* [Indianapolis, 1961], pp. 43–44, 113). Pendleton had been misinformed about Harrison's return to the United States. Harrison's letters of 7 January, 20

February, 24 April, and 19 August from Cadiz leave no doubt that he was still in Spain (NA: PCC, No. 92, fols. 393–410).

[6] Pendleton's meaning would have been clearer if he had begun the sentence by writing, "A strange story from Baltimore informs us." See Pendleton to JM, 20 May, n. 10; 17 June 1782, n. 4.

[7] See Randolph to JM, 27–29 June 1782, and n. 4.

[8] See Randolph to JM, 20 June, and n. 48; 5 July 1782. Although Pendleton undervalued the achievement of the General Assembly at its May 1782 session, "important Bills" reforming the tax system would await enactment until the legislature reconvened in October of that year. See Hening, *Statutes*, XI, 112–29, 140–45.

[9] This word is taken from the version in the *Proceedings of the Massachusetts Historical Society*. Either Pendleton or Peter Force's clerk inadvertently wrote "no" instead of "a."

Motion To Pay William Lee

MS (NA: PCC, No. 36, I, 349, 351). In JM's hand. Docketed: "Motion of Mr. Madison seconded by Mr. Izard for drawing a bill in favour of Mr. W. Lee July 2. 1782."

EDITORIAL NOTE

On 12 April 1781 William Lee had written from Brussels to the Committee on Foreign Affairs of Congress, requesting a settlement of his account as American commissioner to the courts of Vienna and Berlin (Wharton, *Revolutionary Diplomatic Correspondence*, IV, 361–63). Exactly five months later, shortly after receiving this appeal, Congress agreed that Lee "appears to be due" 42,189 livres, and authorized Morris, "as soon as the state of the public finances will admit," to pay that sum, "with interest at the rate of six per cent. per annum" from "this day," 12 September 1781 (*JCC*, XXI, 931, 955). After being asked by Robert Morris to discharge this debt, Benjamin Franklin replied on 30 March 1782: "No demand has been made on me by Mr. Wm. Lee. I do not know where he is, and I think he did so little for the 3,000 guineas he received, that he may wait without much inconvenience for the addition" (Wharton, *Revolutionary Diplomatic Correspondence*, V, 26, 278). Ralph Izard, who seconded JM's motion, had been favored by Congress with a full settlement of his accounts as a foreign agent (*JCC*, XVIII, 1086, 1145). By authorizing the payment of 42,189 livres, Congress had fulfilled William Lee's hope that his salary and allowances would be calculated at the same rate as those of his friend Izard (Worthington C. Ford, ed., *Letters of William Lee*, III, 844).

[2 July 1782]

That the Superintendt of Finance[1] draw bills on the Minister Plenipo: at the Ct. of Versailles in favor of William Lee Esqr. for the Sum of 42,189 livres tournois with Interest thereon from the 12 day of Sepr last,[2] the same being the balance due to him from the U. States[3]—inserting in such bills a proviso agst. the payment thereof[4] in case the debt sd. have been previously discharged by the sd. Minister Plenipo: [—] and that the Secretary of Foreign Affairs transmit the bills so drawn to William Lee Esqr.[5]

[1] Following this word, JM wrote and deleted "be directed to."

[2] See the editorial note for the reason why Congress specified this date.

[3] At this point JM made a caret to signify where the passage from "inserting" through "Plenipo:," which he wrote on a separate page (fol. 351), should be placed.

[4] Instead of "thereof," JM at first wrote and struck out "of them."

[5] Immediately following the adoption of this motion, Congress directed the secretary for foreign affairs to inform Lee that he should "apply for payment of the monies due to him to Mr. Benjamin Franklin" (*JCC*, XXII, 369). Upon receiving a copy of the resolution, Franklin, with obvious reluctance, accepted Lee's account but warned him that the money would not be available before 12 April 1783 at the earliest (Wharton, *Revolutionary Diplomatic Correspondence*, V, 595, 610; Worthington C. Ford, ed., *Letters of William Lee*, III, 882–83, 886–87, 888–89).

Virginia Delegates to Benjamin Harrison

RC (Virginia State Library). In JM's hand, except the signatures of Bland and Lee. Addressed to "His Excellency. The Honble B. Harrison." Docketed: "Virga Delegates Lr. July 82[.] July 2d 1782."

PHILADA. 2d July 1782.

SIR

We had the honor of receiving your Excellency's favor of the 22. Ultimo[1] by yesterday's mail.

All the late intelligence from Europe which has not been already communicated, is contained in the gazettes herewith enclosed.[2] From the west Indies we have received no certain advices of late date, nor even yet any official advice of the event of the 12th. of April.[3] At New York the Enemy, we are told, are industrious in disciplining their army, and substituting oeconomical arrangements in place of the expensive abuses which have prevailed there.[4]

We have the honor to be with the highest esteem & respect Yr. Excelly's obedient & humble Servants

J MADISON JR.
THEOK: BLAND JR.
A. LEE

[1] *Q.v.*

[2] These may have been the issues of the *Pennsylvania Packet* for 27 and 29 June and 2 July 1782. See JM to Randolph, 2 July 1782, and nn. 8 and 11.

[3] The Battle of the Saints.

[4] This and "the Languor and Inertion of the several States in sending on the Recruits to the Army" were the subjects emphasized by Washington in his brief letter of 24 June 1782, read in Congress three days later (Fitzpatrick, *Writings of Washington*, XXIV, 384–85; *JCC*, XXII, 357 n.). So effective were Sir Guy Carleton's reforms, particularly in rooting out corruption and favoritism, that one observer credited him with saving the British treasury two million pounds sterling a year (Thomas J. Wertenbaker, *Father Knickerbocker Rebels*, pp. 162, 249).

To Edmund Randolph

RC (LC: Madison Papers). Unsigned but in JM's hand. Docketed, "James Madison. 2d July 1782." The cover is missing. The italicized words are those that JM wrote in the official cipher.

PHILADA. 2d. July 1782.

MY DEAR SIR

The confidential & circumstancial communications in your favor of the 20th. of June[1] have afforded me much pleasure. Those which relate to the scheme of *garbleing the delegatetion* were far from surprizing me. In a conversation with Mr. J. before he left Philada.[2] it was our joint inference from a review of certain characters & circumstances that such a scheme would be tried. The prevailing temper of the *present delegatetion is too little flexible to the factious and vindictive plans*[3] *of a particular member of it*[4] to be relished by *him and his adherents. No delegate* who refuses to *league with him in the war against the financeir*[5] must *expect to be long at ease in his post. The* disappointment *in the affair of the flags will increase the venom against the minister.*[6] *The first* conversation *I had with the doctor after his return*[7] clearly *betrayed how much it rankled in his bosome.*

No addition has been made to our foreign intelligence in the course of the past week. Some of the republications from the European papers herewith sent[8] throw light however on the general state of foreign affairs. Those which relate to Ireland in particular are very interesting.[9] The Empress of Russia appears by the Memorial of her Ministers to be more earnest in forwarding a reconciliation between England & Holland than is consistent with the delicate impartiality she has professed as Mediatrix,[10] or with that regard which we flattered ourselves she felt for the interests of the U. States.[11]

One article of our late communications from France was that the interest *on the certificates is no longer to be continued* and that provision *mu[st]*[12] *be made* within ourselves. This has caused great commotion & clamour among that class of public creditors, against Congress, who they beli[e]ve or affect to believe have transferred the funds to other uses.[13] The best salve to this irritation, if it could with truth be applied, wd. be a notification that all the States had granted the impost of 5 PrCt. and that the collection & appropriation of it would immediately commence.[14] It is easy to see that the States whose jealousy & delays withhold this resource[15] from the U. S. will soon be the object of the most bitter reproaches from the public creditors. Rhode Island & Georgia are the only States in this predicament, unless the Acts of Virga. & Maryland should be vitiated by the limitations with which they are clogged.[16]

No step has yet been taken in the instructions prepared before your departure. I expostulated a few days ago with D[oct]or W[itherspoo]n[17] on the subject & prevailed on him to move in the business, but his motion only proved the watchfulness & i[n]flexibility of th[os]e who think they advance towards their own objects in the same proportion as they recede from those of Virginia.[18] I have since shewn him the report and he is a confirmed advocate both for the innocence & expediency of it.[19]

We are even at this day without official advice of the naval event of the 12 of April in the W. I.[20] nor have we any advices of late date from that quarter. There is little room to hope that the misfortune of our ally will be repaired by any subsequent enterprizes.

Congress are much perplexed by the non-appearance of Connecticut at the time appointed for the meeting of her Agents & those of Pennsylvania. We wish to avoid leaving her any pretext to revive the controversy & yet the reasons for her neglect cannot be pronounced sufficient. Her adversary professes a strong jealousy that she means by every artifice to parry a decision during the war; and it[21] cannot be denied that appearances but too well authorize it.[22]

[1] *Q.v.*

[2] Joseph Jones left Philadelphia on 2 May to return to Virginia (JM to Randolph, 9 April 1782, n. 6).

[3] Randolph erroneously decoded JM's 202.5 as "feelings" rather than "plans." See also Burnett, *Letters*, VI, 378.

[4] Arthur Lee. See Randolph to JM, 20 June 1782.

[5] Robert Morris. See Randolph to JM, 16–17 May 1782, n. 17.

[6] See JM to Randolph, 4 June; Randolph to JM, 15 June 1782, and n. 3.

7 Arthur Lee had resumed his seat in Congress on 27 June 1782 (*JCC*, XXII, 354).

8 Immediately after "sent," JM wrote and struck out "will throw light on sundry." He certainly enclosed a copy of the *Pennsylvania Packet* of 27 June and possibly also copies of the same newspaper for 29 June and 2 July. These included excerpts from debates in Parliament as late as 16 April 1782.

9 The resolutions of 14 March 1782, agreed upon by delegates from fifty-nine military volunteer corps of the province of Connaught, declared that "no power upon earth has any right to make laws to govern this kingdom, except the king, the lords and commons of Ireland; and that we will at the risque of our lives and fortune, resist the execution of all other laws, for we do consider as absolute slavery, that of being governed by a foreign legislature, over which we have no controul" (*Pennsylvania Packet*, 27 June 1782). See JM to Pendleton, 23 July 1782, n. 9.

10 As long as the United States was at war with Great Britain, Americans obviously could not credit Tsarina Catherine II with impartiality if she succeeded in decreasing the number of Britain's enemies.

11 The word "regard" replaces a heavily deleted passage which may have been "attention to American interests." Indifferent to "the interests of the U. States," the tsarina had no intention of offending London by recognizing prematurely the independence of the new nation (Frank A. Golder, "Catherine II. and the American Revolution," *American Historical Review*, XXI [1915–16], 92, 96). Under a 3 April date line from The Hague, the *Pennsylvania Packet* of 27 June 1782 reported that, on their return trip from London to St. Petersburg, two of the tsarina's envoys had addressed a memorial to the States-General urging the Netherlands to agree to an immediate truce with Great Britain, since the latter power was ready to negotiate a peace treaty restoring to the Dutch their "rights of free trade and navigation, which neutral nations enjoy, and especially those who have acceeded to the principles of the armed neutrality." The Netherlands recognized the independence of the United States less than three weeks after the Russian envoys presented this memorial (Report on Salaries of Representatives Abroad, 28 May 1782, n. 11).

On 20 May 1784, about seventeen months after agreeing upon a truce, Great Britain and the Netherlands signed a definitive treaty of peace wherein the Dutch ceded Negapatam to the British, relinquished exclusive trading rights in the Far East, and failed to gain recognition of the principles of the League of Armed Neutrality of 1780. On the other hand, Great Britain returned all other possessions conquered from the Netherlands during the war (J[ohn] Holland Rose *et al.*, eds., *The Cambridge Modern History of the British Empire* [8 vols. to date; New York, 1929——], I, 781–82; *Papers of Madison*, II, 56, n. 3; III, 45, n. 9; 205, n. 3).

12 JM erroneously encoded the last two letters of this word by using 42, signifying "only," rather than 421, the symbol for "st."

13 After La Luzerne, upon instructions from Vergennes, had informed Robert Morris that the French government would no longer provide money with which to pay the interest on loan-office certificates, a committee of Congress recommended on 13 June "that no more bills of Exchange be drawn or issued for the interest of loan office certificates; but that the said interest be paid out of the revenues to be granted by the several States for funding the public debts." The threat of this action, which Congress delayed taking until 9 September 1782, after all efforts to have the states pay their financial requisitions and to induce Rhode Island and Georgia to accept the 5 per cent impost amendment of the Articles of Confederation had been unavailing, caused the "great commotion & clamour" mentioned by JM. With Morris' encouragement, the "public creditors" in Philadelphia addressed memorials to Congress and appointed a committee "to make one common cause" with all holders of loan-office certificates "so that they might be able to have influence on all

the legislatures in the several states" (*JCC,* XXII, 302 n., 321, 329, and n., 352, and n., 365, and n.; XXIII, 553–55; Wharton, *Revolutionary Diplomatic Correspondence,* V, 442–43; *Pennsylvania Packet,* 4 and 6 July 1782; William E. O'Donnell, *Chevalier de La Luzerne,* pp. 191–92; Clarence L. Ver Steeg, *Robert Morris,* pp. 123–24).

[14] See *Papers of Madison,* II, 303–4; III, 13, n. 11; 77–78; 128, n. 5.

[15] JM substituted this word for a deleted "benefit."

[16] For Virginia's "limitations" upon her acceptance of the impost amendment, see *ibid.,* III, 349, n. 7. The act of the Maryland General Assembly, which was not presented to Congress until 15 July 1782, was "clogged" with similar provisos (*JCC,* XXII, 388: NA:PCC, No. 70, fol. 509; W. H. Browne *et al.,* eds., *Archives of Maryland,* XLVIII, 158, 213).

[17] In the dispatch sent to Randolph, JM wrote only "D—or W—n." Many years later, while preparing the letter for publication, JM filled out the abbreviations (Madison, *Papers* [Gilpin ed.], I, 145–47).

[18] See Motion Concerning Peace Negotiations, 17 June 1782, and n. 1.

[19] See Report on Instructions on Peace Negotiations, 7 January 1782, editorial note, and n. 30. The "report" to which JM refers was entitled "Facts and Observations in support of the several Claims of the United States not included in their Ultimatum of the 15th of June, 1781." This lengthy essay had been drafted by Randolph with help from JM's Report on Instructions on Peace Negotiations, 7 January 1782. As early as 22 April 1782 Randolph had written Governor Harrison: "I was instructed by my brethren in the delegation to obtain access to the entries of the council before the revolution. A report is prepared for congress in the form of an instruction to the ministers of the united states, who are to negotiate peace, in which the affair of western territory is pretty fully discussed. But we supposed, that the subject would receive considerable illustration, by consulting those entries. With the permission of the executive therefore I will collect such information from them, as applies to the present case" (Burnett, *Letters,* VI, 332).

[20] The Battle of the Saints.

[21] Following "it," JM wrote and struck out "must."

[22] In accordance with the ninth article of the Articles of Confederation, Congress on 14 November 1781 had adopted a committee report, drafted by Randolph, calling upon Pennsylvania and Connecticut to send agents to Congress on 24 June 1782 for the purpose of presenting the respective claims of their states to the Wyoming Valley, located in that part of Northampton County which was to become Luzerne County in 1786 (*JCC,* XXI, 1115–16). Although the four "counsellors and agents" and the "solicitor" of Pennsylvania appeared on the appointed day, Eliphalet Dyer was the only one of the three Connecticut agents on hand. He was also a delegate from his state in Congress (*JCC,* XXII, 345–47). See JM to Randolph, 16 July 1782, n. 22.

Congress waited for two days and then took two motions under advisement—one by Dyer to postpone the hearing until "the 25 or 26 of July," and the other by Thomas Smith of the Pennsylvania delegation, reading "That the State of Connecticut, not having appeared by their lawful agents, agreeably to the resolution of the 14th day of November last, therefore Congress will, on the day of next, proceed to nominate three persons out of each State, in order that due proceedings may be had on the dispute mentioned in the said resolution, agreeably to the 9th Article of Confederation" (*JCC,* XXII, 351–52). On the following day, with the Connecticut delegation alone in dissent, Congress refused to postpone a decision of the controversy "until after the termination of the present war," as requested by "the governor and company of the State of Connecticut." Thereupon, Bland moved "That the sense of the house be taken, whether the reasons for the non-attendance of the agents from Connecticut . . . be sufficient." No doubt JM would have supported this motion, but it never came to a vote (*JCC*, XXII, 355–57, 359, 361). Connecticut, it will be recalled, was opposing Virginia's title to the Northwest Territory. See Observations Relating to the Influence of Vermont and Territorial Claims, 1 May 1782.

The delegates from Connecticut succeeded in preventing a further consideration of the issue until 16 July 1782. This was the day after Jesse Root, who served Connecticut both as a delegate and agent, had resumed his seat in Congress (Burnett, *Letters*, VI, 376–77; *JCC*, XXII, 386, 389). See also Report on Mission To Inform States of Financial Crisis, 22 May 1782, and n. 2.

Motion on Commissaries of Prisoners of War

MS (NA: PCC, No. 149, I, 480). In JM's hand.

[3 July 1782]

That the Secretary at War be authorized to appoint proper persons to take charge of the prisoners of war at the said places until the said[1] Commissaries shall be discharged from their arrests, or Congress shall otherwise direct[2]

[1] Following "said," JM wrote and deleted "trials shall be had."

[2] On 3 July the secretary at war informed Congress that the commissaries of British prisoners at Lancaster, York, and Reading, Pa., were reported to be disobeying orders and exercising "independent, uncontrollable power." His informant had alleged that the commissaries, in spite of positive instructions to the contrary, had allowed the captives "to work in the boroughs, towns and country," thus enabling many of them to escape. Following the reading of Benjamin Lincoln's communication, John Rutledge moved that the secretary at war be empowered to try the accused "commissaries and assistant commissaries" by courts-martial. Apparently JM then added to Rutledge's motion a second paragraph, as given above. Congress or Charles Thomson altered its phraseology by inserting "And" at the beginning, and "and he is hereby" between "be" and "authorized." Before voting upon this resolution, a second resolution was paired with it—to authorize Lincoln, "in the absence of the Commander in Chief," to try by courts-martial all persons charged with disobeying "any orders which he is empowered to issue" (*JCC*, XXII, 321, 372–73).

For further action in 1782 by Congress on the same general subject, see *JCC*, XXII, 382, 403; XXIII, 785, 867. See also Virginia Delegates to Harrison, 2 April 1782, n. 5.

Report Revising John Adams' Instructions

MS (LC: Madison Papers). In JM's hand. Docketed by him: "Report of the Committee consisting of Mr. Madison, Mr. Duane, & Mr. Clymer, relative to the instructions of Mr. Adams–July 5th. 1782." Above these words JM wrote "for Appendix." Also as part of the docket, Charles Thomson noted, "8th. Last part recommitted." If JM thereby meant to recommend the inclusion of the report in the appendix of the journal when published, his suggestion was not followed. See *Journals of Congress, and of the United States in Congress Assembled. For the Year 1781 [–1782]*. Published by Order of Congress. Volume VII (Philadelphia: Printed by David C. Claypoole. M,DCC,LXXXI [1782]).

[5 July 1782]

The Comittee appointed to revise the instructions of Mr Adams &c,[1] recommend.

That the Minister Plenipo: at the Hague be instructed, in case no definitive steps shall have been taken by him in the proposed Treaty of amity and commerce with the U. Provinces, to engage them if possible, in an express stipulation to furnish an[n]ually to the U. States, a loan of , with an interest not exceeding , the principal not to be demanded within years[2] after the conclusion of the war, and the payment of the interest to be suspended during the war; or in case the U. Provinces shall refuse to stipulate such a loan, that the said Minister endeavor to obtain[3] their engagement, to authorise & countenance a loan from their subjects[4] & to guaranty if requisite the due payment of the interest & repayment of the principal by the U. States.[5]

That in case Definitive steps shall have been taken in the proposed Treaty, the said Minister Plenipo: be instructed still to represent to the U. Provinces the great advantages which would result as well to them as to the U. States from such pecuniary succours to the latter as would give stability to their finances, and energy to their measures against the common Enemy:[6] and to use[7] his utmost address to prevail on them either to grant directly the loan abovementioned, or to support by such responsibility as may be[8] necessary the applications made[9] to individuals for that purpose, on the part of the U. States.[10]

The[11] Committee beg leave to observe that in the Treaty between the U. S. & M. C. Majesty, it is among other things stipulated that the subjects of the parties "may by testament, donation, or otherwise dispose of their goods immoveable as well as moveable, in favor of such persons, as to them shall seem good, and the heirs of the respective subjects, wheresoever residing, may succeed them ab intestat[o] without being obliged to obtain letters of naturalization":[12]

That the plan of the proposed Treaty between the U. S. & the U. P. with which the Minister Plenipo: of the former is furnished, extends this privilege to the subjects of the[13] latter, under a general stipulation of the same privileges as are allowed to the most favor'd nation:[14]

That as it is not probable that the U. P. have granted, or will grant this privilege even to the most favored nation, the said treaty if executed in its present form, will engage the U. S. in a concession which will not be reciprocal: and which[15] if reciprocal, would not be equally beneficial to the parties.

That in the opinion of the Committee it is at least questionable whether the extension of this privilege to the subjects of other powers than of France, and Spain[16] will not encroach on the rights reserved by the federal articles to the individual States:[17]

That without enquiring into the inconveniences which may result from an indefinite permission to aliens to hold & transmit real estates within this Country the apparent reluctance[18] of some of the States, notwith[standing] the special clause in the federal articles with respect to France[19] & their favorable disposition towards her, to pass the proper laws on this subject,[20] renders their compliance in case of[21] a similar engagement to another power, extremely precarious:

That in order to avoid these difficulties & consequences, the Committee[22] recommend further:

That the sd. Minister Plenipo: be instructed in case no steps [inco]nsistent therewith, shall have been taken, to decline stipulating to the subjects of the U. Provinces any right or privilege of holding any real estates[23] within the U. States.[24]

[1] Congress had appointed the committee on 3 July (NA: PCC, No. 186, fol. 40). On 29 December 1780, for John Adams' guidance, Congress had adopted a detailed "Plan of a Treaty of Amity and Commerce between the United States of America and the United Provinces of the Low Countries" (*JCC*, XVIII, 1206–17).

[2] On 8 July 1782, without filling in the blanks, Congress referred the first two paragraphs of these recommendations to Robert Morris (*JCC*, XXII, 374).

[3] This word replaced a deleted "engage."

[4] Taking advantage of "the express" that "is to go off this evening," Livingston wrote unofficially to Adams on 4 July: "I need not urge the propriety of availing yourself of your present situation to procure a loan. You may easily convince the government of the validity of the security which it is in the power of a growing country, as yet very little encumbered with debt, to give. That security will derive new force from our being a commercial people, with whom public credit is almost invariably preserved with the most scrupulous attention. . . . I see the people of

the United Provinces are struck with the importance of forming a commercial connexion with us when ours with Britain is dissolved" (Wharton, *Revolutionary Diplomatic Correspondence*, V, 592–93).

[5] Instead of "by," JM at first wrote and crossed out "on the part of." The committee proposed that Adams seek to have the government of the Netherlands guarantee her citizens who might lend money to the United States against loss resulting from default by Congress in paying the stipulated interest or in repaying the principal.

[6] In the letter quoted in n. 4, Livingston had assured Adams that a loan from the Netherlands of "a twentieth part of what Great Britain expends annually in her attempt to enslave us, would be more than sufficient to enable us to defeat all her attempts, and to place our affairs on the most respectable footing."

[7] Before this word, JM struck out "urge them to."

[8] Between "support by" and this word, JM originally wrote "any responsibility he thinks."

[9] After "made," JM deleted "for that."

[10] On this same day Adams was sending to Livingston copies of a contract dated 11 June 1782 but ineffective until ratified by Congress. Under the terms of this proposal, three banking houses of Amsterdam offered to lend five million guilders to Congress for ten years at an annual charge of 5.5 per cent. Adams remarked in his letter, "If we get a million and a half by Christmas, it will be more than I expect" (Wharton, *Revolutionary Diplomatic Correspondence*, V, 594–95). Congress agreed to the contract on 14 September 1782 (*JCC*, XXIII, 579–80).

[11] On 8 July Congress recommitted the remainder of this report. See Report on Treaty with the Netherlands, 12 July 1782.

[12] The portion of this paragraph enclosed in quotation marks is partially an extract from, and partially a paraphrase of, Article XIII of the Treaty of Amity and Commerce between the United States and France (*JCC*, XI, 429–30). The expression "ab intestato" means "without a will."

[13] After "the," JM wrote and deleted, in succession, "parties" and "former."

[14] Article VI of the "Plan of a Treaty" with the Netherlands (n. 1, above) corresponds in subject matter with Article XIII of the treaty with France (n. 12, above). There was one significant difference, however, between the two articles. The latter, unlike the former, qualified the reciprocal privileges extended to the citizens of the two countries by stipulating that although the nationals of either could inherit property in the other, they might be prohibited by France, the United States, or the individual American states from residing in the country where their property lay (*JCC*, XI, 430; XVIII, 1209–10).

[15] After this word, JM heavily deleted a word which appears to have been "even."

[16] The words "and Spain," were interlineated by someone other than JM.

[17] See n. 14, above. In this paragraph JM was referring to the portion of the sixth of the Articles of Confederation which reads: "No state shall lay any imposts or duties, which may interfere with any stipulations in treaties, entered into by the united states in congress assembled, with any king, prince or state, in pursuance of any treaties already proposed by congress, to the courts of France and Spain" (*JCC*, XIX, 216). This clearly did not bar Congress from extending to other governments every reciprocity already exchanged with France. In drafting the paragraph, JM also had in mind the second of the Articles of Confederation, which reserved to each state "every Power, Jurisdiction and right" not "expressly delegated to the United States, in Congress assembled" (*JCC*, XIX, 214).

[18] Between "within" and this word, JM at first wrote "the U. States the." He changed the first "the" to "this," substituted "Country" for "U. States," and interlineated "apparent."

19 "France" was substituted by JM for a deleted passage which appears to have been "the Treaty with his M. C. Mjsty."

20 Virginia was not among the states to which JM referred. Besides ratifying the Treaty of Alliance and the Treaty of Amity and Commerce with France, the General Assembly had not discriminated by law against subjects of friendly powers engaging in commerce, buying, selling, and bequeathing property, or seeking access to the courts of the Commonwealth (*Journal of the House of Delegates,* May 1779, pp. 32, 34; Hening, *Statutes,* IX, 207–8; X, 122–23, 129–30; Boyd, *Papers of Jefferson,* II, 289–90; III, 11–12). See also Randolph to JM, 21–24 May 1782, n. 22.

21 JM interlineated "their compliance in case of" over a deleted "it extremely probable."

22 After "Committee," two words are heavily deleted. They may have been "resolved to."

23 Following this word, three excised words appear to have been "in fee simple."

24 On 17 July 1782 Congress rejected a revised version of the last seven paragraphs of this report. See above, n. 11. On 23 January 1783 Congress ratified the treaty of amity and commerce which John Adams had concluded with the Dutch on 8 October 1782. Article VI provided that citizens of either republic could inherit "sucessions," real or personal, devised or left *ab intestato* in the other (Samuel F. Bemis, *Diplomacy of the American Revolution,* pp. 169–71; Wharton, *Revolutionary Diplomatic Correspondence,* V, 803–5; *JCC,* XXIV, 64–82). The formal exchange was made at The Hague on 23 June 1783 (Hunter Miller, ed., *Treaties and Other International Acts of the United States,* II, 59).

From Edmund Randolph

RC (LC: Madison Papers). Unsigned letter in Randolph's hand. Addressed to "The honble James Madison jr. of congress Philadelphia." Docketed by JM, "July 5th. 1782."

VIRGINIA JULY 5. 1782.

DEAR SIR

If before the receipt of your favor of the 25th. Ulto. I could have doubted concerning the policy of the act against British merchandize, the artifices of the enemy and the parricidal villainies of some of the citizens of America, therein enumerated, would wipe away every scruple. I have confidence, that in the exhortation, about to be made by congress to the people,[1] caution will be used, so as not to create a belief in Europe, contrary to truth, that congress have any reason to consider the consumption of British manufactures, as a symptom of a returning desire for a political connection.

This intelligence, if it has reached Williamsburg may affect congress in another, unexpected form. Coffin's[2] contract for the tobacco seems doomed to perpetual obstruction. The ship, called the New-York, which is one of the flags, destined for the reception of the tobacco, covered by the passports, has been employed, as is suggested, in selling to a merchant in Wmsburg. large quantities of British goods. This conduct has spoiled her, in the opinion of some, of her immunity from seizure: and she is now in the custody of the marshal, to be finally adjudged next monday.[3] An express has just left me, having brought a summons for my attendance, as counsel, at the trial. Altho' my hesitation to say, whether a flag, which abandons the sacredness of her character by illicit commerce only, not by active hostility, is liable to condemnation, might have prevented me of itself from undertaking the cause of the libellants, yet when I reflected that Mr. Morris's schemes might be deeply wounded by a confiscation, and the united states thereby much intangled, I agreed to go to the court upon the express condition of advocating or not advocating the libel at pleasure. But in order to obtain the facts before my departure from home, I wrote to Mr. Daniel Clarke, the agent for loading the british vessels,[4] requesting information on the subject. He returned the inclosed answer.[5] The purport of that answer will be the occasion of my declining the side of the question, offered to me, unless it should wear a very different complexion from what it now does. But I am apprehensive that a jury, impressed by an opinion, that the enemy are daily meditating the diffusion of their wares, will prove stern to the flag, against the law of nations, and the necessities of the united states.[6]

The French legion marched from Richmond yesterday morning, at which time the remainder of the army left Wmsburg. They have preserved the character of peaceable soldiers, and their absence will be regretted. We must pass by the irregularities of a few individuals, as being inapplicable to the body of the army.[7]

On tuesday the assembly completed their session. They passed fifty five acts; the most capital of which I mentioned in my former letters.[8] The recruiting act, revenue act, and the act for the erection of separate courts in Kentuckey are, as I have already stated them to you.[9] But I will forward them immediately after printing.

The resolution, appointing the committee for the patronage of western territory; have never exchanged a letter on the subject.[10] Mr. G. Mason will enter into the discussion, I am told, if he approve the acts of the present session. Mrs. Jefferson has been too near her flight to a happier station, to suffer her affectionate husband to do more than lament the prospect of a separation. (She is now within the reach [?] of medicine). Of Dr. Lee I have not heard a syllable since his setting off for Phila. Dr. Walker has supplied a few rough materials only.[11] I am pursuing the inquiry: but wait for the movements of my elders in the nomination.[12]

Upon reviewing some of the papers, which I collected in 1780, I am inclined to think, that the white inhabitants of Virginia will be found on the census, directed to be taken by a late law, to amount to a much larger number, than even Massachusetts contai[ns.] For in that year the militia might in round numbers be estimated at 50[?],000.[13] The principles then, which you well know, can easily be applied, when you recollect, that no person is liable to militia duty, but between the age of eighteen and fifty. My computation is equal to 250,000 whites[14] at least.[15]

I wish, that on future occasions of[16] speaking of individuals we may us[e] the cypher, which we were taught by Mr. Lovell.[17] Let the keyword be the name*[18] of the negro boy, who used to wait on our common friend Mr. Jas. Madison. Billy[19] can remind you, if you should be at a loss for it.

There can be no necessity for this process in the communication of intelligence, merely public: but a private hint would be no secret to any person, having access to the cypher of government.[20]

*probably *Cupid*

[1] See JM to Randolph, 18 June, and n. 7; 25 June; Report on Illicit Trade, 19 June 1782, and nn. 8 and 11.

[2] See Lee to JM, 16 May 1782, n. 7; *Journal of the House of Delegates,* October 1782, pp. 86–87. Ebenezer Coffin (1763–1817) was a son of the Boston Loyalist merchant, William Coffin, Jr. (b. 1723), who apparently accompanied the British troops when they evacuated the city in March 1776 (W[illiam] S[umner] Appleton, *Gatherings toward a Genealogy of the Coffin Family* [Boston, 1896], pp. 43, 45; *Proceedings of the Massachusetts Historical Society,* 1st ser., XVIII [1880–81], 226; 2d ser., X [1895–96], 163). By the next year in New York City, the father had formed Coffin and Anderson, a firm with which the British army contracted for supplies (Fitzpatrick, *Writings of Washington,* XIII, 186, 190, 283). "Anderson" may have been Alexander Anderson, master of the flag-of-truce ship "Fame" (n. 3, below; NA: PCC, No. 20, II, 293). Either William Coffin, Jr., or his son, Ebenezer, was probably the "Mr. Coffin" who, in the spring of 1780, had come to Hampton, Va., from New York City in a flag-of-truce ship freighted with supplies for British prisoners of war (Boyd, *Papers of Jefferson,* III, 318).

Although the father's later career is obscure, Ebenezer Coffin was one of the merchants-capitulant in Yorktown in October 1781 (NA: PCC, No. 20, II, 305). Shortly thereafter, as the representative of all of them, Ebenezer engaged George Eddy of Philadelphia to conclude an agreement with Robert Morris. On 11 February 1782 Congress had empowered Morris to act on its behalf in this matter and instructed Charles Thomson to issue passports to the flag-of-truce ships which would come from New York to Virginia for the tobacco owed to the merchants (NA: PCC, No. 75, fol. 376; *JCC,* XXII, 70–71). On 20 April 1782 Rear Admiral Robert

Digby, commanding the British navy in North American waters, authorized the "Fame" and "New York" to proceed to the James River, take the tobacco aboard, and return to New York Harbor. According to Digby's passport, Coffin was aboard the "New York" as "Agent or Supercargoe" and as one of the consignees of the expected cargo (NA: PCC, No. 20, II, 309).

[3] That is 8 July. For the action taken by Governor Harrison upon the arrival of the flag-of-truce ships, "New York" and "Fame," in Hampton Roads on 8 May, see Lee to JM, 16 May 1782, n. 7. In mid-June the Virginia General Assembly had reluctantly permitted the vessels to load tobacco (Randolph to JM, 15 June 1782, and n. 3). The governor's initial opposition to the contract between Robert Morris and the traders-capitulant of Yorktown had been intensified during the spring of 1782 by frequent reports that masters of flag-of-truce ships and a few British merchants who had remained in the Yorktown neighborhood ever since the surrender of Cornwallis were engaging in illicit trade with Virginians (McIlwaine, *Official Letters*, III, 163, 207, 232; *Journals of the Council of State*, III, 86, 89 n.). On 29 July 1782 Harrison ordered all flag vessels in Virginia to be detained pending further instructions from him (*ibid.*, III, 129). See also *Calendar of Virginia State Papers*, III, 219, 233, 236, 244, 246, 250–51, 257. The indefiniteness of the expression obliges "a merchant in Wmsburg." to remain anonymous.

[4] See Randolph to JM, 21–24 May, and n. 3; Pendleton to JM, 17 June 1782, n. 19.

[5] Not found.

[6] For the outcome of the hearing before the Virginia Court of Admiralty, see Randolph to JM, 18 July 1782.

[7] See Randolph to JM, 10 May, and n. 18; 18 July 1782. For the Duc de Lauzun and his legion, see Jameson to JM, 26 January 1782, and n. 2. This contingent of Rochambeau's army began its northward march by moving to Petersburg, Va., late in June. Acomb, *Journal of Closen*, pp. 206 ff., furnishes a detailed account of the plan of march and the route followed by the French army. Both the Virginia General Assembly and the residents of Williamsburg expressed to Rochambeau their appreciation for the signal services which his troops had rendered to the Commonwealth and for their "strict discipline." The address of the General Assembly on 25 June, published in the *Virginia Gazette* on 29 June, was reproduced in the *Pennsylvania Journal* on 10 July 1782. Although Governor Harrison shared in these manifestations of gratitude, he was much concerned because the French took with them on their northward march many Negroes owned by Virginians and Carolinians (McIlwaine, *Official Letters*, III, 255, 257–58, 263, 265–66). See also Harrison to Virginia Delegates, 6 July 1782.

[8] See Randolph to JM, 15 June, and n. 5; 20 June, and nn. 28, 32, 39, 40, 42, 48; 27–29 June 1782, and nn. 8 and 12. The *Virginia Gazette* of 6 July 1782 lists the fifty-five statutes by their titles. See also Hening, *Statutes*, XI, 9–103.

[9] See Randolph to JM, 20 June, and n. 48; 27–29 June 1782.

[10] See Randolph to JM, 1 June 1782, and n. 3.

[11] See Randolph to JM, 16–17 May 1782, n. 6. In the sentence in parentheses, Randolph clearly wrote "now" but probably intended to write "not."

[12] See Randolph to JM, 1 June 1782. Of the five members of the committee appointed to draft a defense of Virginia's title to the Old Northwest, Thomas Walker was the eldest and Randolph, the youngest.

[13] See Randolph to JM, 20 June, n. 28; JM to Randolph, 16 July 1782, and n. 5. On 27 July 1780 Governor Jefferson had written that "after all probable deductions," Virginia could raise 45,000 militia (Boyd, *Papers of Jefferson*, III, 509). Randolph may have overestimated the number of Virginia's white inhabitants as compared with those in Massachusetts, at least if the five counties in Maine are

included. According to the federal census of 1790, there were 442,117 whites in Virginia and 469,294 in Massachusetts (Department of Commerce and Labor, Bureau of the Census, eds., *A Century of Population Growth from the First Census of the United States to the Twelfth, 1790–1900* [Washington, 1909], pp. 201, 204).

14 Although the editors are unacquainted with Randolph's "principles" of computation, he apparently multiplied 50[?],000 by 5. He took the age range between "eighteen and fifty" from "An Act for speedily recruiting the quota of this state for the continental army," probably enacted on 13 July 1780 by the Virginia General Assembly (*Journal of the House of Delegates*, May 1780, pp. 79, 84, 85; Hening, *Statutes*, X, 258).

15 After this sentence, Randolph so heavily deleted about seven lines of text that the following rendition of them may not be wholly accurate: "If so, our advantage in contributing to continental expenses according to the rule of the Confederation [?] will not be so great, as we supposed, when we controverted the wish of some of the Eastern gentlemen who contended for the quota of money being regulated by white populations. For I am almost convinced, that our white numbers, if they amount to 250,000. . . ." Instead of "white" before "populations," Randolph probably should have written "whole."

16 Randolph may have intended to write "when" rather than "of."

17 James Lovell, a delegate in Congress from Massachusetts. He, Randolph, and JM had been together in Congress between 16 July 1781 and 23 January 1782 (Burnett, *Letters*, VI, xlvi, liii). For Lovell's expertness as a cryptographer, see *ibid*., VI, 223–24, 241, 328 n., 384, n. 2.

18 This asterisk and the footnote are in JM's hand. Since in his reply of 16 July (*q.v.*) JM readily understood the key word to which Randolph referred, the adverb "probably" suggests that JM added the footnote many years later, when he was editing some of his correspondence for publication.

19 Cupid, mentioned in the footnote, was probably a servant of the Reverend James Madison. Billy may have been JM's body servant, although his owner was James Madison, Sr. (Orange County Personal Property Tax Book, 1782, MS in Virginia State Library).

20 In the last two paragraphs of this letter Randolph suggests that, although they can safely continue to use the official cipher when writing to each other about governmental affairs, they should more securely disguise their comments about individuals by employing the little-known Lovell code. Messages written in it were inscrutable unless the particular key word used in their encoding was known. See Edmund C. Burnett, "Ciphers of the Revolutionary Period," *American Historical Review*, XXII (1916–17), 331–32.

Benjamin Harrison to Virginia Delegates

FC (Virginia State Library). In the hand of Archibald Blair.

COUNCIL CHAMBER July 6th. 1782

GENTLEMEN

Our Assembly has passd a Law for the seisure of Brittish Goods on Land but the Execution of it is suspended untill other States shall do the same[1] I beg the favour of You when this happens to give me information that proper steps may be taken to enforce the Law here. your favor by the last post[2] came to hand too late for the Assembly[3] I have some reason to suppose that the practice of running Goods from New York is takeing place here. a stop shall be put to it if possible.[4] I think the Act for raising 3000 Men will produce them it gives a bounty of twelve pounds specie to each recruit and forty Shillings to the recruiting officer every person refuseing or neglecting to pay the tax imposed for this Bounty is to be sent a Soldier for three Years.[5] The French Troops are now on their March to the northward. they have with them many Negroes that I have good reason to think belong to North and South Carolina if you give the Gentlemen from those Countries notice of it they may be reclaim'd when the Army gets to Philadelphia[6] we have no arrivalls nor nothing new from the South.

I am very respectfully Your most obet. servt.

[1] See Randolph to JM, 16–17 May, and n. 8; 21–24 May, and n. 2; Report on Illicit Trade, 19 June 1782, and n. 8.

[2] See Virginia Delegates to Harrison, 25 June 1782.

[3] The legislature had adjourned on Tuesday, 2 July.

[4] See Randolph to JM, 5 July 1782, and n. 3.

[5] See Randolph to JM, 20 June, and n. 48. Harrison's meaning would be clearer if he had written "as" after "sent."

[6] See Randolph to JM, 5 July 1782, and n. 7.

From Joseph Jones

RC (LC: Madison Papers). Addressed to "Honble James Madison jr. Philadelphia." Docketed by JM, "July 8. 1782."

Spring Hill 8th. July 1782.

Dr. Sr.

I intended when I left Richmond to set out for Philadelphia about the middle of this month[1] but from a manoeuvre of Mr. Ross's in settling the balance due from Mr. Braxton and which had by the Executive been ordered to me I am disappointed of the means necessary for the Journey and am left to my own resources wch. I am determined shall not be applied to public use farther than is unavoidable, I mean in the line of my appointmt. to Congress—when I shall be properly furnished and I see a prospect of continued supply I may perhaps revisit Philadelphia. at present it depends on Mr. Ross, who instead of furnishing me money or Bills as promised has settled Mr.

Braxtons balance of abt. £200 by transmiting me your order on me given to Whiteside for the money I procured before I left Philadelphia and which the Govr. and also your Letter informed me was paid. This order I expect was taken by Mr. Whiteside as a voucher to transmit to Mr. Ross.[2] The disappointment however considering the violent heat of the weather proves agreeable on that acct. tho' I could have wished to have gone northward before the commencement of the sickly season.[3] I have never heard from Mr. Solomon whether the Waggoners delivered him the Tobacco they carryed from here.[4]

The French Army are on their March,[5] the Legion came over to Falmouth yesterday and the Infantry are expected to be there next Thursday.[6] Ct Rochambeau on his way quartered at old Mr. Hunters the night before last.[7] Mrs. Bland was a few days past Col. Dangerfiel[d's][8] on her way to Philadelphia. she intended Dr. Lee shod. have escorted her but the Dr missing her Letter occasioned a disappointment.[9] when I saw her she was in doubt when she should proceed and by whom be attended.

One of the Ships sent for the Tobacco I am told has been seized & will be proceeded agt. in the Admiralty—the cause, having on board a quantity of Goods wch. was sold or offered for Sale to some of the Inhabitants.[10] I believe they came well provided for such a trafic but this step will probably suspend all further commercial intercourse.

If Mr. Ross puts me in a situation to proceed you shall be informed. in the meantime you will not omit your inquiries abt. a lodging shod. I have occasion for one.[11] We have had a great drought & the hottest weather for the Time of the year I ever experienced. our Crops of small grain short & not so good as usual.[12] Randolph I understand will be up in the fall.

Yr. Friend

Jos: Jones.

[1] See Jones to JM, 1 July 1782.

[2] Before leaving Philadelphia for Virginia, Jones evidently had gone into debt by borrowing money from Cyrus Griffin and Haym Salomon and by purchasing goods on credit from Baker, Potts, and Company.

While serving as commercial agent of Virginia, David Ross had conducted much of the state's business in Philadelphia through Whiteside and Company. In Virginia, Carter Braxton, planter, merchant, and public official (*Papers of Madison*, I, 164, n. 2; 180–81; 181, n. 3; 269; III, 139, editorial note), bought and sold commodities, especially tobacco, both on his own account and that of the state.

Early in June 1782, after receiving from Ross a bill of exchange on Whiteside for over $220, Jones forwarded it to JM, with a request that he use the money to pay Baker, Potts, and Company if Griffin would be content to wait longer for his due (Jones to JM, 25 June 1782). After Jones learned that this remittance had fallen into the hands of mail robbers, he asked Ross to supply a duplicate draft and also to fulfil his promise to place an additional sum to his credit in Philadelphia, so that he could return to Congress. Ross's delay in responding to these requests may have been influenced by the decision on 11 June of the Council of State to authorize him in his private capacity to give Carter Braxton and his business associates nearly £200 sterling for a large consignment of tobacco (*Journals of the Council of State*, III, 106–7). On 2 July, for a reason now indeterminable, Braxton paid Ross £220 18*s*., which the latter on that day placed to Jones's credit with Whiteside and Company (Papers of David Ross, MSS in Virginia State Library; see also JM to Jones, 28 May 1782). For Ross's subsequent action enabling Jones to go to Philadelphia, see Jones to JM, 16 July 1782.

[3] In his journal for 2 July, Closen made note of the "excessive heat" gripping Virginia "for more than six weeks," which "compelled us to order the troops to march at 1 a.m." (Acomb, *Journal of Closen*, p. 208). From mid-July to mid-September ordinarily encompassed the "sickly season," when victims of malaria suffered with the "ague."

[4] This episode is unidentified, but Ross, as commercial agent for Virginia (or Braxton), may have consigned tobacco to Haym Salomon in payment for loans by him to delegates who had pledged their overdue salaries as security.

[5] See Randolph to JM, 5 July 1782, and n. 7.

[6] The Duc de Lauzun's mounted legion formed the van of the French troops. Falmouth, on the north bank of the Rappahannock River in Stafford County, was opposite the considerably larger town of Fredericksburg on the south bank in Spotsylvania County. The "next Thursday" was 11 July 1782.

[7] The wealthy bachelor, "old" James Hunter, Sr. (d. 1785), lived in his "Mansion House" close to his iron foundry on the outskirts of Falmouth. His cousin was James Hunter, Jr., whose mercantile firm was now established in Richmond (*Virginia Magazine of History and Biography*, LVI [1948], 4, 18, 20; *William and Mary Quarterly*, 1st ser., XXVII [1918–19], 74). On 4 July Rochambeau and his staff left the slowly marching French troops near Newcastle, a no longer extant town in Hanover County, Va., in order to reach Philadelphia on 13 July for a conference with Washington (Fitzpatrick, *Writings of Washington*, XXIV, 425, 430–31; Acomb, *Journal of Closen*, p. 208; *Virginia Gazette*, 3 August 1782).

[8] Mrs. Theodorick Bland, Jr. (d. 1803), nee Martha Daingerfield, was a sister of William Daingerfield (d. 1783), whose plantation, Belvidera, was in Spotsylvania County on the Rappahannock River about seven miles below Fredericksburg (Edward Miles Riley, ed., *The Journal of John Harrower, an Indentured Servant in the Colony of Virginia, 1773–1776* [New York, 1963], pp. 172, 174; *Virginia Gazette, and Weekly Advertiser* [Richmond], 18 January 1783; *Patrick Corran* v. *Corran's Executors & Heirs* [U.S. Circuit Court, District of Virginia, Ended Cases, 1821, MSS in Virginia State Library]).

[9] Arthur Lee probably passed through Fredericksburg at least a week before Mrs. Theodorick Bland, Jr.'s, arrival there, for he resumed his seat in Congress on 27 June (Jones to JM, 25 June 1782, n. 15).

[10] See Randolph to JM, 5 July 1782, and n. 3.

[11] See Jones to JM, 25 June 1782.

[12] See n. 3, above; Pendleton to JM, 1 July 1782.

Virginia Delegates to Benjamin Harrison

RC (Virginia State Library). In JM's hand except for Arthur Lee's signature. Addressed to "His Excelly. Governor Harrison." Docketed, "Virga Delegates Letter July 9th 1782."

PHILADA. 9th. July 1782.

SIR

Your Excellency's favor of the 29th. of June inclosing a letter to Mr. Irwin & a bill of exchange in his favor from Mr. O. Pollock[1] was received this morning.

The defect of intelligence which rendered our last so uninteresting[2] still continues. In particular we are uninformed of the state & dispositions of the fleets in the West Indies. The report which circulates is that those of the French & Spaniards have left Hispaniola, the former to convoy the Trade of that Island[3] towards Europe, the latter to return to the Havannah.

We have the honor to be with great respect & esteem Yr. Excys. obt. & hbe servts.

J. MADISON JR
A. LEE

[1] See Harrison to Virginia Delegates, 29 June 1782, and n. 5.

[2] See Virginia Delegates to Harrison, 2 July 1782.

[3] JM interlineated "of that Island." The *Pennsylvania Packet* of 4 July printed a report from Charleston, S.C., to the effect that of the twenty-one French ships which arrived at Cap Français, Haiti, about 15 May, most had been in a "very shattered condition." In the 9 July issue of the same newspaper, under a Salem, Mass., date line of 20 June, was an item about an American merchantman which recently had entered that harbor after sailing from Cap Français with a convoy bound for France. Although the delegates could not have seen the issue of the *Packet* for 11 July 1782, it told of the capture by the British of several transports filled with Spanish troops who were being convoyed back to Havana after forcing the surrender of New Providence Island in the Bahamas. See Report on Foreign Dispatches, 20 March 1782, nn. 5 and 6.

To Edmund Pendleton

RC (New York Public Library). Unsigned letter in JM's hand. The cover is missing. Docketed, "James Madison Esqr. July 9. 1782."

PHILADA. 9th. July 1782

DEAR SIR

The betts which your favr. of the 1st. inst: says are still laid on the subject of the naval combat of the 12th. of April, are a proof rather of the fashion of the Country than of uncertainty as to the event. Altho' no official accts. have been recd. on the part of our Ally, those which have been published on the other part with the numberless corroborating incidents are too powerful for the skeptical mind.[1] The last *report* from the Cape is that the Fr: & Span: fleets had parted the former with the Trade towards Europe, the latter towards the Havannah.[2] You will observe that this is no more than a report.

The same defect of authentic information applies to every other quarter. The first arrival from Europe will I hope enable me to feast your starving curiosity with a treaty, with Holland, and a prospect of all its salutary consequences, particularly to the Tobacco States.[3] This hope however is not founded on any other facts than those which I have heretofore communicated to you.

[1] See Pendleton to JM, 1 July 1782, and n. 4.

[2] See Virginia Delegates to Harrison, 9 July 1782, and n. 3.

[3] See JM to Randolph, 4 June, and n. 6; Virginia Delegates to Harrison, 25 June; Report Revising Adams' Instructions, 5 July 1782, and nn. 1 and 24. JM foresaw that a commercial treaty with the Netherlands probably would assure the southern states of a far larger unrestricted foreign market for their surplus staples than the British navigation acts had permitted prior to 1776. For John Adams' explanation of some of the provisions of the treaty and for its text as ratified by Congress on 23 January 1783, see Wharton, *Revolutionary Diplomatic Correspondence,* V, 804; *JCC,* XXIV, 68–78.

To Edmund Randolph

RC (LC: Madison Papers). Unsigned letter in JM's hand. The cover is missing. Docketed by Randolph with his own name only. The italicized words are those written by JM in the official cipher. Late in his life JM or someone by his direction bracketed the first and third paragraphs of this letter, thus designating them for inclusion in the first edition of his papers (Madison, *Papers* [Gilpin ed.], I, 147–48).

PHILADA. 9th. July 1782.

DEAR SIR

Your two favors of the 27th. were recd. this morning.[1] I sincerely regret that any reports should have prevailed injurious to the patriotism of Williamsbg. and particularly that my name should in any manner whatever[2] be connected with them. I *informed* Mr. *Jones that the minister of France* had been made somewhat *uneasey by some accounts from Virginia and desired him to enable me to remove it by proper enquiries.*[3] It must have been a very gross mistake that could have *built the reports in question on this letter even if* its *contents had been known.* You saw I presume *the letter.* I think I wrote you *a letter to the same effect but I am not sure.*[4]

The dearth of intelligence which has rendered my late letters so uninteresting, is not yet removed. It is reported that the French & Span: fleets have left the Cape & each other, the former to convoy to a safe distance the trade of that Island, the latter to resume its inactivity & security at the Havannah.[5] This however is mere report. The next arrival from Europe will I hope render[6] my correspondence more valuable. I am exceedingly impatient for the conclusion of a Treaty with Holland. The commercial spirit & views of that nation must produce the most salutary effects to the U. S. & to those especially whose staple is Tobacco.[7]

The trade with the Enemy at N. Y. has at length I am told produced spirited & successful exertions among the people of N. Jersey for suppressing it.[8] The same alarm & exertions seem to be taking place in Connecticut.[9] The ordinance of Congress against collusive captures on water has not yet passed. The mode of proof & the distribution of the effects, occasioned some diversity of opinion, & a recommitment ensued.[10] I am not very sanguine that any thing of efficacy will be done in the matter. Notwithstanding the supposed danger arising to the bank from the exportation of hard money to N. York, a dividend of 4½ PerCt. for the first half year has been advertized to the Stockholders.[11] Will not this be very captivating to the avarice of the Dutchman[12] in case his apprehension shall be removed by a Political connection between the two Countries?

Mr. Jones writes me that he proposes to set off about the 20th. instt.[13] When will you follow him?

[1] Judging from JM's comments later in this paragraph, he meant that he had received Randolph's letters of 27–29 and 29 June 1782 rather than two dated the 27th of that month.

[2] JM interlineated "in any manner whatever" above two or three words too heavily canceled to be legible.

[3] See JM to Jones, 28 May 1782, and n. 15.

[4] See JM to Randolph, 28 May, headnote; Randolph to JM, 29 June 1782, and n. 3.

[5] See Virginia Delegates to Harrison, 9 July 1782, and n. 3.

[6] Instead of "render," JM at first wrote "enable."

[7] See JM to Pendleton, 9 July 1782, n. 3.

[8] See JM to Randolph, 18 June 1782, and n. 7.

[9] JM may have derived his information from the *Pennsylvania Journal* of 6 July, which printed a proposal made by the inhabitants of Farmington, Conn., on 21 June

that delegates from all the towns in Hartford County assemble in convention on 16 July to devise measures for executing the law of the state prohibiting trade with the enemy.

[10] See Report on Illicit Trade, 19 June 1782, n. 11.

[11] The Bank of North America announced in the *Pennsylvania Packet* of 6 July that stockholders of the institution should call there "any time after the tenth" of July to receive a 4.5 per cent dividend for the period 1 January through 30 June 1782.

[12] JM expressed an opinion of the Dutch which had been prevalent in England ever since the commercial wars of the seventeenth century. In 1701 Daniel Defoe summarized his countrymen's prejudice against certain foreigners by writing,

> Rage rules the *Portuguese*, and Fraud the *Scotch:*
> Revenge the *Pole;* and Avarice the *Dutch*

("The True Born Englishman," in *A True Collection of the Writings of the Author of the True Born ENGLISH-MAN* [2 vols.; London, 1703–5], I, 4). For agreement by some of JM's contemporaries with this characterization of the Dutch, see *Papers of Madison,* II, 182, 230; III, 34, 43.

[13] See Jones to JM, 25 June 1782.

Benjamin Harrison to Virginia Delegates

FC (Virginia State Library). Addressed to "Virga. Delegates." The handwriting is that of Archibald Blair through the word "Counties" in the first paragraph. The copying was completed by Thomas Meriwether.

VIRGINIA IN COUNCIL July 11th. 1782

GENTLEMEN

When Count Rochambeau was about to leave this State He call'd on Government for 1000 Men to garrison the Towns of York & Gloucester. his request has in part been comply'd with[.] about 520 Men are sent down and the Neighbouring Counties have orders to hold 600 more in constant readiness to throw themselves into the Town on the shortest notice.[1] General Washington has also written to me desireing that I woud comply with any requisition that shou'd be made by the Count[2][.] as the expence attending this Garrisson will be extreemly great I thought it proper to aprize you of it that if necessary proper steps may be taken for our obtaining credit in our quota of this Year for the expenditures[.] every step is taken to lessen the expence as much as possible.[3] the extravagant mode of feeding them with specific articles furnish'd by the Country is laid aside and they are now supported by contract with a compleat continental ration for tenpence, this perhaps may be thought high with You but we look on it as moderate.[4] If the Financier[5] does not approve it He may take it on Himself after december at which time the Contract will end. You have a resolution of the Assembly enclosed disaproveing the alteration of the mode appointed by the confederation for opportioning each States quota of tax &c.[6] it shou'd have been sent you sooner but thro the neglect of the Clerk of the House of delegates it did not get to me till the 8th. instant.[7]

[1] See Randolph to JM, 5 July 1782, and n. 7. By letter on 24 June to Governor Harrison, Count Rochambeau expressed his intention of immediately moving all his troops, except for a small contingent which would remain for a short while, primarily to guard the fortifications and surplus matériel. The next day Harrison and the Council of State decided to transfer almost all of Colonel Charles Dabney's "Legion" of state troops from Portsmouth to Yorktown, except for a few to be stationed at Hampton. At the same time the governor took steps to have four hundred militia from nearby counties attached to Dabney's command at Yorktown and to alert six hundred more militiamen from five other neighboring counties for service in that town or in Gloucester in case of an emergency. Harrison appointed General Edward Stevens to command this entire force and asked the General Assembly to furnish the means for supplying these troops "with provisions & other necessaries" (McIlwaine, *Official Letters*, III, 254–55, 257–58, 265–66; *Journals of the Council of State*, III, 113–14; *Calendar of Virginia State Papers*, III, 206–7).

[2] In a letter to Harrison on 5 May, received by him on 25 June 1782, Washington informed Harrison that "the Count de Rochambeau will soon put the french Troops in motion" and asked for sufficient militia to guard the equipment, stores, and artillery which necessarily would be left at York and Gloucester (Fitzpatrick, *Writings of Washington*, XXIV, 222–23, 226; *Journals of the Council of State*, III, 113).

[3] See Virginia Delegates to Harrison, 23 July 1782, and n. 3.

[4] See Virginia Delegates to Harrison, 23 July 1782. The decision to provide food for the state troops of Virginia by contracts with private suppliers, insofar as possible, rather than by impressments or by taxes paid in kind was reached on 18 January 1782 (McIlwaine, *Official Letters*, III, 133; *Journals of the Council of State*, III, 29). Having defined the basic ration on 4 November 1775, Congress about ten months later made it commutable for approximately nine cents (*JCC*, III, 322; V, 780). On 25 December 1781 Congress abandoned its efforts to maintain a fixed ration in an inflationary economy and ordained "That the superintendant of finance be authorised and directed to ascertain the value of a ration, from time to time" (*JCC*, XXI, 1013). Several laws enacted by the Virginia General Assembly during the Revolution implicitly or explicitly authorized the executive of the Commonwealth to provide troops of the state line and militiamen with the continental ration whenever they were called to active duty and assigned to continental service (Hening, *Statutes*, IX, 34, 295; X, 296–97, 419, 467). In these instances the cost of the ration was charged to Congress.

[5] Robert Morris.

[6] See JM to Pendleton, 7 February 1782, and n. 6.

[7] John Beckley. On the manuscript of the resolution is a notation, apparently in Harrison's hand, that the copy did not reach him until 8 July (NA: PCC, No. 75, fols. 363–65). The Virginia delegates presented the resolution to Congress on 24 July 1782 (*JCC*, XXII, 413). See Virginia Delegates to Harrison, 23 July 1782, n. 1.

Amendment to Motion on John Laurens' Mission

MS (NA: PCC, No. 36, I, 347). Docketed, "Mr. Blands and Mr Scots Motion July 12. 1782." In Bland's hand, except for the passage written by JM and designated in n. 2, below.

EDITORIAL NOTE

The background and outcome of Colonel John Laurens' mission as a special minister of the United States to France have already been summarized (*Papers of Madison,* II, 207, n. 2; 239, n. 4; 259–60; 260, n. 9; III, 244; 245, n. 5; 247; 248, n. 2; 249; 250, n. 4).

Shortly before Laurens reached L'Orient on 9 March 1781, the court of Versailles had granted the United States a "free gift" of six million livres (Wharton, *Revolutionary Diplomatic Correspondence,* IV, 278, 281). Franklin proposed and Vergennes agreed that Laurens should use about two million livres of this total to purchase military matériel in France and that the rest of the specie should be shipped to America (*ibid.,* IV, 418–19, 605–6). Insisting that the two million would not suffice to re-equip Washington's troops, Laurens pressed for an additional grant. In Franklin's opinion, Laurens "*brusqued* the ministers too much," but they consented to have the king's treasury stand as security for the repayment by Congress of a potential loan from Dutch bankers amounting to an additional ten million livres (*ibid.,* IV, 355–59, 361–66, 391–92, 660–61). Louis XVI also agreed to advance this sum "as soon as possible," if the "loan should meet with difficulties" (*ibid.,* IV, 418). Although Laurens by 15 May had been notified "of the total refusal of the Dutch to countenance" the loan, he assumed that he was authorized to draw at once against the ten million as guaranteed by France (*ibid.,* IV, 416, 688–89, 692). Prior to embarking for the United States on 1 June 1781 with 2,500,000 livres in specie and a part of the matériel, Laurens arranged with Franklin and Vergennes to have his secretary, Captain William Jackson, bring 1,500,000 livres to America as soon as he could complete the mission (*ibid.,* IV, 545–46, 605–6, 692).

By acting hastily Laurens created the long-lasting and complicated problems reflected in the present motion. After purchasing from Commodore Alexander Gillon for £10,000 goods for which the latter had been unable to pay, Laurens arranged with Gillon to transport them and other supplies to America (*ibid.,* IV, 382–83, 485, 781; Report on Foreign Dispatches, 20 March 1782, nn. 5 and 6). Although Vergennes had expected that the king's gift of money would be used to purchase French wares, Laurens and Jackson bought heavily, including some goods of British origin, in the Netherlands (Wharton, *Revolutionary Diplomatic Correspondence,* IV, 383, 484).

News that Jackson had bought beyond the limit of his funds and, with

Gillon, had also chartered two merchant vessels to transport the goods, reached Franklin soon after Laurens sailed for America. Lacking money to cover these unanticipated bills, failing to persuade Vergennes to come to his financial rescue, and recognizing that the credit of the United States was in jeopardy, Franklin informed Jackson that the 1,500,000 livres would have to be used to help satisfy his creditors rather than be taken to the United States (*ibid.*, IV, 467–68, 484–85, 493, 522–23, 605–6). Following an acrimonious exchange of letters with Franklin, Jackson sailed with Gillon in August 1781 and finally reached Philadelphia on 28 February 1782 (*ibid.*, IV, 529–31, 543–46, 546 n.; NA: PCC, No. 41, IV, 445–59, and especially fol. 451; JM to Randolph, 29 May 1782).

Jackson necessarily had left in Amsterdam the military stores for which he could not pay and the two vessels wherein these goods were stowed. Both the suppliers of the articles and the shipowners looked to Franklin for remuneration and heavy damages for non-fulfillment of contracts. Gillon's creditors further complicated matters by seeking their due through "arresting" some of the goods bought by Jackson as Laurens' agent (Wharton, *Revolutionary Diplomatic Correspondence*, IV, 705, 827; V, 514). At the time of the present motion and for many months thereafter, Franklin, Adams, and Thomas Barclay were still endeavoring to disentangle these transactions, effect settlements with the claimants, and thereby release for shipment to the United States the articles abandoned by Jackson in the Netherlands (*ibid.*, IV, 835, 838; V, 114, 159–60, 163, 219, 514; Report on Foreign Dispatches, 20 March 1782, n. 6; *JCC*, XXV, 574).

In the meantime John Laurens had arrived in Philadelphia on 2 September 1781 and reported to Congress that Jackson would return before long in Gillon's ship, bringing the balance of the specie and matériel (Wharton, *Revolutionary Diplomatic Correspondence*, IV, 685–92; *JCC*, XXI, 932). Jackson, however, having quarreled with Gillon, disembarked in Spain and reached Philadelphia empty-handed in the following February. While in Spain Jackson had written apologetically to Franklin, admitting that his distrust of Gillon and his refusal to permit the money to be carried on Gillon's ship had been completely warranted (Wharton, *Revolutionary Diplomatic Correspondence*, IV, 546 n.).

Although Gillon had much to account for, he was greeted with acclaim when, after his West Indian exploits, he docked his frigate and prizes at Philadelphia on 29 May. He, too, had been aggrieved by Franklin (JM to Randolph, 29 May 1782; *JCC*, XXII, 309). By then Congress had received from Franklin at least two letters which included brief explanations of his dealings with Jackson and Gillon (*JCC*, XXII, 141 and n., 150–51, 290–91; Wharton, *Revolutionary Diplomatic Correspondence*, IV, 825–28; V, 218–19).

Ralph Izard began his term in Congress on 7 June, and Arthur Lee resumed his seat on the 27th of that month (Lee to JM, 24 May, n. 4; Jones to JM, 25 June, n. 15; JM to Randolph, 2 July 1782). They and Franklin's other foes in Congress probably welcomed the opportunity to embarrass Franklin by having a committee investigate his conduct. In a letter to Samuel Adams on 6 August 1782, Arthur Lee designated Franklin's withholding of the 1,500,000 livres from Jackson as equivalent to "an absolute robbery" (Burnett, *Letters,* VI, 428–30).

[12 July 1782]

That Col: Laurense's letters & reports to Congress[1] concerning his Mission to the Court of France and the loans & donation in Specie obtaind from that court and the disposition made by him respecting the said Donation & loans—and respecting the purchases and Contracts made by him on the Credit thereof—and for freight &.c.[2] [or by others & paid for out of monies obtained from the Ct of France on his application] be referred to a[3] Committe[4] to make strict enquiry into the Causes of detention of the money goods &c and report thereon to Congress[5]

[1] These letters and reports, dated 11, 19, and 20 March, 9 and 24 April, 15 May, 2 and 6 September 1781 are in NA: PCC, No. 165, fols. 53–262, *passim.* Most of the letters are printed in Wharton, *Revolutionary Diplomatic Correspondence,* IV, 278–79, 317–21, 355–57, 685–92, 700–701. For the receipt by Congress of these letters and reports on various dates between 28 May and 7 September 1781, see *JCC,* XX, 550, 577, 693, 751; XXI, 928, 940.

[2] Below and to the right of "&.c.," JM placed a caret and then wrote at the bottom of the manuscript the succeeding passage through "application." This passage was made a bracketed insertion within the motion. Following "obtained," JM wrote and deleted "by him." The purpose of JM's amendment was clearly to inquire into Jackson's and possibly Gillon's conduct as well as Laurens'. JM probably struck out "by him" as tending to accept one version of a subject to be investigated.

[3] This word is interlineated above a deleted "the."

[4] As originally written, "Committe" was followed by "Just Chosen to make strict enquiry into the Causes of detention of the money goods &c and report thereon to Congress." Although ink lines were drawn through this passage, it was then repeated with the exception of "Just Chosen." The deletion of these two words and the substitution of "a" for "the" (see n. 3) raise a question to which the printed journal provides no answer. Between the time of drafting and of introducing the motion, Bland and Scott either discovered that the committee to which they expected their motion to be referred had not been appointed, or that it would be more appropriate to have the proposed investigation made by a committee appointed solely for that purpose. The journal for 12 July fails to note any committee "Just Chosen" to which this investigation appropriately could have been assigned (*JCC,* XXII, 383–86).

[5] The editor of the *JCC* entered the motion as adopted by Congress in the journal for 12 July before the entry of the version introduced by Bland. Besides a few unimportant changes, chiefly in punctuation and capitalization, the adopted motion placed "on the credit thereof and for freight &c." in parentheses, and deleted the brackets enclosing the passage contributed by JM (*JCC,* XXII, 384).

With Bland as chairman, and Jonathan Jackson (Mass.) and David Howell (R.I.) as the other members, the committee named to prosecute the inquiry was anti-Franklin in outlook. The committee's report, written by Bland, first read to Congress on 26 September and finally spread upon the journal on 1 November 1782 (NA: PCC, No. 19, III, 449–56; *JCC*, XXIII, 700–705), was characterized by JM on 15 October as "shameless" and "unfair" in its treatment of Franklin, and as "one of the signal monuments which party zeal has produced" (Burnett, *Letters*, VI, 508). See also Report on Congressional Inspection of Departments, 17 June 1782, editorial note.

Report on Treaty with the Netherlands

MS (NA: PCC, No. 25, II, 121–23). In JM's hand. Docketed: "Report of Committee for revising the instructions to Mr. Adams. July 3. Mr Madison Mr Duane Mr Clymer Delivered and read July 12. 1782. Entd. Monday the 15h assigned for the Consideration–July 17. 1782 Question on the resolution passed in the negative."

[12 July 1782]

The Committee to whom was recommitted the report relative to the Instructions of Mr. Adams[1]–Submit the following remarks and resolution–

They observe that in the Treaty between the U. S. and his M. C. M. it is among other things stipulated that the subjects of the parties, "may by testament, donation or otherwise dispose of their goods *immoveable*[2] as well as moveable, in favor of such persons as to them shall seem good; and their heirs wheresoever residing, may succeed them ab intestat, without being obliged to obtain letters of naturalization["].[3]

That the 2d. Art. of the proposed treaty between the U. S. & the U. Provinces with which the Minister Plenipo: of the former is charged, contains a general stipulation to the subjects of the parties, that they shall enjoy mutually the same commercial exemptions and privileges, as are or may be allowed to the most favored nations;[4] under which general stipulation, claims & expectations may be excited in the subjects of the U. Provinces, of an entire equality under the laws of the U. S. with the subjects of his M. C. M.

That the 6th. Art: of the said proposed Treaty proceeds farther and expressly stipulates that the subjects of the parties may by, Will or otherwise dispose of to such persons as to them may seem good, the effects, moneys, debts, or goods *immoveable* as well as moveable which they have or ought to have, within the dominions of either of the partys and their heirs altho' not naturalised, shall freely & quietly take possession of all the said goods & effects whatsoever, according to the laws of each Country respectively: in such manner however that the wills & right of entering upon the *inheritances* of persons dying intestate, must be proved according to the law in those places where such person may happen to die; any law, statute custom or right whatsoever notwithstanding.[5]

That in the opinion of the Committee it is not altogether clear that the stipulation of the right above stated to the subjects of his M. C. M. does not encroach on the rights reserved by the federal articles to the individual States;[6] And very clear, that on extension of it to the subjects of other powers than of Spain, will be chargeable with such encroachment;[7]

That without enquiring into the inequality of this stipulation, as it will probably be exercised by the Citizens of the U. S. and the subjects of the U. P. or into the inconveniences which may result from an indefinite licence to aliens to possess real property within the U. S. The Committee infer from the repugnance shewn by some of the States to such an indulgence to the subjects of France, notwithstanding the special clause in the federal articles relative to that country[8] and our peculiar relation to it, that the compliance of the States with a like engagement to another, power, will be extremely precarious.

That in order to avoid these difficulties & consequences, it appears to the Committee expedient to resolve as follows; viz

That the Minister Plenipo: for negociating a treaty of amity & commerce with the U. Provinces of the low Countries, be & he hereby is instructed, so to vary the tenor of the 2d. & 6th. Articles in the plan of treaty transmitted to him, as to exclude all right or pretext in the subjects of either of the Contracting parties, to acquire, or hold within the dominions of the other party, any real property or estate of inheritance whatsoever; and to be careful not to admit into any other parts of the said Treaty, any terms or expressions from which such right or pretext may be inferred: provided that the said Minister Plenipotentiary be at liberty to depart from this instruction in case he shall have taken steps towards a conclusion of a Treaty with the U. Provinces, which in his opinion are inconsistent therewith.[9]

1 See Report Revising Adams' Instructions, 5 July 1782, and n. 11.
2 That is, realty.
3 *Ibid.*, and n. 12.
4 *Ibid.*, and n. 1; *JCC*, XVIII, 1207–8.
5 See Report Revising Adams' Instructions, 5 July 1782, and n. 14.
6 *Ibid.*, and n. 17.
7 *Ibid.*, and n. 16.

[8] *Ibid.*, and n. 17.

[9] *Ibid.*, and n. 24. On 17 July 1782, "the yeas and nays being required by Mr. [James] Madison," every state delegation except New Jersey's rejected the resolution. Arthur Lee's and Bland's adverse votes overrode JM's "ay." Of the twenty-nine delegates in Congress, only six favored the proposal (*JCC*, XXII, 396).

Virginia Delegates to Benjamin Harrison

RC (Virginia State Library). Written by Arthur Lee except for Theodorick Bland's signature. Docketed, "Virga Delegates Letter July July 16th 1782." Although JM did not sign the letter, it clearly was written on his, as well as Bland's and Lee's behalf. The omission of his signature may be explained by the comment at the close of JM's letter to Pendleton of this date (*q.v.*).

PHILADELPHIA July 16. 1782

SIR,

We had the honor of receiving your Excellencys Letter of the 6th.,[1] together with one of the same date from the Clerk of the Council, enclosing the Resolutions of the Assembly on the Supplies requested from his most Christian Majesty.[2]

The Resolutions we immediately transmitted to the minister of France.[3]

We shall inform your Excellency from time to time, of the proceedings of the several Legislatures touching the seizure of british Goods. That of N. Jersey has lately passd an Act for this purpose.[4]

It gives us very great pleasure to be informd, that an effective Law is at length passd, not only for the good of the Service, but because, tho' many other States are equally deficient without equal reason, yet the whole odium is centerd upon Virginia.[5]

We have informd the Delegates of S. Carolina, of what your Excellency mentions. Those of N. Carolina are not here.[6] Still we are without any intelligence from Europe or the Islands. Genl. Washington & Count Rochambau are at present in this City, to consult on the operations of the Campaign.[7]

There is a report here from N. York that the Enemy have evacuated & burnt Charles-town, & sent the garrison to the W. Indies.[8] Sir Guy Carelton is so desirous of retreiving the Soldiers we have taken, that he offers, if we will exchange them for Seamen, to stipulate that they shall not serve against the United States during twelve months.[9] But he will find this artifice, somewhat too shallow for his purpose. Lippencut is not, nor is it expected he will be, given up.[10]

We have the honor to be, with great respect, Yr. Excellency's most obedient & most humbl. Servts.

THEOK: BLAND JR
A. LEE

[1] *Q.v.*

[2] Neither Archibald Blair's letter nor its enclosure has been found. For the "Resolutions," see Harrison to Virginia Delegates, 8 June 1782, and n. 3.

[3] La Luzerne.

[4] See JM to Randolph, 18 June, and n. 7; Report on Illicit Trade, 19 June 1782, n. 8.

[5] See Randolph to JM, 20 June, and n. 48; Harrison to Virginia Delegates, 6 July 1782. Lee means that, in view of the fact that Virginia in 1781 had been a main theater of the war, she could not be as justifiably blamed as many other states for delinquency in filling her quota of continental troops.

[6] See Randolph to JM, 5 July, n. 7; Harrison to Virginia Delegates, 6 July 1782. Present in Congress from South Carolina were Ralph Izard, Arthur Middleton, David Ramsay, and John Rutledge (*JCC*, XII, 390–92). For the North Carolina delegation, see Harrison to Virginia Delegates, 12 April 1782, n. 4.

[7] See Jones to JM, 8 July 1782, n. 7. Washington reached Philadelphia on Sunday, 14 July, one day after Rochambeau's arrival in that city. Their principal conference was on 19 July (Fitzpatrick, *Writings of Washington*, XXIV, 430, 433–35, 471; *Virginia Gazette*, 3 August 1782).

[8] The rumor, which was reported in the *Pennsylvania Packet* of 16 July, had no foundation in fact.

[9] See Report on Fish and Fuel for Naval Prisoners, 1 July 1782, n. 1. Besides making this offer in his dispatch of 7 July 1782 to Washington, Carleton expressed his willingness to have the American seamen return to naval service as soon as they were released (NA: PCC, No. 152, X, 629–32). This at best was a small concession, because, after their incarceration in British prison ships, few sailors were physically qualified for duty. In a letter of 9 July to the president of Congress, Washington commented: "notwithstanding the plausibility of the terms on which Sir Guy Carleton proposes the exchange of American Seamen for British Soldiers . . . it must still be obvious, that it would amount to nearly the same thing to have the Prisoners so exchanged employed against our Allies in the West Indies, as it would to have them acting against ourselves on the Continent" (Fitzpatrick, *Writings of Washington*, XXIV, 406). On 15 July Congress referred this letter and Carleton's offer to a committee consisting of John Witherspoon, JM, and John Rutledge (*JCC*, XXII, 388 n.). For its report on 12 August 1782, see *JCC*, XXIII, 462).

[10] See JM to Randolph, 1 May 1782, nn. 17 and 18.

From Joseph Jones

RC (LC: Madison Papers). Undocketed and cover missing.

FREDERICKSBURG 16th July 1782

DR. SIR.

Having occasion to go to Town I recd. your Letter of the 9th.[1] and thank you for the trouble you have taken about a habitation for me and my family. Mr. Ross[2] has this day put it in my power to go forward and if the health of Mrs. Jones and my little boy will permit and her inclination and the heat of the weather does not interfere to prevent it I shall probably see you in less than a month. If good lodgings with the use of a Kitchen can be obtained it will answer tho' not so conveniently as a House with furniture but I intreat that neither be possitively engaged untill you hear from me again as by that time I shall better know Mrs. Jones's determination. present my compliments to friend Griffin and give him my thanks for his trouble in assisting you abt. a House.

I inclose an order from Mr. Ross on Mr. Whiteside for the Bill lost and also a Bill for three hundred dollars wch. be pleased to negociate and pay Mr. Griffin and also Messr. Baker potts & Co. Ironmongers in second street near Arch Street £110[?] I owe them.[3]

The French Army have all passed Rappahannock at Falmouth. the last division will move Tomorrow from that place. their progress through this part of the country furnishes some of the Inhabitants with Cash to pay their Taxes. about 500 convalescents remain at York.[4] I expected Mr. Lee wod. have been with [you] some time past but hear by Col. Monroe he only lef[t] Chantilly about ten days ago.[5] make my Complimen[ts] to inquiring friends and believe me

Yrs very truly

JOS. JONES.

[1] Not found. In his letters of 25 June and 8 July 1782 to JM (*q.v.*), Jones had asked that accommodations be found in Philadelphia for his family.

[2] See Jones to JM, 25 June, and n. 12; 1 July; 8 July 1782, and nn. 2 and 4.

[3] See Jones to JM, 8 July 1782, n. 2.

[4] See Randolph to JM, 5 July, and n. 7; Harrison to Virginia Delegates, 11 July 1782, n. 1.

[5] See Jones to JM, 8 July 1782, and n. 9. James Monroe had been misinformed, because Arthur Lee was in Philadelphia by 27 June. Lee's estate of Chantilly was on the Nomini River in Westmoreland County, Va.

To Edmund Pendleton

RC (New York Public Library). Unsigned and cover missing. Docketed by Pendleton, "James Madison, jr. Esqr. July 16th. 1782."

PHILADA. July 16th. 1782

DEAR SIR,

Your favor of the 8th. instant[1] escaped the danger of late incident to the post; the robbers having removed to the Northward for the purpose of attacking the Eastern mail which fell into their hands near Trenton last week. It is said to have been the identical party.[2]

I am not yet so happy as to be able to transmit the expected intelligence from Europe, no vessels having arrived from that quarter or from the W. Indies. Our only news is a report that Charlestown has been evacuated & burn[ed]; of which you will be a better judge than I am.[3]

Genl Washington & Ct. Rochambeau met here on Saturday evening.[4] The object & result of their consultations belong to the military cabinet.

Genl Carlton in a correspondence with Genl W. yesterday laid before Congress[5] complains much of legal proceedings agst. adherents to the British cause, as Traitors, adopts the maxim that "in a civil war between people of one empire there can *during the contest* be no traitors at all." and asks a passport for Genl Robinson & Mr. Ludlow to confer & settle arrangements on that idea.[6] He at the same time and from a similar policy, proposes in order to remove our objection agst. exchanging B. soldiers [and] Amer: seamen, that the latter shall be free & the former restrained from serving *agst. the 13 Provinces* for one year, within which he is sanguine an end will be put to the calamities of the present war.[7]

Other parts of the letter which speak of Lippincut make it probable that Asgil will at last be left to expiate the guilt of this mu[r]derer.[8] Having less time for perparing for the post than I usually devote to my friends I must conclude abruptly with begging an excuse for the defects which render this scarcely legible or intelligible.

[1] Not found.

[2] See Harrison to Virginia Delegates, 8 June, n. 1; Report on Mail Robbery, 19 June, and n. 3; Jones to JM, 25 June 1782, and n. 4. The interception of the mail, allegedly by "about Twelve Men," occurred at noon on 10 July at Penn's Manor, approximately eight miles south of Trenton, N.J., on the road to Philadelphia. According to the account in the *Pennsylvania Packet* of 18 July, the "armed villains" informed the postrider that they had robbed "the southern post, a few weeks ago in Maryland." See also Burnett, *Letters*, VI, 385 n.

[3] See Virginia Delegates to Harrison, 16 July 1782, and n. 8. JM evidently meant that, if the report was true, Pendleton would probably have been so informed by his nephew, Captain Nathaniel Pendleton, Jr., an aide-de-camp of Greene.

[4] JM was misinformed. See Virginia Delegates to Harrison, 16 July 1782, and n. 7.

[5] *Ibid.*, and n. 9.

[6] Two Loyalists, who had been taken into custody from aboard a British flag-of-truce ship docked at Elizabethtown, N.J., were charged with "High Treason" and convicted by a civil tribunal of that state. In a letter of 20 June 1782 to Washington, after declaring this verdict to be a measure "of the most fatal Extremity," Carleton continued: "In a Civil War between people of one Empire there can, during the Contest, be no Treason at all, or each party assuming the other to be Traitors, shall be able, by the same or different Laws, some made even during the very Contest, to effect more Carnage than by the Sword." Carleton suggested that Lieutenant General James Robertson (*ca.* 1720–1788), royal "Governor" of New York, and Captain George James Ludlow (1758–1842) of the 1st Regiment of Foot Guards meet with Washington or with his representatives for the purpose of placing "these Questions for the future, on the Ground of some mutual good Understanding" (NA: PCC, No. 152, X, 617, 621–24; Fitzpatrick, *Writings of Washington*, XXIV, 420 n.). In his reply on 22 June to Carleton, Washington disclaimed any control whatsoever over the civil authorities of a state (*ibid.*, XXIV, 372; NA: PCC, No. 152, X, 625–27).

During most of the Revolution American captives in Great Britain were charged with high treason, denied the right of a writ of habeas corpus, and imprisoned at the king's pleasure. Carleton's proposals reflected the change of policy embodied in a parliamentary statute of 25 March 1782 whereby Americans were to be incarcerated or detained "according to the custom and usage of war, and the law of nations" (Olive Anderson, "The Treatment of Prisoners of War in Britain during the American War of Independence," [University of London] *Bulletin of the Institute of Historical Research*, XXVIII [1955], 63–83). Carleton's phrase, "Ground of some mutual good Understanding," no doubt embraced a hope that at the end of the war Congress would enable Loyalists to regain their citizenship and property by taking the requisite oaths of allegiance.

[7] See Virginia Delegates to Harrison, 16 July 1782, n. 9.

[8] See JM to Randolph, 1 May 1782, nn. 17 and 18.

To Edmund Randolph

RC (LC: Madison Papers). Docketed by Randolph, "July 16. 1782." The cover is missing. What may have been a brief complimentary close and signature are too faded to be legible. The italicized words are those written by JM in cipher, except in the one instance mentioned in n. 10. For the passage which he encoded in the Lovell rather than the official cipher, see n. 27. Many years after writing the letter, JM or someone at his bidding indicated by brackets that the first two paragraphs should be published in the first edition of his papers, but the letter appeared in that compilation with only the last two paragraphs omitted. The passage in the Lovell cipher was not decoded (Madison, *Papers* [Gilpin ed.], I, 149–52).

PHILADA. July 16th. 1782

DEAR SIR

Notwithstanding the defensive professions of the Enemy they seem to be waging an active war agst. the post riders. The mail for the Eastward on wednesday morning last shared the same fate which the Southern mail did a few weeks ago and it is said from the identical villains.[1] This operation has with drawn them from their Southern stand, and secured the arrival of the mail which brings your favor of the 5th. inst:[2] I fully concur in the change of cypher which you suggest and understand the reference for a key-word.[3] I have been in some pain from the danger incident to the cypher we now use. The enemy I am told have in some instances published their intercepted cyphers. On our first meeting I propose to prepare, against another separation, a cypher framed by Mr. Livingston[4] on a more en[lar]ged and complicated plan than ours, of which he has furnished me several blank printed copies.

Your computation of the numbers in Virga. tallies very exactly with one transmitted by Mr. Jefferson in an answer to several queries from Mr. M—s. It is as accurate as the official returns to the Executive of the militia would admit. His proportion of the fencibles to the white souls is stated precisly as your computation states it.[5]

You will continue your information on the case of the flag and send me the acts of the Legislature as fast as they are printed.[6] Will you be so good also as to obtain from the Auditors a state of the balance due on the principles established by law, and let me know when & how it is to be applied for? as also what chance there is of obtaining a regular remittance of future allowance?[7]

Genl. Washington & Ct. Rochambeau met here on saturday evening. The object of their consultation is among the arcana of war.[8]

A dispatch from the Commander in cheif communicated to Congress yesterday a late correspondence between him & Genl. Carlton, principally on the subject of two traitors who under the cover of a flag of truce exposed themselves to arrest in New Jersey, and had sentence of death passed upon them. Genl. Carlton among other observations on the Subject, says that "In a civil war between people of one empire, there can during the contest, be no treason at all"—and asks a passport for Genl. Robinson & Mr. Ludlow to confer with Genl. W. or persons appointed by him, & to settle arrangements on this idea. Gel. W. declines the conference observing that the proposed subject of it is within civil resort. Whereupon Genl. Carlton asks—Am I to apply to Congress to admit persons to conferences at Philada.? can any deputation be sent by Congress to your camp to meet persons appointed by me? or will you Sr. undertake to manage our common interest?[9] The drift of all this need not be pointed out to you. As a counterpart to it, the British Genl. proposes, in order to remove all objection to an exchange of Soldiers for seamen, that the latter shall be perfectly free; and the former subject to the condition of not serving *agst. the 13. Provinces* for one year, within which period he is very sanguine that an end will be put to the calamities of the present[?] war.[10]

The same despatch informs Congress that a party of the Enemy have lately made a successful incursion upon the settlements of Mohawk, have reoccupied Oswego, and are extending themselves in to the Western Country.[11] However little these movements may coincide with a defensive plan, they coincide perfectly with ideas which will not fail to be urged at a pacification,[12] Messrs. Montgomery & Root returned yesterday from their Eastern deputation. They have not yet made their report.[13] The former complains that several *of the States* are *appropriating the taxes which they lay as their quota of the eight million*[14] *to internal uses—He owns that the knowledge he has obtained of the case*[15] has *changed his mind on that head* and *that if the ground was to be trodden over again he should take a very different part in Congress.*[16] *He adds* that the current opinion is that a vessel arrived at Quebec brings a *royal charter* for *Vermont.*[17] that the people there are *in much confusion* and *many of them disposed to reunite* with *N—Hamshire.* A letter to Mr. Livingston from Mr. *Livermore*[18] corroborates this good news. It imparts that a very unexpected turn had taken place in the temper of the people *between the river* and *the ridge*[19] that they were *petitioning New Hamshire to be restored to* that *state* and that measures would be taken in concert with New York for that purpose.[20] The revolution in the *sentiments of M—g—y*[21] may be owing in part *to the new relattion in* which *Pennsylvania stands* to *Connecticut* which he says is governed on this occasion by interested *individuals.*[22] The controversy between Pena. & Connecticut will I suppose be now resumed & put into a course for decision, the return of Mr. Root having removed the cause which suspended it.[23]

In the beginning of this month Committees were appointed in pursuance of a previous Resolution for such an appointt. every half year to examine into the proceedings of the several executive departments & make report to Congress. This plan was adopted not only to discharge the general duty of Congress & to satisfy their constituents, but also that[?] such reports might shelter in some degree faithful officers from unmerited imputations & suspicions, as well as expose to just censure those of an opposite character.[24] For reasons which will occur to you *Doctor Le*[*e*] *wa*[*s*] [*se*]*n*[*t*] *into* the department of Finance.[25] The [*Do*]*cto*[*r*] is endeavouring I am told Contrary to the object in view to go into an investigation of the *cont*[*r*]*ac*[*t*]*s in trade* allowed by Congress. All the movements of *D*[*o*]*cto*[*r*] are pointed directly or circuitously either to *Moris o*[*r*] *Franklin*[26] This cypher I find is extremely tedious & liable to errors.[27]

Genl. Carlton in his letter to Genl. Washington above quoted, says with respect to Lippincut only that the Ct. has passed their judgment and that as soon as the length of the proceedings would admit, a copy should be sent to him.[28] It is inferred that this murderer will not be given up, and consequently a vicarious atonement must be made by the guiltless Asgill.[29]

Our expected news from Mr. Adams is not yet arrived,[30] nor any news whatever from Europe. The same continues to be the case with [respect ?] to the W. Indies. The reports for several days have turned on the evacuation & burning of Charleston.[31] If there be any truth in either of them, you will have heard a confirmation before this reaches you. The former is as probable as the latter is otherwise, unless it may have been the effect of chance, or the hand of some desperate refugee.

You never touch on the time of your visit to us, a point on which I am you know not a little anxious. Mr. Jones is detained I perceive by a mode of supply from Mr. Ross which has only a retrospective efficacy.[32]

[1] See JM to Pendleton, 16 July 1782, and n. 2.

[2] *Q.v.*

[3] See Randolph to JM, 5 July 1782, and nn. 17, 18, and 19.

[4] Robert R. Livingston. Which of the several codes used by the secretary for foreign affairs in 1782 was given to JM has not been determined (Wharton, *Revolutionary Diplomatic Correspondence*, V, 53, 74, 405, 460). In a letter of 20 August 1782 to Randolph, JM stated that the four sheets of "the printed cypher of Mr. Livingston," being too large to go by the postrider, could not be sent until a "private conveyance" became available (LC: Madison Papers). JM and Randolph did not employ this code in their correspondence later in 1782.

[5] See Randolph to JM, 5 July 1782, and nn. 13 and 14. In response to a query from Barbé-Marbois ("M—s"), Jefferson had estimated the "Whole Militia of the State" of Virginia in 1780–1781 as 49,971. In 1782 he believed that there were 296,852 "free inhabitants" and 270,762 slaves in the state (Thomas Jefferson, *Notes on the State of Virginia*, ed. by William Peden [Chapel Hill, N.C., 1955], pp. 82–90).

[6] See Randolph to JM, 5 July 1782, and n. 3.

7 See Jones to JM, 25 June 1782, and n. 9.

8 JM was misinformed. See Virginia Delegates to Harrison, 16 July 1782, and n. 7.

9 See JM to Pendleton, 16 July 1782, and n. 6. Carleton hoped that he might negotiate directly with Congress, separate the United States from France, and keep the "Provinces" within the British Empire.

10 See Virginia Delegates to Harrison, 16 July 1782, n. 9. JM underlined rather than coded the italicized passage in this sentence. He suggested the "drift" of Carleton's tactics by emphasizing that the general had used the word "Provinces," not "States."

11 Washington included this news in his letter of 9 July to Congress (Fitzpatrick, *Writings of Washington*, XXIV, 405). During the summer of 1782 Joseph Brant, leading about five hundred Indians, again ravaged the Canajoharie and German Flats (now Herkimer) neighborhoods of the Mohawk Valley (Francis Whiting Halsey, *The Old New York Frontier* [New York, 1913], p. 309). Following General John Burgoyne's surrender in the autumn of 1777, the British had abandoned Fort Oswego at the confluence of the Oswego River and Lake Ontario. They briefly reoccupied the post two years later and once again garrisoned it and strengthened the fortifications in the spring of 1782 (Crisfield Johnson, *History of Oswego County, New York* [Philadelphia, 1877], p. 40; Jean N. McIlwraith, *Sir Frederick Haldimand* [Toronto, Canada, 1910], p. 157).

12 Following this comma, JM may have written five or six additional words to complete the sentence. If he did, they have entirely faded except for a few ink dots and lines. The passage comes at the bottom of the second page of this four-page letter. Without indenting, he began the third page with "Messrs." He probably expected Randolph to infer that, by "extending themselves in to the Western Country," the British hoped to keep the friendship and trade of the Six Nations of the Iroquois and to retain the region after the war, if the peace negotiators applied the principle of *uti possidetis* in defining boundaries.

13 See Report on Mission To Inform States of Financial Crisis, 22 May 1782, n. 2.

14 See Report on New Hampshire Requisition, 25 March, n. 3; Harrison to Virginia Delegates, 6 April, n. 6; Motion To Inform States of Financial Crisis, 20 May 1782, and n. 3.

15 After this word, JM inadvertently repeated 94, the cipher for "of."

16 Although leaving the impression that Joseph Montgomery had changed his mind about how states should use their income from taxes, JM probably meant that the delegate from Pennsylvania had become an opponent rather than an advocate of admitting Vermont as a state (Burnett, *Letters*, VI, 450, 501; *JCC*, XXII, 108–14). See n. 22, below.

17 By using 213, the figure for "van," rather than 619, standing for "ve," JM erroneously coded this word. Although "the current opinion" appears to have been in error, the refusal of Congress to recognize the independence of the "state" of Vermont and heed its request for admission to the Confederation had led influential Green Mountain men to resume negotiations with British agents in Canada.

Lord George Germain still hoped to convert Vermont into a royal province, but, probably with good reason, Sir Frederick Haldimand, governor and commander-in-chief of Canada, suspected that "Governor" Thomas Chittenden, Ethan and Ira Allen, and their colleagues were manifesting a willingness to place Vermont under King George III merely as a strategic move to prevent an invasion by the British and to force concessions from New York, New Hampshire, and Congress. Haldimand's faint hope of success almost completely disappeared in June 1782, when he received orders to suspend all offensive operations (*Collections of the Vermont Historical Society*, II [Montpelier, Vt., 1871], 198–99, 230, 263–68, 273–76,

283–86, 288–89; Hiland Hall, *The History of Vermont, from Its Discovery to Its Admission into the Union in 1791* [Albany, N.Y., 1868], pp. 360–61, 366–78, 398–402).

[18] Not found. Both Robert R. Livingston and Samuel Livermore, chief justice of the Superior Court of New Hampshire, favored an "equitable solution" based upon the premise that "it was wrong to attempt to govern people against their will" (George Dangerfield, *Chancellor Robert R. Livingston*, p. 118; Motion Concerning Documents on Vermont, 3 April 1782, editorial note).

[19] That is, the watershed in Vermont dividing streams flowing into the Connecticut River on the east from those flowing into Lake Champlain, Lake George, or the Hudson River on the west.

[20] For the background of the Vermont, or New Hampshire Grants, controversy, see JM to Pendleton, 22 January, and nn. 5 and 6; 7 February, n. 4; 2 April, and n. 2; 23 April, and n. 7; Motion Concerning Documents on Vermont, 3 April, and editorial note, and nn. 5, 6, 8; Motion on Letter of Vermont Agents, 20 April, and n. 3; JM to Randolph, 23 April; 1 May, and nn. 15 and 16; Observations Relating to the Influence of Vermont and Territorial Claims, 1 May 1782, and n. 6.

In the spring of 1782 Vermont residents of four towns on the west bank of the Connecticut River made known their desire to submit to the jurisdiction of New Hampshire, and residents of three towns west of the Green Mountains manifested their readiness to acknowledge the authority of New York. There was "much confusion" because each of the "seceding" groups was opposed by many of their neighbors as well as by the "legislature" of Vermont, which on 13 June 1782 passed "an act for the punishment of conspiracies against the peace, liberty and independence of the state." In October, after the opposition of the three western towns had been quelled by armed force, the Superior Court of Vermont severely punished the leaders of "the Yorkers." On 21 June 1782 the New Hampshire General Assembly discouraged the discontented memorialists in the eastern Vermont towns by agreeing to heed their plea only if the "generality of the Inhabitants" east of the "heighth of land" expressed a desire to re-declare their allegiance to New Hampshire, and if that state and New York could amicably divide Vermont between them (Hiland Hall, *History of Vermont*, pp. 392–97; *Collections of the Vermont Historical Society*, II, 270–74, 277–78, 286–87, 295–99; Nathaniel Bouton *et al.*, eds., *New Hampshire Provincial and State Papers*, VIII [Concord, 1874], 943).

[21] Joseph Montgomery.

[22] See JM to Randolph, 2 July 1782, n. 22. The Susquehannah Company of land speculators was organized in Connecticut in 1753. They based their claim to a large area in northeastern Pennsylvania upon the boundaries of Connecticut as defined in its colonial charter and upon a purchase of land from the Six Nations of the Iroquois. Among the prominent members of the company in 1782 were Eliphalet Dyer and Jesse Root, who were delegates from Connecticut in Congress (*Pennsylvania Archives*, 2d ser., XVIII, 2–4, 22, 102). For the genesis of the company, see Julian P. Boyd, ed., *The Susquehannah Company Papers* (4 vols. to date; Ithaca, N.Y., 1962–), I, lviii–lxxxix.

If the company achieved its purpose, the area of its claim would be transferred from the jurisdiction of Pennsylvania to that of Connecticut, or even be accorded separate statehood. In the face of this threat, Montgomery reversed his position on Vermont's similar effort to gain separate identity at New York's and New Hampshire's expense. See n. 16, above. In 1786 Ethan Allen came to the Wyoming Valley and allegedly declared that "with one hundred Green Mountain Boys, and two hundred Rifle men he could make that a new State in defiance of Pennsylvania" (*Pennsylvania Archives*, 2d ser., XVIII, 109; Edmund C. Burnett, *The Continental Congress*, p. 649).

[23] See JM to Randolph, 2 July 1782, and n. 22.

[24] See Report on Congressional Inspection of Departments, 17 June 1782, and n. 5.

[25] See *JCC*, XXII, 370. Arthur Lee was a member of the committee, under James Duane's chairmanship, "to enquire fully into the proceedings of the department of Finance, including the several branches of the same." See Report on Congressional Inspection of Departments, 17 June 1782, editorial note.

[26] For Arthur Lee's enmity toward Benjamin Franklin, see JM to Pendleton, 23 April, n. 10; Randolph to JM, 16–17 May 1782, and nn. 13 and 17.

[27] In using the Lovell cipher to encode the thirteen italicized words in this paragraph, JM made eleven alphabetical errors. See Randolph to JM, 5 July 1782, and nn. 19 and 20. A copy of the key to this code is in the University of Virginia Library.

[28] Carleton's letter, from which JM "above quoted," had been written on 20 June. In the present paragraph JM is referring to Carleton's letter of 7 July, informing Washington that Lippincott's court-martial had been held but not divulging its outcome (NA: PCC, No. 152, X, 631). With his dispatch of 9 July to Congress, Washington had enclosed copies of Carleton's two communications (*JCC*, XXII, 388 n.).

[29] For the affair of Lippincott, Huddy, and Charles Asgill (*ca.* 1762–1823), see JM to Randolph, 1 May and n. 17. JM borrowed from Christian theology the phrase "vicarious atonement," meaning that Christ by his death on the cross had paid the penalty for the sins of all men.

[30] See Virginia Delegates to Harrison, 25 June and n. 3; JM to Lee, 25 June 1782, and n. 3. On 29 August 1782 Livingston wrote to John Adams, "Near five months have elapsed since I have been favored with a line from you" (Wharton, *Revolutionary Diplomatic Correspondence*, V, 677). Adams had written faithfully, but his dispatches had been delayed in transmission. Thus Congress lacked official word from him that the States-General of the Netherlands had recognized the independence of the United States on 22 April 1782. See JM to Randolph, 23 July 1782.

[31] See Virginia Delegates to Harrison, 16 July 1782, and n. 8.

[32] This comment indicates that JM had received Jones's letter of 8 July (*q.v.* and its n. 2). See also Jones to JM, 16 July 1782.

From Edmund Randolph

RC (LC: Madison Papers). Unsigned but in Randolph's hand. Undocketed and cover missing.

RICHMOND July 18. 1782.

DEAR SIR

In my letter of the last week but one, I anticipated the cause of my failure to write by saturday's post.[1] The trial of the flag-ship, whose defence I undertook, added to the debt, due from me to my connections by friendship and blood, detained me in Williamsburg until the afternoon of that day.[2]

The ship[3] was indeed acquitted upon principles of law. But I fear, that the "chasm" in the testimony, by which her acquittal was affected, did not proceed from her innocence, so much as from the non-attendance of a witness.[4] I fear, too that she imported a considerable quantity of merchandize. Nay, if it had not been for my aversion to interrupt the schemes of Mr. Morris in the management of finance,[5] and my apprehension, lest the enemy should be clamorous and troublesome, if she were condemned without the most direct and pointed evidence–I was so well satisfied with my suspicion[s] that I would have laboured strenuously for confiscating her. For every avenue not explored for the [conta]mination[6] of british goods–an evil, which, if it stood single and unmixed with public benefit, arising from other considerations, I would not countenance upon any allurement of lucre whatever. But the forbearance of my temper in this respect was really worn down, when I was informed, that another of the flags, the sloop Good Intent, was basely violating her character. She was permitted to go as far as Boyd's hole[7] on Potomack; but went up to Alexandria without licence. The distance between those ports of the river is about sixty miles. She had on board a very liberal cargo, besides four anchors and four cables for ships; the having of which plainly indicated a design of stealing vessels, after the example of another flag ship[8] from Charlestown. I libelled her without hesitation. Her fate will be decided on friday sevennight, and will probably be adverse.[9]

From what cause has it proceeded, that the notification of the birth of a dauphin reached the hands of our governor on monday last only? Mr: Livingston, from whom the official intelligence did at last come, ought surely to have sent his dispatch, announcing that event by the post, rather than on opportunity, by Winchester: which was the route of the letter.[10] Some apology seems necessary for the involuntary omission of our executive to celebrate it, unless the address of the assembly to Ct. Rochambeau has made amends.[11]

Mr. Ambler[12] informs me, that there is not a single letter or paper from Phila. by the mail of to-day. This circumstance deprives me of the pleasure of acknowledging the receipt of any letter from you later than the 2d. instant,[13] and induces a belief, that Sir Guy has been again on the highway.[14]

The inclosure relates to the claim of an honest man, and zealous whig, for salary &c, as an attendant on the hospital here. I represented to him the impracticability of having his account immediately paid off, and the difficulty of obtaining, what he is willing to receive as a substitute for actual payment, a certificate. I must however intrude this business upon your attention so far, as to beg you to have the doctor's[15] demand, placed upon a footing, equally respectable with that, on which demands of a similar nature have been placed.

A late incident will probably try the fortitude of our judiciary, by calling upon them to say, whether a law, contrary to the constitution, is obligatory. The power of pardoning is delegated to the governor by the act of government, under two exceptions only: the one, where the prosecution may have been carried on by the house of delegates, the other when the law shall otherwise particularly direct. [In ei]ther of these instances the house of delegates is declared capable of pardoning. The law against treason, passed at a session, subsequent to the one, which formed the constitution, strips the governor of all authority to pardon in cases of treason and vests that in the general assembly, and thus interchanges with the senate the peculiar rights of the other branch of the legislature.[16] Three persons were attainted of treason at the last session of the general court,[17] and a vote of pardon was entered into by the delegates. This vote was submitted to the senate for their concurrence, and was negatived by them.[18] But the friends of the condemned have procured the suspension of execution in order to try at the next general court the force of their opinion, that the vote of the delegates is an actual pardon, in spite of the disagreement of the senate.

It is a wonderful mistake, that the French have diffused much specie thro' the lower country.[19] The inhabitants had been too great sufferers under the ravages of the enemy,[20] other states had been too active in throwing in their supplies, and the zeal of the contractors had been too ardent, to leave any portion of the french crowns, open to the pursuits of our countrymen. But let it be remembered; that the citizens of Wmsburg. and its neighbourhood do almost universally regret their departure. Equal condescension in commanders, and good order in soldiers were never yet known in any army. As justice and policy united in dictating a compensation for the small destruction of houses, which took place in consequence of their stay in Virginia, so has that compensation been marked by liberality. The president of the college was paid very handsomely for his library, and 1500£ were allowed for his house.[21]

I have not seen Dr. Coste's oration in return for the degree conferred on him by our university.[22] But I am informed, that he rallies the mode of rearing children, our diet, and in short the whole system of our education with great acrimony: Among other examples of the ill effect of our diet, I am told that he says, that it causes "*ventrum prorumpere.*"[23]

[1] See Randolph to JM, 5 July 1782. By "saturday's post," Randolph meant that of 13 July.

[2] Both Randolph and his wife Elizabeth were natives of Williamsburg (Moncure D. Conway, *Edmund Randolph,* pp. 36–37; Randolph to JM, 11–13 April, n. 2; 16 August 1782, MS in LC: Madison Papers).

[3] The "New-York." See Randolph to JM, 5 July 1782, and n. 3.

[4] Unidentified, but Randolph may have meant "any witness."

[5] See Ambler to JM, 20 April 1782, n. 4.

[6] With the exception of "For every" and "for the," the words to this point in the sentence are a doubtful rendition of what Randolph wrote. The brackets mark a hole in the manuscript.

[7] Governor Harrison had authorized four flag-of-truce vessels, sent from New York City to Virginia to load tobacco in accordance with the agreement made with the traders-capitulant of Yorktown, to ascend the Potomac as far as Boyd's Hole in King George County, Va., about eighteen miles east of Fredericksburg (*Calendar of Virginia State Papers,* III, 195; McIlwaine, *Official Letters,* III, 259).

[8] This was the brigantine "Maria." On 10 May 1782 five members of her crew had deserted at Hampton, Va., seized the sloop "William and John," and departed in her for New York City. Off the coast of New Jersey they were captured and carried into Egg Harbor. The Court of Admiralty of that state condemned the prize and ordered its sale. The new owner renamed the ship the "Dove," freighted her with naval stores, and set sail for New London, Conn. A British man-of-war captured the vessel and brought her to New York Harbor. In the meantime Governor Harrison had ordered the detention of the "Maria" at Hampton and written to Carleton demanding reparation or the return of the vessel and cargo. When the "Dove" arrived in New York, Carleton immediately complied. Thereupon, on 26 July 1782, Harrison released the "Maria." In December of that year Carleton sent Washington 187 guineas "and a half and one Dollar" to enable Harrison to recompense the owner of the "William and John" for the loss of his vessel and her cargo (McIlwaine, *Official Letters,* III, 234–35, 239–40, 271–72, 279, 281, 312–13, 327; *Journals of the Council of State,* III, 124, 128, 136; *Calendar of Virginia State Papers,* III, 227, 249; Fitzpatrick, *Writings of Washington,* XXV, 407 and n., 410, 454, 469).

[9] For exceeding the "limits of her permit" and having British merchandise aboard, the "Good Intent" had been libeled at Alexandria (Randolph to JM, 6 August 1782, MS in LC: Madison Papers). The Court of Admiralty ordered the confiscation and sale of the vessel and her cargo (*Calendar of Virginia State Papers,* III, 248; McIlwaine, *Official Letters,* III, 267).

[10] See Harrison to Virginia Delegates, 19 July 1782. Robert R. Livingston's circular letter of 14 May, misdirected by his office to "His Excellency George Harrison Esquire Virginia," had finally reached the governor on 16 July, after going to Winchester, Va., and from there to the state war office in Richmond, where it was opened and resealed (MS in Virginia State Library).

[11] See Randolph to JM, 5 July 1782, and n. 7. On 4 July 1782 Harrison "gave an entertainment" in Richmond. Among the thirteen "patriotic toasts" drunk on that occasion was one to "The Queen and Dauphin of France: May he inherit the virtues of his illustrious father" (*Virginia Gazette,* 6 July 1782).

[12] Jacquelin Ambler, Virginia state treasurer.

[13] *Q.v.*

[14] That is, the mail might again have been intercepted by the supposed agents of Carleton. See JM to Pendleton, 16 July 1782, and n. 2. When JM's letter of 9

July reached Randolph is unknown, but he acknowledged its receipt in his letter of 6 August 1782 to JM (MS in LC: Madison Papers).

[15] Dr. William Carter, who died in 1799 at "an advanced age" (*Virginia Argus* [Richmond], 14 June 1799), was a native of Williamsburg and a hospital surgeon in the southern department from 1 July 1776 to 31 July 1781. Despite JM's efforts in his behalf, Carter seems to have procured no direct relief from Congress. On 26 May 1784 he asked the Virginia General Assembly for nearly five years' back pay, with allowances for depreciation. A certificate for the balance was authorized to be issued and charged against the United States (*Journal of the House of Delegates*, May 1784, pp. 21–22, 27; Gwathmey, *Historical Register of Virginians*, p. 135).

[16] The Constitution or Form of Government of Virginia, Article IX. The second exception was "where the prosecution shall have been carried on by the House of Delegates" (Hening, *Statutes*, IX, 115–16). The General Assembly in its session of October 1776 enacted a law "declaring what shall be Treason." The third article of this statute, besides specifically denying to the governor and council the authority to pardon anyone convicted of treason, reserved that prerogative to the legislature (*ibid.*, IX, 168). On the other hand, Article IX of the Form of Government, although authorizing the legislature to deprive the governor and council of their pardoning power, clearly stipulated that it should thereafter be exercised by the House of Delegates rather than by the General Assembly as a whole.

[17] See Randolph to JM, 15 June 1782, and n. 2. The three men were James Lamb (d. 1785), Joshua Hopkins (d. 1795), and John Caton, all of Princess Anne County. Although the House of Delegates at the May 1782 session responded favorably to a petition to pardon the men, the Senate refused to concur, and the House took no further step in the matter before adjourning, except to determine to let it "lie." Thereupon "the friends of the condemned," believing that they were supported by the action of the House of Delegates upon the petition to pardon and no doubt aware of the constitutional issue mentioned in n. 16, above, appealed from the verdict of the General Court to the Court of Appeals. When this higher tribunal affirmed the attainder, a second petition for pardon was laid before the General Assembly at its October 1782 session. By a statute, enacted on 3 December 1782, Lamb and Hopkins were pardoned and banished from the state, and Caton was pardoned with the proviso that he serve in the continental army. The three men apparently returned to Virginia after the war, but only Lamb seems thenceforth to have avoided trouble with the law (Minute Book, House of Delegates, May 1782, pp. 73, 82; *Calendar of Virginia State Papers*, III, 193; *Journal of the House of Delegates*, October 1782, pp. 18–19, 51, 58, 60; Hening, *Statutes*, XI, 129; John Harvie Creecy, *Princess Anne County Loose Papers, 1700–1789*, *Virginia Antiquary* [1 vol. to date; Richmond, 1954], I, 90, 115–16, 133, 149–50; Gwathmey, *Historical Register of Virginians*, p. 139). See also David J. Mays, *Edmund Pendleton*, II, 187–202; Daniel Call, ed., *Reports of Cases Argued and Adjudged in the Court of Appeals of Virginia* (6 vols.; Richmond, 1824–33), IV, 5–21.

[18] This action is not recorded in the fragmentary manuscript minute book of the legislative session of May 1782.

[19] For contrary opinions, see *Papers of Madison*, III, 262; Pendleton to JM, 15 April and 22 April 1782.

[20] That is, to have commodities to sell to the French army between September 1781 and July 1782.

[21] See the Reverend James Madison to JM, *ca.* 2 March, and n. 7; 15 June 1782, and n. 14.

[22] See the Reverend James Madison to JM, 15 June 1782, and nn. 7, 9, 10.

[23] Abdominal flatulence.

Benjamin Harrison to Virginia Delegates

FC (Virginia State Library). In the hand of Archibald Blair.

RICHMOND July 19th. 1782.

GENTLEMEN.

I enclose you a copy of the direction of a Letter dated 14th. May which came to me from Winchr. three days ago which I shou'd not have open'd but for its being frank'd by Mr. Livingstone, I am really concernd that so little care should have been taken in Communicating the Birth of a Dauphine to me,[1] it may perhaps induce a belief in the Minister and french Court that it is a matter of no joy to the State, and that we are grown at least luke Warm in our attatchment to our illustrious ally. I know of no other way to satisfy the Minister, that his not being sooner complimented on the joyfull occasion by the State was not oweing to either Negligence or want of Attatchment, but by begging the favor of you to make Him fully acquainted with the circumstances and requesting Him to make them fully known to the French Court—the Letter that I have the honor to send Him on the occasion you will please to deliver Him at the same time. I prefer the mode of complimenting his Most Christian Majesty by Letter rather than by address, haveing ever look'd on the Latter as highly improper and too great an acknowledgement of the inferiority for the Sovereingnty of a State the Way to become great and to make others think so is not only to act in Character but to shew the World that We claim & will support a Rank amongst the Nations of it.

A Report has prevaild here that Mr. John Todd of Kentuckie was in Philadelphia—last Winter was twelve Months—[2] and that during his stay He associated himself with those who were for seperateing that Country from a dependance on this and was deeply concern'd in the measures taken at Philadelphia to bring that event to pass, if either of you know any thing of this I shall be much obliged to You for the communication.[3] no letter or papers came by the last post from Philadelphia, we are much at a loss for the reason of this.[4]

I am &C.

[1] The "copy" has not been found. See Randolph to JM, 18 July, and nn. 10 and 11.

[2] That is, in the winter of 1780–1781. The editors have inserted the dashes to clarify the meaning.

[3] See *Papers of Madison*, I, 277, n. 4; III, 21, n. 1; 275, n. 8; Jefferson to JM, 24 March, and n. 5; Pendleton to JM, 27 May, and n. 11. Colonel John Todd, Jr., who had held important civil and administrative positions in the county and district of Kentucky and the county of Illinois since 1776, was appointed by Governor Harri-

son and the Council of State on 6 July 1782 to be chief judge of the Supreme Court of Judicature of the District of Kentucky (Thomas P. Abernethy, *Western Lands and the American Revolution*, pp. 166, 202, 248–49; *Journals of the Council of State*, III, 118). For a year or more before he was slain by Indians on 19 August 1782 at the Battle of Blue Licks in Kentucky, Todd had become increasingly critical of George Rogers Clark for his ineffective military defense of the settlers south of the Ohio River, and for his opposition to the efforts of many Kentuckians to gain greater autonomy or even separate statehood (Thomas P. Abernethy, *Western Lands and the American Revolution*, pp. 251, 264–65; *Calendar of the Virginia State Papers*, III, 130–31, 300–301). No evidence has been found that Todd visited Philadelphia in 1780–81. In a letter of 15 April 1781 he offered to go there if Congress favored his application to be continued as surveyor of the Illinois country, now that he had heard of its cession by Virginia to the United States. The College of William and Mary had appointed him to that office in 1778. On 12 June 1781 Congress decided to let his letter "lie on the table" (NA: PCC, No. 56, fol. 97; *JCC*, XX, 632).

[4] See Randolph to JM, 18 July 1782.

From Joseph Jones

RC (LC: Madison Papers). Addressed to "Honble James Madison jr. Philadelphia." Docketed by JM, "July 22. 1782."

SPRING HILL 22nd. July 1782

D. SIR.

The reason why Williamsburg and its neighbourhood was mentioned as the place supposed to be alluded to by the[1] correspondent of a certain Gentleman,[2] proceeded from my mentioning to Mr. H—d—y,[3] what had been communicated and his observing that he supposed it proceeded from a report that had been circulated of a pet.[4] set on foot in Wmsburg. praying the legislature to accept any reasonable terms that shod. be offered, but which had been suppressed upon Ct Ro—h—b—u's[5] sending one of his Aids to remonstrate to the partys on the imprudence of the measure which suspended all further proceedings in the matter. this Mr. H. mentd. as a report he had heard but doubted its truth. I asked some other Gent. if they had heard any thing of it and wished to know if there was any foundation for the report supposing what had been communicated must have proceeded from this report. I was the more desirous to learn the truth that if it was a misrepresentation the character of the people there might not bear the aspersion but my inquiries served only to convince me the report respecting the pet. in Williamsburg was groundless and as I imagine the people there suspected the intelligence communicated might proceed from the above misrepresentation and thinking themselves in some measure injured by the Report, they took up the matter in the manner the paper I inclosed to you exhibits. they supposed your communication to me was local as I mentd. the matter as from you, but in general terms in the manner you s[t]ated and it was the previous report only that fixed it on Williamsburg, and which the Governors certificate in consequence of application to him clears up. I sent you the paper that you might be satisfied the report as to Wmsburg. and its neighbourhood was groundless, and my inquiries lead me to suspect no other part of the Country as manifesting a disposition to precipitate matters.[6]

We have some agreeable reports from our quarter since the last post. Your Letter wch. I expect by the post today[7] will I hope confirm them. The evacuation of Chs. Town, a successfull attack of the Dutch upon a British Convoy in the Baltic & the accession of the 7th State of the U. provinces to the Treaty with the States of America.[8] The first and last are probable and have been expected; and I am not disposed to discredit the other, especially when I reflect on the bravery of the Dutch in the few conflicts they have had with the British since the commencement of hostilities.

The last week I requested you not to engage a House or lodging positively.[9] It is yet uncertain whether Mrs. Jones will accompany me. The approaching sickly season may determine her to undertake the Journey though opposed by almost every other circumstance. she is at present indispos[ed by] a very common disorder prevalint at this [t]ime, sore or inflamed Eyes. Joe has gone through it, probably it will be my turn next. By the next weeks post my determination shall be conveyed to you; as to a House or lodgings, if the latter and Mrs. Jones shod. not be with me, I presume I can be accommodated at Mrs. House's.[10] Have you heard any thing of Cyrus[11] shod. he be apprehended let him be confined in prison untill I come up unless an opportunity presents itself of shiping him for the Wt. Indies where if I recover him I mean he shall be transported & sold. Be pleased to inform Baker potts & Co. of the remitance for them by the last post.[12] I burthen you with trouble but cant help it.

Yr. &c

J. Jones

[1] Following "the," Jones either deleted a word with strokes of his quill or superimposed a word upon the one he first wrote. Neither the former word nor the latter is legible.

[2] La Luzerne.

[3] Probably Samuel Hardy (*ca.* 1758–1785) of Isle of Wight County, Va. Soon after graduating from the College of William and Mary in 1778, he had been ad-

mitted to the bar. He represented his county as a delegate in the General Assembly in 1778 and 1780–1782. At the time of the present letter Hardy was a member of the Council of State. From 6 June 1783 until his death on 17 October 1785, he served as a delegate from Virginia in Congress.

[4] An abbreviation of "petition."

[5] Rochambeau.

[6] For the general subject of this paragraph, see JM to Jones, 28 May, and n. 15; Randolph to JM, 29 June, and n. 3; JM to Randolph, 9 July 1782.

[7] In his letter of 16 July (*q.v.*), Jones had acknowledged receipt of JM's letter of the 9th. No subsequent letter from JM to Jones, prior to the latter's return to Congress on 5 September 1782, has been found.

[8] See Virginia Delegates to Harrison, 25 June, and n. 3; 16 July 1782, and n. 8. Jones perhaps should have written "North Sea" rather than "Baltic." He may have heard of this action from someone who recently had been in Baltimore. On 13 July two merchantmen had docked there after a voyage to St. Croix, where their captains were told that in the North Sea a Dutch squadron had captured a 74-gun British frigate, a sloop, a cutter, and several transports (*Pennsylvania Packet*, 20 July 1782).

[9] See Jones to JM, 16 July 1782.

[10] See *Papers of Madison*, II, 92, n. 8.

[11] See Jones to JM, 1 July 1782, and n. 4.

[12] See Jones to JM, 25 June, and n. 12; 16 July 1782.

Virginia Delegates to Benjamin Harrison

RC (Virginia State Library). In Arthur Lee's hand, except for JM's signature. Docketed, "Lr. from Virga Delegates rec'd Augst 1st. 82 July 23d. 1782." The cover is missing.

PHILADELPHIA July 23d. 1782

SIR,

The Letter of the 11th. with which your Excellency honord us, came safe with the enclosd Resolves, which we shall lay before Congress[1]

The Super-intendant's[2] Contract, for the main Army, is ten pence pensylvania curry. per Ration, which is 25 perCt. less than what your Excellency mentions.

We shall make the application, you recommend, to Congress.[3] No Instructions have yet reachd us on the important points, which were stated to the Assembly for that purpose.[4]

The inclosd Paper[5] contains all the late Advices from Europe, Congress not having receivd any Dispatches. But we have no doubt of our Independence having been acknowlegd by the States-general.[6]

We have the honor to be, with the most perfect respect, Your Excellency's most Obedt. Servants

J MADISON JR.
A. LEE

[1] As a reply to resolutions of Congress of 20 February, the Virginia General Assembly on 28 May–7 June adopted two resolutions which the delegates laid before Congress on 24 July 1782. In the first, the legislature declined to authorize an alteration in the mode prescribed by the Articles of Confederation for the allocation of financial quotas among the states. In the second, the General Assembly, to assist Congress in basing the proportionate quota of each state upon its ability to pay, directed the Governor in Council to appoint "proper Persons" to supply the next session of the legislature with an estimate of "the Losses and Injuries sustained" during the war "from obstructed Commerce and the Enemies Cruisers within the Bay of Chesapeake and the depending Rivers" (NA: PCC, No. 75, fols. 363–65; *JCC*, XXII, 83–86, 413; JM to Pendleton, 7 February 1782, nn. 5, 6). On 1 August 1782 the Executive appointed Colonel Thomas Newton, Jr., and seven other commissioners to assess these damages (*Journals of the Council of State*, III, 132).

[2] Robert Morris.

[3] For "the application" and the subject of the preceding paragraph, see Harrison to Virginia Delegates, 11 July 1782, and n. 4. Harrison's letter was presented to Congress by the Virginia delegates on 24 July and referred to a committee under Ezekiel Cornell's chairmanship. On 27 August, after obtaining the advice of Morris and Benjamin Lincoln, secretary at war, this committee recommended that a continuation of the garrisons at Yorktown and Gloucester, "at the expence of the United States," was "inexpedient," and that Governor Harrison should be asked to send Morris an accounting of the cost of these troops, so "that such order may be taken thereon as shall appear just." Congress adopted these recommendations (NA: PCC, No. 20, II, 277–84; *JCC*, XXII, 415 n.; XXIII, 531).

[4] See Virginia Delegates to Harrison, 14 May 1782, and n. 13.

[5] Not found, but probably the *Pennsylvania Packet* of 20 or 23 July 1782.

[6] See Virginia Delegates to Harrison, 25 June, and n. 3; JM to Randolph, 16 July 1782, and n. 30. Much European news, including unofficial word of the recognition of the independence of the United States by the Netherlands, had reached Philadelphia on 19 July, when the ship "St. Helena" and the brigantine "General Gist" arrived from L'Orient (*Pennsylvania Packet*, 20 July; *Pennsylvania Gazette*, 24 July 1782).

To Edmund Pendleton

RC (New York Public Library). Docketed by Pendleton, "James Madison Esqr. July 23d. 1782." Cover missing.

PHILADA. 23. July. 1782.

DEAR SIR

The sterility of my late correspondence will be compensated by the contents of the inclosed paper,[1] which besides other interesting particulars sufficiently confirms the recognition of our Independence by the States General.[2] Among the numerous good consequences of this event to us I wish the people of Virginia not to be inattentive to its influence on the value of their staple,[3] which it is probable will be an immediate object of speculation.[4] Other particulars not yet republished from the foreign papers are the capture of 1 if not 2. French 74s. with a number of transports on their way to the E. Indies, by Admiral Barrington[5]—the capture of a British Frigate, with some transports by a Dutch ship of war[6]—the capture of the rich island of Ceylon from the Dutch by Admiral Hughs, & of Negapatam another of their important possessions on the coast of Coromandel, with two ships richly laden with oriental productions.[7]

The language of the New Ministry is not a little novel & extraordinary. They seem to consider themselves as they really are, the creatures of the people, not of the crown and address their whole conduct to the temper of the former, with as much assiduity as their predecessors did to the latter. The popular & oeconomical principles which they urged out of office, are the basis of their plans in office. They are excluding contractors &c from the legislature—abolishing sinecure appointments—pruning the civil list—arming the Militia and even patronizing a scheme of equal representation. In the last particular they met with great obstacles & Mr. Fox had the mortification to find himself in a minority on the question for appointing a committee to bring in plan for the purpose.[8]

Ireland is reaping a large share of the harvest produced by our labours. Besides a free trade & a free legislation, the shackles are taken off the poor Catholicks in the articles of their religious worship & the tenure of real property.[9]

Genl. Washington is still here.[10] My last contained all the information I can give you relative to Lippencut & Asgil, Carlton preserves his taciturnity.[11] It is said that a fleet of transports is just arrived at the Hook, and that they have troops on board. This has brought to life again the supposed evacuation of Charleston.[12]

Adieu

[1] Not found, but probably the *Pennsylvania Packet* of 20 or 23 July 1782.

[2] See Virginia Delegates to Harrison, 25 June, and n. 3; JM to Randolph, 16 July 1782, and n. 30.

[3] Tobacco.

[4] See JM to Pendleton, 9 July 1782, and n. 3.

[5] On 20 April 1782 in the Bay of Biscay Captain John Jervis, commanding the 80-gun "Foudroyant," a ship in the fleet of Vice Admiral Samuel Barrington (1729–1800), captured the 74-gun "Pégase." On 23 April the 90-gun "Queen," commanded by Captain Sir Frederick Lewis Maitland, forced the 64-gun "Actionnaire" to strike her colors. Ten other vessels in the French convoy, which was bound for Mauritius and the East Indies, were also taken (William L. Clowes, *Royal Navy,* IV, 80–83, 114; *Pennsylvania Journal,* 20 July; *Pennsylvania Packet,* 30 July 1782).

[6] See Jones to JM, 22 July 1782, n. 8.

[7] JM appears to have heard a distorted version of a letter, written in Madras on 13 October 1781, from which the *Pennsylvania Journal* published an excerpt on 24 July 1782. Although JM may have seen the entire dispatch, the excerpt states only that Sir Eyre Coote, having defeated Haidar Ali, planned to lay siege to Arcot, and that the fleet of Vice Admiral Sir Edward Hughes (*ca.* 1720–1794), in co-operation with British troops, intended to invest the Dutch garrison at Negapatam, about 160 miles south of Madras on the Coromandel Coast of India. Although the British had captured Negapatam in November 1781 and forced the Dutch at Trincomalee, Ceylon, to surrender about two months later, their operations on land and sea during 1782 were either unsuccessful or, at best, indecisive. They were driven by the French from Trincomalee on 31 August 1782 (*Cambridge Modern History*, VI, 469).

[8] See JM to Randolph, 14 May 1782, n. 2. There was acute rivalry in the ministry of the Marquis of Rockingham between the joint secretaries of state—the Earl of Shelburne, who had domestic matters as his principal province, and Charles James Fox, whose sphere of administration was foreign affairs. JM's summary of the policy of the ministry exaggerates the extent of the reforms. Ten days after Rockingham's death on 1 July, Shelburne became head of the government and Fox resigned (*Cambridge Modern History*, VI, 457, 459–62).

[9] See JM to Randolph, 2 July 1782, n. 9. Late in May 1782 the Irish Parliament repealed Poynings' Law of 1495, which had barred that legislature from convening or passing any legislation, except money bills, without the prior consent of the King in Council. Early in June the British Parliament repealed a statute affirming the right of Great Britain to legislate for Ireland and forbidding the Irish House of Lords to interfere with the judgment of Irish courts. Upon presenting a Declaration of Rights for the third time to the Parliament of Ireland on 16 April 1782, Henry Grattan had accompanied his eloquent affirmation of loyalty to Great Britain with the words: "Shall the colonists of America be free and the loyal people of Ireland slaves? No—I know the gentlemen of this country too well. I know they won't submit" (*Pennsylvania Journal*, 24 July 1782). The *Pennsylvania Packet* of 27 July reported that on 4 May 1782 the Lord Lieutenant of Ireland had proclaimed, by authority of the King in Privy Council, that Irish Catholics thenceforward could have their own schools and possess landed estates. During the ministry of Lord North, many but not all of the restrictions on Irish trade had been removed.

[10] See Virginia Delegates to Harrison, 16 July, n. 7. Returning from Philadelphia, Washington reached his headquarters at Newburgh, N.Y., in the evening of 27 July 1782 (Fitzpatrick, *Writings of Washington*, XXIV, 438).

[11] See JM to Randolph, 1 May, nn. 17 and 18; JM to Pendleton, 16 July 1782. The *Pennsylvania Journal* on 20 July 1782 reported as almost certainly authentic the news that the British court-martial had acquitted Lippincott.

[12] See Virginia Delegates to Harrison, 16 July, and n. 8; JM to Pendleton, 16 July 1782. Twenty-eight "sail of victuallers from Cork," convoyed by two British frigates, had arrived in New York Harbor on 18 July (*Pennsylvania Packet*, 27 July 1782).

To Edmund Randolph

RC (LC: Madison Papers). The letter lacks a complimentary close and signature. Words italicized in the next to last paragraph of the letter were written by JM in the Lovell cipher. The cover is franked by "J. Madison Jr." and addressed by him to "The honble Edmund Randolph Esqr Richmond." For a time the cover was used as a wrapper for a number of letters, because it is docketed by Randolph, "J. Madison jr Letters written in 23d of the month of July 1782." Before "Letters," Randolph deleted "Several." Upon making this change he probably added "23d of" but neglected to substitute "on" for "in" and to strike the terminal "s" from "Letters."

PHILADA. 23 July 1782.

DEAR SIR

I have at length the pleasure of presenting you with certain tho' not official intelligence of the recognition of our Independence by the States general.[1] This event with other interesting particulars is contained in the inclosed Gazettes.[2] among its salutary consequences to this country I hope the people of Virga. will not be inattentive to its influence on the value of its Staple on which it is very probable Speculations will be attempted.[3]

The Language & measures of the present administration will furnish you with copious matter for reflection. If we had recd. fewer lessons of caution agst. sanguine expectations, I should with confidence explain them by a scheme for a general pacification and for fathering on their predecessors[4] all the obnoxious conditions which the public distresses may expose them to. If this solution were a just one it ought at the same time to be remembered that the triumph of Rodney[5] may give a new turn to their politics. It appears from the paper from which the inclosed intelligence is republished that this event had reached London, that it was received with great rejoicings, but that the public were still haunted with fears for Jamaica.[6] Other articles not included in the paper herewith sent, are, the capture of 1 if not 2 French 74's with a number of Transports for the East Indies by Adml. Barrington,[7] the capture of a British frigate with some transports by a Dutch ship of war,[8] the capture of the valuable Island of Ceylon from the Dutch by Admiral Hughs, & of Negapatam another of their important possessions on the Coast of Coromandel, with 2 ships richly freighted with spices & other oriental productions.[9] Ireland is likely to be indulged in every thing. In addition to a free trade & a free Legislation, they have obtained the assent of the Ld. Lieutt. to an act of Parliament for emancipating the Catholics from the shackles on their religious rights, & on their tenures of real property.[10] Your philanthropy will be gratified by my adding as other proofs of the progress of light & freedom, the abolition of the inquisitorial jurisdiction in Sicily, the only part of the Neapolitan dominions where it was in force, and the inefficacy of the Pope's visit to Vienna in checking the liberal innovations of the Emperor in his ecclesiastical polity.[11]

The[12] news from Holland has much emboldened the *enemies of France.* [D]*octor Lee declared* that it ought to be considered as the *epoch of our emancipation.*[13] Yesterday I was reminded *by Izzard*[14] that *Franklin was interested* in restoring the *backlands t*[o] *the crown.* Soon *after I was shewn by Lee a proposition for reconsidering the* commission & *instructions for peace.*[15] The plan is to *exclude F—n* & [*J*]*y*[16] & *to* with*draw* the others[17] from the *direction of F*[*r*]*ance.* The *notes* of *M—s*[18] *are also* to be *attacked.* These and some other *symptoms* strongly *portend a revival* of *party heats.* I earnestly wish we had *your aid* in *repressing them.*

General Washington is still here. I have nothing to add to my last on the subject of Lippencut & Asgil. It is said that a fleet of transports is just arrived at the Hook, & that it has troops on Board. This revived the idea that an evacuation of Charleston has taken place.[19] I hope you will not neglect the request in my last touching pecuniary matters.[20] My wants begin again to be very pressing & I hear nothing of remittances. I hope your silence by yesterday's mail has not been the effect of ind[isposition?]

1 See Report on Salaries of Representatives Abroad, 28 May, n. 11; Virginia Delegates to Harrison, 25 June, n. 3; JM to Randolph, 16 July 1782, n. 30.

2 Not found, but they probably included the *Pennsylvania Packet* of 20 and 23 July 1782.

3 See JM to Pendleton, 9 July 1782, and n. 3.

4 The ministry of Lord North. See JM to Pendleton, 23 July 1782, and n. 8.

5 In the Battle of the Saints. See JM to Pendleton, 23 April 1782, n. 3.

6 See JM to Randolph, 11 June 1782. The *Pennsylvania Packet* of 25 July 1782 published news from London under an 18 May date line, telling of the concern about the safety of Jamaica in spite of Rodney's victory in the Battle of the Saints.

7 See JM to Pendleton, 23 July 1782, n. 5.

8 See Jones to JM, 22 July 1782, n. 8.

9 See JM to Pendleton, 23 July 1782, n. 7.

10 See *ibid.*, n. 9. William Henry Cavendish (later Cavendish Bentinck) (1738–1809), Duke of Portland, had taken the oath as Lord Lieutenant of Ireland on 14 April 1782 (Sir F[rederick] Maurice Powicke and E. B. Fryde, eds., *Handbook of British Chronology* [2d ed.; London, 1961], p. 166).

[11] The source of JM's information about the two matters mentioned in this sentence has not been determined. He may have heard, prior to its publication in the *Pennsylvania Journal* of 24 July 1782, the report that Charles III of Spain planned to abolish the royal Inquisition in Spain and his dominions, including the Two Sicilies. Although the report was incorrect, the sovereign did reduce the prerogatives of the inquisitors. In March 1782 Pope Pius VI visited Vienna in an unsuccessful attempt to induce Emperor Joseph II to rescind his Patent of Tolerance (June 1781), which extended limited civil rights and freedom of worship to Protestants and Greek Catholics (*Cambridge Modern History*, VI, 635–36).

[12] The bracketed letters in this paragraph signify errors in JM's coding.

[13] Arthur Lee meant freedom from dependence upon, and obsequiousness to, the court of Versailles.

[14] Ralph Izard.

[15] See Comments on Instructions to Peace Commissioners, 24 July 1782.

[16] Benjamin Franklin and John Jay.

[17] John Adams and Henry Laurens.

[18] Robert Morris. For his notes, see Virginia Delegates to Harrison, 19 March, n. 1; Randolph to JM, 20 June 1782, and n. 42.

[19] For the information mentioned in this sentence and the preceding three sentences, see JM to Pendleton, 23 July 1782, nn. 10, 11, 12.

[20] See JM to Randolph, 16 July 1782.

Comments on Instructions to Peace Commissioners

Printed copy (Charles Thomson's "Debates in the Congress of the Confederation, from July 22d to September 20th, 1782," *Collections of the New-York Historical Society*, XI [1878], pp. 64–65). This edition was made from a transcript rather than from Thomson's manuscript (*ibid.*, p. xi) and will be referred to hereafter as Thomson, "Debates." Both the manuscript and the transcript are lost.

EDITORIAL NOTE

As JM had predicted in his letter of 23 July 1782 to Randolph (*q.v.*), Arthur Lee presented his "proposition" to Congress the next day by moving: "That the Commission of 15th. June 1781 appointing ministers plenipotentiary to negociate a treaty of Peace with G. Britain, together with the Instructions given to the said Commissioners–be re-considered" (NA: PCC, No. 36, I, 355). Bland attempted to second the motion, giving his reason for so doing, but was forced to withdraw on a technicality. After Jonathan Jackson seconded the motion, John Lowell opened the debate by supporting "the propriety of a reconsideration" (JM to Randolph, 30 July 1782; Thomson, "Debates," p. 63; *JCC*, XXII, 415). The following is Thomson's summary of what JM said in opposition to the motion.

[24 July 1782]

Mr Madison objected to it.[1] He took notice that the motion before the house went much farther than the reasoning in support of a reconsideration. That the reasoning was confined entirely to the impropriety, inexpediency and dangerous consequences of one single clause in the instructions;[2] that the motion was pointed against the ministers as well as against the instructions; that nothing was said to show that the appointment was improper and that therefore he could not agree to the motion.[3] But waiving this he should object to the motion if confined to the instructions; as to the objection started[4] on account of an amendment to the original instructions which was carried by seven states,[5] he apprehended the articles of confederation did not require the vote of nine states for the purpose of making peace;[6] but even admitting it did and that there was an error or defect in the instructions by reason of the amendment, admitted by seven votes on the 11th June 1781, yet the passing them afterwards on the 15 of the same month which appears to have been done without dissent, and the confirmation of them by the act of the 31st of May last removed every defect or error which the admission of the amendment might have occasioned.[7] That before gentlemen condemned the instructions they ought to consider the times & circumstances in which they were passed. Here he went into a detail of the critical situation of affairs in America in June 1781, the interposition of mediating powers, the rejection of the motion for joining other persons in the Commission with J. Adams, the unfortunate difference between him & the Cot de Vergennes & the information given that the court of F. had not a full confidence in Mr Adams prudence & management.[8] Upon the whole he did not think it prudent or proper to reconsider the instructions; that they could not be productive of any ill consequences and that the reconsidering and altering them might interrupt the harmony which at present subsists between the U. S. & F., might abate the zeal she has hitherto shown in our favour & that our affairs were not at present in such a situation as to warrant so hazardous a step.[9]

[1] That is, to a reconsideration of the instructions to, and the appointment of, the peace commissioners, Adams, Franklin, Jay, and Henry Laurens. Although Jefferson had also been named to the commission, he declined the appointment on 4 August 1781 (Boyd, *Papers of Jefferson,* VI, 113, 114 n., 240). For the election of these commissioners, the adoption of their instructions, and the subsequent efforts in Congress to alter the commission's personnel and instructions, see *Papers of Madison,* III, 133; 147–54; 168–70; 188–90; Instructions on Peace Negotiations, 7 January, and editorial note, and nn. 5, 30; Report on Fidelity to French Alliance, 31

May, and editorial note; Motion Concerning Peace Negotiations, 17 June, and n. 1; JM to Randolph, 2 July 1782, and n. 19.

[2] JM referred to the "clause" directing the commissioners to be at all times governed by the "advice and opinion" of "the ministers of our generous ally, the King of France" (*JCC*, XX, 651; Burnett, *Letters*, VI, 389–90).

[3] Bland and Lowell so far had spoken only against the "clause," but the resolution also challenged the appointment of the commissioners.

[4] Thomson may have written, or intended to write, "stated."

[5] JM refers to a roll-call vote on 11 June 1781, whereby the acquiescence of seven state delegations served to amend the proposed instructions of the peace commissioners by limiting their freedom in the manner summarized in n. 2, above. Of the Virginia delegates, Bland had opposed, but JM, Jones, and Meriwether Smith had supported the amendment (*JCC*, XX, 626–27).

[6] JM erred, granting that his remarks were summarized accurately by Thomson. The ninth article of the Articles of Confederation stipulated that Congress should not "enter into any treaties . . . unless nine states assent." A treaty was virtually indispensable for "making peace." JM may have differentiated between the ratifying of a treaty, which clearly would depend upon the approval of at least nine states, and amending the peace commissioners' instructions, which in his opinion would require only "the votes of a majority of the united states in congress assembled" (*JCC*, XIX, 220).

[7] Shortly before JM spoke, he listened to the reading of the journal of Congress for 11 and 15 June 1781 (Thomson, "Debates," p. 64). The record for 15 June justified JM's remark that the instructions appeared to have been adopted "without dissent," because a tallied vote on them had not been required by their opponents on that day (*JCC*, XX, 651–54). Although all of the nine states then represented in Congress had agreed to the instructions, individual delegates almost certainly voted against them (*Papers of Madison*, III, 154 nn.; *JCC*, XX, 626–27, 650; Burnett, *Letters*, VI, 115–18, 119–20, 121–22, 124–25, 129). How a reference to "the confirmation" of 31 May 1782 could strengthen JM's position is not clear, since on 25 May only seven states had as many as two delegates present in Congress, and no more attended during the next six days (Burnett, *Letters*, VI, xliii–liii; *JCC*, XXII, 300, 311–13; Report on Fidelity to French Alliance, 31 May 1782, and editorial note).

[8] The citations in n. 1, above, are in point here. See also *Papers of Madison*, III, 154, n. 5; William E. O'Donnell, *Chevalier de La Luzerne*, pp. 123–24, 237.

[9] Thomson closed his entry for 24 July 1782 by adding, "Sundry other members opposed the reconsideration & at last an adjournment was called for which was agreed to" (Thomson, "Debates," p. 65; *JCC*, XXII, 415).

Benjamin Harrison to Virginia Delegates

FC (Virginia State Library). In the hand of William Tatham, assistant clerk of the Virginia Council of State, and directed to "The Virginia Delegates in Congress."

VIRGINIA IN COUNCIL July 27th. 1782.

GENTLEMEN

A Mr. Linctot of the Illinois was appointed Indian Agent in that Country by Governor Jefferson on behalf of this State. It appears by his Accounts and some Letters of Colo. Broadheads who commanded at fort Pitt that he also acted in the same capacity (tho' not regularly commissioned) for the continent. I wish to be inform'd whether he has received anything for that service, and beg the favor of you to make the necessary inquiry.[1] The feeding the Garrison of York Town embarras's us exceedingly I request you will attend particularly to it, and use your endeavours to get them taken off our hands, or a resolution pass'd that will enable the State certainly to obtain credit for the expenditures, which is so highly reasonable that no just objection can be made to it.[2] A vessel from Providence[3] is just arrived the Capt. reports that he call'd at Savannah, that the Enemy had evacuated it, and that Waine[4] was in possession.[5]

I am Gentlemen &c.

B. H.

[1] Daniel Maurice Godefroy de Linctot (*ca.* 1740–*ca.* 1783) was a Canadian who had served as an ensign in the French army during the French and Indian War. By the outset of the Revolution he and his older brother (d. 1778) lived at Cahokia and, as fur traders, had gained the friendship of many of the Indian tribes in the upper Mississippi Valley. In 1779 the French habitants at Cahokia chose him to command a company of militia. Thereafter, and perhaps even earlier, he supplied food and other commodities to the troops of George Rogers Clark. According to Clark, Linctot also rendered a signal service by persuading Indians either to make war on the British or at least to remain neutral. On 5 August 1779 Clark commissioned Linctot as Indian agent in the Mississippi Valley west and north of the Illinois River (George A. Brennan, "De Linctot, Guardian of the Frontier," *Journal of the Illinois Historical Society,* X [1917–18], 323–66; Louise Phelps Kellogg, ed., *Frontier Retreat on the Upper Ohio, 1779–1781* [Madison, Wis., 1917], p. 176 n.; Clarence Walworth Alvord, ed., *Kaskaskia Records, 1778–1790* [Springfield, Ill., 1909), pp. 163, 177–78; James Alton James, ed., *George Rogers Clark Papers, 1771–1781* [Springfield, Ill., 1912], pp. cvii, 150, 297, 301 and n., 328–29, 341–42, 355, 363; *ibid., 1781–1784* [Springfield, Ill., 1924], pp. 28 n., 230, 243–44).

On 17 February 1780, when Linctot was in Williamsburg trying vainly to obtain a full settlement of his accounts, Governor Jefferson rewarded his "courage, zeal and attachment" by appointing him Indian agent in the "northwestern department." For this service he was to receive "the pay of five shillings in silver money by the day and the rank and rations of a major" (Boyd, *Papers of Jefferson,* III, 296). By then Linctot had established his residence at Vincennes, but he spent much time in the Ohio country and at Fort Pitt, still cultivating the friendship of the Indians and also their assistance on Clark's proposed expedition against the British post at Detroit. Linctot apparently was not recompensed by Congress for co-operating closely at Fort Pitt with Colonel Daniel Brodhead (1736–1809), continental army commandant of the "western district" (*ibid.,* III, 296, 322–23, 479; IV, 113–14, 180, 249–50, 283, 479, 600; V, 320; *Papers of Madison,* II, 292, nn. 3 and 7; III, 209, 210, n. 4; McIlwaine, *Official Letters,* II, 88 and n., 89, 95, 103, 105, 106; Clarence W. Alvord, ed., *Kaskaskia Records,* p. 163; James A. James, ed., *Clark Papers, 1771–1781,* p. 388).

When Harrison wrote the present letter, Virginia had neither paid Linctot's salary and rations nor remunerated him for most of the expenses incurred during his negotiations with the Indians. His expense account was referred for audit to the commissioners of Virginia for the settlement of western accounts, but he or his assignee received by June 1783 the salary and ration money due him from 17 February 1780 to 18 January 1783. The latter date appears to have marked the termination of his appointment as Indian agent. His death seems to have occurred between then and 30 April of that year (McIlwaine, *Official Letters*, III, 63, 70, 280–81, 285, 389, 399; *Journals of the Council of State*, II, 389; III, 175, 269; *Journal of the House of Delegates*, May 1783, pp. 64, 72–75; October 1783, p. 82; James A. James, ed., *Clark Papers, 1781–1784*, pp. 28–29, 159, 230, 253, 278–79, 380–82).

[2] See Virginia Delegates to Harrison, 23 July 1782, n. 3; McIlwaine, *Official Letters*, III, 270–71.

[3] New Providence Island in the Bahamas.

[4] Brigadier General Anthony Wayne.

[5] On 27 July 1782 the *Pennsylvania Journal* announced as almost certainly true the departure of the British garrison from Savannah. Although the ship captain who informed Harrison has not been identified, the news appeared in the *Virginia Gazette* of 3 August. Complying with General Carleton's orders, the British had evacuated the town on 11 July 1782 (John Richard Alden, *The South in the Revolution, 1763–1789* [Baton Rouge, La., 1957], p. 266).

Note for Report on Prisoners of War

MS (NA: PCC, No. 19, VI, 399).

EDITORIAL NOTE

Having received Washington's letter of 9 July enclosing copies of his correspondence with Sir Guy Carleton concerning a possible exchange of American seamen for British soldiers (Virginia Delegates to Harrison, 16 July 1782, and n. 9), Congress on 15 July referred these dispatches to a committee comprising John Witherspoon, JM, and John Rutledge (*JCC*, XXII, 388, n. 3; Fitzpatrick, *Writings of Washington*, XXIV, 405–6, 441). The report of the committee, delivered on 29 July, is in Rutledge's hand (*JCC*, XXII, 421–22, 422, n. 1). Although JM wrote the note, given below, on the docket of a committee report of 12 August (*JCC*, XXIII, 462), he intended his suggestions to be of service to John Rutledge in drafting his recommendations of 29 July 1782. See n. 4.

[29 July 1782]

Report of the Committee to whom was recommitted the later's[1] report on the letter of General Washington submit the following Resolution for consd.

That the[2] Congress have always been & still are ready to concur in a Cartel for an exchange of Prisoners on equal & just principles as far as human[3] and approve of the measures taken for that purpose by the Commander in cheif.

That a copy of this Resolution be transmitted by Genl W. to the British Commander in cheif at N. York.[4]

[1] JM canceled "later's."
[2] JM canceled "the."
[3] JM canceled "as far as human."
[4] The entire draft was canceled by diagonal and vertical ink lines. The printed journal of Congress erroneously includes the draft as a portion of a report struck out by Congress on 12 August (*JCC*, XXIII, 462).

On the same page used by JM, Rutledge jotted down in much abbreviated form some expressions which he incorporated in the third paragraph of the recommendations submitted to Congress on 29 July. In these recommendations JM's influence is shown in the first paragraph reading, "That Congress always have been ready & willing to agree to a General Cartel, for the Exchange of Prisoners of War, upon just [&] reasonable terms," and in so much of the sixth paragraph as reads, "R. That the Comder. in Cheif be directed to transmit these Resolves to Sir G. C." (NA: PCC, No. 28, fols. 83–85; *JCC*, XXII, 421–22).

On 29 July Congress, apparently without debate, referred these recommendations to a new committee comprising John Lowell, Ezekiel Cornell, and JM (*JCC*, XXII, 422 n.). This committee never reported, perhaps in some measure because Lowell left Philadelphia for his home in Massachusetts on 6 August (Burnett, *Letters*, VI, 431). The next day Congress assigned a dispatch, written by Washington on 3 August about the cartel, to a committee on which JM served under John Morin Scott as chairman. On 8 and 9 August, when further word on the same subject from Washington reached Congress, the Lowell and Scott committees were discharged, and all documents relating to the issue were referred to a new committee headed by Arthur Lee (NA: PCC, 186, fol. 48; *JCC*, XXII, 456 n., 460, n. 2; Fitzpatrick, *Writings of Washington*, XXVI, 455, 466–67; Thomson, "Debates," 103–4). Although Rutledge was a member of this committee, the portions of his report of 29 July influenced by JM bear no resemblance to the resolutions about a cartel included by Lee among the recommendations which his committee submitted to Congress on 12 August 1782 (*JCC*, XXIII, 462–64; Thomson, "Debates," pp. 105–6).

Comment on Settlement of Foreign Accounts

Printed copy (Thomson, "Debates," pp. 69–70). See Comments on Instructions to Peace Commissioners, 24 July 1782, headnote.

EDITORIAL NOTE

Although Congress on 28 May 1782 had resolved to appoint a commissioner "to liquidate and finally settle the accounts of all the servants of the United States, who have been entrusted with the expenditure of public monies in Europe," nothing had been done since that date to fill the office or to determine the salary of the incumbent (*JCC*, XXII, 306; Report on Salaries of Representatives Abroad, 28 May 1782, and n. 4). When the matter was revived on 25 and 29 July, Arthur Lee and other delegates who suspected that Franklin had been guilty of financial irregularities urged Congress to repeal the above resolution (*JCC*, XXII, 416–17, 421; Burnett, *Letters*, VI, 379, 389; Thomson, "Debates," pp. 65–66, 69–70). According to Thomson, Edward Telfair opened the way for debate on 29 July by moving that the commissioner's annual stipend should be four thousand dollars.

[29 July 1782]

Mr Madison was for sending a person or persons to liquidate but not with power finally to settle the acct.[1]

[1] The debate terminated with the adoption of a motion, offered by Bland and seconded by John Witherspoon, to have the resolution, quoted in the editorial note, referred to a committee. Its members should "define accurately the powers with which the said commissioner is to be entrusted, and prepare instructions for the execution of those powers, to confer with the Superintendant of Finance." John Morin Scott, Arthur Lee, and John Rutledge were first named to do this, but JM took Scott's place on 29 August. The committee's report, in Rutledge's hand, was submitted on 3 September and adopted on 18 November 1782. Although Thomas Barclay, already in Europe, was chosen to be the commissioner, a decision about his salary was postponed until the difficulty and duration of his task should become known (*JCC*, XXII, 421, 421 n.; XXIII, 728–30, 773–75).

From Edmund Pendleton

Tr (LC: Force Transcripts). Addressed to "The Honble James Madison Esqr Philada." Another copy made from the manuscript is in the *Proceedings of the Massachusetts Historical Society*, 2d ser., XIX (1905), 157–58.

Caroline July 29th 1782

Dear Sir

I am sorry to find by yr favr of the 16th that the Robbers of the Mail seem to be a regular train'd band, who may probably return to their Station on this side Philada[1] to divert the Attention of those who may seek them; should this be the case, they will have a bad bargain in mine, not worth the trouble of reading. The report of the burning and evacuation of Charles Town[2] had reached Us, before Yours came to hand, but I believe it came from the Northward,[3] Accounts from No Carolina[4] speak of it as a thing in Agitation rather than done. I mean the evacuation, for they say nothing of the burning, which I hope is not true.

I am sorry poor Asgil is at last likely to suffer for another's crime; however the sacrifice is necessary, and just on our part, let them answer for the misapplication of the punishment, who alone might have saddled the right horse.[5]

The introduction of Genl Carlton's maxim[6] at this time probably looks forward to an important event, in which I always supposed the Interest of American Loialists[7] would make a considerable point of discussion. I wish he may prove prophetic in the period in which that event will take place, tho' perhaps we may differ widely in the grounds of his hopes. I am sorry for his proposition for exchanging Prisoners in a mode which would enable them to employ them agt our Allies, & appropriate others to the War here,[8] as it betrays an Opinion on their part that they may still Insult our understandings with impunity, if not wth hopes of Success.

My Nephew Mr. Edmund Pendleton jr[9] has lately lost a young negroe man about 22 yrs old, five feet eight inches high, rather thin made, is a little bow legged, and has a down look when spoke to. he run away last summer & having plunder'd a party of Troops, they whip'd him so severely that he lay up for two Months & reclaims[10] the apparent Marks of it on each shoulder. He reclaim'd him twice from the French Troops as they Passed, & therefore suspects that he finally rode ahead of them to join them in Maryland & Pennsylvania, He stole a fine horse belonging to a Mr Allan[11] & a valuable Mare from a Neighbour, but I can discribe neither. Will you do me the favour by application to Count Rochambeau or other French officers, to endeavour to recover him if he should have joined them, & in case you succeed, to have him confined in Goal[12] 'til my nephew can send for him, unless you can sell him for £ 100[13] specie, which tho' much less than he would sell for here, my Nephew would rather take than be further troubled with him. The fellow's name is Bob. I have not described his dress, as he stole variety of Cloaths from different people.[14] I would not have troubled you with this request, but knew not how otherwise to get the application made.

I am as usual My Dr Sr Yr very Affe friend

EDMD PENDLETON

[1] See JM to Pendleton, 16 July 1782, and n. 2.

[2] See *ibid.*, and n. 3.

[3] The word "southward," appearing in the Massachusetts Historical Society's version, is probably an error.

[4] Not identified.

[5] See JM to Randolph, 1 May, and nn. 17, 18; 16 July 1782, and nn. 28, 29.

[6] See JM to Pendleton, 16 July 1782, and n. 6.

[7] This misspelling may be chargeable to Peter Force's clerk, since the word is correctly spelled in the Massachusetts Historical Society version.

[8] See Virginia Delegates to Harrison, 16 July 1782, and n. 9.

[9] After attending Donald Robertson's Latin school and the College of William and Mary, and being tutored in law by his uncle, Edmund Pendleton, Edmund, Jr. (1744–1827), was admitted to the bar in 1765. His estate, White Plains, was near his uncle's plantation in Caroline County. During the next decade Edmund Pendleton, Jr., became locally prominent as a practicing lawyer, as acting crown attorney, and as county attorney for the Commonwealth. A committee clerk in the House of Burgesses in 1773, he was clerk of several committees during the revolutionary conventions and was thereafter clerk of the committees of Privileges and Elections and of Propositions and Grievances in the House of Delegates for years. A member of the county Committee of Safety, 1774–1776, he was chosen by his neighbors at the outbreak of the war to lead a company of militia and had risen by 1780 to command all of the militia of Caroline County. He was the executor of Edmund Pendleton's estate upon his uncle's death in 1803 (*Virginia Magazine of History and Biography*, XLI [1933], 85; David J. Mays, *Edmund Pendleton*, I, 140, 141, 300, 339 n., 348 n.; II, 18, 44, 171–72, 287–88; T. E. Campbell, *Colonial Caroline*, pp. 235, 243, 266, 289–90, 344–45, 370, 467; Gwathmey, *Historical Register of Virginians*, p. 615).

[10] Pendleton probably wrote "retains," as shown in the Massachusetts Historical Society version.

[11] Either Erasmus (d. *ca.* 1812) or Thomas (d. *ca.* 1814) Allen, who were farmers in Caroline County (Personal-Property Tax Books, 1783–1815, Caroline County, MSS in Virginia State Library).

[12] "Gaol" in the Massachusetts Historical Society copy.

[13] "200" in the version cited in n. 12.

[14] Having been recovered for $20.00 from a French lieutenant in Baltimore, Bob again escaped and upon his recapture was confined in the jail of that town. Pendleton apparently informed JM later that the slave was once more at the plantation of Edmund Pendleton, Jr. (David J. Mays, *Edmund Pendleton*, II, 183, 383 n.; Pendleton to JM, 19 and 26 August, 2 and 9 September in *Proceedings of the Massachusetts Historical Society*, 2d ser., XIX [1905], 159–63; JM to Pendleton, 24 September 1782, MS in New York Public Library). In the meantime JM had sought the aid of Barbé-Marbois and of Lieutenant Colonel John Jameson in apprehending Bob (JM to Pendleton, 3 September and 24 September 1782, MS in New York Public Library).

Comments on Public Faith and Credit

Printed copy (Thomson, "Debates," p. 73). See Comments on Instructions to Peace Commissioners, 24 July 1782, headnote.

EDITORIAL NOTE

On 21 October 1780, by a vote of six states to three, Congress had adopted a plan for reorganizing the continental army. This reform would result in displacing or, in the language of the day, "deranging" many worthy officers. Therefore, in justice to them, Congress included among the resolutions embodying the reform a pledge that these supernumeraries, beginning on 1 January 1781, would be entitled to half pay for life (*JCC*, XVIII, 894, 896–97, 960–61; Edmund C. Burnett, *The Continental Congress*, p. 641). Owing largely to the failure of states to honor their financial quotas, this promise remained unfulfilled.

On 17 July 1782 Pelatiah Webster and William Judd, then in Philadelphia, memorialized Congress on behalf of forty-five deranged continental army officers of Connecticut. After Secretary at War Benjamin Lincoln substantiated the facts stated in the petition, Congress referred the documents to a committee comprising Ezekiel Cornell, Joseph Montgomery, and Thomas McKean. On 30 July 1782 they recommended only that "it is not expedient at this time to grant the prayer of the memorialists." During the ensuing debate Cornell and Montgomery added that the petitioners, recognizing the emptiness of the public treasury, would be satisfied to have "Certificates given for the sums due, payable, with interest, at a future day." Thereupon, although Congress decided to postpone acting on the committee's report, Theodorick Bland and Arthur Lee asked Congress to resolve that to make such "a partial arrangement" with the supernumerary officers "would be inexpedient." Abraham Clark then arose to call into question the binding force of the pledge of 21 October 1780—especially since it involved finances—on the grounds that it had not been sanctioned by the minimum of nine state delegations, as required by the Articles of Confederation (*JCC*, XXII, 404, 404 n., 418, 418 n., 423; NA: PCC, No. 19, VI, 491, 493, 495, 499, 503; Thomson, "Debates," pp. 70–72). JM's speech, in refutation of Clark's argument, is summarized below.

[30 July 1782]

Mr Madison combated the objection of Mr Clark; the doctrine it intended to establish was dangerous and if admitted would sap the foundation of a credit, and might be attended by the most ruinous consequences; that the States were as much bound by acts of Congress, which passed by a majority of votes, before the ratification of the Confederation[1] as they would be now by the number of votes required by the Confederation: that on this rested the treaties and alliances already made[2] and the instructions given to our ministers abroad to enter into other treaties and alliances; on this rested the money borrowed and the debts contracted, at home and abroad, for the payment of which the public faith was solemnly plighted & for which the States must provide funds, that the fixing of the pay of the army rests solely with Congress & that the States are bound to provide for what is stipulated and granted to the officers and men, whether to be paid then, at certain periods & in certain sums during service only, or while in service and for years or lives after the termination of the war;[3]

[1] On 1 March 1781 (*JCC*, XIX, 213–14).

[2] Although JM's general position is undoubtedly valid, the Treaty of Alliance

and the Treaty of Amity and Commerce, both concluded between France and the United States, had been ratified unanimously on 4 May 1778 by the eleven states then represented in Congress (*JCC*, XI, 457).

[3] According to Thomson's "Debates" (p. 73), several other members spoke after JM had concluded his remarks, but "at last an adjournment was called for & the house broke up without coming to a decision." See Comments on the Cost of the War, 31 July 1782.

Virginia Delegates to Benjamin Harrison

RC (Virginia State Library). In Theodorick Bland's hand, except for JM's and Lee's signatures. Addressed to "His Excellency the Governor of Virginia." Docketed, "Virga Delegates Lr., July 30. 82 July, 1782." Cover missing.

PHILADELPHIA July 30th. 1782

SIR,

We deliverd the Letter to the Chevalier de la Luzerne, enclosd in that your Excellency honord us with on the 19, together with the apology you desird for your Congratulations, on the auspicious event of the birth of a Dauphin, having arrivd so late[.][1] The Minister expressd his satisfaction in recieving it.

The Secretary for foreign Affairs[2] will pay proper attention in future to your Excellency's Address. Due enquiry will be made by the Post-master-general,[3] into the miscarriage of our Letter of the 9th. ult. of which we now send a Copy.[4] We shall make all possible enquiry concerning Mr. J. Todd & his proceedings here.[5]

That part of your Excellency's Letter of the 11th. relating to the expence of garrisoning York & Glocester, was laid before Congress, & referrd to a Committee, which has not yet reported upon it.[6] We shoud be happy to hear, from time to time, of the success of the recruiting plan.[7]

It is so confidently reported here, that a fleet of 13 Sail of french Ships of war, with 4000 land Forces & a numerous Convoy, are arrivd in the Chesapeake;[8] that we cannot help congratulating your Excellency on an event, which promises so much to our State & to the Union.

With sentiments of the[9] profoundest respect, We have the honor to be Yr. Excellency's most Obedt. & most Humbe. Servants.

THEOK: BLAND JR.
J. MADISON JR.
A. LEE

[1] See Randolph to JM, 18 July, and nn. 10 and 11; Harrison to Virginia Delegates, 19 July 1782.
[2] Robert R. Livingston.
[3] Ebenezer Hazard.
[4] See Virginia Delegates to Harrison, 9 July 1782. The copy, in the hand of Arthur Lee, is certified by him to be a "True Copy from the Book" (Ms in Virginia State Library).
[5] See Harrison to Virginia Delegates, 19 July 1782, and n. 3.
[6] See Harrison to Virginia Delegates, 11 July; Virginia Delegates to Harrison, 23 July 1782, and n. 3.
[7] See Jameson to JM, 23 March, and n. 5; Randolph to JM, 20 June 1782, and n. 48.
[8] In his journal on 28 July 1782, Baron von Closen, then in Baltimore, noted that Rochambeau had just received "dispatches from M. de Vaudreuil, who had passed by the Capes of the Chesapeake on the 25th" on his way to Boston, where he would obtain supplies for his thirteen ships. "The *Néréide*, a frigate of 40 cannon, entered the bay and sent some packets to Hampton, after which it rejoined the fleet" (Acomb, *Journal of Closen*, p. 216). The delegates evidently had read the *Pennsylvania Packet* of 30 July 1782, which left the impression that Chesapeake Bay was the destination of these vessels. They had sailed from Cap Français, Haiti, on 3 July.
[9] Bland inadvertently repeated "of the."

To Edmund Randolph

RC (LC: Madison Papers). Docketed by Randolph, "July 30. 1782." Cover missing. The italicized words are those written by JM in the Lovell cipher.

PHILADA. 30th. July 1782

MY DEAR SIR

I was not mistaken in my *intimation that an attack would be made on* the *last commission* and *instructions* relative to *peace*[.][1] *on Wednesday* last the *motion was made by M—r Lee* and *seconded* by *Bland* at *first but* afterwards *by a member from Mas:* the *rule for reconsid—n* so requiring.[2] Not a word *was said* against *the* [word] underscored in the third line.[3] The arguments on the other point were drawn from a source which need not be pointed out to you.[4] An *adjournment arrested the debate*[.] An intended *renewal was announced but has not yet taken place.*[5]

I have found means hitherto of parrying the *attack on* the *notes of Morris*[.][6] My *colleagues have repeatedly* pressed the necessity of an *act of congress* for *ratifying the convention* on that subject be*tween* him and the *assembly* os*tensibly for the security of* the latter, but *really* to bring the *subject before congress*—At present *Bland seems* to decline the object as having an *ill tendency*[7]

If any mail has failed to bear witness to my punctuality, It has not been caused by any default in me. I am the more at a loss to account for such a miscarriage, as it does not appear that any outrage has been repeated on the post.[8] I shall notify the fact to the Postoffice here, and think it will not be amiss for you to urge an investigation upon the Post Master at Richmond.[9]

The letter inclosed in your favor of the 18th. from Docr. Carter has been sent to the Auditors.[10] As far as my attention may be necessary, his case will recieve it.

A Capt: of an American Vessel is just come up with an account of the arrival of a French fleet off the capes of Chesapeak, with a body of Troops on board.[11] Many persons are so sanguine as to expect that this armament is destined agst. New York and that it will immediately possess itself of the Harbour of that place, before the arrival of a superior enemy can prevent it. Altho' the troops on board seem to favor such a conjecture, there are improbabilities which with me outweigh that circumstance.[12]

I am not enabled to make any addition to the intelligence from the Netherlands conveyed in my last.[13] You will find by the inclosed paper that a Vessel is arrived at Boston from France, which brings some loose accounts. private letters tell us that Majr. Franks was a passenger in her.[14] From him we shall probably receive further advices with respect to Europe in general, and ample ones from Madrid. I add to the paper of this morning two others of prior date which detail some interesting proceedings in the B. & I. Parliaments not published in the paper transmitted by last post.[15] Some paragraphs of the Courier de L'Europe contained in neither of them, make it very probable that the New Ministry have been feeling the pulse both of Dr. F. & the Ct. of France.[16] We are very much surprised that none of these important transactions should yet have come officially either to Congress or to the Chevr. de la Luzerne.[17]

My situation obliges me to remind you of my late request touching pecuniary matters.[18] If the interposition of your endeavors shall be necessary, to hasten a supply, it will I assure you be a very acceptable instance of your friendship.

1 See JM to Randolph, 23 July; Comments on Instructions to Peace Commissioners, 24 July 1782, and editorial note.

2 As recorded by Thomson in his "Debates," p. 64, Bland's second on 24 July of Arthur Lee's motion to reconsider was declared to be out of order, because Bland

"had acknowledged he had voted agst the instructions." Thereupon, "after sometime," Jonathan Jackson of Massachusetts "gave it his second."

[3] In the third line of the manuscript, JM underscored the ciphers for the word "commission." See the second and third sentences of JM's Comments on Instructions to Peace Commissioners, 24 July 1782, for his stress upon the inconsistency between the wording of Lee's motion and Lowell's and Bland's speeches supporting it.

[4] The "other point" was the adoption, by a vote of fewer than nine state delegations, of an amendment to the proposed instructions to the peace commissioners. See Comments on Instructions to Peace Commissioners, 24 July 1782, and nn. 5, 6. By "source," JM may have meant Arthur Lee.

[5] *Ibid.*, n. 9. Although neither the printed journal nor Thomson's "Debates" mentions an announcement of intention to resume the debate, a motion by John Lowell on 2 August 1782 confirms the accuracy of JM's remark (*JCC*, XXII, 428).

[6] JM apparently refers to Robert Morris' notes, mentioned earlier in this volume (Virginia Delegates to Harrison, 19 March, and n. 1; Randolph to JM, 20 June, and n. 42; JM to Randolph, 23 July 1782).

[7] See Randolph to JM, 16–17 May, n. 18; 20 June 1782, n. 42. In a letter of 30 April, Morris had promised to accept his notes "at the treasury of the United States in discharge of any debt due from Virginia." Consequently, on 1 July 1782, the General Assembly in its "permanent revenue" law, erroneously citing Morris' letter as of 29 April, declared that the notes would be receivable in payment of taxes (MS in Continental Congress Papers Collection, Virginia State Library; Hening, *Statutes*, XI, 68–69). The journals of Congress furnish no evidence that Bland and Lee had "pressed" Congress to ratify the agreement.

By "ill tendency" Bland may have meant "bad politics." The Virginia General Assembly might view with displeasure an unsuccessful effort by the delegates, acting without instructions, to have Congress ratify what in effect was a contract between Morris and the Assembly. On the other hand, ratification of the "contract" by Congress probably would offend Bland's and Lee's usual allies, the delegates from Massachusetts, because the depreciation of Morris' notes in that state was subjecting them to attack (Clarence L. Ver Steeg, *Robert Morris*, pp. 118–19).

Many years later JM or someone at his bidding designated, by the use of brackets, the first two paragraphs of this letter for publication. Although JM's directive was heeded in Madison, *Papers* (Gilpin ed.), I, 155–56, Gilpin was unable to decode the ciphers. Gilpin further erred by including in the letter the final two sentences of the seventh paragraph and all of the eighth paragraph of JM's dispatch of 16 July 1782 to Randolph.

[8] See Randolph to JM, 18 July 1782, and n. 14.

[9] The postmaster at Richmond was James Hayes, Jr., the publisher of the *Virginia Gazette, or, the American Advertiser.*

[10] See Randolph to JM, 18 July 1782, and n. 15. The auditors were William Geddes, William Govett, and John Dyer Mercier (*JCC*, XXII, 60, 260).

[11] See Virginia Delegates to Harrison, 30 July 1782, and n. 8. The "Capt:" was probably Charles Lyon, who had been a Philadelphia shipmaster at least as early as 1750 and had registered his brigantine "Nancy" in that city in 1774 (*Pennsylvania Magazine of History and Biography*, XXV [1901], 123; XXVIII [1904], 488). Sailing under the protection of the French fleet from Haiti to the Chesapeake Capes, he had disembarked at Baltimore and proceeded overland to Philadelphia, arriving there on 29 July (*Pennsylvania Journal*, 31 July 1782).

[12] Among the "improbabilities" may have been the unlikelihood, because Rochambeau's troops were still in Maryland and Washington's army along the lower Hudson River was weak, that the French fleet would endeavor to control New

York Bay with no prospect of receiving effective support from the land. As late as 6 August 1782 Washington had not heard officially of the French fleet's arrival off the American coast (Fitzpatrick, *Writings of Washington*, XXIV, 473, 497).

[13] See JM to Randolph 16 July, and n. 30; 23 July 1782.

[14] The *Pennsylvania Gazette* of 30 July 1782 reported the arrival at Salem, Mass., on 16 July of the ship "Thomas" after a month's passage from Nantes. David Salisbury Franks (*ca.* 1740–1793), a native of Philadelphia, was a merchant in Montreal when the city was captured by the Americans in 1775. He entered the continental military service and eventually became a lieutenant colonel. At Robert Morris' request, Washington in July 1781 granted Franks an indefinite leave of absence to enable him to carry secret dispatches to John Jay in Madrid. After further service as a member of Benjamin Franklin's staff, Franks embarked in mid-June 1782 for the United States as a courier to Congress. In 1784 he bore to the American commissioners in Europe a copy of the definitive peace treaty with Great Britain ratified by Congress. Thereafter he served for three years in successive consular and diplomatic posts until his straitened finances necessitated his return home. His subsequent efforts to secure a federal appointment were unsuccessful. For at least two years before his death in Philadelphia from yellow fever he was an assistant cashier of the Bank of North America (Hersch L. Zitt, "David Salisbury Franks, Revolutionary Patriot [c. 1740–1793]," *Pennsylvania History*, XVI [1949], 77–95; *Publications of the American Jewish Historical Society*, I [1893; 2d ed., 1905], 76–86; IV [1896], 81–87; X [1902], 101–8).

[15] Besides the *Pennsylvania Packet* of 30 July, JM may have sent Randolph the issue of that paper of 25 July, the *Pennsylvania Journal* of 24 and 27 July, and the *Pennsylvania Gazette* of 24 July 1782. These all printed extracts of debates in the British or Irish Parliament on various dates between 22 March and 10 May 1782.

[16] JM was referring to an unidentified issue of the *Courier de l'Europe*, published in London, 1781–1788. The *Pennsylvania Journal* of 24 July told of a British agent in Paris engaged in conversations with Franklin, while the issue of 31 July of the same newspaper mentioned other British agents meeting with John Adams and Henry Laurens in The Hague.

[17] Congress did not hear from Jay until 2 August; from John Adams until 11 September; from Franklin until 17 September; and from La Luzerne, communicating information sent to him by Vergennes, until 24 September. These dispatches vary in their dates from 9 April to 5 July 1782 (NA: PCC, No. 185, III, 36, 41, 42, 43; *JCC*, XXIII, 594, 597).

[18] See JM to Randolph, 16 and 23 July 1782.

Comments on the Cost of the War

Printed copy (Thomson, "Debates," p. 75). See Comments on Instructions to Peace Commissioners, 24 July 1782, headnote.

EDITORIAL NOTE

On 31 July 1782 Congress resumed the debate begun the day before on the problem of how, in view of an empty treasury, to fulfill the pledge of 21 October 1780 to remunerate with half pay for life the continental army officers "who should continue in service to the end of the war or be deranged" (Comments on Public Faith and Credit, 30 July 1782, and editorial note, and n. 3; Thomson, "Debates," pp. 73–74). On 31 July 1782 Jesse Root moved that "every State which shall settle with the officers belonging to their respective lines in regard to their half pay aforesaid and cause the United States to be exonerated therefrom *shall be discharged from contributing any thing towards the half pay of officers in the line of any other State.*" Recognizing that, if this proposal was adopted, a state which, in proportion to its population and wealth, had furnished fewer officers than another state would be able to discharge its obligation with comparative ease, Theodorick Bland moved to replace the italicized words in Root's motion with, "Shall be credited in their annual quota to the amount of the half pay of the officers so settled with." JM's remarks, as summarized by Thomson, were obviously a rejoinder to Root and Bland and also to Eliphalet Dyer, who had spoken on behalf of Root's motion (*JCC*, XXII, 424–25; Thomson, "Debates," pp. 74–75).

[31 July 1782]

Mr. Madison. All charges of war are by the Confederation to be paid out of one treasury. The motion violates this article of the Confederation;[1] the amdmt is more conformable to it; but still does not meet his approbation.[2]

[1] The eighth article of the Articles of Confederation stipulated that: "All charges of war, and all other expences that shall be incurred for the common defence or general welfare, and allowed by the united states in congress assembled, shall be defrayed out of a common treasury" (*JCC*, XIX, 217).

[2] Root's motion, if modified by Bland's amendment (see editorial note), would still not have conformed with the eighth article of the Articles of Confederation. See JM to Pendleton, 7 February 1782, n. 5. JM was probably influenced in his stand by the recent refusal of the Virginia General Assembly to sanction a proposed change in the wording of the eighth article (JM to Pendleton, 7 February, n. 6; Harrison to Virginia Delegates, 11 July 1782). After JM completed his remarks, and at least thirteen other members of Congress expressed their views, a motion was adopted "to postpone the farther consideration of the subject" until 1 January 1783 (Thomson, "Debates," pp. 75–79; *JCC*, XXII, 425 and n.).

INDEX

NOTE: Persons are identified on pages cited below in boldface type. Identifications made in earlier volumes are noted immediately after the person's name.

The Papers of James Madison

DESIGNED BY JOHN B. GOETZ
COMPOSED BY THE UNIVERSITY OF CHICAGO PRESS
IN LINOTYPE JANSON WITH DISPLAY LINES IN
MONOTYPE JANSON AND CASLON OLD STYLE
PRINTED BY THE UNIVERSITY OF CHICAGO PRESS
ON WARREN'S UNIVERSITY TEXT, A PAPER WATERMARKED
WITH JAMES MADISON'S SIGNATURE AND MADE EXPRESSLY
FOR THE VOLUMES OF THIS SET
PLATES PRINTED BY MERIDEN GRAVURE COMPANY
BOUND BY RAND MC NALLY IN COLUMBIA BAYSIDE LINEN
AND STAMPED IN GENUINE GOLD